# PRISONERS OF THE
# THIRD REICH...
## A Sapper's Story

### W.E. WELBOURNE

# Introduction

Enduring the hardships of the Great Depression, a young 'Arty' Dawson knows full well that a conflicted world is heading for another war. In 1933, the nineteen year old joins an engineering Militia Unit in his home town of Waratah, Newcastle.

Six years later, as a trained Sapper, he is among the first of the Aussie diggers to answer the call to assist Britain in its hour of need. His Unit, the Second First Company, Royal Engineers Sixth Division, sets sail on the Orcades in the first convoy, leaving Sydney on 10 January, 1940.

Arthur realises the dangers of being killed or maimed, but he is determined to do all in his power to return home in one piece. Arriving at the nearest war zone in the Middle East and North Africa, these ANZAC forces sweep through Libya, from Egypt to Benghazi, defeating superior numbers and heavily armed Italians ... the first Allied land victories of World War II.

Redirected from North Africa to Greece to help the Greeks face the overwhelming German advance, the Anzacs, lacking supplies, are forced to retreat south and evacuate from Kalamata. Arthur and fellow diggers of his Battalion are crammed on board the transport ship, Costa Rica, which is bombed and sunk off Crete. Rescued by destroyers, they are taken to Crete to bolster the island's defences.

The invasion of Crete begins on 20 May, 1941 when German airborne forces overrun the Allies' gallant resistance. A counter attack begins on the outskirts of Chania, halting the German advance long enough for thousands of troops to cross the mountains to the evacuation beach at Sfakia on Crete's south coast.

Over four successive nights from 28 May, British and Allied Warships from Alexandria evacuate 11,000 troops, using the cover of darkness to avoid detection.

The evacuation abruptly ends on 1 June, 1941, when the Germans outflank the Australian rear-guard holding the ridge above Sfakia. The Germans capture 5,000 hungry and abandoned Allied troops and Arthur is one of those unable to escape. Four years of harsh captivity lay before them.

Arthur begins his grim incarceration in Skines POW camp on Crete, before being transported via Athens and Thessaloniki by train in overloaded cattle trucks to Stalag VIIIB at Lamsdorf, in the historic region of Silesia. The lost years sees Arthur endure the mental and physical hardships of three hair raising escapes, and three and a half years on a working party at the saw-milling township of Mahrisch Trubau, the German name for Moravska Trebova, in the historic Sudetenland, now part of the Czech Republic. From here Arthur makes his final dash to freedom, escaping to American lines, when German soldiers flee from the advancing Russian Front in 1945, during the last days of the Third Reich.

Arthur's survival is largely due to luck and the forces of family love, combined with the cooperation and support of his comrades, as well as the unexpected and significant life-saving help from the Red Cross. Importantly, in keeping his spirits alive in the darkest of times, Arthur finds secret love from unexpected quarters.

This remarkable true story of a quintessential Aussie bloke, my uncle, could not have been written without privy to our episodic family records and Arthur's war diary, detailing his courageous experiences as a soldier serving his country.

W.E. Welbourne

# Table of Contents

Chapter 1. Family Pastimes ................................................................ 1
Chapter 2. The Great Depression – Family Survival ........................... 9
Chapter 3. The Militia Engineers ....................................................... 30
Chapter 4. Training and Leave – Palestine ......................................... 40
Chapter 5. Training and Leave – Egypt ............................................. 60
Chapter 6. The Western Desert Campaign ........................................ 90
Chapter 7. The Greek Campaign ..................................................... 131
Chapter 8. The Crete Campaign ...................................................... 177
Chapter 9. POW Days – The Greek Experience .............................. 214
Chapter 10. On the run in Greece .................................................... 247
Chapter 11. Escape No. 2, again in Greece ...................................... 300
Chapter 12. Welcome to Stalag VIIIB, Germany ............................. 364
Chapter 13. Working Party Days at Mahrisch Trubau: Episode 1 ..... 401
Chapter 14. Working Party Days at Mahrisch Trubau: Episode 2 ..... 454
Chapter 15. Working Party Days at Mahrisch Trubau: Episode 3 ..... 510
Chapter 16. Escape to Freedom ....................................................... 547
Chapter 17. Freedom – England ...................................................... 586
Chapter 18. Homeward Bound ........................................................ 618
Chapter 19. An Unexpected Reunion .............................................. 637

## Chapter 1

# Family Pastimes

I THINK OF MY FATHER, Thomas Edward Dawson, as an unsung hero. He is quite a phenomenon before us kids come into the picture. He was born at Coal Cliff, a little village on the South Coast near Wollongong and south of Sydney, New South Wales, in 1881. In his bachelor days, his activities cover the whole spectrum of what is considered the desirable leisure pursuits of the time. There being no radio or television, these activities involve the sport and entertainment of the day. My Dad becomes a superb athlete and excels at football and swimming. In football, he helps to introduce the new code of Rugby League.

He tells me that before Rugby League began in the Hunter River District and Newcastle, there were two branches of Rugby Union, with Headquarters at Newcastle and Maitland. The Newcastle branch was called the Northern District Rugby Union and the Maitland Branch was called the Hunter District Rugby Union. However, when Rugby League takes over, both branches merge and are called the Newcastle Rugby League. My father was chosen to represent in the first Maitland District and Coalfields team to play against a Newcastle Rugby League representative team.

In entertainment, my father tries just about everything. He acts in plays, sings comic songs, does conjuring and tap dancing, and even dabbles with the trapeze. One of my earliest memories is of a trapeze he sets up as a swing in a large tree in the backyard of the house where I was born. It is for the use of my sister Clare and myself.

The commercial entertainment of those times is provided mostly by plays. The most prestigious of these usually come from overseas, mainly Britain. One such production is a drama called Silver King which played a full season at Newcastle's most noted theatre, The Victoria, in Perkins Street. For its season, my Dad is the understudy to its lead actor, Julius Knight, an eminent English actor.

My Dad wrote plays of his own. Later in life, we kids were privileged to view some on rare occasions when he chose to open his two large trunks, one wooden and one metal. They were crammed to the brim with his writings, sheet music, costumes, and all paraphernalia connected to his activities that he had collected over time. Sadly, they no longer exist.

He becomes a great ballroom dancer. Together with my Mum, the pair win many competitions. They excel at the Waltz, the premier dance of those times. Competition was so keen, and poise, style and balance so important, that sometimes eggshells were glued to the heels of their shoes. Crushed shells meant automatic disqualification, as the correct style required the dancers to be always on their toes.

All of my Dad's activities were competitive, with rewards for a winner being a gold medal. For football, it was a skullcap in the club colours, decorated with an ornate silver tassel. My Dad won so many gold medals that he had some linked together and made into bracelet for my Mum.

My Dad thinks the world of Mum. They first meet in a park when she is 18 years of age and he 12 years older. He was looking for the thinnest woman he could find because his mother, Emma Major, was a big fat person and a crazy spiritualist. His father, William Jewett Dawson, and Emma migrated from England and they eventually raised a family of five boys and three girls, and settled in the Coalfields at Kurri Kurri. When spiritualism split them up, Emma stayed at their home and my Dad went to live with his oldest brother, my Uncle Tom in East Lambton.

Naturally, his former activities cease when he marries my Mum, Ivy Fullick. Our knowledge of his former life is only by hearsay, with very rare exceptions, when he will show us kids a trick or two.

As a married man, my Dad knuckles down to the business of providing for his family. He is a medium tall man, good looking, well built, fair and erect, with some presence. Yet he is humble and his credo is: never boast, and never brag.

Both my parents came from mining families. My Dad worked at the mining game as that is where most of the local work was. He also worked extensively at the local abattoirs, mostly as a digester man. This is a smelly, not very pleasant job, involving the boiling down of all the waste products and turning them into blood and bone fertiliser.

In the manner of the day, our family lived in rented accommodation. If you worked in the mining game, renting is almost universally the norm. Firstly, a mine will be established, then some rows of Company houses will be built close by for its workers. Then follows the small businesses to cater for their needs and, quite quickly, a small township will have been established. If, and when, the coal deposits are worked out, the mine will close, and the Company will move on to establish somewhere else. Then, the whole process will begin all over again. Those renting will be free to move on, also.

In the township of Lambton, where us kids were born, the local mine was almost worked out. The workforce had dwindled to almost nothing. Still the township had established itself into a thriving community, with all the relevant infrastructure intact—roads, parks, schools, and businesses so that there was other work as well. So, with its close proximity to the port of Newcastle, Lambton became a suburb of that town. Together with a range of other suburbs similarly placed, a fairly large important district had been established.

My Dad was working at the local abattoirs located about five miles from where we lived. In the manner of those times, such a distance was not considered excessive. You either walked to and fro from the place, or rode a push bike. He also became a member of the local Volunteer Fire Brigade.

The Brigade Headquarters was centrally located in the town, about a quarter of a mile from our house. My dad would run to the station house whenever the alarm was sounded by somebody ringing the large bell. First to arrive, usually my Dad, would haul a large hand-drawn hose reel, mounted and finely balanced, on two large carriage wheels. Late arrivals would fetch up the rear with a horse-drawn tanker. The reel men, hopefully joined by another helper, would set off at a trot towards the scene of the fire. With the whole town now alerted by the fire bell, several kids would have gathered also. As the reel men trotted along, the kids would hang onto the back, so then they had the extra weight of the kids to pull along as well. While less than satisfactory, it was the best that could be done in those times. Luckily, fires did not occur very often.

In our family, six kids were born. Roy, the first born, died of pneumonia at the age of two and a half. I, the second born, then aged one, became the oldest by default. Then came Clare, then Jean, then Dorothy, then Ted, the last born and named after our Dad, who chose to be known by his middle name of Edward.

When there is just Clare and me, a mini crisis occurs. One early evening, just after dark, my Mum tells Clare to do something but she refuses. Mum insists and Clare replies, "I won't. I won't." A frustrated Mum takes Clare by the hand and up to my Dad. Mum says, "Ted, you'll have to chastise her for being naughty."

Chastisement in those times meant a dose of the strap. My Dad unbuckles his belt from around the waist of his trousers, takes Clare by one hand, and proceeds to give her several cuts around the legs. Clare cries and covers up as best she can, but not very successfully. A number of red welts appear on Clare's legs, together with a slight trickle of blood. Shocked, my Mum immediately grabs Clare from Dad's grasp.

In a perverse female way, my Mum now begins to berate my Dad. She says, "Look at what you've done! You've drawn blood. You're never to chastise them again." My Dad says nothing, but is clearly astounded at the outcome of what is supposed to be a minor bit of discipline. Us kids will go onto adulthood. There are times when an exasperated Mum will be pushed into pleading, "Ted, do something." But my Dad will just quietly evade the issue, leaving my Mum to deal with our indiscretions, in her own way.

Also in his bachelor days, my Dad took up voluntary Military service. The local Unit was a Scottish Infantry one with a grand, resplendent uniform. It was one of the costumes he kept in those trunks of his. Here again, his prowess shone out. At his first try in the rifle shoot, he beats all comers, thereby earning his marksman's badge and several gold medals as well.

In those days, a gold medal was the general trophy award. But they were given sparingly. To earn one, a person had to be the best of the best. And our Dad had them laid on. But, to us kids, they didn't mean much and we just didn't think about them. When we walked down the street the grownups would say, "Gidday Ted. How's things?" They were just being friendly. Wasn't this the way with all Dads? That's the way we saw it, anyway.

I loved to visit my Grandma's place, especially at Christmas. It was a family tradition to meet there, year after year. All my Aunties, Uncles, and Cousins would be there, and us younger kids would have a great time together. There was scope to play, and many interesting things going on around us.

My Grandma's place was situated in what was known as Plattsburg, a sort of suburb of Wallsend on its northern outskirts, and adjoining what is now known as Maryland. Her house in Fletcher Street stood on a corner block, roughly of about one acre in size, which was about the average size block of her few neighbours as well. At the bottom of her street was Wallsend Race Course and opposite the Course was the Race Course Hotel. On occasions, my Grandfather would give me a billycan and sixpence, and send me to the hotel for sixpence worth of beer for him.

Fletcher Street was a well-formed gravel road, with deep ditch gutters on either side. My cousins, Frank and Jim, and I used to catch crawchies in little watery pools, left behind by rain, in those gutters.

The house, still with a small section of original timber slab construction, too good to replace, was not overly large, but still fairly roomy. It contained lots of family trinkets and treasures, including my favourite, a very large volume of The Family Bible. Just inside the front cover was a section set aside for the recording of the family history of births, deaths and marriages. It fascinated me to find my own name recorded there. The heavy volume had two large ornate brass clasps to seal it closed.

Apart from my Grandma and Grandfather, it was a home to two of my uncles, Pat and Tom, and my Aunt Phoebe. Pat, a confirmed bachelor, was a miner, and worked on the South Maitland coalfields. During the week he boarded at Weston, returning home at weekends and holidays. Tom, going steady but not yet committed, worked on the steam trams, firstly, as a conductor and lately as a driver. He was permanently based at home. Aunt Phoebe, a confirmed spinster, also based at home, helped Grandma.

As my cousins, Frank and Jim, lived in Wallsend, it was my custom to stay at my Grandma's a couple of days before Christmas and through until the New Year. With my cousins staying over too, we generally piled in for the night, three to a bed. Always, there would be hi-jinks and shenanigans before we settled down for the night. Our antics caused my Grandfather to declare in mock despair, "One boy's a boy, two boys are only half a boy, and three boys are no boy at all."

The kitchen, the hub of the house, was big and roomy, and at the rear of the house. Its main feature was a big open fireplace in which a fire was always burning— coal-fuelled, of course, as free coal was one of Pat's perks for being a miner. Perched squarely on one side of the fireplace was a big, square, cast iron, box oven. The heavy door opened to show a single shelf, halfway between top and bottom. To cook in the oven, part of the fire would be raked into the space immediately beneath it. Pot and pan cooking would be done on top of the fire proper.

Using her expertise, my Grandma could do wonders in that oven, from cakes to baked dinners; and her daughters were nearly as good, including my Mum. We kids did our bit, making toast. We would put a slice of bread on a long-handled fork and hold it close to the heat.

Aunt Phoebe was responsible for keeping the fireplace spic and span. The plastered-over brickwork at the back of, and surrounding, the fireplace was always painted with whitewash. The box oven was painted with stove black. In front of the grate was a heavy rug, Aunt Phoebe's speciality. She made them from a chaff bag with strips of cloth woven through it, in a coloured pattern. Embers sometimes fell from the grate, singing the rug. If it started to look a bit tatty, she would make a new one. She banked the fire down before going to bed at night, and was first to stir it into life again in the morning.

Just outside the side door of the kitchen was an underground well. It was about fifteen feet in diameter and covered by a sturdy timbered frame. The well was brick-lined, cool and dark. Us kids were sternly forbidden to venture onto the cover. But, by peering through cracks we were able to see its structure, its still-water level, one or two frogs, and of course some tadpoles. Water drawn from the well was almost icy cold on the hottest day, crystal clear, and tasted delicious.

Just behind the house complex, the yard was fenced in half. In one section was a cow bail and small dairy, with the remainder being taken up as a poultry run. The poultry consisted of both ducks and fowls, and there were coups to house them. There was a special coup to house the birds selected for Christmas dinner. They were not allowed to run free, and were specially fattened for the big day. A further fence served to contain the poultry run, and in resplendent isolation, was the dunny.

It was my Grandma's custom to keep a house cow— a Jersey, of course, for they gave the richest and creamiest milk. She was a docile, obedient beast, even to us kids. She would feed placidly while being milked, by my Grandma of course. Occasionally, a well-directed stream would find its target of an eager young face.

The next-door neighbours were bachelor brothers, named O'Hare. Their block was entirely covered with stone fruit trees, their speciality. For two shillings, we could have a wicker shopping basket filled with peaches, plums, nectarines and apricots, ripened on the tree and delicious. Occasionally, we might get lucky and be given a nectarine from their own special tree. These were about the size of an average grapefruit, and soft, sweet and juicy. Always only one though, and given with an air of regretting such an impulsive gesture. As this was the era of B.F.F., before fruit fly, there was never a mark or blemish on any of their fruit.

Then there was our special Christmas treat. My Grandma owned a small wooden keg, in which she made ginger beer, just for us kids, only at Christmas though. The keg would be set up in the cool dairy, to mature and be ready for the big day. Though the sight of its wooden spigot of a tap, ready to pour, was tantalising, our upbringing prevented us from helping ourselves. Still, Grandma had the uncanny ability to know when our thirsts needed slaking.

As the population of those times fed predominantly on beef and lamb, a poultry dinner was reserved only for a special occasion— always at Christmas, but seldom for any other time. Technology had not evolved to a point where a bird came in a plastic wrap, prepared and ready, so that part was always done at home. Uncle Pat usually performed the beheading and hanging up to bleed. Then it was my Grandma's turn. Although the chosen birds, by now, had become almost pets, she just went ahead plucking and cleaning.

Then comes the big day and the feast is magnificent. With all the aunties, uncles and cousins, sometimes there are as many as three sittings, always plenty for all. Then on the New Year, a dance was held in the Church Hall for all the grownups, entrance fee sixpence. The badge of adulthood, is being allowed to attend that dance.

As my two cousins and I were still youngsters, we remained at home in the care of my Grandfather. Everybody else is at the dance. At the appropriate time, and when we are in our pyjamas ready for bed, Grandfather would sternly order us to go out to the coal heap and command, "Water the nags." This we dutifully did.

# Chapter 2

# The Great Depression – Family Survival

I HAVE STARTED SCHOOL; OUR family has started to grow and increase, and it is a happy caring household we live in. My Mum and my Dad have their friends; there are other kids around for us to play with; and there are relatives, not too far away, whom we regularly visit. Our lifestyle, though not grand, is immensely pleasing. Then disaster—my Dad is put out of work.

As the oldest child, I only dimly sense that there is a crisis. Ted, our youngest, has recently been born. Something has to be done to curb our already sparse expenditure, and my Dad has to somehow find another job. My Mum and Dad tackle both these problems as best they can. But my Dad cannot get any other work. With the situation now critical, my parents decide they have no alternative but to move to where work might be found. The decision is taken to move to Caledonia. This multi-talented Dad of ours, who has taken on the burden of providing for a wife and family, uncomplainingly, decides to leave the scene of all his triumphs to try and start anew elsewhere.

Caledonia is the last stop, on the privately owned South Maitland rail line, before Cessnock. While Cessnock is a fairly large township, the Caledonia area is virtually virgin bush. Anybody proposing to live there, has to build their own housing. The custom is to take out a Miners Right for five shillings and sixpence from the Mines Department. This entitles the holder to squat on a piece of Crown land, while presumably prospecting for minerals.

With a young family, and one of them a new born baby, my Mum insists there was no way she can live rough in the bush. My Dad will have to build us a house. While he is doing this, we will live in our rented house in Lambton. The sooner the Caledonia house is completed, the sooner we will be able to leave Lambton, thereby saving the rent.

Building your own house is not a common occurrence, but it is not a rarity either. But it is always in the outlying bush areas, never in the settlements. Depending upon the skills of the builder, the construction either becomes a humpy or a house. Of course, much depends upon the quantity and quality of materials you are able to scrounge.

Now begins a period when we are to be without Dad. He is away camping and building at Caledonia. Sometimes he might come home for a short period at the weekend. Sometimes it might not be for weeks at a time. In the meantime, my Mum carries on as best she can. While we miss our Dad, to us kids, life is pretty much as normal. Those of us of school age go to school and enjoy the normal kid's games and pastimes with other kids around us. Finally, it is time to move to Caledonia. To me, it is rather exciting and something of an adventure.

My Dad's brother, our Uncle Charlie, lives and works at Abernethy. Our family has spent some holidays with him and his family on several occasions. Abernethy is an important mining area in virgin bushland, a number of miles east of Cessnock town. A good road links the two places. This road passes close to the Caledonia Rail Station. Having stopped there on our way to Uncle Charlie's, we have some familiarity with the area. We find that our house is set across this road, and somewhat back into the bush fringe, in line with a couple of nearby houses.

Our house is similar in construction to the other houses. Bush timber is used for the framework. The roof is corrugated iron. A large corrugated iron tank mounted on a railway sleeper provides the water supply which is gathered from the rain runoff from the roof. The frame is covered with brattice, a kind of sacking used extensively in the mines as screens. These screens are subject to heavy wear and tear, and are quickly discarded and replaced by new stuff. Lots of it can be found on mines' rubbish heaps. When used in housing, it is painted over with a heavy coating of whitewash which makes it impervious to the elements. Cooking is done on a fire in the open, as is the boiling of clothes in the washing process. As soon as possible, a cast iron fuel stove will be purchased and installed inside. A small outhouse set some distance back is obviously the dunny. With no sewerage service, my Dad will have to dig a hole and bury the pan's contents down in the bush.

From a short distance, our house, with its white painted walls, looks neat and trim. Us kids have some idea of this kind of living through our holidays at Uncle Charlie's. It is a new experience and like those holidays, a bit exciting. What my Mum thinks, she doesn't say.

My Dad has done a good job, considering the limited resources available. He has tried to please my Mum. Initially, there are two rooms, one for sleeping and the other for living, dining or whatever. Now that all the family is together again, my Dad can direct his energies to expanding the complex. The big project now is to have a large room with a kitchen and cast iron stove at one end, and the bulk of it for dining and living. The room, now providing these services, will become a bedroom. Thus, our house will make provision for a bedroom for my Mum and Dad, a bedroom for us kids, and a large kitchen and general living room. The floors at present are dirt. Later, my Dad plans to put floor covering in the bedrooms. The dirt floors are hard packed earth, encouraged to stay so by sprinkling spent bathwater on them. The resulting surface is compact and can be swept tidy with a broom, leaving a finish as clean as any wooden floor.

There is no electricity, so kerosene has to serve for lighting. Lamp globes (the glass shield that protects the wick section) can be made to last longer by first boiling the globe in water. This is a trick passed on from family to family. At night, the soft mellow glow from the lamp, coupled with the surrounding dancing shadows, is very pleasing and restful to our eyes. Compared to our former lifestyle, this new way of living has a slight touch of adventurous magic to us kids.

In moving from our former home at Lambton, we lose our second sister Jean. She is to stay temporarily with our Aunty Emma. Our Aunty Emma had married our Uncle Bill who had lost a leg in the First World War. Though married for some years, they have no children of their own. Having despaired of the situation changing, our Aunty Emma persistently plagued our Mum to allow one of us kids to come and live with them. While Mum has consistently resisted the idea, continuous pressure from Aunty Emma wears her down so that she gives in. Aunty Emma's choice is of Jean, who will be allowed to live with them, but only until we get settled in our new home.

Us town kids rather enjoy the freedom and space of our new surroundings. There is a neighbour next door, the James family, with one son about our age. They are English. Further along, towards Cessnock township is another family, the Kirwins. They are a typical Australian bush family, with a large brood of kids, both boys and girls. The father is a long, lean, somewhat dark man who keeps five or six draught horses and several drays. He can always be seen, astride his horse, with a whip over his shoulder, the handle to the front and near to hand, and with the long leather thong trailing down his back. Their home is a large rambling establishment, with corral type enclosures made from bush poles, for the horses. There are lean-tos for the drays and the harnesses. The house is fairly large, to cater for the big family. All of these houses are the same type of construction as our own. While the area around the houses, and in front of them to the main road is clear and open, immediately behind, the bush is thick and dense.

How the rail station came to be named Caledonia, it would be hard to say. To me, Caledonia has the hint of exotic faraway places. Still, most of the places around had been named by expatriates as a nostalgic reminder of favourite areas back home in the "Old Dart". Almost certainly, this had been the same with Caledonia.

Once settled in, those of us kids of school age, will have to go to the public school at Aberdare, some three to four miles to the west, on the outskirts of Cessnock, walking of course. This will take care of Clare and me, while Doss and baby Ted will stay at home. My Dad will continue to improve our home and, in between, will be looking for work. This takes place in 1923, at the beginning of the Great Depression.

From the outset, school to me proves a piece of cake. I am always near to, or at the top of the class. Mr Simpson, my teacher, naturally enough, gives me favoured treatment because of this. It is the custom of the day for the teacher to donate books as end of year prizes, to be given out just before the Christmas break. They will be for first, second and third, and are eagerly contested. First prize usually is a Boys Own Annual type, and greatly coveted by all. This is to become almost my exclusive property.

Meantime, my Dad is still unable to get work. We live on dole payments. I suppose we really can be considered disadvantaged, utterly poor and truly needy. But nothing like this occurs to us. My Mum can do wonders with the supplies we have; and always, although our appetites are young and healthy, our bellies are full. As for clothing, while it may not be very grand, it always seems adequate to us. All households own a sewing machine of some sort, and any mending is quickly attended to. My Mum is especially good at this.

My Dad continues on with our house improvements. Our large kitchen, dining, cum living room, now has a fuel stove plus chimney installed at one end. Fuel for the stove is either coal or wood. Coal can be gleaned from the nearby rail line. It is just a matter of taking a hessian bag and picking up small lumps that regularly fall off the coal hoppers on their way to the export loading point at Newcastle. If coal becomes scarce, there is always plenty of wood in the nearby bush. With the stove in place, all cooking etc. can be done inside and under cover.

To further improve our main living area, my Dad now decides to build the walls of railway sleepers. Constant maintenance on the rail line sees the timber sleepers regularly being replaced by new ones as they begin to wear. The old sleepers are just left lying beside the line, discarded and unwanted. My Dad uses them to do the job. Firstly, he has to fetch them home, one by one, until he has sufficient to do a section of the wall at a time. Without any means to transport them, each and every one has to be carried on his shoulder. Being tough hardwood, they are extremely heavy, and the distance carried could be within a radius of almost a mile.

My Dad's building method is to stand each sleeper on end along the wall line. The cracks between each sleeper are covered by strips of tin, cut from discarded kerosene tins, and nailed into place. Brattice again covers the walls, so the finished appearance is as before. The inner wall surfaces are pasted over with sheets of newspaper.

Now settled in, we carry on with our new life. School occupies most of my time during the week, with plenty of playtime at the weekends. As kids will, we quickly became friends with the Kirwin kids. I became friends with the two older boys, Sonny, about thirteen or fourteen, and Jack, about eleven.

These two are regularly sent into the bush by their father to cut bakers' wood. And I am happy and eager to go with them, whenever I can. In these times, all bread baking is done in wood-fired ovens. The supply of bakers' wood is a fair and legitimate business, and the supply and sale of wood is partly the means of the Kirwins making a living.

The wood has to be well dried and smoke free, and the billets of regular size and length. It is sold at so much the dray load, usually paid for by cash on the nail.

With plenty of deadfalls in the nearby bush, supply is no problem. We three will set off with the tools to do the job, a cross cut saw, and a maul and steel wedges. We will cut the logs in proper lengths, then split them into billets, using the maul and wedges.

I am happy to help with the work, and the two boys are happy enough to show me how. Working together, as they have to, finds them always in fierce argument. The saw will jam in the cut and each will blame each other, claiming the other was the one who curved the saw, rather than keeping the cut true and straight. Then, "You pushed the saw, when you should only have pulled." And when splitting, "You put the wedge in the wrong place, and now it's jammed." Either one will work with me as his partner, without the least problem, even though my performance might not be as good as his brother's.

When cut, the billets are stacked where they lay. Then we will move onto the next log. When it is judged that we had enough for a dray load, one of the boys will go back home, harness one of the horses, hitch on the dray and drive it to the loading site, where we will load up.

The bakery is in the Cessnock township area, quite a distance from where we live. With us three perched on top of the load, it is a long slow journey to the delivery site. Then we all will unload and stack the billets neatly on the bakery pile, that is in the open, near and handy to the ovens. One of the bakery staff will pay Sonny in cash, then we will head back home.

To get to Cessnock, we have to pass through Aberdare. There is a hotel on the main road there, about halfway between. Mr Kirwin, the boys' dad, spends most of his day there and, is pretty much an alcoholic. On the way in, we will pull up there. Sonny will report to his dad, who will come out of the pub and inspect the load. Satisfied that all is in order, he will return to the pub. On the way back, we will again pull up. Mr Kirwin will again come out; Sonny will hand over the cash and Mr Kirwan will disappear back into the pub.

Mr Kirwan is a bit of a martinet, and the whole family are scared of him, including the two boys. While he doesn't exactly object to me being with the boys, he doesn't exactly approve either. So, I only make the trip into the bakery, just the once or twice.

We like the freedom of our bush surroundings. We kids can run around barefoot, and there is plenty of space for us to indulge in our games. We can build cubby houses out of the gum tree branches, and explore pretty much as we wish. The climate can be very cold in mid-winter and fiercely hot in mid-summer.

One winter's morning we wake to a magical fairyland. There has been an extremely heavy frost during the night and everything is covered with half an inch of snowlike ice. The utterly still forest looks exactly like those English Xmas cards we have become so used to. In summer, of course, there always is the risk of bushfires. Thankfully, while they do occur, mostly they remain a fair distance away.

Clare and I carry on with our schooling. Doss is getting close to starting, and baby Ted is beginning to run around. Jean is still living with Aunty Emma, who resists all my Mum's pleas to allow her to come home. My Dad is still unable to get work.

My schooling now takes a somewhat radical turn. The education policy until then has been – advancement, according to age. Now it is to be – advancement, according to ability. I am assessed as being a good performer and am moved up three classes. This puts me in line to sit for the high school examinations, and I have just six months to prepare. Suddenly, I am struggling.

Coupled with this pressure, I also have to decide on what my probable career will be. At the age of ten, this, of course, will be decided mostly by my Mum and Dad. This situation is forced upon us because I have two choices of High School—Cessnock High, which covers schooling only up to third year, giving qualifications for trades apprenticeships and general work; or Maitland Boys' High, with schooling up to the fifth year, giving qualifications to go on to University and the professions.

This has to be a tough decision making time for my Parents, particularly for my Dad, struggling with his own work situation. We opt for Maitland Boys' High. For myself, I am happy because it gives me time. If I am good enough, maybe a way can be found for me to go on. If not, then I can still drop out after three years. For my Mum and Dad, I guess they can see how limited the prospects are. Cessnock is a large town, serving a purely coal mining area. With too many people vying for too few openings, any alternative choice just has to be taken.

I sit for the Maitland Boys' High exam and just scrape through. I am committed. In order to go to school, sees me catching a train from Caledonia to Maitland, change there, and wait for a connecting train to Victor Street Station in East Maitland. Then I walk up to "the school on the hill", put in my day's schooling, then do the same journey in reverse in the evening. After arriving home, there will be homework to do by lamplight on the kitchen table, after tea. While an Education Department pass allows me to travel free, the days in winter often see me leave home and return in the dark.

My sister Doss has started school in Cessnock, but she is proving quite a handful. After picking a fight with other kids in the playground, my sister Clare is often called in by a teacher to sort her out. My Mum's attempts to influence Doss to change her ways, doesn't get very far.

I have been continuing my schedule for about a year when my sister Clare becomes seriously ill. She is suffering from extreme pain in her right arm. And trips to the Doctor sees him as mystified as to the cause as my parents are. In desperation, my Mum insists on Clare being transferred to Cessnock for treatment.

With Wallsend being my Mum's family location, there are family members who can oversee her treatment. The Doctor is known to my Mum and is someone she trusts. The hospital too, is a good one. She is admitted there for treatment which is to be long and excruciatingly painful. The diagnosis is tuberculosis of the bone and the treatment involves scraping out the wound and insertion of tubes for drainage. Clare is to spend most of her time in hospital, in excess of two years. She will be allowed only minor breaks of a couple of days away from the hospital on some special occasions. Absence of funds sees most of these breaks taken in Wallsend. Only rarely is she able to make it back home. The time to return sees a very broken hearted and inconsolable Clare leaving behind a badly upset family. Her schooling at this time, mostly has to be put on hold.

At last my Dad gets a job as a digester man at Foggit Jones factory in Maitland. Obviously, the thing to do is to leave our bush surroundings and move closer to the job. With my schooling and Clare's treatment as added factors, it is even more so. My Dad seeks and finds fairly cheap rental accommodation in Bourke Street, Maitland.

We are, by now, confirmed bush kids. Suddenly being transferred to big city living, is a pretty exciting time. I begin to have trouble maintaining interest in my school work, while brother Ted finds a great liking for hitching a ride on the sanitary cart. Unlike living in the bush, the sanitary chore no longer has to be performed by my Dad, as somebody does it for you. My sister Doss goes to school, this time seemingly, with much less aggression than she showed at Cessnock. My sister Jean is still living with Aunty Emma, and seemingly, unlikely to return home for the present. Clare, of course, is mostly confined to hospital.

While ours is a pretty closely knit family, it is not demonstratively so. It is just our way of living. My Mum and Dad combine as a team, guiding and mentoring us kids. While Mum delivers most of the lectures and ultimatums, it is tacitly understood that my Dad is in total agreement. He also, is our breadwinner.

When we move to Maitland, our house is sold to somebody else. While it isn't exactly legal, it is the custom. This is because the Crown land, occupied by Miners Right, is not yours to sell. You find somebody willing to buy, and do the deal. No legal business is necessary. At the time of our moving, several other families have settled nearby, under the same conditions that we had. In time, all this type of settling will be sorted out, with the area eventually becoming a suburb of Cessnock.

As we settle in at Maitland, we begin to find out a few truths. The bargain rents, we are paying, is because of the location of our rented premises. This is a flood prone area, with this being the dead end lower section of Bourke Street, the worst section of the lot. There is also a social stigma attached to being "one of the Bourke Street mob", with only the poorer families living here.

I struggle with my schoolwork, with my progress almost stagnating. With third year coming up, I will soon have to decide whether to leave, or go on to fifth year. If my rate of progress doesn't improve, my decision will be made for me. Meanwhile, there are other distractions to occupy my time.

Just up behind our home, on reasonably higher ground, there is a long established, wholesale fruit and vegetable market. There the local produce is sold to dealers by auction. The surrounding district, being rich in top quality soil, is greatly renowned for its fruit and vegetables. The market days of Mondays, Wednesdays and Fridays are always very busy times.

For surrounding farmers, the practice of selling is to bring their goods by dray load into the market during the early hours of the morning. They will unload, set it out on display, with everything being ready for the auctioneer for an early morning start. Generally, the farmer will be on his own and will need some assistance to unload. Us kids, living nearby, provide this labour. We will approach the farmer, ask if he wants a hand, then, if accepted, pitch in and help. Payment always is with some of the goods for sale. We therefore, always carry a hessian chaff bag with us, to cart home our couple of cabbages, or pumpkins or whatever.

To be part of this auction, means turning out something like three o'clock in the morning. Being up half the night is not conducive to being ready to front up for school. So, I have to do some heavy persuading to get my Mum's permission. She will be torn between what I should be doing and the lure of free vegetables—often with a regular win of enterprise over school. I am able to vary my jobs so that we get most of our produce for free.

Most of what is on sale is laid out for the dealers' needs. The quantities involved make the sale lots out of the question for an average family, although anybody can bid. The goods there are for sale to all comers. The trick, for bargain buying, is to organise several families wanting the same kind of produce, bid for the lot, then share the goods and the cost. On occasions, I might not be able to get somebody to share the cost of something we particularly need. I will buy it, nevertheless, and then hawk the surplus round the neighbourhood, thereby getting my money back and getting our goods for free.

Another gig I became involved in, comes about by my association with one of the Bourke Street kids. He was a bit older than me and works as a paper boy, selling papers and magazines to the train travellers on Maitland Railway Station. Also, he works several nights a week as a lolly boy at the local picture theatre. As a result, he always has money in his pocket, and some prestige because of it. For various reasons, there are several casual vacancies, from time to time, when some of the other boys don't turn up. I am close by and available, so he will arrange for me to fill in. Quickly, I am becoming almost a permanent as a lolly boy.

These activities cut more and more into my school time. Then, when I do go to school, instead of buckling down to homework, I seek to be out in the street playing with the other kids. I am almost fourteen, a time when I will be eligible to leave school if I wish. I guess for my Mum and Dad it is a pretty worrying time.

Whilst my Mum and Dad want better things for me, this requires me to continue on to fifth year. My market day activities sees me happy enough to give that angle a go. But, whilst I like my school, my interest is waning somewhat. Finally, my Mum has had enough and cries quits. She says, "That's it. You're finished at school, but don't think you're going to spend your time hanging about here. You're going to have to go to Business College." The sudden decision takes me by surprise. I'm not really sure whether I want to leave school, or not.

There is a local Business College just up in the main street. The fees are reasonable and it is convenient. My Mum sends me up there in care of her brother, my Uncle Tom, who happens to be visiting. I may have handled things myself. But, I suppose she wants to be sure I haven't been sufficiently corrupted by going through the motions, and not actually attending.

I find the class to be a one teacher show, of sixty to seventy pupils, both boys and girls. They all are here with the same ideas as myself—as an alternative to school, and with the hopes of getting sufficient skills to enable us to embark on a business career, anything better than a labourer.

We are to be taught shorthand, typing and business procedures. There are text books to study, and, with our note pads, pens and pencils, we all look the part. Actually, with such a large class, our male teacher can only start us off on something, then leave us to our own devices.

But, for the girls, it is different. He has a penchant for sitting with his arm round a girl, giving her his undivided attention to the exclusion of everybody else. After a period of this, he will move on to another girl, and repeat the manoeuvre. For us boys, more and more, we are just going through the motions, and virtually setting our own agenda.

I don't have the heart to tell my Mum that it is just a charade. I know it means a lot to my parents for me to carry on. I continue in this fashion for about six months, then comes a lucky breakthrough.

My older cousin, Dulcie, is Office Manageress for W.S. Bacon Ltd, a carrying firm, also specialising in Customs and Shipping work. They need an office boy, and, with my (supposedly) newly acquired Business College skills, it seems that I will fit the bill.

I get the job, much to the relief of my parents, I suppose. However, as the firm operates from premises in Watt Street, Newcastle, I will have to travel there and back, each day, from Maitland.

Now that I have a full-time job, I can no longer carry on with my market day routine. I can still dabble in the lolly boy thing and continue to do so. Then we have a flood. Luckily, this flood is not a full blown one. But it is sufficiently bad enough to show what it can do. And it almost costs my Dad his life.

The Hunter River, which runs immediately behind the Maitland business district, has become a wide, swift flowing and turbulent torrent. In its usual fashion after days of rain, it has spread across low lying areas, roads and farms. Debris, including much farm produce is picked up and swept into the river proper. As usual, the locals gather on the river bank at the back of the business houses, watching and trying to gauge, if and when it may be necessary to evacuate.

While some water is lying around at the bottom end of Bourke Street, our house and others around us, are still relatively okay. My Dad decides to join the watching locals on the river bank to assess the situation. He arrives home a couple of hours later, carrying a water melon. Questioned as to 'how-come', a chastened Dad, rather sheepishly, tells us the story.

Simply, the melon had been floating past amongst the debris. My Dad just dives in and retrieves it. Aghast, my Mum scolds him for being so foolhardy, and asks about the risks. My Dad admits he has misjudged these, and the river had almost got the better of him. If he had not been such a superb swimmer, he will have drowned. The effort takes so much out of him that it was some time before he recovers enough to come home. We all know of my Dad's great love of watermelon, and understand his being unable to resist the temptation. And, now that it is all over, at least he has his melon. But has he? Upon being cut open, it is found to be a jam melon, suitable only for making jam. My Dad had risked his life for nothing.

I have been working at my job for almost a year. I am being trained as a Customs and Shipping Clerk. I work office hours and am allowed an hour for lunch. We have morning and afternoon tea. I handle the mail and the banking. My work takes me daily down to the nearby wharves, checking shipping manifests, and to the Customs House, submitting customs entries. I have joined the lending library and use my travelling time to and fro from Maitland, to devour such books as takes my fancy. I am well pleased with, and thoroughly enjoying, my new career.

My Dad has his work at Foggit Jones. My Mum runs our household and I have my job. My sister Clare is spending most of her time in hospital; my sister Jean is still with Aunty Emma; my sister Doss is going to school and my brother Ted is just about ready to start school. While our family life has settled into a fairly smooth pattern, there are aspects of it that don't sit too well with my Mum and Dad.

There is the forced separation from my sisters, Clare and Jean, and the difficulty of doing something about it. While my situation appears to be taken care of, there is the schooling prospects for Doss and Ted. Whilst the local schools are good enough, there is the fact that our neighbourhood has a doubtful reputation and this may rub off onto us as well. Then there is the flood problem. We have been lucky once, but Maitland is notorious for the severity of its floods, and next time— well anything may happen.

My Mum and Dad decide that we will move. And it will be closer to where we regard as our origins. It will be closer to work for me, but my Dad will now be the one to do most of the travelling.

My Dad seeks and finds a house he can buy, by paying it off as rent, in Waratah. It is not very grand and is tucked away in a lane, running between a main roadway and a minor street. Therefore, it is cheap and the owner is prepared to do business without a solicitor, thereby saving legal costs. While it is a little run down, it is reasonable and my Dad can do it up as he finds time.

We settle in at Waratah. The family unit is now my Dad, my Mum, my sisters Clare and Dos, my brother Ted and me. Clare has finally been discharged from hospital, her left arm is in a permanently stiff, bent position at the elbow joint. All she had to do is try and catch up with two years lost schooling, and cope with an awkward disability. My sister Jean is still staying with Aunty Emma.

Jean's situation has changed a little in that, now, Aunty Emma has a son of her own. He has been born during the time in which Jean's short stay of a few weeks has stretched into years. My Mum thinks that now we are settled at Waratah, and that Aunty Emma has a son of her own, she will be agreeable to Jean coming back home. But still not so—Jean has become so used to the setup that she now regards Aunty Emma as her Mum, and us kids as her cousins—and, with Aunty Emma's attitude strongly fostering these ideas.

At Waratah, I am able to ride backwards and forwards to work on the firm's push bike. As I use the bike daily in my duties, this is an acceptable extension. Clare, Doss and Ted go to school and my Dad travels to and from his work at Maitland by train.

We have been sailing along for about a year and have completely settled in at Waratah. Then another crisis comes—another Maitland flood. This time it is a big one and the rail line has been cut across the Hexham flats. With no trains running, my Dad cannot get to work.

His work as a digester man, though lowly in status, is vital in clearing up the waste products, and thus keeping the factory operating. If he isn't there, somebody else will have to do the job. In these hard times, it could mean that my Dad will lose his job. Somehow, someway, he has to get to Maitland.

My Dad and Mum discuss the pros and cons. My Dad decides to set off on his push bike to try and get through. If he can, he will stay in Maitland and board there, until the trains started running again. The factory site is on high ground, so will not be affected. If he cannot get through, then he will be back home again. We will just have to wait and see if he comes back or not.

Away he goes and he does not return. It is a couple of days before word finally comes through. Then it is second hand, relayed to my Mum by a phone call to a friend. He is safe in Maitland, boarding with a work mate. To get through the flood, he had walked along the rail line, sometimes with water up to his chest, carrying his bike on his shoulder. Across the Hexham flats, that would be something like one and a half miles. From then on, he was mostly able to ride his bike.

We have worried about him, but at least to me, I have complete faith in my Dad's ability to get through. In about a fortnight, the flood subsides and my Dad comes home again.

The Depression is really biting by now and Foggit Jones is really struggling to keep going. For weeks, the rumours persist that the factory is no longer viable, and will have to close down. Finally, the decision is taken and my Dad is again out of work. A return to the Caledonia set up is no longer viable, as I am working here, and there are prospects for the girls to get at least something better in this area. My Dad will just have to register for the dole.

With the entire country in the Depression, many families have to rely for their very existence on the dole. Payment is to be assessed according to family size, with the man of the family having to work the equivalent number of hours on council community works before receiving that payment, usually two to two and a half days per week.

With some work time, and a lot of free time, it is a soul deadening experience. For a young bloke, once deemed as being too old to be part of a family, he is required to travel from town to town to pick up his dole payment, in order to prove that he is actively looking for work—no travel, no payment.

Much effort is put into trying to find ways of supplementing the food supply— grow your own or work for payment in food. Those people in work think themselves to be a privileged class. But, they are ever mindful of the fact that there are plenty of others out there, willing and hoping to replace them, and for less money. Quite a lot of blue collar type workers are signing for award wages, but gladly accepting less than they sign for, again conscious of those others, hoping to replace them.

With my Dad's efforts and some handouts and, with me and my job, my Mum seems always able to keep us fed. While our living style is certainly not very grand, it still is adequate and satisfying to us. On the strength of my Maitland lolly boy experience, I am able to get to work at the local picture theatre doing the same work. That also helps a little. Then another disaster.

One day there is a knock at our front door. A man standing there asks for the owner of the house. My Mum brings my Dad to meet him. The man asks, "Are you the owner of this house?"

My Dad says, "Yes."

The man replies, "No, you're not—I am. I've just bought this house from the previous owner, and you are now tenants renting from me. You can continue to live here, but must pay your rent to me—not him."

This drastic news stuns both my Mum and Dad. It takes days to sink in. My Dad, an honourable man himself, just cannot believe that anybody can pull such a stunt. That hard-earned rent is no longer buying us a home. It is dead money going down the drain, and there is nothing we can do about it.

Meantime, my firm is going through a phase of change. A family business, whose members have passed on or reached retirement, employ a Manager to run the show. Their accountants, whose offices are nearby, keep a regular check on things. Now the Manager receives an offer of a job elsewhere, that is more to his liking. So, he takes it, leaving our office staff of just two ladies and me. And one of the ladies is my cousin Dulcie. The ladies will have to run the office and I will have to handle the customs work, until a replacement Manager is hired.

While I am completely familiar with the general shipping entries, the customs duty payable on shipping imports is a tricky business, needing a lot of expertise—the kind of expertise that made our former manager's services so valuable. There is a customs duty manual, setting out the percentage of duty payable on a vast array of imports. But it is cumbersome and takes time to wade through. Moreover, Regulations require that this type of work can only be handled by an adult… (21 years). As I am still not quite 17, without special dispensation, that will rule me out. For the moment, we will have to use the services of a specialist firm of customs agents.

Another crisis hits our family early one afternoon when our Aunty Emma arrives with my sister Jean and a small suitcase. There is something in her manner that tells my Mum that this is not just an ordinary visit. And so, it proves. Our Aunty Emma, a person being used to having her own way, says simply, "I've brought your daughter back."

My Mum has aimed and asked for this for a long time. The years had passed and she had quietly resigned to having lost Jean. Now, out of the blue, this is a bombshell. Aunty Emma offers no explanation for her change of mind. In due course, she ends her visit, leaving behind a totally confused and bewildered Jean, who had just reached her teens.

The transition for Jean is severe. She has moved from a fairly affluent household to a drastically poor one. Where before, she has enjoyed her own room and quality clothing, she now has to share with her two sisters, possibly reluctant to allow her to fit in.

Meanwhile, I have my own particular worries. The viability of the firm begins to look doubtful, as a replacement manager cannot be found. Then, out of the blue, the firm is sold. I expect we can carry on somehow, because the customs import work is only a small part of the business, which has a large storage warehouse at Islington, a busy fleet of delivery vehicles, both motorised and horse-drawn, and their drivers. It seems that we still have a thriving business. Maybe the new lot will let me carry on as before.

For a while this happens. The new owners are a family firm of coal traders. The older of two sons has been selling and delivering bags of coal to local households—a dirty, unpleasant job. He dons a suit and occupies the Manager's Office, taking over the running of the firm. He begins accompanying me on my daily rounds of the nearby wharves and Customs House. As my boss, he has me explain the everyday routines and duties.

After several weeks, and having got the hang of things, he tells me that the woman running the coal company office is leaving, because she was about to have a baby. He proposes to move me out there in place of her. His brother is the Manager and I will run the office. This is ominous. Close to 17, I am due for a pay rise. If the usual happens, I will be sacked on my birthday and replaced by a fifteen-year-old. A replacement will be easier to hire for a coal company office than to a customs and shipping office.

The move is made. The lady stays on for a couple of weeks, showing me the simple routine required. Meanwhile, another bloke has been hired for the town office to do the work that I had done. He is a former schoolmate of mine. He offers to stand down when he finds that he has taken my job. I tell him to forget it. If it isn't him, it will be somebody else.

I am in the coal office for a couple of months before being sacked. I come home and tell my Mum and Dad. My Mum goes to see the Town Office Manager to try and get him to rehire me. He has contracted to rebuild a local road. He offers me a job as a tally clerk on this job, which will run for several months, then that will be it. In due course, the road job finishes. Then, I am truly out of work. The family income is now minus what I had been able to contribute.

I am too old to be considered a dependant of my Dad, thereby enabling him to claim extra dole payments. He has a perfect right to kick me out and tell me to make my own way, on the track with the other young blokes. He doesn't, and I don't think it even occurs to him. Certainly, it doesn't to me, and I don't offer to move on. For this is my family; we've always been together, and this is how it is going to continue.

In the meantime, Jean has somehow made a reasonable adjustment after being dumped by Aunty Emma. My brother Ted is progressing well at school and showing great promise at schoolboy rugby league. This pleases my Dad greatly to have his son perform well at one of his great sporting loves, and at which he, himself, had excelled.

With the work situation, as bad as it is, most people turn to sport as a relief to their woes. Those unable to participate physically, become avid and fanatical spectators. The two great sports are cricket in the summer, and rugby league in the winter. This fanaticism spreads even to regular Interschool competition and also Interstate contests. It is at Primary School level that my brother Ted is showing such promise. Ultimately, he is selected to represent the entire District at Interstate level.

To say that my Dad is pleased and proud would be an understatement. But, as is his way, he keeps it mostly to himself. Then, once again, heartbreaking disaster as each lad is responsible for his own expenses. That means he will have to pay for his full uniform of boots, shorts, socks, and jersey, plus travel expenses. Our household just doesn't have that kind of money, nor the means to be able to raise it. Almost certainly, my brother Ted will have to rule himself out.

For a week or so, there is much heartache and wrestling with the problem, hoping that somehow a solution could be found. Then, when all hope has just about faded, a local official, alerted to the problem, goes to the town's Royal Hotel and calls for a whip around the bar. Sufficient funds are raised and my brother Ted is able to fulfil his dream. For my Dad, there is an immense sense of gratitude, tempered by the humiliation on having to rely on others to fulfil what is his parental duties. Again, he keeps his feelings to himself.

We continued on with our battling lifestyle, conscious of the general hardships around us. We are happy enough in our own ability to combine as a family and to get by.

There is a Militia Unit of Field Engineers with Headquarters at a Drill Hall, just around the corner from where we live. Recruits are paid for their attendance for a couple of hours training per week. My Dad sees this as a source of a little income, so he joins. A uniform is also supplied by the government. Just after my Dad joins, I too, join the Militia.

At long last, I finally land a job as a milk delivery roundsman for the Hughes family, the local dairy farmers. It doesn't pay much, but it does provide free milk. I am assistant to their son, Jack. We start at 1.00 am and finish at 7.30 am for the morning round; then again at 1.00 pm, finishing at 3.30 pm for the afternoon round. The morning round is for a full seven days per week. The afternoon round is for five days, with a small one hour run on Saturdays, but none on Sundays.

The demands on me physically in my new job are tough for a month or so. It demands that I cover quite a few miles per day at a trot. Gradually, I become accustomed to the exercise and grow to love the open-air life. The Hughes and I get on famously and became almost like family. While the job itself can be done by any reasonably fit young bloke, and there are plenty out there perhaps better equipped than me, it has been me whom they had chosen and I am deeply grateful—both for my Mum and Dad's sake and for my own self-esteem. After a couple of years with the Hughes family, I attain my majority (21 years of age) and receive a pay rise to twenty-five shillings per week.

Meantime, my Dad has found that a different Militia Unit holds their training nights on a different night to the Engineers Unit near us. My Dad figures out that if he joins this one too, he will have the advantage of two separate rates of pay. Provided he fulfils his commitments in both places, he sees no reason why this cannot be done. So, he joins the other Unit as well.

Obviously, this double enlistment business cannot last. Sooner or later, my Dad will need to be in two separate places at the same time, such as the annual fortnight's camp where all Units work together. But my Dad manages to carry it off for about eighteen months before being found out. The Regular Army blokes in charge of the two Units, sort out the problem quietly, with no penalty to my Dad. He does have to resign his enlistments though, which was no big deal, for he is over-aged for enlistment and had lied about his birth date in the first place.

I continue with my milko's job and my Militia training. It seems certain that a new War is soon to start. I resolve, that when it does, I will enlist. While I know that my family probably will be against this, I also know that, as I am of age, I do not need parental permission.

The probability of War, ever so slowly, begins to have an effect on the industrial situation. Production of steel begins to climb marginally and that means more jobs. It also means a fierce competition for those jobs. Male workers, both young and mature, will have to get themselves registered at personnel offices and be available when needed. This raises a problem for me.

I love my milko job, although the pay is lousy. It has a carefree air about it that suits me fine. While I know that the Hughes family has grown to depend on me, I also know that, sooner or later, I will have to move on. But, it will not be until I can secure a proper paying job. Such a job will require me to start immediately, without being able to give notice. I just cannot do that to the Hughes family. Also, there is my contribution to our family finances to consider. I decide on a rather drastic solution.

I will give a fortnight's notice to the Hughes family, while accepting another milko job that is on offer. I will then quit the new employer, without notice, when real job prospects are right. While I am upset at quitting the Hughes family, I temper my feelings by remembering that I will be quitting anyhow, once War breaks out.

I also get some solace from focusing on a good turn that I have been able to do for the Hughes family. I rescue one of their good milking cows from a situation that almost certainly will have ended in its death. Each day, after the midday milking, the cows are grazed on the nearby Braye

Park hillside. This area is pitted with broken ground and holes. A cow, jostled by another of the herd, falls in and becomes wedged in one of these holes. With no means of being released from the trap, I erect a tripod and winching gear over the hole, using equipment and skills I have acquired from the Field Engineers. The result—no harm to the cow, and everybody is pleased.

My new job has an attraction that pleases me. Instead of a horse and cart to work from, this one is from a motor bike outfit and I get to be its driver. The distraction though, is that I am required to collect the accounts.

I work at my new job for about eighteen months. It becomes abundantly clear that, if I am to land a proper job, I will have to present myself at a time that clashes with my milko duties. While prospects for work in the industries is improving slightly, and I know it will be a gamble, I will have to take a chance. So, I quit and concentrate full time on looking for work. It is a slow process and many tricks are tried to gain preference over all the other blokes. My Dad is trying too, but, as an older person, he finds that the younger men are gaining selection. Gradually, I begin to get some casual work, then finally a full-time job.

Our family prospects begin to look up. Although my Dad is still engaged in his dole work, I have a proper paying job; my sister Clare is working in an office job at the Co-op Store; my sisters Jean and Doss are working as housemaids at the Mater Hospital; and now my brother Ted has secured an apprenticeship at the B.H.P. My Mum, of course, runs our home.

# CHAPTER 3
# The Militia Engineers

IN 1933, AT THE AGE of 19, it is obvious to me that another World War is in the making. I decide that I will be going to this War. My next decision has to be, in which of the services. While realising the dangers of being killed or maimed, I am also determined to come back in one piece, so my choice has to be the one that offers the least risk.

I think about the Navy but say no. When they sustain a hit, it is a big one with not much chance of survival. Well what about the Army? There are lots of drills and route marches with heavy packs and my physical size to consider. At five foot six, maybe a half an inch more, and a weight of nine stones seven, I do not fancy my chances much at hand to hand combat. That leaves the Air Force. They hop into their planes, fly off into action, where it is skill against skill, then return to the fairly comfortable quarters. That's what I will do, I will become an airman.

To become a pilot requires academic qualifications that I do not have. And the selection process makes it very tough for those who do. The easiest way to get around and all that stuff is to transfer in from some other service. That might be easy in wartime, but, for the moment, it seems that my best bet will be to join the Militia, get as much training as I can, then be ready to transfer on the outbreak of war.

Just around the corner from where I live in the Newcastle suburb of Waratah, is a Drill Hall and the Headquarters of the First Field Company of Engineers. It is convenient and handy, so I join. I find it to be a Specialist Unit that teaches skills, other than just weapons and their uses. This, surely, will make me more acceptable when I make my transfer.

With the depression biting hard at that time, the Drill Hall, and what it has to offer, becomes something of Mecca. I had started work as a custom shipping clerk at 14 years of age, and then made redundant at 17 after the sale of the company I worked for. At 19, I have been unemployed for two years. Now I have a sense of having somewhere to belong. I absolutely love the training and can hardly wait for each Tuesday evening and Parade night to come around. Fortnightly camps, each year, are something else again. Every special course that comes up, I take it. Then there is the pay and a uniform. So now, I have a little extra clothing and a pair of boots to wear.

As Newcastle is an industrial town, the Officers and NCOs, given their civilian background, are proficient and know their stuff. The Drill Hall is staffed by two regular Army men, one is a big likeable Englishman and the other, Bill Monkhouse, a quintessential and competent Australian. The Englishman obliges by teaching all things military, such as semaphore with flags. After a couple of years, he is replaced by Vic Marinier, another good bloke. Training consists of knots and lashings, erection of the various military type structures, and trestle bridge building. And of course, there is weapons training and drill movements.

Also in attendance on Tuesday evenings is a specialist transport training group, which retires to their own small area at the eastern end of the Drill Hall. Horse-drawn transport is still the order of the day, but it is not practical to have horses on hand for only a few hours each week. Therefore, they are only on hand for annual camps of two weeks' duration. Warrant officer, Jack Griffiths, ably assisted by Sgt Peter Lyall, handles this part of the training. There is always a steady stream of men waiting to join this section, with it being seen as a bit of a rort, just sitting around yarning. But the Unit is top-quality in every way.

NCOs handle most of the hands-on training, with Officers acting as overseers. Lectures of a military aspect, such as gas warfare, are always conducted by an Officer. Annual camps of a fortnight's duration, usually at Liverpool, give us a chance to hone our skills and to synchronise with other military formations. The nearby Georges River allows us ample scope for bridge building. Liverpool is the New South Wales State's main training area, where selected personnel are trained for promotion to NCO ranks.

One of the annual camps at Liverpool results in an escapade that is retold many times in our Unit. A small group, after a hard day in the field, decide that, being so close to the big city, they just have to see the bright lights. They hightail it to the rail station and go into Sydney. First stop is to the fairground at Luna Park, but that soon pales. After a few drinks, they realise they are just about out of money. They have just enough to get back to camp, but it is still only about 6 o'clock. Their group's banker, Sid Welbourn, points out that they just have time to place a bet on the last race with the pub's S.P. Bookie. They decide to give it a go. Sid puts all their money on a horse ridden by a jockey known by the name of Last Race Cooky, who has the habit of scoring in the last race of a meeting. It wins, and the bookie pays out at good odds. Now, the next stop will be at King's Cross to see what it has to offer.

Still early in the night, nothing much is happening. The group straggles on, somewhat weary. One of them lags a little behind the others and is accosted by a Lady of the Night. This chap is a very thin man of whom it has been said, that if he turns side on, he will cast no shadow. Naturally, he has been nicknamed Don Athaldo, the bodybuilding muscleman of the era. The Lady says, "Hello soldier, are you looking for a naughty girl?"

Don replies, "Yes, can you tell me where I'll find one?" The Lady takes a long hard look at Don, then turns on her heels, no longer interested in these country hicks.

Their energy, now mostly gone, they head for the rail station and make it back to camp. This story is retold many times, with much play on Don's masterly handling of a Lady of the Night.

With our Drill Hall becoming more and more the focal point of our activities, permission is sought and granted of its use for social evenings. An orchestra is hired and dances are conducted for a small entry fee. Girlfriends, wives and unattached daughters become supporters. The timber floor is worked over to give it a good dance surface. Several successful unions emanate from this intermixing. One of the town's biggest social events of the year is the Military Ball, held at the town's premier dancehall, the Palais. Always four or five of the debs' partners are supplied by our Unit.

Naturally, we have our own song we refer to as The Engineer Song. Its words are:

> Australian Engineers are we,
> Australian Engineers are we,
> We will always stick to shovel and pick,
> Australian Engineers,
> From heart to heart and hand to hand
> The R.A.E. will always stand,
> To make and break is the motto that we take
> Australian Engineers.

The personnel of our Unit are many and varied, too numerous to mention. But I remember Jack Griffiths whose family owns a condiment date factory in Islington. For bivouacs and camps, Jack always comes up with a goodly supply of pickles and sauces to augment Army rations. The two inseparables, 'Pee Wee' White and Reg Jobber are the two best cooks in the Army. They can perform miracles with anything. The Sappers, and general personnel, all work well together in a harmonious team. One, Sid Welbourn, becomes my brother-in-law when he marries my sister, Jean.

As we move closer to World War II, training begins to intensify a little. Always, however, there is the bugbear of a shortage of money. One camp is a case in point. We move from our base at Waratah to Nelsons Bay under canvas. The exercise is for a seaborne landing at Fingal Bay. Some Infantry formations are to take the role of enemy troops for this landing. We, the engineers, are to set up a water supply, and act as defenders. We set up camp at the fringe of housing and where virgin bushland begins. In order to get through to Fingal Bay a local truck, a huge man-diesel, and its driver, has been hired. We get our gear through, build an elevated platform, and by using a waterproof tarpaulin as a holding tank, we fill it with clean water. Several trips in the truck are needed to achieve this. We have hardly finished when word comes through, that the Infantry landing has been cancelled, through lack of funds.

We now have to dismantle it, and take the gear back. A couple of Officers, not wishing to see all that work go for nothing, decide to take a bath. They climb into our tank, after stripping off, and start splashing around. Somehow the ropes holding the tarpaulin in place become loose, the sides collapse and the water rushes out. There they are, all soaped up and stranded!

My last annual camp, before the War, at Liverpool is in the midst of a very hot summer. Live firing ignites some of the scrub. Hot westerlies fan the flames into a full-scale bushfire. We have just got it under control and we collapse in some shade for a breather. Suddenly a loud call from my Section Officer, John Mather, rings out for 'Corporal Dawson'. He has a habit of calling for me when he wants something done. I hoist my weary frame off the ground, and, grumbling to myself, I make my way to where he is standing some distance away. I cannot see anything that still needs to be done. Upon reaching him he says, "Here, get this into you." It is a cold bottle of beer. He has two cases for his men. We are miles from anywhere. How he has managed to conjure them up, I will never know. But I am eternally grateful to him. Any further calls for "Corporal Dawson", thereafter, are answered very smartly.

From 1938 onward, there is an influx of new recruits, as we are obviously heading towards war. The Great Depression is still rolling along, only slightly dented by the approaching events. Hardships are endured and the toughness of everyday life have created a strong, self-reliant type… and our bunch of men is typically these kinds of people. When War is declared in 1939, I have served six years, and risen to the rank of Corporal. As for the Air Force, I never give it a second thought. I am hooked on being a Sapper.

Quite a few of our lot go to the Hamilton Depot when enlistment opens. A group of about twenty of us are intent on joining up. By now, I am fairly cluey in the ways of the army. I have always had trouble remembering numbers, so I stand back while observing procedures. I insinuate myself into the line-up in order to be allocated one that I can remember. It is N X 777. All I have to do now is square myself away with my family. My Mum, Dad, sisters and brother have not been told of my intention. My mum insists that I say goodbye to her Mum, my Grandmother. She cries and I cannot placate her. She says that she will never see me again. She is right. I never will.

We are called to go into camp at Ingleburn and, on the day, we wear our Militia uniforms to denote we are Engineers. Upon arrival, we ask for the Engineers lines and move in— our bloc of about twenty includes one Officer, Jim Hay, a couple of NCOs and the rest are plain Sappers. Everything is chaotic, so we pick an empty hut and move in. We are accepted without question. With the exception of Jim, we know that we will all have to start from scratch. The Commanding Officer, from a Sydney-based Field Engineer Unit, has already been appointed. Naturally, in selecting the hierarchy to run the Unit, he sticks with the people he knows. And, in the main, they are good. The remainder of the personnel, that dribble in over the next few days, are a wide and varied lot. Our new Unit is the Second First Field Company, Royal Engineers, Sixth Division.

Government regulations have been enacted, debarring certain occupations from enlistment. As most of us Newcastle blokes are working in the steel industry, myself included, in reality we are ineligible to enlist. We, therefore, have to lie in such a way that will qualify us as a Specialist Unit and also for enlistment, so I declare my occupation to be a rigger.

The C.O. is busy setting up the mechanics and organisation of the Unit, so the early initial training is very rudimentary, with a few early NCO appointments running things. We men get to know each other as mates, and it becomes very evident, that most of us have stretched the truth quite a bit in stating at our occupations. We are all a bunch of liars. This must have filtered through to the C.O. for he calls in a couple of Technical College Inspectors to check our claims.

As a rigger, all they can test me on is knots. I can tell, instantly, that I know more than they do. I show them a couple of military hitches that they do not know. They pass me, and, to the best of my knowledge, not one person is culled as a result of their testing.

For everybody now, it is the time to break loose, to free ourselves of the shackles. Now is the chance to try something different. And this we do. There is much jockeying to fit into the various job categories as take our fancy. Some can pull it off and some cannot. In our Newcastle group, we have two of the best cooks in the peacetime Militia, in Pee Wee White and Reg Jobber. This time they want nothing to do with cooking, and we respect their wishes and keep their secret. This, despite the crew, who elected themselves, being the lousiest managers of food ever brought together.

Like the others, I take the opportunity to focus on the direction I want my military career to take. With my clerical background, I could easily land a cushy job in the Headquarters Section. Paper handling and records are very vital at this time, and they are having trouble filling such positions. The perks are no marching or drilling, and quarters a bit better than the average. But I decide not to. I want to have a hand in whatever is being done, and I want to be part of that doing. As for promotion, I am quite content to sail along, and to wait and see what happens. I know my training gives me an edge, if I want to do something about it.

The rest of the Country is trying to come to terms with being at War, while we are going through the motions. The local press label us 'Five Bob a Day Murderers', which does not go down too well with us. It is even more resented, when we later find out, that the First World war men got six bob a day. They get us on the cheap. We counter with the song, that we bellow out each and every occasion:

> We're a bunch of Blamey's Bastards,
> The Second A.I.F. are we
> Bread and jam for breakfast
> Greasy stew for tea
> Sweating on Parade at this damn drilling
> While the mug Militia's in the bar swilling
> We do all the work, we do all the killing,
> Scum, scum, Militia can kiss me bum
> We're woolly and wild, we're nobody's child,
> We're fighting fools,
> We and the Canteen are dry as hell
> The Second A.I.F. are we.

With only a few weeks together, our group is still only a bunch of nondescript soldiers and definitely not a Unit. At Christmas 1939, we are given leave and word has filtered through that this will be final leave pre-embarkation. We are happy for we are impatient to be off. We head back to our Waratah Drill Hall for one more time. Each of us is presented with a leather wallet with an inscribed silver shield in the corner, by the Sergeant's Mess.

We have been cautioned that everything is to be hush hush. We are to make our move in the middle of the night. We will quietly slip out of the Country without anybody knowing; our people will only know, after we are safely at sea.

We march as quietly as we can to the rail siding in the Liverpool area. There is much activity with engines puffing, carriages being shunted and railway men moving about. With all our gear and the number of Units, it looks as if the entire Division is moving out. It is daylight before the carriages begin to move.

Immediately, after clearing the loading area, the embankments on both sides of the track are lined with wildly cheering people. Obviously, our secret move is known to at least some people. The further we go, the thicker the people. And it continues right through to the wharf area, where big crowds are kept back by barriers and the police. So much for secrecy, the whole world knows.

We sail in the First Convoy on January 10, 1940. Our ship is the Orcades, a classy Cruise Liner, hastily converted to transport troops. Officially, she is known as the U2. Our Unit has scored former First Class accommodation, so it seems our C.O. has some clout. My cabin is a former two berth, converted to four by mounting extra bunks on top of the existing ones. My cabin mates are Harry Bassford, Joe 'Blackadder' and Dick Fennel. Dick is a Newcastle bloke and 'Joey' is a Geordie, from the north of England, who migrated to Australia. We embark our ship which moves out into the harbour while the rest of the loading on other ships is being completed. For the rest of the day, small craft circle us continuously with people calling out, trying to make that one last contact. We sail next morning for an unknown destination.

There is much speculation as to our destination. With both hot and cold weather gear in our kits, we have no idea. The ship turns south after clearing the Heads. That means we will be turning into Bass Strait, crossing the Bight and heading off from West Australia. Still no clue. Maybe we will pick up other ships from Victoria, South and West Australia. There are plenty of bets to be had. My own view is that it will be in the Middle East. I figure that the Top Brass, having gained experience in the First World War, will be of the opinion that this is where the Australian role will be. Particularly, with the New Zealanders coming into it, the ANZAC concept will be irresistible.

Now that we are at sea, there is time to turn our sloppy formation into a Unit. A Field Engineer Company has a Headquarters and three Work Sections. Each Work Section has three Sub Sections. Each Sub Section is seen to be capable of being detached, and sent away on the job, and work independently from the Unit. The C.O., his 2.I.C., the Sergeant Major and various clerks make up Headquarters Section. Each Work Section has a Lieutenant in charge with a Sergeant as his deputy; each Sub Section has a Sergeant or Corporal in charge, with a Lance Corporal as his deputy. With around 10 men to a Sub Section that leaves eight Sappers. There are Specialist classifications for Sappers, which give them higher rates of pay.

Now the fun begins… Headquarters picks itself, but the Sections and Sub Sections are a different matter. Trying to stick with mates, or taking advantage of pay rates, sees much manoeuvring. New appointees seek to handpick their teams. First No.1 Section and its three Sub Sections, A., B., and C., are filled. Then No.2 Section and its three. Halfway through No.3 Section, there are not many of us left. My Newcastle mates have been scattered throughout the Company. Still only acquaintances, none of us know much about each other. I look at who is left over with much interest. There is a fellow standing some distance from me and, as our eyes meet, we seem to strike some sort of rapport. His name is 'Taffy' Towers, who will become a good mate. We go into the same Sub Section, Sub Section C of Section No. 3. We are the bottom of the heap. I become Lance Corporal and deputy to a Corporal Chandler.

A German-armed raider is supposed to be out there lying in wait for any unwary shipping. Despite this, the trip is mostly uneventful. There are exceptions. Our Unit puts on a food strike that becomes a bit of folklore. We line up for tea one night to be greeted by cheese and macaroni pie. Healthy, hungry young men with appetites sharpened by the sea air, view this apparition with disgust. There are loud grumbles with most of the troops deciding grudgingly to make the best of a bad job. But not the 2/1 Field Engineers. We sit and refuse to budge until given some decent tucker. It takes two hours, but eventually some bully beef, pickles and bread and butter are broken out from stores, and we declare ourselves satisfied.

Later the ship's Army Commander, Colonel England, calls all personnel to the ship's public address system. He warns the few nurses aboard to stay away as what he has to say is not for female ears. He starts by saying, "You men, because you have put on uniform, think you are soldiers. Let me tell you that you are not one little hair on the real soldier's arsehole. Many times, in the future, you will wish you had that same cheese pie." He continues on for some 15 minutes. When he finishes, we consider ourselves well and truly ticked off. And we respect him for it. Later, after a successful breaching of the wire at Bardia, he passes through our crews at the Tank Trap. He recognises us from our Colour Patches and cannot resist calling out, "How would that cheese pie go now?" And we cannot resist calling back, "Bloody good Sir."

Another incident is when an infantry man goes overboard in some heavy weather. It is about mid-morning, with swells of about 30 feet. His small face and head can be seen as he shoots astern at tremendous speed. About half a dozen lifebuoys are thrown to him, and the ship heaves to. There is instant reaction from the Navy. Battleship Ramillies appears briefly on the horizon; destroyers dash about and semaphores flash, while we are ordered to get underway again. The Navy with their lower profile are finding it much harder going in this bad weather than we are. Somehow, he is picked up and returned to us at our next port of call, Colombo.

After Colombo, there is Aden, the Red Sea, and the Suez Canal. There are some who think we might still continue on to England, but not too many now. Early one morning we disembark at El Kantara bound for Palestine. The Ship's Captain is on hand and he shakes hands with every last one of us. He wishes each man well and hopes he will be back in the next few months to take us all back home.

# Chapter 4

# Training and Leave – Palestine

Our trip from El Kantara to our camp is by rail in cattle trucks much like box cars. For just about all of us, this is our first experience of a foreign country and we crowd the open doorways taking it all in with much interest. The fact that it is mainly flat open country, sparsely populated and with not a lot to see, doesn't matter much. It is a welcome change to the open sea. Then again this is Palestine, the Holy Land, and surely that means something.

The Unit is housed under canvas at a place called Quastina. We are able to accommodate a full Sub Section to a tent and thereby get to know each other very well. We are very busy settling in and this keeps us fully occupied for a few days. There is the fascination of observing a few Arabs and their ways and colourful dress. Then with whetted appetites to see more, we seek to venture a bit further afield. But this is forbidden.

We are vaguely aware that there have been some Arab-Jewish skirmishes going on before we left home. Now that we are in Palestine we find that the troubles are quite serious, and that there is a strong British military presence to keep both sides apart. British Army Units are stationed permanently in the Country and it is subject to Military rule. And we are required to abide by that rule.

A strong guard system has to be mounted and care has to be taken of one's rifle and ammunition against theft. But, being hundreds of miles away from any actual War Zone, it makes such precautions fretful and irksome, and quite foreign to our former rather easy-going approach.

For a week or two now, the Arabs and Jews seem to have lost interest in each other. The men take this as a sign that a bit too much has been made of the situation in order to keep us under control. They begin to get restless. Somebody says, "Why haven't they sent us to Egypt instead of Palestine?" After all, our mob spent plenty of time there in the First War. Somebody else mentions they have heard that the Egyptians have refused to accept us, but they will take the Kiwis, who are now already there. It seems that we are not very welcome in this part of the world, and that leave will be a bit hard to come by. General Wavell, the British Army's Commander in Chief in the Middle East, tells us bluntly that the Egyptians will not have us in their country because of the shenanigans of our forefathers in the First World War.

One or two hard heads decide to do something about it, and slip away from camp. We are many miles from Tel Aviv, the capital and nearest city. But somehow, they manage to wrangle a lift and come back with glowing accounts of the delights and amenities to be had there. Contrary to our belief, there is little evidence of British Army controls, and that the British soldiers are able to visit there when they are on leave.

This is downright discriminatory in our eyes and that makes us fret even more. Schemes to beat the system just have to be worked out. Reg Jobber comes up with probably the best of them. Reg, now Sergeant, has his men smartly turned out and he forms them up as a squad in the Company lines. He informs them that they are the town Picquet and will be going into Tel Aviv. The fact that they have no transport, as well as no authority, will have to be overcome once they clear the Company area. He says that he will pick out a meeting spot once they get there and also a rendezvous time; then it will be every man for himself. He warns them to stay out of trouble, or the whole scheme will be blown.

With so much activity going on, this is just another squad going somewhere to do something. They march smartly through the camp and down to the main road. They give a smart 'eyes right' to the Guard on duty and wheel along the road in the direction they want to go. Once clear of the camp area, they wait for the first transport to come along. It is a truck and Reg stands in the middle of the road with his hand up in the stop signal. The truck contains two Pommy Officers and Reg just says, "Sir, we're the town Picquet; we have to get to Tel Aviv, and we have no transport. Could you give us a lift?"

"Certainly Sergeant," says the Officer. "Get your men aboard and stand to one side while they all clamber in the back." Well, they have a good night and reckon that if they ever get caught, it will be definitely worth it.

These clandestine bouts of shooting through are triggered by several things, as well as the nature of the men themselves. Back home, our safe arrival in Palestine has been well publicised in the press as a triumph against that armed Raider lurking somewhere in our way. So, while Britain needs the publicity, and everybody knows, then why can't we have a bit of leave?

Here we are now, working fairly hard during the day and needing to relax a little in our down time. Our still, very raw new camp isn't able to provide us with any amenities, so leave seems the only alternative. Then there is the food problem. Our lousy cooks, if anything, are getting worse. The chance to visit a proper eating house is beginning to become a necessity.

My Sub Section crew are coming through as a pretty special lot. There is Taffy, Lenny Cope, Harry Bassford, Joe 'Blackadder', 'Wog' Ewings, 'Moby' Dick, Bill Parkes, Frankie Potter and our assigned driver, Tess Tickle. A few men from other Sub Sections manage to spend time with us as well, such as Jock Deirden, Ayrt Onyons and Dave Bennett. Most have seen moderate to very hard times and are solid and dependable. They knit together almost like family. A group, such as this, practically makes their own rules. When they make up their collective minds to do something, it usually is done.

For myself, I know I am accepted, for they call me 'Arty'. If not, I probably may have been given some savagely biting nickname to live with. And I feel privileged. Anyway, by now, Taffy has appointed himself as my minder. And, once more, as he has fought for the Australian Welter title under the name of Billy Richards, I am not likely to have too much trouble.

With a permanent military presence in the Country, there is also a permanent instruction facility. Sergeant Instructor is sent to us on an assignment. He is English, fits in well, and he is a thoroughly likeable bloke. He knows his stuff too, except that it is trench systems and things like that, mainly World War I ideas. We all feel there is little place for those this time, and that we are being mucked about.

While our NCOs have the right credentials, their Field Engineering know-how is practically nil. They just have to blunder along as best they can, trying at the same time, to train their men who instantly can see this lack of knowledge. And immediately, the men will question any doubtful instruction. Taffy sometimes will urge me to tell them how to do it. I try to keep him quiet by telling him that it is not my place to tell a superior ranked man how to do his job. But Taffy will say loudly, "Go on, tell 'em. Just let 'em start something. I'm right behind you." This, of course, can only serve to get me off side, if I speak up or not. It is in this atmosphere that we get word that we have to prepare for a very important visitor. It is the C.R.E., Commander of the Royal Engineers, the top ranked Pommy Engineering Officer, and we will be required to put on a display for him.

It is to be a full Section job, and each Section is left free to decide what its display will be. There is a bit of jealous rivalry among the Section Lieutenants at this time, with each trying to achieve a bit of ascendancy in the promotion order. With a crisis on hand, our Lieutenant calls us altogether and asks for any ideas.

I have taken part in quite a few of these types of the exercises back in the Militia and I know exactly what is expected… some spars lashed together with ropes and some block and tackle lifting gear. There are several standard formations and they demonstrate the skills of a Field Engineer Unit. I hang back and wait for somebody to speak up. I don't want to poke my bib in. Also, with Taffy's frequent urgings, I feel I am already too far offside.

Nobody is forthcoming, so I finally speak up and say, "Sir, we have the gear. Why not put up a standing Derrick? He asks me if I think I can do it, and I confirm. He says, "You better show us how." I tell them what gear I need, and the Section Sergeant organises the gangs to fetch it. I have chosen a Standing Derrick as our exercise because, once the gear is laid out, the work is fairly simple. It's just a matter of brawn and the job looks pretty impressive.

A Standing Derrick is a long pole, similar to a telegraph pole, with a block and tackle lifting gear fixed near its top. Holdfasts are used to raise it into position and to secure it when erect. None of the blokes have seen anything like this before and I have to show them what I want. I do the layout and they do the work. And they work with the will. When everything else is ready, there comes the crucial part of lifting this huge pole into the erect position. I give the order, the men begin to haul, and up she goes without a hitch. Our Lieutenant is impressed, but still not too sure. He asks me if I think I can do it again tomorrow. I assure him, "Yes, no problem," and we lower the pole back down on the ground.

When the C.R.E. arrives next day, the holdfasts are fixed and everything is laid out. All we have to do is raise the pole and secure it in position. The Lieutenant orders the Sergeant to commence and he orders me to raise the Derrick. I give the men the order to haul. I have instructed them that a steady pull is all that is needed, but in their enthusiasm, they go to it with will and the lifting tackle whips about alarmingly. It is dangerous for anybody to get near it until the pole is erect. Once again it is in position and everybody is pleased. The C.R.E. makes suitable comments to the Officers grouped about him, then away he goes. While our mob think that it is a great show, I know he must have seen dozens of these displays, and will not have been fooled in the least. Our inexperienced first time, just has to be plain to see.

With leave, still unavailable, we grumble a fair bit, but just have to put up with what is available in camp. Since we have arrived, there has not been action on the part of the Arabs or Jews at all. Whether our presence has made the difference, it is hard to tell. One thing our leave position does achieve however, is a big improvement in our camp canteen services. There is a good supply of toilet requirements, razorblades etc., and we begin to get supplies of Aussie beer.

On pay nights now, my crew will just look at each other and somebody will say, "Let's have a session." We will move off in a body to the canteen and each will buy a bottle of beer. We will move some tables and chairs together and just sit and drink and talk. It is always good natured and there is never ever any incident.

On occasions, one or two of the mates from other Sections or Sub Sections will join us. Taffy tries to instruct me in the art, but I'm a poor drinker. Anyway, they are far too seasoned for me, and all I can manage to do is to get sick. When this happens, he will support me, get me to my bunk and safely tuck me in, then rejoin the others.

After a while, they figure out that the constant walking back and forth to get another bottle is only wasting serious drinking time. From then on, they each buy a case, set it down beside their chair and just reach down for a refill when needed. On occasions, they are known to back up for another case.

I, of course, have backed out by now, and the pace begins to catch up with the boys, too. One or two begin to get cunning and hide a bottle or two away in the tent for the next morning hangover. After a quick reviver, they are bright and happy and ready to go again.

After one session, they hide away a few too many bottles. I warn them to take it easy or they will be well under again. I leave them and go about my business of washing, eating and getting ready for Parade. They are a happy lot when I leave them and, when I miss sighting them in my comings and goings, I begin to worry. Where are they? In the army, drink is a self-inflicted wound and you just have to front up to Parade, no matter what. But they don't show up, and have shot through.

They claim that they have enjoyed their day in Tel Aviv and have had something decent to eat. Of course, they have to be charged for being Absent Without Leave. AWOL and the punishment meted out is several days detention. This raises a problem… we have no Detention Centre built yet. Orders are given to set one up, and who better to build it than the prisoners themselves.

As the new Detention Centre is for themselves, they set to it with a will. A tent is erected and surrounded by barbed wire. They are directed to collect their gear and move it. A Sentry is posted, and toilet and washing functions have to be performed under escort.

They immediately can see the advantages in the situation, and exploit it to the full. Their food is brought to them and, when they feel like a stroll, they just call out for an Escort. They just sit on their tails while everybody else toils away at training. And, in the afternoon twilight, their friends will wander over for a yarn while leaning on the barbed wire. Anything they need, tobacco, papers, matches or even a beer, is on hand. A few strands of wire are no deterrent. When they return from detention, they reckon it is the best holiday they have had so far, and is well worth it.

My brush with authority is a little bit different. As Lance Corporal, I'm detailed to duty as Acting Corporal of the Guard. In taking over the guard duties from a previous Guard, we are handed over a detainee who has just been brought in. He is 'Albo' Bowers. His crime is being AWOL, and causing a disturbance.

Albo is a well-liked and amiable bloke, and a bit on the short side. Taffy knows him well from back home, and tells me that our Albo has won the Australian Welter Title. He has taught some boxing skills to a few of our would-be fighters, aboard ship on our way over. On this occasion, he has tangled with a Pommy Regular in a bar at Tel Aviv, been picked up by Military Police and brought back to camp under escort. He has to remain under guard until tried and sentenced. The rumour is that the Pom is big, just over 6 feet tall, and Albo chopped him to pieces. In any case, there isn't a mark on Albo. With no other facilities available, Albo, for the moment, just occupies a corner of the Guard Tent.

About 8.30 PM, just after the new Guard has settled in, we are alerted to a disturbance well back in the camp lines. It is alleged that somebody with a few drinks aboard has gone berserk, and he is waving a bayonet around. It appears to be somebody from a different Unit.

In the tent at this time is the Corporal drafted to Acting Sergeant of the Guard, three or four of the men, Albo and myself. The Corporal is on duty, while I am not. Those men off-duty have taken the opportunity to do their own chores, visit the canteen or whatever. The Corporal decides to take available men with him to attend to the trouble, leaving just Albo and myself in the tent. I, of course, will be on duty until the Corporal returns.

They have been gone about a quarter of an hour when I spot the Orderly Officer heading straight for the Guard Tent. One of the most important permanent guard posts is the Guard Tent itself. A Guard has to be on duty there at all times. I cannot mount the position myself and be in charge inside the tent at the same time. Half aloud I say, "Oh hell! What's going to happen now?"

Albo sizes up the situation as quick as a flash. He says, "Leave it to me." He quickly grabs a rifle, affixes a bayonet, and rushes into the Guard position. He manages to get there while the Officer is still a little way from the tent. He stands at ease and comes smartly to attention for the Officer's entry. The Officer looks hard at him, but I cannot tell if it is because of the person, or of the little flurry to get into position at his approach.

The Officer asks me if everything is in order and I tell him that the Sergeant of the Guard and a small party is attending to a disturbance in the Camp Lines. Other than that, all is well. He lingers for a few minutes, reminding me of some special instructions regarding some of the Posts, and then leaves. Once again Albo comes smartly to attention.

With the Officer gone, we can relax. Albo comes back into the tent, unhooks the bayonet and places it and the rifle back from where he has grabbed them. I thank him, saying that he has saved us from a fair bit of strife. With this small crisis is over, a few of the off-duty men begin to drift back. Now Albo is faced with a crisis of his own. He says, "Look mate, I'm bustin' for a piss." I turn to detail one of the newly returned men to go with him as escort. Albo says, "Look, you're shorthanded and I don't need anybody to come with me. I'll just go for a piss and I'll be right back."

I look at him. He has helped me out when he needn't have. He now seems sincere in his promise to come straight back, although I'm prepared to concede that he might dally just a little bit. What can I do? I owe him, so I say, "Okay."

The off-duty men are now mostly back at the Guard Tent where they will sleep for the night, ready to be awakened to stand their shift. The Corporal's companions return to tell me that in subduing the man with the bayonet, the Corporal has received a bit of a nick. He is having it attended to at the RAP, the Regimental Aid Post. If it is serious, I might have to be on duty all night myself. The man concerned is indeed from another Unit. He is allowed to be carted away by his mates, and there the matter is dropped. There is no need to cause inter-Unit animosity by an official complaint.

I am well into my duties, when the Duty Officer can again be seen heading for the Guard Tent. Obviously, he is steaming. What has gone wrong now? The regular Guard is at his post and I'm satisfied that I have everything under control. I just wait. He ignores the Sentry's salute, storms up to me and demands, "Where's the Prisoner Bowers?"

Oh hell! I have completely forgotten about Albo. It dawns on me that quite a fair bit of time has elapsed since I gave him permission to go to the toilet, even allowing for a bit of visiting. I say, "He wanted to go to the latrine Sir, so I sent him."

"Under escort?" demands the officer.

I stutter a bit… "Yes Sir," I lie.

"Then, he must've given his Escort the slip, for he's down on the main road trying to hitch a lift into Tel Aviv."

The Officer takes a couple of men and hurries off to round Albo up and bring him back. Being the NCO on duty, I have to stay at the Guard Tent. As the Officer is leaving, he says, "If the silly bugger has to shoot through, why does he have to do it on the main road right outside the C.O.'s tent?" Why indeed?

It is a very chastened Albo who is returned to the Guard Tent. Later, when I get the opportunity to talk to him, I ask, "What has happened?" He says he got talking to a couple of blokes at the latrine. Apparently, they were about to shoot through and they say to Albo, "Why don't you be in it, too?" On the spur of the moment he says, "Okay," and away he goes.

I say, "But Albo, you promised. You gave me your word."

Albo hangs his head and says, "Yeah, I know. I'm sorry."

The Officer demands to know who the Escort has been. All I can say is that there were several men in the tent at the time, and I have turned to one of them, saying, "You go with him. I'm not sure who I have detailed?"

This is not good enough. The C.O. demands to know the full details. He is incensed at the blatant act of trying to go AWOL, right outside his quarters. Then too, Albo has to be dealt with on the other charges involving the assault claims from the British Authorities. The Officer tells me I had better get my facts right for the full court hearing to be held in the morning by the C.O. himself.

The hearing is very proper and very regimental. I am marched in and asked to give my version of what has happened. All I can do is stick to my story of the night before. I add that I have tried to locate the Escort, whom I had detailed, but am unable to find him. Therefore, I have to take the full responsibility for this failure of duty myself. Failure to recognise is still reasonable plea in our Unit, as Officers, NCOs and men are still trying to get to know each other.

I am found guilty of allowing a prisoner to escape. The penalty is a severe reprimand. And that is how it is entered in my pay book. I am pleased with one thing though... I am not fined. I have allotted the greater part of my pay to my mother back home, and just cannot afford the loss of money.

Albo belongs to another Section, and I do not see him very often. When I do, I always look at him reprovingly and shake my head. I will just say, "Albo, you let me down." Always he is very contrite and says, "I'm sorry, I'm sorry. I didn't mean it." He owes me one and we both know it. For myself, I am content to leave it that way.

Our training is continuing, but it seems mostly Infantry stuff. We do erect a couple of concrete pill boxes and then blow them up. We aren't getting much in the way of Field Engineering though. There is no sign of Arab–Jewish troubles and we wonder if there has been anything much to worry about in the first place. Our cooks seem to be finding more ways to render our food inedible that can be thought possible, and still there is no sign of leave. Then at last, there's a breakthrough.

There is a small Jewish village, called Rehovat, just a few miles along the road to Tel Aviv. We will be permitted to go there on leave. It is a small village, serving a small community and in no way geared to cope with a sudden influx of troops. We find that in half an hour we have covered just about everything. It is just a poor substitute for the real thing, and we quickly lose interest in going there.

Then comes an intriguing request that spreads through the Unit like wildfire. One of our men has made an official application for permission to marry. The man concerned has organised a job for himself as a Cook's helper, but spends the greater part of his time running a fairly big two-up game. When working for the Cooks, he usually cleans the pots and pans and attends to the fires. He mostly appears untidy and smeared a bit from his chores. He is a tall, dark and lean bloke, who, when dressed up, can look quite presentable. But this happens so seldom, that we just cannot figure out how he can be seen as instantly desirable and marriageable material.

The lady concerned has to present herself at our Orderly Room in connection with the application and, she is a beauty. Officers and Staff fall over themselves in a bid to make her welcome. Her prospective husband is summoned from his duties in his usual untidy state, while details are taken down. There is no kissing or holding hands, just two acquaintances standing side-by-side. As soon as the details are completed, he goes straight back to his duties without even a backward glance. The lady dallies awhile, being fawned over by the Orderly Officer, before driving off in a private car.

She is a mature good-looking woman in her late twenties or early thirties. She is a Jewess from Rehovat. She is smartly dressed and totally feminine. She returns quite a few times in connection with the application, remains about half an hour, and attracts much attention from the staff. Her man will be summoned, and on occasions during a two-up game, is known to say, "Bugger her. She can wait," until he is summoned again. He, in the meantime, makes no special effort to get to Rehovat, beyond what seems to be necessary meetings at a café table with her and a couple of other civilians.

There has to be an angle and, for a while, we can't figure it out. Then the penny drops. Hitler has been deporting quite a lot of German Jews on a couple of ships to any country which will take them. Nobody will, citing in the main, that they have no papers. Germany won't issue any, so they are forced to roam the world. Finally, in desperation, they run their ships ashore on the beach at Tel Aviv and scatter into the countryside. Without proper papers, they are stranded here. Some are reputed to have quite large fortunes and investments in different countries, but only available to them if they can get there and establish their identities. This proposed union has to be a legal angle to overcome this problem.

The marriage does go through, but, to the best of my knowledge, is the only one of its kind. The perks, if any, for our bloke, are completely invisible and unknown.

At long last, proper leave does come through and the monotony of isolated military life is lightened by the touches of civilian living. We are able to go on one-day leave to Tel Aviv and then Jerusalem. The modern everyday life of a large city like Tel Aviv makes us feel civilised again. There are cafes to eat and drink in and the beach is a good one. In Jerusalem, there is the fascination of a very ancient and Biblical history. Those almost forgotten Sunday School stories now come to life at the scenes of some of those happenings. There is the Via Dolorosa, the Way of the Cross, along which Jesus was driven before his crucifixion. There are the marked stopping places. There is the Dome of the Rock, an Islamic

Temple covering the stone upon which Abraham is said to have prepared to sacrifice his son to God.

We are duly impressed and, in due course, when we are permitted to take extended leave periods of up to a week, we explore more and more. Life seems to become almost normal. It is a welcome break to the rigours of camp life. But it only brings trouble to Joey 'Blackadder', by now christened 'Jock' because of his accent. He is a Geordie, not really a Scotsman, but that is close enough for our mob. While most of us take time out to find something to eat and see the sights, he settles into a corner of a grog shop and just drinks. While our lot always sticks together, pretty much as a group, somehow Jock always seems to get left behind when the last bus leaves for the trip back to camp.

Zealous Pommy Red Caps, (Military Police), are quite happy to pick up an Aussie, even though he is causing no trouble, charging him for overstaying his leave and putting him in their cells for the night. The next morning our Unit will be notified, a charge laid and a cranky C.O. will give him a stiff term in the Glass House, (Military Prison). This is a tough Military Prison, run for and by the Pommy Military authorities. We have none of our own, so Jock will be returned to their tender care for his punishment.

Upon his return for the first time, we gather anxiously around, quizzing him about his ordeal. We find him quite happy and relaxed. His punishment has consisted mainly of intensive and expensive, Parade Ground drill. He is happy with that as long as there are no fines. Fines will limit his beer money.

Several other Aussies are there in the same boat, and they are formed into a squad and taken over by a tough Sergeant Instructor. He barks his orders and they pretend to try, but are pretty sloppy. "Alright,' he says, "You'll just have to stay there until you get it right."

For the squad, this is no big deal. While they are there, so also is the Sergeant. Anyway, a fair amount of what they are doing, they will have been doing anyway, back at camp. If Jock feels like a spell, he will ask the Sergeant, respectfully of course, to explain or demonstrate a tricky manoeuvre. And usually, the Sergeant will oblige. Well, they are only a bunch of dumb Colonials, aren't they? And they need to be shown.

Thereafter, we worry no more about the Glass House. Others in our crew even give it a try themselves. The only upset people are the C.O. and a few with ambitions to higher rank, at being forced to be involved with our lots day-to-day training. Our squad does tend to be judged as being very low on the totem pole.

One incident makes our C.O. even more cranky than usual. Jock has just returned from his latest Glass House stint to find that the C.O. of a nearby Unit has requested the loan of him for his soccer team.

Our C.O. has wanted to make things really tough for Jock, this time. But grudgingly, he feels he has to oblige his good friend, the other C.O. Our Unit is too small to carry a team of our own. So, our C.O. succumbs to some heavy persuasion by the other bloke. Sporting competitions are very popular between Units.

Jock is an extraordinarily gifted soccer player and his prowess has somehow become known to a few. He does not race madly about the field. He just positions himself, and has an uncanny knack of having the play come to him. He then bangs in the goals with monotonous regularity. So, this is Jock, a gifted man, whose choice is anything but that.

He is medium tall, strong and sturdy, and slightly hump-backed— a condition acquired by years of pick and shovel work. His movements are precise and measured, without expending any surplus energy. He has a quizzical half-smile, half-grin, and his eyes will twinkle in silent amusement, while he stands there in resigned acceptance of our badgering. His voice and brogue is soft and musical, and, what he has to say is short and always to the point.

He has taught me how to shovel. To the average person, most labouring work requires all brawn and no brains. Actually, there are techniques involved that require the insight of an expert. Shovelling is an example. Try it sometime… attack a heap of lumps of coal, or clods of earth, and see how soon you will want to cry quits. Be amazed at how small an amount, you come up with, on your shovel, no matter how much vigour you apply. Jock shows me how.

I quiz him as to how he has acquired his knowhow. He had been working full time in a clay pit for a brick-making company, digging out the clay by hand. In those days, a manufacturer would not use expensive machinery for the job. Manual labour is dirt cheap and there is an endless supply. Is it tough? You 'betcha'. In summer, you absolutely fry in the confines of the open, airless pit, and in winter, you freeze. For Jock, joining up is a welcome change.

I ask him, "How come you have ended up in Australia?" After some probing, he tells me.

He is a married man with four kids. He has lived in a small town in the north of England, where he had a regular job and a fairly happy life. He comes home from work, one day, to find that his wife and kids have disappeared. Weeks of enquiries and searching follows, and he finds that she has fled to Scotland, with another man. A frantic Jock sets out to find them.

Some months later, he tracks them down to where they have lived, only to find that they have migrated to Australia. Still searching, Jock decides to do the same. Two years after landing, he finds where they are living and turns up on her doorstep, while the bloke is at work. He begs her to come back to him, but she refuses, telling him that it is all over, and she never wants to see him again.

Jock leaves, gets a job in the brick pit, boards in a single room in a pub, and spends his spare time drinking. A couple of years later, as the Depression begins to bite, she turns up on his doorstep, baby in her arms. The bloke has cleared off and left her, and she pleads for Jock to take her back. He says, "No!" He has had enough. She goes away, and he settles down to his one room, his clay pit and his drinking. He never sees her again. Then comes the War.

The British Military Establishment has a permanent School of Instruction set up at a place called Sarafand. Our Australian Establishment takes advantage of this by sending along regular intakes for training. As a Lance Corporal, I am selected for one and sent to a Junior Leaders course for a fortnight.

The place itself is very big, with a huge Barracks Square in its centre. The Pommy way is an eye-opener. The Training and Instructors are the very best. However, the training is all Infantry stuff, with no Field Engineering. All it does for me is bugger up my voice. We are called upon to shout orders at each other across the Barracks Square. Instead of a budding Sergeant Major, my voice cracks and I have to drop the volume.

We ask the instructors about what has happened during the troubles between the Jews and the Arabs. They tell us of what has happened at Sarafand.

They say the Arabs have a penchant for creeping in and snatching a Sentry. They will take him away and hand him over to their women. These playful ladies will disembowel him, and fill his stomach with stones. They will then cut off his genitals, stuff them in his mouth, and sew his lips together. They will hand his body back to their men, who will return and leave it in the centre of the Barracks Square... all this, without being seen. The impact on morale can only be imagined.

Back in camp, the cooking situation is becoming a crisis. When the Orderly Officer attends the Men's Mess at meal times and asks if there are any complaints, he is inundated. He will write them down, take them back to the Head Cook, who will then promise to do something about it. No improvement is forthcoming, and the whole process will be repeated.

The Military Establishment is fairly tolerant with regard to the cooking setup. As long as the men are fed properly, they are allowed to run things pretty well their own way, with a minimum of interference. The Officers' and the Sergeants' Messes are fed and looked after, separately, from the Men's. While they might know that the men are having problems, they are not likely to know how serious the problems are.

The Head Cook has gathered a large staff around him. Once they see he hasn't much of an idea of how to tackle the job, they lose interest themselves. They are only putting in a half-hearted effort, and often go missing when they are most urgently needed. With mostly wood fires used for cooking, the pots, pans and utensils quickly go dirty. Attempts to clean them are not very sincere, and the assisting Helpers become as crummy as them. Realising they are stuck in a rut of their own choosing and, being unable to see a way out, they seek to forget their problems by getting stuck into the grog. On occasions, because of camp duties, one or two men have to attend the Cook House for a late meal. They can see some of the Staff cooking up some pretty tasty snacks for themselves, stuff that is unavailable to them.

Finally, the men feel they can stand it no longer, and a delegation goes to the C.O. and asks him to get rid of the Cooks. To do so, he would have to have suitable replacements. By now, the fact that my Newcastle mates,

Pee Wee White and Reg Jobber, are good cooks, is a fairly open secret. They are the logical ones to take over.

There are a few snags however. In the first place, will they be agreeable? Then there is the matter of rank. Reg is now a Sergeant while Pee Wee is a Sapper. As Cooks, Pee Wee has always being in charge. Of course, they can always be ordered to take over, but it would be much better if they can be persuaded. You just don't replace one reluctant crew with another.

They are both pretty happy with their present status and agree to take on the position, if the vexed problem of rank can be solved. Pee Wee solves that by saying, "Let the ranks stand." He is a single man, while Reg is married with children. Reg allots most of his pay home and needs the money. They will work together as they always have, except in this case, Reg carries the rank and Pee Wee doesn't.

The change is immediate. The helpers now have direction on what their duties are and somebody to see that they are carried out. Once their job is done, their free time is their own. There is now no risk of having to fill in for somebody else who hasn't shown up. And the men insist that the food has improved one hundred percent.

The displaced Cooks try for a period to fit into the Unit, but with little success. The rest of the men feel that they have been used by these blokes in a pretty cynical way, and just aren't prepared to accept them in any other capacity. They apply for, and are granted, transfers to other Units.

The Italians have been making some warlike noises for a while, but we aren't taking too much notice. Here in Palestine we consider that we are too far from their sphere to have anything at all to worry about. Then, out of the blue, comes an air raid on Haifa.

Haifa, one of the three main cities in Palestine, is many miles to our north and much too far to be considered as a leave venue. For the Italians to get there, from their bases, the planes would have to overfly areas they can much more easily attack, including ours. While reports claim that there has been no damage, the Ities have demonstrated that they can easily raid us, if and when they want to.

Our blokes quickly dismiss the happening as of no consequence. They figure that, if the Ities are serious, they will mount more attacks. But, the days pass and none come, and we reckon that it is just a one-off thing. The top Brass however, take things more seriously. They eventually come up with the idea that, if the Ities want to immobilise us, they can easily do it with little risk to themselves by an airborne gas attack.

We think this is farcical, but the Brass persist and issue orders that every man has to have his gas mask with him at all times, with no exceptions and no excuses.

We all have been issued with gas masks, but, considering the antipathy to the use of gas on all sides, we regard them as a very unnecessary precaution. We therefore, use them as a receptacle for all manner of things. The haversack, along with its soft rubber facemask, is ideal for use as a pillow. But it comes at a cost by taking up space, and we have to find another storage for the odds and ends. And, to add insult to injury, we undergo the Gas Drill.

We hope it will be a five-minute wonder, but the Brass are serious and persist. While we think that it is sufficient to comply with the order on parades and work details, some men have been ticked off for not having gas masks with them at the showers and the latrines. Day after day, at least half a dozen men will be caught out, without their gear, in what seems to us as petty disciplinary orders.

While we are becoming more frustrated at official persistence in following the gas idea, they are becoming equally frustrated in our refusal to accept it as a serious possibility. Finally, it is announced that an Officer, designated as the Gas Officer, will call a Gas Alert sometime during the next week. The day and time will be known only to that Officer. Upon the call, a General Parade of the whole Unit will have five minutes to assemble on the Parade Ground. Anybody, no matter who, found without his Gas Mask will be put on a serious charge.

They mean business and we will just have to be careful. For a few days, nothing happens and we begin to relax a little. Maybe it is just an idle threat to get us onside. Then the alarm sounds and everybody rushes. The Gas Officer has chosen a time for the maximum amount of confusion. It is just before dark and after tea, when everybody is taking it easy. Men are at the Canteen, in the Wash House doing some laundry, or in the Recreation Hut writing a letter home. Officers are in their Mess having a few drinks.

Even with a few minutes of extra leeway, there is much trouble in getting the full parade assembled. It is evident too, that there is a fair catch of culprits without their masks. The C.O. at the head of the parade, and surrounded by his Officers, orders Section Leaders to take the names of the offenders. He then proceeds to give us a stern lecture on the perils of disobeying orders.

As he warms to his speech, it is obvious to the assembled men that he has been imbibing himself when the alarm sounded. He is well into his stride when there comes a stirring in the front row of the assembled men. One of them has taken two paces forward and stands rigidly to attention. This is the official procedure to be followed by a man wishing to speak, and, the Officer in Charge must give him that permission.

The C.O. carries on for a moment, before appearing to notice the man. The man is a noted hard-head in the Unit and just cannot be ignored. Besides, he is militarily correct in his demeanour.

The C.O. pauses and says, a little testily, "Yes Riley, what is it?"

"Please Sir," says Riley, "Can I ask you a question?"

The C.O. again says, "Yes. what is it?"

"Please Sir, are you immune to gas?" asks Riley.

It then becomes apparent to the whole Company that the C.O. himself is without his respirator.

There is a stunned silence for a few moments, then the C.O. turns on his heel, gives orders for the Parade to be dismissed, and stalks off with as much dignity as he can muster. Very few will have the guts to confront their C.O. publicly in such a manner. But Riley is one of those few. He does us a big favour too, for, somehow after that, all the gas nonsense just fades away.

Our Training has not yet taken in what is, more or less, an integral part of an Engineer's job, that of Bridging. The advancement in military techniques sees little need for the old type hand-built trestle bridges with poles and ropes. The new types consist of prefabricated sections that can be slotted together and rushed into position, wherever required. These sections theoretically, are held in reserve, then transported by truck when called for. Actually, at this stage of the War, such types of bridging are very hard to come by. But somehow, some have been found and we are to be given training in their use.

The usual natural barriers to be crossed are rivers. The only river in Palestine is the Jordan, of Biblical fame. It is too far north of our present camp, so for training purposes, the whole Unit has to move to a campsite near Haifa.

It is a welcome change of scenery and there are scarcely any other troops in the area, bar ourselves. It is a nice city and the locals are quite friendly. The bridging work is a pontoon folding boat assembly which I have seen and used on the Georges River back home. Most of the men have not seen it; but, we just muddle through, picking things up as we go along. While here, we get first-hand accounts of that sole Italian air raid. There is no damage and the locals are mystified at what all the fuss is about.

The bridging course finishes and we return to Quastina. Now our No. 3 Section is detached and sent into camp, on the coast, near Ashkelon. Our job is to set up a Rest and Recreation Centre there for the whole Division. We build a few huts and set up showers etc. and Taffy, our only plumber, rigs up the water supply.

There is a superb beach there and we make full use of it. We enjoy our stay immensely. Close by, there is evidence of a fortified camp, dating back to the Crusader times. There are marble columns, about one foot in diameter, set horizontally into the embankment. Ships, apparently, tied up to them, for there are deep grooves, worn into the marble, from the chafing of mooring ropes.

While here, Taffy is called away for a day to do a plumbing job at another worksite. He returns with the roll of sponge rubber to use as a mattress, and he tells tales of the wonderful amenities to be had there.

The place is the General Hospital, and they are building a race track. A race track! The mind boggles at the mere thought of such an amenity. "But that's nothing," says Taffy. "They have a gymnasium and facilities for all kinds of sports. It's a real Country Club there." As for the sponge rubber… it had covered the floor of the wrestling ring. It has been knocked off, cut up and distributed amongst the workers. As they come from far and wide, there is very little chance of the culprits ever being traced.

Next, we are called upon to set up a camp for some new arrivals from Australia. "Good God, have we been over here long enough for another contingent to catch us up?" We have the job completed before somebody thinks to ask, "What Unit is it?" And that is only on the day of their arrival. The answer is… "the Military Police."

That does it! Our driver, Tess, is an alcoholic. He is totally harmless and, when on leave, he concentrates on getting quietly drunk. On several occasions, he has been lumbered by the Military Police and reckons that they pick on him as an easy mark. He sees the opportunity to get his own back.

It is a terribly hot day with a nasty Khamsin, a desert wind, blowing. He throws three or four shovels of fine sand into the tray of his empty truck. He sets off and collects a load of them from the railhead. He drives them, round and round, on the roughest road he can find, while the back draft swirls the dust around inside the truck canopy. He bounces over the roughest potholes, claiming he backtracked over the best of them several times.

The sorry, bedraggled mob, that falls out over the tailboard of the truck, has to be pitied. While we are in cool shirts, they are in heavy winter khaki in midsummer. The fine sand has impregnated their clothes and kit, and become ingrained in their skin and hair. An unrepentant Tess refuses to lower the tailboard to make things easier for them. When at last they speak, they ask if conditions are often as bad as this. Cheerfully, we tell them that this is a good day.

Tess is an easy-going, non-violent, and generally non-vindictive man. But this is one time he happily proclaims that he has got his own back.

Now comes word of another move. This one is supposed to be a secret, but the rumour is that we are bound for Egypt. Each Sub Section has its own truck by now, and we are becoming an expert at breaking camp. While the stand-to is in the middle of the night, Moby Dick reckons that we will not move before 8 o'clock. He refuses to leave his bed before its time to go. We let him have his head and just drop the tent around him. In half an hour, we are packed and ready, and then comes the long wait.

Moby is right. We don't move until 8 o'clock and we heave him and his bed onto the top of the load, the last aboard. We move off in convoy, bound for Egypt.

# Chapter 5
# Training and Leave – Egypt

In terms of training, we know we have a lot to learn. As far as Palestine was concerned, we feel that that was the theory part of our training, and we have gone about as far as we can go.

Now is the time to get on with the practical part, and we just can't wait to get into Egypt. To us, Palestine had become a bit of a backwater. This move is in the right direction, giving us a feeling of being welcome as part of the team. After all, the Italians seem to be stirring up a bit of excitement.

While our essential equipment is a bit slow getting to us, at least we now have most of our transport. Each Sub Section has its own truck to carry its complement and work gear. Now we move out in a truck convoy bound for El Kantara and the Suez Canal.

We cross into Egypt and to a nearby rail station. We are to travel to our campsite, outside of Cairo, by train. On the station, we are entertained by the famous gulli-gulli men – travelling conjurers and magicians who make coins and small chicks appear and disappear at will. They are damn good and we are fascinated. We reward them a few coins for their tricks.

We arrive at our camp which is ready and waiting for us. We are instantly conscious of the difference to Palestine. Now we are in the true desert area. Close to the Nile River everything appears lush and fertile with many trees growing, as well as the crops. Outside of that narrow band nothing grows and it becomes instant desert. We are located in the desert fringe.

The local population too, is now different. They are all Arab and lots of them. Apart from the standard flowing robes, there's a strong sprinkling of Western dress. Those in the Western dress generally are the more affluent class. We now have to adjust to a slightly different people, other than what we thought would be the same.

Leave is available from the outset and we make good use of it. We see the famous sights of the Pyramids and the Sphinx, including the burial chamber inside the Pyramid. The hawkers, the camel rides, photos and postcards— we sample them all. We begin to get to know the little cafes which abound.

Egypt has long been a popular and well sought after destination for tourists from all over the world. Alexandria in the north and Cairo, the capital, are as sophisticated and modern as any city anywhere.

With modern hotels, bars, cinemas etc., there is a dedication to leisure that suits us fine. With Cairo being a prominent world commercial centre, all tastes are catered for. We have none of the eating adjustments that we had to endure in Palestine.

With the strong military presence here, all sorts of entertainment have been organized, especially for the troops. Almost nightly there are big tombola and housie games with big cash prizes. There are regular dances at Ezbekieh Gardens, with good music and a sprinkling of young local girls as likely partners.

The Egyptian lasses are good looking and shapely, with light olive complexion that seems to enhance rather than detract from their beauty. They mostly wear modern dress and will hold their place in any city in the world.

A strong garrison of British Troops has long been stationed here, and the Kiwis have preceded us by at least six months. This means that our chances of meeting up with a 'nice' girl at the dances are not very good. Anyway, we have an aversion to organized entertainment, much preferring to go our own way. It is much more interesting finding your own way about.

The earthly Red Light district is always our first priority. Although confined to a particular area, there is an openness about it that we find intriguing. There is not the remotest suggestion of illegality; it is just like any other thriving business. The sights and sounds and the aggressive salesmanship of the girls, always draws us like a magnet. Close by are a number of bars where we can eat and drink. They have an atmosphere and price more suited to our liking, rather than the up-market more posh places, frequented by more affluent visitors.

Our first leave is spent getting to know the hang of the place. Once this has been accomplished, we just cannot wait for the next. However, unlike Palestine, where the troubles have caused leave to be spaced out a bit, our next leave comes a bit too soon. It finds Taffy, Lenny Cope and me, broke.

There are several days still to go until pay day, so we make frantic efforts to borrow from those still in funds. This is fruitless and we know that, if we stay in camp, we will be saddled with hated chores. We just have to get away somehow.

The classic way is to volunteer for the town Picquet, whose job is to round up the drunks and strays. They wear a bayonet in its scabbard as a symbol of their role, but it is unheard of for anybody to make use of it. The usual thing is that once you get to town, you take the thing off, stow it in a safe place, and make yourself scarce until it's time to return to camp. But, even this out is denied to us, for we have wasted so much time, trying to borrow money, that all Picquet positions have been filled.

No matter, we will proceed as if we are actually going on leave. Trucks take us to the rail station where we will go by train into Cairo. Once we get there, we will see if we can figure out something.

At the station, we mill around, but cannot come up with any ideas. We have to purchase a ticket to get us onto the platform. One of us might be able to evade the officials, but three of us is just out of the question. I rake through my pockets, once again, and come up with a few coins. I go to the ticket office and ask for three tickets to as far as they will take us. It is to one stop further down the line, but still far short of Cairo.

The journey is short enough to make us wonder if the ticket seller has put it over us. We alight at Maadi, a place we have never heard of. We feel it is just as well we have not gone on to Cairo; as Cairo, without any money, is just too bad a situation to think about. Here, we will spend a quiet few hours wandering about, then go back to camp the best way we can. Even if it means forcing our way onto a returning train.

We amble off the station to find we are in a very pleasant place indeed. We have stumbled onto an exclusive and very large Country Club with first class sporting facilities. There are beautifully kept and extensive playing fields for cricket and football, as well as other sports. It is the social centre for well-to-do foreigners living permanently in Egypt. With a large commercial and diplomatic community to cater for, the place is busy at all times. At the moment, there is a cricket match in progress between a Pommy regimental team and what appears to be a local club team. With nothing better to do, a least we can settle down and watch the game for a while.

We take up a position beside a small grandstand that is well patronised by Gentlemen and Ladies. Taking in the scenery, we loll back on a raised grassy bank. Apart from ourselves, there is not a uniform to be seen anywhere.

After about half an hour, the ever-restless Lenny gets up and decides to have a look around. He returns, a short while later, with two bottles of beer. "Here," he says, "Get that stuck into you," which we do with gusto.

The three of us soon polish them of, then lay back in a more amiable frame of mind. After a period of quiet, Lenny decides it is time to make another foray. He disappears and back he comes again with some more bottles. And so, it goes on.

When questioned as to where the goodies are coming from, he is rather cagey. As far as we can work out, he has come across some unattended supplies and just helps himself.

As the liquor begins to work, we cannot resist applauding— all in good taste of course, and in keeping with the tone of the place. With cries of, "Good shot Sir," and "Well played," some of the ladies sitting on an open-deck area just above our heads, chatting among themselves, look down in some amusement.

Smiling back, we doff our hats and gallantly bow. They laugh, ignore the game, spend their time waving and calling to us, as we do to them. They are young, probably married, French and very chic. There is no suggestion of any liaison; they are just happy to relieve their boredom with a little mild and provocative flirtation. We sense this and keep the game going. And so, it goes on, well into the afternoon.

French is one of the subjects I have studied back home in High School, not that many years ago. I rack my brain trying to remember something of what I have learned. But the odd word or two, that I can recall, is of no help here.

Finally, the cricket match comes to an end and the players stroll leisurely off the field. Spectators and other players walk out to meet them and there is a good deal of hand-shaking and milling around. Our French sirens, whose menfolk are probably part of the team, suddenly disappear. A Pommy Army truck draws up, obviously to transport the Regimental team back to their base.

Now we are at a loose end, stranded with a lot of time to put in. Our leave does not terminate until midnight. Our only hope is the Pommy truck, so we approach the driver and NCO in charge and ask for a lift. "Sure Aussie," the friendly Poms say, "We're going right into the city, and we'll drop you off anywhere you like."

After a short delay, while they change from whites into uniform, we are on our way. In due course, we pull up in the city centre. We climb down, thank our benefactors and wave them goodbye.

Now what to do! The whole night is before us and we don't have a brass razoo. We have to come up with some funds somehow. It is useless finding our mates and trying to borrow. We have already tried that and they are almost as skint as we are. Short of stealing, it looks like we have had it. Then Lenny says, "I know, I'll sell my teeth."

Taffy and I think he must be going bonkers, but he explains that the gold inlays in his teeth, which is a big feature of his smile, is on a dental plate. We will go down to the gold market, sell the gold, and have sufficient funds to enjoy ourselves. Lenny is very confident of getting a good price.

We set off for the gold traders, already imagining how we will spend the pound or thirty shillings, or maybe even two pounds, we feel certain we are going to get. We choose a small open-fronted establishment whose proprietor, a man in his mid-thirties, has a reputable and honest look. We explain our wants, hand over the plate, and then comes the snag.

He explains that in order to value the gold, he will have to weigh it. That means he will have to break up the plate to get it free. "Are we prepared to go to that extent?"

It is Lenny's decision to make and we leave it to him. He has thought that his only inconvenience will be a couple of gaps where the inlays are. He studies his plate for a long few seconds, then says impulsively, "Oh bugger it, go ahead!" and hands it over to the dealer.

As the dealer sets-to with his pliers, Lenny confides to us that, almost certainly, we will get our higher guess of about two pounds. And the reason? His plate has been made up for him by his cousin who is a dentist. As gold is not generally available back home, Lenny had provided two gold sovereigns for the job. Therefore, the value is there.

Once the gold is free, the dealer carefully weighs it on a small set of scales in front of us. Then he announces his price. He offers five shillings. Lenny is thunderstruck. Obviously, his cousin has cheated him badly with the inlays, and a furious Lenny promises to even the score when he gets home.

With the plate broken up and useless, we have no alternative but to proceed with the deal. Five bob, however, is too low a figure for our needs, so Lenny asks him to reweigh the gold and begins to haggle for a better price.

The final figure the dealer comes up with is seven shillings and sixpence, and he is most unhappy and only very grudgingly agrees to go that high. We take it and leave, not really knowing if we have been diddled or not. The man's whole demeanour, however, suggests he may kick himself for being so soft.

In these times and in this place, a little money goes a long way. But, seven and sixpence split three ways is just expecting too much. In no time at all, we are flat broke again. With four hours to fill in, we wander down to Ezbekieh Gardens to watch the dancing. The dance pavilion itself is in a beautiful setting beneath huge and graceful trees. With no rainfall to worry about, the building is virtually an open-air one. The night is soft and balmy and the music first class.

We edge our way just inside the entrance and stand there, taking in the scene. The large dance floor area is surrounded by small individual tables and chairs. They are dotted about so the patrons using them can have a reasonable amount of intimacy, in twos or fours.

The couples, using the tables, are exclusively British Regular soldiers and their girlfriends. There are no casuals looking for a partner. All the girls have been brought to the dance and will go home with their soldier boyfriends. Any attempt to infiltrate will be sternly rebuffed. A strong Military Police Post is just outside and doubtless will insist that good order be maintained. It is here that our town Picquet has to report and standby.

While most of our blokes on Picquet duty have scattered, the bloke on standby is Cocker, one of the best-liked blokes in the Unit. He apparently has volunteered, thereby freeing the others.

Cocker is chunky, medium tall, and sporting a walrus moustache. He has spent some time in the Islands, north of Australia. So, his mate, Burkey, in his dry humour, reckons that Cocker has been involved in Blackbirding. Cocker just grins and says nothing, and is immediately accepted as a worthy character.

We immediately spot each other and, after eyeing us over expertly, he walks up and says fiercely, "Now don't you bastards start anything." Then, turning to me, "I'm holding you responsible for keeping these two in line." While he is only a Sapper and I am a Lance Corporal, the issue of who ranks in authority, in this case, doesn't matter.

It has been a long day and, by this time, we are looking a bit tatty. His practiced eye can see this, and I suppose he has good reason to be a bit wary. We assure him there is nothing to worry about, and that we have everything under control.

There are three distinct levels of drinking capacity in us three. I am a light or poor drinker, Lenny is fair to middling, and Taffy a seasoned one. Cocker has chosen me as the responsible one, purely because I am the soberest.

The music starts once again and the couples arise from their tables and swing into dance. It is tranquil and soothing and, as they glide around the floor, Lenny decides to go for a walk. He is gone for about ten minutes and returns with two bottles of beer.

Once again, he tells us, "Get that into you." It has been some time now since our last drink, and we are dry and grateful. After downing the beer, we suddenly think to ask where it has come from. All Lenny can say is, "Just hang on for a bit and watch."

By this time, the music has stopped and the dancers have returned to their tables. As is usual for a dance social, the couples just sit conversing together, having a drink and a nibble at some nuts or confectionary, while waiting for the next dance to start. Liquor is very strictly controlled with bottled beer only available for purchase, as well as soft drinks, which is what most of the girls are drinking.

Once again, the music starts and the couples rise to their feet and move out onto the dancefloor. With the tables almost vacated, Lenny moves off. As we watch, he moves swiftly from table to table, pausing only long enough to scoop up any full bottles of beer. When he has enough for one each, he returns to where we are standing.

The whole process is done so smoothly that it is practically unnoticed by anybody but ourselves. To me, however, it is obvious that we will not be able to get away with this sort of stunt for long. The dancers, after finding their bottles gone, will be watching closely for how it is being stolen.

We drink the spoils, giving very little thought to possible consequences. The music again stops and the dancers return to their tables to chat, drink and nibble. There is no indication from any of them that anything is amiss. Embolden by his success, Lenny repeats his manoeuvre as soon as the dancers move out onto the floor. He is just as smooth this time as before, but with one little difference. He has been seen. Luckily, for us, it is by Crocker.

Crocker, very prudently, has decided to keep an eye on us just in case. He may have missed the previous attempts, but this time he doesn't. Cocker moves swiftly but carefully, so as not to attract any attention, and herds the three of us outside the entrance. He berates us soundly for our stupidity, pointing out that there will be a riot if the Poms wake up to what is happening. Lenny protests feebly that we can give it a few more goes before that happens. But Cocker is adamant, saying, "That's enough! You're not going back in there, so make yourselves scarce until train time."

There is a large open foyer at the entrance to the hall. With seating scattered about, a sprinkling of men are already gathering and just lolling at ease. Their money spent, they are waiting for transport to take them to the station for the ride back to camp. There is an equal number of Aussies and Kiwis, but no Poms. The Poms' Barracks are in a different direction.

We just stand there, trying to make up our mind as to our next move. The night is well on, and a return to base is reasonable, but our problem is that we have no money and no ticket. While pondering this, onto the scene staggers a very drunk Kiwi. He lurches from one group to another, mouthing off to everyone in turn in a most offensive manner. Swaying and scarcely able to stand, he pauses in front of each group, swearing belligerently as if daring them to start something. Because of his state, they just ignore him.

Frustrated, he tries a bit harder when moving from group to group. Still nobody takes notice. Then he spots us three in the centre of an open space and turns on us. Singling out Lenny, he lets him have a particularly vitriolic burst.

A surprised Lenny, momentarily taken aback, says, "What's the matter with you mate?" With everybody else ignoring the Kiwi, up till now, he has no option but to move on. Now that Lenny has spoken back, the Kiwi has somebody to focus all his attention on, and he isn't going to let Lenny go.

In an attempt to avoid a confrontation, Lenny sidesteps to the right and moves round to one side of Taffy and me. The Kiwi lurches around immediately, keeping him face to face. Lenny moves back in the opposite direction and the Kiwi turns again to face him.

Suddenly, Lenny's patience snaps. It has been a long day and some trying things have happened to him, culminating in the denial of a good source of free beer. Putting up his hands in a fighting stance, Lenny says, "Come on, you want to fight, eh? Let's see what you can do."

With fists at the ready, Lenny dances round and round the Kiwi. He, in turn, tries hard to rotate and keep Lenny in front of him. With his body turning and his feet finding it hard to follow, his alcoholic state is such that he can barely stop from falling over. Though serious, the antics of both of them look ridiculous.

I have just about decided that the episode has reached a stalemate, when Lenny let's go with a right-hander that catches the Kiwi on the chin. It is not a power blow, more of push than a punch—just a probing shot. The bewildered Kiwi immediately flops on his backside, just sitting there, and not really knowing what has happened.

Suddenly, there is a flurry of movement from the entrance of the Hall as Cocker charges straight up to us. He pushes, herds and shoves the three of us out onto the roadway. There is an M.P.'s truck parked at the kerb. He heaves and hoists us in the back while telling us, "That's the finish. I've had enough of you bastards. You're going back to camp."

Cocker's swift action is effective and timely. With both Kiwis and Aussies assembling for a trip back to camp after a day's leave, the potential for trouble is explosive, if either side thinks one of their own is being victimised.

Cocker climbs in the front with the driver, ordering him to head for the station, with us three still sprawled in the back. Upon arrival, he herds us along the platform to the exact position for boarding the train. It is then I tell him that we have no money and no tickets.

He says fiercely, "I ought to have bloody well known," then orders, "Stay here and don't move." He hurries over to the nearest ticket window, purchases three tickets, comes back and thrusts them into my hand. Half-ordering and half-pleading, he says, "You, I can trust. Don't let these other two bastards out of your sight. Get them back to camp and see that nothing further happens." I assure him that we are okay now and he can leave it to me.

He leaves us and, after a short wait, the train arrives, and we get on board. Lenny is bubbling and happy. He cannot shut up about his victory. Over and over again, he keeps repeating how he has gone about it—of how he has taken on that obnoxious Kiwi and taught him a lesson. The Kiwi had started it and Lenny had finished it.

We arrive at our home station, together with a lot more of our blokes. As we all climb aboard our Unit trucks for the trip back to camp, there is a great deal of laughing, chaffing and boasting. Lenny, of course, has to retell his mighty feat for the umpteenth time. We make it back with still about an hour to leave deadline. It has been one of the most memorable leaves we three have ever been on, and it has cost us practically nothing. As for Lenny, he finishes his day a truly happy man.

The episode with the French girls intrigues me and, in the next few days, I have a word with Rex Scanlon. Rex, a South Australian man, has some French ancestry and speaks the language. I explain how I have found it difficult to remember my schoolboy French. "Not to worry," says Rex, "There is only one phrase that you have to remember—voulez vous promenade avec moi?" Even I know the translation of it. Harmless enough, it just means, 'will you take a walk with me?' Why can that be significant? Rex explains that it is the classic and well-known approach of anyone requiring the services of a prostitute.

I protest that, although the ladies we were talking about were flirts, they were also decent. They probably would not know that. "Don't worry," says Rex with conviction. "They would know." So, my education has been advanced just a little bit further.

Now comes word of another move. It is to be a Unit only job. We are to set up a new camp outside Alexandria. This will be our first real job as an Engineer Unit, and we are happy to be able to function under our own steam.

The designated spot is bare and featureless desert. It is some distance from Alexandria, but fairly close to the fertile sections of the Nile with their network of irrigation canals. It is called Amariyeh.

Our first priority is to set up our own camp. Our tents go up fairly quickly as we are pretty experienced by now. One extra feature, we aren't too sure about, is the slit trenches. We are told they are necessary as protection against air raids on Alexandria.

They have to be joking, don't they? We are much too far away to be in any danger from bomb bursts. We've heard so little about air raids that we consider them to be only a remote possibility. The slit trenches, therefore, are only rudimentary and for appearance's sake.

We have finished our evening meal and are relaxing after a good day's work on our first evening. It is just softly dark on a moonless night with myriads of stars twinkling in the sky. Across the flat landscape the city lights of Alexandria are bright and glowing. At least, they don't seem to be worried about any air raids.

We have been yarning and sitting around for about an hour when suddenly the lights in Alexandria quickly begin to turn off. Whole sections of the city are black in seconds with others following like a wave. Then we catch the faint sound of a siren from afar. An air raid is actually about to occur.

We gather together outside to watch the action. This is our first experience of actual warfare. Then we catch the drone of highflying aircraft. They are very, very high and are passing over us on their way to Alex. They will have to pass over us again, to return to their bases.

Now searchlights stab out, and their beams begin to sweep back and forth. We speculate about the Ack-Ack crews being able to get a hit. It is said they are well-trained and sighted, with a Pommy Sergeant in charge, and Egyptian forces as Gunners. It is also said that the 'Gypos' are excellent ground soldiers, but not so good under fire.

Now the planes are over the target, and Ack-Ack bursts begin to appear in the sky. Bombs are dropping, but there is little evidence of any resultant blasts. The searchlights are having difficulty locking onto any planes, while the Ack-Ack guns appear to be also having difficulty reaching the extreme height of the planes.

Alexandria is a very important Mediterranean seaport and we know there will be a fair amount of the Med. Fleet in the Harbour. We also know that they will make it damn tough for any attackers. It seems that the Ities are coming in at a height that will protect them from receiving any casualties, while the Navy and Ack-Ack crews are preventing them from achieving any worthwhile hits. It is a bit of a Mexican standoff.

The resultant show is spectacular and entertaining from our point of view. Now the planes have finished their bombing run and turn for the run home. We can only tell this by the searchlight beams and Ack-Ack bursts for, although we can hear the engines, we can see no planes.

The planes are directly above us on their return when some hefty thumps on the ground close by, startle us. What the hell can that be? The Ities aren't bombing us, so it must be something else. Then we twig what is happening. The Gypo gunners are following the planes with their fire, but in their excitement, they are not setting their fuses. Instead of bursting in the air, the shells are arcing over, and landing in our vicinity. Suddenly, there is a mad scramble for those inadequate slit trenches. And, with the raid over, nobody wants to go to bed until the trenches are made long enough and deep enough.

Our main jobs, in the construction of this new camp, are the setting up of a large volume reservoir and a series of supply tanks, connected by a four-inch water main. The reservoir is to be sited in a large rocky outcrop, while the supply tanks, spaced at regular intervals, are to be built out of stone. The connecting pipeline is to be underground.

The actual labour force is largely Arab, while the planning and supervision is our responsibility. We are being called upon to set up a small township and, although being virtually inexperienced, we have to meet our problems and overcome them on the way. That we are able to do this is quite a triumph for the Unit, but, on the way, it results in some rather strange goings on. Each of our blokes is allocated a task for which he is responsible. Sometimes he might have one or two others to assist, but the actual work is done by 'his' gang of Arabs who are usually referred to as Wogs.

At first, their Wog teams are picked, willy-nilly, from the pool sent to us by the authorities. With this large pool, pushing and shoving to be chosen, we have to work out a more orderly way. We search for and find a likely man among them to be named a foreman. The man selected is physically big and speaks reasonably good English. He has an air that suggests he is good boss material. Although an Arab, he is not local and, therefore, likely to select without playing favourites. We give him favoured treatment, and in return we get orderly and good choice of men available.

Now that order has been achieved, each Wog crew becomes permanent. Every morning their Boss will arrive in a truck with the canvas stripped back, pick up his men and take them to their work site. They love to climb to the highest point of the pipe frame canopy, and it is some sight to see their truck bowling across the desert with their white robes flowing like sails in the breeze.

In very short time, a genuine affection grows between each boss and his crew, and they eagerly seek each other out at the start of every day. Where before the term Wog has been used in a more or less derogatory manner, it now becomes used less and less, and only with the real pride of My Wogs.

We begin to learn a few things from them too. There is almost a total lack of machinery in their work practices. While we are used to having to make do, we still don't have to resort to methods that have long become a way of life for them. In mixing concrete, we watch with interest as they prepare to do the job of preparing very large batches by hand. They work in a gang of six, one is the shovel hand, and five are the rope men. The shovel is a large round mouth with a short, thick and heavy handle. The blade is almost two feet across at the top and the same in length. The handle is a straight shaft without a hand grip. They tie a stout rope at the junction of the blade and handle, then take up their positions.

Not knowing what to expect, this all seems very primitive and not very productive to us, until they start working. Then we are astonished to witness what seems like a minor miracle.

They start a rhythmic chant; the shovel man digs the blade in vertically at the back of the heap and the rope men give a short hard pull. At the end of the pull, the shovel man digs the blade again into the back of the heap, and again the rope men pull. This to and fro movement is maintained effortlessly and quickly with the shovel man selecting the best spot to dig in his blade. No machine could have turned out a better mix or as quickly. And, as for the chant, they loved to sing it, and we loved to hear it.

Then there are the stone masons. Our elevated tanks are constructed of stone from a large heap being dumped on site. These men with a few hand tools, which they carry in a wicker or straw woven carryall, will work away selecting a chunk of stone and fitting it into place. As the tanks rise steadily in height, the symmetry of finish is something to see.

We have a few experienced bricklayers in the Unit and they are used as bosses of the stonemason gangs. But nobody knows anything about stonework, so the Arabs have to be left largely to their own devices. For the most part, our blokes have the good sense not to interfere. But, one bloke finds their ways a bit hard to take.

He is a young bloke, trained in the hard school back home, where the ability to lay a certain number of bricks per day has to be guaranteed, before he can be considered for a job. The necessarily slower selective process needed in stonemasonry is a bit hard for him to take. He feels his crew are deliberately delaying the job and putting it over him.

He cannot take it any longer when they regularly break off their work to pray. He tries ordering them back to work. However, when this isn't getting anywhere, he resorts to more drastic measures.

To pray they adopt a prone position, facing towards Mecca. Then they bow several times in succession, touching the ground in front of them with their foreheads, while reciting verses from the Koran. The act of bending over automatically raises their backsides on high. This is too tempting a target for our bloke. So, if he catches anybody at it, he just lays in with his big army boot.

While this does not endear him to his crew, it has the effect on cutting back the praying incidents remarkably. We are not aware that their beliefs require them to go through this ritual at least five times a day. And, when only a few appear to be ritualistic, it does seem as if they may be malingering. All in all, however, relations between the Gypos and us, are very harmonious. Each crew boss tries his best to give little extras to his men in any way they can. They in turn appreciate any act or gift.

We are now working pretty well together as a Unit. Rank doesn't mean a lot. What counts is the expertise to get the job done. It sees Taffy, a Sapper and plumber in civilian life, calling most of the shots in the building of the reservoir and the pipe connections. He enlists Dave Bennett as his offsider, another Sapper and a favoured drinking mate. Together they will indicate what they want done, then the NCOs and/or Officers will see that it is.

One funny incident occurs at the reservoir. In the laying of the inlet and outlet pipes, Taffy gives his instructions and goes away to do something else. He returns to find that our Section Lieutenant, Rodger, has altered his instructions.

While Taffy has directed that the inlet pipe has to come in over the top and the outlet from the bottom, Rodger has decided that both will be in the bottom. Taffy argues with Rodger and tells him he can't do that, pointing out that the pumps would have to work overtime to force the water in against the weight of the head. Rodger won't be moved. When Taffy begins to argue, Rodger just drops one shoulder and points to his Lieutenant's pips. He says, "See those? They say the inlet goes in the bottom." And in the bottom, it goes.

My job is to map the layout with the help of Bryce Johnson. Bryce is one of the Headquarters Section clerical staff who has been a draftsman in civilian life. While he does the pencilling, I shoot the bends and angles with a prismatic compass. This is a new experience for me and I'm not sure if I can get it right. I wait anxiously while Bryce retires with all our figures and goes to work on the plan. Wonder of wonders! It comes out perfectly.

Our leaves here are great. We find we prefer Alex to Cairo and, with leave being plentiful because we are so close, we soon find a few favourite haunts. A little out of the mainstream and more to our liking is the Cap D'or, the Long Bar and a couple of spacious Arab cafes.

At the Cap D'or we get good quality beer accompanied by a variety of snacks. The beer we pay for while the snacks are free. The snacks are never standard and differ greatly, totally different to Army food—the change is wonderful. The Long Bar is much the same, but the emphasis there is on cocktails rather than beer.

The Arab cafes sell good beer and very potent local liquors such as Arrack. We mostly aren't into the heavy stuff and generally stick to beer.

The attraction here though is the very large bowl of peeled prawns that is placed on the table when you order your first drink.

Another feature is the appearance of the Arab hawker with oysters to sell. If you elect to buy, he will squat on his heels beside your chair. He has one large basket of unopened oysters and a small one of fresh limes. He will open an oyster, cut a lime and squeeze the juice onto it, then hand it to you to eat. They are delicious and very, very cheap, and he will keep them coming as long as you feel like eating.

The Red Light District here is in an area called Sister Street. With Alex, having been an important seaport for hundreds of years, the district is well established and patronised. The ladies are even more aggressive here in their salesmanship than we have so far encountered. For those not wishing to indulge, they are prepared to put on an exhibition for a price.

We are close to finishing our job when the whole of my No. 3 Section is given a new assignment. We are to move into the nearby Nile Delta, itself, and build a series of concrete Pill Boxes. They will be strongpoints to protect against hostile attack.

With the strong concentration of Allied forces in Egypt, we do not consider there to be much danger of such a happening. Still somebody does, so we are named to do something about it. As it is being done with the cooperation of the Egyptian Government, we are sent to a village called Kom el-Hanash, or Hill of Snakes.

Kom el-Hanash is at the end of a branch rail line and ideally placed as a depot for our supplies. We are given an open area in which to set up our camp and get quickly into the job. As we expect to be here for a while, we will have to build adequate facilities, probably the most important will be the latrine.

Our Section Lieutenant, Rodger, decides the latrines will be deep pit type, with fully enclosed seating and an automatic drop lid. If done properly, they will be completely flyproof and therefore disease free. To do the job, he picks Lenny.

Lenny has been a drainer back home and Rodger's choice is probably a fair one. Lenny however, doesn't see it that way. All the time he is working he keeps muttering to himself about how he is going to get even. He speaks a lot about it to Taffy and me. We try to tease him out of it, but it is several days before he gets back to being his usual bouncy self.

A wealthy Arab landowner has a large residence nearby and, as far as we can make out, he is the big noise around here. Any Egyptian cooperation required, he seems able to provide. Rodger seems grateful to liaise with him as much as possible. In return we are accorded the greatest goodwill.

The Commander of the Royal Engineers, or C.R.E., provides the planning and arrangement of supplies. Arab labour will do the work while two of us will be in charge of the actual construction. There are about half a dozen Pill Boxes to be built. I am one of those in charge of construction.

On our first morning, Rodger loads us onto a couple of trucks to take us out to the worksite. He leads the way in his utility driven by his personal driver. Firstly, he has to stop at the landowner's residence to pay his respects. As he pulls up, the landowner walks out to greet him. Accompanying the landowner is a large German shepherd dog of top pedigree. The dog obviously is a much indulged and greatly favoured pet. It also has a gentle and amiable nature.

While the two men are talking, we look the place over with interest. It is a two-storey construction with an open verandah running the full length of the upper storey. There are some six or eight women attired in the filmy native dress, lolling at ease on the verandah. As they obviously aren't working women, we assume they must be the man's Harem. We eye them over and they eye us back, talking and giggling amongst themselves as they do so.

In the meantime, the dog pauses firstly at his master's side then wanders over to Rodger's ute. He circles it, sniffs at the driver, then suddenly leaps up into the tray. It puts its head first on one side of the cab, then on the other. After deciding which side it likes the best, it settles down on its haunches and just sits there.

Rodger now takes leave of the landowner and begins walking back to his ute. The driver looks first at the dog and then appealingly at Rodger. With the dog unmoving, Rodger turns back to the landowner for help. He just waves his hand airily, like a king granting largesse to the poor, indicating that if that is the dog's wish, then so be it.

Rodger, still unsure, climbs into his ute and tells his driver to move. As the ute begins to pick up speed, the dog settles with its head forward and without a backward glance. From that moment on, it adopts us totally.

The ute cannot move without him. And it remains so for our entire stay at Kom el-Hanash.

While none of us have had actual experience in building Pill Boxes, we know enough about concrete work to tackle the job with confidence. The sites have been chosen and an Egyptian Engineer has established the levels with a theodolite. We have a set of plans to work to, so it is just a matter of following your nose. Besides, if anybody strikes any trouble, we will just help each other out.

Each morning we travel to our site, put our gang to work, then just idle the day away with nothing to do, but just be there. The weather is marvellous, the surroundings are idyllic, and we get lazier and lazier. Sometimes my crew get a bit cheeky amongst themselves at my expense. They know I don't understand their lingo and their antics make them feel bold and daring. Still they work well, so I affect not to realise what they are driving at.

When the Civil Engineer arrives to check levels, however, they are on their best behaviour. Although the Engineer is only a little man in stature, he speaks sharply, and those big men on the construction are instantly servile. He speaks excellent English and tells me to let him know if they give me any trouble. While I have the power to get rid of any of them, I know that their attempted cheek is just a little game amongst themselves, so I ignore it.

The Engineer travels from site to site in a ute with his theodolite mounted on its tripod laying carelessly in the back. I know that none of our professionals would treat a precision instrument in such a fashion, and I can only hope his levels are somewhere near the mark.

Still, he is a friendly and likeable man and I enjoy talking to him. One afternoon he arrives at my site just before knock off time and when he finishes his check, we stroll back to our vehicles together, talking.

He slips his arm easily into mine, so that we are walking arm in arm. I am appalled. In our culture that sort of thing is strictly for people with homosexual leanings. I cannot offend him by disengaging, so I just pray that none of our blokes catch me at it, for they will make my life hell.

We talk mostly of the differences in our customs and beliefs. I mention that our fellows find it hard to come to terms with their practice of being allowed four wives. He claims that with his culture it is a necessary thing.

Perceiving my non-understanding of his meaning, he goes on to ask me how many times a night does an Australian man indulge in intercourse.

I suppose I should tell him that I have no idea, and that our people generally do not discuss that sort of thing. Also, that I, myself, am not married. But I know that this type of prudish attitude is totally incomprehensible to his open outlook. In the end, with my pride coming to a fore, I mumble my answer, "Maybe once or twice."

"Well you see, an Egyptian man goes eight times," he replies easily, "So then, it's necessary for us to have four wives." I am dumbfounded. Maybe he is having me on, but his straight forward matter-of-fact tone seems to make that highly unlikely. Reluctantly, I believe him.

While struggling to come to terms with this astounding piece of data, we reach our respective vehicles and say goodnight. I have disengaged my arm before being seen by any of the others, and thankfully am spared their comments.

I am quiet all the way back to camp, just turning things over, and trying to come to terms with the problems of the Egyptian man. In my mind's eye, I can see his nightly procession, first from one bed and then to another, until all his wives have been serviced. Then he has to do the whole damn thing all over again. Good God! How does he ever get any sleep?

With our excavations starting to shape up, materials for the next stage have to be assembled. Rodger tells us that several rail wagons of river gravel for concrete will be arriving and will have to be unloaded without delay. The load comes from far up the Nile valley and will be shunted onto our rail spur. All other work will have to stop while this is done. The country does not hold much rolling stock, so the wagons have to be unloaded.

When they turn up, Rodger has already departed for a session with the C.R.E. (Commander of the Royal Engineers). Our Sergeant, Reg Jobber, has to take charge, knowing only that the gravel has to be unloaded. There are tons of the stuff and, with no mechanical devices of any kind, there is no alternative, but to do the job by hand.

Our Arab labourers are left to their own devices on the sites, while we set-to, shoulder to shoulder, with shovels. It is hard and tough, taking us quite a while, and we are damned pleased when it is finished. As we rest on our shovels taking a breather, Rodger returns. With the confidence of a job well done, Reg informs him that the trucks are empty and ready to be picked up.

Rodger surveys the scene and tells us it is no good. The gravel is too close to the line and will have to be moved back at least ten feet. The protests are loud, long and bitter, but Rodger is adamant. Trying to soften the blow a little, Rodger says he thinks he may have been able to arrange a football match for us.

Rodger, a New Zealander by birth, is mad keen on Rugby. He has declared that he likes nothing better for a Saturday afternoon than to mix it in a good hard game. Although an odd game or two has been played amongst ourselves, there is little interest, opportunity or enthusiasm to play on a regular basis. Anyway, while a friendly match may be okay, we really are here for a different purpose.

We ask him who the probable opponent may be. He thinks it's an English Regiment, but he isn't sure. It may be a Welsh Regiment. We ask him if they are any good. Again, he isn't sure, but their front row has played for England.

This is typical of Rodger. He is so keen himself that an ordinary game is not good enough. It has to be against the best that he can find. To us it is just a minor side show. If it gets us away from irksome duties, then fair enough. But we are enjoying our present activities, and feel we are doing something important.

Then there is the question of players. We can muster only three or four, including Rodger himself, who may loosely be described as experienced. The rest will have to come from one Section of a very small Unit, while the opposition had a whole Regiment to pick from. They, being stationed here on a permanent basis, sport is a big part of their leisure activity. Regimental matches are played on a regular basis.

Rodger has overdone it this time. Still, with the importance of the work we are doing, he might not be able to get permission for the match to go ahead. We know, however, that Rodger is quite capable of going ahead without permission. Our only hope is that his proposal is only a "maybe".

Thinking and arguing over the pros and cons of a "maybe" football match has at least achieved its purpose. Magically, all the gravel has been moved to where Rodger wants it.

Following the advent of the gravel, the cement and reinforcing rods soon follow. One or two of the sites, including my own, are almost ready for the pouring of the concrete base. Some other sites are located in positions where access is difficult. The only way to reach them is to cross a fairly wide canal. This will require building a bridge.

This proposal gets some very derisive remarks from our blokes. The gist of these is— "Fancy this lot being trusted with building a bridge. The first truck to use it will end up in the canal." I let my blokes know that we have built quite a few bridges back home in the Militia, without any problems.

Rodger takes the matter up with the C.R.E. and arrives back to inform us that the materials for a Bailey Bridge will arrive at our campsite in the next day or two. Our training to date has not included such a thing, and most of the blokes are mystified. I am able to tell them that the bridge is a box girder arrangement that fits together like a meccano set.

A short while ago, a Corporal Chester, who is a specialist reinforcement, moves into our Unit. He is a West Australian known by the name of 'Billie Blue'. He is a quiet and likeable bloke. Now the word goes out that he is an expert on the Bailey Bridge. At least, if Rodger and Sergeant Reg know little about it, Billie has the expertise. I have, too, but then, I am only a Lance Corporal. And, while the fellows are aware that I know something about the bridge, those in charge do not.

When we arrive in camp a day or so later, it is no surprise to find a pile of box girder material, heaped up where it has been unloaded. We all give it a quick once over, then go about the business of washing up and getting ready for our evening meal.

We are all seated in the mess tent and well into our eating, when the call goes out over our noisy din, "Lance Corporal Dawson, report to Corporal Chester." Mystified, I rise and go outside. There, grouped around the box sections, stands Billie, Reg and Rodger. They have been sorting out the sections.

I go over not knowing what to expect and, for a moment, the three just stand there and say nothing. I stand at attention, but do not salute as I am bareheaded, and I say, "Sir, you wish to see me?" Often, we just walk up to Rodger and speak to him man-to-man, and just as often he does so to us. Sometimes, however, there are formal occasions that require the proper approach. I have the feeling that this is one of those occasions.

For another moment, he says nothing, then pointing to a section, he blurts out, "What's that?" I am dumbfounded. Obviously, Billie the expert, isn't quite the expert that he is reputed to be. It means that yours truly is the only one with any experience to speak of.

I haven't made a big noise about my Militia training, nor have I tried to keep it quiet. I am not chasing a promotion, as I have this feeling of wanting to be part of the normal goings-on, in whatever happens to come up. I don't fancy the idea of ordering somebody else to do a particular job, especially if it turns out to be dangerous. It seems to me, rightfully, that I ought to tackle it myself.

We have been together for long enough now for most of our blokes to be aware that I have had a fair bit of training. Whether or not these three are aware of it, I just don't know. For Rodger to have called me out seems to indicate that he has some inkling. So, in reply, I tell him, "It is a Horn Beam."

The Horn Beam is an odd shaped part with a large wheel mounted on it. He asks again, "What's it for?" I explain the bridge is assembled on one side of a gap and the Horn Beam is mounted on the end to be launched toward the other side. Being a pretty weighty structure, it will tend to dig into the bank on the opposite side and be difficult to move. With the Horn Beam and its large wheel mounted, that end can be wheeled into place without much effort.

"Oh," says Rodger, "I see; well carry on," dismissing me to go back and finish my meal. It is with very mixed feelings that I return to the Mess. I have to admire Rodger's approach. He has come straight out and asked, whereas, most others in his position will have covered up, bought time, and consulted a manual.

Everybody wants to know what he wanted me for. I have to tell them something, so I say, "He wants to know what one part is used for." That is sufficient to raise all those doubts again. Now, everybody is sure that the job will be a proper mess.

Next day, all other work is suspended and all available manpower is ordered onto the bridge building job. We load all the sections, transport them to the site, and prepare to proceed with the assembly.

As usual Rodger is away at the C.R.E.'s Office, leaving Sergeant Reg and Corporal Billie in charge. The chain of command sees Sergeant Reg ask Corporal Billie what he wants done, then giving the appropriate order to the men. The men will then look at me and, if I seem to agree, they will do it.

Now and then, the order will be wrong and I will say, "Don't do that, let's do it this way." Understandably, Reg is becoming frustrated and furious because the blokes are taking little notice of him before they check with me.

Once or twice he threatens to put me on a charge when something really blatant happens. But I know, as well as he does, that he won't do that. Firstly, he is too good a bloke, and secondly, it will make him look pretty bad.

And so, it goes. Somehow, someway, we get the damn thing together and get it across the canal. The canal is both wide and deep, so it is no mean feat. Apart from a few bruises to both bodies and egos, everybody is pleased with the result.

As we depart, I spot a serious flaw. The bank seats are not level. The one on the far side is about nine inches lower than the one on this side. The bank seats are where the bridge ends sit on the bank. When level, they support the load evenly across its length. With one end lower, the weight tends to be thrust towards that end. Under the circumstances, I decide to keep this error to myself. Besides, I know that only a few loads are needed to go across it. Surely, it will hold together for this limited use.

A day or two later, it is the weekend and Rodger is invited by the Landowner to a day's entertainment on the Sunday. We all are intrigued but have no way of knowing what is involved. Rodger departs very early and we just have to wait until the day is over to find out. He arrives back just after dark, and after the evening meal is over. He is staggering and is obviously affected by liquor. It is just as well his driver is with him as he is incapable of driving himself.

We find out from his driver that the Landowner and some of his friends have taken Rodger to a marshy area well up the Nile for a day's duck shooting. They have provided everything—food, liquor and guns. While a good many birds have been taken, it seems that Rodger has been largely unsuccessful. However, he does arrive home with a pair of ducks.

He hands them in at the kitchen and asks for them to be prepared for his evening meal. The somewhat miffed cooks, seeking to put off the unwanted task, point out that it may take some time. Rodger says, "No matter, I will wait."

Lenny happens to be in the kitchen at the time and says, "Leave it to me. I will do a good job."

Rodger says, "Okay," and wanders off to his tent.

The cooks are happy to have the job taken out of their hands, giving Lenny access to the kitchen and leaving everything in his hands. By no stretch of the imagination can Lenny be regarded as a cook. There has to be an ulterior motive of some sort, involved in his volunteering.

Lenny comes back to our tent a couple of hours later and tells me about it. He says that he plucked the birds, but still left a few feathers on. He left all the innards in and the heads on. He put them on to cook, but took them off before they were fully done. He served them up without any further trimmings.

I ask him if Rodger said anything, but Lenny says, "No, he was still pretty much affected by the grog." Lenny stayed long enough to see him start eating and then left.

I protest mildly saying, "That seems a bit rough!"

But Lenny says, "No way. He deserves it."

When I press as to what he means, Lenny says, "Serves him right. That'll teach him. He'll know better than to put me on digging shithouses again. I hope the bastard chokes."

Needless to say, Rodger didn't choke and, although a little worse for wear, he fronts up next morning, seemingly without any ill effects.

A day or two later, Rodger arrives back from his usual visit to the C.R.E. to tell us that the Rugby match is definitely on and set down for next Saturday. He hasn't mentioned it for a while now and we all have thought that it has died a natural death. Since he has committed us, we have to somehow come up with a team. Of course, we can all refuse to play, but that seems a bit drastic.

We now have to seriously consider what we are up against. The British Army Regiments are some of the oldest and most famous in the world. Their personnel are full time professional soldiers and, because of their training, just about the best there is. British Empire commitments see them manning full-time military establishments in various places around the world, ready to be called upon at any time, with Egypt being one of those places. And their involvement in sport is one of the releases from the intensity and tedium of their training.

Sport for them is actively pursued at all times. It is pushed and encouraged right throughout their ranks. Inter-Unit, inter-Regiment and inter-Service competitions are regular activities. With spacious barracks and top class facilities, these men are almost akin to professional sportsmen.

On the other hand, our team has to come from a very diverse group of about forty blokes. Rodger is about the only experienced player we have. There are a couple who have filled in occasionally in a couple of games, myself included. But most of our blokes haven't even seen a game played and have no idea of the rules.

Somehow, we coerce, chiack and urge a team together, just blokes who grudgingly agree to give it a go. We will rely on Rodger to lead us and just gallop around, hoping not to get into too much trouble. For a couple of days before the game, we continue our work. There is no training whatsoever.

On the day of the match, the whole lot of us climb aboard our trucks and head for the ground, which is the Welsh Regiment's Sports Oval, adjacent to their barracks. We have not seen it before and have no idea what to expect. Rodger has left for his meeting with the C.R.E., but promises to meet us at the ground.

We get there to find it a quality playing field, level and well-grassed. That is a good sign. We can hit the deck without worrying about the rocks and stones. On one side of the field there is tiered seating stretching along from the halfway line. Most of it is already occupied by Welsh supporters.

There is scarcely a uniform to be seen, with most of them being clad in mufti. We get the impression of a sea of white casual dress which, in itself, is almost a uniform. A large bloc of what is obviously Officers is in the foreground, with the other ranks spaced around them. It looks as though they have turned out in force specially to honour us.

We mill around in a group waiting for Rodger to show up. We expect to be able to wait for him before the game commences, but the Welshmen are ready and passing the ball around among themselves. We think we best get ready too.

The Welshmen are properly attired in regulation jerseys with the Regimental emblem on them, and socks and football boots. In contrast, we have to resort to our khaki Army sweaters, regulation shorts and Army boots.

Emulating the opposition, we make a brave attempt at passing the ball amongst ourselves, but our inexperience and unpreparedness is so obvious that we quickly stop. We waste as much time as we can waiting for Rodger, but finally, the Referee walks out and calls the two teams onto the field. Our moment of truth has arrived.

The referee and linesmen are from the Welsh Regiment. The referee is a long lean Officer, very agile and obviously very competent. He calls the two Captains together for the toss. Rodger is our Captain, but he is not here. We just nominate the bloke nearest and tell him, "Righto, you call." We still hope Rodger will show.

With the toss decided, we now sort ourselves out into forwards and backs. This is done with a lot of verbal instruction of, 'You go here," and, "No, I want you to go there," amongst ourselves. With an extra man co-opted into Rodger's spot, finally we are spaced out into some sort of order. While Taffy has chosen to be a centre, I have chosen to be a breakaway as I have had a limited bit of experience in this position.

The whistle blows and the game is on. As Rugby is a running game, in five minutes flat our condition is blown and we are hard put to keep up. The one or two of us, who have some experience, try to instruct the others on the run.

With cries of, "Tackle him! Kick!" and, "Pass the ball!" or whatever, we gallop from one end of the field to the other. Try as we might, there is no way we can stem the relentless tide.

Whenever they get the ball, they score. Whenever we get the ball, we go down in a flurry of arms and legs, and they get it back from us. We try to slow the game down, but the only way we can achieve this, is for somebody to drop to the ground and feign to be injured.

Our side is made up of blokes who have some football experience, but all in an amateur way. The trouble is that it happens to be in the other codes of soccer, Aussie Rules and Rugby League. If they try to do something in the style of game they are used to, they only end up more bewildered than ever. Taffy has played some Rugby League and, the first time he gets his hands on the ball, he attempts to run with it. He is quickly tackled and hangs onto the ball, thinking to get up and play it Rugby League style.

But in Rugby Union, when tackled, you must release the ball while both sides ruck frantically for it with their boots. With those boots flying round his head and body, Taffy and the rest of us quickly get the message. When you go down, don't hang onto the ball!

Somehow, someway, we manage to last until the halftime whistle. We drag our weary and aching bodies off to the sideline, grateful for the chance to rest and recover. Suddenly we catch a familiar figure striding towards us. It is Rodger. As one, we rise to our feet, surround him, and begin to abuse him roundly.

The gist of our quite loud complaints is, "Where the hell have you been?" and "Why didn't you get here on time?" and "You ought to know better than to pull a stunt like that," and much more in the same vein.

All the time we are heckling him, Rodger is attempting to explain and to apologise at the same time. He is sorry, but the C.R.E.'s meeting has taken much longer than expected and, because of its importance, he really could not get away.

This spontaneous pantomime takes place squarely in front of the panel stand, and is plainly audible to all. Rodger, with his tall and gangly build, moustache, beak-like nose and nasally twang caused by damage at his beloved Rugby, is no fashion plate. All this talking, explaining and waving of arms, tends to make him look slightly ridiculous.

God knows what the Welsh personnel think of these crazy antics. The solid block of Officers, surrounded by their other ranks, certainly are not able to understand the easy familiarity and seemingly disrespect as practised by our lot. In any case, they observe, but make no comment.

Now it is time for the second half to commence. As replacements are not allowed, Rodger, still unable to play, has to take a seat in the stand, where some of the Officers move to make way for him.

For this half, we adopt slightly different tactics. We decide to concentrate on trying to stop them scoring rather than trying to score ourselves. We have learned a little bit about this rucking business, and while the ball is locked inside these melees, it does tend to slow the game down a bit. As soon as the ball goes to ground, we rush to form a solid group, with our Army boots kicking and lashing out at the faintest sign of it. Our wild, indiscriminate tactics are disconcerting to the sophisticated techniques of the Welsh.

We manage to slow down the scoring avalanche a little bit, but in doing so, first one, then two, and finally three of our opponents, have to be assisted off with bad leg gashes.

Never, at any time, is there any intention from either side to indulge in illegal practice. They don't need to; any harm, which we cause, comes from our ignorance which they can readily see. They make no attempt to retaliate, but just carry on with the game. Despite being three men down, they still manage to run through us and score at will., although not with the same momentum as before.

At long last, the final whistle is blown and we troop off. We have been soundly beaten and don't even bother to check the score. We are glad just for the game to stop. As we stand there in a group, Rodger comes down and informs us that we all have been invited back to the Welsh Headquarters for a clean-up and dinner. This invitation on its own is worth all the effort and lost sweat we have put in.

There is one big problem though. What about our dog? The ever-present German shepherd is with us and we just cannot leave him. This doesn't faze the Welsh one little bit. They say to us, "Please, bring him along." Our dog is equally welcome.

The Welsh take us in and give us a marvellous meal. It is an exhibition of what can be done with Army food. Of course, we have to eat in the Men's Mess, a vast place, together with all of their Unit, while Rodger eats with the Officers.

While we are eating our fill, our dog is also being taken care of. The Orderlies dish up the food for everybody from very large baking dishes. These have been brought in from the kitchen and placed on a serving table at one end of the Mess Hall. One of the baking dishes, about a quarter full with enough in it for five men, has been placed under our table where our dog can eat undisturbed.

We are greatly impressed by the hospitality and comradeship shown to us by these men. Our style is much more laid back and easy going than theirs. We have great respect for their skills and knowhow, but feel that they stick too rigidly to rules and regulations. We feel that our way is better. This little interlude, however, makes us feel truly comrades-in-arms.

With the meal ended, it is time for us to leave. It is early evening and now dark. The sporting afternoon and its aftermath has whetted our appetites and, an early return to camp is distinctly unattractive. We ask Rodger to grant us leave to go into the city. He says, "No, I can't do that."

As one, we surround and verbally harass him. We argue loudly that we have been working damn hard without let up, and have done everything that he has asked of us. He has let us down badly for not turning up for the game, and he owes it to us. Besides it is Saturday night.

We have him cornered and have no intention of giving up. He puts forward a few feeble protests which we quickly howl down. Finally, accepting the inevitable, he says, "Alright, but the deadline is eleven o'clock." We know that we will have no trouble extending that to our usual midnight.

As we joyously prepare to go on our merry way, Rodger says plaintively, "That's alright for you, what about me? How am I going to put in the time?"

Leave facilities for Officers are distinctly separate from those of other ranks. Rodger is the sole Officer with us, and it is unthinkable that anyone should have to go on leave alone. We cannot go without him, so the only solution is for him to come with us and we tell him so.

He is rather reluctant about this radical plan. We argue and convince him that we will regard it as a one-off thing and no advantage will be taken. There is only one proviso—he will have to take his pips off and appear to be a Private.

He thinks about this for a moment, then agrees. He will be away from the haunts where Officers associate, and it is most unlikely he will be recognised. Although he has sanctioned our leave, we have no passes, so it is unofficial. Being with us, he can see that we do not get involved with anything that might attract the wrong kind of attention.

We set out and what a great night it is. Rodger finds that our style of enjoying ourselves is much more akin to his own personal tastes. For Rodger and his fellow Officers, it has to be much more formal and discreet, and their establishments are tucked away from prying eyes.

The most notable difference he finds, is in the brothel area. He claims that the prices quoted in the open places are less than half those quoted in their area. He claims that the talent available is much more diverse and generally more attractive. This claim seems a bit hard to believe because of the greater numbers passing through our areas.

All good things come to an end and finally, it is time to return to camp. Despite the debacle of the Rugby game, the day has turned out to be something we will remember for a long time. Still, enough is enough, and we aren't too worried if we are never called upon to play another game. I think Rodger feels pretty much the same.

In the next couple of days, our Pill Boxes go to the stage of pouring the concrete bases. Firstly, it's Les Lawrence's, who is slightly ahead of me, and then mine. It is fascinating to watch the Arab mixing gangs in action again. Their chanting, their rhythmic action, their speed and ease of working.

Les starts to put the wall reinforcing rods into place and I am about to start on mine, when suddenly a halt is called. We are to drop what we are doing and move on. With a buzz of excitement, we find that we are to form up with the rest of the Unit, and prepare to move up the Western Desert. We are to move against the Italians. We are going to War!

Practically, the whole of the Sixth Division is to be involved, so it is to be a major do and not a minor one. The planning for this movement is the reason for the C.R.E.'s conference that had prevented Rodger from taking part in the Rugby match.

Quickly, we load up and move out. We never give these Pill Boxes a second thought, and I haven't a clue if they will ever get finished. As a matter of course, we have to leave behind that temporary member of our group, the Arab Landowner's German Shepherd. Whether he manages to settle back into his former routine, after the excitement of dashing round in Rodger's ute, we will never know.

# Chapter 6

# The Western Desert Campaign

W<small>E MOVE OUT IN CONVOY</small> onto the Coast road. This road follows closely to the shoreline, all the way from Egypt right through into Libya. It is a good road and has been the main connecting link between the two countries.

We keep together as a Unit, although aware that we are only a small part of a much larger movement of men and equipment. We make good progress and stop just on dusk. We move off the highway into scattered positions and camp for the night. We are only a couple of hundred yards from the seashore and lots of the men from the combined convoy take the opportunity to have a dip. Although it is winter and the water is cold, we enjoy it greatly. In our minds is the sober realisation that this may be the last opportunity for anything resembling a bath for some time to come.

We are pleased and eager to be getting on with the job that we have come for, to secure Egypt. We are quietly confident with our own abilities, yet a little apprehensive of the unknowns that lay ahead. We speculate quietly amongst ourselves of what we might expect, then turn in for an early night.

Some intelligence information, we have, suggests that we do not have the total support of the local population, all because a very beautiful Italian Courtesan who has tremendous influence over Egypt's King Farouk. And, to this extent, the King would sooner have welcomed the Italians into his country, than the British. If this is so, then the Italians will be aware that we are on the move and will take steps to do something about it. We will have to be watchful, just in case.

The Italians have pushed into Egypt, taking some coastal towns. These initial warlike moves by the Italians are probably an attempt to prove to Hitler that they are not just lame ducks hanging onto his coat tails. With exotic sounding names like, Sollum, Sidi Barrani, Mersa Matruh, they have made a big deal of these outstanding successes. Also, they have built a new fortress on their own side of the border called Fort Capuzzo. In reality, these places are just fly specks on the map, notable only because of the fresh water that is available there. It seems that local officials have abandoned the towns when threatened by the Italians, rather than fight for them.

Prior to our movement, the British and Indian forces have forced the evacuation of the Italians from these places, just as quickly as they had run over them. The British and Indian forces now have the Italians holed up in their Fort Capuzzo.

We move out early next morning, headed for Sollum. If the Ities are to have a go at us, it will be from the air. We have faith enough in our own Air Force to be able to counter any threat, and we are unworried as we speed along.

The country hereabouts is true desert. The road traverses a very narrow coastal plain, ranging from a few hundred yards to barely a quarter of a mile wide and completely flat, to a craggy, rocky escarpment soaring straight up, seemingly to a thousand feet or more. There appears to be very, very few places where it may be possible to get from the plain to the top of the escarpment.

When we near one of the overrun and abandoned settlements, we encounter shot-up and burnt-out vehicles and other debris abandoned by the Italians as they cleared out. The towns themselves are no more than a cluster of about half a dozen flat-topped, cell-like houses of concrete construction. Sollum is the same, but is considered of some importance because of its proximity to the border. It also has a good supply of fresh water, tapped from an underground source.

We take up residence just outside Sollum, itself unoccupied. The fortified town of Bardia, some fifteen miles away, has installed a large naval gun with firepower that can just reach Sollum. There is a well-constructed zigzag roadway, climbing from the plain to the top of the escarpment here. The gun can keep the waterpoint and the pass in range. But mostly, the gun has to be fired blindly as, once the shells drop below the rim, the gunners cannot tell if they are on target or not. With this uncertainty, they resort to firing a few rounds at a time for about half an hour, a couple of times a day. Our blokes christen the gun Bardia Bill. The gunners develop a routine so that we have a fair idea of when it is about to fire. This is important to know, as we are to draw from the waterpoint to supply our surrounding troops. The trick is to get in and get out between firings.

We take over the dugouts and caves previously occupied by the Italians. There are two very large and very roomy caves that are ideal. Inside we are protected from the biting winds and are fairly snug from the cold nights. But, the trouble is that the Italians have left a few friends behind. The place is infested by fleas. We clean them out as best we can, but a lot of our blokes elect to bed down outside in rocky shelters. They reckon the cold is preferable to the fleas.

During the day, we are putting in our time by ranging out around the area, looking for anything useful abandoned by the Ities. They have abandoned quite a lot of gear, and our people are only too willing to press into service anything that will help at all.

A group is detached under Sergeant Rex Scanlon and given a roving commission. They have a compressor truck and jackhammers, and work with the Infantry. On top of the escarpment, the country is solid rock and covered by a thin layer of fine sand. Wherever the Infantry wants to set up a gun position, the gang will dig a pit for them.

There is some competition among the scavenger crews, and a lot of speculation about a monetary return for recovery of anything valuable. Lenny reckons that such booty is a prize of war, and that there are laws insisting on the finders being paid a percentage of its worth.

We come across a couple of light Fiat tractors one day, and Lenny insists on driving one back to camp as his personal prize. We check it out for booby traps, find it okay and start it up. The Ities have just walked away from it, with the key still in the ignition.

There is fuel in the tank, but we do not know if there is enough to get us back to camp. We, therefore, have to dawdle along, with the tractor just behind. We can't leave Lenny on his own. It has just turned dark when we arrive back.

Sergeant Reg has just pulled up in a utility, ahead of us. He asks us to come and give him a hand with Bill. I ask, "Why? What's the matter with him?"

He replies, "Oh, haven't you heard?"

I explain about being delayed by Lenny and his tractor, and he tells me that Bill has had his head blown off. A party had gone into the waterpoint in Sollum when Bardia Bill dropped one over the escarpment unexpectedly. They heard a whoosh, just before the shell burst. Bill had moved in a different direction to the others and copped it. Nobody else has been hurt. Reg has just returned from collecting the body.

I know that we have two Bills in the Unit. One is more nuggetlike than the other, so we differentiate by calling them Big Bill and Little Bill. I ask Reg, "Which one is it?" And he says, "Big Bill".

Shocked into silence, we help as best we can, then make our way back to our digs. I am alone, walking along and thinking of Big Bill as we have known him. I round a rockface and bump into somebody coming the other way in the dark. It is Big Bill and I nearly drop. I blurt out, "You're dead."

"Not yet," he replies calmly. I then realise that it is Little Bill who has been killed. Without a head, we had no way of knowing who it could be.

Little Bill is our first casualty. He was a married man with three or four kiddies. All the way over on the boat he bemoaned the fact that he had enlisted. He claimed that he would never see his wife and kids again. He kept it up so much that we christened him Calamity Bill, and, try as we might, we could not talk him out of it. It is uncanny and sobering to find his prediction to be so true.

As we are the only Unit in the immediate vicinity, we don't take any special security precautions when we're out scavenging. We just leave our personal gear behind in camp. There are always a few men left behind in camp, such as the cooks etc., and so this seems a reasonable attitude to take. But, some of the blokes in the rock shelters out in the open begin to complain of losing valuables from their packs while they're away.

Once the word came through that were moving out, many had taken the precaution of stocking up on essentials at the canteen; things that will be hard to get where we are going—razor blades, tobacco, cigarettes, papers and matches. It is these valued items that are disappearing.

At first, it seems that the losers have just mislaid their things. But, as more begin to complain, it is obviously serious. We cannot understand how it is happening. Finally, Sergeant Reg decides to do something about it. He chooses a party of about half a dozen blokes and scatters them in positions among the rocks, with rifles at the ready. Then they settle down to wait.

It is a long wait, but finally five or six khaki clad figures appear and make for the rock shelters. They begin to handle the packs there when Reg rises from his position and orders them to stand still. They panic and turn to run. A shot is fired with a bullet passing through the fleshy part of one man's arm. They immediately begin to fall to their knees and beg for mercy.

Reg and his men are beside themselves with anger. It is touch and go for a while as to whether they might shoot the lot on the spot. Gradually, as things calm a little, Reg demands to know who they are and where they are from. They are from a Cypriot labour Battalion that has moved into the area, unbeknown to us.

Reg detaches one of them and gives him explicit orders. He is to return to his Unit and fetch the Sergeant-in-Charge and bring him forthwith, while the others remain here. No hanky panky, otherwise our Unit will have no compunction in wiping their Unit out.

The man scuttles off and returns together with his Sergeant. He is a Pom and has no knowledge of what his men have been up to. When confronted with the evidence and proof, he begs Reg not to go any further with it. He points out that his men have had the fear of God put into them and certainly will not try anything like this again. He gives his personal guarantee that he will ensure that it doesn't. Also, with the forthcoming build-up and set-to with the Italians, nobody can afford the time nor trauma of sorting out this kind of mess. Reg takes some convincing, but eventually agrees to drop it. He warns, however, that if anyone of their Unit is sighted near our area, he will be shot on sight and no questions asked.

A build-up for the coming push appears obvious. Some storage dumps of various kinds, including food, begin to appear. My crew manage to get up onto the escarpment to take a good look at what is left of Fort Capuzzo. It looks for all the world like a fort from one of those Foreign Legion movies that had been popular in pre-war days. Now it is nothing more than a sorry mess. It looks as if our Artillery has given it a round or two, for there are gaping shell holes in what is left of the walls. Any thought of such a point of defence being of any use in modern warfare is just ridiculous.

On our way back, we drive down the pass that drops from the escarpment to Sollum. Its real name is Halfaya Pass. Naturally, it is christened Hellfire Pass by our blokes. The road is good, but the twists and turns are hair raising. I am glad when we get to the bottom.

An examination of some of the storage dumps turns up some small unbranded crates. Each is found to contain two crocks of rum. A little sampling helps to relieve the tedium of waiting for the show to begin.

The C.O. and Officers have been involved in quite a few Headquarters planning sessions. We wait for the outcome, expecting some role, but just hoping that they don't get too carried away and volunteer for some death or glory mission. When we are finally told the plan, it is sobering enough. We will supply teams to go in with the Infantry, blow the barbed wire with Bangalore torpedoes, and knock down the Tank-trap to make a road through for our tanks and transport.

Our target, Bardia, is typical of the small towns dotted along the Mediterranean Coast of Libya. It is situated on a small harbour, barely more than an indentation in a very rugged and rocky coastline. Mussolini has had quite a few years to fortify and strengthen the place. Access from the sea is difficult and dangerous because of the ruggedness. Access from the land will have to be across miles of dead flat landscape that gives no cover for an invading Army. A series of in-depth fortifications push out some miles from the town in the form of below-ground bunkers, and the whole lot is surrounded by an anti-tank ditch.

Patrols and aerial surveillance have given us some knowledge of what we have to face up to. Now, further patrols go out to measure specifics that are necessary info for our task—such as, the width and depth of the Tank-trap and how far it is from the Trap to the barbed wire.

Everybody turns to preparing and learning for the coming job. This will be our first and most important test, and nobody wants any slipups. There is a general feeling that we owe it to those men who have gone before us in the last set-to, and we just cannot let them down.

Of the two allocated tasks, the easiest to prepare for is the Tank-trap job. Basically, it is just a pick and shovel job to turn a ditch into a shallow depression. The only precaution needed is to avoid clanking the tools together on our way in. That noise will carry far across the desert at night.

The Bangalore torpedos are a much more complicated setup. Most of the blokes have not even heard of such a thing before. When told it is a pipe filled with explosives that rip a great hole in barbed wire defences, they just accept the fact without question. They ask, "Where do we get them?" There's none available, so we just have to make our own.

Our Officers, all trained engineers in their own right, gather all the materials needed for the job which requires a mixture of civilian and military materials. The pipes are standard lengths of two-inch galvanised steel water pipes. These sections, about five feet long, will be sealed with wooden plugs at each end, one with a hole in it to let the fuse come through. The civilian materials are gelignite, standard fuse and detonators. The military materials are gun-cotton primers and fuse instantaneous detonating, called F.I.D.

Each pipe has a piece of F.I.D. running its full length in its centre. This is surrounded by gelignite tamped into place. At about every foot, a gun-cotton primer is threaded onto the F.I.D. And then a detonator is attached to the last primer, with a piece of standard fuse, ready to be lit by a match.

Making up the torpedos is a tricky business. A very long wooden tamping rod is made for packing the gelignite into place. We pack about a foot and then thread on a primer. Care has to be taken with the primers—if we handle them too roughly, they might explode. We find that the hole of the last primer is too big to take the commercial detonator, so we wrap it with cigarette papers to ensure a firm fit.

For safety-sake the pipes will be made up without the detonator and lighting fuse. They will be fused on the night, at the start line. Two pipes are needed to do the job, but an extra one will be taken by each team as a spare. With six teams, that means eighteen pipes have to be made up.

The information gathered indicates that it is about fifty yards from the Tank-trap to their barbed wire which is about fifteen feet in depth, and then there's a further fifty yards to their strongpoints. We do many tests on lighting the fuse to gauge the length required. It has to be long enough to enable the wire team to light it, and then get back to the safety of the Tank-trap. Finally, we're sure that we have the right length.

We build replicas of the barbed wire and the Tank-trap, and practise on them. The Tank-trap job is fairly easy. More difficult is the Bangalore torpedo job which requires one length of pipe to be pushed right through the barbed wire and protrude from the far side. The second pipe, or trigger, overlaps the first one by one and a half to two feet. This one will be lit and the detonation will cause the other to explode simultaneously. All our practices are dry runs. We will just have to wait for the night to see the results of the explosion.

After a few practice runs, we try again at night. Finally, we decide we are as good as we can be without doing the actual job. Then comes the selection of teams. The Bangalore teams are to be of eight men, with one being the leader. The Tank-trap teams are to be of six men, with one being the leader.

Six Bangalore and six Tank-trap teams will be required in all. As Lance Corporal, I expect to be in one of the teams. In the wash, I am to be the leader of one of the Tank-trap teams. The Senior NCOs immediately select their teams, but I'm not accorded that right. My team is allocated to me from men, here and there, within the Unit.

We move against Bardia in early January, 1941. It is midwinter and bitterly cold. Even heavily clothed, the desert wind cuts through us like a knife. We are clad in heavy wool long johns and singlets, full uniform and overcoat, and topped with a sleeveless leather jerkin which arrived only a couple of days ago.

We are in position close to the start line in plenty of time. The wind troubles us that much that we decide to put our picks and shovels to work. We dig a large saucer like depression and climb in, with feet in the centre. As we lay back waiting, we are below ground level and spared the torment of the wind.

We talk quietly amongst ourselves, but think mostly of the job ahead and the build-up to it. There has been much radio propaganda from the Italian side of how their gallant defenders of Bardia are surrounded by hordes of bearded, murderous Australians. They will never surrender and will fight to the last. Soon we will know.

It's time to get ready and we stir from our friendly hole. A few men move amongst us with crocks of rum for anybody who feels he needs a shot. Those who do, take very little and mostly to ward against the cold. The mere smell of it is more than I can stand, so I have none.

We line up on the start line which extends for a thousand yards. We will move straight ahead in single file columns of firstly, an Infantry column, then an Engineer Bangalore party, then an Infantry column, then an Engineer Tank-trap party and so on, right along the line. There comes the order to move and the whole front sets off walking in. Almost immediately, all hell breaks loose.

Our side opens up with a terrific barrage from land, sea and air. The Ities reply furiously with everything they have. Multi-coloured tracers fill the sky in reds, greens, pinks and mauves. It is the greatest fireworks display that any of us have seen, and it is all lethal.

We are about halfway to the Tank-trap when there comes an explosion some yards to my right amongst our columns. It seems like a shell has landed there. In the flash of the burst, I sight Sid Malcolm with one end of a Bangalore on his shoulder with the other end dragging on the ground. It seems that one of his team has been taken out. As the flash is fading into darkness again, I just glimpse the lead man on the next pipe stoop and pick up the dragging end, while Sid presses doggedly on.

We continue on without further mishaps and reach the Tank-trap. We crowd in where we have to wait for a few minutes while the Bangalore teams do their job. We find the contours of the Tank-trap are as expected, but the trench is not as deep. The hard rocky substructure of the terrain prevents this.

We are able to see the barbed wire entanglement from our position and then, also, something serious. Just slightly to our left, and just beyond the barbed wire, we detect one of the Italian strongpoints. Whether we have strayed offline, or whether it has been pre-planned, we are now in a dangerous spot. If they become aware of our presence, they can cause merry hell with our attack.

We can make out some sort of a gun emplacement, but most of the installation is below ground. Then we hear faint voices as they talk among themselves, followed by some movement around the gun pit.

A couple of our teams are still in the tank-traps and are unaware of the danger. Our blokes raise their rifles ready to take them on, but I order my crew to hold fire. I try to influence the others in the Tank-traps to do the same. For the moment, they seem unaware of the situation. But if we open fire, they will definitely know.

I reason that if we do, then the Ities will phone through to their Headquarters who could react by calling in artillery fire. We are still only at the Tank-trap and they could kill our attack before we even get through the barbed wire.

Before I can get my message across to the other blokes, one of them fires off a single shot. Instantly, all movement ceases. We wait for further signs, but there are none. Nor is there any hostile fire coming our way.

Now it is time for the Bangalore men to do their job, They go out, lay their charges, light them and return to the Tank-trap to wait for the blow. The explosion comes, then the okay is given for the Infantry to move in. They pour through the gaps and fan out. The attack is properly underway.

Now it is our turn. I spot two familiar figures as we shape up to hoe into the lip of the tank-trap. They are Cocker and his mate Fatty. They have attached themselves to the Infantry and are going in with them, unarmed. I call to Cocker, "Where the hell are you going?"

He just waves back and calls, "See you later." The pair obviously have some scheme in operation and I will just have to wait until they return to find out what it is.

Ever more Infantry are coming through now. As one batch goes through, we signal and call out for them to investigate the nearby Itie strongpoint. One man detaches himself and moves cautiously over. He finds what seems to be the only means of getting across and then searches for an opening. He finds one, pulls a grenade pin, drops it down, then stands back for the blast.

A few seconds later a stick with a white flag tied to it appears from a nearby hole. It waves cautiously backwards and forwards a few times and the Infantryman moves in to urge the holders out. They clamber out slowly and gather in a knot around him. The last few are carrying out a wounded man on a stretcher. There are eighty-two Italians in that strongpoint and, with such a large number to one man, we keep watch in case he needs some backup.

He doesn't, but now he clearly becomes quite irritated. He's only just got going and is stuck with this lot. His mates are well ahead and he will have to go like hell to catch them up again. We can see his dilemma and call out to send his prisoners across to us. We will shuttle them through for him. This he does, then disappears on his way.

We have time to examine their strongpoint later, and find it to be a mini fort. It is completely surrounded by yet again another tank-trap. This one, however, is wide and deep and constructed of concrete. It is impregnable by tanks. It is roofed over by thin pine boards the same colour as the surrounding sand. These boards have been doubled in one spot only, just sufficient to carry the weight of a man. It is here that our Infantryman has crossed over.

Inside the strongpoint, we find their living-quarters and storerooms are in tunnels and caves, all below ground. They are amazingly well-constructed and, protected by the tank-trap, are almost impossible to get at. In the emplacement is a small calibre, quick-firing cannon, set up and ready to fire. A mounted machine gun is alongside as cover, also ready to fire. It is here that we had seen enemy movement. There is a bullet hole in the outer jacket of the machine gun, certainly from that one shot fired by one of our blokes. That one shot has been enough to make the Ities decide not to fight.

We turn back to our task as the first trickles of prisoners begin to come through. They march along with their hands up and here and there is a white flag. I suddenly realise that they are an abundant source of free labour. I turn to my blokes and say, "Grab a few of these and put them to work."

One of my men is Bill Collier, a big dark Queenslander, He says, "Leave 'em to me. I hate these bastards. I'll make sure they work." I stand back watching, until I'm sure that Bill isn't driving them too hard.

I observe the ever-increasing flow of prisoners. Suddenly, from a knot of about half a dozen, a strong Australian voice calls out, "Any of you blokes from Footscray?"

"No," I answer, "We're all New South Welshmen here. Why?"

"Well, I've got a fish and chip joint there," he replies.

"Well what the hell are you doing here?" I ask.

"Aw, I went home on a holiday to visit the folks and Musso grabbed me, and put me in the Army," he answers.

Then he wants to know what will happen to them. I cannot really tell him, but suggest that seeing he has been captured by Australians, he might even end up in Australia. "You bloody beauty," he says. "That'll do me," and he goes happily on his way.

Another Itie shows me that he has been wounded. A bullet has passed through the fleshy part of his upper leg. I take out my field service dressing and bind it up for him. I tell him, as best I can, to show it to the first doctor he comes across, somewhere behind us. It is a clean wound and not bleeding. He is able to get along alright, and two of his mates stick with him. He is grateful and does his best to show it before moving off.

Our job is just about completed now, so I give the word to tidy up and call it quits. Our Italian prisoners have worked well and quite happily. Because of their help, we have made the job a bit more elaborate than we would have on our own.

Just then, Bill spots a few more Ities coming through, a little distance to our right. He says, "I'll go and grab this lot, too." I explain it is hardly worth it as we are just about finished. But he insists, so I let him go.

He pulls them up about fifty yards away, begins talking to them and waving his arms about. He makes no attempt to bring them back to the job. He just stands there in deep conversation. I am puzzled as to what is going on, as I know that he cannot speak their lingo.

Finally, he makes his way back to us, very slowly, shaking his head in bewilderment. He has sent them on their way and I cannot figure out why. As soon as he comes within earshot, I ask him, "What happened?"

In deep amazement he tells me, "That bloke almost is my father-in-law. I was engaged to his daughter." Bill goes on to say that the man was a Queensland cane farmer and, like the Footscray man, had gone home to Italy on a visit and been forced into the Army.

Bill takes no further part in the tidying-up. He has lost interest. He just sits there on the side of our mound of dirt, deep in thought. I send our co-opted labourers on their way, while we relax and take it easy.

Bill had been in Sydney when the war broke out, so he enlisted there. If he had joined in Queensland, we would never have met him. The reason he was in Sydney is because he had got somebody else's cattle mixed-up with his own—so he claims. Therefore, he was needed for a few questions by the law. That may account for the broken romance. Then again, it may have been another one of Bill Burkey's fanciful tales.

The sound of battle has moved well away from us now, and everything is relatively quiet. More and more prisoners are coming through in a steady stream. Everything has gone off well, and it looks as if the whole affair has been a huge success.

As far as I can tell, there are no injuries to our blokes other than that caused by the explosion amongst the Bangalore team on the way in. Later, we chide the Artillery by claiming the explosion had been one of their drop-shorts. For myself, my ears had found it impossible to cope with the intense noise of the barrage until they had become muted. I am pleased, and figure that my ears have somehow adjusted themselves to the pressure, and will, in due course, right themselves.

An injured Infantry man, with his head swathed in bandages, comes wandering by. He strolls over to show us his smashed tin hat, still marvelling at his great good fortune. The entire crown is blasted from the inside out and, by rights, his head should have gone with it.

At daylight, a lone Military Policeman, armed only with a service revolver, has stationed himself in the nearby Tank-trap. He is directing the streams of prisoners back towards Sollum. We are impressed, for we think their main job is to keep us in check when on leave.

There are large batches of prisoners now, in groups of something like two thousand being escorted by two Infantrymen. In a couple of instances the Infantrymen are so drunk on the Itie liquor they have found, that they are being supported and half-carried by a prisoner under each arm, while other prisoners are carrying their weapons for them. Still there is no danger, for the prisoners have only one place to go, and that is Sollum. There is no future in trying their luck out in the Desert.

By mid-morning Pee Wee and Reg, our cooks, get a cooked meal to us in hot boxes. They have worked long and hard, preparing and getting it to us. We have completely forgotten about hunger until our meal arrives. We eat ravenously and that lukewarm stew tastes like a banquet fit for a king.

We are not called upon for any more tasks and, later in the day, we pull back to the campsite, a short distance from the outer perimeter. It is almost dusk before Cocker and Fatty find their way back to join us. They have had a big day and are almost exhausted. They are laden down with heavy suitcases, filled with souvenirs and loot. There are ceremonial daggers and swords, automatic pistols, medals, rings, watches, money and trinkets, and anything you can think of.

We press them as to where it all came from. They say they just went along with the Infantry until there was some resistance. Then they just stood back while it was cleaned out. As the Infantry moved on, they went into the now empty quarters and gave them a thorough going over, collecting anything they fancied before hurrying onto the next point of resistance.

It has taken three or four days to subdue Bardia and, by the time all resistance has ceased, it is estimated that between thirty and forty thousand prisoners have been taken. Loads and loads of quality guns, transport and equipment have been taken. Anything that can be put to use is commandeered.

The Italian resistance had been fierce wherever their Black Shirt Division troops were, but mediocre elsewhere. It seems that those leather jerkins we were wearing, were mistaken for bullet-proof vests. When the Ities saw them, they just lost heart.

With Bardia out of the way, obviously, we will be onto our next target of Tobruk. Now that we are rolling, momentum will be kept up without delay. The word is that Tobruk is much stronger than Bardia, and will be much harder to crack.

We figure that the Italians will have learned a few things from Bardia, and will come up with a few surprises for us at Tobruk. The first of these is quickly in evidence in the shape of a new type of anti-personnel bomb which we call a Thermos bomb.

We call them Thermos bombs because they are shaped like a Thermos flask. They are scattered over an area indiscriminately by being dropped from aircraft. They have a cap that is dislodged in the drop, exposing a tiny propeller. The propeller activates the firing mechanism so that upon landing they are ready to explode. They are so sensitive that anybody walking nearby will set them off, and the resultant blast is deadly. Several desert areas leading up to Tobruk are seeded with the things, and we are given the task of dealing with them.

We pack up and move to a site closer to our job scene. By now, moving camp in the desert is simple. The whole Unit is completely mobile, so it is just a matter of rolling up your bedroll, throw it aboard your truck, climb on and go. When you get there, you lay out your bedding somewhere near your truck and you are in business again.

The things we have to contend with are the cold, the sand and the wind. Each individual sets himself up to cope against these as he sees fit. I have developed my own particular technique. I will dig myself a slit trench, wide enough, long enough and deep enough for me and my bedroll to fit in comfortably. I line it with Italian ground sheets which I have acquired, spread my roll, and roof it over with another ground sheet if need be. With our Army issue blankets being of top quality Australian wool, I am as snug as can possibly be.

Rodger, our Section Lieutenant, is given the task of dealing with the Thermos bombs. He selects a party of about ten and they set off. They find the area and can plainly see them scattered about. They are so sensitive to vibration that the only safe method of dealing with them is to set them off. And, the safest way to do that is to get fairly close and fire at them.

Rodger and Sergeant Reg direct the men to spread out and get down into a prone position. Reg is on one knee supervising their placement when Rodger orders him, too, to get down. Rodger reminds Reg that exploding bombs are no respecter of persons. With everybody placed, Rodger gives the order to fire. Shots ring out followed quickly by the explosion. Everybody is safe except one. Rodger himself has forgotten to get down. The wound, though serious, is not fatal. The men put him aboard their truck and take him back to camp. From here he is sent back to hospital in Cairo.

Another device becoming increasingly more evident to our patrols, probing the approaches to the Tobruk perimeter, is an anti-personnel landmine. Several of these are retrieved and brought back, so that every man in the Unit can familiarise himself with them. They are about the size and shape of a standard tin of jam, with a spring-loaded metal plunger protruding from the top. When primed, a small metal slide holds the plunger in the ready-to-fire position. From the slide, cords radiate out in a circle. The mines are secured in one of the low salt bushes that abound in the area. With the cords stretched out and secured to other bushes, they are difficult to locate, especially at night.

For safer handling by the Italians, there is a hole through the plunger, just above the metal slide. A safety pin through this hole enables the mine to be set up with any amount of rough handling. Once in place, you withdraw the pin and it is ready to fire. Like the Thermos bomb, the casing is filled with metal fragments, capable of making a nasty mess.

Our method of neutralising them is to put an ordinary nail through the pinhole. This renders them harmless and we can take them away and disarm them at leisure.

Constant pressure is being kept on Tobruk by bombing and shelling. Patrols keep probing while supplies build up. Bardia has been such an outstanding success that it is considered unnecessary to change anything for the assault on Tobruk. Our Unit's role will be exactly the same.

Again we will supply Bangalore and Tank-trap teams. In addition, teams will work through the night of the attack, clearing away landmines and booby traps right through to the Tank-trap. This time, I have copped the Bangalore job.

Once again, I am denied the choice of selecting my own team. And, because of the Units extra involvement in clearing landmines, I am informed that two of my team of eight will be from a Pioneer Unit, on loan for the job. I complain loudly and finally gain the concession of being able to select two of my own choices.

I should have shut my big mouth. By being allowed only two, I have very little leeway. I now have to make a choice, without appearing to make favourites. If I had let things stand, I would have been spared this kind of decision. As a backup to myself, I have to have somebody resolute enough to get the job done. The actual barbed wire party has to be me and two others. If we are knocked out, then another three will take over. This means that a man of strong character, capable of leading, has to be back in the tank-trap ready to take command.

My first thought is my good friend and 'minder' Taffy. He is ready to back me in anything. In fact, his willingness to cause and get into trouble, as well as his generally undisciplined approach, keeps me busy trying to curb him, without appearing to do so. This characteristic has him considered by some Officers, NCOs and men, as not being reliably responsible.

There is a hard core of men in all Units, who, because of the Great Depression, have had a very tough battle for several years, just to survive, before joining the Army. They are cunning, resourceful and have worked out their own code of what is right and wrong. Rough living conditions mean nothing to them and, as long as their food is plain but wholesome, there will be no complaints. With a regular supply of money in their pockets, often for the first time, they drink, gamble and get up to any mischief their fertile imaginations can dream up. If their shenanigans get them into trouble with the authorities, well so be it. They generally accept their punishment without complaint. Occasionally, they might whinge that the penalty is rather harsh for, what is to them, a relatively harmless indiscretion.

The city-based survivor is usually just a little bit wiser than his country-based counterpart. Moreover, he has access to more lurks, often on the fringe of the law or just beyond. If he has connections or influence, he might even be in regular employment.

In our kind of circle, these hard-living blokes tend to gravitate together. They just barely tolerate Officers and NCOs, regarding them as not-very-necessary evil. The rest of the men often become confused and undecided as to whose lead to follow.

In my own case, I have had a tough time in the Depression too. But I have had the advantage of being able to stick it out in a small town, and in the middle of a loving and caring family circle.

Taffy is from an inner Sydney suburb, and is a plumber in his own right. He is on good terms with most of the hardheads and is accorded some respect because of his fighting days. There are three loves in Taffy's life—his wife, his daughter and me. Two of them deserve it. Taffy and I are totally opposites, but our friendship stays firm just the same.

For both our sakes, I finally decide against Taffy. If the slightest thing goes wrong, and there are dozens that can, somebody will claim that his unreliability was responsible.

From the leftovers available, after the other leaders have taken their pick, I choose Lenny and Bill Parkes. I tell Lenny that he is to be my number two man at the barbed wire. Lenny automatically assumes that means he is second-in-command. Actually Bill Parkes, or Sparks as we call him, is my true second-in-command.

Sparks is a medium tall, grizzled and taciturn man, of few words and economy of action, and as steady as a rock. I can rely on him to do what is wanted.

Lenny is pleased with the importance of his role, and a little bit daunted as well. He expects to be able to stand back and tell somebody else what to do. But I quickly let him know that his job will be a lot more hands-on than that.

I tell Lenny that if anything happens to me at the wire, then he is to see that the job is done. Privately, I know that if I get knocked out, then, almost certainly, he will too; and, probably the third man with us as well. He is one of the two men from the Pioneer Unit, called Davidson, who is needed as a carrier. If our wire party is knocked out, it will be up to Sparks and his backup crew to finish it.

Our fuse man is Paddy, a short gregarious little bloke, everybody's friend and nobody's enemy. He has a battered looking face, with a nose that appears to have been flattened by a truck. His voice, affected by that nose, is thick and guttural. It is rumoured that he and some others had been removed from a ship in Brisbane by the authorities, en route to the Spanish Civil War. Upon the outbreak of World War II, he has joined immediately and ended up in our Unit.

In choosing Paddy I take into consideration that he is a smoker, and the fused detonators have to be packed into the primer with cigarette papers for a proper fit.

Shelling and bombing have been kept up to keep the Ities guessing as to when the assault will take place. Part of the Navy's contribution is a Monitor, a ship of Battleship dimensions with a shallow draft, enabling it to get into places, inaccessible to conventional heavyweights, and to use its sixteen inch guns.

With time for the assault on Tobruk to commence, we move into position. We are in plenty of time and, as at Bardia, it is bitterly cold with the night wind keen and biting. Without picks and shovels to dig a hole, this time we have to endure it. The two men from the Pioneer Unit join us and I put them into their positions in our lineup. I choose the most likely looking one of the two to come out to the wire with me. After our job is done, both men have to rejoin their Unit and carry on with the assault.

Our orders are to fuse the Bangalores at the start line before moving off. But my mates' experience at Bardia show that it is better to fuse them at the Tank-trap, where there is still sufficient time, and less likelihood of the fuses being dislodged on the way in.

But, we are so cold here, that I decide we shall do our fusing at the start line. It will occupy the blokes while we wait and, besides, I am following orders. So, Paddy and the boys knock out the wooden plug and thread the fuse through the hole; they pack the detonator in the primer, and then knock the wooden plug firmly back into place.

Our clearance teams have been busy most of the night. They have laid out a start line of a thousand yards in marking tape and have cleared land mines right up to the Tank-trap. Officially everything is clear, but, upon checking with the fellows myself, I am told there were so many mines here that our guys could not carry them all. They think they have cleared all of them, but some they have had to leave behind. They warn us to be careful.

We line up as we did at Bardia and the rum does its rounds. Then it is time to start walking in. Again the fireworks are brilliant and spectacular, and the noise deafening. Beneath the canopy of fire we plod on in relative quiet, with the targets well ahead of us.

The flat terrain is covered fairly loosely by low clumps of saltbushes. As I lead my team along, I keep a wary eye out for anything that may have been missed by the clearance crews. We are about halfway in when, suddenly, I spot a circle of cords radiating out from the edge of a bush, just two paces in front of me. It is dead in our path and there is no way we can go around it. I instantly halt my crew and gingerly move forward to inspect the mine. If it is armed, I'll have to deal with it. I have some nails in my pocket, just in case.

The mine itself is now clearly in my view. I bend over, cautiously, and stretch out my hand to feel for the hole in the extended plunger. As I am crouched over, with my hand about to make contact, a runner, from somewhere on my right with a message for somewhere on my left, charges straight across in front of me. Without even noticing, he rips straight through and breaks the circle of cords. One second he is there, the next second he is gone. Nothing happens, so I give the order to move on.

For one shocked split second, I had died. Then, in the next split second, I have surged into life again, feeling damn foolish, but very grateful. The mine must have been one of those neutralised, but left behind. The runner never knew how close to disaster he had come. He appeared and was gone so quickly, that I didn't have a chance to speak to him.

This interlude has dropped us behind a little, and now we have to hurry to get into position. I keep alert for any further sightings, but we make it through to the Tank-trap without further incident.

We still have some minutes to go before it is time to go out to the barbed wire. I gather the crew together, checking once again that everybody knows what is expected of him. Then another emergency arises. The fuse to one of the Bangalores has dislodged and been lost, somewhere behind us—perhaps where and when I had called a halt at the mine. I immediately put Paddy to work to re-fuse it.

I now have a problem over which of the pipes to use. The key pipe is the trigger, the one whose fuse is to be lit. If I stick with the two I have, I cannot be sure that they too haven't worked loose from the primer. I decide to use the one that Paddy is re-fusing as the trigger.

I tell Paddy of my intention and urge him to be certain that it is a proper job. While he is working, I take Sparks to the front edge of the Tank-trap to spy out the barbed wire. We can see it fairly well from where we are and I feel satisfied that Sparks will be able to tell if he is needed to take out the backup team.

Meanwhile, Paddy fusses over his task, while the others hold the pipe steady for him. Finally, he declares the fuse is ready. My two helpers and I get ready for the dash to the barbed wire, as the final minutes tick away.

Then it is time. The wire is about fifty yards from the Tank-trap and we waste no time getting out there. I lead with one end of a pipe, then Lenny with the tail of mine and the front of the other, then Davidson from the Pioneer Unit with the tail of that one.

We drop to the ground at the edge of the wire. I quickly push first pipe right through, so that it protrudes from the far side by about a foot. With Lenny now by my side, we smartly push the second into position, so that it laps the tail of the first by about two feet. To ensure a proper placement I roll this one away from and then back, so that they are now hard against each other. Davidson is right behind us in support.

I ready my matches to light the fuse in the approved Army fashion. This requires the match to be placed on the forty-five degree-angled-cut of the fuse end, and struck with the matchbox striker. I take hold of the fuse, feel for the end, and know immediately that I am in big trouble. The fuse end cut has been made with a blunt knife, so that the end has not properly severed. This semi-attached end has been pulled away, leaving frayed ends of casing, and allowing the fuse powder to spill out. I have no alternative but to press on.

I position the match as best I can and strike it with the box. As it sputters alight, Lenny jumps to his feet and prepares to dash back to the tank-trap. I order him to stay put, and he drops to the ground behind Davidson. The match flickers and dies, with the fuse refusing to light. I try again, this time with a couple of matches, hoping that a wider spread of flame will do the trick. Once more, it refuses to take. Meanwhile, Davidson, sensing the problem, moves into position alongside of me and just vacated by Lenny.

We have been out at the wire longer than expected, and the Bangalores on either side are getting close to exploding. If that happens, we three will be chopped to pieces, as well as the wire. Resisting the urge to panic, and steadied by Davidson's calm reliance on my decision, I get ready for one more try. This time I take a bunch of six or eight matches, strike them in the orthodox manner, and hold them under the fuse end. Davidson holds the fuse steady and, with both hands cupping the very bright flame, he feeds it directly onto my small fire.

The reflected brightness on such a dark night should have given us away to the Italians, if they had been on the alert. We cannot be worried about that now and just carry on. For a long moment nothing happens, then comes a very faint splutter of burning powder. Immediately, I give the order to clear out, and we scamper back to the Tank-trap with Lenny leading the way.

The rest of the crew are relieved to see us, as they worry at our long absence. Sparks is just about ready to take out the relief crew. All I can say is that we have had trouble with the fuse. I am still not sure whether our attempt to light the fuse has provided a genuine take, or whether we have just lit some loose powder caught in the frayed ends.

The Lieutenant-in-Charge of the Infantry column alongside mine is anxious to get going and asks if he can carry on. All I can tell him is, "No, there is still one more Bangalore to go."

As I wait for the blast, all I can do is recap on what has happened. By rights, I should have delayed longer to make sure it was properly lit, but I had just run out of time.

Again the Lieutenant asks me for the Okay. I check my watch and am shocked at how much time has elapsed. I have held them back for more than a quarter of an hour, when the burning time for the fuse is approximately one and a half minutes. I have either missed the blast or the Bangalore has failed to explode. I give the word and off they go.

Anxiously, I watch the column of advancing men in the dim light and see them negotiate their way through the wire. Whether it is through my gap or somebody else's, I cannot tell. I will just have to wait until daylight to find out.

It is time for the two men from the Pioneer Unit to move on also. I shake their hands and thank them for their help, particularly Davidson. He has been a tremendous tower of strength to me out there. He is a good man to have in a crisis. Now, all I can do is wish him well. If I never see him again, he leaves me believing that we have been successful in our job and that he will have the quiet satisfaction of his part in it.

Now that the first wave of Infantry has gone through, I query Paddy about the re-fusing. He claims to be totally mystified and is adamant that he has done everything by the book. He wonders if we got the pipes mixed up, but I have been very careful and am certain I had used his pipe. While I know Paddy well, he is from another Section of our Unit, and I am not familiar with his general work. I just have to take his efficiency for granted.

Our attack, by now, is well under way and is an exact copy of the Bardia operation. The Barrage is heavy, but aimed somewhere well ahead of us. The multi-coloured Italian return fire streams up into the air, with planes seeming to be their target. A Lysander spotter plane is again circling low down just ahead of us, completely oblivious of anything the Italians can throw at him. The parachute flares he drops hang in the air, seemingly forever.

Further along to our right comes the heavy rumble of moving vehicles and several tanks come into view. They are Italian tanks captured by our blokes at Bardia, and pressed into service for this job. They have our kangaroo motif stencilled all over them in white, so that there can be no mistake as to who is using them now.

Without exception, they all break down, most of them just making it through the wire. One fails just on the brink of the Tank-trap and I make a mental note to have a good look at it after daylight. The disgusted Infantrymen abandon them where they stop and carry on by foot.

Cocker and Fatty have again managed to attach themselves to an Infantry Section for their souvenir foray. They give us a cheeky wave on their way through. And now comes one of the strangest sights that is possible to see on a battlefield.

There is a short gap between the first wave of troops and the second. Now the second comes into view, but unlike the first that advanced spread out in a skirmish line, these march in at Company strength in columns of threes. They are fully equipped for battle with all gear, plus tin hats. Their C.O. is leading in front, but in front again is their Padre. He is bareheaded and clad in a white surplice that reaches almost to ground level. Around his neck and hanging almost full length is his gold-trimmed purple stole. He has an open Bible in his hands and is reading aloud from it, in the dim light of an approaching dawn. We watch open-mouthed as they steadily come into view, and just as steadily move out of sight.

I keep staring out at the wire, trying to see if my Bangalores have exploded or not. Gradually it gets lighter, until finally, I am able to see. The two pipes are still there, lying in position. They had failed to fire. I am furious and disgusted at my failure. I order my crew out to the wire to retrieve those offending pipes. We will cut the hole with our hand cutters. I am determined that the job will be done, although the need is not so urgent now. While the others collect pipes, Sparks and I cut the barbed wire. It is surprisingly easy to cut and we peel back large sections of the wire in seconds. The job is done in a few minutes and, for all the effort that has gone into the Bangalores, it hardly seems worthwhile.

I order the now useless but still dangerous lengths of pipe, together with the spare, to be taken well away from the area, and dumped further along the Tank-trap. One thing I notice in cleaning up my failure is that the front of our advance had converged inwards upon itself. If the Italians had been on the ball, they could have chopped us to pieces.

With the action having moved well ahead by now, things are relatively quiet. Still upset at the failure of my job, I decide to wander along and take a look at that tank. I want to be by myself, and use it as an excuse to be alone in my misery.

I intend to climb all over it, inside and out. It is the first chance I have had to get close to one and I am curious. As I get closer I can see a twisted metal object under the track closest to me. It is a badly mangled Italian anti-tank mine that has failed to explode. I immediately abandon my attempt to explore the thing. And I can only marvel at the great good luck of that temporary crew who had abandoned it.

Great streams of Prisoners are again coming back and being shuttled through to our rear. By midmorning our senior Officers come through to our positions. It is now time for the team Leaders to report, regarding their missions. As the only failure, I have been dreading this. But when my turn comes, all I can do is tell the C.O. of my problems in getting the fuse to light. I tell him how finally I had to virtually light a fire under the fuse end in my two cupped hands. I hold them out in front of him in demonstration. As I do so, I look down at them, suddenly realising I am wearing woollen mittens. If I had lit the fire in my two hands, surely they will be scorched or marked in some way. But there isn't a blemish on them. Hastily, I drop my hands to my sides, hoping he will accept my story for the truth it is. The C.O. accepts my report without comment, and I am not badgered in any way.

The Hierarchy are over the moon with the outcome of our efforts at both Bardia and Tobruk. In the welter of so much success, my little effort is hardly even noticed.

The pressure and stress has given me a king-sized headache. My tin hat seems to be pressing ever harder down onto my skull. We are given the job of clearing anti-tank mines and there are hundreds of them. We just stack them in big piles ready to be carted away later. I just go about my tasks mechanically, and am very pleased when the day is over.

The pattern of fighting at Tobruk has been almost the same as for Bardia. It has taken a day or two longer for the fighting to finish, and here the prisoner tally is between forty and fifty thousand. Tobruk has been better fortified, with their in-depth strongpoints stretching right back into the town.

Our pattern of pressure and advance continues with our next objective being Derna. This time however, instead of being the spearhead, we remain behind in Tobruk. We are given a spell. The Unit moves into what has been an Italian artillery strongpoint called Fort Palastrino. It is time to totally relax, feed-up, clean-up, take it easy and lick our wounds. It's time for a proper general bludge. Our job requirements are practically non-existent, and we have time to have a good look at what has been captured.

Palastrino, like all Italian strongpoints is mostly underground. The caverns and storage areas have been cut out from solid rock by those master workers in stone and concrete. The surface perspective is bare, flat and bleak with practically nothing visible to indicate that an installation is there. They seem well-nigh impregnable and our ease of its capture seems unbelievably remarkable.

My Sub Section takes over a fairly long, low wooden hut as our quarters. It has a row of single iron beds, side by side, sufficient to accommodate all of us. The Italians have moved out, leaving all their personal gear behind. There is all manner of things and we just help ourselves to whatever takes our fancy. I confiscate a mauve, blouse-type, windcheater. It has a silver zipper front and two silver zippered breast pockets. Short little silver chains hang from each zipper to activate the catch. It is a high fashion garment, and I fancy I would be as pleased to own it back home as I am here.

There are family picture albums containing snaps of quite beautiful wives and sweethearts. And in the manner of soldiers anywhere, there are some of quite pornographic nature. All in all, it is much better here than making a hole in the ground.

A refrigerated truck is found, tilted to one side just off the road. It is full of sides of beef still frozen solid. Using the truck itself as storage, Pee Wee and Reg with the aid of a butcher in the Company, take just what is needed. For a while we live like kings.

There are large supplies of Italian foods such as dehydrated vegetables that only need the addition of water in the cooking. There is a plentiful supply of coffee, and bottles of mineral water. A gully is found containing great quantities of wine in very large wooden barrels. It is nicknamed Cognac Valley.

We turn up for breakfast one morning to find Pee Wee and Reg under the influence, but still functioning. They have a row of large wooden barrels lined up with the heads stove in. As well as our regular fare, we have a choice of beverages to wash it down. We can opt for Chianti, red wine, white wine, Cognac, coffee, tea or cocoa. Using a saucepan as a ladle, they are dishing out the wine in large quantities.

There are weapons of all kinds lying about, ranging from revolvers through to light machine guns and quite heavy stuff. There are grenades of all kinds as well as prepared Molotov cocktails—bottles of petrol with a grenade wired to its base. You grasp the bottle by the neck, pull the grenade pin, then hurl it at your target. The bottle smashes, spilling its petrol everywhere, then the grenade explodes at about the same time and the resulting fire is spectacular and very hard to quench.

Naturally, we have to try these weapons out. Anything we consider useful, we will put to use. The weapons themselves we find are quality stuff, but the ammunition is a different matter. A reasonable amount of it is faulty and fails to fire.

There is an abundant supply of revolvers of a long barrelled type, similar to those used by cowboys in Western films. Everybody has to try his hand at a "quick draw" with one of these. When attempting to fire one, you often can pull the trigger on the same cartridge for as many as twenty times without getting it to fire.

For myself, I have obtained a nine millimetre Beretta automatic pistol that I am very happy with. At all times, I carry it in its holster, strapped to my waist, as my personal weapon. The ammunition for this seems good.

A few of the fellows develop a habit of wandering down to Cognac Valley, having a few snorts and testing some of the arms lying around. A small group are throwing grenades one day. One of them pulls a pin, draws his arm back for the throw and bumps his arm on a rocky outcrop. The grenade is a contact grenade and explodes instantly, blowing his hand off.

His mates bring him back to camp and his stump is bound. He is given a shot and made ready for evacuation to hospital. Although still on his feet, he is a little woozy. As he boards transport for the journey, his parting remarks are, "Well at least I should be able to get a job as a lift driver back home."

One day a Pommy Transport Sergeant turns up and asks if we have seen some of his men. We are mystified and ask, "Why?" He says he has been told they were last seen in Cognac Valley, drinking with one of our blokes. He has tried there, but his men have gone, and their truck has gone too.

As we are talking, we notice a truck slowly making its way towards us, across country. There are no roads and the whole area is heavily pockmarked with holes, craters and emplacements in the rocky and sandy ground. It lurches violently from side to side, seemingly in great danger of overturning. It comes to a barbed wire fence and ploughs straight through at the same leisurely pace. Finally, it rolls to a halt in front of us. It is a Pommy truck and it is being driven by one of our blokes who, to the best of our knowledge, doesn't know how to drive.

The Sergeant asks where his men are and the driver says, "In there," pointing to the back of the truck. We go round and look over the tailboard. There are six men scattered across the floor of the truck, and all unconscious. They are clad in shirts, shorts, socks and boots, and have plenty of exposed skin area. Almost every square inch of that exposed skin is stripped, exposed and bleeding.

We ask the driver how they got in that state and he is just as mystified as we are. Obviously, their rough journey home has thrown them about so violently that that has caused the damage.

We ask our bloke, "What happened?"

He says, "Well, I was sitting around and just talking and drinking. And, one by one, they passed out. When the last one passed out, I had nobody to talk to, so I decided it was time to come home. They are all good blokes and I just couldn't leave them there. So I picked them up, one by one, and rolled them in, over the tail board. I didn't know where their camp was, so I have brought them home to ours."

"Why haven't you taken a proper road?" we ask.

"I wasn't sure which one it is, so I decided to take a short cut."

The Pommy Sergeant is ropeable. He rants on about the punishment he is going to inflict on his blokes. We argue their case with him, pointing out that we are in the field and, as long as they do their job, they should be allowed to relax a little. Besides, the punishment, unwittingly meted out by our bloke, will make them very sick and sorry for some days to come.

In the end, he seems to mellow a little. He climbs into the driver's seat, and sets off for home with the still unconscious men in the back. His own driver follows behind in their ute. But this time they take the proper route.

Lenny has acquired a motor bike in good running order and he spends a fair bit of time ranging out across the desert looking for souvenirs. Souvenirs to some people are something interesting to take home, while to others, they are just something to sell. Lenny is definitely the latter kind.

I notice that he always seems to go off in the same direction. I chide him about it, pointing out that one-going-over is enough to find whatever is worthwhile souveniring. I ask, "What have you found interesting out there where, obviously, there appears to be nothing?" Then he tells me.

He has stumbled on a small Italian outpost of ten or twelve men. They know of the surrender, but are well-stocked with provisions and intend staying put until these run out before turning themselves in. They offer to surrender to him, but Lenny has a better idea. They can stay there and carry on with their original plan and they can occupy their time searching for marketable souvenirs to turn over to Lenny. In return, Lenny will keep them supplied in the one thing they are short on—cigarettes.

Lenny offers to take me out to meet them, but there are a few things I have to consider against that idea. First, is my status as Lance Corporal. If I go, I will have to bring them in as captives. That will scotch Lenny's souvenir plan. Then there is the thought of bouncing across the desert on the back of a motor bike which is being driven by a novice rider. After the Pom's experience, I decide, "No thanks".

So each day, Lenny goes out to his souvenir hunters. He has a fine meal with them, but comes back with precious little. They are in an isolated area, away from most of the installations, so are unable to come up with anything of note. In the end, I think Lenny's hunters get more out of him than he does from them.

Due to wear and tear and natural attrition, the Unit is understrength in full NCOs. It has been the practice to transfer in, the odd one or two Officers needed, from outside the Unit. Now there are strong rumours that the required makeup will come from promotions within the Company itself.

While natural progression suggests that appointees to full status will come from the ranks of Lance Corporals and Lance Sergeants, it still leaves openings for those ranks also to be filled. Some appointments will have to be filled from the ordinary ranks. There is much jockeying to find out who and when these promotions will take place.

My Sub Section mates are very vocal in asserting that my name has to be on top of the list. Privately, I'm not so sure. There is that failed Bangalore torpedo job to be taken into account. Then, it isn't my style to try any lobbying as some are prepared to do, quite blatantly. While the extra money will be handy, my personal feelings have me wanting to be close to my mates.

In anticipation of my promotion, my good friend, Harry Bassford, begins calling me The Little Corporal. When I look at him askance, he solemnly assures me that that is the nickname of Napoleon. Again, I am not sure, whether or not, I am being got at. But it keeps me from getting too bigheaded.

In the midst of all the speculation, Taffy and Dave wander in one evening and assert to me, "Well, we've fixed it. Your name should be on the board tomorrow, promoted to Corporal."

In dismay, I ask, "What the hell have you been up to?"

They have been down to Cognac Valley having a quiet drink, and they got round to discussing the probable appointments. As a result, they decide to confront the C.O. and tell him who they should be. As Taffy puts it, "We've just been to the C.O. and abused the shit out of him. We told him Arty Dawson has got to be promoted to Corporal before any of those other bludgers." All the time Dave is nodding his head and interjecting verbally in agreement.

I groan at the thought of what might have occurred and say, "You pair of buggers have probably cruelled any chance that I might have had. Anyway, what did he say?"

"Nothing," replies Taffy belligerently. "What could he say? He knows it's true."

I know them too well to think it might be some kind of joke. I know they enjoy a rather easy-going relationship with the C.O., because of their work. But this is pushing things a bit too far. I think of going to him and try to explain. But how? He might think that I have put them up to it. In the end, I do nothing.

Next morning, the notice board is the focus of much attention from my blokes. The orders appear and, sure enough, there is my name, among others, promoted to Acting Corporal. "There you are," says an unrepentant Taffy, "I told you so. If it hadn't been for me and Dave, you'd have missed out."

But in the end, I think it is the C.O. who scores the most, for he leaves me in charge of my old crew. Discipline may have been better served, had I been moved to another Sub Section. Maybe he figures, that with such an unruly lot, it will be poetic justice to leave me to find out how to sort them out myself. I know it cannot be done physically. I will just have to try common sense and guile. But, under the circumstances, I cannot complain.

With the appointments made, the newly elevated men immediately appear in public with brand new sets of stripes sewn on their sleeves. Headquarters must have anticipated promotions when we set out on this campaign and brought their stripes with them. There is certainly nowhere here to obtain them.

As for me, all I can do is take some stripes off a discarded Italian uniform. They are smaller and totally different to ours, but it is the best I can do. This doesn't make me exactly popular with my Section Commander who, himself, has been promoted to Acting Lieutenant.

No time is wasted in putting the new appointees to work, with myself being detailed as in charge of water supply for the following day. Enquiries regarding these duties find that all that is required of me is to ride upfront with the driver of the water truck and deliver one load to the Italian prisoner-holding compound.

This job is being done on a regular basis and all I have to do is follow the daily routine. A couple of men do the work and the driver knows the pickup and delivery points. The truck itself is just an ordinary truck with a large tank riding in the back.

The watering point is marked by a small hut with a large diameter galvanised pipe rising from the ground in front of it. The limited supply is strictly rationed and controlled by a permanent twenty-four hour guard. Only authorised personnel are allowed to draw from it. The presence of water here is one of the reasons for the importance of Tobruk.

My driver moves into position under the overhead arm, with its short length of dangling hose. The Guard Sergeant unlocks the valve controlling the flow. My men man the tap and guide the flow into the tank. When full, they turn off the flow and remove the hose, scarcely losing a drop. I sign for the delivery, climb into the front passenger seat while my men ride in the back. We move off in a direction that I haven't been before. As I lean back in my comfortable seat, I can only think that this Corporal business is a piece of cake.

As I have no idea of where I am going, I just sit back and leave it to my driver to get us to the prisoner-holding compound. There isn't much to see as the whole area is flat and featureless, without vegetation and only rock and sand showing. After we have been travelling for about ten minutes, I become aware of a strange distant sound.

It is an alien sound and I cannot make it out. It grows gradually louder and is coming from the direction in which we are heading. Then I recognise the singing is of Italian light opera style, not the heavy stuff. In this God forsaken place, it is beautiful. And the closer we get, the more beautiful it sounds.

I am mystified as to its origin and half-imagined that somebody must have found a gramophone and some records. Still, it sounds too good to be recorded music. Then my driver says, "It's the Italian prisoners." But I find it hard to believe, as there is nothing to see.

Then suddenly there they are. The terrain has been rising ever so slightly that it has been unnoticed. Now as we clear the crest, the whole camp, if you can call it that, comes into view. The Guards' encampment is just to one side of the prisoners' enclosure. The enclosure is a medium-sized, rectangular area, surrounded by an ordinary barbed wire fence. There are no buildings of any kind and it looks for all the world like a temporary, cattle-holding pen.

Inside the enclosure is an almost solid mass of about two thousand of the sorriest looking, most bedraggled bunch of men that anybody can see. They are dusty, dirty and unclean. Because of the cold, they wear forage caps with the flaps pulled down round their ears and fastened under their chins. Their long overcoats trail almost to the ground, and a grey blanket is draped round each man's shoulders.

Yet, it is from this unlikely lot that this glorious singing comes. I am close enough to get the full power of their voices. It is magnificent and I am enthralled.

As my men prepare to discharge the water, I walk over to speak to the Guard Sergeant. He and about half a dozen of his men are constantly moving up and down, exhorting the Italians to sing.

I ask him, "How on earth can you entice them to sing?"

He says, "We just have to. If they ever take it into their heads to just lean against the fence, the whole damn thing will collapse. We've just go to keep them occupied."

I know that, because of our policy of clearing the prisoners out of the area as quickly as possible, their stay here will be very brief. So the rough conditions they are putting up with now, will soon be over.

Once the water is discharged, we all climb back on board and leave. As we go further and further away, the sound of their singing gets fainter and fainter, until it ceases. Due to the normal rotation of duties, I never manage to get back there again. But the memory of that experience will last for a long time.

By now, Derna has been taken, then Benghazi. The front has moved on to El Agheila. Practically all of Cyrenaica is in our hands. The rapidity of our advance has surprised everyone. Then our Unit gets word to move up again. This pleases us for, although we have enjoyed our relax and stay in Fort Palastrino, we are just as anxious to get on with the job.

We leave Tobruk and head westwards on to Derna, where we turn left and inland. The road begins to climb up yet another steep escarpment. On top of this escarpment, we enter a totally different world. Here the land is fertile. There has been heavy rain and the county is dotted with neat little farmhouses. There are trees and grass growing as well as crops and gardens. In the farmhouses are Italian civilian families going about their daily business. For us this is different. Up to now, we have not had to cope with non-combatants. Somehow, we will just have to work around them as we get on with the business of war.

On our first day here, we pull up at some empty brick buildings on the side of the road near the town of Barce. We will stay here for a few days, awaiting further orders. With rain about, we can use their shelter rather than just doss in the open as we are used to.

As we are in transit, awaiting to move on, there is nothing to occupy our time. We just sit around in idleness. There are a few Infantry Units in the area in somewhat the same position. To curb any ideas of mischief, somebody in authority comes up with the idea of holding a sports meeting.

All this athletics stuff doesn't appeal to us at all. Besides, we haven't anybody much in the way of talent to consider. Then I remember my Newcastle mate, Tex Ramsay. Tex had confided in me that at a sports meeting back home, he had done the hundred yards in ten seconds, bare foot.

Tex is a good mate of mine from our pre-war Militia days. He has come into the Unit as a recent reinforcement, so he is not-well known to the other blokes. He had joined up after us and was in Palestine for training when the Desert Campaign started. Not wanting to be left out, he, and a few others, just took off. They hitched rides all the way until they reached the fighting zone. Tex just turns up one day, more or less asking for a job, and, as we are a few men down in strength, the C.O. accepts him while sending through the paper work to make it official.

I spread the word that we do have a possible contender for the hundred yard dash. A few of the blokes become interested, then dream up a scheme to make a financial killing. They will gather up all the money they can within the Unit and back our dark horse to win.

They reason that, as we are on service, there won't be proper gear around. Almost certainly the others will run in sandshoes, and, when our bloke turns up in bare feet, it will be seen as a disadvantage. We should be able to get good odds.

On the day of the event, just Tex and a couple of the blokes to handle the betting, present themselves. The contestants wander around allowing themselves to be seen, and, as expected, our bloke appears to be a forlorn hope. The bets are made, then the runners are called to lineup.

Immediately, our blokes know they are in trouble, for in the centre is a runner clad in full professional gear, including spiked running shoes. The race is run and the professional wins easily. Then his Infantry sponsors reveal the fact that he was a Stawell Gift winner. So, instead of taking the others, we have been taken ourselves.

When Tex and the backers had left for the meet, they did so with the enthusiastic well-wishes of most of the Unit. There were words of encouragement and pats on the back. After being beaten, their return is virtually ignored. There will be little spare cash for most until somehow or other another payday can be wangled.

We leave our temporary stopover and move on near to Benghazi. We have to pass through Barce where we look for signs of shops, bars etc., but there are none. It is just a rural town. Our guys have established some store dumps there, and we see lots of military traffic passing through. As the roads are all dirt roads, they are deeply rutted and bad. We are pleased to get to our destination.

We find our new quarters to be a collection of neat wooden buildings, fully lined and comfortable. Once again our C.O. has managed to have us set up just a little bit better than average.

We quickly settle in and are given the responsibility to run a short railway between Benghazi and Barce. With just an Engine crew and a couple of others needed for the job, again, the majority of the Unit has very little to do.

I have taken to wearing my mauve jacket most of the time, despite the lamentations of my Acting Lieutenant. While he does not order me not to, he lets me know that he is displeased and considers it to be unmilitary. I fob him off as much as possible by pointing out my tunic is also unmilitary with its bodgy stripes. Anyway, there is not much chance of a ceremonial parade out in the field.

For the moment, with the front having consolidated some distance ahead, there seems to be a temporary halt. There are patrols and skirmishes and some aerial activity. But things in our Sector are very quiet. We seek permission to visit Benghazi. After coming this far we want to see the place. We also reason that there certainly will be some sort of commercial activity there, if only in the way of a couple of bars.

Quickly, a leave of sorts is organised. We climb down from our truck in an open Square in what proves to be a very neat but rather small town. The enclosed harbour is also rather tiny and there are several small ships sunk at their moorings, whether by hostile action or scuttling we are unable to tell.

There are absolutely no civilians in the place at all, other than a handful of Arabs. The Arabs have small bottles of lolly water for sale from boxes they have set up in the Square. There is no way of cooling them. The odd one has a bottle or two of hard liquor as well. This is of a type unknown to us and highly suspect. Very little trading is done, firstly, because we have no interest in their wares and secondly, because they want to trade in Italian currency.

It is obvious that the place had been a thriving commercial centre with many businesses operating around the Square. Surely somebody has stayed behind and traded on. But it takes us next to no time to find that nobody has. And they have not just walked out taking whatever they can. They have stripped the whole town clean—the goods, the fittings, everything. Not even a chair remains.

Thoroughly disillusioned, we give up and prepare to board our truck and head back to camp. As we are passing what has obviously been a large shop of some kind, we spot a large steel door set into a large wall surface. It can only be a doorway into a strongroom and this, certainly, has been a jewellery store.

The door has not been forced and gives no sign of having been tampered with. The only way to find out if anything has been left in there is to get that door opened. And this will require blasting it open, either by a professional or a very good amateur.

We feel certain that the owners are relying on the security of their strongroom for protection, and have left a goodly portion of their stock behind. They probably intend returning to it as soon as the fighting stops. To get at the contents will require a blast, a quick grab and a scatter, before the MPs intervene, a hit-run affair. This is one leave we are quite happy to get back to camp from. The only thing worthwhile remembering is the question of that strongroom.

One or two are foolish enough to have bought a bottle of that suspect liquor. It is a clear liquid, like water to look at, and put out in small soft drink bottles. The label names it as Grappo. My own crew of very hardened drinkers won't even touch it.

We awake the next morning to some very sobering news. One of fellows has died during the night and was found dead in his bed. We all know that we are not exactly on a picnic over here. But it doesn't seem right for it to happen like that.

While we are all still shaken by the news, my Acting Lieutenant calls me in and orders me to arrange the funeral. I try to talk him out of it, claiming a Sergeant will be more suitable than a Corporal and besides, I do not know the procedures. He is adamant, however, and I am stuck with the job.

The Acting Lieutenant makes the official arrangements through our Company Headquarters. They cover the paperwork, the gravesite, and a Padre for the Service. There is an Official War Cemetery at Barce. My job is to get him there and to see him buried.

Now that I cannot get out of it, I make my own plans. I know that one of our blokes has worked with his father in England, building coffins, as an undertaker. His name is Les Lawrence. I order Les, himself a newly promoted Lance Corporal, to take a couple of men and construct a coffin. I take him to one of the spare wooden buildings, and, pointing to the beautiful tongue and grooved pine board lining, tell him to rip it out and use all he needs for the job. This they do and finish the task later in the day.

With the coffin completed, our comrade is placed inside for his last journey the next day. His mates have removed his personal belongings and these are handed into Company headquarters. The necessary notification to the next-of-kin will be done through the proper channels.

The next day, I arrange a Utility to carry the coffin and a truck to convey about eight of his mates to the funeral. For the Padre's convenience, we are to arrive at the grave site at about eleven. We set out allowing plenty of time and, on this occasion, I wear my tunic, and not my zippered jacket.

With the Ute leading, we follow along what has now become a deeply rutted and dusty road. Our dead comrade had been one of the most vocal complainers about the rough rides experienced up here. This one is to be his worst. Several times the coffin bounces violently from the tray of the Ute and hard up against the overhead pipe canopy. Each time I expect the coffin and body to be thrown out the back. If that happens, the box will be smashed and Les's good work gone for nothing. Luck is with us and we finish the journey without losing our load.

At the grave site, the hole has been dug, and the bareheaded Padre is ready and waiting for us. After a few words with him regarding our comrade, we just gather round and the service begins. I have not considered having a firing party, so the ceremony proceeds more or less as if it is in civilian life.

At the completion of the short service, I thank the Padre for his help and the men set-to and fill the hole. Almost certainly, this is the only person buried, while on service, in a coffin.

With the service over, we remember that Barce is a Supplies Headquarters and that, almost certainly, means canteen supplies as well. We have been in the field for a couple of months now and have been unable to get any of the basic necessities. The thing that irks us most of all is the failure of our beer ration to find its way to our Unit. I decide to seek out the Wet Canteen Supplies Depot and see what we can do about it.

After a little searching, we find the place and I decide to take the bold approach. I tell the Sergeant in Charge that I have been sent by my C.O. to pick up our Unit's beer supply. I tell him that we have missed out for some months now, and the C.O. is concerned as to why this is so. How come they have fallen on their job?

These hard-headed men have heard most of the hard luck tales by now and are very careful of not being ripped off. He says there is no way he can release any without the proper requisition signed by the C.O. This is a standard answer, so I say, "Give me a form and I will sign it on his behalf."

The Sergeant demurs a little, then says, "Okay." As long as the Sergeant has a signed requisition, he is in the clear. By demanding that the ration is for our entire Unit, I have made my request as near to legitimate as possible.

Now comes the scramble to pay for it. We have to chip in from among ourselves to find enough money. This makes the Sergeant edgy as, under normal circumstances, our C.O. will have provided the cash out of Unit funds. I explain this away by telling him that we have just come from a funeral after burying one of our mates, and did not know that their depot is here. And, therefore, we have neglected to bring the funds with us.

We load up and quickly get out of there before he changes his mind. The trip home is made much more carefully than the outward one, and we make it back safely without any breakages. I insist that the beer be distributed in the manner of a normal issue of one bottle per man. Those, who have contributed to the cost, are reimbursed.

We are given a great welcome back in camp. We have sent our Comrade on his way, in a fit and proper manner and, as a bonus, we get to drink his health as well.

A few days later, persistent rumours begin to circulate that the strong room has been cracked. Nobody seems to know by whom, or at least they are not saying. Then a mate lets slip that it is amazing how small an amount of explosive was needed to do the job. A detonator with a short fuse was placed in the keyhole. Just sufficient gelignite was packed around it to seal the hole and hold the detonator in place. The fuse was lit and those concerned stood with their backs to the wall on either side of the door. After the bang, the door swung open of its own accord. Those involved make a dash inside, scooping up whatever they can lay their hands on, then quickly exit before the MPs come running.

The unconscious inflections in my mate's voice, as he tells me the tale, makes me pretty sure that somebody else, other than my mate, has done the job. Whether he has been a spectator or not, well that is another matter.

Initially, there is no sign of any of the proceeds. After a few days, discreet words begin to circulate that, for an interested buyer, maybe a few items can be forthcoming. Nobody seems to know the source, but a stated intention of purchasing will bring forth half a dozen items for a private selection, sometime later.

I have accumulated a few souvenirs of medals, badges etc., and I intend sending them home by post. I decide to include a few gifts for my family and lady friend. I let it be known that I would like to buy something and, in due time, my mate turns up with a selection. I choose a small propelling pencil, a wristwatch and a ceremonial dress medal. For me the price is very cheap and I have no way of knowing where they came from. I take the whole lot to my Acting Lieutenant to be franked, put them in a small biscuit tin and get Taffy to seal it with solder. I sew the whole package in cloth from an Italian ground sheet, put the appropriate labels on and send it off home. In due course, I receive word of their safe arrival.

Our Unit is becoming browned-off with our comparative inactivity and are impatient to get moving again. After reaching El Agheila, our front just seems to get bogged down. We are told of a few German planes having appeared there, with one or two being shot down by ours. In one instant, the pilot had bailed out, but his 'chute had failed to open. When found, his body, encased in his flying suit, was just like a bag of jelly.

We feel we are losing our advantage and giving the enemy a chance to get stronger. Then comes word that we are to be pulled back and be committed to something else. Wild speculation has us being sent to all sorts of places, even to England to prepare for the Second Front. Our C.O. has been gone for a couple of weeks now, with rumour suggesting that he is in Cairo. Maybe this is what this is all about.

The Section is assembled with our Acting Lieutenant giving us orders for the journey. The whole Unit will move out in convoy and keep going with as few stops as possible. Our destination is just outside Alexandria, and we are required there as soon as possible. Each truck is to maintain its position in the convoy at all costs.

He takes me aside to tell me that those are the orders given to him and what he is expected to enforce. If there is to be any trouble at all, he expects it to come from my unruly lot. He puts me on notice of dire consequences to myself if anything untoward happens.

We set out on that long journey and in two days we are back at Mersa Matruh. We have travelled over 700 miles. I have some minor friction with my mob, but manage to keep them under control. Besides, everybody is hoping for a bit of leave.

Our stay at Mersa is to be brief, with movement to follow onto our former camp outside Alex, as soon as it is cleared. Other troops are moving up and taking over positions as soon as they are vacated. A few of these fresh new men meet us at Mersa and eagerly question us as to what they will have to deal with up there.

One of these men sits talking to us and is open-mouthed at the amount of weaponry we have. Everybody has a revolver of some sort at least. I have my Beretta automatic strapped on and there are several of those long-barrelled cowboy types lying around. First sight of one of these makes them irresistible. Movie pictures have long featured them as the cowboy's standby. You just have to pick it up, feel its weight, spin the chamber, aim and fire.

A group of us is sitting around, tired after our long drive, so the man is cautious not to fire it. Then somebody tells him that the Italian ammunition is faulty and, although the chamber is full, it is unlikely to fire anyway. Reassured, he tries a few tentative firings, taking care with his aim. When nothing happens, he gets bolder and a bit careless. Suddenly the gun fires, and Fatty, one of our souvenir scouts, receives a bullet through the fleshy part of his upper left arm.

As the wound is not serious, I tell the man to scram back to his own lines. When our Acting Lieutenant comes to investigate, I pass it off as an unfortunate accident with the bodgy Italian ammo. I also claim that the gun has been destroyed, for possession of them is rather frowned upon. For the shocked and furious Fatty, it means he will not be going with us.

Our C.O. now rejoins us and is seen to be wearing a medal ribbon on his jacket. It is for the Distinguished Service Order, and a lot of the men are furious. They say, "We did all the work and he gets all the glory." With a beer ration on tap, somebody takes the liberty of informing him of their displeasure. Thankfully, this time it is neither Taffy nor Dave.

Next morning, he orders a full Company Parade. He addresses the Parade saying, "You will see that I have the honour of wearing the D.S.O. I want you to know that it is not my D.S.O. It belongs to the Company. I am wearing it on your behalf. We have also been awarded six Military Medals, which are to be distributed at my discretion. All this is for the very good work you have just completed."

The Company takes it in, mostly in silence. They still aren't greatly impressed. It just doesn't seem the right way to gain a decoration.

Our Unit moves on to camp outside Alex., and catch up with some of the things we have been missing. Here we are served up a belated Christmas dinner, several months late. It is marred somewhat, for no matter how hard the Cooks try, the food still contains its quota of desert sand. Then, what we have been waiting for—leave is granted.

After several months up in the desert, we just cannot wait to be let loose in Alex. Everybody has their priorities, but nobody will overstay their leave. With a general movement so close, it is unthinkable to be left behind.

We split up in our little groups and head off in whatever direction takes our fancy. Everywhere we go, the locals make a fuss of us. The successful Desert Push has been well publicised and they are keen to show their appreciation.

My mates and I head straight to a large barber shop. We all climb into a chair, lounge back and order the works. The staff, happy to oblige, busily fuss over us. We are given a haircut, a shave, a shampoo, hot towel treatment and an ultraviolet face massage. It takes about an hour and a half and when it is finished, we feel on top of the world.

We now set out to visit some of our favourite haunts. First there is Sister Street and the girls. Some will indulge and some will just look. Then it's to the Cap D'Or and the long Bar, and one or two of those good Arab cafes. There is no need for food for, in all of them, an endless supply of the tastiest snacks of many varieties, comes with the drinks. The change from camp food is wonderful. Just to sit there, lounge back, and forget the sand and flies, is heaven.

Finally, it is time to return to camp. Midnight is the deadline and everybody tries to spin it out to the last moment. I arrive back to bad news. Taffy is in hospital. He has been knocked down by a taxi in the blackout. He had left us during the day and gone off with some of the others. He had been trying to cross the road when hit. He is the victim of a new game the Cabbies have dreamed up—knock a serviceman down and go through his pockets. With our departure imminent, there is not a thing I can do. The report I get says that he is a bit knocked about, but otherwise in a satisfactory condition.

Then our Unit moves to a small rail spur for a short journey to the docks. A few lone Arab traders appear with bottles of Scotch for sale. Mindful of the purchases made prior to moving up the desert, which turned out to be coloured water, a couple are enticed aboard, only to be tossed off as the train gets underway. It is satisfying to see them roll over and over down the sandy embankment, then jump to their feet in fury, with nothing hurt but their dignity.

We arrive at the docks for a night-time loading. We will sail under the cover of darkness. We are headed for Greece. We have no fears about the trip for we are supremely confident that our Navy is in complete control of the Mediterranean. The whole Contingent is now seasoned, blooded troops, supremely confident in their ability to take on anything that is thrown at them.

For me, the sobering thought is that I have lost my minder. With Taffy left behind, I am without my backup.

# Chapter 7
# The Greek Campaign

THE TRIP ACROSS TO GREECE doesn't worry us in the slightest. The big threat in this area comes from the Italians and we have them, well and truly, on the run. Our navy is in control of the Mediterranean and we have a strong Air Force to back them up. This should be a pleasure jaunt and so it proves.

We don't even bother to look for comfortable quarters, but just lounge and loll about the open deck. Moby Dick and Sparks just flop where they have been standing, and quietly resume their never-ending game of crib. An idle moment is never wasted by these two. They just get on with their game, anytime and anywhere. One of them carries a thick and dog-eared pack of cards in his pocket while the other carries the board. The ritual is always the same. One will pull his tobacco tin out, select what he needs to roll a cigarette, and hand the tin to the other. He, in turn, will take what he needs and pass the tin back.

All the time they will be having a quiet dig at each other saying such things as, "It's about time you bought a new pack of cards. These are bloody terrible." Or, "This tobacco tin is just about empty. See you get the bloody thing filled." And, "These are lousy cigarette papers, you've got. Where the bloody hell did you get them from?" The back and forward wordplay will be answered in kind. Each ignores the others insults and gives back as good as he gets.

Then they will light their cigarettes and, using the spent matches as crib board pegs, get on with the game. The slight digs will continue while we all watch. There is an affinity between these two that is well-nigh perfect. Their oblivion to anything other than their game has a tremendous calming effect upon us. Surely, no enemy will dare interrupt such a ritual.

We arrive at Piraeus at this new unknown country. We are buoyed up by the expectation that we are going to enjoy our stay here very much. Conditions will be totally different to anything we have experienced so far. There will be new people, a new language, and a welcome change to the Western Desert.

The Port area is neat and picturesque. We are met at the wharf by fleets of trucks ready to transport us to our camp area. These quickly load and get underway. We stare with interest as we begin to traverse the streets. The local civilians come into view and they are just as interested in us as we are in them.

As the trucks are canvas-covered, we crowd the tailboard for a good look. The people are all in modern clothing—not like in Palestine and Egypt where there is a considerable mix of native dress. And the girls are decidedly pretty too. It looks very much as though we are going to enjoy our stay in Greece.

As we drive along some of the girls, in twos and threes, stand on the narrow pavements and openly beckon us to come to them. A few instantly decide to take up the challenge and prepare to drop off the moving truck. The driver, becoming aware of their intentions, speeds up, making this move impossible. The girls, for their part, laugh and talk excitedly together and display great interest in these antics.

This beckoning we are to find out later is not the invitation we think it is. It is the Greek style of waving in welcome.

Our camp is on the outskirts of Athens and has just been newly set up. We are under canvas, but quite comfortable. Everything we see, we like. Our surroundings are green and fresh and there are even trees. After the bleak desert, this seems like a mini heaven. A day or two later, it begins to rain—real rain, where, if you are not wearing your groundsheet, you will even get soaked. And the smell of it all is just too wonderful. Whatever may happen in the future, worries us not at all. We are supremely confident of the outcome.

Leave is quickly forthcoming and we begin to explore with interest. We find a little coffee house that specialises in fresh cakes. We haven't seen anything like it since we left home. We order a plateful and they are all kinds—some with cream in them, others iced over with pink icing with a cherry on top. Oh boy! Do we indulge!

The red-light area is much more discreet and harder to find than in Egypt. The blatant salesmanship of the ladies there is totally different to that of the ladies here. Still, once found, business is pretty much the same. The Madam-in-Charge just stuffs the proceeds into a little drawer in the table where she is sitting.

Lenny's eyes bulge when he observes this pile of money and, instantly, he comes up with a scheme to get his hands on it. I am to create a diversion by claiming the Madam's attention, while he grabs the drawer and runs. While I can see that the initial snatch is quite feasible, I am aghast. This is robbery and my upbringing and principles of honesty rebel at the idea. I quickly veto it. Lenny's only reaction is, "Oh well. It is just a thought."

Damn him! Now I am not sure whether he has been serious or not. I have the feeling that he is testing me out to see how far he can manipulate me. I know from experience that he is an expert at it. Now, I miss Taffy, for he has the faculty of keeping Lenny's wild schemes in check.

Lenny takes the opportunity to unload the three radio sets which we had liberated from a small settlement up in the Desert. He had intended selling them in Egypt, but our leave time had been too short for him to do anything about it. We find a small out-of-the-way tavern and offer a demonstration and possible sale to the owner. While radio music is popular, the owner is reluctant. But Lenny is persistent. Lenny plugs it in, switches on the power, and blows out the set. He has not taken into consideration that the settlement, from where the sets came from, is supplied with electricity from a power generator and, therefore, of a different voltage to the town's supply.

What to do now? They are not saleable and, if found in our possession by the Unit Hierarchy, it may get us into all sorts of trouble. In the end, Lenny manages to get the tavern owner to take all three sets off our hands by persuading him that a good local radio mechanic can easily make the conversion.

Our reception by the locals is wonderfully friendly. The only bugbear is the struggle to communicate and this is accepted on both sides with great humour. We quickly pick a few phrases in Greek which help maintain our friendship—this, despite a vague rumour that Greece is fifty percent pro-German.

There seems to be only two real cities in the country—Salonika in the north and Athens in the south. These two cities, in every sense, have every modern facility, whilst the rest of the country seems to be mostly rural.

The Greeks are justly proud in that they have just completed a major Airport to serve Athens. This is very timely in view of the coming conflict. They point to the fact that men and women have applied themselves with picks, shovels and baskets to carry the soil in order to get it completed.

We, in turn, have some misgivings to think that a major project has to be carried out in this way. We can only hope that the Country is indeed prepared for what is to come.

After a week or two in the Athens' area, we are on the move again. While our short rest has been enjoyable, we are now to move right up to the mountainous northern border region. As yet, we have no idea of what we might be committed to. There is no fighting within Greece itself. The Greeks have belted the Italians on the Albanian frontier, pushing them back to Albania. What our role is to be, remains to be seen.

It is early spring and the weather is sunny and pleasant. The countryside is green and beautiful, and there is fresh sparkling water everywhere in little streams and springs. This trip is more like a holiday.

More than ever now, I am wearing my mauve jacket. My Acting Lieutenant complains mildly that I should be in proper military attire. I counter by saying that, if he is prepared to issue me with the proper chevrons to replace these bodgy Italian ones, I will gladly consider wearing the proper gear. We both know that he does not have such an item.

On this first day, we have to traverse a very high mountain pass at Bralos. I feel especially privileged as I loll back beside my driver while we pass columns of our Infantry marching over it on foot. Our Field Engineer status provides us with our own transport, while our comrades have to do it hard.

At the top of the pass we can see for many miles ahead. The road at the bottom of the pass goes straight ahead for some distance until it reaches the town of Larissa which we can just see. We are to turn off and camp for the night, just below the pass.

My Sub Section, being one of the least favoured, naturally cop one of the least favoured drivers. A liar much like the rest of us, he had claimed vast experience in order to get the job. Once there, his inexperience is patent to all. And he improves very little as he goes along. His name is Dalley, and Lenny has christened him Lord Dalley.

At the top of the pass, which is said to be some three thousand feet high, and with a winding tortuous road to the bottom, Lord Dalley decides to do the descent in neutral. When I notice this, I tell him, "For God's sake, put it back in low gear." He tries, unsuccessfully, all the way down the pass. As we gather momentum and the truck begins to sway, my crew react by screaming and hanging over the tail board, ready to jump. With a solid rock cliff face on one side and a sheer drop of thousands of feet on the other, a jump has to be the last resort.

The winding nature of the road seems to slow us down on the bends just sufficiently for us to make it round. Somehow we make it to the bottom with Lord Dalley riding the brakes and still trying to get back into gear.

We shoot off the bottom of the pass at tremendous speed, and fly up the straight stretch of road towards Larissa, before he manages to get the truck under control. We turn around and come back, and the guide chides us for missing the turn off. I just say, "Sorry, we didn't see you."

The guide says, "No wonder, at the speed you were going." I no longer feel pity on the Infantry, for having to do it on foot.

Our whole Unit is to spend the night here, in a close compact camp. There is lush green grass everywhere and water close by for drinking and washing. After the Desert, it is almost idyllic. The sun is beginning to set and is followed by a long soft twilight. Smoke and steam from the cooking fires, together with the smells, waft lazily into the fresh night air. As it darkens, lanterns are lit. Then a couple of Greek lads, of about twelve or thirteen, wander over, attracted by these strangers in their land.

We are attracted to them too, and soon friendly encouragement from the fellows has them at ease. We feel we want to give them something, but are at a loss at to what might be appropriate.. With the Unit being on the move, part of our ration tonight is Army biscuits. Somebody tentatively offers the lads a few of these. They snap them up and eat them with gusto.

We are only too pleased to keep them coming as we regard them as hard and tasteless. It seems too, that food here is not all that abundant.

The lads, for their part, feel that they have to do something in return and offer to sing to us. We encourage them to go ahead and, there are these three Greek lads, surrounded by a fair group of us, singing in sweet clear voices. We don't understand the words of course, but we like the tunes. The lad most favoured by them seems to be called Garoydo Mussolini. We gather that it is a derisive dig at the Italians whom every Greek despises. Following their great success against them in Albania, the Greeks consider themselves far superior to any Italian, and feel obliged to show it.

It is quite late by the time the lads call it quits and wander off home. In this friendly land it is deemed unnecessary to mount anything much in the way of a guard. War, for the moment, seems very far away and remote.

In the morning we move on again. As is his want, My Acting Lieutenant singles me out; he warns me to maintain my position in the convoy and see that my misfits do not get up to any shenanigans. He is a bit sensitive about his own position, and is of the opinion that, if there are any problems, they will come from my lot.

Actually, he and I get on pretty well. It is just that he is a little bit stuffy in his ideas, and I am a little too much my men's way. I know that the reasons for his attitude are sound and, we both know, that mine leave a little to be desired—especially for a NCO in charge of a Sub Section. But, I feel that, as long as the blokes do what is expected of them, then tight discipline does not matter too much.

Moving in convoy is a strange thing in that the movement order calls for maintaining steady speed, usually at thirty-five miles per hour. The leading vehicles have no trouble with this and travel along quite sedately. But, each vehicle in succession has to travel a fraction faster than the vehicle in front of it, just to maintain its position. At the tail end of the convoy the last vehicle has to travel at between forty-five and fifty, just to keep up.

My Sub Section C is the last Sub Section in Section Three, and the last Section in the Unit. As such, we always travel near the tail of the convoy. Under the circumstances, there is little trouble we can get into, even if we want to.

The journey north is pleasant and agreeable. There are sunny days and a few spring showers. The roads are good and the countryside interesting, while the scenery is diverse. There are mountains and valleys and some plains. For camping sites, we will just pull off the road for the night. If the weather is good, we will sleep in or under the truck. If it is bad, we will pitch a tent.

I have taken over Taffy's bedroll as my own. It contains a piece of sponge rubber matting that had been stolen from the wrestling ring way back in Palestine. To set up my bed, all I have to do is untie a piece of rope and roll it down. To get ready to move, I roll it up again and retie with my piece of rope. At night, I string the rope between two handy points and hang my clothes over it, ready to put on again in the morning.

Keeping clean is no problem, for there are small streams and springs everywhere. At one such place, we are able to indulge in a natural shower. A stream, said to be from Mount Olympus, has formed a small waterfall about eight to ten feet high. The stream cascades into a large bowl worn into the native rock. The bowl is about twelve feet in diameter and about chest-deep at its centre.

We strip off and wade in. It is so intensely cold that we can only stay long enough to get wet and then have to come out to soap up. Then follows another dip in to wash off, followed by another quick dash to dry off. It is wonderfully invigorating and it has us jumping out of our skins.

During convoy, I manage to stage a pseudo breakdown, once or twice, in a reasonable sized town. While Lord Dalley goes through the motions of cooling down an 'overheated' motor, I manage to buy some loaves of freshly baked bread. They are large, round, wholemeal loaves, and are very welcome.

We now begin to approach a solid block of very high mountains. They mark the border between Greece and Yugoslavia. They are rugged and snow-capped and, we believe, the only way through them is by mountain passes. It looks like ideal country to defend and we feel pretty sure that anybody will have a hard time getting past us.

As we get closer, we can see a bank of what looks like smoke, hanging in the air, and about two thirds of the way up the mountain. Our road climbs up through it and, when we get there, we find it is a cloud. We continue on, so it looks as if our positions will be above the cloud line.

At last, a halt is called and we spread out into what is to be our permanent camp. We are high in the mountains and the terrain is very rugged. The peaks ae still some distance above us, while rocky outcrops give an abundance of cover. The road continues on and disappears from view. Pockets of snow lay about further up above us.

Snow is a new phenomenon to most of us, and, as soon as we are able, a few of us take time out to go and have a look-see. It is a long hard climb and almost straight up. We find the snow to have set in banks of ice, and that pristine white colour has turned to a dingy grey in close-up.

From up here we have an even greater appreciation of the area we are taking over. The more we look, the more certain we become that it will be well-nigh impossible to dislodge us. We feel sure that the going will be so difficult for an attacker that a handful of men will be able to hold off an Army.

For the next day or so, we are given a roving commission to traverse and familiarise ourselves with the surrounding roads and tracks. This involves coming back down the mountain and scouting the flat lands below. We are not sure what our role may be, but, if we have to go somewhere in a hurry, it will be a big help if we know where we are going.

We are on one of these forays and are returning to base in the early afternoon. While still a few miles from the foot of the mountains, I become aware of a solid block of movement, dead ahead of us. We know this area is totally isolated of both people and animals and, at first, I cannot make out what it may be.

As the gap between us narrows, I become aware that it is people. There are thousands of them and they are spread right across the flat fields as well as the road. They are all on foot, just hurrying along, making no noise. It is uncanny.

As the human tide and our truck come together, all we can do is pull to a halt at the roadside. For a moment it is impossible for us to advance any further. They just surge around and pass us, ignoring us completely. They are all civilians loaded down with suitcases or anything they can carry. They are intent in putting as much distance as possible between themselves and whatever is behind them. They surge on and on, and it is four hours before we are able to move on again.

The stream has now become a trickle. I realise that they are Yugoslavs fleeing their country and that this is just the vanguard. Fleeing civilians, cluttering up battle zones, will make it very difficult for us to fight a war. I just have to get back and let our people know what we have encountered.

We arrive back to find the whole Unit packing feverishly and preparing to break camp. I hurry to my Acting Lieutenant with my story, as well as to find out what is going on here. He tells me that the Germans have overrun Yugoslavia and are now in complete control. We are under orders to pull out and move back as soon as it is dark.

"Why?" I want to know. "We've got a marvellous positions here. Why can't we take them on here? We've got a distinct advantage." Then comes the bad news. They have broken through the Greek forces, well over on our flank and there is a real danger that we can be cut off. We have no alternative but to pull back.

Everybody feels bitter and frustrated. We cannot expect to have positions as good as those we now have to abandon—and without a fight, too. It goes against our grain to pull back. We aren't used to it and don't like it. How have they managed to get through the Greeks?

While we know the Greeks are regarded as good tough fighters, we now learn of some of their limitations too. They have practically no transport other than a small amount of horse-drawn stuff. Everywhere they go they have to march. If a man goes on leave, he has to hand his rifle to the man taking his place. Other arms are in very short supply also. If a breakthrough comes, it takes a long time to rush in reserves to plug the gap. Sadly, they are able enough, but they just aren't equipped enough to fight a modern war.

Nevertheless, we are, and we have Air Force backup as well. Or do we? Then comes the nagging worry of that modern airfield outside Athens. It is their latest and greatest. But it had to be constructed with manual labour. Does anybody know of any other airfields in the country? Nobody seems to, so all we can do is hope.

Our troops are good enough; we have already proved that. But then, so too have the Greeks. Our gun supplies and transport are top class, and we have augmented all that with lots of Italian stuff that we had captured up the desert. But that Italian stuff is a bit tricky and unfamiliar, with the machine guns and field guns working quite well, but plagued with faulty ammunition.

Our own stuff cannot be interchanged with the Italian. It has been made abundantly clear from the beginning that any Units electing to use Italian arms as supplement to their own, have to ensure that they also carry an adequate supply of ammunition. Our Stores supply none at all.

All the desert men have done experimental firings with different Italian guns and, whenever a stoppage occurs, it almost always is due to their bodgy ammunition. Nothing like this has ever happened with our own. While we cannot bring ourselves to abandon the stuff, we cannot rely on it either. It will just have to be a backup of last resort.

I have commandeered an Italian light machine gun, together with several clips of ammunition, and carry it in my truck. It is somewhat similar to our Bren guns, but much lighter in weight and much less robust. Several of my crew and I have our Beretta automatic pistols, but, because of this ammunition thing, we cannot put too much reliance on the stuff. So we have to cut and run.

We hope our Air Force will get cracking and be helpful. We hope our arms are sufficient and good enough to hold them out, although there is some worry and misgiving. This Greek caper has lost its holiday atmosphere and is beginning to sound a bit ominous. Somehow, we are starting to get a slight feeling of being trapped.

When you retreat or make a strategic withdrawal, you do so under very adverse conditions. We now have to make our way down that mountain road, in the dark, with little or no lights, and, with the rocky cliff face on one side and the unprotected drop on the other. I am also 'blessed' with the dubious talents of Lord Dalley as my driver. He is prone to ask me, "Am I near the edge? Will I give it a go?"

I answer frantically, "Stop! Back up! Swing to the right!"

In due course, we make it to the bottom of the mountain, with the road now continuing on fairly flat terrain, back the way from which we had come. We are in Convoy and it is just a matter of keeping to the truck in front of you. We drive on and on, fighting against sleep and not knowing where we are to stop. Much later, in turn, we pull off the road. This will be our campsite for the moment. But first we will have to disperse our trucks before we can settle down.

This is to be the regular pattern of our behaviour. When required to move, we will do so only after dark. Always it means travelling at night, and only moving into cover before dawn. Sometimes we might stay in one position for a couple of days. At others, it may be each and every night. It all depends on a particular Sector that allows us to delay and hold the Germans in check.

Each and every day the German presence becomes more and more evident—their planes in particular. They just take over the skies. Initially, we wait expectantly for our lot to rush up and take them on. But this does not happen. None of our planes show up at all. Bitterly, we come to realise we will have to face up to this encounter without aerial support of any kind.

There are several types of German planes being used, but the one that bugs us most of all is the Stuka. It is a dive bomber type. A flight of fifteen or twenty is the norm. They will peel off, one after the other, over a target and, in a steep dive, release a bomb and then climb back into position for another go. Once all bombs have been released, they will swoop down to shoot what is left, with their machine guns.

To create as much panic as possible the Stukas are equipped with screaming devices on their wings and on the bomb fins. At first, we think this is childish, but they soon start to get to us mentally. A plane will peel off at the start of the dive, and the screaming will become ever more loud until, at the release of a bomb, it has risen to a crescendo. Then the scream of the bomb will take over until the bomb hits its target and bursts. These screaming demons seem to be aimed at the back of your neck, so that you have an almost irresistible urge to claw your way into the ground, as deeply as possible, to get away from them. In time, we learn to assess our possible danger from the loudness of the screamers.

At the outset of our withdrawal, things are pretty much a scramble. Whenever our Infantry takes up new positions, they are more intent on hitting back than preparing for rapid disengagement. They tell us of one of their first encounters.

They had dug in on the forward slope of some hilly ground. These were scattered positions, some yards apart, but each able to support the other. Each position contained about six to eight men. While being on guard against the Germans, they also had to watch out for any of our stragglers. During the night, some of the forward positions were observed by those at the back, to climb out of their strongpoints and advance towards the Germans, then disappear from sight. They had not returned by daylight and investigations pieced together what had happened.

Some Australian stragglers had stumbled up during the night, calling softly as they came, "Can you tell me where the 16th Brigade is? We're lost.", or variations on that theme. Somebody would stick his head up and call softly back, "Over here." The stragglers would circle the position, then suddenly reveal they were not Australians. They were Germans dressed and talking like Australians. They would order their captives to climb out and march them back to German lines, without a shot being fired.

Our blokes are furious at having fallen for such a sneaky trick, and fiercely determined to shoot without warning ANYBODY approaching at night.

Falling back involves delaying the enemy as much as possible. That means blowing up roads and bridges or any good targets. That's where we come in. This is our Unit's function. One of the first blow-up jobs is a small road bridge. It will not be a big obstruction in itself, but it will delay them at least a few hours. They will have to approach with caution to see if it is defended, then clear the gap.

The laying of charges is a pretty straight forward job, with enemy activity still some distance away. The actual blowing up will be performed by a party of three or four men. They will wait until the last possible moment to do so, then scamper to their ute, hidden close by, and speed away from the area.

A small rearguard of our side will be delaying their troops as much as possible to allow the others the maximum chance to get away. The blow party has to give the rearguard every chance to get away also. This means they have to get the okay from the rearguard that there is nobody left behind them— and actually, almost in sight of the Germans, before they light the charges. It needs some fine tuning and responsible judgement to get the timing right and some steady reliable men to carry it out.

Our Number Three Section is given this job and our Acting Lieutenant selects the men to be left behind, while the rest of us are to clear out. His choice is good, and the men accept it without demur. They all are men, whose general behaviour is frowned upon, by him, as being unruly and disruptive. One of them, Burkey, struck by the oddity of the choice, decides to say something about it.

"You know," he says, "You've got no time for us. You reckon that we're just a bunch of drunken no hopers. Yet, when you want something done, you know who to call on, don't you?"

The Acting Lieutenant replies cheerfully, "Of course, I choose you because I know I can rely on you."

This job goes off without a hitch, but another one, a day or two later, almost comes to grief. This is a double blowing up job, where the rear one is some distance behind the other. Our Unit handles the front one, while a different Unit handles the rear one. Our blokes fire theirs, race back to the other one, only to find it has already been blown. Our blokes are now cut off, and the Germans are right on their tails.

Meanwhile, our whole Unit has pulled back and dispersed to a new campsite. Word comes back to us of what has happened. Two of the men, in the missing party, are my Newcastle mates—Les Thomas the driver, and Moby Dick. We all feel pretty bad about it, and curse the supposed panic of the other Unit in doing their part prematurely.

All that night and well into the morning of the next day, a fairly gloomy pall hangs over everybody when there is no news or sign of them. We just stand around in knots waiting for some tidings. The worst affected is Sparks. He had been with me on the Bangalore job in Tobruk and is Moby's crib-playing best mate. He always is a taciturn man and says very little. Now he just paces up and down in an agitated state, saying not a word.

We chide him in our usual rough manner, saying, "Wearing out boot leather isn't going to help things." But he ignores us and continues on with his pacing up and down.

It is about eleven o'clock when a figure comes striding towards us. He is smiling and jaunty and, unmistakably, Moby Dick. Bill halts in his tracks and just stares open-mouthed. Moby marches straight up to Sparks, adopts his usual slouch, one thumb hooked into his belt and says, "Gidday Sparks." We are all as pleased as hell at his return and, for a moment, there is dead silence. Then suddenly, Sparks bursts into the greatest tirade of swearing and abuse I have ever heard, all launched at Moby. We can only stare, open-mouthed. He goes nonstop for about five minutes. It is the greatest torrent of words we have heard from him since we have known him.

Moby is just as surprised and open-mouthed as we are. He just stands there not knowing what to say. Then suddenly Sparks stops. He reaches into his pocket, pulls out his tobacco tin, holds it out at arm's length to Moby and in his normal voice says, "Here, have a smoke." Instantly, they both relax and just stand there swapping words as if nothing has happened.

Apparently, when they had found themselves cut off, a resourceful Les turned off the road and slammed across open fields, looking for a way out. He came to the railway line about half a mile away and forced his utility up onto the tracks. He bumped along over the sleepers until the ute broke down and could go no further. They abandoned it and struck off back towards the road. They were now in an area of extensive swamp through which they had to wade and force their way. Finally, they reached the road and were lucky enough to hitch a ride on one of the last remaining trucks bringing out the rearguard. Because our Unit had moved, it took a bit of time for them to find us. The whole party is safe, but minus a ute.

The pattern of our lives now, while confused, is pretty simple—a day or two here, then drop back to another location. We concentrate on keeping the Unit together with each Sub section sticking pretty close to their truck. A few jobs that come our way, usually only call for a couple of men and are quickly completed.

The Stukas are above us every hour of daylight. With no opposition, they fly as close as they like. We hate them passionately and, in our frustration, we often loose off a few shots from our rifles. This has absolutely no effect. But, because of their activity, there is very little cookhouse activity either. In the main we just grab something to eat, whenever and wherever we can.

One afternoon coming on dusk we pull up close to a solitary farmhouse. It is one of the very few we have seen and appears to be deserted. There are a few chickens scratching about and a couple of nice fat ducks paddling on a pond. One of my crew mentions that a nice roast chook dinner will be very acceptable right now. We agree that a roast will be out of the question, but we ought to be able to come up with a stew.

I select a likely looking duck, pull out my Beretta and shoot it. At least I think I do. The damn duck just floats there on the pond as if nothing has happened. I think that I must have missed, or the ammo is faulty. I raise my pistol for another try, when suddenly the duck rolls over on its side—dead.

Now all hands turn to cleaning the bird, cutting down a petrol tin for a boiler and getting rid of the petrol taste. With some onion for flavour, we put it on to stew. We have to rig a shelter so that no light can be seen from outside.

One of my crew, Bill Heaps, claims to have had some experience of cooking birds and predicts that we will be in for a long wait. He claims that ducks take much longer than fowls to cook. Now he tells me. Why hadn't he told me before?

Indeed it is a long wait. It gets later and later, and I begin to worry that we might get called upon to move out. We are feeling hungrier by the minute too. Finally, we can wait no longer. Bill Heaps is right. It is only about half done. We tuck away and there is plenty of gnawing and chewing. At least, it is something different. But we all decide that it will be better to stick to our dry rations, until we have the time to do a better job.

Another blowing up job sees us in some hilly country, where the road winds round two spurs, and passes through a narrow flat area a little over half a mile wide. The target is a small bridge over a river bed, about five hundred yards ahead of the right-hand spur. The road leading to the bridge continues on, winding around the right-hand spur, and obscuring it from enemy view. It then continues on for almost a mile, before clearing another long ridge at right angles to the road.

Although I am not included in the team, I am there to see the placement of the crew and to take in the terrain. It is a pretty good spot, with plenty of open ground in front of the bridge. This will give the men ample time to recognise our rearguard from the enemy, before setting off the charges. Then it will be a quick dash to our ute, hidden behind the spur, followed by a fast getaway up the road, using the ridge as cover.

With jobs allocated, I return to our camp area, a couple of miles behind this particular front. I have hardly got back when Jimmy Hay hurries up to me, and tells me that he has a job, and he wants us to get into right away. Jimmy is Second in Command of the Unit, and is from our Newcastle-based contingent. He and I have had much experience working together in our Militia days. He is one Officer, whose judgement, I have some respect for.

He wants us to return, from whence we have come, and help lay out a mine field. A Sergeant-in-Charge of one of the other Sub Sections is carrying out the job, and he needs some assistance. I am surprised about this, for we have seen no sign of such a job going on, even though we have just left there.

We return, and, just as we clear the ridge, almost a mile from the hill spur, there is a large dump of landmines in wooden cases placed on the left-hand side of the road. They have appeared from nowhere, between the time we had left and returned. We can also see the other men working feverishly across the fields at right angles to the road. The dumpsite is quite a distance from the worksite.

We hurry down and I tell the Sergeant, "We are here to help. What do you want us to do?" He tells me they have completed the task on the open side, and are now working on the side sheltered by the hill spur. He gets one of his men to demonstrate the arming of the mines, and for us just to follow in the same pattern.

The mines are domelike with a spring-loaded lid. The fuse, about the size of a man's thumb is thrust into lace from the underside. They are then armed and ready to do their job. It is simple and straight forward, just place them into position. The demonstrator is a bit reckless in forcing the fuse into place, so I decide we will keep some distance from him, just in case.

We have no problem following the pattern as it is clearly visible. The mines are to be placed in a narrow band, stretching on either side, and at right angles to the road. The band is about six to eight feet wide, and several hundred yards long. The mines are fairly thickly laid, being no more than two feet apart and in staggered rows across the width of the band. We set to and just follow the pattern set by the others.

As we work, I begin to assess the military aim of our job. The road itself has not been mined. With mined stretches on either side, it seems that the object is to force the enemy to use the road. If that is the aim, then you will have field guns in position to beat the hell out of him. But I have seen no sign of any guns. If there is to be no stand or opposition here, then the minefield is nowhere near extensive enough. It should have had much more depth than just that narrow band. The Germans are fairly close and we can expect them to make contact fairly soon. Maybe our mines are just a stunt to make them think we are going to make a stand here. If so, it is pretty amateurish and, with troops as competent as theirs, they will charge straight up that road the instant they realise there is no opposition. Then, all this will be for nothing.

The Sergeant is some distance away from me, so I cannot question him in any way. There is nobody else in authority overseeing the job, so I can only conclude that it is he, who is deciding what the pattern will be. The only experience in minefield layout, that most of us have had, is the disarming other people's. The more I see of this one, the more I think it is a useless exercise. There is no attempt to even hide the mines. A couple of blokes just go along and dig small depressions with a shovel, and then the arming crew will drop a mine into each hole. There is little or no attempt to cover them with dirt.

After about three-quarters of an hour's work, the job is completed—at least as far as the Sergeant is concerned. He declares, "Righto, that's it. Let's get out of here."

There is still a very large dump of unused mines just in front of the ridge and well back up the road. I say to the Sergeant, "How about those? What are we supposed to do with them?"

He replies, "They're none of your business. Just leave 'em."

This appears to me to be patently stupid. But the Sergeant is in charge, and there is nothing I can do. Those mines had been rushed up between our first departure for camp and our return to help with the laying. I now have visions of the Germans using our own mines against us.

We hightail it back to camp, pleased to be well out of the area. As we pull up, Jimmy hurries over and enquires if the job has been completed. When told it has, he asks what has been done with the surplus mines. When told that they have been left behind, he becomes greatly concerned. Then he says, "They must not fall into the hands of the enemy. You'll just have to go back and get 'em." So once again, we turn around and go back, from whence we have come.

This time, some three or four hundred yards before the ridge, there is ample evidence of shell bursts and a few bodies are scattered around. Ominously, the bodies are of our side. We have heard nothing of an engagement and are taken by surprise. We approach the ridge with caution, leaving our transport under shelter and continuing on foot.

From this side of the ridge we are out of sight, and able to walk the few yards to the crest, in a fairly open manner. But once we get near the crest, from where we will be able to see what is in front of us, we become much more cautious.

We drop to our knees and edge our heads over the skyline. There, about a hundred and fifty yards away is the dump of unused mines, just as we had left them. The long stretch of road leading down to the spur of the hill, including the fields to either side, are completely devoid of any sign of life.

I say to the Sergeant, "If we are to pick 'em up, we need to drive the truck alongside the dump, sling 'em aboard, and get out as fast as we can." The Sergeant, as leader, is turning the idea over in his mind—no doubt thinking of the driver's reaction to being told to drive over the crest and thereby making himself a prime target when, suddenly, he notices some activity, where the road rounds the spur.

It is some three-quarters of a mile away, but we can plainly see a knot of about a dozen men setting up a heavy machine gun in the centre of the road. They are Germans. Obviously, they are there to safeguard their comrades behind them who are bridging the gap, which we had created by blowing the bridge. Our minefield is a couple of hundred yards in front of their present position but, at this moment, any protection for us, seems pretty meagre indeed.

The Sergeant says, "Well, that's it. We've got no hope of loading those mines now. The best thing we can do is get out of here."

While everybody is only too anxious to agree, I say, "Well, what's the chances of destroying them?" Nobody is willing to consider the idea, thinking it to be too dangerous. I persist, suggesting that it will be possible for someone to crawl up to the dump, using it as a cover to screen him from being sighted by the mob below, then arm several mines and prop them up against the crates. Then, using our rifles, we can fire from our present positions and hopefully set them off. It just might set the whole dump off in any resultant explosion. At least, it is worth a try.

The Sergeant will not consider it. I suppose the racket we may make will focus their full attention upon us. With our small group, being the only lot of our side, still around here, they may give us hell. He gives the order to get out, and everybody scrambles quickly back to the truck. The driver wastes no time in getting us under way, and making a speedy retreat out of the area.

We arrive back at camp, where Jimmy rushes up and shakes hands with every man in turn. He declares how pleased he is that we are back, as he never expected to see us again. This is quite a jolt. The Sergeant reports that our mission is unsuccessful, because the Germans were in sight.

The business of giving ground gradually, and being more and more harassed by Stukas, is getting all of us very edgy. Day after day, we watch for our planes to give us some relief, but they never come. Food is a bit of a problem for, with this constant shifting about, it is difficult for stores to find us. Any transport movement is gleefully set upon by Stukas. Movement by night becomes the norm. But driving is a nightmare, with little or no lights and the ever-present danger of going over the edge of a cliff. Trying to keep awake and alert has everybody bug-eyed and weary. Tempers are frayed and, although nobody becomes openly hostile, Lord Dalley threatens to shoot me.

Each Sub Section sticks close to their truck and, although part of the whole Unit, it operates and keeps pretty much to itself. For camping, we will choose a position where we can duck for cover when the planes come over. Our light Italian machine gun is always at the ready, in case we can get a chance to fire back. Although this is a fairly useless exercise, just hitting back gives us a tremendous psychological boost and immense satisfaction.

Lord Dalley is just a shade more panicky than the rest of us, and is very quick off the mark. He has developed the habit, at the first alarm, of springing to his feet, sweeping the machine gun up into his arms, turning and running for cover. He almost always is quicker off the mark than anybody else.

As he sweeps up the gun and turns, the muzzle will traverse an arc that sweeps across the whole of our group. The danger to all of us is considerable, as a good sort of bump is sufficient to start the thing firing. I, therefore, order him not to touch the gun anymore.

He draws a lot of comfort in just the feel of the gun when the alarm goes and, to be told not to touch it, makes him very resentful. He mutters, half aloud, that if I try to stop him, he will shoot me. I tell him that it will have to be in the dark, and from behind, as I doubt he will be game enough to do it from in front. We are all tired and bad tempered, and things are easy to say. The whole gripe stops there, and never goes any further.

While there is plenty of fighting in Greece, there is very little in the way of a set battle. For one thing, we cannot afford it. Our blokes have to just hold and delay, then fall back to the next natural barrier for another stand. Always the threat of being outflanked, spurs us on to another move.

We are in some high country south of Aliakmon River for yet another pause. The main road, through a pass, is almost a mile away, on our right. While we are in perfect peace here, the pass is being subjected to a sustained and heavy pounding by the Stukas.

From our positions, we have a great view across an open valley for about twenty miles. About fifteen miles away the Stukas and their support personnel have taken over some flat grassy fields. They are operating with three flights of between fifteen and twenty planes per flight. They are operating a shuttle service so that a flight is over the target at all times. So, while one flight is bombing, the flight they have just relieved is on its way back to reload, while the third flight is ready to take-off fully armed.

They maintain this terrific, continuous pounding, all afternoon. It is obvious that there must be a special reason for paying so much attention to this one particular target. And there is, for our Sixteenth Brigade has been cut-off and are stranded on the other side of the river.

There has been a bit of a buzz about, that we are here for a special purpose. What it is, nobody seems to know. Now it turns out, that we are to get the Brigade across under the cover of darkness.

This is achieved by building a trestle bridge. While the men are safely brought out, a lot of their transport has to be abandoned and left behind. Only part of our Unit has been used for this particular job, and I am not one of them. For a moment, I pause to reflect, "I have spent six years training in the Militia building trestle bridges of all types and the one instance, where my training may have been of some use, I am not even called upon."

Jobs here, jobs there, some of them are just plain damn silly. One night, we are sent to a rail siding after dark to take some supplies somewhere by truck. We find that the supplies are steel pickets which are used for erecting barbed wire entanglements for fixed positions of defence. As we are constantly dropping back, our positions are anything but that. Still it is a job we have been told to do, so do it we will.

The truck and driver is from another part of the Unit. We only have to supply labour with the driver knowing the destination. By the time the pickets are loaded, we have between three and four tons aboard and the vehicle is overloaded. We pack the load across the body of the truck so that there can be no sideways movement. But there is a fair bit of space both in front of and behind the load. But if we crash, the pickets will be flung everywhere and my crew riding in the back with them will be chopped to pieces.

We set off with me riding in the front with the driver. He is a good competent driver and we carefully creep along, mostly by instinct rather than by the light from our headlamps. The road is fairly straight for a while but then it begins to twist and turn as we begin to climb. It is inevitable that we shall come to grief and we do so on an S-curve after rounding a small shoulder.

As we come into the bend, he drives just a little too close to the road edge and the front and rear offside wheels drop over. Because he is going slowly, he is able to stop immediately and we just balance there. Nobody is hurt, but we all have to be very careful getting out, in fear of causing it to roll over. Once we are on solid ground, it is obvious that we cannot do anything more tonight. We cannot tell how deep the drop is and we cannot possibly unload it, until it is safe to do so. We hitch a lift home and leave the truck just as it is.

In the morning we return with the Transport Corporal to see if we can salvage the truck. In daylight we are able to get a good look at the situation. We have been pretty lucky, thanks mainly to the driver. Although the drop is nothing like some of the precipitous stuff we have come across, it still is some seventy to eighty feet. The truck may have rolled over and over and, the damage to the fellows inside, just cannot bear thinking about. There is a general underlying fear of being injured in some way, and having to be left behind in some obscure first aid station or hospital.

The position of the truck is pretty tricky. Because of the bends in the road, it is very difficult to tow out and our vehicles are not heavy enough anyhow. I assess that I will be able to get it out okay with the gear we have by using ropes, blocks and tackle and a couple of holdfasts. This is the sort of stuff that I am good at and the Transport Corporal says, 'Go ahead."

We begin to set up, and are working away, when a heavy transport vehicle comes along. He stops to see what we are up to and the Corporal asks for a tow. He gets a steel cable hooked on but, as we have already assessed, the angle of the pull is extremely difficult. He persists, however, and, instead of rolling out, the truck is dragged virtually sideways. Our driver is able to drive it back to camp but, two days later, it has to be abandoned. That sideways drag has damaged the wheels too severely.

A day or two later, we are moving in daylight when we come across a sorry sight. The road has been bombed and there is a single large crater in the centre. As the road is fairly flat, all it needs to get around the crater is to turn off over a moderately bumpy bit and back on again. Judging by the wheel marks, most traffic has managed this alright. But, when we arrive, one truck has rolled onto its side while trying to negotiate the bumpy part.

A couple of trucks before us have skirted the bloke in trouble and continued on. When we arrive, we can see the driver's dejected figure sitting forlornly by the roadside.

The closer we get, the more familiar the driver seems to become. Then we realise that it is Tess, one of our best drivers and, therefore, one of our trucks. We pull up and I go over to him and say, "Come on mate, we had better get you back on your wheels." Where before he was totally without hope, he now springs to his feet brimful of confidence again.

I put the crew to work, unloading Tess's truck, while instructing my driver to move into position for a strong pull. With the loss of some transport, the drivers have been rostered round a bit and, today, I have the services of one of the better drivers.

I get him to back up to the wheeled-side of the fallen truck, and at a right-angle to its centre. I take a stout rope and fasten it to the chassis on the downside, pass it over the steel pipe canopy affixed to the truck tray, then fasten the end to the back of my truck.

We are helping a mate and our willing workers have everything ready to go in ten minutes. I rehearse with my driver what I want done. I want a strong hard pull at the beginning to get Tess's truck to start to rise, followed by a sudden hard brake as it gets onto its wheels. I give the signal and my driver does just that. Presto, the truck is back and ready to go. Quickly we reload and Tess is on his way.

We have been losing, on a regular basis, bits and pieces of equipment, both large and small. And to achieve this minor success gives me a good feeling. I feel that this is a victory, a poke in the eye to the Germans, and it makes me feel happy for a long time.

A steady feeling of resentment and helplessness is creeping into our innermost thoughts. We are being pushed around, and can do nothing much about it. We had sped through the country like conquerors. But now we are dropping back almost as quickly and, seemingly, with our tail between our legs. For our Unit, there is frustration in having to move without seeing much happening. There are other Field Engineer Units and the occasional blowing-up jobs are spread around. With that seeming to be the main activity now, there is not much else we can do.

It is not that we are fearless and spoiling for a fight. It is not like that at all. In the main, we are jittery and jumpy, and the Stukas do their damndest to keep it that way. Moving about in daytime is hell. All you want to do is get under cover and stay there. These damn Stukas seem to be permanently camped just above us, so close that you feel you can reach out and almost touch them. They bomb and shoot up anything that moves. I pity the Supply Corps men whose job it is to ferry supplies forward from base. Their lives must be hell on earth.

Also, it's tough for the Infantrymen. Their job is to hold the enemy back, while giving everybody else the chance to clear out, before they can clear out themselves. This constant fighting, then breaking off and relocating, gives them very little chance for eating and sleeping. Of course, their job of taking the brunt is spread around between them. But the burden is steadily worsening for all.

We are in a quiet spot one day when I come across a small group of Infantrymen resting. There are about ten of them and they are close together in a small circle, seeming to draw comfort from each other to the exclusion of anybody else. Their eyes are large, wide and sunken, and they are unshaven and dirty. They are just slumped there, almost in total exhaustion.

I just stand there, a bit fearful of approaching, as they are oblivious to anybody else. Then one of them looks at me and suddenly calls out, "Arty!"

I move forward and say, "Hugh? Hugh Howie? Is that you?" And indeed it is.

Hugh Howie had been a Corporal in our Unit and one of the original members. While on training in Palestine he had become disenchanted and frustrated with the way things were shaping and asked for a transfer to the Infantry. While a transfer under those circumstances is usually very hard to achieve, in his case it had been granted. I have not seen him since then, until now.

I ask him how he is faring and what they have been up to. His pent up feelings burst and he is glad to open up, especially to someone he feels will understand.

He says, "Arty, we've been charging bloody tanks with fixed bayonets. Can you imagine anything as stupid as that? We've got nothing to hold 'em. It's bloody hopeless. We've lain in our trenches and let the tanks roll over us, then jumped to our feet, climbed onto the back of 'em, and dropped grenades down the turrets. But the bastards won't beat us. We'll see to that."

Then we talked back and forth about their trials. He claims that, man for man, they feel that they have the Germans' measure. But those tanks are the hard things to combat. I ask about anti-tank guns and he says that they haven't seen any. I tell him that I have a Boys anti-tank rifle and will give it to him if he wants it.

"What? Those bloody things," he says, scornfully. "I wouldn't have one of those at any price. They're bloody useless. I bet you've got no rounds for it."

"Only two," I tell him. Then we both agree that they are not worth carting around.

There are three Boys anti-tank rifles in our Unit, one for each Section. Each Section nominated one of its Sub Sections as being responsible for the thing and, if you were unlucky or not-too-well thought of, then you ended up with that chore. I cop it for my Section.

The gun itself is a beautifully sculptured piece of blue steel that makes you feel you just have to take it into your hands. The barrel is about four feet long and has a bulbous contraption at the muzzle called a flash-eliminator. The breech is fairly conventional and the bolt rather complicated with several pieces assembled together to help with the shell extraction. The butt is rather big and shaped to a man's shoulder, and shielded with a very thick, curved pad of sponge rubber. It fires an armour-piercing type cartridge or shell of about fifty calibre. To fire it you lay prone, legs together and your toes dug in, unlike that of a normal rifle where your legs are spread apart. It has a small tripod for support and you grasp it tightly, pulling it into your shoulder as firing it tends to make it walk away from you. It is very heavy and, frankly, I cannot see it being of any use to an Infantry at all. Ammunition is very hard to come by, and we only have the one issue that came with the rifle itself. By the time a sprinkling of the Unit personnel have had a test firing, there is precious little left. That's why I only have the two rounds.

I have been one of those to test it, and I find that the explosion drives you back a little, even with your toes dug in. The sponge rubber-lined butt takes most of the recoil. The trouble is that it takes a little time to sight and to pick an aiming point and, with a moving tank, you get only one chance. Theoretically, the shell should pierce the outer armour then burst inside, spraying the interior with metal fragments. We have not been given instruction on an aiming point on the target and feel that the sloping contours of the turret will deflect the projectile, rather than it getting through.

The gun comes in a large, long, narrow wooden crate, into which it is fitted neatly in special chocks. My crew use the crated rifle as a seat when we are moving about. This is about the best use we can see to make of the thing. At the time, this was the only weapon the pundits had come up with for the Infantry to defend itself against tanks.

We leave Hugh and his mates to get whatever rest and food they can before having to front up to the Germans again. The obvious exhaustion, both mentally and physically they are feeling, makes me wish that our Boys anti-tank rifle really could perform as it is meant to.

Close by, a small battery of twenty-five pounders has been set up, with their crews ready to fire. This is the first time we have had an opportunity to see them working, and we pause to have a look. We had been under their field of fire at Bardia and Tobruk, but never anywhere near their firing point.

The gun crews go about their business, oblivious to anything but the job in hand. We, the spectators, keep prudently out of the way and just watch. The spiteful and deadly crack, as each shell goes on its way, makes me silently exultant and I say to myself, "Cop that, you bastards! That's one for Hugh." I just hope there is something in there for those tanks as well.

We watch for a little while and envy the Gunners' satisfaction at being able to slam something back at the Germans. But we cannot appreciate being unable to see any havoc caused. Their spotter is out in front somewhere, calling the range and finding the targets. But the Gunners are unable to see any hits. To us this is very disappointing, but then this is how Gunners have to work. The only counter that the enemy has, is to use his own heavy stuff and to put his tormentor out of business. The probability of a reply is sufficient inducement to make us move on.

We hear of the bombing of a small town in Central Greece that badly upsets the Greeks. While the bombing of towns is a grudgingly accepted fact, this one is significant because it occurred in the middle of an earthquake. Greece is in an earthquake belt and tremors are reasonably frequent. For one to occur and coincide with a bombing raid, is just a freak accident—but not so to the Greeks. They feel and claim that the heartless Germans should have been able to see an earthquake in progress and to call the raid off. They are bitter about the inhumanity shown.

We move through the town just after the event, and are interested to see for ourselves what the devastation is like. As luck would have it, the whole Unit stops for a breather, in and around the place, so a sprinkling of men climb down for a short look. As the stoppage is only a brief one, most keep close to their truck. But, one or two venture a bit further. One of them is Cocker.

It seems that all Greeks have deserted the place and, with most of the houses badly damaged, it is easy to see why. I follow a short distance after Cocker, and come across some Military Police and a couple of Infantrymen. They have three prisoners under guard.

The prisoners are silent and pretty glum looking. I ask their guards who they are. The guards claim that they are fifth columnists and a closer look seems to bear this out. Your average Greek is of medium height and nuggetty, wears rough workaday clothes, is of dark complexion and always has several days growth of stubble on his face. When he shaves, it is usually once a week or sometimes longer.

All these prisoners are six foot or over, very fair and slim, wear city-type clothes, although far from any real city, and are neatly clean-shaven. I ask what their captors intend doing with them. "We'll attend to them before we leave," is the ominous reply.

As this is only a very limited stop for that lot as well as us, those prisoners' future look very short indeed. I am not prepared to argue the point about it, even if I could. Those men have had some pretty bitter experiences forced upon them in this campaign and will have to make their own decisions on what to do. Whether they relent and spare the prisoners is something we won't know, for we are moving on before them.

I venture a little further along the street and meet Cocker coming towards me. He tells me he has come across a wrecked small shop with some goods still in it. I ask him if it is worthwhile investigating. He says there are a few jars with some lollies in them, but not much else. "Here," he says, "Here's a zipper purse you can have, that came from there."

I take the purse and examine it. It is made of leather, small and just with the one pocket. I stick it in my pants pocket and go to look for some lollies. When I locate the place, it is a mess. But there are two jars of lollies still on the shelf. They are acid drops, and red and white bullseyes. I reach for the bullseyes to see if they are edible. Suddenly, a Greek man appears from nowhere and intervenes. Although I cannot understand what he says, it is obvious that he is pleading with me not to take anything. He must be the owner. I will have helped myself if there was nobody to claim them. But now, I am pleased enough to leave them alone. It is only later, and after we have left, that I remember the purse. It is still in my pocket.

This latest withdrawal is a long one. We have been pushed back and shoved around in a manner that keeps us tired, hungry and cranky. While the Stukas are always with us in daytime, we have developed our own strategies to cope. When on the move we will just roll to a stop, then it's everybody out and scatter. With a dispersed target, they seem to think that it is hardly worthwhile to attack. Once they have gone, then it's back on the truck and away again. However, the stresses, the bombings and the fears, have affected some quite badly and it sometimes takes a while to get everybody reassembled.

Night journeys are the safer, but they have their own particular problems of unfamiliar roads and poor lighting. They also cut into your sleeping time. On this leg we have done a little bit of daylight travelling and then continued on for most of the night. In doing so, we have travelled back over the Bralos Pass. It is a nightmare journey and we only pull up just a few hours before dawn. We are too dog-tired to seek good cover so, with most of the Unit bunched together, we rely on the cliff overhang to keep us safe.

We are back on the flat ground behind the Pass and, with a very formidable natural barrier between us and the Germans, we feel fairly safe. As well, there are a lot of our troops between us and them.

In the pitch black of the few hours before dawn, we just roll out our bedrolls alongside the truck in our familiar routine. I take enough time to string a light rope between two fixed points, as is my usual habit. Although it is only about fifteen inches above ground level, it is high enough for me to hang my beloved jacket over and keep it off the ground. When I awake my jacket will be reasonably dry and not wet from ground moisture.

We have passed out into a deep sleep, or so it seems, when we are startled awake by frantic cries from some of the more panicky members of the Company. The usual aircraft approach warning of, "Here they come!" rings out. This is always the signal to scatter and take cover.

Struggling to come awake and bring my senses into focus, I find that it is daylight and I can hear the drone of approaching aircraft. I think, "You bastards, won't you give us any peace?"

Automatically going through the motions of disentangling from my blankets and reaching for my boots, I get a sudden urge of pent-up anger and stubbornness. I say to myself, "Damn you! I'm not going to run away."

Swiftly my thoughts run through my chances by staying put. Because of the cliff overhang, machine-gunning is almost impossible. So it will have to be bombs. Bombs burst upwards and out, clearing the ground by two to three feet before shrapnel starts to fall. I am confident enough that they will not be able to get a direct hit, again because of the overhang. So, if I lay face down and hug the ground, I should be able to avoid being hit. That's what I will do.

With most of the men running for shelter, I will be on my own. Some will be a fair way away, with others not so far, just enough to be safe without taking any risks. Then I hear a voice calling out, "Come on

Dawson, get out of that bloody bed." It is Cocker. He had bunked down close to our position and now sees that I have not moved.

I call back, "Bugger 'em. I'm staying put."

"Alright," he says, "Suit yourself," and moves off.

Now, their sounds tell me that the Stukas are directly above and not very high either. I am pretty busy flattening myself against the ground and not prepared to have a look. Then I hear the ominous sounds of bombs on their way. And then they hit. There is a stick of about eight or ten of them and they are awfully close. I hang on for a few seconds before gingerly raising my head. They seem to be going away now, but maybe they are only circling before making another run. If so, I will have to stick it out, as it is too late to find shelter now. Maybe my blanket will protect me from stray fragments.

When I'm sure, from the fading sounds, that they have indeed left, I half-raise to take stock. Firstly, I have not been hit. That is a welcome feeling, although I do feel a bit foolish for having taken the risk. Looking for any damage, the first thing I see is a small mound finely-powdered, mauve dust. My jacket! My beloved jacket has been utterly destroyed and is now nothing more than fine dust. My feeling of rage is instantly tempered by the realisation that splinter responsible has missed my backside, my highest point, by barely a half inch.

I stare stupidly at that small pile, hardly believing that it has happened. I would have expected that the material may have been shredded, and something left, but this is just dust. The destruction is total. Then I realise that the Germans have played a dirty trick on me. They have used daisy-cutters, anti-personnel bombs. They have a much lower trajectory and hug the ground more closely. Instead of going for the trucks, they have deliberately gone for the people they carry. Then I think of Cocker and, intuitively, I know he has been hit.

When I stayed, I knew his pride would not let him go very far away. He would have stayed close and those bombs were very close. I stir further and call to some of the returning men, "How is Cocker?"

A small knot has quickly gathered and somebody calls back to me, "He's copped it. He must have been bent over watching them. A splinter caught him in the middle of the back, passed right through his body, and out the top of his head."

Then, as an afterthought, I blurt, "He wouldn't have felt a thing. It must have been over in a second."

I am stunned. He is my friend. I count him as a mate and now my behaviour has got him killed. It is useless trying to tell myself that it is his decision to make, whether to go or stay, and no concern of mine. I know that the way I have played it out has made the end result almost inevitable. I feel bad, too bad to go and see him. Some of the other blokes dig a hole, collect his personal effects, and roll him in. it is only yesterday he had given me that small leather purse. I will feel guilty every time I touch it.

We are now about halfway down Greece, in an area that is a formidable, natural barrier. It is very mountainous and difficult to cross other than by road over the Bralos Pass and the railway that cuts through, close by. The railway has to pass over a very steep gorge which is spanned by an extremely high bridge, the legs of which spider way down into the depths below. It is a good place to make a stand and, blowing up the Pass and rail bridge will give us plenty of time to get out.

With the decision having been taken to hold here, at least for the time being, our Unit moves back a little to an area where we can be much more dispersed—where we will be much less of a target than we had been where Cocker had been killed.

Activity here is pretty quiet for a day or two. There is searching for back trails that may give the Germans a chance to bypass our proposed blowing-up jobs. There is the selection and sighting of gun and defensive positions while, all the time, German planes probe overhead.

Our senior Divisional Engineer Officer, Colonel Lucas, is out reconnoitring in his ute and he has stopped about halfway up the Bralos Pass. His party consists of his Aide, his Batman and his Bren-gunner, as well as himself. A Stuka appears from nowhere and proceeds to shoot them up. The Bren-gunner takes him on and dies at his gun, while the Colonel is seriously wounded.

We really hate those planes, but can do nothing about them, while they harass us at will. Then, one time, we manage to get a little of our own back. Each of our Sections has a tripod-mounted Bren-gun for anti-aircraft protection. Our Section's Bren-gunner is Jim Atkinson, a very likeable country man. He is a good shot and always goes into action whenever planes appear. Despite our fire, their planes do exactly as they please.

Just after the Colonel's incident, Jim is sitting beside his ute, cleaning his gun. He has just finished and clipped on a full magazine when a reconnaissance plane comes into view. It is a Storch monoplane, similar to our Lysander.

These things will stooge around at a hundred to a hundred and fifty feet, seemingly impervious to ground fire. They are cheeky and taunting, but this one runs out of luck.

Jim just raises his Bren-gun, rests the barrel on the gunwale of his ute while sitting on the ground, and commences firing. He aims just ahead of the plane and allows it to fly into his field of fire. We can clearly see the pilot at the controls. Suddenly he sits bolt upright, then falls facedown into his instrument panel.

Jim has loosed off a full magazine and, with some tracers to indicate, we can follow the line of fire. He has killed the pilot, although the plane is virtually undamaged. This is probably the only way to down one of these things. The plane noses straight down and crashes a little more than a hundred yards from us. It instantly bursts into flames and burns fiercely while its ammunition begins to pop and explode.

The whole Unit goes wild. They cheer and whoop and dance. This is the first success we have had against those hated planes. The pilot's body can be seen, but it is twenty minutes before we can get anywhere near it because of the heat.

Joe Blackadder finally manages to drag it clear by driving a pick into the body. While one or two protest at this method, claiming it to be inhuman, the rest point out that he is dead anyway. And, as we are to be here for a few days, we just will not be able to stand the smell of barbecued pilot, hanging over the place. He is buried nearby to his plane.

When the fire is out and cool, we decide to camouflage the site with trees and bushes. But before that, we have a good inspection of the plane to find out why they are so hard to down. We find that there is a solid piece of armour plate that practically encases the pilot. It is about three-quarters of an inch thick, curved from underneath the pilot's seat, up behind his back, then over the top of his head. The only vulnerable spot is the pilot himself. Even after the fierce heat of the fire, bullets make no impression on the armour plate.

A rough goat track has been discovered that winds high over the mountains and down onto our side. As a possible method of bypassing our defences, it has to be put out of commission. Another part of the Unit is given the job. They select a spot, high up amongst the peaks, which is ideal. As a truck cannot get near the spot, all gear will have to be man-handled the rest of the way. My crew is called in to help.

The track is fairly rugged, although the footing is not too bad. The chosen position, when we get there, is next to a mountain meadow. A deep trench has been dug, along a rock wall, and at the side of the track. The explosion should blow a large section of the track away, making it impassable.

We have three very large cases of gelignite and about half a case is enough to do the job. I ask, "What will happen to the rest of it?" I am told that it is intended to use the lot. We have the stuff here so we might as well get rid of it. With that amount of explosive, it should be a spectacular blow.

As the work proceeds, I look around and am enthralled at the sheer beauty of our surroundings. The winter snow has melted in the spring thaw and has become a small lake in the meadow. The surface of the water is absolutely still and mirror clear so that the surrounding peaks are perfectly reflected.

The fresh spring grass is dotted everywhere with new field flowers running down to and beneath the water's edge, so that it is difficult to determine where the grass stops and the water begins. It is a fresh, clean, silent and beautiful place, seemingly far removed from the sacrilege of human presence. For us to even be here, makes me feel as if we are a horde of vandals in a sacred place. And to think we are about to desecrate it with our explosion. I cannot bear to witness the final destruction and leave before the charge is set off.

The few days pause behind Bralos is very welcome. The constant moving about and being menaced by planes has us very jittery. The stress of the constant harassment affects us all, with some handling it better than others. Some of the worst affected refuse to ride in the trucks. They insist on riding on the footboards to act as plane-spotters. At least, this rest allows some nerves to settle down.

After a couple of days of relative quiet, we are called together by our Acting Lieutenant. He announces we have a job to do. We are to patrol the main road back from the Pass to ensure that it remains open and useable. Each Sub Section will be responsible for a stretch of about five miles. Any change in orders will be relayed to the first Sub Section, who will pass it onto the next, and so on, down the line. Joe Blackadder and his crew will be first in line, then me and my crew, and so on.

I do not worry much about who comes after me, other than to know that there is someone. If there are any changes, Joe will get them to me and then I will find the next lot.

Personally, I just consider this chore to be something dreamed up for the sole purpose of keeping us busy, just giving us something to do. Up to now there has been very little road damage done by the Germans. Why should there be? They are following us so closely behind that they will be using the roads themselves in next to no time. And, with no roads to retreat on, we will be forced to make a real stand. That would be a situation that the Germans will be happy to avoid.

We move off and I decide to take up a position about midway along my patrol area, off the road and under some cover, from where I will be able to keep my whole Section under observation. I do not want to move about unnecessarily. I find a reasonably good spot and settle down to wait.

About midmorning I observe Joe's truck travelling towards us. I signal to him, indicating our position, and he comes to inform me of a change in orders. Just after dark, the Infantry will be pulling out. We are to pull out with them and join in the convoy. Joe goes back to his beat and I set off to inform the next lot.

We head south on a road that is completely devoid of traffic. We have been mobile for about fifteen minutes when a village comes into view. The area is wide and flat with the road stretching straight ahead for some distance. The road passes through the village which is evenly spread on both sides of it.

This village looks a bit more prosperous than the usual run, and is neatly and attractively laid out. It is completely walled-in with high plastered walls facing onto the roadway and stacked stone walls, about chest high, running down the sides and along the back. This has the effect of dividing it into two parts. Trees, shrubs and gardens can be glimpsed over the stone side walls. Beyond and off to the right is a cluster of taller trees, suggesting a small forest area.

We are almost at the edge of the village, and barely have time to take this in, when a sharp burst of aerial gunfire is clearly heard by all. It comes from the direction of the tall trees, although, as yet, no plane has been sighted, nor have we heard one.

Instantly, our driver pulls to a halt. The cry goes up, "Everybody out!" and there is a mad scramble to get clear. This is, by now, a well-practised routine. But, while this is going on, there is a fair bit of chiacking directed towards the footboard spotters for their failure to alert the rest of us about the presence of aircraft. Most of it is aimed at Big Tom, a West Australian, who is giving back almost as much as he gets. Tom, a good bloke, is a bit wooden-headed and stubborn, and can always be provoked into an argument.

We all make for the nearby stone walls, aiming to keep them between us and any possible danger. As we move, a Stuka shoots into view from the far side of the village. He climbs, seemingly from ground level, and spots us at the same time as we spot him. Instantly, he readies to have a go at us and instantly, we press into the shelter of the stone walls.

Unable to draw a bead on us, he quickly banks and attacks again from our rear. Just as quickly we scramble over the wall, again placing it between us and him. Again frustrated, he banks sharply and makes another run. Once more we jump the wall, placing it between us and him. His banking and diving and our wall jumping continues for about eight times, like some crazy game of tag. Finally, he breaks off, probably because of a shortage of fuel.

He never once is able to get a shot at us. He might have used all his ammunition during that firing we had heard and has nothing left. In that case, he may have been having some sport at our expense. We are pleased enough to see him go.

We make our way back to the truck and climb aboard. He has ignored our vehicle which is just sitting there on the side of the road. Now, it is time to find our next Sub Section and pass the message on.

We clear the village to find the country is wide, and open, and flat. And we find that the cluster of tall trees beyond the village is set back some three-quarters of a mile from the road. It is the only cover available. About halfway to the trees, and well out in the open, we find our next Sub Section truck, standing stationary, with a few of our blokes clustered around it. Instantly, I know what the Stuka has been firing at.

I direct my driver to take us over to find out what damage has been done, if any, and to relay the change of orders. I find a shocked and stunned group, minus their Sergeant. Their driver has been killed and two men are badly wounded, with identical wounds of a bullet through the shoulder.

I demand to know where their Sergeant is. A still-stunned second in command, Lance Corporal Les Lawrence, can only tell me that he has gone off somewhere with our Acting Lieutenant.

I then demand to know how the hell they have come to be caught so far out in the open. Les says that the Sergeant had taken up a position alongside the stone wall just off the road. After the Sergeant had gone, Les began to worry that they were a bit too vulnerable there, so he had decided to move his crew to a position under the shelter of the trees. They were halfway across when the Stuka had caught them.

What can I do now? This Sub Section is now immobilised and the change of orders still has to be passed on. There are two wounded men to be taken care of and one to be buried. The second in command has just given an order which ends in disaster and he is in shock. I decide to take charge.

The first consideration has to be the wounded men. They are Paddy Meenan and a Newcastle mate, Keith Davidson. Their wounds are very close to the arm joint and it is unclear how much damage has been done. They are lying flat on the bed of the truck, being attended to and being made as comfortable as possible by a couple of their crew.

Their truck is undamaged, so it will have to be their transport. The driver, however, is the dead man. His name is Keith Viney. He is sitting upright at the wheel, with his hair stirring gently in the slight breeze, and seemingly without a mark on him. He is reputably the youngest man in the Unit, putting up his age to join up. He would only be about seventeen. Nobody else can drive.

I have to get these blokes into hospital and I have no idea where one is. I am certain that there will be one in Athens.

At the time, not too many people have acquired driving skills and it is regarded as a specialist's job. I have a couple of men in my crew who can handle it, so I'll have to use one of them. I need somebody with the initiative to get the job done, so I choose George Wade.

My instructions are simple, "Get these blokes into hospital in Athens. Drive fast, but remember their comfort. Stop for no one. Once there, you're on your own. If possible, try to rejoin the column, but you will have to use your own judgement. See how things are there and then decide what to do."

I instruct Les to take a couple of his men to remove and arrange the burial of Viney so that George can get underway. He will also have to remove and take charge of Viney's personal affects and hand them into our Headquarters when reporting the circumstances of his death.

I will have to push on and try to relay the change of orders. My crew will stay here and help Les with the burial. Meanwhile Joe Blackadder is unaware of what has happened and will be expecting to make contact with me when it becomes time to move out. I ask for a volunteer to make the long walk back to tell Joe about our situation. It has to be a walk, for there is no other transport. Lenny volunteers.

With George already on his way with the wounded, now it is my turn. I instruct my crew that they are to stay here under the cover of the trees until I get back. But if somehow that is impossible, then Lance Corporal Les is in charge. Then it is absolutely vital for them to make contact with Joe, so that they will not be stranded.

Everybody sets to, without a quibble. They all are just glad at having something to do. With Lord Dalley driving, he and I set off to find somebody in the next group to relay the orders. I don't care who it is, as I am mostly interested in getting back to my men.

We drive fast along a deserted open road. I instruct Dalley to keep an eye on the mileage indicator so that we have an idea of how far we have gone. We keep a keen eye open for any cover where some of our Unit may have taken shelter. We speed along and there is nothing. I am thinking, "Something must be badly wrong." I am getting more anxious the further we go. But luckily, there is still no sign of aircraft.

We have travelled about fifteen miles when we spot a utility on the side of the road. It is the Acting Lieutenant's ute. It has run off the road and into a ditch and is canted at an angle. We pull up to inspect it, and we find that it has been badly shot up. There is neither blood nor signs of anybody having been hurt. It has been abandoned and just left there.

I decide that I will look no further, and I head back to my men. It looks as if our Unit has just cleared out and abandoned our three Sub Sections. We should have met up with somebody long before this. In any case, it is now obvious that Joe and I are on our own. With no Unit clout, somehow we will just have to find our way into the Convoy and stay there.

I arrive safely to my crew, with still no planes about, and find that all the tasks have been cleared up. I put everybody in the picture and emphasise how vital it is that we and Joe's crew keep together. We all realise that our position is pretty serious. We have no idea where, or how far, this withdrawal will take us.

What had started out as an easy day, has now turned into a busy one, and it is afternoon now. We have totally abandoned any pretence of patrolling the road. While under cover, I am churning over in my mind of what is in front of us and how to tackle it. Since it concerns Joe as well, it irks me a lot at not being able to work things out with him. Then there he is. When Lenny had got through to him, he has decided to come through and see the situation for himself. I heave a huge sigh of relief. At least we will now be working together.

We discuss a strategy for breaking into a nose-to-tail column of the Convoy after dark and without authority. We will have to be on the side of the road, ready and waiting. Joe's driver will force his way in and hold up the column. Then I will come in, in front of him, and we will be underway. We are a bit desperate and just hope that it will work. As it turns out, the Convoy is under way earlier than expected and comes along just on darkness. With still plenty of light, we lumber into position. Joe goes through his manoeuvre and I swing into position ahead of him. The Infantry has made way for us without any trouble. It has been a piece of cake. We are on our way and all we have to do is stay with them. But what a nightmare that turns out to be.

Complete darkness is upon us very quickly and, with just a pinpoint of light showing from our headlamps, it is essential that we keep our nose as close as possible to the tailboard of the truck in front of us and hope that Joe does likewise. It is slow cautious driving with the fear that a sudden stop from in front could cause a crash. While the pace is slow enough not to put much danger on any of us, the prospect of having our truck immobilised is frightening.

On and on we go throughout the night. Here and there are some dim figures on the side of the road, guides pointing us on our way. Somewhere we will have to negotiate a stretch of high country. The winding road conditions of a cliff face on one side and a deep drop on the other, upwards of a thousand feet, scares the hell out of us. Several times while negotiating a bend, our outside wheel appears to be going over the edge. I, the spotters and Dalley himself, spy the danger at the last minute. With us calling frantically to him, he stops.

A very tired and very stressed Dalley, pushed to the point that he doesn't care anymore, asks me, "Will I give it a go?" meaning, Can he continue on?

Urgently, I order, "No... back up a little more and give it a bit more lock." Always this is a difficult manoeuvre, with the column behind us now stationary and close up on our tail. Each time he shuffles back a foot or two, and each time we manage to make it round. Then we hurry up to catch up with the man in front again.

By daylight it appears that we have left the hilly country and we are able to see and drive faster. For the good of all of us, I decide I will give Dalley a spell. I have a good driver in my crew who can relieve him, named Bill Heaps. But Bill is not a designated driver. I can order the changeover, but it will be better if I can persuade Dalley, as the truck and its care is his responsibility. This I am able to do and, at the first opportunity, the changeover is made.

The Convoy rolls steadily on with stoppages made only for essentials, such as fuel. Along the roadside we spot some mules wandering about and a couple of them lying dead in the ditch. The dead have been machine-gunned, almost certainly from the air. These are big, strong, fat animals, totally different to the small, scrawny donkeys, used widely by the locals. Obviously, they have been abandoned and turned loose by the Unit which had brought them here. It seems pretty certain from all the signs that we are moving on to a full scale evacuation. That makes it even more essential to keep our place in the Convoy.

To me the situation looks pretty gloomy and I cannot help but think of that other evacuation that took place, not very far from here, in the

First World War at Gallipoli. It was supposed to have been achieved in a masterly fashion. Here, it is beginning to look like a bit of a bloody shamble.

About midmorning we can see a group of Greek soldiers a short way ahead, on the side of the road, apparently signalling for the trucks ahead of us to stop. None do and, as we near them, I instruct Bill to keep going also. One of them, in desperation, walks into our path, trying to stop us. I again instruct Bill to keep going, an action which will have required him to swing around the Greek. Moved by compassion, Bill stops.

The Greek immediately moves to the driver's side door and pours out his tale in English. He has a badly wounded comrade close by, who has to be moved to hospital immediately, or he will die. He pleads for us to take him aboard and get him there for them. I shake my head firmly and declare that I cannot. I am in a Convoy and cannot leave it. They will have to find some other means of transporting him. Bill fidgets uneasily in his seat, while the stunned and shocked Greek steps back. I then order Bill to drive on.

I am angry. Why me? I feel I have already had too many tough decisions to make. I am conscious of the heartless image I feel that I have been forced to portray. Bill, for his part, is silent and drives on.

Although I believe strongly that I have to keep in the Convoy and keep going, I am uneasy. If only it had been someone else's decision to make and not mine. I feel resentful at Bill for having stopped, when I told him not to. He has forced the issue on me. His silent and unspoken hint of disapproval at my decision does not help either. Then I think, "What if it has been a con?" Greeks are notorious at exaggerating. "What if they had been using a slightly wounded man just to bum a lift?" Anyway, it is too late now and we just do not have the time to sort the situation out.

Not much is said as we continue on. Gradually, day gives way until once again it is night. Still continuing, it must have been close to midnight when we are subjected to a series of stops and starts. As we get nearer to the reason for it, we find that we at a crossroads manned by Military Police. They are splitting the Convoy here, sending some to the left and the others straight ahead.

When our turn comes, I am asked the name of our Unit. I tell them and I am ordered to proceed straight on. This sorting out divides the column, so that roughly half go to the left and half continue on. Maybe we will catch up with our lot somewhere along the way. Boy, will I have something to say, if we do!

There are now some sizeable gaps between us; and, with the road in fairly flat country, we are able to speed along and make good time. When daylight comes, we are pretty much on our own. We speed on and the only thing that interrupts the quietness is a solitary plane, very high up, that ignores us completely. We know it has to be German, but it is not interested in us at all.

At midmorning we begin to pass through a seemingly deserted village when, in its centre, three Australians led by a Lieutenant, waves us to a halt. The Lieutenant has his service revolver in his hand and is waving it about as he says, "What the hell do you think you're doing?"

Too tired to bother about courtesies, I ask, "What seems to be the trouble Sir?"

He says, "Don't you know you're giving our position away to that spotter plane up there?" I patiently explain that I am a Field Engineer Corporal under orders to patrol the road, and ensure that it is useable for our traffic.

This is stretching the truth a bit, as those orders applied only to the stretch behind Bralos, which is now many miles from here. But I am prepared to use my last orders as an excuse for my conduct, particularly if it seems necessary to allow us to keep in the Convoy. This cuts no ice with the Lieutenant and, although he does not question my orders, he says, "Get this bloody thing off the road, or I will shoot you here now." And he means it too.

Without arguing further, I climb down and tell Bill to stay put until I find suitable cover. Joe and I turn down a side street to see what is available. We find a spot that will take two trucks and then return to find the trucks gone.

The Lieutenant and his men also, are nowhere to be found. Saying aloud, "Now what?", it seems we have no alternative but to search for our trucks. Maybe the Lieutenant has sent them on and left us stranded, or just moved them on somewhere out of sight. We begin walking along the road leading out of the village, while looking on either side for possible hiding places for the trucks.

We walk maybe two hundred yards, when we observe a truck coming towards us from the opposite direction in which we are headed. It is my own truck, and I am very pleased to see it, as is Bill to see us. I ask him, "What has happened?"

Bill tells us that the very furious Lieutenant had ordered him on as soon as we started looking for some cover. "We cleared the village and waited for a few minutes. We started making our way back cautiously to find you, when we both spotted each other."

We climb aboard, turn around, and continue on our way. There is no further sign of the Lieutenant or any of his men. We just continue on feeling pretty low and dispirited. We just have to keep going and try to pick up whatever information we can on our way. We are told that the check-point we passed during the night, where many had been directed to the left, was the direction to an embarkation point. It led to an open beach with transports waiting offshore. The troops were being ferried out to them in the ships' boats and, in the middle of proceedings, the Stukas had arrived. Several transports were sunk and, or, set on fire, and the ships' boats were shot up, as well as the troops assembled on the beach. It is a proper shambles. The Port of Piraeus is just about wiped out with ships sunk everywhere, as well as a couple of hospital ships. "God!" I think, "If Keith and Paddy have made it through to one of those, they will have no chance of saving themselves by swimming, not with a bullet through the shoulder."

It seems that the Germans are now fully aware that we are trying to quit the country. Wherever we go, it is only reasonable to expect that they will try to head us off. Our prospects do not look too bright. As for where we are headed, all we can find out is that it is as far south as we can go, to the extreme tip of the country, and this brings on another worry. To get there we will have to traverse the Gulf of Corinth. We know that it is a very large slab of the country at the bottom of Greece, and to the southwest, separated from the mainland by a very deep and precipitous gorge. This gorge cuts right through, making that area a virtual island. The only way across this natural barrier is by a couple of bridges. The Germans know this also, and will certainly try to secure these bridges, more than likely, by using paratroops. We might have to fight our way through.

A little further on, we are told that they have indeed tried this caper by sending in a paratroop force. Our Infantry has gone in and wiped them out, and now the area is considered reasonably safe. For all the confident assurances, we still feel that there may be small groups who have managed to evade our defenders. Anyway, there is nothing to stop them from giving it another try.

We approach the area with great concern, only to pass through it without any trouble. We still have a long way to go. But, once past this bottleneck, we feel a fair bit safer. We have been spared the attention of the Stukas for some time, and can only conclude that they are busy elsewhere. We know they haven't gone completely. They might be a bit off our track now, but they will find us again in their own good time.

I, personally, am now at a pretty low ebb. The strain and the nightmare events, the lack of food and sleep, and the necessity to press on regardless, are all bearing very heavily on me. All the others are pretty much the same and, although there is no talk between us as such, we instinctively know how each other feels. We all have this absolute compulsion to push on and get there somehow. The usual good-natured dissention of why this or why that, is completely gone. The urge to reach our destination, wherever it might be, has us united as one. Then we are told that we are heading for Kalamata.

Kalamata means absolutely nothing to us. We have no idea whether it is a town, a port, or even an open beach. We have no idea how we will recognise it when we get there. We just have this blind faith in efficient roadside guides who have kept us heading in the right direction. Somebody will be there to tell us what we are to do.

Finally, we arrive at an area where we are directed off the road and under the shelter of a large belt of trees. There is no sign of any water and indeed, no sign of any town. Many have arrived before us and many more are still arriving. A busy group of senior NCOs and junior Officers are instructing all arrivals on what is expected of them.

All trucks are to be moved well back to a separate area. The driver and an offsider are to remain with them. All other personnel are to stay grouped together and keep to a defined assembly area. The whole lot is under cover and nobody is to move around. It is absolutely essential that the Germans be unaware we are here, so there is to be no movement of any kind. Contact is being made with the Navy and it is hoped that we will be able to evacuate tonight. To be ready, we will have to abandon all our gear, except for a small pack containing only essentials and our personal weapons. Every group will have to have an Officer-in-Charge and he will be the only one to give the order when to move.

We are immediately at a disadvantage. We are a small group without an Officer. We will have to search for one who also is with a small group and who may be prepared to take us under his wing. This could be a tall order and if we cannot pull it off, we may be left behind. Joe immediately takes this task upon himself and sets off to see what he can do.

I am pleased to leave it to Joe. The two of us are equal in rank, but I only have those bodgy Italian stripes to indicate mine. But then, it had been me who had confronted that agitated Lieutenant who had wanted to shoot me back in the village. If I run into him and he recognises me, it might kill our chances altogether. I have another problem also: What to do about the Boys anti-tank rifle? It certainly is not a personal weapon, nor is it a major one like an artillery field piece. I cannot leave it intact to be taken by the Germans. The only way to make it inoperable is to remove the complicated bolt, strip the bolt down into its several pieces, then get rid of those pieces.

The Boys anti-tank rifle had been left in its crate in the truck. We are now separated from the truck by a fair distance and with a veto on us moving about. However, big Tom has volunteered to remain with the driver as his offsider. I have instructed him to do the job and to make sure that all the parts are scattered widely and impossible to gather together again. Short of blowing it up, which we cannot do, it is the only thing I can think of. At the appropriate time, those two will rejoin us and I will know for sure that the job has been carried out.

Joe returns to tell us that he has found an Officer who is willing to include us in his party. We move over to where he is and settle down. Everything is now in place. All we have to do is wait. There is no sign of any others of our Unit, so we can only think that they have been caught up in the shemozzle of that other embarkation point. It just doesn't bear thinking about of what may have happened to them.

From where we are now, we can catch a glimpse of some water. We appear to be on one side of a very wide bay or inlet. Of course there is no way we can inspect our surroundings and there is no sign of any locals. We are part of a very large body of men, hidden from sight and just waiting under the shelter of trees and undergrowth. The average Australian usually finds it impossible to ignore the challenge of going anywhere he is forbidden to go. But in this situation our position is so grave that not one man disobeys his orders.

As the day wears on, we just speculate quietly amongst ourselves as to our chances. Then in the early afternoon, word comes through that contact has been made with the Navy. An evacuation attempt will indeed be made tonight. With this news comes final instructions on what procedure we are to adopt.

The drivers and offsiders will drain their vehicles' sumps, then run the motors until they seize. They will then move down to their representative groups. Just after dark and at a given time, each Officer will form his group up in a single file and move up to a start line. When given the signal, each group will march steadily straight ahead onto the wharf area. [So, there must be a wharf there, that we still cannot see.] At the wharf, we will be met by Destroyers which will not be tied up. The Destroyers will remain in position for fifteen minutes during which time the troops will stream aboard. After fifteen minutes, the Destroyers will head straight out to transports waiting out in the bay. The Destroyers will again wait for fifteen minutes there while the troops stream off. Then the Destroyers will head back for another load. At no time will they tie up, so if anybody gets caught at the wharf or the transport, he will have to stay put until the next round. If everything goes according to plan, it is hoped that the Convoy will be well clear of Greece by daylight.

Some more waiting follows and some more speculation about the execution of the embarkation plan. It is said that the plan has been evolved by General Blamey himself. If the Navy does not show up then we are stranded. Our trucks will be useless and we will have nowhere to go.

Just before dusk comes the sound of a plane. Watching, we sight a huge, lumbering Sunderland Flying Boat sweep in and land on the far side of the bay. Instantly, a small launch shoots out from nowhere and heads straight for the plane. Quickly, a number of figures can be seen scrambling aboard and, just as quickly, the launch returns to shore. The plane, whose motors have not stopped running, turns about and, after a very long take-off, rises into the air and disappears. Obviously, our top Brass are getting clear. We can only wish them luck. If their plans for us succeed, then they deserve it.

It is fairly late when the drivers rejoin us and soon it's time to move into position in our single files. I glance along our ranks, taking stock of my crew. The only jarring note is big Tom. He is carrying that heavy, awkward, Boys anti-tank rifle on his shoulder. With the Lieutenant at our head, I quietly berate him as fiercely as I can. He has deliberately disobeyed my orders. No way can the bloody thing be accepted as a personal weapon. If the Lieutenant chooses to take exception to it, our places may be at risk. But the Lieutenant, for his part, takes no notice. He has other things to think of.

Big Tom is quietly defiant at my bitter tongue bashing. With no alternative but to accept the situation, I end up saying, "Alright, you brought the bastard, you carry it. You'll get no help from any of the rest of us." And he knows I mean it. For the first time, he begins to think that maybe he might have made a bit of a mistake.

We are now moving steadily ahead in columns of single file, and with the files stretched closely to our left and right. In only a few minutes we are on an extensive and bare wharf area. A Destroyer is in place and we quickly step onto its deck, not wishing to miss our allotted fifteen minutes. The deck and wharf edge are practically on the same level and, with the ship's rail down, it is the easiest thing in the world.

We crowd ahead as far as we can, making way for those behind us. We are close up to some deck superstructure and I tell Tom to put the Boys anti-tank rifle down alongside it. This he does while the Destroyer begins to get underway and head out into the dark of the harbour.

Quickly the dark gloom gives way into the shape of a ship, and we are at the gangway leading up its side. Those ahead begin to scramble up and we begin to move with them so as not to delay proceedings and have to wait for the next trip. Tom is reaching down for the Boys anti-tank rifle when I order, "Leave it." I make the sudden decision realising it is as safe there as anywhere. It is useless to us and is a burden to carry. The ship can keep it as a souvenir, or chuck it overboard. At least the Germans won't get it.

Tom straightens up and for once obeys me. As we move along, a sailor hurries along the deck on some particular duty and spies the Boys anti-tank rifle. He calls to us, "Hey, you've forgotten your weapon." We, for our part, just shrug our shoulders and look blank. We hurry onto the gangway and start to climb. The sailor pauses for a moment, then goes about his business. And that's where the Boys anti-tank rifle ends up.

Once aboard, we just move ahead anywhere. We crowd into passages and alleyways, anywhere at all. We just take up a vacant position and flop. The exterior of the ship is blacked out, but inside there is a blaze of light and we can see each other clearly. What a motley crew of unwashed brigands we look!

Some sympathetic ship's crewmembers direct us to large boilers of tea and cocoa, somewhere below. We line up in droves, gorging on the almost forgotten, exquisite luxury. And there is a never ending supply.

Sated somewhat on tea and cocoa, we move back to our possies and try to settle down. Our ship is the Costa Rica and our Convoy is to sail direct for Alexandria in Egypt. We are as good as home. Sometime during the early hours of the morning, the engines begin to throb and we are underway.

## Chapter 8

# The Crete Campaign

WITH THE SHIP UNDERWAY WE try to settle into some sort of sleep. We are not very successful. We are too exhausted for proper sleep and it just comes in fits and starts. We are hungry too. While some have managed to scrounge a little something, our lot gets nothing—and, there does not seem much prospect before breakfast, if then.

Almost certainly, this rescue flotilla will have been rushed together in a hurry, grabbing practically anything that can float. Probably, with only skeleton crews to man them, there will be little or nobody spare to prepare food for such a huge influx of starving and hungry men. We might not get much until we get to Egypt.

It is about 4.00 am when we start to move and, with still a few hours before daylight, we feel we just have to stay put before being able to take stock of our surroundings. For myself, I just start to feel bad. I have this heavy feeling that is just weighing me down. It isn't a sickness. At least, I do not think so. It seems to be something connected with our present position. It worries me and I cannot shake it off. It just seems to get worse by the moment. It feels like I have made a wrong decision that will bring us big trouble. But, with circumstances having made decisions for us, there is nothing I can do. I just feel somehow trapped.

At the very first signs of daylight, I go out on deck to size up the situation which is, more or less, from a sense of self-preservation, rather than an exercise on behalf of our crew. Still, while I am looking after me, I am looking after them too. First thing to take stock of, is our ship, the Costa Rica.

It seems that she is a medium-sized ship, normally engaged in trading around the Dutch East Indies. She is equipped to carry some passengers as well as cargo. As such, she is a fairly slow reliable boat that will be flat out making ten knots. She will be about the slowest ship in our Convoy.

Looking around there is not very much to see other than the ocean. We are clear of the land but, with the Convoy widely dispersed, it is possible to get the impression that we are virtually on our own.

Now, with more men stirring, there is a quietly efficient setting-up of weapons. These are seasoned Infantrymen. All the make-believe bullshit is long gone. It gives me a lift, just to be part of them. Of course, with the restrictions imposed for our evacuation, other than rifles, all we have is light machine guns such as the Bren.

There are no mounts for them, so the men have to improvise. There are overhead frames on the fore and aft decks, where canvas awnings are spread under which passengers can loll about while cruising in the tropics. The men just cut pieces of rope and suspend their guns from these frames. They work out the right height and field of fire and, when satisfied, settle down and wait. I can see no protective armaments on the Costa Rica at all. The men on the guns just stay put and their mates act as look outs. It now seems a good time to try for some breakfast.

Naturally, there will be a queue. To find the beginning or end of it is like a Chinese puzzle. With men snaked out in every corridor and passageway in the ship, no matter which way I go, it seems to be the wrong way. Suddenly alarm bells start ringing. It is 7.30 am and we are under attack.

The Stukas have found us and are intent on doing their best to prevent our escape. Our gunners, ready and waiting, are just as determined to drive them off. The Navy and every ship in the Convoy has now opened up. The Stukas are pressing in as close as they dare. The tremendous cacophony of sound from the guns and the falling bombs seems to be concentrated solely on our ship which shakes and rattles from stem to stern and in every rivet.

We, quite naturally, want to get up there to see what is going on. It is unthinkable to be trapped inside if we are hit. Just as quickly, it is obvious that it is far too dangerous to step out there. Our gunners, while following a target, just sweep everything before them. Wire strays and the funnel are being chopped. Even the people on the bridge are at risk.

We just have to hang on and hope. Every bomb blast seems to be closer. Ouch! That one almost certainly is right alongside. It had to be a very close near miss. I know that a near miss can disable us from the concussion alone. If that happens, will the Convoy Commander decide to abandon us in the interests of the safety of the others?

Then the firing eases off and then it stops. We have made it through. The ship's engines are still turning, so she mustn't have sustained any serious damage, and we are still on our way. A quick glance on deck shows cartridge cases everywhere, otherwise everything is intact and nobody hit.

We know, of course, that this is only a respite. Now that the Stukas have found us, they will be back. The only thing that will stop them is, if they lack the range. We have no idea from where they are operating, so no way of calculating when we will be beyond their reach. Now orders go out barring everybody from the deck except the gunners. There must be no interference to their ability to instantly react.

Nobody wants to go too far down inside the ship, so we all gather just below the main deck. Here, there is a wide passageway down both sides and across each end. A piano is placed across one corner. As the former passenger cabins fronted on the passageway, it was evidently their intended gathering place. There is no lounge as such, as the passageways skirt a huge open-space that goes straight to the bottom of the ship. This is the cargo hold and, quite obviously, cargo was the primary function of its trading. Passengers were just a sideline.

From where we are gathered, there is no real protection of any kind from a direct hit. Still, neither is anywhere else on the ship. We just gather there, fully apprehensive and trapped, just like sardines in a can.

Quite soon comes another attack. Again comes the crashing thunder of combat, and again the great relief when the attack breaks off. The attacks continue, with a break of about twenty minutes to half an hour between them. Soon we begin to differentiate, commenting, "Nah! That one didn't even get close." Or, "Jesus! That is the nearest one yet."

Someone sits himself at the piano in the corner and begins playing in between the bombing runs. Soon a few start to sing and then we all join in. With everybody singing, we continue right on through. As the crescendo of the battle rages, we counter by bawling at the top of our lungs. It is the only way left to show our defiance. It is like a scene from a crazy madhouse at each peak of a bombing run. There is the pianist, bouncing around and thumping at the keyboard, while a thousand or more mouths are forming the words of the song, and, none of this sound can be heard because of the overwhelming crashing roar of the battle overhead. As the battle sounds wane, the piano and singing sounds cut in at full volume without missing a beat.

About midday, word goes out that ammunition is beginning to run low. A plea is made for every last round we have—even that solitary, maybe forgotten one tucked away in a pocket somewhere. It is absolutely vital that the guns be kept firing. It is the heavy screen of fire that prevents the planes from making an accurate bombing run.

There is no respite. It seems that those bloody planes might chase us all the way to Egypt and, soon, we will be unable to defend ourselves. Then, after a raid that seems to have no more effect than quite a few others, one or two ship's Officers come hurrying through in a manner that suggests to us that something is on. Maybe one of the other ships has sustained a hit.

While there is a bit of confusion going on, it seems to me that it's a good time to slip away and try to get in line for some food. There has been a vague rumour that an attempt will be made at providing a midday meal, and that it might be lambs fry. The mere thought of that sends me into drools of anticipation.

Once away from our singing community area, I find myself on my own. I have barely started to look for the likely food source when the ship's Officer comes hurrying through. He directs me to make my way up on deck as the ship is disabled. Her engines have been thrown six feet out-of-line by a near miss. It is only then that I realise, they are no longer turning. His mission is to see that nobody is left below decks.

On my way up, I grab my few meagre remaining possessions, which include my rifle, and go out onto the deck. The deck area is packed with men and everything is orderly. There is no pushing or shoving and everybody is calm. It is almost as if this is just another training exercise.

The ship is listing over about twenty-five degrees on the side where I am now. With the opposite side being higher, attempts are being made on this side to free the lifeboats from their davits, ready for launching. Some men have made the decision to strip off, go overboard on the high side, swim clear and wait to be picked up. Some of my blokes tell me that Lenny has elected to take this course. I think, "Trust Lenny. He'll always take the course that can best be expected for looking after number one." Still, in this situation, it has to be every man for himself.

A couple of Destroyers are moving in close. We are all donning the standard ship's life jackets with the bulky pack that sits on the chest and the back part which ties around the waist with tapes. The falls of ropes from the davits now hang free and are dangling down the side of the ship. As the ship's boats begin to be freed, there comes a hail from the now very close Destroyer, "Don't touch those boats!" With that the Destroyer moves smartly alongside.

This manoeuvre damages some of the boats by the Destroyer's upper superstructure, and because of the Costa Rica's lean. This lean has our ship's deck level, not much higher than the Destroyer's deck level. With both ships heave to, there is a regular rolling together and apart in the sea swell. There is some grinding as they come together.

With the Destroyer's small size against the bulk of our ship, it does not look too safe a place to be. But the Navy men just take it all in their stride. The sailors now hurry into position, in line with the Destroyer's side. They take hold of those dangling falls of rope, and then call to our men lining our ship's rail to climb up and prepare to swing across onto the Destroyer.

The first few climb onto the rail and take hold of the ropes which are fastened securely to the ship's davits. The loose ends are held by the sailors. As the two ships roll together, the sailors will give a great heave. The men clutching the ropes will swing out and drop to the Destroyer's deck. Hey presto! Not even your feet get wet.

Everybody quickly sizes up what to do. With the men nearest the rail going first, there is a steady stream making the swing across. Sometimes the timing is a bit out and somebody will be caught out of position, just as the ships roll apart. Those persons have to wait briefly until the ships swing together again. Eagerness to get across and slippery Army boots trying to balance on the rail, make these moments a bit hair-raising.

My position in the lineup is about eight rows back from the rail. I just have to wait patiently for my turn. Now a call goes out for everybody to discard their lifejackets, and it is obvious why. The Destroyer's narrow decks need every inch of space in order to cram us aboard. Four men can fit into the space of two fitted in lifejackets.

As the rows in front of me begin to thin, I start to move forward. I am clutching my rifle in my hand when suddenly the realization comes home to me. If I go into the water, my rifle will take me straight to the bottom. Those in front of me seem to have no weapons or have discarded them. I can sling mine across my back for the swing across, but it will then take up valuable space on the Destroyer's deck. I have no ammunition for it, so it will best for me to leave it behind. I lean it against the cabin wall, at my back. Leaving it gives me a great sense of loss. It is such a good rifle, with only the recoil of a .22.

Then it is my turn. I mount the rail and get into position. The ships begin to roll apart, so I wait. While apart, the distance is at least twelve feet and terrifying. I glance down at the water and an army greatcoat s floating and swirling in the surge. I cannot tell if there is a body in it, but if there is, it will assuredly be dead, for nothing could survive the grinding when the two ships come together. Then the ships roll back and, in seconds, I am on the deck of the Destroyer.

Along with a couple of my crew, we cram together in a position just astern of the funnels. We are anxious to know what will happen now. We are told that we will have to be put ashore. With her decks crammed full, our Destroyer cannot manoeuvre or fight which she will have to do, if we are to make it through to Egypt. Instead, we will be dropped off on Crete.

Wasting no time, she quickly gets up to full speed and leaves the scene. I cannot see a thing for her bow wave, which is about two feet above the level of my head. I glance at my watch to find it is two-thirty. We have been under attack, almost continuously, for seven hours. Then I realise that the air raids have stopped. Just one more will have caught us in the middle of a rescue operation and seen us absolutely slaughtered. The tally of planes downed during the fight is judged to be about fifteen.

Our feelings are mixed during our dash to Crete. We are glad to be spared of any further pounding, but conscious that we are still in the danger zone. We are bitterly disappointed at not having made it safely through to Egypt. Still we have managed to get out of Greece and that is really something to be grateful for.

We learn later that our old Costa Rica was very reluctant to die and was sinking only very slowly. Faced with the problem of what to do with her, the Navy decided to sink her. So they stood off, pumped a few shells into her and sent her to the bottom.

With our Destroyer's speed suddenly slackening, we realise that we are almost there. We sail quite sedately round a point and into a long and fairly wide bay. There is a fair-sized wharf heading out from the land, about halfway along. This will have to be our landing point There are several ships spaced around the bay and close inshore. One of them is a Navy Cruiser sitting at anchor beyond the wharf and deeper into the bay. It all looks very calm and serene. We are told that this is Souda Bay. (Souda Bay? How very much like Suvla Bay of Gallipoli fame.)

By now there are other Destroyers following us in, and soon all of us oddbods are streaming onto the wharf. As quickly as we are cleared, the Destroyers head back to rejoin the Convoy. There is a fair amount of milling around while the throng endeavours to sort themselves out. Nobody apparently, knows of our arrival. We are on our own and will have to make whatever contacts we can, and upon our own initiative.

For the Infantry boys it won't be such a big problem. Belonging to large, well-defined Units, their locations can be found easily. For our little group, it is a different matter. We do not have a clue where our Unit might be. There is a fair chance that our mob isn't even on the island. For all intents and purposes, we are as good as lost.

Our only missing member, Lenny, has now rejoined us. But what a different Lenny it is. When picked up, after swimming away from the Costa Rica, he had been taken naked down to the engine room to dry out. There, one of the sailors had given him a civilian suit that he kept especially for going on shore leave. It was a lightweight material, cream coloured, and, although the jacket fitted rather well, the trousers were just a little too tight for Lenny's roly-poly figure. He had bent over to put some shoes on and the seat had split almost to the waist band. For the life of me I cannot help but be amused at Lenny's inconvenience. Under the circumstances it is no big deal at all, yet Lenny is deeply embarrassed and continually doing his best to hide the split from everyone. He keeps close to me as if, somehow, he might be shielded. He is destined to have to live in that suit for at least a fortnight before finally being able to get some bits and pieces of proper uniform.

Everybody else has disappeared and we are on our own. We look around for Unit destination signs, but there are none. There is a total absence of personnel around the wharf area. The reason might be explained by what now becomes obvious to us. Those ships, carefully dispersed around the Bay, are all wrecks, even the Cruiser. They certainly look alright at first glance, but they all are aground. The Cruiser is sitting upright, but firmly on the bottom. One good thing about it... if they look alright to us, then they certainly will to the Germans from the air.

Walking off the end of the wharf, we find that the main road servicing it, passes at right angles, continuing on to our left and right. Which way to go? To the left seems to be out into open country, while to the right seems to be towards habitation in the direction of the capital, Chania. Whichever way we go has to be tackled on foot, and we really are in no condition to go very far.

There are now about twenty-five of us, and we automatically keep to our regular formations: that is, my crew with me, Joe's crew with him and, what is left of the other lot with their Lance Corporal, Les Lawrence.

Now everybody wants to have a say in which way we should go. I reason that we should look for some kind of headquarters to find out if, indeed, our Unit is on the island. If it is, then we will get the right directions. If not, then somebody in authority will make a decision as to what is to be done about us. Also, we might wrangle some transport or some food. I reckon any headquarters are more likely to be in the Chania area than somewhere in the open.

Others are opposed to going anywhere near a headquarters, reckoning that all we will get there is a load of bullshit. "Look at the lack of organisation that has led to our present plight," they reason. The main consensus is to look for our Unit and be damned to the Brass.

While we are arguing, a couple of uniformed men come walking along the road from our left. Joe and a couple of others go over to them to see if they can give us any information. No, they haven't heard of the 2/1 Field Engineers. They are not sure of anything much, nor where anybody is for that matter. Then one of them says, "Hang on, there is an Engineer Unit along there," pointing to the left.

"About how far?"

"Oh, maybe a mile."

"Any idea who it is?"

"No, but I think it's Australian." The other bloke doesn't know anything about it at all. They go on their way, leaving us still arguing.

Joe feels pretty sure that this information is on the right track and feels that we cannot dally any longer as the day is coming to an end. I am reluctant to head off in what I consider the wrong direction, but feel we all have to stick together as a group, right or wrong. But I absolutely dread the thought of maybe having to retrace every inch of that journey.

We set off, really in no condition to go very far, plodding and grumbling on our way. Each step, I take, convinces me that I am going the wrong way, and that makes my journey all the harder. With night closing in and no sign of any group or personnel, we have no way of checking our whereabouts. As time goes on, after what seems hours, I finally call a halt. I suggest to Joe that I think we have gone much further than a mile and, now that it is dark, we can quite easily miss the camp and pass it by. I decide, therefore, that my crew and I will stretch out on the side of the road and wait until daylight. But, the crews of Joe and Les Lawrence decide to press on a little further before they call it quits.

We move slightly off the road and sink gratefully onto the grass. The weather is fairly mild so we should not be too badly off. But there will be nothing to eat. We have done pretty poorly for food for several weeks now and are really hungry. This is our main problem. We just curl up and sleep the best way we can. At first light, stiff and sore, we get going again. There is a slight, hilly spur alongside where we had stopped, and where Joe had continued on round it, and out of sight. I wonder how much further he had continued before he, too, had had to call it quits.

We round the spur and immediately sight a group just off the road, about a quarter of a mile away. The nearer we approach, the larger this lot appears to be. It just cannot be Joe. Then some of them begin to take familiar shapes, and we realise that it is our Unit. I had erred, and badly, in not continuing on with Joe. We turn into the camp area and, instead of an expected fond welcome, we are treated with loud chiacking and cries of, "Where the bloody hell have you been?"

I had intended to front up to my Acting Lieutenant and the Sergeant, and demand to know why they had pissed off and left us. Appearing to be a responsible and efficient leader would add plenty of weight to such a demand. But, now that all the reports have already been presented by Joe and Les, instead of appearing to be a returning prodigal son, I stand out as a tardy, don't care leader, not much better than the rabble around me.

I am resentful, too, at the fact that nobody had sought to come out and get us last night, and take us into camp. I know this is too much to expect of Joe and his boys, as they were too far gone. Still, some of the others could have come out and got us. But then, Joe's vague directions to locate us, "somewhere along the road", would unlikely get any volunteers. It is not a great homecoming but, at least, we are all together again.

I do demand and get some explanation from my Acting Lieutenant. It seems that he had been ordered to pull out and link up with the rest of the Unit, when it pulled out earlier on that particular day.. "Well why the hell didn't you let us know?" I ask. He claims that he was ordered to leave, and knew that we would pull out with the Infantry. "Well what about the Sergeant?" I quiz.

"Well he was with me when the order was given, so he came along too."

His explanation sounds a bit lame and less than satisfactory, still it will have to do. How had they got to Crete? Much the same as us it seems. Where the MPs had split the column, they had been turned left while we had been sent straight on. They had been involved in the shambles of an evacuation on the open beach. Somehow they had made it through to be offloaded on Crete.

As a Unit, we are now no better than a bunch of men, just dumped on the roadside. We have no gear, no transport and no shelter. Contact with headquarters is rudimentary. We are receiving some rations of a sort, but anything else is out of the question for the moment. The influx of virtual refugees has created some chaos and until, who is who and what is what can be sorted out, no real organisation can be achieved.

In this sort of vacuum, all we can do is while away our time. The weather is good, each has a spot to doss down and there are no air raids. The reprieve from the latter alone seems like a gift from heaven. Lack of food is the one thing that has us bothered. Officers, NCOs and men alike are all in the same boat. Unit administration is practically non-existent. We gratefully welcome a couple of quiet days to get some of the trauma of our recent hard times out of our system.

In this atmosphere, I am mildly surprised to be summoned to report to the C.O. I usually make it a point not to actively cultivate the top Brass, so I am unsure what it may be about. I find him, sitting cross-legged on the grass. I snap to attention, salute and say, "You wish to see me Sir?"

He pauses for a moment, then says, "It's about your appointment to Acting Corporal. It's been recommended to me that the appointment be not confirmed. What have you to say?"

His statement hits me hard. It is almost as if I have been hit between the eyes with a hammer. For a moment, I rock on my feet with an overwhelming impulse to turn and bolt. And this I almost do. Somehow I manage to control myself and strangle out, "Well Sir, you're the C.O. You'd better do what you consider best for the Company."

I suppose my distress is pretty evident, for he reacts in a sympathetic and compassionate manner. Instead of deciding there and then, he says, "I will let you know later, what my decision will be."

I ask, "Would that be all Sir?"

He answers, "Yes, you can go now." I about-turn and march smartly away.

I am pretty confused and upset, and very glad to get away from the interview. I return to my dossing spot, where my mates want to know what he has wanted me for. So I tell them, repeating in parrot fashion, "It has been recommended that my appointment to Acting Corporal be not confirmed."

Their reaction is almost as stunned as mine. Their vocal comments are very pointed. Their consensus is, "It's a bloody shame. It's that bloody crew of yours. The sooner you get away from them the better."

Over the next few days, I am in a kind of limbo. If we had had any duties to perform, it may have been easier to get it out of my system. As it is, all I can do is keep to myself as much as possible, and have a good hard think about my actions and attitudes.

I chew over my failings. Starting from my appointment, there was some controversy. Taffy and Dave had fronted up to the C.O., while pretty inebriated, and insisted that he had to include me in his appointments. When it had been posted, I used bodgy Italian stripes, and still do, to indicate my new rank. For much of the time, I had worn my flash mauve jacket, instead of my regular jacket, until it was destroyed when Cocker was killed. Then there was the failed Bangalore torpedo business at Tobruk. And what about allowing Albo to escape? I had received a severe reprimand for that, as well as an entry in my pay book.

I have to admit that there are quite a few instances where my conduct is not exactly up to standard. And I am close to my crew, and they do take advantage of it. Still there are things that they would do for me that they would not do for anybody else.

I try to look for some plusses in the mess. Those failings are no big deal, and there are perfectly reasonable excuses as to how they had occurred. There have been very few situations after my appointment that anybody could take exception to. But then, nothing outstanding either. Still, the other appointees had fared little better and, while general wastage created the need, there was not much talent available, other than mine, to fill the gaps. Perhaps the C.O. will let the matter drop. But, as the proposal is now generally known, my position will be difficult until I live it down.

A day or so later, we are on the move again. This time the Unit is to move closer to Souda Bay, an area where some use might be found for us. It is just a matter of get up and start walking, for we have little or no possessions and no camp to break up. I have sought to get an inkling to my own standing, by taking note of the general attitude when I'm told to do something. I will know if it is to be as a Sapper, or Corporal, needing to organise something. Under these circumstances I just cannot tell.

The area, we move to, is just above the wharf and on the south side of the Bay. It is about halfway up on rising ground and gives us a marvellous view of the entire surroundings and for some distance beyond, mostly towards the west of Chania. As before, we just pick a dossing spot, with the whole Unit being contained within a small radius. I choose a position alongside a low stone wall, around which I pile some loose stones that will give me a certain amount of cover.

Once in position, we study the layout of our surroundings with interest. The Bay itself is moderately large and fairly long, running from east to west. Opposite to us on the north side of the Bay is a peninsula with rising ground, somewhat steeper than on our side. To the west and towards Chania, the ground is reasonably flat and cultivated in small patches, here and there, and dotted with groves of olive trees. To the east is the entrance of the Bay.

We ferret out what information we can over the next few days. Souda Bay is the reception point for all supplies. As a protection against aerial attack, five Bofors anti-aircraft gun emplacements are scattered around the Bay. They are manned, around the clock, by crack and efficient Pommy crews. As for planes, that is a different matter.

It seems, that at one time, there had been a very strong presence of fighter aircraft here. The top Brass had decided that they could be better utilised in Egypt and had removed them. A token force of three Hurricanes was left behind. When a German flight had suddenly appeared, these Hurricanes attempted to scramble. One was destroyed before it could get rolling, another managed to get halfway along the runway before it was destroyed. The third managed to get airborne and shoot down two of the Germans, before it too was shot down.

This was supposed to have happened two weeks ago, but there still has been no replacements sent in. And it doesn't look as if any are going to be. It appears that our only protection will be those Bofors. Those Stukas, that we hate so much, once again will be able to do as they please.

With nothing much to do, small groups start walking into Chania, in the hope of being able to buy some food. Despite being the capital, we find Chania to be hardly anything more than a reasonably sized village. There is little we can get there, and the hike back is pretty tiring.

We spend a quiet and blissful fortnight, basking in the warmth of the early spring sunshine, and getting some of the effects of the recent hard times out of our systems. Then the peace is shattered by an air raid. A few planes appear, flying rather high, and drop a few bombs. They appear to be aiming at the Cruiser. The Bofors go into action and they clear off.

With only an occasional raid, we do not have to put up with anything like the intensity of the pounding we had to endure in Greece. Still, the mere sound of aircraft engines approaching, no matter how far away, is enough to rekindle all the old anxieties. Those amongst us, who have reacted the most before, now find those old fears almost intolerable.

There is little or no shipping in the Bay. Now and then, a small freighter will slip in, laden with supplies. She will be unloaded by a Cypriot Company, apparently a labour Unit, then just slip quietly back out to sea. While we know for sure that any shipping will be under Navy protection, no Naval vessels enter the port. There are one or two Motor Torpedo Boats often moored at the wharf, but their bulk is so small that, in the shadows from high above them, it is well-nigh impossible for aircraft to spot them.

In an effort to find something useful for us to do, Jimmy Hay decides to take a party out to those beached ships and see if there is anything salvageable in them. Jimmy, by now Second-in-Command, has managed to get the use of a small landing craft. We will be looking mostly for arms and ammunition. Maybe some of their deck guns are still serviceable.

Jimmy selects a small party of NCOs, and I am one of those included. I do not know much of what to make of that. Either he does not know that my appointment is under question, or does not care. As one of our Newcastle contingent, I know he is quite capable of taking the latter view. In any case, I am not about to make any fuss about it, so I just go along.

There are about ten or twelve of us in the party, with a steersman-operator who comes with the boat. We head fairly smartly across to the far side of the Bay, and to a ship that is nose-in to the shore. It seems that when a ship is disabled, it is just cast adrift and allowed to beach itself. Remarkably, this has resulted in them appearing to be strategically dispersed and undamaged. From the air, the port will appear to be much more busy than it really is. This will account for regular bombing attempts on ships already sunk.

We have no idea how we will get on board, nor whether we will be able to move about if we do so. With nothing said, I think we are all hoping that there will be no more air raids while we are there. While there is no sign of any direct hits, we cannot help feeling very vulnerable. As we swing alongside, we find the water so clear that we can plainly see the bottom. Directly under the free floating stern is a huge aerial bomb. It is much bigger than the usual Stuka stuff and, straightaway, Jimmy gives the order to turn around and head back home. His verdict is that it could be a delayed-action type, and just isn't worth taking the risk.

A day or two later, word comes through that defence of the island is to be under the command of General Freyberg, a New Zealander. This depresses us a bit, for after being driven out of Greece, it seemed that the strategically sensible thing to do would be to abandon this rather small outpost. Crete is within easy bombing range of the German held mainland, making the cost of keeping it supplied with men and materials so daunting. In particular, the pressure on our overworked Navy, to keep the sea lanes open, is almost unbearable.

Then comes a summons from General Freyberg for all available Officers and NCOs, to attend a meeting. This is most unusual. Ordinary rank and file, such as us, rarely ever see or come in contact with a General. Again, my status has me wondering if I should be one of those to attend. After a bit of thinking I decide that, while that there isn't a word to the contrary, then my present rank still must stand. Besides, I am intrigued and want to find out for myself what he has to say.

A fairly large gathering of several hundred personnel assemble in the early afternoon in an open area not far from our position. General Freyberg stands on a slight rise and urges everyone to move in close so that we can all hear what he has to say.

He says that the Germans are expected to make a strong effort to take the Island. They cannot afford to have it as a potential threat on their back doorstep. They can only come at us by sea or by air. If they try the sea approach, our Navy will stop them dead, so we have nothing to worry about there. Therefore, they will have to come at us by air, and we will be ready and waiting for them.

He expects the aerial assault to be by bombing and softening up, then the use of paratroops. They will have to gain control of a landing field to do any good, so he says we will concentrate all of our forces around the three landing fields on the Island, at Heraklion, Retimo and Maleme. There are British, Australian and New Zealand forces on Crete and they each will be charged with the defence of a landing field. The British will look after Heraklion, the Australians Retimo, and the New Zealanders Maleme. We cannot expect much in the way of weapons, as our forces are heavily committed in Egypt. Still, every effort will be made to get us our fair share. But, as these will have to come by sea, they will be subject to the availability of ships and Navy priorities.

It all sounds straight forward and simple enough, and it is very heartening to be privy to the proposed strategy and its aims. It is a nice touch to have the defence handled by a set of national groups, as mixed forces quite often lead to some confusion in the heat of battle. All we can hope for, now, is that the Germans have not dreamed up some tricky way of being able to land away from one of the airfields, and take us by surprise.

The terrain and layout of Crete, however, would make this practically impossible.

We return to our lines and settle down to wait. As in Greece, all flying here will be in daylight because there is no opposition. For a while, nothing much, other than reconnaissance flights, takes place. Very gradually, activity begins to increase while, now and then, a lone freighter will slip in.

Each time planes appear, the air alarm is sounded and everybody will take cover. When a freighter is being unloaded and the planes appear, the Cypriots will take off, and it is impossible to get them back to work again. This would see the freighter caught at the wharf, half-unloaded and very vulnerable. The delay, in its timetable, cannot be afforded. So the top Brass have decided to dispense with the Cypriots, and hand the job over to us Engineers.

The small amount of shipping coming in makes the job itself very easy. But, as a plane will always try to nail a ship at the wharf, we worry that one day it might get lucky. Anybody caught down in the hold will not have sufficient time to get clear, between the first sound of the alarm and the plane's arrival.

Some of the gear coming in seems to make these trips hardly worthwhile. It is mostly captured Italian munitions and obsolete American rifles. Faulty ammunition is the problem with the Italian stuff, while the Yankee rifles pose a different threat. They are Springfields and, by the way they are greased up, have obviously been stockpiled since the end of the First World War. While they are better than nothing, they are totally unfamiliar to us. We know how to open the bolt and insert a cartridge, but the sighting system is different. While our sight is U-shape theirs is a C-shape. We can hardly ask the Germans to hold still, while we get a couple of shots off to get the hang of it. A further complication is that the ammunition for the Springfields is not interchangeable with our trusty 303's.

There is a large force of seasoned and battle-hardened troops, in good positions, to defend the Island. They are backed up by a very large group of hardy Greek soldiers, who have made it through to Crete. Then there is the no-nonsense Cretan people themselves. This is the plus side—all with a hotchpotch of weapons, needing a hotchpotch of ammo to serve them and making supply problems a nightmare. It will be a tricky situation when the crunch comes.

The crews needed for unloading are only small and, with our numbers, often we will stand by and not be needed at all. Our camp positions are about three quarters of a mile above the wharf, so it is an easy, leisurely walk to and from the job. The weather is consistently fine and clear, and it is all very pleasant. With the Bofors protecting the port, we only bother to clear from the wharf during an air raid, then quickly return to the job.

Now and then, there will be the odd few who will go aboard ship and return to Egypt. There are reasons of course—maybe for medical or service movement, which we have no knowledge of. One bright morning, about nine o'clock, about five of us are just coming onto the job. There is a small freighter at the wharf, and its unloading has just completed. Three English Officers are pacing up and down talking, and obviously waiting to embark.

Our two groups have just passed each other, when Lenny spots a large open crate filled with tin hats. It is sitting there, waiting to be moved. He says," Go on Arty, grab one. You've got no head gear at all." We all pause as I put one hand on the crate and look in.

I am just about to say to Lenny, "The frontline blokes need to be fixed first." But before I can touch any, one of the English Officers breaks from his pacing, and he marches straight up to me. With one hand on his revolver, he says. "If you put your hand on anything, I will shoot you where you stand for looting."

He pauses for a moment, grimly determined, while I just stare open-mouthed. Then he turns and marches back to his companions, and they continue their pacing. With the narrow wharf, we are under close observation by the other. All we can think is, "What a stupid and ridiculous attitude to take!" Once again, one of my own side has threatened to kill me and, quite obviously, he means to. I seem to be under as much danger from our lot as from the enemy. With the freighter moving and their going aboard, I don't know whether to be pleased or sorry. Almost perversely, I wish I had tested out his resolve.

A freighter arrives, this time containing a small Unit of troops. They are British and part of the Welsh Regiment. As regular troops, they arrive with all their weapons and Unit trappings.

My crew and I are just coming onto the job and most of them have already departed. There is still a lot of their gear in the hold and we will be working to get it out. As we near the bottom of the gangway, a Junior Officer comes hurrying up and asks who is in charge.

Rodger, one of our Lieutenants, is supervising and is standing up on deck at the head of the gangway. Normally, I would have called up, "Hey Rodger, somebody wants to see you." But, as I am in front of a British Officer, I reason that I had better observe the niceties. So instead I call up, " Excuse me Sir, there is an Officer here who wishes to speak to you."

Rodger puts his head over the rail and peers down at us. In a very loud voice he calls down, "How many Pips has he got?"

"One Sir," I reply.

"Well, I've got two. If he wants to see me, tell him to come up here," is Rodger's reply.

I turn, apologetically, to the British Officer and shrug my shoulders. Without another word, he hastens up the gangway.

This Officer's mission is to get priority unloading, for the Mess silver. It is in a special box and is clearly marked. We are deeply incensed at this request. The whole Island is standing by waiting for invasion, and this lot want us to give priority to eating utensils. To top it off, such luxuries are denied us. We haven't even the facilities to cook a meal, and are just dossing on a hillside. These freighters too, are facing big risks, running the gauntlet to get what they can to us for the coming battle.

The Mess silver is unloaded alright, but I'm pretty sure it is only at a time suitable to the unloaders. On the way to camp we pass a high stack, just clear of the end of the wharf. It is a big mound of hand insect spray guns. Gee! If we run out of ammunition, I suppose we can always attack the Germans with insect spray. But, if things run true to form, I'll bet that while the insect guns are here, the spray will be back in Egypt.

The Bofors guns are troubling the Germans and they begin flying regular patterns, trying to pinpoint their positions. For a time, they have no success. But finally, the inevitable happens. They find and destroy one. With this success, they step up their efforts, while the well-sited Bofors men do their best to keep them at bay. It becomes a deadly cat-and-mouse game and we are enthralled as it is played out around us. Then another one goes and then another. Finally there is only one emplacement left. As each one is lost, the wharf area becomes less and less secure. Each alarm sees us take a bit more care now in getting clear.

One freighter caught at the wharf goes very close to being hit. We clear the wharf while the ship eases out into the Bay, with Rodger still aboard. Some of the blokes say that the ship's Engineer is a New Zealander, as is Rodger. The pair get together and go to the Officer's cabin for a few drinks. This appears to have turned into a session. They either are oblivious of the raid, or just don't care. A short time later the ship sails out of the Bay, without returning to the wharf. Rodger is still on board. The comment by most of us is, "Half his luck."

On another day, a Tanker is hit. She was standing a short distance off the wharf at the time and the resultant damage was only to the ship itself and its cargo. We were off-duty at the time, back in camp and, with a grandstand seat, we watched the whole proceedings.

We watched the plumes of black smoke as the bombs hit, then the red flames of the fire. Following the explosion we see the intermingling of red and black clouds climb up, and up, and up; and, although it seems impossible to go higher, still they climb. We stare, fascinated by the sight. Our distance from the scene makes it all a fairly soundless spectacle. Suddenly, the noise reaches and rolls over us in an horrendous blast. It knocks us clean off our feet.

This was the only Tanker to come into Souda Bay during our time there, and her crew cast her loose, allowing her to drift onto the far shore, just like those other wrecks. There she is allowed to burn herself out.

The one remaining Bofors gun has the Germans worried and they try their best to pinpoint it. It is manned by a top-class crew who are determined not to give themselves away. The lives on both sides depend on each being able to outsmart the other. The Bofors is a deadly, efficient gun. But, the need for it to be able to traverse in any direction, means that its emplacement has to be fairly open. Its main method of concealment is by camouflage. If located, it doesn't stand much chance.

At first, the Germans fly back and forth in a conventional grid fashion, tempting the Bofors gun to fire and reveal its position. Our gunners refuse to fire while they are under observation. The frustrated Germans decide to try a new tactic. On this particular day a flight of about eight or ten planes appears overhead. Forming up into a circle, they fly very low, over the gun's approximate position. Nose to tail, round and round, they fly, at almost point-blank range. We watch in fascination while the deadly game is played out. How we sympathise with those gunners. They must be sorely tempted to go for it. Still they give no giveaway sign. Then, a flaw in the German plan begins to appear.

While concentrating for signs on the ground below, the last plane in the circle drifts ever so slightly away from the plane in front of it. Imperceptibly, a gap begins to open up. With growing excitement, we watch as this slim chance starts to emerge. Wider and wider it grows until suddenly the plane's crew becomes aware of the danger. Instantly, it speeds up to try and close the circle once again. This is a fatal decision for the plane now places itself well clear of the one in front and the one behind. This is the chance the gunners have longed for.

Instantly, the rapid firing Bofors gun spits out a clip of about five shells and, just as quickly, ceases fire. Our gunners must have been tracking the flight the whole time, for they are in position to do their job at the split second the opportunity presents itself.

The shells slam home and instantly the plane lurches out of formation, losing height rapidly. It plunges towards the ground on the far side of the Bay. In the last few seconds before it hits, a couple of parachutes appear. At that low altitude, they have no chance, and they go straight down without opening. Then follows the crash and a big ball of flame.

The instant the plane hits, the whole area erupts. Every single man watching the drama being played out, leaps to his feet. They dance and howl, caper and roar, cheering like maniacs. The universal feeling is, "Cop that you bastards! That's one for us."

The sustained hammering we have suffered from the German planes over the past few months, has given us a deep and abiding hate of them. Often in frustration, we have slammed off a few shots from our rifles as a relief to our pent up feelings. Although we know it is a forlorn hope, there is always the chance that we might get lucky. Now, to see one downed by a gun really equipped to do the job, is oh so sweet, and just too much.

The circling planes are stunned at the loss of their comrade, but still cannot find the Bofors gun emplacement. They never do find it, and that is the last time it fires. Whether they have run out of ammunition, or have just decided to quit, we never find out.

There is a general feeling of expectancy nagging at us now, as we wait for whatever might happen. Then, word goes round that the sick and wounded, as well as anybody else considered unnecessary to the coming encounter, are to be cleared from the Island. A ship steams in to cover this task, and what a ship! It is an almost brand new Dutch luxury liner of about sixty thousand tons. It is called the Nieu Holland. She is bigger than the Orcades that we had come over on. She towers high above the wharf and presents a huge potential target. We are on tenterhooks that the Germans might mount a raid and find her.

While these evacuees are genuine cases, a small sprinkling have manoeuvred and contrived to get themselves included. One of these is Lenny. Ever the conman, he has managed to fake the symptoms of a sexual disease.

With the ship only there for about two hours, the last man aboard is Tex, one of my Newcastle mates. He has been ordered out, but badly wants to stay. He greatly fears aerial bombing and much prefers to take his chances here. I walk with him to the bottom of the gangway, talking to and persuading him all the way. A very reluctant Tex climbs the long set of steps up the ship's side, still unwilling to go. There are many who gladly would have swapped places with him.

Then comes a night when our sleep is greatly disturbed by the sounds of Naval gunfire out to sea. Sometimes close, sometimes further away, it waxes and wanes for most of the night. We know that something major is happening, and next morning we seek to find out.

We learn that the Germans have tried a seaborne invasion, only to be intercepted by our Navy. Of about fifteen enemy ships, all have been sunk except three. These are disabled and in flames, and are drifting back towards the Greek mainland, but not expected to make it. There are stories, for days after, of bodies being washed ashore at different points along the coast.

With very little shipping activity, we just watch and wait. The days are bright and sunny. About nine o'clock on a clear bright day like any other, we become aware of the heavy sustained sound of approaching aircraft. These sounds are quite different to what we have become used to and, instinctively, we know that this is what we have been waiting for.

We scramble to our vantage points and stare out to sea. Into sight comes a massed column of heavy transport planes heading in towards Maleme aerodrome. Old Freyberg has been dead right. The Navy has whipped them at sea, now they are trying by air. While apprehensive at the coming battle, we know that our preparations are as good as they can be. With our blokes ready and waiting, this will be a sorry day for the Germans. They will be made to pay dearly for what we have had to take in Greece.

The planes' approach is quite blatantly arrogant. They act as if they own the place and that this is just a display for some visiting General. As well they might, for the only defence we have against them is the men waiting on the ground.

Our vantage point, high on the hillside, seems to put us on about the same height level as the planes they are using. We have an absolutely clear and unimpeded view of the whole proceedings. We can see the open doorway in each plane's side, and the paratroopers ready and waiting for the word to jump.

In front of us there are some small garden patches, then groves of olive trees, then the capital Chania. Beyond Chania and slightly to the southwest is Maleme aerodrome, about four or five miles from where we stand. The aerial armada sweeps in from the sea, just beyond Chania and proceeds on to Maleme. Over Maleme the paratroopers stream from their planes, with the skies instantly filled with white canopies. The transports continue on in a wide circle, heading back towards us and then heading back out to sea, after passing over the olive groves. In a continuance of the drop, more parachutists spew out over the groves.

With the skies above filled with paratroopers, it is now the turn of the defenders. As for that nearby drop over the olive trees, we immediately dismiss them from our thoughts. We know something that they do not. Under those trees are camped elements of the Maori Battalion. Famed for their prowess with the bayonet, we know that those Germans never will have a chance.

At Maleme, where the bulk of the defence is placed, they have a field day. It is a duck shoot. We can see the suspended men, suddenly stiffen and then sag as the bullets thud home. While we can observe everything happening in the air, we cannot see any of the ground action. Still we know that if anybody does land, they will be quickly taken care of.

For most of the day the action is fairly hectic. Stukas sweep in trying to support any of their side who may need them, while we, the defenders, wipe out any resistance we can find. The olive grove lot is as we predict. Many Germans are impaled or hung up in the trees and those who make it to the ground are quickly taken out by the Maoris. There are very few survivors.

By nightfall, it is obvious that the paratroopers have copped a beating. In their conquest of Europe, they had only to appear in the skies to cause panic and confusion amongst defending or unready ground forces. At least that is how it appears to us. Here, where our troops are ready and waiting, the element of surprise is lost. They do not know how to cope. Again, that is how it appears to us. During the night, we stand at the ready with our Springfield rifles, just in case some manage to get through. We do not really expect any, and none appear.

But, in the morning, again on a bright, clear and sunny day, they come lumbering in, just as before, at the same time and on the same flightpath. We knew they would. Once committed, they just have to keep coming. It comes down to who will crack first... them or us.

Whereas yesterday, they came in at a height of about a thousand feet, today they practically halve that. Realising that they have been too vulnerable, hanging there, drifting down, the shorter drop gives them a better chance to reach the ground. This tactic brings the planes themselves into range and our blokes are able to rake them as well. Paratroopers are now being killed inside the planes before they can jump. From here on, they concentrate on the aerodrome only. They have given the olive groves away. At least that is one place they have conceded defeat.

At this lower height there is a regular pattern of parachutes plunging straight down, without opening. Intrigued, I watch for this happening and estimate that it is at the ratio of one in ten.

Again it is a hectic day with the massive drop continuing throughout the morning. Confusion follows on the ground, with our blokes cleaning up wherever necessary. The confusion makes any attempts by the Stukas to support their lot, less than effective. It is a daylong ebb and flow that again only ceases at nightfall.

As for the ground action, we are too far away to see or know anything. We just have to judge by the signs, and whatever information we can glean. While we have complete confidence in our lot, we are not stupid enough to misread those signs. We can tell that the action has slowed considerably from about two hours before dark. Thereafter, it's only sporadic stuff that quickly peters out, ceasing entirely before nightfall. Again we stand to, and again nothing happens.

In the morning, at the same time and on the same flightpath, they again sweep in. They have elected to maintain their lower height level. The regularity of their timing, the flightpath and the height, makes our blokes readiness and preparedness very much easier. Again we give those paratroopers a murderous reception.

Today we become aware of a new innovation in the Germans' strict routine. After the drop, as soon as the transports have cleared the land on their way back to Greece, a figure can be seen working busily at the open doorway in the side of each plane. He is dragging bundles to the opening and pushing them out to drop into the sea below. We can plainly see that the bundles are the bodies of dead men.

Later we find out that when the transports returned, laden with dead and injured on the second day, those paratroopers waiting to board, refused to do so. With a continuous shuttle service vital to any hope of success, they have been forced aboard with threats, and at the point of a gun. Presumably, without the presence of dead bodies to indicate how hot the battle was where they were going, there would be much less trouble getting the paratroopers to enter the planes.

Again in the morning, the latest attack comes with the same timing and same procedure. For a couple of days, it seems that a bit of urgency is creeping into the Germans' attitude. The paratroopers are their top troops and they are copping a belting. How long can they afford to keep pushing on while losing so many men? Then what about our side? We just hope that our meagre supplies will hold out.

We begin to hear of some of the happenings in the ground fighting. It seems that they have a good system of signalling to their aircraft when they need support. They will lay out a German flag and a large arrow pointing to where they desire bombing and strafing. A similar system prevails for when they need supplies. They will then retire a short distance from the signs and let the Stukas do their stuff. As soon as our blokes catch on to their system, somebody will crawl out and reverse the arrows. This results in our blokes dining on fresh sandwiches and hot coffee, while watching the Stukas shoot up their own men. There are all sorts of wonderful things in those supply canisters too, such as submachine guns and even collapsible motorbikes for scooting around on.

Of course, there are plenty of problems for our side too. We are told of some nightmares with that Italian ordinance. Many of the field guns have no sights, so our blokes have to resort to putting blobs of chewing gum on the barrel to get some sort of aim. And that faulty ammunition results in some shells roaring from the muzzle quickly on their way, while others barely clear the gun and drop harmlessly to the ground.

Food is not very plentiful and has to be the kind where a man can snatch a quick bite in between the fighting. This makes those misdirected German food canisters all the more welcome. Other than that, a real meal is not on.

With the Germans just having to keep coming and being unable to vary their pattern, gives our blokes an edge. As long as the attack has to be in one place and our blokes can concentrate there, we can nail them. Man for man, we are certain that our blokes have their measure. The key thing is going to be supplies. In manpower and supplies, we can holdout against theirs and win. The problem is: Will the Germans crack before our supplies run out?

Since the fighting began, no ships have arrived for us to unload. Then we are notified that a ship will be arriving at night time, and it will have to be cleared quickly. It will contain a Force of three thousand British Commandos and their supplies.

You beauty! The news gives us a big lift. These specialist troops will be ideal for mopping up any paratrooper ground pockets. This proves more than anything, that we are winning. I am one of the crew detailed to help with the unloading.

It is somewhere about midnight, when we are ferried out to the ship which is standing out in the Bay. In the pitch dark we cannot see her until we are almost by her side. There is a long gangway, the standard ship's type, leading up the side, with a small dim light at the top. We scramble up and onto her deck, and look around with interest. She looks brand new, is a Navy ship, not a freighter, but has us puzzled as to her type.

The Commandos are already ashore, and their gear will have to follow. With the ship not at the wharf, this will be a new procedure for everybody. It seems that everything will have to go over the side onto a landing craft far below. In the dim light of a shaded Arclight, the landing craft seems to be at least thirty feet below us, and lifting and rolling in a very light swell.

We mill around a bit, unsure where to begin. I take the opportunity to talk to a nearby sailor and ask him about the ship. Her name is the Abdil and she is a minelayer cruiser, a completely new type. I ask whether their Convoy has been under attack on the way over. He says, "We do not travel in a Convoy. We always travel alone and aircraft do not worry us, as we can do better than forty knots." When I marvel at this, he invites me to stay aboard and go back with them.

What a thought! I say, "Thanks, but I can't do that."

He says, "Suit yourself, but we'll be back for you in a couple of nights anyway." I just cannot make any sense of that, at all.

Meanwhile, there is a bit of arguing going on where our lot is gathered at the ship's rail, above the landing craft. A party is needed to go over the side, down onto the land craft to receive and stow the stores. The sheer drop into the lightly rolling craft, with its unstable footing down there, in the dark and without even a rope to hang onto, is daunting. Nobody is keen to lead the way.

A sailor in a uniform suggests a Petty Officer be in charge of breaking out the stores and handing them over to our lot for the unloading. He is trying to bully and shame somebody, or anybody, into making the descent. Our lot has been through too much to fall for that kind of trick, so we ignore him. The frustrated sailor is getting more agitated by the minute. There is a small knot of Army Officers standing around, looking on as well. One of them asks, "What seems to be the trouble?"

I speak up and say, "The men think it's too dangerous to go over the side like that, and risk being crushed between the ship and the landing craft, Sir."

None of the Officers attempt to throw their weight around to order somebody to go ahead. Perhaps they can see these hardheads may respond by saying, "You lead Sir, and I will follow." The truth is that nobody, including any sailors fancy the idea of making that descent. I, as an NCO, could be expected to lead the way. But, taking full advantage of my doubtful status, I am very happy to play the role of a not-too-brave Sapper.

The Petty Officer, faced with making a deadline, attempts to get things moving. He calls for assistance to lower a wooden ramp over the side and down into the landing craft. It is about three feet wide, and long and heavy. All our crew quickly lend a hand, swing it into position, push it out, counterbalance it for a moment, then let it thud down into the craft below.

With the ramp in position, the Petty Officer attempts to make the first drop. It is a sealed container of Army biscuits. They come in a metal container about two feet by three feet, and are not overly heavy. The ramp is constantly moving up and down, with the uneven motion between the two ships caused by the swell. The Officer releases his hold and allows the ramp to slide. It has barely travelled two feet before the container rolls off and plunges into the sea. There it floats away and is quickly lost to sight.

This is no surprise to any of us, for we can see that this will happen to every package, unless somebody is below to steady it down. Then Big Tom speaks up and says, "Watch out, I'll have a go." Big Tom, who had given me a hard time over the Boys anti-tank rifle incident at Kalamata, cannot bear to watch any longer without doing something.

He moves into position at the top of the ramp, crouches on his haunches with his feet under him. Facing downwards, he holds onto the ship's rail for a few moments, then lets himself go. Protected by his Army boots and, with his arms outstretched for balance, he slides a few feet then is quickly and safely in the landing craft.

This breaks the ice. With the demonstration of a successful technique, I am the next to try it. I am careful to copy Big Tom's method exactly and, like him, I am quickly, although a little roughly, in the landing craft also. A couple more follow and we have a crew to catch and stow. The supplies flow quickly and at a good pace, and not another thing is lost overboard.

With all the stores safely transferred to the landing craft, we set off for the shore. Upon arrival we quickly get stuck into the unloading. We are as anxious as anybody to get the job over and done with. All the stores are in open boxes and cartons, in what seems to be one-man loads. They look as if they have been thrown together in a hurry, probably with the idea that they might have to be unloaded in a hostile area. This amuses me, for we are in what we consider is a perfectly safe area.

There are no Commandos to be seen, nor a representative of any kind. All we can do is stack everything in a heap on the open shore. While I accept that the Commandos are probably trained to get stuck into things straightaway, I just cannot see that being the case here. We are too far away from the actual fighting for that.

With the unloading completed, the landing craft takes off, and we are left there alone with the heap of stores. Most of the blokes head back to camp, and I take one last look over the opened packages. There are boxes of canned food in special one-person packs, as well as some familiar looking weapons. The weapons are American Thompson submachine guns, or Tommy guns, seen so often in American gangster films.

Left unattended, I know that a good proportion, if not all, of this will just simply disappear. Everybody has been doing it hard in the way of food for some time, so I know very little of that will be left. I am about to follow the rest of the blokes back to camp when I think, "Damn it! The stuff's going to be knocked off anyway, so I'll grab a bit to take back to my mates." I begin to stuff a few tins inside my shirt. Then I think, "I may as well grab a weapon too," so I pick up a Tommy gun and three drums of ammunition.

My lingering and looting has left me well behind the other blokes, so I hurry and try to catch up to them. With my shirt full of canned food, and carrying a very heavy load of the Tommy gun and ammunition, this is rather difficult. I struggle for a while, then call out to them to hang on, as I have a shirt full of food. I figure that will make them wait.

Just as I call out, a couple of figures loom up in the pitch dark on my left. Startled, I turn to see that the leader is my C.O. He is the one I had to front up to regarding my appointment to Corporal. I am caught red-handed with a stuffed shirt and a uniquely special gun.

There is nothing I can do, so I just stand there. He continues on, asking in passing, "Job finished?"

"Yes Sir," says me.

He replies, "Carry on and get back to camp."

Obviously, he can see what I have been up to and chooses to ignore it. I am humbly grateful. Feeling very chastened, I hurry on after the others.

It is daylight by the time we get back to camp. We have had a full night, are tired and looking forward to catching up on some sleep. The camp is astir and I can see my Acting Lieutenant walking towards me. "Hello!" I am thinking. "The C.O. must have got onto him to give me a ticking-off for pinching from the Commandos." I prepare myself to have a go back at him.

His words are totally unexpected. Quite calmly he says, "It has been decided to evacuate. All of us are to make our way over to the south side of the Island, where we will be picked up." I cannot believe it and look dumbfounded. We have been on top of the Germans, so what the hell has gone wrong?

Although he is in charge of our full Section, of which my lot are just a small part, he probably knows little more of the situation than I do. But he is the bloke in front of me, and he is the bloke to vent my frustration on.

I am bitter and feel cheated. I should not have been on Crete in the first place. If it had not been for the Costa Rica being sunk, I would have been in Egypt. It was a pretty hairy evacuation that has got me this far, and now I have to face up to another one. While the efficiency of the first one had been top-class, it will be expecting a bit too much for the same kind of luck in the second, especially once the Germans cotton on to the fact that another evacuation is underway.

I rail at him, saying that all our night's work has been for nothing. All those stores will be left behind for the Germans, and I am damn glad that I have pinched what I have. I only wish that I had taken more. And what about those three thousand Commandos? They will have to join the queue without firing a shot. If the situation is this bad, those stupid bastards should not have allowed them to land. They should have remained on the Abdil and not landed at all. As a matter of fact, if I had known the situation, I would have stayed aboard myself.

I am recklessly defiant when I throw in that last little bit, and he is patiently calm and reasonable. He replies, "As a matter of fact, I didn't expect to see you come back."

I am completely surprised at his tone and the calmness of his attitude, but I cannot resist replying, "Oh yeah, and if I had, you'd be the first bastard to charge me with desertion."

Well that is the situation and, with small knots of men already moving out, I have no choice but to do likewise. There is no transport, so we will have to hike all the way. How far, nobody knows? Where to, only a vague somewhere on the south of the Island?

I hurry to my hole in the ground to collect my meagre belongings, then join the others. I am glad I have the Tommy gun; it gives me a sense of security. Firstly, I'll have to figure out how the damn thing works. I cannot expect a possible target to wait for me to find out.

I sit down and start to examine it. It is the first real look I have been able to take up to now. The cylindrical drum magazines are full of .45 calibre copper-jacketed slugs. Any one of them is capable of causing a gaping wound. Continuous fire would probably chop a man to pieces. I have no idea how many slugs a magazine contains and do not have time to find out. But I figure it is anything from fifty to a hundred, if those gangster films are anything to go by.

I work out the bolt mechanism and how the magazine attaches to the gun. I find the cocking lever and the safety catch. It should be a simple matter of cocking the bolt then pressing the trigger, either in short bursts or continuously until the magazine runs out.. With such powerful slugs, I probably may have to keep a firm grip, or the recoil may make it jump all over the place. There is one or two fitments I cannot quite get the hang of, but I figure that I have worked out enough to get by.

My dallying has seen me left well behind by the others. Now I will have to hurry to catch up. With the morning advancing, I can hear aerial gunfire behind me in the Souda Bay area. The Stukas are on the prowl, and I well know the drill. They will fly barely a hundred feet up and shoot anything that moves.

Now I can hear a solitary Stuka, unmistakeably heading in my direction. I will have to scramble quickly to take cover. For a moment, my eyes dart about, assessing what direction it will be best for me to run. Then I blow up. I have had a gutful. I am not going to run and hide from those bastards anymore. I have my Tommy gun and I will take him on. I have the advantage because I know he is coming. He is looking for a target, but will not know one is there until the last minute.

Just here the road takes a slight bend around a low rocky spur. I hurry over and sit on the ground with my back against the rockface. Cradling the

Tommy gun firmly under my arm, with the butt on the ground and the muzzle angled upward, I spread my legs for a better balance. With finger on the trigger, I am faced to take him head on.

These preparations take just seconds, and I wait for him to come into view. Suddenly, I realise that the sound of his motors are receding and not advancing. He has turned back just a split second before coming into view. He must have been low on fuel. I feel badly cheated.

Suddenly, I realise how stupidly ridiculous I must have looked just sitting there. I scramble quickly to my feet, eternally grateful that I am alone and that nobody else is aware of my silly posture. I hurry to catch up with my mates, feeling as deflated as a pricked balloon.

Much later, I find that I would be lucky to have fired more than a couple of shots. One of the fitments I have not been able to figure out is a butterfly key that folds flat on the centre of the magazine drum. This key winds up a clockwork-type spring whose tension is needed to feed the ammunition continuously into the gun.

I soon catch up with some of the blokes, and we just continue on in the general direction that everybody is heading. We talk as we hurry on, speculating as to what has gone wrong and what are our chances. We use the road while everything is quiet, but swing into the shelter of olive trees whenever the sound of approaching planes can be heard.

The olive groves prove to be dubious shelters anyway, for we come across several with bodies of our dead scattered around. The Stukas have taken pot luck and shot them up anyway.

One poor bloke had taken up a position that seemed completely safe. He had placed the solid trunk of an olive tree between himself and the line of fire. He had stood upright and had been killed in that position. His body is still there, caught in the fork of the tree, half-slumped, half-upright.

It is a grim sight, but all we can do is hurry on. The strain is beginning to get to me. This damn Tommy gun and its drums of ammunition is getting heavier by the minute. I cannot just chuck it away, but it is making my condition poorer all the time. For several months now, we have all been short on food, grabbing some when and where we can, often going without. The little I had pinched off the Commandos has gone nowhere. We had been up all night unloading, and now have had to keep going all day.

With a few mates alongside, I struggle on, but, by mid-afternoon, I am almost in a stupor. We come to a spot where some soldiers are standing to. They are just assembled there in a small knot. I ask them what they are up to, and they tell me that they are the rearguard. I say, "Here, you can make better use of this than me," and thrust the Tommy gun and drums of ammo into the hands of one of them. The surprised soldier just stands there while I continue on, much lighter and almost with a new lease of life.

It is quite dark when at last a halt is called. The forward elements of our Unit, with some of our Officers, have stopped by the roadside and collected us together as we come along. Jimmy Hay has been very active in this. Now that we are all together, the decision has been taken for us to rest for the night then get going early in the morning.

The several hundred of us just spread out on the grassy verge and just sink gratefully down. We are all too tired to worry much about food. In any case, it will only be something that a man has managed to hang onto himself. I sink immediately into a deep sleep. About half an hour later, I am partially roused by somebody calling my name.

It is one of my Newcastle mates, Arthur Swain, and he is calling, "Artie, Artie Dawson, where are you?" I am so damn tired that I refuse to answer. He goes on for several seconds while I roll over, trying to blot out the sound. Then he gives up and, I again, fall into a deep sleep. I know nothing further until daylight.

I awake, greatly refreshed, but to a disturbing situation. About half the Unit has disappeared during the night, among them Jimmy Hay, the remainder of the Officers, as well as Arthur Swain. So that's what Swainy had been calling me for. Somebody had taken the decision to keep going and, with the men scattered about, the only way to make contact was by calling them by name.

Oh well, it is too late to do anything about it now. The rest of us will just have to keep going and hope we can make contact later. With all of us together as a Unit, we can command some consideration in evacuation priorities. Now, we are no more than individuals, trying to get off the Island.

After the night's sleep, I feel somewhat refreshed and in better shape to keep going. We now know that we are making for a small fishing village called Sfakia. We know only that it is on the southwest coast. What will be there waiting for us, if anything, we will just have to wait and find out.

We move off, intermingled with men from many different Units. All are consumed with the one idea—to get to Sfakia as soon as possible.

One bloke, who walks with us for a short while, is badly handicapped. Both his hands have been blown off. Despite this, he paces it out with the rest of us. He just swings along with his blackened, unbandaged stumps, dangling. We are a bit nonplussed at his acceptance as normal, at what is completely abnormal. So I ask him, "How did you lose your hands?"

His answer is matter-of-fact and clear. He just says, "Mortar bomb."

I ask, "Are you in any pain?"

He answers, "No, can't feel a thing."

One ridiculous, but unspoken, thought keeps teasing me: How does the poor bugger get on when he wants a piddle? I guess he will just have to ask someone nearby to do the honours for him.

We keep going all day and it is late afternoon when, at last, we reach a spot where the land seems to just fall away beneath our feet. There, far below us, are a couple of small houses. This has to be Sfakia. It seems to be almost a thousand feet below us, almost straight up and down. The only way to get down there is by using a couple of twisting, winding tracks, cut out by goats.

It is a daunting descent but, with the prospect of evacuation as a spur, we are only too happy to make the try. Thank God, we don't have to do it in the dark! Once down there, the land is fairly flat, with only a narrow area between the high ground and the sea's edge. There are plenty of trees for cover, so we shall be well-sheltered from the air. There is already a surprising number of men scattered about.

We look for the missing members of our Unit, to find that a good proportion of them had got off the previous night. Arthur Swain was not one of them. He had become separated from the others in the dark and missed out. I console myself by supposing that that's what may have happened to me, had I heeded his call.

The procedure for evacuation is that we will form up in single file, then march to positions further along the shore to our right. Ships' boats will come in during the night, then ferry us out to Warships waiting offshore. The job has to be completed in time for the Navy to be well clear of the

Island before daylight. A halt will have to be called at a certain time. Those missing out will have to wait for the following night.

We wait expectantly for the night's evacuation to commence. Officers-in-Charge have the men lined up in plenty of time, with minimum of delay, in order for a maximum number to be cleared. There are too many men standing by for all of us to go tonight. So a lot of them do not even bother to get into the lineup. We happen to be some of those who will have to stay behind. Naturally, we are not too happy about it, but I can see the wisdom of not overcrowding the embarkation point.

We sweat it out, just talking, and envying those who have made it into the lineup. We promise ourselves all sorts of good things when we make it through. At least there is still no sign that the Germans have become aware of what is going on.

Next day is clear and fine and, restless and edgy as we might be, we just have to wait for another nightfall. While the overhead cover is marvellously dense, we still feel obliged to keep our movements to a minimum. And while we feel reasonably safe, the problem nobody wants to think about is: How many nights do we have left?

Some disturbing rumours start to circulate that the evacuation procedures are not so hot. There is talk that the Officers-in-Charge have underestimated the numbers that can be moved, and that some ships' boats have been waiting at the water's edge for men who do not show up. Supposedly, they have to leave virtually empty. Obviously, the slickness and efficiency of the Kalamata evacuation is not likely to be matched here.

There is no food of any kind, unless a person has something he has managed to hang onto. For the greater majority of us, it has already been several days without a bite. With empty stomachs gnawing at us and the uncertainty of our position nagging also, it is hard just to sit and wait. I decide to inspect for myself the beach embarkation point. It gives me something to do, and it might give me a pointer as to what position to take in the lineup.

I say nothing to anybody else and just wander off at what seems an opportune moment. The site is several hundred yards from where we are gathered—not too close and not too far away. Several guards are posted to see that nobody crowds the spot. This is mostly unnecessary for everybody realises how vital it is to make it appear unused and deserted.

The approach is parallel to the seashore, with the going underfoot a little rough, but not too bad. There are some medium sized, sea-rounded boulders which we will have to negotiate in the dark. The beach itself is slightly pebbly and not very wide. It looks as though only a couple of ships' boats will be able to beach there at a time. That is a serious fault and will slow down proceedings considerably. Obviously, a good spot in the lineup is imperative.

Having seen all I want to, I manage to casually turn away and head back, just as one of the guards begins to move in my direction. Rejoining the others, I tell them that we just have to be in a good position to join the lineup when it is being formed. During last night's evacuation, in some instances, men had opted to drop out in order to stick with mates. It had all been fairly friendly with no pushing and shoving. Tonight, I feel we will be unable to afford those kind of courtesies.

Just before sunset, there comes the sound of a single approaching aircraft. We can tell it is not a Stuka and we watch curiously to see what it may be. We catch a short glimpse of it through the tree canopy as it levels off to come in and land. It is a Sunderland Flying Boat. I know instantly what is happening. This is a repeat of Kalamata. The Sunderland will be here to evacuate General Freyberg and his senior staff. There is a short delay during which the motors never cease turning, then a sudden accelerated roar as it revs up for take-off. Again we get a short sight of it between the trees, this time heading back towards Egypt. It looks as if we don't have much time left.

Well before dark, there is a lot of casual moving into favourable positions, preparedly to being called to form a line. Nobody wants to be accused of pushing in, while nobody wants to risk being left behind. My mates and I do the best we can, but we still have to settle for places well down the line.

With the general exodus from the other side of the Island, the assemblage here is of all kinds and types of Units. A sizeable group of a particular Unit may have some clout, especially if it has some Officers to put its case. In our case, all our Officers must have made it through on that first night, for there is none to be seen now. We are just groups of individuals hoping for our turn to come.

There is still fighting going on, of course, and those of us here understand and accept that first preference for evacuation has to be for those fighting the rearguard. The decision of how and when to disengage, then make it through to the boats, will be a tricky one. We all sense that there will be a lot of confusion and boats will be leaving without a proper load. We just hope it will be possible to correct this imbalance.

As soon as it is time, the line forms quickly. Then comes the word to move off. Edgy with excitement, we talk softly amongst ourselves, while advancing in the darkness. Bill Collier is in front of me and, as he is six foot two, I have an easy mark to follow.

There are stops and starts all the way, with sometimes small knots of men being led straight past me. They must be some of the rearguard. The night seems to stretch on to eternity. Finally we reach a position where we can actually see the beach. There are two ships' boats side by side and men are quickly climbing in. With the line splitting in two, we move to the right-hand one. It seems to have the most room anyway.

With Bill and I talking about the first things we are going to do when we land, we are as good as on our way. The left-hand boat is just about full when an Officer comes hurrying down. He calls out, "Is there a doctor here?"

A figure stands up in the boat and says, "Yes, I'm a doctor."

I can see and recognise that he is Doctor Gunther, a doctor we regard as our Unit Doctor. The Officer calls back, "We need somebody to stay with the wounded. Will you please come with me?"

Without a word, Doctor Gunther stands up, threads his way through the men in the boat and steps back onto the beach. I am thinking, "You poor bastard! What a hard thing to have to do!"

Without hesitation, Bill steps over the gunwale and into the boat. I cock one leg over the gunwale to follow when the Sailor-in-Charge of the boat drops his arm between the two of us and says, "Sorry, that's all for tonight. But don't worry, we'll be back again tomorrow night."

Bill turns and shakes hands with me. He says, "Don't worry, I'll have one set up for you in the Long Bar," a favoured haunt of ours, and we farewell.

With proceedings over for the night, all we can do is watch the ships' boats disappear into the darkness. All I can think is, "God, they could have made room for one more! And what about Doctor Gunther's seat? They hadn't put another man in when he stepped out." But it is over and we will just have to sweat it out for another day. A very disappointed lot straggle back to spend what is left of the night under the trees.

Dozens of conflicting thoughts go through my mind, making sleep very hard to come by. "Why have they called it off so soon? With much of the night still to follow, it cannot be the time factor. Maybe it is a shortage of ships. Don't tell me they are stupid enough to go to all the trouble and then not have enough ships!"

After the big letdown, I remember the Sailor's promise, "We'll be back tomorrow night." We will just have to believe in that.

With no food and nothing to do but wait, we do not bother to stir from our flop-down spots until quite late in the morning. It is another fine sunny day and about 9.00 am a couple of Officers can be seen approaching. They are still some way off and are saying something to the knots of men as they pass.

The men for their part just stand there, talking seriously together. Obviously, what has been said is pretty important. We wait expectantly to hear what it is and, when they arrive, it is simple and to the point, "Well chaps, we are sorry, but we are now all Prisoners of War." To our howls of disbelief, they reply, "We surrendered two hours ago. All acts of war have now ceased. If there is anything you don't want to fall into the hands of the Germans, get rid of it now. They will be here shortly."

We are stunned. The import of the message is too serious to have been a joke. With the urge to just take off and disappear, we are unsure of what our status might be if we are hunted down. Then, where can we run? Although large, this still is only an Island. Somebody calls out, "Does anybody know the date?"

Somebody else calls back, "The first of June."

"Good God!" I am thinking, "I've got a birthday at the end of the month and I'll be a Prisoner of War."

# Chapter 9

# POW Days – The Greek Experience

It is almost impossible to accept the actuality of being a captured prisoner. As yet no Germans have appeared and, for the moment, it just seems like some fanciful dream. In weighing up the pros and cons of what might happen to us during our service life, we had imagined many things, but never the possibility of being taken prisoner. We are shocked, totally unprepared, and unsure how to proceed.

For the moment, the advice to get rid of anything we don't want the Germans to get their hands on, seems like a sensible move. There is a well nearby, just the ideal place to dump things. Quickly this is pressed into service.

Those Commando boys we had helped to unload, are much disliked by the Germans, because of their clandestine activities and hit and run tactics. Commandos have a standard issue dagger which incorporates a knuckle duster into the handle – a wicked looking thing which they are prepared to use effectively. Daggers and insignia quickly disappear.

As Germany and Italy are allies, it seems prudent to get rid of all things Italian as well. Automatic pistols begin to follow the daggers. I pull out my Beretta from its holster and look at it. It is a beautiful piece of work and I have carried it, strapped to my waist, ever since Tobruk. I just can't bear to chuck it down the well.

I look around for somewhere safe to hide it, and spot a small boulder firmly set in the ground. I prise it out of its setting, dig a hole underneath, just big enough to accommodate the gun and its holster, then carefully place the boulder back into its former position. My bodgy stripes go down the well.

Most of us have not eaten for several days now, and for several months have been getting by the best way can. We are in fact starving and can only hope to get something from the Germans.

There has not been the slightest sign of any local inhabitants since we have been here. But a little donkey tethered under the trees nearby indicates that they cannot be too far away.

In our hungry state that donkey means food. In minutes it is killed and carved up, with only the head and hooves remaining. Fires are lit, with groups here and there, trying to cook their pieces as best they can. In most cases the ravenous men cannot wait. They are just grabbing the meat off their fires and tearing into it, practically raw. Most can only watch as one donkey doesn't go very far.

Somewhere along from us, a plane appears and fires a few shots. A Paratrooper rushes out, holding a German flag in front of himself, warning the plane to ceasefire. It veers away and disappears, leaving us in peace.

Now German troops appear and, herding us together, they set us to climb up that almost perpendicular face with its winding goat tracks. We are to head back from whence we have come. For the moment, there is no heavy-handed stuff from our captors; just enough verbal urging to get us moving in the right direction.

We group together in patches of friends and Units as much as possible. The remnants of my Unit, between thirty and forty men, are assembled together by our Company Sergeant Major. They are of various ranks other than Officers. All our Officers have managed to get away. With the C.S.M. leading and me next in line, we start to tackle the stiff and arduous climb. It is very tough going and, in our weakened state, we are almost exhausted when we reach the top. By now, more German troops have arrived at the edge of the high ground and one of them is standing right where we scramble over the edge. He has three huge packs, obviously very heavy, on the ground beside him. Just as obvious, these packs are destined to be delivered far down below.

As our C.S.M. straightens up, the German grabs him by the arm, points to the packs and down the goat tracks. The C.S.M. with long practiced ease, stands to one side and orders the next two in line to do the job. The next two in line are myself and George Wade. I have no intention of doing that climb again if I can possibly get out of it. So, looking blank, I ignore the C.S.M. and continue on. Taking his cue from me, George does the same. A completely surprised C.S.M. just stares open-mouthed.

The frustrated German now grabs the C.S.M. roughly and indicates that he is to do the job. He grabs another man as a helper and sends them both on their way. The German takes the other pack himself. It is a lousy trick to pull on the C.S.M., but at least it brings home to him that in this Prisoner of War business, rank doesn't mean very much. I do apologise to him later, and he, being the good bloke he really is, just shrugs it off.

In knots and groups we straggle off, back towards Chania. A few Germans are in charge and march along with us. Our abiding problem is food, or the lack of it. We are actually starving. While none is forthcoming at the moment, our captors promise that this will be rectified when we reach where we are going.

Along the way we try getting the grain from heads of barley and wheat growing close to the road. But being half green, we can't separate the kernels from the husks. And we can't chew them as is, for the husks have tiny barbs that cut into our mouths. Without success, we try begging bread from Germans bivouacked by the road.

Here and there, signs of fighting begin to show up, mostly of bodies scattered about as they had fallen. Grimly enough, they all are of our dead. We again come through the olive grove where I had spied the dead man caught upright in the fork of a tree. He is still there, only now he is black and the body has swollen about four times its former size. His uniform seems set to burst under the pressure.

It is a nightmare journey, with most of us plodding mechanically in a daze. The German NCO and his men keep urging and cajoling, doing their best to keep us moving. They claim we are headed for a permanent camp where there will be food.

At long last we are approaching the outskirts of Chania. It is just before nightfall and we begin to pass an area of lush vegetable gardens spread out on both sides of the road. There is about half an acre on each side filled with such things as potatoes, tomatoes, carrots, marrows etc., just about ready for picking. Our column, spread out over a hundred yards, suddenly splits cleanly down the centre, with each side charging straight into the gardens.

Nothing has been said, but it happens so spontaneously that it seems like an expertly planned manoeuvre. The guards react immediately with the NCO firing several shots in the air from his revolver. There is no way that the warning will have the slightest effect on this ravenous tide.

The whole process takes only about two minutes, with the men sweeping off the road, making a quick grab, and sweeping back on again. The difference, however, to the garden is dramatic. Where before there had been beautiful lush green crops, a few moments later all that is to be seen is utter devastation, with not a thing left.

We continue on a short distance and come to our destination. It is Skines, a detention camp set up by our side for captured Italians. They have been turned loose by their allies, the Germans, while we are marched in. The role of the jailer just changes hands. The weather is fine and mild, so we just select a spot and flop, leaving it until the morning to get our bearings. It is here that I get my first food as a POW. Counting carefully back, I realise I have gone seven days without a single bite.

The Italians have worked diligently to make this camp liveable. There are trees within the compound and tents are scattered about to take advantage of the shade. There is a reasonably large assembly area, but for the most part the rest is grassed. They have built an underground latrine, then covered it with branches and topped with soil. The grass has started to grow on top and, although it is open to the elements, the whole aspect is pleasing to the eye. However, a latrine is a latrine, and the smell soon gives it away.

Our digestive systems have taken quite a beating over the last several months and a good latrine system is extremely important to us. I do not know if our people designed the layout or the Italians themselves. But the result to the naked eye is almost of a holiday camp.

We now start to get ourselves organised, mainly on a Unit basis, with our senior NCOs becoming responsible for food distribution. The day's rations are split up according to the Units and their numbers, with the NCOs doling out to each individual. Depending upon what is doled out by the Germans, this system works without a hitch.

The methodical Germans begin to record our statistics. They want our name, rank, Army number, Unit and civilian occupation. We decide to lie about our occupation so that any work we are allotted is somehow tied up with food. We, therefore, mostly declare ourselves as farmers.

As we lineup to give these particulars, I happen to be behind one of our Unit who is big, rough, but normally an easygoing man. When asked for his details, he gives his name, number and then his Unit. "Ah," says the German, while consulting a list by his side, "Your Commanding Officer is Major Torr."

"Yes," says our man in a deep and heartful resentment, "And you wait till I get the bastard."

The German, whose English is very good, is completely nonplussed by this exchange, while our man makes his feelings abundantly clear. The German next asks for an occupation.

"Strapper," says our man.

"What is that?" asks the German.

"Never you mind," says our man, "Strapper it is, and that's what you put," all the time stabbing the air with his forefinger to emphasise the point. The subdued German, just writes it down, passes him on, then turns to me.

Each day, groups of Germans will turn up, seeking volunteers for working parties. Mindful of the service maxim of never volunteer, we begin to be tempted by the promise of extra food. There are bodies to be buried that have been laying out in the hot sun for several days. As it is close to midsummer, the smell is almost unbearable. As a counter, the Germans are giving out strong cigars while engaged on this necessary but unpleasant task. Being a non-smoker, I look for something more agreeable.

I go on a short stacking job as one of about twenty men. The food return is negligible, but on the way back it does offer a chance to escape.

We are traversing an area of thick reedy type grass, along a single file track. The height of this grass is seven to eight feet, well above our heads. It is a twisting track that winds in and out. I am in the centre of the file with a German at the head and another at the tail. We come to a tight bend where, for a moment, I am out of sight to anybody. For a second I am tempted to dive into the dense cover at my side. I reject the idea. It would have meant dodging and hiding and relying on the locals for food.

While I feel sure they will help, I am also sure there is a fair chance of being recaptured. My common sense tells me that if that happens, reprisals will be savage to any helpers. It's the only way an occupation force can keep control. And I would still be stuck on an Island from which the British Navy has been unable to get me free. How else will I be able to get away? All in all, it seems the best idea to return with the others.

Then I meet a young Infantryman who has just returned from a job. He tells me that they want the same lot for the next day, plus a few more. He says these Germans have taken over a warehouse full of Army tinned food and have co-opted a Pommy Army cook to cook for them. The Pom has kept our blokes supplied with food all day. The job is easy, just repainting some old Army trucks. It is painters they need. Straightaway, I become a painter and I am accepted as one of the crew for the next day.

The trucks turn out to be British Army Bedfords, as used in the Western Desert. They have camouflage markings with some details painted on in Arabic as well as English. They have somehow found their way to Crete and are now a little worse for wear. The Germans want the Arabic writing, and some of the other lettering, redone. They want a signwriter, not a painter, and this is a bit beyond me. I have to fill in an entire day as if I know what I am doing. Somehow I am able to do this without using one drop of paint.

The Pommy Cook is magnificent. He plies us with morning tea, lunch, afternoon tea and a little to take back with us. The tea itself is big mugs of strong, sweet, white and hot, Army style tea. There are biscuits and fruit to go with it. Lunch is big helpings of Army canned meat and vegetable stew, (captured from us of course), plus heaps of fresh local vegetables, followed by canned peaches and cream. We feel bitter that the Germans are faring so well on our food, when we have been deprived for so long.

After morning tea I have trouble with lunch. Our hunger is so strong that we cannot knock anything back. We just keep stuffing it down. The compassionate Pommy Cook keeps bringing us bits and pieces all day. Come to think of it, I'm too busy eating to do any painting.

My stomach is feeling overfull by midday and, by mid-afternoon, I know I am in trouble. But I cannot stop eating. The discomfort becomes a feeling of distress by the time we are to return to camp. If there had been no transport, I don't think would have been able to make it.

The young Infantryman, who has told me about the job and the food, is worse than me. It is his second day and, when he gets back, he collapses by the latrine. I manage to make it back to my position, but by eight o'clock I am rolling around in agony. My stomach and intestines feel as though they will burst. Visits to the latrine make no difference to the pain. Somehow, I make it through the night with some easing by daylight. I am completely useless all the next day and not much better for several days after. My poor mate is semiconscious for two days and lay by the latrine for a week, before recovering enough to move back amongst his friends.

The rations distributed by the Germans are mostly bread and some fresh local fruit. It is never ever at so much per man. It is always a bulk issue for the whole camp, to be split up and issued as best as can be arranged. Senior Unit NCOs try to keep a fair distribution system, but with the lopsided numbers per Unit, it is always a difficult job. Always there are disgruntled men, spurred by their great hunger, certain that they are being discriminated against.

There is not much water at the camp so the Germans take us to a nearby beach for a swim, in small parties, during the day. This is truly a welcome break. The Pommy prisoners especially enjoy it. They are greatly taken in by the golden sand and clear water, so unlike their own. They ask us Aussies if we have anything like it back home. When we tell them that we have hundreds of miles as good or better, they just smile in disbelief.

A nearby well helps us to replenish our drinking water. The water level is about fifteen feet below ground level, so we have to lower containers on a string or rope. By now we have all managed to scrounge a container of some sort, be it jam tin or whatever. String is a different matter. Sometimes it has to be bootlaces strung together for the job. I manage to get hold of a galvanised bucket and am able to help some of those without string to get a fill. With these activities and the all-important daily food distribution, our time passes reasonably and pleasantly. Given the warm balmy weather, the tensions, that we have been under for so long, begin to ease. We find that we have great rapport with the Paratroopers to the extent that we can sit down and discuss frankly, various aspects of the fighting.

They claim that they consider it unfair for us to have fired on them while they were in the air and drifting down. They think we should have waited until they were on the ground before opening up. We argue strongly against that idea. We point out they had been delivered right on target, fresh and ready for battle. As defenders, we just had to take whatever advantages we could get. To do otherwise, would have been militarily stupid. They consider our case, gravely and seriously, and without rancour. They refuse, however, to believe that ours are standard and regular troops. They insist that we had to be regiments of specially trained sharpshooters, as the German losses had been so severe.

One of the great propaganda blurbs put out by the Germans is that Max Schmeling, the former World Heavyweight Champion, had joined the Paratroopers. We ask if Max had made the jump with them. Several of them grin and look knowingly at each other as they reply, "No, he was wounded in the foot on another jump." We gain the impression that Max's wound may have been self-inflicted. We know that the Troopers had the habit of spraying the ground with their Tommy Guns as they drifted down. Maybe that's how it happened.

They claim that they cannot understand us Australians. We live so far away on the other side of the world, where the issues are of no consequence to us. "Why do you fight for the British?"

We just reply simply, "We are British. England is our Mother Country, so we fight."

We cannot see the Germans keeping us indefinitely on Crete. Any movement will have to be back to Greece, and onward from there to wherever it is decided to send us. This will require shipping, but may take some time, as we know that most of it has been destroyed. We are fiercely hopeful our Navy will intercept us and we will again be free.

From the moment of our capture, every one of us has an overwhelming feeling that an immediate bid will be made to free us. We only speculate how it may happen. We only hope there will not be too much gunfire, as we do not wish to be killed in this way.

Small groups begin moving out from time to time, and news filters back that some shipping has been found. We know that this can only be minimal, because of the size of the parties and the time lapse between departures. This worries us, for we realise that small boats will be hard for our Navy to find and, therefore, they will have a good chance of slipping through.

When it becomes our turn, a group of us are told to grab our belongings and move to the Souda Bay area. We arrive there to find the harbour not much different to when we last saw it. There are a couple of German Motor Torpedo boats and a couple of Greek Caiques moored at the wharf. The Caiques now fly a German flag at the stern and they have a quick-firing gun mounted as protection. We are to sail in one of these.

A Caique is a broad beamy vessel of about fifty tons. It has a fairly powerful diesel motor located near the stern. A small boxlike wheelhouse is mounted there too. Most of the ship consists of a very large hold capable of carrying a fair amount of cargo. With a stout deck running the full length, they are a solid no-frills workhorse.

Between three and four hundred of us crowd aboard, with us POWs down the hold and our Escorts occupying the deck area. To use the latrine, we have to ask permission, climb out of the hold and hang over the rail. As almost all of us have bowel problems, there is a constant stream coming and going for the whole trip.

We get underway during the late afternoon of a fine sunny day. There is no attempt at evasive tactics, just a confident straight voyage through. We are bitterly disappointed at the non-appearance of our Navy. We cannot believe that they have more important business to attend to than our rescue.

The sea is calm and peaceful. As evening approaches, our Escorts try to badger and cajole us into singing. There is no way we will be in that, considering the plight we are in. So they start to sing some of their marching songs. This gets our backs up and, here and there, some of our fellows start to sing some of our popular songs. Gradually a few more join in until finally, all of us are singing.

As everybody joins in, the Escorts crowd round the hold, sitting on vantage points and listening. Finally, we have exhausted our repertoire. Somebody says, "They want us to sing. Let's give these bastards something. Let's sing the National Anthem." We stand to attention and defiantly bellow it out at the top of our lungs. As the first notes ring out, every German aboard springs to attention, salutes, and remains so until the last notes die away. They then bade us a goodnight and we all settle down. The rest of the trip is uneventful.

We arrive at Piraeus to find the harbour in shambles, completely crammed with sunken ships. With its funnels still showing above the water, there is the unmistakeable Red Cross markings of a hospital ship on one of them. I immediately wonder, with some foreboding, whether my two wounded mates had been aboard when it sunk. There is no evidence of any attempt to clear up the mess. Our boat weaves through to a tiny space dockside, where we are able to disembark. We are marched off through the town, with no idea where to.

As we march along, the local Greeks crowd the footpaths lining our route. When we first arrived in Greece, we were fairly spic and span and a well presented Army, and we were greeted by cheers of welcome. Now, we are a dishevelled unkempt lot, clad in bits and pieces of clothing, some even without footwear. This is the type of effect the German propaganda machine does its best to highlight. The unspoken message is: See, this is what happens to those who oppose the might of the German Army. We don't like being used like this, but there is nothing we can do about it.

The Greeks, for their part ignore the propaganda message and indicate they are stoutly behind us. They are calling out a message to us and, because of our limited knowledge of their language, it takes us a little time to make sense of. Phonetically, it sounds like, "Den peirazei George, deka or dekapente imera." Deciphered it means, "Never mind George, in ten or fifteen days."

According to their scriptures, this war and its ending has been predicted in the Bible. According to that timetable, we only have ten to fifteen days to wait before it will be finished, and we will be free again.

As we march along, we certainly look a sorry lot. We have few possessions, are unshaven, unwashed and, in some cases, shirts are rotting off our backs. Most have no hats as, at the time of capture, the standard headgear had been tin hats. These have had to be dumped in a pile. One man has somehow managed to scrounge some headgear that causes some laughter among the Greeks. It is a tall, round, black, brimless hat, as worn by Greek Priests. It is the oddest sight of many oddities.

Another man, limping along, is carrying a small dog. He must have suddenly decided that there is no future for it, so he suddenly turns and thrusts it into the arms of a startled Greek, then marches on as before.

The dog has been one of many kept by the Italians as pets in Tobruk. Shell-shocked and aimless, they had been left to defend for themselves. The man had taken pity on this one, cared for it, nursed it back to health, and taken it with him wherever he went. He must have been deeply attached to it for, after what we have been through, it is amazing it has lasted this long. There are many among us who quite gladly would have killed and eaten it long before.

When we finally reach our destination, we find it to be a former Greek Army Barracks, somewhere on the outskirts of Athens. They are located in a fairly spacious area and appear to be a holding point before our moving on further. They are relatively undamaged, but without much in the way of facilities. The scattered buildings are completely bare and empty. There are a few taps with running water, but nothing in the way of bathing facilities, other than a couple of horse troughs in the open. As this is Athens, there is a sewerage system. The trouble is that the toilet is a bare patch of concrete with a hole about six inches in diameter in the centre. To use it, one has to squat on his haunches. In our weakened state, it is impossible to do this without toppling over, usually into one's own excreta. The psychological hurt to our pride is very deep.

There are a fair few men already in the camp when we arrive and, as we wander about getting our bearings, we come upon a confrontation between a Prisoner and some German NCO Guards. The Prisoner is browbeating the Germans very effectively, so we gather round to see what all the fuss is about. He is a New Zealand Doctor and is surrounded by panniers marked with a Red Cross to indicate medical supplies.

He very soundly berates them, quoting the Geneva Convention to emphasise his demands. He insists they are forced by it to set him up in proper quarters, care for and maintain his instruments contained in the panniers, provide him with transport to go anywhere he needs to do his job, and that the Germans themselves have to provide the means and the labour to do this.

The Germans are completely nonplussed and baffled as to how to handle the situation. With us enjoying their discomfiture, the Doctor becomes ever more vocal. They offer to move him to another camp for Officers, saying that this one is for other ranks. He flatly refuses saying that, as a Medical man, he should be free to come and go anywhere among the Prisoners to attend to their needs. Finally, they give up and walk away.

The next day our Doctor friend circulates round, inviting Prisoner NCOs to a meeting. We assemble round him in the open, with him standing on a high point. A couple of Germans hover in the background, keeping an eye on things.

He begins by indicating at those Germans and saying, "Don't think these bastards don't know what we're saying. Almost certainly, they all speak English and will report back what goes on here. Never say anything within earshot that you don't want them to know about." He goes on to say we have all sorts of rights and privileges under the Geneva Convention and should insist vigorously that the Germans stick to them. "Wherever they fail, we should carefully take note, and insist on our right to contact the authorities of the Swiss Red Cross." He urges us to watch out for our men, and see that they are treated decently also.

His uncompromising insistence on what are our rights gives us all a lift. Throughout the short time we know him, he seems to be always arguing some point or other with the Germans. The Geneva Convention is a vague, largely unknown document to most of us. We know it dictates the rules of conduct between Prisoners and their Captors. But we do not know what these rules are. Anyway, it will depend on the goodwill of the Captors. What we do know is that it will be very hard to match the resolute courage of the Doctor.

After only a few days, we are notified to prepare to move on further north. As we assemble, our Doctor, surrounded by his gear, refuses to budge. He demands that the Germans be responsible for transporting his precious panniers. He wants cast-iron guarantees that not one item will be lost or destroyed in transit. How the Germans accomplish this I do not know, for he refuses to allow any Prisoner to be used as a carrier. As we move out, the Doctor marches with us, leaving his panniers stacked together, and still threatening the Germans.

This movement is totally different to anything we have experienced up to now. This is a movement of Prisoners by their Captors, and they mean business. Armed German soldiers, about four paces apart, march on either side of the column. The streets we traverse are packed on both sides by Athenians. This time there are no cries of, "Don't worry George." They are completely silent.

Still, their hostility to the Germans and their sympathy towards us is patently obvious. Here and there, somebody will risk a show of support by holding up two fingers in a "V" for Victory sign, used by Churchill. A Guard will then charge into the crowd, clubbing the offender with his rifle butt. Any crowding on the roadway meets with the same treatment.

One very pregnant woman, obviously very close to giving birth, is a little slow to move back. As the Guard passes, without unslinging his rifle, he drives the butt into the pit of her stomach. The woman instantly collapses while the surrounding people rush to her aid. Those of us, who see this incident, are seething at the senseless brutality.

The "V" signs are still appearing, but people are trying to show us without being caught by the Guards. The Guards are still catching some and they now change their tactics. After catching the offender, he will be then forced into the column of marching Prisoners.

Finally, we arrive at our destination. It is a railway siding where covered wagons, similar to cattle trucks, are ready waiting for us. While we are moving to board the wagons, the Athenians, who were forced into the column, are lined up in front of the Officer in Charge. He has his men force them to make a "V " sign at full arm's-length above their heads. As their arms begin to sag, a rifle butt forces them to fully extend it again. This continues the whole time we are loading. What happens to them after we leave, I do not know. Hopefully, this may have been considered punishment enough, and then they are let off.

With the trucks loaded, we finally get underway. We are surprised to be going by rail as we know that we have blown the vital bridges in Central Greece. We speculate as to whether we had botched the job or whether the Germans are so good that they have repaired them already.

A couple of hours later, the train pulls to a halt and we are all ordered out. We are to remain there for the night. At daylight, the next morning, we start marching over Bralos Pass to the rail siding on the other side. We have one day to complete the trip. Obviously, the bridges are still down and we had made a good job of it.

As we move off to march, our Doctor friend refuses to move. His panniers are unsighted and he refuses to believe German promises that they are being taken care of. Finally, he moves off too, still threatening.

We have to travel cross-country to the foot of the Pass, traverse the Pass, then cross-country again to the rail junction on the other side. It is a march of close to fifteen miles. In our weakened state, it will be a formidable journey and tax us to the limit. We wonder what will happen to those unfortunates who can go no further and fall out. One consolation is that our Guards will have to march every inch of the way.

There is some semblance of order at the start, but before long the column begins to stretch out. By the time we reach the bottom of the Pass, we have already had a couple of rest stops. Each time, we find it difficult to get moving again. The Guards seem to fit into our pattern of movement, and our fears of the fate awaiting stragglers dies away.

Before our capture, we had travelled over the Pass several times. Indeed, this is the Pass that my driver, Lord Dalley, had elected to coast down the other side in neutral. Some Infantrymen had done it on foot, but that was when they were reasonably fit.

About halfway up there had been a modern strong, steel trestle bridge, spanning a very deep impassable chasm. We had blown this in our retreat. I am professionally interested as to how the Germans have overcome this barrier. But for the moment, all I can do is concentrate on keeping going.

As we begin to climb, our pace drops to a plod. Our mates around us quietly urge us on when we begin to struggle. Each man now can only concentrate on putting one foot in front of the other. Finally, we come to the bridge site. It is still down, a beautiful clean job. However, there is a small goat track, which circles past the head of the ravine and cuts into the cliff face. This had been so precarious that we had not even considered it as an alternative. But the Germans had gone to work with picks and shovels, and have managed to make it barely useable for a truck by slowly inching forward around the bad spot.

Our already low spirits fall a little further, when we see this. We can now only concentrate on getting to the top, and look forward to the downhill trek on the other side. We are grateful for any rest stops, but the effort to get going again after dropping out of our plodding rhythm is almost too much for many. This prompts some to elect to keep going, while some, who stop, just cannot get their legs going again. They are left behind to catch up later, with even the Guards ignoring them.

A long time later, I catch up with a man who had been left. He tells me how the column had just moved, leaving him completely alone. Hours later, just on dusk, some Greek shepherds, returning home with their flocks, find him. They half-carry and half-drag him back to their house. The woman of the house whips him up a hot stew made from a tin of our Army M&V—meat and vegetable ration. She had quite a stack of food stowed away, rescued from one of our abandoned food dumps, left behind in our retreat.

When he becomes mobile again, they fit him out with old civilian clothes and a homespun peasant shoulder bag, and send him out each day with a flock of sheep and goats. For months he would leave each morning with some bread and boiled eggs in his bag. With a long wooden staff he would follow his flock, returning each night to a hot meal and a secure bed. Sometime later he becomes bored and decides to move on. He ends up in a town, is rounded up, and becomes a POW again.

Plodding on, we make it to the top and down the other side. The cross-country trek to the railhead is a nightmare. The last five miles of our journey is done in a daze. It is almost dusk when we reach the siding. My mate and I stand under the loco watering point, dousing ourselves in the cold water. After recovering a little, we collapse by the track, not stirring until the last of the stragglers arrive and we are ordered to board the train. Most of us have very little recollection of the trip to Salonika. We are a pretty subdued lot by the time we disembark and march into Salonika No. 1.

Each holding camp for prisoners is a former Greek Army barracks. All are fairly dilapidated with some worse than others. None have bathing facilities other than a few horse troughs out in the open. Toilets are a hole-in-concrete slab-types. All buildings are completely bare, with concrete floors. You just grab a body space and call it your own. Food is a bread ration with very little else. Complaints about food or conditions always bring the same response. This is only temporary. Things will be much better when you get to where you are going.

There are two prison camps in Salonika and we name them No. 1 and No. 2. In No. 1, where we are now, we just crowd in together. There are several different nationalities, with a fair-sized representation from India. We focus on learning the ropes as much as possible from those who have arrived before us. They tell us to keep away from the barbed wire fence as a man has been shot there.

The barbed wire fence consists of two panels about ten feet high and about ten feet apart. The space between is piled in chest-high, coiled loose wire. Inside the compound, about six feet from the fence is strung a single strand of wire about a foot above the ground. This strand is known as a tripwire, with everybody being warned not to step over it, or they will be shot.

It seems that one man had washed his shirt. He sought to hang it on the fence to dry. A guard was standing watching and the man held it out in front of him, seeking permission to hang it there. Receiving no reaction, the man took it as an agreement and stepped over the tripwire. The Guard raised his rifle and shot him. He fell against the wire fence and hung there on the barbs. His body was left hanging there for several days as a warning to others.

One day, I observe one or two Indians with their heads down searching across a small stony area within the camp. From time to time, they pick up a stone, examine it, sometimes discard it and search for another, but always walk off with a stone. I suddenly realise that these men are probably from the Indian Frontier and use a smooth stone to wipe their backsides. For us, paper is an almost impossible thing to procure, and it adds to our woes.

In our weakened state, we form the habit of going from one place to another, then sitting down, preferably with a wall to lean one's back against. It is customary to spend most of the day like this soaking up the sun. One midmorning a group of about six or eight of us are relaxing like this, adjacent to the toilet. We are spread around in a semicircle, sitting on the ground with legs spread and leaning against a convenient wall.

We are yarning together, fairly quietly, but making practically no movement. As there are no doors, we can see directly into the toilet. From the hole in the centre, a small head appears and looks around. Boldly, a large rat scampers out and does a small reconnoitre. He is quickly followed, one after the other, by about ten of them who run off in different directions investigating. They keep close to the sewer hole, and fascinated, we watch to see what they are up to.

Then one more appears out of the hole. While the others are ugly enough, this one is downright repulsive. He has lost most of his hide off one side and part of the head, and the area has regrown some skin or scar tissue. No hair grows on this area. It attempts to follow the others, but has a lopsided gait and cannot run straight.

Watching, we feel our skin crawl at this hideous sight. The whole pack are scouting round, when there comes the sound of footsteps and a bloke comes round the corner into sight. There is instant reaction and they all make for the sewer hole. The ugly deformed one cannot make it and searches desperately for a hiding place. Suddenly, it finds one and bolts up the pants leg of one of the fellows sitting in our semicircle..

While we have been talking, this fellow has raised one leg slightly, bending at the knee. Because of his skinny state, the hanging pants leg looks like a large drainpipe. The rat claws its way up to the knee and firmly clings there. The frantic man jumps to his feet, dancing and stomping, trying to dislodge the thing.

It takes some seconds before the thing disappears down the sewer hole. The exhausted fellow collapses into his former sitting position badly shaken. The thought of having to squat over that hole is almost more than we can take.

We remain at Salonika No. 1 for only a short time before being moved to Salonika No. 2. Salonika No. 1 seems to be the Prisoner Administration Centre, with everybody passing through here. Salonika No. 2 is a holding camp from which groups are transported on to Germany. Movement from No. 2 is dictated by the availability of transport.

We find that Salonika No. 2, if anything, is more dilapidated than any barracks we have encountered, so far. There are several large bare buildings of more than one storey. We just move in wherever we can, again laying claim to a body space.

In getting this far, necessity has forced us into certain patterns. Trying to stick together as a Unit is too unwieldy. The universal pattern is to form partnerships of twos and threes. Occasionally, it may go to as many as five, and there is the odd person, here and there, who elects to go it alone.

Having a partner and mate seems to lighten the burden. There isn't a lot to share, apart from fears and bad experiences, but at least we can look out for each other and, if the worst happens, then somebody would be able to pass it on.

I have formed a partnership with George Wade. George is a Sapper from my Unit and we know each other well. We have similar likes and dislikes, and we decide to stick together if we can. Although I am Acting Corporal, the difference in rank doesn't mean much.

There are no Officers in this camp. Indeed, apart from our New Zealand Doctor friend, we haven't seen one Officer since our capture, As for the Doctor, we lost sight of him round about the Bralos Pass area. For all we know, he could still be there, surrounded by his panniers.

Again we take stock of our new camp. It covers a fairly large area, completely bare of vegetation. The grounds are slightly eroded in some sections and surrounded by the standard barbed wire enclosure. There are Guard towers about fifteen feet high, set at regular intervals.

Apart from the Barracks buildings, there is a medium sized building at the lower end of the compound, just beyond the parade ground. This is the cookhouse. Rations are distributed from there and, the fact of its existence, gives us hope that we might get a meal from there.

These Barracks have been served by horse drawn transport, and a large cluster of stable buildings are located at the rear. The German Occupation Forces are also mostly using horse drawn transport and are using these stables for their horses. Access to the stables is by a road through the centre of the camp.

Amenities are as bad as ever. There are no showers, just a few taps and a couple of horse troughs in the open. The few toilets are the hole-in-the-concrete type, no doubt with their colony of rats as well.

The only formal requirements by the Germans are for two check parades per day, one in the morning and one in the afternoon. Everybody has to attend these. Other than that, the main event is the distribution of rations.

Our state of health is now very poor due to the prolonged shortage of food. Complaints to the Germans bring the response that they are having trouble getting supplies through due to Partisan activity along the supply routes. While we are happy that the Germans are having problems with the Partisans, it doesn't help our situation. We just have to try to do something about it.

Some trading, of treasured personal possessions for bread, begins to take place with individual Germans. Most favoured trade items are gold rings and wrist watches. Almost in all cases those sorts of things are treasured gifts from loved ones at home, presented as a going away present on our departure overseas. I have a pocket watch on a chain, given to me by my Mum and Dad, and a gold signet ring from my girlfriend.

I can no longer wear the ring as my fingers have shrunk so much that it just falls off my hand. I carry it, tied in a knot, on my watch chain. I decide that I will try to trade my ring. While trading seems to be fairly widespread, it is supposed to be clandestine. The first problem is to make contact with a possible trader. This is partly solved when the Germans call for volunteer work parties to help in the stables. George and I both decide to join one of these parties. We figure this will give us a double chance to make contact.

We have no idea what work is required, but suppose it will be cleaning out the stables. We both manage to get chosen by claiming to be farmers used to working with horses. Because of our health, we plan to go out only long enough to make our trade, then beg off sick.

Some of the fellows from our Unit get word that we propose to go out on the stables' working party, and a group approach me to do a trade on their behalf. They have a gold ring and will be willing to settle for a loaf of bread. This enables us to change our plan. We decide to aim for two loaves, but be prepared to settle for no less than a loaf and a half. Any extra would be for our commission and I will keep my ring for later.

When we arrive on the job, we are assigned to our various tasks. As this is an ongoing thing, we are expected to report for the same job each day. This is good, as it brings us into contact with the same Germans, making our trading deals easier.

My job is blacksmith's helper, while George is doing some cleaning. Most of the others are sitting down cleaning harnesses. I am required to hold up a horse's hoof for shoeing while the Smith does the job. I have seen a horse shod before and know the procedure. But in our country the Smith holds the hoof over his knee himself. Now I am required to do it for him.

The horses here are huge beautiful animals, said to have been confiscated from farms in France and Belgium. While I have seen many large draught horses at home, these are larger again. Their legs and hooves are massive, and I doubt my ability to pick up and hold one long enough for the Smith to do his job. Still I am here and I have to give it a go.

With the first horse already tethered alongside the forge, I walk up and place my hand on its shoulder in the approved fashion, letting it know that I am there. Then I run my hand down its leg to the fetlock and take a good grasp of the hair. Tugging gently until it takes its weight off that leg and lets me raise it, I move my leg into position underneath. With the horse being familiar with the procedure, it has been relatively easy. As long as I can maintain my balance while the Smith works, we will be alright.

However, once, I just happen to get the horse off-balance in an uncomfortable stand. It objects by working its leg backward and forward with some vigour. With me hanging on, this results in me being thrown around like a rag doll. From now on, I let it adopt its own stand. By and large, I manage to cope.

Removal of the old shoe, cleaning the hoof, and fitting of a new shoe, allows some pauses between. During these pauses, friends of the Smithy will stop and have a yarn with him. I take advantage of these stoppages also.

Between shoeing horses, while the Smith takes a break, there are some handouts. Sometimes a cigarette or a piece of bread, occasionally a drink of coffee. There are Germans willing to trade, too. The German we do our business with is a Private and seems a genuine straight forward fellow. I show him the ring and he promises to do his best. He doubts his ability to make it two loaves, but will get back to us the next day.

Following a working pause, we have a yarn with a group cleaning harnesses nearby. There are about ten in this group, all from a West Australian Unit and there is one fellow amongst them, whom I am certain, I know. But I cannot see how this is possible, as I have not had any contact with West Australians outside the Army. So, I am certain it has been in a civilian capacity.

He recognises me as well, but is equally nonplussed as I am. We begin to crosscheck with names, home towns etc., and it all becomes clear. His name is Noel Lumby, and had lived just a couple of miles from where I did back home. Without actually knowing each other, we had passed each other often. He had gone to West Australia looking for work. War broke out and he joined up there. His group are a very cohesive and supportive group, and it is great to be around them.

We return to camp after work, and I report on progress with the ring owner. I show him that I still have it in my possession. While it is necessary for me to have the ring to do business, it is also a very great act of trust for the owner to leave it with me.

At work next day, our German says that as the bread has to come out of his ration and what he can scrounge from his mates, he will only be able to make it a loaf and a half. While making expressions of unhappiness at such a "poor" deal, privately, it doesn't sound too bad. It means a loaf, (what he wants), for the ring owner, and half a loaf for George and me. The German will bring what he can tomorrow and the rest the following day, as that is ration day.

Satisfied with progress, the day passes, much the same as the one before, and I take some time out to chinwag a bit with Noel and his mates.

The following day the German turns up with three chunks of bread, a little more than half a loaf, saying this is the first payment. He will receive two loaves tomorrow, which is his ration, and one of these will be the final payment.

He then argues that, as he has been fair to us and made a down payment, we should let him have the ring, as proof that we are not going to cheat HIM. I tell him that I am reluctant to do this as the ring does not belong to me, and how am I to know that HE will not cheat ME. He calls one of his mates over and, with the mate confirming it, he promises to come good the next day. Otherwise the deal is off.

This puts me in a dilemma. I am very reluctant to hand back the bread. I have told the owner of the ring that the deal is set. I cannot give him the down payment, as it is less than his agreed selling price. If the owner catches me coming home tomorrow with a full loaf after giving him the down payment, then he will know that I have negotiated a better deal than he has been aware of. As it is his ring, he might demand the full payment, and George and I will get nothing for our trouble.

I just cannot give the bread back, so, grudgingly, I hand over his ring. I make the second German swear to keep faith, threatening that if not, then, I will report it.

That night George and I eat the down payment. It is to be our commission anyhow, and we keep our fingers crossed for tomorrow. Of course, the ring owner only knows that he is to get a loaf of bread the next day.

As soon as we arrive at work, I look for our man but cannot see him. This does not mean a lot, as he is mostly based in another area and passes through, from time to time, on his duties. As the day wears on and there is still no sign, I begin to have misgivings.

George's job gives him more freedom of movement than mine, so he circulates round trying to catch sight of our man, or his guarantor mate. But with no luck, at the end of the day, we have to return to camp, still without seeing them. I have to tell the ring owner, no luck today, but everything is set for tomorrow.

Next day, two very anxious men make a very determined effort to locate either of the two German traders. Finally, we find a man we have sometimes seen our trader with. Asking where our man is, we are told he had gone back home to Germany the previous day, on leave. After leave, he will not be coming back. He will be posted to another area.

That night, I have to tell the ring owner that I have been tricked. There is no ring and no bread. He curses me soundly as a stupid bloody fool, and I can only agree with him. As we have already eaten the down payment, I have nothing to offer in recompense.

I am half-tempted to give him my ring in exchange. But his ring, although gold, was not as good a quality as mine. That is why the owner was prepared to accept only one loaf for the deal. Some innate cunning, forces me to ride out the storm and save my ring for another, perhaps more valuable, trade. After this disastrous episode, we beg off sick and do not return to the work party.

We have formed a talking friendship with a chap who stands out as a little different to most of the others. He is a quiet, serious, country style man, in his thirties. He has managed to hang on to most of his kit, other than weapons. In the tough marches, while most of the others throw away anything they consider surplus, he has doggedly persisted in keeping his. He has become a familiar sight, plodding on with a full pack. While we consider this a bit silly, we all admire him for his persistence. He is on his own and has not formed any partnership.

We have a favoured spot where we meet each day, just to talk. Being too weak to walk much, we just sit in the sun with our backs against a wall and legs sprawled out. He eventually confides to us that he intends to trade his wrist watch. It is a good watch and we agree that he should be able to get two loaves of bread. Two loaves is the ultimate in trading. We warn him to be careful of cheating and tell him of our experience.

A day or two later when we are flopped in our usual positions, he tells us that he has managed to make his trade, and shows us his newly acquired bread. He heeded our warning and made sure the bread was here before he handed over his watch. The bread the Germans use is a different type to what we are issued with. Where ours is round like a cow pat, theirs is like Vienna loaves we are used to back home, in size as well as shape. For his watch, our friend has scored two of these.

We congratulate him on his success and ask him how he intends to eat it. He says he will eat one loaf tonight after lights out, and put the other in his kit to supplement his daily ration. We say good luck to him. He does not offer any and we do not expect any. It is taken for granted that any gains from the trading of personal possessions, belongs to that person only.

Next day we head to our usual spot, wondering how he has fared with his wonderful feast. He is not there and, after a reasonable time, he still doesn't show up. As he is bunked down in a different building to us, we begin to ask others, if they know where he is. Finally, we get the story. He had eaten his loaf, lapsed into a coma, and died.

This tragedy upsets us deeply, and our already low spirits sink a little lower. By this time, men are beginning to die each day. The cemetery is just across the road from the camp, and the daily quota will be buried in the late afternoon in time with the afternoon check count. A German Guard of Honour will fire a volley over their graves. With morbid curiosity, we will count the number of volleys to estimate the number of deaths. Towards the end of my stay in Salonika No. 2, it varies between three and five per day.

Our poor diet keeps us in a prolonged state of very poor health. Our cookhouse and staff seldom have anything much to cook, and their duties are mainly distributing our daily ration. On one occasion they come up with broad bean soup. This consists of broad beans boiled in a large boiler of water. It is vegetable water really. It has a bit of colour in it, and some people even get a few of the beans. But the crop has been destroyed by beetles and inside each bean seed are four or five tiny black beetles.

On another occasion, a thin soup has some tiny bits of meat in it. Speculating as to how this can be, a rumour quickly spreads saying that one of the horses has died. The preparation and cooking of this meal is kept very quiet and low key. After the stripping of the meat, the bones are placed in the fires and partly burned before dumping. They are raked from the fires, loaded into a wheelbarrow and trundled across the lower end of the parade ground to be dumped by one of the cooks. In this seldom frequented area of the camp, a couple of our blokes see this strange sight. They stare in disbelief and start to walk towards the man and his barrow to take a closer look. Their interest spurs others who do the same. Realising that this is indeed something to do with food, the walk becomes a trot, then a run and finally a stampede. The cook and barrow are knocked over by the hungry mob, and the whole lot disappears in seconds.

Once, we are given a small helping of cheese that, obviously, has been in a fire. What has been rescued is squashed and melted into charred foil paper, and is difficult to prise free. We presume that Partisans must have intercepted a supply train.

A couple of times, instead of bread, we are issued with a type of biscuit. It is similar in appearance to our Sao biscuit, but rock hard. It is about five inches square by about one inch thick. You cannot break it or bite it. You just have to keep gnawing at it or soak it in water. We much prefer the bread.

The bread loaves, shaped like cow pats, are about ten inches in diameter. They are issued out at one loaf per so many men. We try to keep the same group together each day, but this is difficult as the number of sharers sometimes varies. On occasions it is seven, sometimes eight and sometimes nine.

This cutting into shares provokes many bitter arguments. Different schemes are devised to try to keep it as fair as possible. We began by using playing cards, with a different card on each wedge; then we tried a distribution of similar cards to each man. You take the wedge indicated by the card you draw. Some objected as they still seem to always end up with the smallest piece.

In cutting, the cutter, while trying to be fair, naturally ends up with some crumbs. Naturally, he scoops them up and eats them. It is decided to do the cutting on a different person's handkerchief each day. The crumbs will belong to the handkerchief owner.

Finally, pieces of three-ply are found and laboriously cut into circles with a nail through the centre, as a pin, and the appropriate number of slots radiating from it. A reasonably accurate cut can be made.

We are physically too weak to stand for long, and this begins to show in the daily check parades. We assemble in military formation, according to our barracks. A Sergeant will be in front in charge of each formation. The Germans require him to call us to attention for the check count, then stand us at ease, but remain standing until the check count is finished. The time lapse between the start and the finish is just too much for some, and more and more begin passing out and crashing to the ground.

It is a curious phenomenon. Firstly, you begin to rock back and forth, gently and almost imperceptibly. Gradually, momentum will increase, until suddenly you will pitch full length to the ground, completely blacked out, sometimes forward and sometimes backward. You always hit hard. You cannot save yourself.

We all try to keep an eye on the man next to us, and ease him down if he shows the symptoms. It can take up to a quarter of an hour to come out of an attack. Anything, from ten to twenty, will pass out on each parade. With two parades a day, the risk of serious injury finally prompts the Germans to agree to us standing only for the count. All other times we can sit.

Most of us are bomb-happy and react violently, diving for cover, at any strange noise. This enables three Germans to engage in, what is to them, a very enjoyable pastime.

These three have the job of carting fodder for the stables, with a flattop truck. They will drive up to the Camp's main entrance where the guard will open the gate for them to proceed through to the stables. After being let through, they will cut motor power, creep up behind some unsuspecting prisoners and suddenly blow the horn. The startled victims will scamper in panic, trying to find cover. Often their weakened legs will collapse beneath them and they will fall down and try to crawl. The three Germans will almost fall out of their cab, laughing. We hate them for it.

We are very pleased when, one day, a German Officer catches them at it. He is a Major in his mid-thirties to early forties. He has been inspecting something in the camp and is walking through when he comes upon them in the midst of their cruel game. He orders the truck to stop and all three to get out and stand to attention. He then publicly berates them in a manner that has them trembling and silent. We, delighted Prisoners, gather round, enjoying their discomfiture. They never try it again.

In the centre of a large open area between the barracks buildings, a square steel plate is set flush with the ground. Investigation shows that it leads into the underground sewer system. It probably is intended as an inspection point, but appears seldom, if ever, used. There has to be an outlet and, therefore, an escape route.

A game of two-up is quickly organised around a blanket that covers the steel plate. With a milling crowd around the blanket, the roving internal German Guard can only see that some strange gambling game is going on. When the Guards continue on their patrol, a corner of the blanket and the steel plate is raised, while a couple of men are sent down to investigate.

It is found that the outlet is well outside the camp, about a quarter of a mile away. It is fairly close to some housing and, when the men emerge, they are spotted by some middle-aged Greek women who quickly grabs them and leads them away. We can plainly see this in the distance.

All the remainder of the afternoon, small knots of men will drop out of sight at the opportune moment. A fair few have gone by nightfall.

At the next morning's check parade, the count discrepancy shows up. The Germans are unable to reconcile their figures. They are worried, but do not know what is happening.

All next day the two-up game and the exodus continues. By now more Greek women have assembled at the outlet, waving their arms towards the camp, beckoning and urging us to hurry. It is obvious that it will only be a matter of time before the Germans twig as to what is going on.

With a sense of urgency creeping in, it is decided to give it a try at night time. This is very dangerous for nobody is allowed outside any building on pain of being shot. As the plate is well out in the open, there is no cover to get to it. Those fellows are on their own and most of us just lay awake, dreading to hear the rattle of gunfire. About midnight comes a flurry of shots, shouts in German and the sound of running feet. We just have to wait until daylight to find out what has happened.

A Guard has seen some movement near the hole. This results in the shooting, but, luckily, nobody is hit. However, a man is caught inside the opening and forced to continue through to show where the exit is. It is daylight by the time they are finished, and the man is hauled off for questioning.

We wonder who it is and dread what might happen to him. As it turns out, it is Bryce Johnson. He and I had worked together mapping the water pipe line in the new camp our Unit set up outside Alexandria in Egypt. Good old Bryce, he is one of the least aggressive men that you can possibly meet. He is more the quiet, studious, academic type. Things have to be bad for a person such as he to take such a drastic risk.

When questioned, he comes up with the only answer he can think of. "It's our duty to escape." The Germans accept this as a proper soldierly response, and return him to the Camp.

After the escape route has been discovered, there seems to be no fuss about the missing men. We aren't sure whether the count discrepancy is just passed on to each succeeding Guard Commander and, thereby, keeping it quiet. But Camp procedures just carry on as before. It is almost as if it hasn't happened.

We settle back into a daily routine of preoccupation with our own problems. George and I try to make it a daily habit of climbing into the horse trough for a bath. The trough is about thirty feet long. We will pick a spot, drop our clothes to the ground, climb in and scrub ourselves with our handkerchiefs. It is about the best we can do with no soap. Most of us are now plagued with dysentery and, an attempt to bathe, makes you feel a little bit cleaner.

The Germans have installed a long boxlike toilet of nine or ten holes. It is much preferred to the hole-in-floor Greek type, for here you can sit down. It is completely in the open and unsheltered in any way and, with the onset of bowel problems, is heavily patronised.

It becomes the habit of spending most of your day lined up in the queue in front of one of the holes. Each queue may contain thirty to forty men, and it will begin forming early in the day and not cut out until dark. The man seated, at any particular time, will be urged to hurry up by those at the head of his particular queue, as the almost uncontrollable urge grips them. The seated man will remain on his seat for as long as he can, before relinquishing it. When he arises, almost always, he goes onto the end of the queue again, in the hope that he makes it to the seat by the time that the next attack hits him.

At night time, in the barracks laying prone, there is some degree of control over the urge. But one man had to go, and was shot. He lay moaning most of the night, with nobody daring to go to his assistance. He had been taken away when we go out in the morning. As he is from one of the other barracks, we never know if he has survived or not.

In our barracks, we are packed in, shoulder to shoulder, with all floor space covered, when sleeping. It is impossible to move without disturbing your neighbour. Yet, in these cramped conditions, an incredible act of thieving takes place.

A man, positioned halfway along a wall has traded for a Vienna-shaped loaf of bread. To keep it safe he wraps it in a towel and sleeps with it under his head. He awakes in the morning to find both end sections missing, and only the piece under his head still remaining. Somehow, somebody, has cut off both ends and taken them, without disturbing him or the people around him. The culprit is never found.

We marvel at the dogged perseverance of one man, a Scottish Pipe Major. On most evenings on dusk, he will march along the Camp perimeter, playing his pipes. All soldiers love the pipes and this man's playing is exceptional. The fact that he can muster the strength to march and still hang onto his pipes, is remarkable.

When rumours seem to suggest that we are pretty close to being moved on, we don't know whether to be pleased or sorry. We find it impossible to accept that we are Prisoners. We are certain that some sort of an attack will be launched to free us. We have not come to terms with the fact that we are expendable. To be abandoned is unthinkable. Therefore, the further we journey into Europe, the harder it will be for our rescuers to get to us.

While this camp is a hellhole, and that the Germans have promised the camps we are going to are much better, we really don't know what may happen. Maybe the Partisans will intercept us and, if they do, will any of us be killed in the attack? Then there are the uncertainties of the train trip in our weakened state. I'm not too hopeful of there being any sort of toilet facilities and, as I have had dysentery for almost three weeks now, the thought of being penned up, not being able to go when I have to, is very depressing.

The rumours become a certainty, and we are to move out in the afternoon of a particular day. There is some milling about with parties trying to organise to stay together as a group. The men of our Unit have broken up as a formation, and are scattered throughout the camp, in their groups of twos and threes. I locate a couple of my Newcastle mates, and attempt for George and I to join with them. One makes it plain that this isn't on, as they are in a group who have escape plans. So, George and I stick together, somewhere in the thousands of men who march to the railhead.

When we get there, the trucks are still being prepared for the journey. There is a large sliding door, centrally located, on both sides of the truck. The one facing us is open and slid back. Their fastenings are on the outside. On both sides there is a small trapdoor, with a hinged flap, located high above the floor. The fastenings for the flap are on the inside and the opening is about three feet long by eighteen inches wide. German soldiers are busy securing these trapdoors by securing barbed wire across the outer opening and with four by two battens on the inside. The battens are fastened with heavy six inch nails, partly bent over and belted deep into the timber.

The Germans give us a stern lecture on what we are allowed to take with us. Any contraband, tools or knives, have to be dumped before boarding. Any escaping attempts will bring reprisals on all, where every tenth man will be taken out and shot. In view of this reaction to what has happened in the Camp, we don't know whether to believe this last threat or not.

Each truck is to take fifty-two men. As we begin to group for boarding, I spot Noel and his mates. George and I manoeuvre ourselves into the group, whom they are with. I hope that, whatever happens, we will at least be with people we know. Privately, I'm not too sure of my ability to make the trip through.

As we move to board, our lot moves towards the truck that still has not been made secure. Once inside, Noel and his mates press close to the still open trapdoor on the far side. The rest of us just cram in wherever we can.

Soon, a German soldier pushes his way in, closes the flap and nails two battens across the opening from top to bottom. He does the same on the opposite side and pushes his way out again. Apparently, running short of time, they decide against barbed wire across the outer opening for our truck. The sliding door is closed and locked, and we are shut in for our trip. In about half an hour the train begins to move. It is just on dark.

Positioning inside the truck, requires that half the number line each side. You lay prone with your legs positioned alongside the body of the fellow opposite, and his legs alongside your body. With everybody lying shoulder to shoulder, we all just fit in.

For the time being, we elect not to fully settle down. A couple of Noel's mates are standing and working away at the battens covering the flap opening. A few more of us stand and peer through the openings and cracks at the passing countryside. Although by now it is pitch dark, there is still something to see.

It is harvest season and people are out there threshing grain in the light of pressure kerosene lanterns. They are working around a stationary belt-driven harvester, feeding sheaves into the machine. This peaceful, workaday, yet idyllic scene, brings a sad emphasis to our present plight. Oh to be out there, just like them, free to come and go!

The fellows working away at those battens have been joined by a couple more. We begin to realise that this is not just idle mischief; these men are working to a definite purpose. With a buzz of excitement, it comes home to us that, without these battens, there is an opening—one that is possible to slip through.

It takes a fair while, but finally they are successful. They have freed the bottom nails and the battens can now be pushed aside from the trapdoor. The flap can be opened and dropped down, exposing the full opening. To conceal the job from any investigation, it requires only to close the flap and slide the battens back into place. A casual glance will be unable to detect anything amiss.

With the way clear, Noel and his mates prepare to go through. It is only a narrow opening and can best be negotiated with a little help from inside. In moments, they begin to drop off the moving train, one at a time.

We know that there is a full carriage of Soldier Guards at the front and rear of the train. We wait anxiously for any reaction from them. There is none. We expect that some of them may be posted as lookouts. Either there is none, or they have missed seeing the drop-offs in the darkness.

Now that the way has been shown, everybody is on their feet and anxious to give it a try. There are dissenters too, and some who feel physically unable to make the jump. Others, mindful of that reprisal threat, wonder what will happen when the Germans find men missing. A couple, determined to give it a go, urge, "Don't wait to find out!"

We are lining up now in front of the opening, in our little groups of twos and threes. The drill is that the person about to go through the opening will get a boost-up from the man behind. At the opening, his pack or gear will be handed to him and he will then make his drop. After each group jumps, the flap will be closed for a few minutes while we wait for any signs from the Guards. As soon as it is judged that they have seen nothing, it is on with the next lot.

There are still some doubts being expressed as to whether, or not, we should be taking the risk; and not knowing what the German reaction will be. A few claim it is unfair to the rest of the Prisoners. As it comes closer to our turn, I cannot contain myself. With a party of three next to go, and then us, I say to George, "We've got to go. A situation like this occurs only once in a lifetime, and we've just got to take it." The last of the three, in front of us, stares at me intently as I speak, but he doesn't say a word. It makes me feel a bit embarrassed, but I am unrepentant.

As we help them up with their gear, I begin to plan, with George, our strategy. I advise him not to drop straight down from the opening as, depending on how we hit the ground, there is danger of rolling under the wheels. I suggest he cling to the outside, work his way round to the buffers, stand there, pick a spot, and jump clear. This is my intention, too.

By now, more than half the men have gone. As we move into position, a young bloke prepares to help us with our gear. He desperately wants to go, but isn't sure if he can make it. He is barefoot and with not much clothing. He is on his own without a mate. I tell him to take his time, and think about it. There is still a long time before daylight.

I elect to go first and will stay put where I land. After jumping, George is to walk back until he contacts me. With the train moving away from us all the time, there is little chance of discovery.

I climb up, swing through the opening and hang my gear round my shoulder. Still clinging to the edge, I begin to work my way round to the buffers. With the toes of my boots, I find a steel binding along the bottom of the truck that gives me a good grip. Within seconds I am standing safely on the buffers. In bright moonlight, I select a flat section, without embankments, and prepare to jump. As I leap, the train slows down. I land on my feet without even falling over. I immediately lay full length beside the track and watch the train pass on. There are no Guards to be seen and no reaction from the rear passenger car.

The exhilaration and excitement of the moment is unbelievable. But it is quickly tempered with anxiety for George. The train has slowed almost to a halt although I am well clear. Maybe there is some sort of a station just up there. If so, I have visions of Guards jumping down, running along, testing fastenings, before climbing aboard again. If George delays his jump much after me, he just might get caught in the act. Then comes the sound of the train moving on, with no fuss or bother. We are safe.

While lying there at the side of the rails, I concentrate on the disappearing train, without paying heed to my surroundings. Now I become aware of voices talking together, and hissing steam from a stationary engine. About a hundred and fifty yards from where I lay, an engine is standing on a side spur. Its crew and shunter are standing on the ground talking together. This appears to be the end of the spur, and it disappears back in the other direction. There appears to be some sort of junction back there that has caused our train to slow almost to a halt—not a station. That means we are pretty well in the clear.

While the engine continues to stand there, I lay prone. Though they appear to be Greek, it doesn't seem prudent to make contact before putting some distance between us and the area. I am sure George will spot them without any trouble. After a short while the loco moves off in the direction the train has taken. George has still not appeared, and the dysentery has caught up with me again. I make a quick dash off to the side and, after what appears to be a short time, return to my position waiting. Then comes the welcome sound of George calling out softly, "Arty, Arty." But it is from behind, not in front of me. He has passed me while I had moved to the side and, after almost giving up hope of finding me, he is making one final search back.

We are deeply grateful to be together again, and would have been devastated to be parted. Our spirits begin to soar, as we realise we are free to go anywhere we please. While providence has looked after us this far, we are determined to make the most of this chance from here on.

# Chapter 10

# On the run in Greece

STANDING ON THE SIDE OF the railway line, George and I are almost floating in our exultation at being free. Until now, our whole thoughts have been occupied with escaping. With this accomplished it is time to concentrate on where we will be heading. The mere fact of being able to make such a decision is heady stuff indeed. To again be in charge of one's destiny, is the ultimate feeling.

There is no real problem about making our decision. We will head for the sea and hope to somehow pick up a boat and get out of the country. With the train having headed North, we know our compass points. We will head towards the East.

With this in view, we look towards the horizon where a line of hills or mountains, maybe about ten miles away, can be seen. That's where we will head for. We are supremely confident that we should be able to make it under the cover of darkness. We will be well out of the way before any German search parties come looking for us.

We plunge off the rail line to be confronted by some kind of garden. There is no sign of habitation, so whoever owns it must live fairly close by. Our first few steps tell us what kind of crops they are. It is a watermelon patch and, wonder of wonders, they are ripe. We select a good one and take it to the edge of the field where we break it open and sit down for a quick feed.

Our spirits soar. We just cannot make a mistake. First the escape, and now instant food. Nothing can stop us. As we eat, I reflect on the knockback we received from our mates in Salonika. They brushed us off, as they have teamed up with others with plans of escaping. Well, while they are planning, we have done it. This gives me some satisfaction. I wonder what they will think in the morning, when an inspection will discover that a few of us have fled.

Wasting no time in polishing off our watermelon, we set off across the open grassy plains. The night is clear and the weather is mild. The conditions are as perfect as if we have been able to choose the time and place ourselves.

We have been walking for about a quarter of an hour, when the familiar gripping pain in my stomach forces me to stop. My dysentery has caught up with me again. Dropping my duds, I squat and reflect on that melon knowing that at least I have had something inside me. This surely will only be a temporary setback, and my innards will quickly settle down.

Again we set off and walk for about ten minutes. Again I am forced to stop. Then it is five minutes, then three. I am shocked to find that the melon is passing straight through, without digesting. I cannot believe this is possible.

It is obvious now that I am in no condition to travel further. Those distant hills, that we optimistically fix as our target, are quite out of the question. We have to find some kind of hiding place, while I still have strength to move.

We veer off to our left where the land appears to be undulating or slightly hilly. It is still the same smooth grassy area, but with a few small folds in the ground. If we had not been seeking a hideout, we would not have noticed it as being any different to what we have been traversing.

Hopeful, but not expecting much, we round a small shoulder and find ourselves in a small natural amphitheatre. Just on one side and near the front, is a circular hut built of straw. It is too well built to be a kid's playhouse, so we figure that it must be a shelter for shepherds.

There is no sign of any animals and the whole area appears deserted. Cautiously, we approach not knowing what to expect. We reach the door opening, peer inside to find it completely empty. There is a layer of straw, strewn on the ground.

Gratefully, we enter and collapse full length on this soft bedding. Once I am spread out horizontally the griping pain becomes less severe. We will give ourselves a few hours rest, then decide on our next move. It has been a very momentous night and we drop into a fitful sleep, not waking till dawn.

With daylight upon us, we consider it prudent to stay under cover, at least for a while. It is time too, to take a hard look at our position. The relationship between George and myself is pretty much as equals. There may have been a slight edge of authority my way, as I am older by a few years and am an Acting Corporal. But in the situation we are in now, these things don't really count. We have a great rapport and can always work out our plans without conflict.

We decide that we will stay here for a bit longer. We will keep inside the hut and hopefully nobody will know we are here. If we are found, there will be no heroics. We will submit without trying to take off and risk being shot. If necessary, we will wait for another opportunity and make a break then.

The heady euphoria, we felt after our escape last night, has almost gone. We feel rather down with the only consolation being that at least we are free. We have had a pretty rough time over the past few months, starting with the Western Desert Campaign, then Greece, then the evacuation, then our capture and finally the slow starvation of the transit camps. Our escape is the big lift that should have put all that behind us. But, due to my condition, now all this is at a risk. Although we don't talk about it, our spirits have taken a hell of a beating and I feel, somehow, that it is partly my fault.

With nothing better to do, we examine our hut more closely. It is beautifully built and quite cosy. While there is little chance of rain in this late summer weather, we feel, if it does happen, the hut will still keep us quite dry. We cannot tell how often it is made use of but guess, because of its neat condition, it is only occasionally.

About nine o'clock, George thinks he hears something and looks out to investigate, while taking care not to be seen. He tells me some Greek civilians have appeared and seem to be headed our way. With no idea whether they might be friendly or otherwise, we have no option but to stay put and see what happens.

Talking together as they walk along, they just head straight for the hut. Upon reaching it, they sink to their knees at the door opening and begin talking with us. They obviously know we are here and their manner is almost like old friends coming to call.

There are two of them. One is about twenty-five and the other about thirty-five. The younger has the bearing of natural authority and the older is respectful to him, like a workman and his boss. There is a difference in their attire, with the younger being dressed as a town Greek and the older as a country or peasant Greek.

We had thought we were well concealed, and that the hut appeared deserted. We are disconcerted that we have been found so easily, but very grateful that it is the Greeks and not the Germans.

We have no understanding of their language, nor they of ours. We just have to make ourselves understood as best we can by waving of arms and pantomime. They take in our situation at a glance and immediately accept that we are English escapees. Being Australian is just more than they can fathom. They can see that I am pretty crook, and are very sympathetic.

They tell us to stay where we are, and they will come back later and take us to a safe place. It will be sometime in the afternoon but before dark. In the meantime they will leave a melon with us to eat until they get back. Then they leave.

With no alternative but to accept the situation, we settle down to wait. I am too scared to touch the melon in case it makes my condition worse. George eats very little also. We begin to recall those rumours we have heard when we first came to Greece, about the Greeks being fifty percent pro German. What if we have fallen in with the wrong kind, and they have gone off to fetch the Germans? As we are in no condition to make a run for it, we will just have to trust them. We put in a fairly miserable and subdued period of waiting.

About two o'clock in the afternoon, they return. This time there are some other Greeks with them. There are now about ten in the party. Our two came to us and are sorry, but understanding that we have been unable to eat the melon. They help me to my feet, and we start off.

They appear to be heading homeward and have probably stopped work early to pick us up. Maybe the garden plot, where we had stolen the melon, belongs to them. Maybe that's why they were so sure of finding somebody in the hut. With the language difficulty, there is no way we can find out.

They deliberately make the pace very slow for my benefit. Often, I have to stop and drop my duds as the pain becomes unbearable. Never once do they pass a remark about it. Always their attitude is sympathetic and understanding. The sturdy Greeks are good and fast walkers. To them, this trip must have seemed to take forever.

Finally, we arrive at a fairly large house, standing alone and quite imposing. It seems to be two or three storeys high and the residence of somebody well-to-do. As our party comes to a halt, I gratefully sink to a sitting position. A lot more Greeks come out and gather round. There are now close to thirty of them, and they obviously are discussing us and what to do about us. The discussion is very animated with the two, who found us, having plenty to say.

By now we have completely dismissed our pro German fears and are quite happy to leave our immediate future in the hands of these people. By great good luck we seem to have landed ourselves in an area that is completely devoid of Germans, or, at least, they are remote and far away. These people seem to not give them a second thought.

Their attitude gives us a lift and already we begin to feel better. We watch with interest as the discussion goes on around us. The younger of our finders is obviously a man of some standing among this lot. He seems to be directing proceedings while our other man has plenty to say too.

After about twenty minutes, everything seems to be settled. As far as we can make out, we are to go with and be taken care of, by the older of our two finders. Our feeding probably will be a community effort, with contributions of each being the reason for all the discussion.

Now that things are finalised everybody relaxes. There is still plenty of talking with everybody being eager to help in any way they can. Somebody comes out of the big house with two coats, one for each of us. Mine, the much more substantial of the two, is black and about hip length. George's coat is of some kind of cotton drill. It has been dyed, rather poorly, in a cross between a blue and purple colour. Both are well worn and, once we put them on, they completely nullify our military appearance. To all intents and purposes, we look like your average Greek peasant. We are pleased and happy with the transformation.

Now it is time to move on to where we are to stay. Our man, whom we find is named Ignatio, leads off with three or four others from the same village. As far as we can tell, it appears that the big house is owned by the landowner and these people farm some of the land on a share basis.

Finally, we arrive at the village which we find later is called Pefkodassos. It is a collection of about ten or twelve houses, side by side, and all pretty much the same. They appear to be mudbrick construction, plastered over and painted white. They have thatched roofs and seem sturdy and sound.

Our advent causes a great amount of interest and Ignatio leads us to his house, talking and explaining to the locals as he goes. He leads us inside where his wife and children greet us. His wife appears in her thirties. There is a daughter about fourteen, a son about ten and a kiddy about two. There is such a procession of youngsters crowding around, we cannot tell if any more belong to him.

We are given food of bread, goat milk cheese and a junket-like concoction of sour milk. We eat cautiously of this unfamiliar fare, but relish every last crumb. I privately ask Ignatio for the whereabouts of the toilet, so I will know where to make my dash. He waves his arm in a wide circle, indicating anywhere outdoors. There just isn't any. As for a bathroom, there isn't one of these either. Nor is there any running water.

After a short while, we indicate we would like to retire for the night. We have had a most eventful day and are pretty well done in. The room is cleared and a bunk made up for us against a wall. Gratefully, we drop off, resolving to take more interest in our surroundings the next day.

With the new day, the house is astir almost from daybreak. Feeling a bit more alert, we stare around us with interest, fascinated with this way of life. The house seems to have three rooms. There is a large room that the entrance door leads into. There is a tiny fireplace on one side, just inside the door. A few sacks, probably of grain, are piled against one of the walls. There is some large earthenware jars also. A small square wooden cover in the floor leads to an underground type of cellar in which is stored their wheat crop. This seems to be the main work room.

To the left, and about half the size, is the dining and living room. It contains a dresser, a small wooden table and three or four wooden frame chairs with woven, plaited, raffia seats. Our bunk, which we both share, is against the wall. This is the room where everybody gathers, both family and friends.

Behind that again is the third room. This is the family's sleeping quarters, into which, of course, we do not intrude. The floor throughout is hard-packed dirt.

We watch with interest the family routine. We want to fit in as much as possible without disrupting their daily life. We are resolved to help anywhere we can, in some sort of meagre payment, for the help given to us.

The daughter's first job is to go outside to where the family cow is tethered. This animal is more for working than milking. She gathers each mound of dung in her hands and kneads it into a round pat. Then she slaps the pat into the house wall where it will dry in the sun. this is used as fuel for cooking.

Some of the family wash in the morning and some don't. The method is to pour a cup of water out of the water container—you empty half the cup into your hands while vigorously rinsing; then empty the other half into your hands for splashing on your face while vigorously rubbing. You don't bother to go outside to do this; you do it in the work room alongside the container where the water is stored.

Their feeding habits are different to ours. Whereas our system is for three meals a day, they seem to have only one main meal at night. This does not mean they go hungry. They just grab bits of this and that as they feel like it.

The evening meal is placed on a small table, in the container it is cooked or prepared in. Everybody gathers round, reaching in with his hand and feeding themselves until it is all gone. At first we feel a bit diffident at this method, but our hunger forces us quickly to become as good a grabber as the others.

The food mainly is bread, vegetables, fruit, goat milk cheese and the junket-like curdled milk. There is little or no meat. When they go out for the day working in the fields or tending the goats or sheep, they usually take a loaf of bread and a few hard boiled eggs in a dilly bag with them. We regard this as the Greek travelling ration.

They are especially kind and careful with me, doing their utmost to clear up my bad stomach condition. One of the neighbours has a Jersey cow which is a practically unheard of acquisition in this part of Greece. Every day she will fetch me a bowl of fresh milk. Ignatio's wife empties it into a shallow dish and puts it on the window sill in the sun. When it curdles to a junket-like consistency, she will insist on my eating it. Often I feel that I would love to drink it before it turns sour, but I persevere under her urging. The taste isn't too good, but it does seem to be working.

Ignatio insists that it is imperative that we look as much like a Greek as possible. We can see how important this is. If we are sighted by strangers, as long as we keep in the background of a group, we should be alright. Then too, if we are somewhere on our own, any Germans will pay no attention to us. While our prisoner status gives us some protection if discovered, for our Greek friends, it may be fatal.

Ignatio points out that our military boots are a dead giveaway. We should wear something more Greek in appearance. Our boots are old and scuffed, down at the heel and with soles worn through. While we are most reluctant to part with them, we feel that we have to agree.

Clothing and footwear is a big drain on the resources of these people. Everything is worn and re-worn as much as possible. Everything is patched until it is no longer able to do so. The coats given to us represent some sort of a sacrifice by someone. Now something for our feet is a problem.

I still have a pair of nondescript army issue sandshoes. Ignatio is satisfied that they will do for me. For George he comes up with a pair of worn black rubber shoes. While much of the attire worn by locals is a mishmash of army and civilian, it is Greek style. This change helps us to blend in a little bit better.

With Ignatio being reasonably happy with our appearance, we try as best we can to pick up their ways and mannerisms and learn something of the language. While we have no illusions of being able to fool a Greek, for any Germans it shouldn't be too hard to fool them.

Now that we are committed to being as much Greek as possible, we are a bit miffed a few days later when Ignatio comes in and clumps around in a pair of boots. They are George's that he has somehow been able to have repaired. They have new soles that are almost threequarters of an inch thick. They are almost as good as new. Ignatio airily passes off the possible danger by pointing out that he is Greek, and can get away with it. We would not be able to.

It is late summer and the weather is warm, sunny and beautiful. Our interest in the goings on around us, and the people, begin to make us lose some of our tensions and we gradually relax. Always somebody will be dropping in, usually with some kind of food. One man has a fair sized tomato patch, just near the edge of the village. The tomatoes are big, juicy and red ripe. His patch is a source of great envy to most of the others. He arrives one evening with a piled bucketful as a gift.

I have developed an almighty craving for tomatoes which indicates to me that I am deficient in the vitamins that they contain. I accept his gift gratefully and stand it in the corner. As we have just finished our evening meal, I silently promise myself that I will guts into them, first thing in the morning.

Almost immediately that he leaves, as is their way, the son picks up a tomato and begins eating. He eats by biting into it, as we will into an apple. One by one, the rest of the family help themselves to a sample. I become a bit alarmed that I may be a few down, if they continue. But I decide, with such a large quantity, there is still plenty left for me. Besides, as I am their guest and they share what they have with me, it is only right that I shall return the favour. Nevertheless, I will make the bucket my first priority in the morning.

As soon as I awake, I go straight to the bucket. It is completely empty. They have scoffed the lot! George and I have not even had one between us. Chastened, I promise myself, I will not be so backward next time. If necessary, I will do the scoffing myself.

Bread is baked in a community oven in the centre of the village by Ignatio's wife. At each baking, enough is made for about a week's supply. This home baked bread is truly wonderful. The mere smell of it, fresh from the oven, is almost more than we can stand. Try as we might, we cannot contain ourselves and, almost invariably, polish off a large loaf at a sitting. After a day or two, when it has lost some of its freshness, our intake becomes a bit more respectable.

With the heavier demand, it sometimes becomes necessary to make an extra baking, halfway between. This is just taken as a matter of course, and there are no complaints. No exception is taken to our intake, though we still feel a bit guilty.

Our tortured stomachs have taken a beating for some months now. With a regular intake of food, plus the difference in the Greek diet from our own, there is a marked effect on our guts. We are plagued with a strong build-up of gas. We find this impossible to control, and any movement causes an involuntary burst. It can roll out of us at any time. The Greek reaction to this bad-mannered display is of extreme disgust, although they fully understand it cannot be helped. We find it hard to reconcile our faux pas, compared with some of their own habits, which seem rather offensive to us.

When anybody has a cold with the resultant snotty nose, they will blow it, Greek fashion, wherever they may be, usually inside the house. Nobody seems to own a handkerchief, certainly not for this purpose. They will place a thumb and forefinger on the top of the nose and blow loudly. At the same time they will flick the resultant mess onto the floor with thumb and forefinger, then wipe these two digits on their clothes. There it will be left to lay.

After a few days we try to tell Ignatio that we really would like a bath. They don't seem to bother themselves, so he probably interprets our request as a desire to swim. Anyway he and a party of others take us by oxen drawn cart to a small river about two miles from the village. We peel off down to our underwear and jump in. Several of the others do the same. We all romp and cavort and have a good all over wash, without soap of course.

Across the other side, about a quarter of a mile away on higher ground, a section of railway can be seen, passing between two hills. This will have to be the one we were using when we made our escape. We do not know whether to be alarmed, or not, at its close proximity. Our Greek friends don't seem concerned, so we relax too.

We had been splashing around for about half an hour when we hear the sound of a train coming. As it comes into view, we can see it has mostly passenger carriages laden with German soldiers, apparently going home on leave. Some are relaxing on the entrance platforms at the end of the carriages, admiring the view.

Our Greek friends make no attempt to hide from them, so we hold fast also. On a sudden impulse, George and I wave to the Germans and they lazily wave back. This cheeky exhibition of bravado provides us with a big lift. It is truly wonderful to watch them fade from sight, while savouring the spiritual high of being free.

Realising that we cannot always call on our friends, whenever we feel like a bath, we look for a simpler method. Close to the village there is a small watercourse with a small trickle flowing through. Here we strip off and sit in the course of the bed. With our handkerchiefs, we scrub ourselves all over and dry out in the sun. Any of our clothing that needs washing, we rinse it out too and spread it out on the rocks to dry. This seems to be a bit of English madness to the Greeks, but as long as it keeps us happy, they don't care.

By now we are beginning to fit more into the ways of our Greek household. I still am having an off-day, but mostly my innards have started to settle down. Often of an evening, some of the people will come to visit and everybody will be crowded into our little room, sitting round and talking.

In this relaxed atmosphere, several young kiddies will be running around, playing with our host's two year old. On one of these evenings, Ignatio's wife is sitting cross-legged on the floor in the centre of the room. Her youngster is running in and out between us, so she just reaches out, grabs him, pulls her breast out and begins to feed him.

This intrigues me very much, for in our society her kiddie would have been considered long past this. And, also during the time we have been here, she has not attempted to feed him before. To complicate matters, she reaches out and grabs one of her neighbour's children, of about the same age and a playmate of her youngster. Pulling out the other breast, she puts him to work on that one. The two of them just nestle in her lap, suckling away, happy and content.

All the time this is happening, conversation just goes on, Ignatio's wife included, without missing a beat. Quite clearly this is considered normal behaviour. To me it seems reasonable to feed one's own child, but not somebody else's. Of course, I cannot tell if there is any milk there. Maybe this is just a way to keep them quiet, as opposed to our method of giving them a lolly.

On one of my off-days, Ignatio wants to take us both away for the day. The plan is to call in at the Big House on the way, and let them see how we are going. With me being off-colour, George goes while I stay at home. When they return in the late afternoon, they have a fair-sized dish of very small fish with them. I ask George where they came from. He tells me that Ignatio took him to a hole in a stream bed, left behind after most of the water had dried up. It was teeming with these small fish, trapped and unable to escape. They had stirred the muddy bottom with a stick and, as the fish came to the surface deprived of oxygen, they just scooped them up.

They are about three inches long and similar in shape and size to a sardine. Ignatio's wife decides to cook them for our evening meal and proceeds to fry them in olive oil. When we sit down to eat, I take the cue from the others who just scooped from the communal pot and hoe in. Poor George cannot quite stomach them in this way and tries to separate the sides from the head, tail and innards, with his pocket knife. Needless to say, his efforts result in him getting only a small portion of the food.

Ignatio decides to do some repairs to his thatched roof. Although it looks sound enough to me, I know that he is a better judge of that. The straw will come from wheat stalks that are in the process of being harvested. But he needs some nails to secure some battens.

He produces a length of fence wire, which he has acquired from somewhere, and puts George and me to work to make them. He produces one himself to demonstrate what he requires, then leaves the job to us. From the hardened piece of steel, we chop them off to length, using a hammer. We straighten this length as near as possible, then hammer a point on one end. The result is supposed to be something resembling our three inch nail. We do as best we can, but to me it looks a poor substitute for the real thing.

Ignatio gets up on the roof and does the nailing. I am glad it is him and not me, for I am sure I would not have been able to drive them in straight. This little exercise drives home clearly to us, just how tough their day-to-day life can be. The many ordinary everyday things that we accept as being part of our normal everyday lives are just not on here.

Our people have been telling us about some other Englishmen who are being taken care of in another village not too far away from ours. They have suggested that they can take us to meet them. In consideration of my condition, they finally decide to bring them to meet us.

We have long since learned that the term Englishmen can mean almost any nationality. To declare oneself to be Australian draws only blank looks. To the average Greek, even the existence of those faraway strange lands seems almost beyond comprehension. For the convenience of everybody we are English. So, when told of these people, we have no idea who or what they may be.

A small party from this other village arrives for the meeting and we are taken to the gathering, just on the outskirts of ours. There seems to be a little wariness in not meeting at our house.

We find them to be two Kiwis whose story is almost identical as our own. We have a happy half hour or so comparing notes. Then it is time for them to depart. After they have gone, our people indicate to us that they are of the opinion that those two are not entirely to be trusted. They assert that the Kiwis are just too friendly with the women folk, especially the younger ones.

There never is any suggestion or idea of us combining together as a group. Our respective villages can cope with a couple extra in their community, but that's all. The least we know about each other, the less chance of any harm being done. George and I owe them nothing, nor they us. We never see them again.

A few days later, about midmorning, we hear some strange goings-on outside our house. All the family line up, just inside the front door, and Ignatio takes off his hat and stands with his head bowed. Now a chanting priest enters, swinging a smoking censer.

George and I stare in astonishment at this religious manifestation. The Priest speaks to no one, keeps on chanting and swinging, and moves through every room in the house. When he covers the whole circuit, he leaves and moves onto the next house. Trailing behind him are two of the young village lads, carrying sacks. In return for the blessing of their homes, the householders stuff gifts of food of all kinds into the sacks. It seems that the Priest repeats this ritual every two weeks. To George and me, it seems like a bit of a lurk.

We have no idea of where the Priest comes from, nor where he disappears to. He certainly is not of our village. He may have some sort of a Parish circuit he is required to cover, but we are unable to find out because of the language problem. Still religious beliefs are always a sensitive issue and it just isn't an area into which we can intrude. We are only guests here ourselves.

With the passing of the days, I am gradually getting stronger. More and more, we are slipping into our people's way of life. Each day we emerge into the beautiful sunshine of yet another perfect day, feeling wonderfully free and relaxed, and cheerfully greeting our neighbours as they go about their tasks. Just as cheerfully, they greet us back.

There is one particular neighbour we have a special feeling for. He is of Yugoslav origin and always is accompanied by his daughter-in-law. They will stride along at a leisurely pace, carrying some hand tools, and return our greeting in a grave almost courtly manner. He name is Arsan and he is always dressed in the Yugoslav national dress. He wears an embroidered waistcoat-like jacket over a shirt and the baggy trousers that goes with it. His boots are knee-length and of leather. He is so colourful amongst the others that we cannot help but take notice.

His daughter-in-law is a buxom, comely woman in her thirties. She is a competent, strong woman, with an air that suggests she will be able to cope with just about anything. Instead of the Greek penchant of dressing mostly in black, she usually wears lighter colours.

Arsan could be anything from fifty to eighty. He is strong and sturdy and appears able to carry on forever. They are as much a part of the village as any of the others, yet obviously different in their nationality. Their air gives the impression that they have always lived here, but then it may have been only since Yugoslavia was overrun by the Germans. We cannot tell, but we like them very much.

Our total acceptance, by our Greek friends, allows us to be involved in another intriguing job that teaches us a little bit more about their ways. Every household has its small flock of sheep and goats. Whenever somebody decides to add meat to the menu, several families will share in one beast. They will take it in turns to supply the beast. After it is slaughtered, it will be chopped into as many pieces as there are participants. After being cut up, then comes the distribution. And that's where we come in.

While all care is taken to make the portions of meat as equal as possible, there's always some better than others. To avoid any arguments over distribution, a system has been worked out. They sit George and me on a log with our backs to the meat. The receivers line up, facing us. Somebody behind us then holds up a portion and we will point to somebody in the receivers lineup to receive that portion. Everybody then goes away satisfied that they have had a fair deal. We too, are impressed with the system, in comparison with the bitter arguments there were over bread portions in Salonika No. 2 POW Camp.

The wheat crop has been harvested and is now ready for threshing. With no machinery available our people just carry on in the age old way. There is a large flat piece of ground at the edge of the village, a sort of village common. The job is done there with everybody pitching in to help. They spread the wheat stalks out in a large circle that covers most of the common. They then drive a short, flat wooden sled over them until the grain is separated from the stalks. They then toss the mixture of grain and chaff into the air, allowing the harvest winds to blow away the chaff and leave only the grain.

It is a picturesque and age-old method that consumes a lot of time. Still, it is a happy period with everybody working and laughing together, and with the satisfaction of a good harvest and the prospect of security for the winter to come.

The tedious and boring work of driving the sled round and round in a circle, is still one of the most important parts of the job. With everybody participating, it doesn't take long before Ignatio tries out first me, and then George, at this chore. The results are hilarious.

The sled is being pulled by a cow and a donkey yoked together. The driver stands on the flat sled with his weight helping to separate the grain from the ears. With a Greek driver, the two beasts plod on without any problems. But in our case, unless we mimic the Greek cries and driving-style exactly, they will suddenly shoot off and we will have a hell of a job to stop them.

After a couple of these unscheduled stops, where somebody has to drop tools, run after and catch the beasts, then lead them back to the circuit, they give us two up as a bad job. We then spend most of our time tossing the grain, separating it from the chaff. We manage this better, although there is quite a knack to it.

The efficiency that the sled achieves in separating the grain, causes me to examine if there is any special help involved. I upturn it to find pieces of metal, glass and quartz embedded all over. Their cutting action helps tremendously, and I am impressed with our people's ingenuity.

This work goes on for a week or more, with all helping with each other's crop. When completed the wheat is stored in the granary beneath the floor of each house. It seems to be a good crop to me, for in Ignatio's case, his is full to the brim, with several sacks besides. As needed, it will be taken to the mill for grinding into flour, a couple of sacks at a time.

With the harvest in, there is a rather a lazy period where not much is done other than regular chores. With time on their hands, the menfolk sit around discussing the happenings in their country, with some stories filtering through from the south. They are openly belligerent towards the Germans and, particularly, the Italians whom they despise. They hint darkly of rifles and grenades, safely hidden away, ready to be broken out when the time is right for an uprising. It isn't a matter of if; it is just a matter of when.

It is bad enough for the Greeks to have to submit to occupation after defeat by the Germans; but the Germans have handed over part of the garrison duties to the Italians. The Greeks naturally take this as a great slight upon their honour, particularly, as they had performed magnificently against the Italians, driving them back wherever they had met. It is galling to have to kowtow to an enemy they despise. Stories are circulating that ridicule the Italians' behaviour. One such story refers to them as tortoise eaters. The fields about are fairly well populated with tortoises. The Greeks themselves will not touch them. Apparently, the Italians consider them a delicacy and catch and cook them in large numbers. The Greeks' scathing scorn for this behaviour is unbelievable.

Apparently, the Germans don't have much time for their allies either. With Germans and Italians both on leave in Athens, some Germans encourage Greek kids to taunt and goad the Italians, provoking them into chasing the kids. The Germans will then step in, taking the kids' part, and beat up the Italians. Stories, such as this, are very satisfying to our people.

With rumours and rumblings, always from some far distant area, of groups preparing for some kind of action against the enemy, all the old belligerence stirs anew. Again comes the threats of breaking out arms hidden in granaries and thatching.

My training tells me that explosives hidden for any length of time are subject to some deterioration. That may mean more danger to the user than his opponent. It is useless to try and tell them, as they have deep faith in their own knowhow and ability.

Rumours, speculation and idle talk, cloud the situation, and give us something to think about. It is pretty idyllic here and we could stay put just drifting along in the village lifestyle, and just let events unfold by themselves. The fairly open-knowledge that escapees are in the area was emphasised by our meeting with the two Kiwis. While the German presence is far away, and seemingly uninterested, they may quickly change this, any time they choose.

There is no telling what sort of crackpot scheme may be devised by the locals, into which we, no doubt, may be drawn into, merely by being here. We are too firmly committed to controlling our own destiny to allow anything like this to happen. While we're reluctant to leave our haven, the urge is upon us to move on.

The biggest single factor on our minds is the knowledge that we will have been posted as missing. While this posting remains in force, nobody will know what has happened to us. We could die, be killed, or simply disappear. And, after a period with no further news, we would be posted as missing, presumed dead. We just cannot put this kind of uncertainty on our families back home. Besides, we owe it to ourselves to keep going, and have a go.

Once we have made the decision to move on, then we will have to let our village people know. My health has improved and I am now practically back to normal. There is still a fair bit of summer before the onset of winter, so, obviously, now is the time.

We inform Ignatio that we feel we have to carry on, try to get out of the country and back to our own people.. To soften the impact, we try to point out that there is some danger to them, while we stay there. He doesn't think much of this, and asks us only to stay one more day, so he can let the people in the Big house know. We agree to this and, so, the commitment is made.

Our plans are very vague and much the same as before. We will make for the coast and try to get a boat to take us to Turkey. We have no maps, so we will just have to follow our nose. From where we now are, we estimate to be quite a few miles from the sea. We figure our village is close to the Greek northern border, where Yugoslavia and Bulgaria come together. Below Bulgaria to the Turkish frontier would be unknown quantity to us. Making for the sea and possibly a boat seems the safest bet. The area we are in must be that which is known as Macedonia.

Try as I might, I can recall very little of my schooldays history lessons about Macedonia, other than that Alexander the Great was born there, and that Macedonia extended right through to the Turkish border.

On the day we leave, Ignatio writes his name and that of the village on the margin of one of our pay books so that we will not forget them. He provides us with a couple of old sacks, to carry what little gear we have and for a bit of food to take with us.

There is no big scene, just a casual wave and a handshake, and away we go. We have nothing to give in repayment for our keep, other than a very inadequate thank you. We have pretty mixed feelings, as we walk away from our haven, no knowing what may be in store, either for us or them.

With the Big house having been informed of our intended departure, we thought somebody from there would meet with us when we pass close by. The only ones to do so are three young women about fourteen or fifteen. Their names are Vera, Nasta and Angela. They are known to George, but not to me. He had met them on a visit on one of my off-days, when I had to stay at home. They greet us warmly and insist on taking us to some nearby fig trees where they climb up and pick a stack of ripe fruit for us to take on our way.

These girls are attractive, very nicely built and at the local marrying age. There are suggestions that some of the locals are actively trying to promote a liaison between daughter and escapee as a means of securing a rich relative in the family. We have no idea whether this is the thinking behind the girls' presence here. Maybe the people at the Big house think that if the opportunity is given, maybe nature will take its course and we will abandon our foolish plans. Maybe the girls just act spontaneously out of their own good hearts.

Anyway, we spend a good hour talking, laughing and eating, before continuing on our way. Maybe things may have been different if there had been two of them, instead of three.

Moving on, it is obvious that we are not going to make much distance on our first day after our interruptions. We come to a channel about six feet wide, filled with water and directly across our path. I gaze at this obstacle and give a half-thought to turning back to the fig grove. Without a word, George strips off and bundles up his clothes. Calling to me, "Come on", he wades across. Quickly, I follow suit and now we are really on our way.

We make fairly good progress across open country after crossing the canal. Towards evening, we decide it is time to try and find a spot to bed down for the night. We turn off towards some folds in the low hills, looking for a shepherd's hut as we had found before. Sure enough, there it is, just where we have hoped it will be. It is not being used at the moment and we will have it to ourselves. We have sufficient food until tomorrow, the weather is warm and balmy and, for the moment, we don't have a care in the world.

On our first night we sleep like babies. My black jacket spreads across me and acts as a marvellous blanket. There is a depth of clean smelling straw to lie on, and the hut is snug and warm. There are a few field mice rustling about, but, as long as we protect our bread supply, they don't bother us and we don't bother them.

We will be living rough from now on, so aren't particularly bothered about bathing. The canal crossing will have to suffice for the moment. Anyway, our intentions are to look and act as much like a Greek as possible. And this requires an unshaven, unwashed look.

With a new day we are ready and eager to be off. We now have a good idea of the direction we want to go. We will just let each day take its course—go where we feel like it and stop where we feel like it. We will beg for our food, when and where we can.

And so our wanderings begin. We actively adopt the lifestyle of a vagabond. All Greeks, particularly in the rural areas, go about their business on foot. Two more, just wandering about, will not be noticed suspiciously.

Our only needs are food and somewhere to sleep. We will cadge our food and just doss down anywhere. The weather is so good that it really doesn't matter if we sleep in the open. The only problem is that all the locals sleep indoors. So, if we don't, then we will have to make sure that we are well hidden.

We have picked up a few words of the language while in Pefkodassos, and feel confident of being a bit more able to make ourselves understood. However, our first attempts are terrible.

We have decided to ask mostly for bread and boiled eggs. We have selected this type of food as the most easily obtainable and less troublesome to the people. We have to ask for our eggs to be boiled as we have no means of being able to boil them ourselves.

Our first use of our new found words just result in blank stares. We just have to go back to our old signs and handwaving. It is laborious and frustrating, but always we are given something.

After a little time, we find that the language predominately used back in our village is not Greek. We think it must be Turkish. Our little enclave had somehow isolated themselves, in this respect, from the surrounding country. They are hundreds of miles from even the remotest suggestion of Turkish influence, and yet, there it is. Maybe, it is a leftover from some ancient times and wars, long past. But, in everything else, they are as Greek as Greek can be.

Always, upon meeting anyone or calling at a house, we identify like "Onglesse". Always they will just stare blankly and not understand. We will repeat it over and over with a dozen different inflections. Then, suddenly, their eyes will light up and they will say, "Ah Engleese", in what seems the same way we have been saying it.

As soon as our identity is established, they become excited and gabble away. Of course, we cannot understand and it takes a little time for them to slow down. Then, we will go about the business of making ourselves understood. With this scenario, meetings are always a lengthy thing.

Our disguise is never so good that it fools any Greek. They can pick us as different, from some distance away. We cannot quite understand why it takes so long to establish our identity. Maybe they are just being cautious. We just continue on our way, once we have established our identity. Usually, we will come upon one, and sometimes two, small villages each day. This takes care of our food needs.

At first, we sleep in shepherds' huts until we begin to get away from grazing country. On one or two occasions, they are being used by young shepherds, who cheerfully share what they have with us. At night they will have a small fire around which we will all lounge, until time to turn in. The cheerful little fire makes it seem very homey.

Gardens become more commonplace, as we begin to come to crop-growing country. With fruits of all kinds being a favoured part of the local diet, most gardens feature a variety of trees and vines. We just move along and help ourselves whenever we feel like it, but trying not to overdo it.

Always there are grapevines, just one or two. Other times, there are rows and rows of them. The grapes now are ripe and luscious. We form the habit of filling two big coat pockets with bunches and just munching away as we walk along.

We have been walking for several days when we meet with a lone Greek man, who suggests a place we should head for, in our quest to get out of the country. He calls it Aeyanoris. He claims it is a sort of sanctuary on the sea coast, where we will be fed and get help to find a boat.

We ask him if he knows of any boats picking up soldiers, and he tells us about the celebrated Poppa Nagouli.

It seems that Poppa Nagouli was a former German submarine that had washed up on the shore somewhere. It had been damaged and the crew were all dead inside. The Greeks had repaired it and are now operating it themselves to rescue any personnel they can find. We digest this information as we continue on, after thanking our informant for his interesting piece of probable folklore.

Trying to put some sense into this improbable tale, we can only come up with the idea that maybe one of our submarines is lurking around, picking up stragglers. Maybe this news has filtered through to the Greek community and, in the retelling of it, the story has become embroiled with the Poppa Nagouli saga.

The Greek man's story is sufficient to build up our hopes, and makes us feel optimistic. We know that the means of contacting such a submarine would have to be very secret. Still, as bona fide servicemen, we feel sure we can find a way. In the meantime we will make for this other place, Aeyanoris, our goal.

Now, when we ask for directions towards Aeyanoris, people seem to know and understand. But they begin to add another word, Athos. This seems to be more favoured than Aeyanoris. To be on the safe side, we use both words.

We have been walking for some days now, and those old sandshoes of mine stink to high heaven. Sometimes, when we bed down for the night, the smell is unbearable. From time to time, I am forced to throw them away outside somewhere. Then I scramble round looking for them first thing in the morning.

The villages, we are coming to, are a bit more substantial than we have met with, up to now. One such place has a large meeting hall and schoolroom. We are invited to stay the night and bunk down on the schoolroom floor. The Schoolmaster has a large Greek/English phrase book. To speak to us he picks out what he wants to say, then shows us the English translation for us to read. In this way he indicates that he has a request, which he hopes we will be able to carry out.

His son is in Egypt and he wants to get a letter to him. This will be impossible through the mails. Are we prepared to take it with us, and hand it on when we get there? I say, "Certainly—just write it out and put his name on the outside. As soon as we get through, he will get it."

He goes away and writes his letter, leaving us touched at his utter faith in our making of a successful escape. Before giving the letter to me, he indicates that he is afraid it may fall into the wrong hands and be traced back to him. I tell him not to worry. In the event of our recapture, I will undertake to destroy it before it can be found. He then hands it to me, and I tuck it away upon my person.

We have a poor overnight's rest. Apart from the discomfort of the bedding down on a wooden floor, there is an all-night noisy party in the next room. About twenty of the local men have gathered together for some reason, and spend the entire night drinking and dancing.

There are no women present, so this do is strictly for men only. The drinking is pretty heavy and the dancing is the traditional Greek style of linked arms and fancy footwork. Often a dance will finish with a leap into the air and a loud shout. It doesn't stop until almost daylight. They just continue on with their party, and ignore us in the next room.

On the new day, our Schoolmaster friend says goodbye and sees us on our way. I again assure him that I will take good care not to let the wrong people get his letter. Privately, I'm not too sure how I will do that. But I have hope that I will have time to do something, if recapture becomes inevitable.

I don't know if last night's party is part of some sort of a festival. But, at the next village, we meet up with two girls about eighteen or nineteen. These two are distinctly different. They are town or city girls back home from Salonika for a visit. They had left their native village to work and live in the big city and their sophisticated manner and style of dress, is worlds apart from this area.

They are keenly interested, and quiz us as best they can, as to our plans, while offering much advice. There are two or three young lads with them, probably brothers or relatives. We all stand around in a group, making heavy weather of trying to communicate. One of the girls asks, "Do you speak French?"

I say, "Sorry, no."

She continues trying to make us understand and will occasionally put in a French word. Now and then the meaning of one of those words comes back to me from my almost forgotten High School French lessons. I immediately show my understanding, and once again she asks me if I speak French.

Again I say, "No."

Looking at me sternly, she begins to wag her finger accusingly, like a teacher to a naughty boy and at the same time saying, "But you must speak French, you understand."

I do my best to explain that I cannot speak the language, but I do know a few French words and one or two phrases. Unfortunately the phrase that springs readily to mind is the one taught to me by Rex Scanlon back in Egypt. It is the seemingly innocent, but fairly well-known approach to a prostitute of, "Will you take a walk with me?" (voulez vous promenade avec moi)

I do not think for a moment, that she will be aware of the subtle meaning behind the phrase. But, as the words leave my lips, she starts waving her forefinger like a conductor's baton. She blurts, "No, no, no, no, no, NO." There is a wave and rise and fall with each "NO", and the last one is firm and decisive.

I cannot help myself. I burst out laughing and cannot stop. The whole idea of propositioning them is so patently ridiculous, it needs no comment. We two are such tattered and dirty specimens, whereas they are beautiful, fragrant and utterly captivating, that the fact they even deign to talk to us is something of a minor miracle.

I laugh so much, I almost become hysterical. When, finally, I calm down, she seems to accept that it is all a misunderstanding. Eventually we part, all good friends, and we go on our way.

We have, by this time, got very close to the coast and, in the late afternoon, we reach a village on the seashore. It seems to be a fishing village, with a few small boats tied at anchor and a few on the sand.

As usual, we walk up to two women we can see talking together and, after identifying ourselves, we ask for food. One of them motions for us to sit down nearby, in the open, while the other just turns and walks away. We can see that the woman, we are left with, is a bit different in some respects. I come to the conclusion that she is a French woman. There is a fire with red embers here, and it appears that this household eats in the open, which is quite unusual.

She produces two fish, similar to our bream, and about threequarters of a pound each. She places them on a wire frame, over the red embers, and starts to grill them. While doing so, she begins to prepare a small table, about two feet square, alongside.

We watch in silent wonder as she goes about her work. She places a white linen cloth on the table, then sets two plates and the proper silver cutlery. She goes back to the fire and urges the grilling along with a straw hand fan. There is no smoke and the fish are cooked beautifully. When ready, she dishes them up on plates and motions us to sit down on the chairs provided. We eat in complete silence. It is delicious and demonstrates to us, sharply, how we have almost forgotten what it is like to eat a proper meal in a civilised style.

For me, it is a very poignant moment and I am very close to tears. I have an almost unbearable longing, just to be at home with my family, and the very sad realisation that they are half a world away. Will we ever get out of this? Will we ever see them again?

We both are very subdued afterwards, and ask if there is somewhere we can bunk down for the night, then we will be on our way. We are shown to a hay shed which is a bit more in keeping with what we have become accustomed to.

In the morning we have a good talk with our benefactor, explaining that we are on our way to Aeyanoris or Athos, only to be told that we are practically there. Pointing to the heavily timbered, rocky, rising ground at the side of the village, we are told that's what we are looking for.

We are warned that it is nearly impossible to get there from this approach, and that there is an easier access further north. Thinking there might be some guard on the easy way, we decide to try from here. We say goodbye to our friend and set out.

The suggestion that it is hard is truly correct. Right from the start the going is very tough. It is rising ground of rocky outcrops, densely packed thickets and thick scrub. We have to force a passage every inch of the way. It is obvious that this is a natural barrier and needs no guarding. For two hours we push on and have made progress of barely threequarters of a mile. It is exhausting, but with the one consolation that nobody will be expecting an approach from this direction.

By midday, when we have covered about two miles, we finally come to a narrow track that leads off along the ridge we are now on. We sit down for a spell, then decide to follow the track to wherever it goes. The bushes and shrubbery are still tightly packed on either side and we have no idea of what we will find ahead of us. We can only move in single file, but, at least, the going is much easier. After about half an hour, the vegetation begins to thin. Suddenly, we come out into open country with a fairly substantial group of buildings spread before us.

We stop to get our bearings, then just stand there taking in the scene. It is an incredibly beautiful and tranquil sight. The spot, where the buildings stand, is a flat area at the base of a great long ridge, stretching ahead until its extreme end suddenly soars up and up into the sky to become a beautiful, lofty, snow-capped mountain.

From the ridge, the land falls away on both sides until it meets the incredibly blue sea. The ridge stretches straight ahead to the east, with the fall to the north steeper, than the fall to the south, which is much more gentle. The whole area is covered with trees and shrubbery, while those single file tracks twist and turn all over the place.

Scattered here and there are old castle-like buildings that conjure up thoughts of knights and medieval times. Each is some distance from the other and there are more than a dozen of them. Miles of land spreads before us, but, from our vantage point, everything seems almost close enough to touch.

Ahead and to the north, several islands can be seen. They seem to have been dropped here aesthetically, purely to enhance the view. We just stand and watch—our eyes going back and forth from the sea on all sides, to the mountain, to the islands, to the castles, and then back to the mountain. Always we come back to the mountain, which draws us like a magnet.

Finally, after almost having to shake ourselves back to reality, we move off again and continue on to the community we have found. We can now see that there are extensive gardens growing all sorts of crops, plus fruit trees and vines spread round the area. We can see numerous people working among the plants and, from their clothes, obviously it is a monastery of some sort.

There are several men in the standard Greek priestly garb, in and around the buildings, and they greet us warmly, almost as if our coming is an everyday event. We identify ourselves in English and they bid us to wait until they send for one of their number who speaks English. When this man arrives, to our delight, he truly does speak English. He has lived and worked in America for more than twenty years. He has returned to his native land, and now has settled in this religious community for peace and quiet. He is a gentle, considerate person, and he explains much of what is a mystery to us.

We have arrived at what is known as the Skite Xenophontos. While not a true monastery, it is a sort of outstation from its parent monastery. Its job is to grow what it can for itself and its parent. Every place on this peninsula of Mount Athos, holds to the tradition of providing food and shelter for the night to any traveller arriving at their gate at dusk. With our immediate needs taken care of, we set about finding out as much as we can.

This peninsula of Mount Athos is a self-governing religious community of monasteries, dedicated to the Orthodox Faith, and set aside by Government decree, centuries ago. The governing body is made up of representatives from all the monasteries and they meet regularly in the only town on the peninsula, Karyes. The sole representative of the Greek Government in the place is a Policeman stationed in Karyes. He, generally, does not interfere with the comings and goings of anybody, but is there merely as a representative of law and order. In principle, we can go anywhere we like, but it may be prudent to steer clear of the town. Then the Policeman could turn a blind eye to the presence of escapees in the place.

No females are allowed on the Peninsula and this extends to animals too, particularly donkeys. They are the sole means of transport, other than on foot, and are responsible for those twisting, winding, single file tracks that go everywhere. There are no roads and no Germans. This is heartening news and makes us feel entirely safe. Even if the Germans change their policy, they would have to come after us on foot, and, we are completely confident of keeping out of their way.

The Orthodox faith is followed by quite a few countries with most of them having monasteries here. There are Greek, Russian, Romanian and Bulgarian ones, each run in their own way, but following the one religion. Of course, the Greeks are the predominant ones, and they caution us to steer clear of the Bulgarians, claiming that they cannot be trusted.

The reason for the Peninsula having become a sacred place and a Monastic centre is said to be because of a visit paid here by the Virgin Mary. She is said to have been on a sea voyage to Turkey when caught in a terrible storm. With the ship being in great danger of foundering, they manage to reach the shelter and haven of the Peninsula. In gratitude at their deliverance by God, Mary declared the place as sacred.

It seems a strange paradox to us that the place owes its existence to a female, yet now all females are banned. Still this is their way, and we are happy to accept it without question.

In peacetime, travellers regularly visit to view the valuable religious artefacts of gold, silver and precious gems, which are a feature of almost every monastery. These have now been carefully hidden away and will not reappear until peace is fully restored. These travellers would come by boat, landing at a Monastery on the south side in about the middle of the Peninsula. From here it is only a short journey by donkey across to Karyes. There are a small number of rooms for these few, but, in the main, visitors are not catered for.

The unique geography of the place, where the three Peninsulas thrust out from the Mainland like three fingers on a person's hand, make boats a much used method of moving around. With Mount Athos being the most northern finger and most developed, the focus of concentration is there. Every Monastery has its boats, and the Monks use them regularly to barter and trade. A major source of trade is a spirit, distilled here, called Raki. Alas! Practically all the boats have now disappeared, having been stolen or confiscated.

The islands, that can be seen from here, are straight ahead. To the east is Lemnos; then slightly left towards the north and a bit further away is the Turkish island of Imbros; then left again and much closer is Samothraki; and then left again and almost due north, and closest of all is Thasos. Imbros is the closest Turkish soil to us, and is about sixty to seventy miles by sea. It is also at the gateway to the Dardanelles. (Shades of Gallipoli) If we can reach there, we are home.

It is a very heady and exciting feeling to stand here in our sanctuary, gaze out across that short expanse of sea, and actually be able to view that bulk of land, where we can be totally and finally free. From our vantage point the water looks so calm, that we are certain we can get there by canoe if necessary.

Our former rather vague plans have now crystallised. Our destination is Imbros and, somehow, someway, we are going to get there by boat. We will just have to figure out the best method of getting a boat ourselves, or getting a boat owner to take us. In the meantime, we will stay here a few days, or until our welcome wears out, and sort out our ideas.

It is a very busy time here right now, with everybody working away to gather in and put down the harvest. We watch with interest their effective methods that are quite strange to us, such as the drying of figs. After gathering, they cut them in half, place them in trays with the flesh part exposed, then place them in the sun for drying. After a few days like this, they will be finished off with an hour in the baker's oven. This is after a bread baking and while the oven is cooling.

Of course, there are grapes to be picked and, as our English speaking friend is working here, we decide to also give a hand. We can converse with him, without taking him from his work.

The grapes are being made into wine and, for this purpose, they are brought by the barrowload to a huge deep wooden vat. A large wide plank is placed across the vat and one of the priests stands there in knee high leather boots. As each barrowload is tipped onto the plank, he stomps and crushes them, then kicks the whole lot into the vat below, stalks and all. To us, this seems primitive and not very effective, but we guess they have been at it long enough to know what they are doing.

They are touchingly grateful for our help in the picking, although we feel that our contribution is so minor as to be not worthy of comment.

The atmosphere is so friendly and helpful and, with the total acceptance of our presence here, one day just follows another, and there just doesn't seem any urgency to move on.

We always are shown a place to sleep each night. Always, it is spartan and rough as in all monasteries. We eat in a communal area with everybody else and, though the food is plain, it is plentiful. Each morning, we emerge to take in that incredible view along the ridge to that fantastic mountain, and to the islands beyond. Everything seems so idyllic that it is very tempting to just stay put, and wait for the War to end.

One evening, just after dark, lamps are lit, and we are all relaxing after the day's work. A Monk suddenly enters, bringing with him an obviously distressed, and almost exhausted, man. The newcomer is an Australian escapee, like ourselves. His small party is somewhere back along the trail, with one of them collapsed from a bad attack of malaria. This fellow has pushed on to try and get some help.

The Monks rally immediately. One of them is a big young strong and hearty man with jet black hair and a beard. He straightaway organises a donkey to fetch the sick man. With a lantern to light the way and a couple of helpers, they quickly set off. They return in about twenty minutes, and the man they bring with them certainly seems in a bad way. This big young Monk works vigorously, with quick bustling efficiency to treat the sick man.

Firstly, he sweeps clear a large table, and lays him full length upon his back. He strips him to the waist, and gathers up about a dozen glass tumblers and several candlelike tapers. Lighting a taper, he then plunges it into a tumbler and places it on the patient's body. The tumbler immediately sticks in place by the vacuum created, raising a lump of the man's flesh. With practiced skill, he does the same with another, and then another, until all the tumblers are spread out on parts of the patient's torso. When all are in place, he begins to rotate them, one after the other, onto other uncovered parts. He releases the tumbler, by placing two fingers of one hand next to the rim of the glass and pressing firmly—and, at the same time, he gently tilts the glass so that air pressure returns to normal. With the tumbler now free, he again plunges the taper in, and moves it to a new location.

He works swiftly for some time and we are fascinated. To me, it is akin to ancient medical practices that I have read about in school history books such as Cupping therapy. I cannot see any value in the treatment, but, not knowing any better, just have to hope it will be effective.

After about an hour the big fellow removes all the tumblers, wraps the patient well in rugs and beds him down for the night. It is a sobering sight to us and brings home how precarious our position is. If we get sick in any way, which would be fairly easy in the state we are in, we will just have to get well the best way we can. Or just die somewhere along the trail.

In the morning we are up early, anxious to see what the sick man's condition is. He has completely recovered. I am not convinced that this is because of the treatment. We have experienced malarial sickness which some men in our Unit were prone to. We know that an attack brings on high fever, and lays a man out. We also know that once an attack has run its course, a man can move around again, as if nothing has happened. We know too, that Greece is a high risk area. While back with our Unit, the appropriate treatment had always been forthcoming. The way things are here, we can only hope that it doesn't strike us.

With the advent of this new lot of escapees, we feel we ought to move on. We don't want to overstrain the resources of our friends and feel that this new lot need to stay put for a while to recover from their ordeal. Besides, we are too far away from the sea here, and, thus, have very little chance of locating a boat.

Announcing our intention, we say goodbye and thank them. They in turn heap us with advice. Their final warning is, "Beware of the Bulgarians." How we will do this, we do not know. In their Priestly garb, they all look alike. So, without warning, we won't know the difference.

Using a well-defined pathway, we plunge off the ridge to the north. This is the way that is the nearest to the sea and keeps us in sight of our objective. We keep going until, some hours later, we approach our first Monastery. Deeply interested, we study the layout of what is the norm in almost all of them.

There are cultivated areas outside the walls of an old time castle-like building. Close up, the Monastery, though substantial, has a slightly decayed and rundown look. There always is a substantial and large gateway leading into an inner courtyard. The gateway is guarded by a heavy wooden door that is closed at dusk, not to be opened until daylight.

The building itself is several storeys high, made of stone, plastered over, and painted white. Well above ground level, several narrow slits and apertures can be seen. One can almost imagine the presence of archers there, on watch to repel any would-be attackers. Obviously, they would have been a real threat when the place was first constructed. That accounts for its castle like appearance. Patches of plaster have peeled away, here and there, giving the building a slightly tattered appearance close up.

Every Monastery has a gatekeeper on duty, located in a tiny chamber on one side of the gate. His job is to watch for and greet any visitors. The ritual is always the same. From his vantage point, he can see anybody approaching well in advance. As you arrive, he meets you at the entrance, presents a tray upon which are two glasses for each visitor. One is a small nobbler size glass, containing a shot of Raki. The other is a standard size tumbler, threequarters full of plain water.

Smiling courteously he will offer the tray to each in turn. The guest takes up the tot of Raki first, toasts the Gatekeeper with, "Ya 'Sou", meaning, "Your health", toss the Raki down in one gulp, then replace the empty glass on the tray. At the same time he will grab the tumbler of water and quickly take a swig to dampen some of the fire.

Raki is a potent fiery spirit that takes a bit of getting used to. Its effect is an overall warm glow, and an instant feeling of wellbeing. For non-drinkers such as George and myself, it is a bit of an ordeal we feel we have to go through, if only to keep onside. While it is bad enough for me to take, it is doubly so for George. He finds it very hard. Maybe Taffy's tuition has had some effect on me after all.

Once this procedure has been followed, then food and somewhere to sleep for the night, soon is arranged. Food always is simple, with bread, black olives, cheese and fruit, being mostly the norm. Sleep, generally, is a corner somewhere on the floor of a room. Always, there are no frills.

Always, we establish who we are and ask for help in locating a boat to take us to Imbros. Always, we receive much sympathy and advice. But, alas, there simply aren't any boats. Maybe the next Monastery will be able to help us.

Day after day, we wander from place to place in this fashion. We visit Monastery after Monastery with strange and exotic names. There is Votopedi, Pantokratoras, Stavronikita, and the head Greek one, Iviron. Quite by chance, we happen to visit a Bulgarian one too. We find it much the same as the others, with nothing apparent to be mistrustful of. In fact, they warn us to be careful of the Greeks.

Then there are the Russian ones. These seem better laid out and newer than the others. This surprises us; there seems to be some support from their country for each Monastery, both in finance and personnel. With Russia, being so staunchly communist, we expected religious support to be totally nil.

From time to time, we come across other escapees on the same mission as ourselves. They seem to be settled in one place, just waiting for news of a boat to be brought to them. Two of these men are an odd pairing. One is a fairly affable Australian and the other a Kiwi, who is thoroughly objectionable. He tell us bluntly to "shove off" as they are expecting some developments any day, and he doesn't want bums like us hanging around, queering their pitch. We are only too happy to move on. The less we see of this bloke the better.

Our wanderings have taken us to a fair few of the Monasteries, by now, and we begin to backtrack and revisit some we have touched at before. We would like to have stayed in the one place, like some of the other escapees, and have the Monks make enquiries on our behalf. But, unless we are invited by them, we have no alternative but to move on. With this being the best plan we can come up with, all we can do is keep on going and hope for the best.

We revisit Pantokratoras where we are immediately recognised and welcomed as old friends. We have gone through the usual ceremony, and are being escorted into the inner courtyard, when, suddenly, a young Priest comes rushing up to us excitedly. He tells us that two boats are due to arrive at any moment and they are going to Turkey.

Our spirits soar, and we are beside ourselves. We will not move from here until these boatmen arrive. We will do our best to persuade them to take us too, as well as anyone else, they are coming for. "How soon will it be before they arrive?" we ask.

"In about two hours," says the young Priest.

Knowing the Greek penchant for embroidering a story, we can only hope that it isn't a false alarm. We are on tenterhooks while we wait, hopefully, but trying hard not to get too carried away. Suddenly, almost on time, the boats are here. There is a narrow opening in the seacoast that widens into a small boat harbour within the Monastery walls. The boats come through on a slight swell, close together, into the calm of the harbour.

They are between eighteen and twenty feet long, high ended, sturdy and look capable seaworthy boats. They are propelled by two oars and a small lug sail. The method of rowing is quite different to what we are used to. Where we sit on a seat and pull, here the rower stands and pushes.

There are two men in each boat. The eldest, and leader, is about twenty-five while the others are between seventeen and eighteen. I feel that the leader cannot be fully trusted, and that the others will follow his lead whatever. Then I realise that this is to be an illegal enterprise, and these blokes are in it for whatever profit they can get. They will be taking some pretty hefty risks, so maybe, they are the right people after all.

As soon as they step ashore, we tell them we are English and wish to go to Turkey. "Can you take us?"

"Certainly," says the leader, while the others gather round nodding in agreement.

We tell them that if they get us through, our government will pay them well for their trouble. We have no idea if this is so, but we decide to meet that problem when the time comes. The only things we still have left of any value are my pocket watch, with a silver chain attached, and my gold ring tied in a knot on one end. I will produce these as our bona fides at the appropriate time, but not just yet. We have no money of any kind.

I thank my lucky stars for having the foresight to hang onto my ring, after that disastrous bread trading business back at Salonika No. 2 transit camp. My fingers are too thin to wear it, and I have prudently kept it out of sight all this time. Currency is virtually of no value here, but anything gold is tangible, and has more trading clout than almost anything else.

Now that these boatmen have confirmed we are to be part of the party, we ask them when they are to leave. They say as soon as they have contacted the rest of the people they have come for, probably sometime tomorrow. There are no supplies of any kind in the boats, and I get the impression that this is their first attempt at this sort of thing.

So this is the position. We have to decide whether to put our trust in a group of not too trustworthy, first time up, would be smugglers. I feel dubious, but realise that we don't have much alternative. We just have to take this chance. We have been roaming about here long enough to know that it is almost impossible to get a boat, and now, here are two. Of course, whoever the others are, whom the boatmen have come for, may cause us difficulties. They may flatly refuse to allow us to accompany them. We will just have to wait and see. I just hope that that objectionable Kiwi is not one of them.

With the boats safely tied up, the boatmen set off, accompanied by a couple of Priests, to make contact with the group they have come for. Of course, we tag along too. Now that we have been accepted as part of the party, at least for a moment, we are determined to make sure not to be left out of the negotiations.

From our observations, it is obvious that these boatmen have come from some distance away, and have been recruited in some way. Messages have been sent out by the ruling Priestly body, and these fellows have responded. This makes us feel better. We feel that somehow this is, more or less, an officially sanctioned operation.

We have been walking for about twenty minutes when we meet a group of about eight or ten coming towards us. Three or four of them are Priests while the others are civilians, probably prospective passengers.

Everybody stops and gathers round, and there is a great deal of talking between the leader of the boatmen and some of the newcomers. One of the Priests seems to preside and appears to be a man of some standing. Three men, reasonably dressed in suits, and obviously Greek, have a fair bit to say too. Another man puts in a word from time to time, but is either leaving the negotiations to others, or having a little difficulty following what is being said. It gradually dawns on me that this man is one of our own kind.

With all the preliminaries settled, the whole party sets off again towards the direction from which the others had come, with us somewhere near the rear. We have been walking for about ten minutes when the man, whom I suspect of being a fellow escapee, suddenly turns back to us and shakes us warmly by the hand.

He apologises for not having recognised us, but says he truly thought we were Greeks and part of the boat party, until the boatmen disclosed who we are. He is an Englishman named, Bob Montefiore, and we are now on our way to meet up with the rest of his party to finish plans for our departure. They have been staying in a place that is away from the Monastery proper, while arrangements for a boat have been going on. They have been there for the best part of a fortnight. The three men in suits are Greek Army Officers and there are three Englishmen, plus Bob and two Cypriots.

We talk animatedly as we walk along, with Bob remarking that the boatmen look rather a villainous lot. But he feels that this is all to the good for our enterprise. He says also that, while he can't speak much Greek, he can speak French, as can one of the Greek Officers. This manages to get pretty good understanding among everybody.

We arrive at the rendezvous with the rest of the party, and now the financial arrangements are discussed. Apparently, this has been worked out in advance with Bob's party and the Greek Officers, who produce a fairly large wad of Greek banknotes. With this open show of payment, it is now time for me to declare my hand. I produce my watch and ring. I say that it is a payment for George and me, and it will be handed over at Imbros.

The boat leader takes hold of my offering and examines it minutely. With his inspection done, he hands them back and nods his head in agreement. He seems more impressed with my offering than the display of banknotes.

Now that we have been accepted as part of the group, all that is needed is to arrange the time and place of departure. It will be tomorrow afternoon at an inlet, just down from and close to where Bob's party are staying. The Monks, who hail from the head Greek Monastery of Iviron, will provision us and see us off. In the meantime, Bob's party will stay where they are. George and I accompany the boatmen to Pantokratoras where the boats are. We, the boats and Bob's party, will all assemble at the cove at the appointed time tomorrow. Then it will be all aboard, and we will be on our way.

We are bubbling with excitement as we return to the boats, and impatient to get going. Already we can see ourselves returning to our Unit and our mates. What a surprise they will get when we turn up! And what a chiacking we will get, for having dawdled so long! They will give us good-natured hell, and we will love every minute of it.

Somehow we get through the night, and are astir early next morning. George and I have a few chores to do and, as the boatmen aren't going anywhere, we tell them we will leave our swags with them until we get back. They readily agree that it will be okay.

We return in about half an hour, and can see instantly that something has been going on in our absence. There are knowing smirks from the young blokes between themselves, and the head boatman has made a not too successful attempt at shaving himself. Although obviously pleased with the result, there are three or four fairly severe snicks that have drawn blood.

I know straight away that they have rifled our swags. One of the very few possessions I still have is a safety razor which we use very sparingly, trying to make it last. They have no possessions, so it has to be my razor he uses for his shave.

We quickly go through our gear to see what is missing. There is precious little in there at the best of times, other than a small store of bread we hoard for emergencies. Most of the bread is gone, but the razor has been returned. I get a little satisfaction to see that, of three or four blades I still have, he has chosen the bluntest one. Thankfully, I am carrying my watch and ring on my person.

We are not in a position to create much of a fuss over this incident. We need them too badly for that. We just repack our swags and sit a little apart from them. We say nothing, but they know that we know, what they have been up to. There is a wary sort of truce between us, until the time comes to move the boats round to the meeting place.

We climb aboard for the short trip round to the cove. We can see that they know their stuff and can handle the boats well. The others are ready and waiting when we pull in and, now, there is feverish activity while we are ready to depart. Several Monks come scurrying down with large wicker baskets filled with food. It needs two of them to each basket. Two baskets are placed in each boat. The whole group is divided so that the head boatman plus one youngster have the three Greek Officers, plus Bob and another Englishman in their boat. In the other boat are two boatmen, two Cypriots, two Englishmen, George and me.

Once aboard we waste no time. We push off while waving goodbye to those very helpful Monks. The weather is fine, the sea calm, and it is about three o'clock in the afternoon. Just before we step on board, the head boatman asks me to let him have my watch so that he can plot the course. He says not to worry as it will be safe in his possession. I know it is possible to use a watch for this purpose, and I also know that it is just a ploy, on his part, to get the watch and ring in his hands.

They plan to head openly for Lemnos which will attract little or no attention as it is part of Greece. Then, under the cover of darkness, they will slip away from Lemnos and make a run for Imbros. This is a run of twenty minutes to half an hour under favourable conditions. With both islands clearly in view from Athos, it obviously is quite unnecessary for any course plotting at all.

He makes his request quite openly in front of the others, and I hesitate, for only a moment, before handing it over. Of course, I could have untied the ring from its knot in the chain and kept it with me. But such a gesture at this time would have been unseemly. It is more fitting to show goodwill from the start of our journey. I plan to give them to him anyway. Now, instead of me carrying them, he will.

With the headman's boat leading, and ours close behind, we soon move clear of the land. There is practically no wind and our sail just hangs loosely. With an almost flat sea, the rowing is relatively easy. At first, the boatmen do the rowing, while we study how it is done. When it is our turn, we all want to appear authentic, in case we are under observation. We knot a handkerchief round our head in the Greek style, so as to complete the picture. Those of us not rowing sit at the bottom of the boat, to keep as much out of sight as possible.

With everyone willing and eager, there are no arguments about taking a turn on the oars. When mine comes, I find their stand-up and push style much easier than our own. As soon as the two boatmen are relieved, they go straight to the provision baskets, pick up a piece of whatever is on top and start eating. In the Greek way it quickly disappears, and they promptly return and select another piece and then another. They keep this up constantly.

We others, of course, know it will be prudent to eat sparingly and conserve what we have. But we are too excited and keyed up to worry much about food ourselves. We feel we cannot deny them their indulgence. There are areas where food is scarce and, maybe, they have come from such a place. There must be drastic hardships of some kind to induce them to take on this kind of risky business. Anyway, it is their boat and we are only the passengers.

The breeze stays away, so, we row the rest of that day, all that night, and all the next day. Just on dusk, we arrive on the west side of Lemnos. So far, we have seen nothing or nobody else for the whole journey. The two boats move to a spot near the bottom tip of the island to wait until midnight, when we will make our dash across to Imbros. Our course will be northeast, and we will be in Turkey well before daylight.

Little is said, and then almost in whispers, as we wait for the time to slowly tick away. It is almost as if we fear that someone will hear us and stop us at this late stage. The boatmen predict that a good breeze will spring up and whip us across without any necessity to row.

Finally, it is time and we move away from the lee of the island. We can feel the breeze and it is strong. In fact, it is too strong. It quickly becomes a gale with a heavy sea running. It is dead against us and, clearly, we have no hope of being able to go on.

We had, at first, welcomed the prospect of a bit of weather, as it would make it easier for us to slip through without being seen. But, the treacherous speed and fierceness, with which this has developed, has caught us completely unawares.

Luckily, we have just cleared Lemnos and are still very close when we have to turn back. To turn around in such a heavy strong sea is an extremely tricky and dangerous manoeuvre. Firstly, the leader's boat makes a turn, and quickly shoots away with the full force of the gale now on his stern. Now it is our turn.

The young lad steering gives all his attention to the wave movement, biding his time to pick the right moment. Every second now the wind force is increasing and the waves getting higher. Suddenly he makes his move. He has timed it so as to use the wave force to turn the boat quickly. For an agonising second, we are broadside to the sea and completely helpless. Then the powerful waves swing the nose round, and we are flying back to Lemnos. In the process we have copped a little bit of slop over the side, but nothing to speak of.

Now, all we have to do is pick a safe anchorage in the lee of the island. This is done without much trouble, and we are all glad to postpone our dash for freedom, at least for another night. The leader's boat has picked a different anchorage, but this doesn't bother us. We will make contact again after daybreak. As soon as we tie up, the lot of us praise our young steersman highly for the skill he has shown. We all know that our safety is due entirely to his judgement. If he had erred, none of us would have survived.

When daylight comes, we set out to see where the others are. They have found a small cove similar to ours, about ten minutes' walk away. We decide to each stay where we are. We will be less conspicuous apart than with us both together. We will keep in constant touch and be on the lookout for anybody nosing around. With the weather remaining bad, and not knowing for how long, for the moment we feel relatively safe.

Food, or the lack of it, now becomes a problem. The baskets of provisions, we have brought from Athos, are practically all gone, thanks mainly to the onslaught of the boatmen. With our large party, we will have to try to do something about it. Our two Cypriots volunteer to explore the area a little to see if they can line up anything. We count ourselves lucky to have them with us, as this is their part of the world and they can move about with impunity.

While they are away, we take stock of our surroundings. There is high ground behind us and rocky outcrops all around. We are able to keep the boat under observation as well as any approach to our position. At the same time, we can slip away virtually unseen if we have to. We have no idea what attitude the locals may have toward us, but feel it prudent to be careful. Anyway, we plan to be on our way as soon as possible.

The Cypriots return to tell us that the high ground levels off into bare undulating country, suitable for sheep and goats to graze. It is split up with deep gullies, twisting and turning about, with narrow tracks formed by the animals. At the top, and a short distance in from the coast, there is a solitary farmhouse. With the family, who live there, they have negotiated the purchase of a goat. They will slaughter and cook it up for us, and we will all assemble there at dusk for the feast.

One of the Poms from our boat sets off to inform the others what we have lined up. When they join us at dusk, we will all go off together to eat. The Pom returns to tell us that the others will join us for sure, except perhaps for their boatmen. They have set off afoot into town to see what they can line up in the way of food. Nobody has any way of knowing when they will be back, but, with their boat still there, we aren't greatly worried.

The others join us at dusk, as promised, and tell us that their boatmen have still not returned. With their cove completely deserted, other than for themselves, they tie their boat securely and are certain it will be safe until their return, even though nobody is guarding it. Their boatmen will have to get by with whatever food they can scrounge for themselves, or go without.

In our case, we just make sure that our boat is secure too. The cove we have selected is fairly wide and deserted like the other, except for a lone boat some distance away. This other boat is identical to our own and appears to be sheltering from the weather, as we are. They are a bit too far away to worry about, and we ignore them while they ignore us. Our boatmen are quiet and seemingly a bit concerned about their comrades. Other than that, they pass no remarks.

When we get to the farmhouse, we find the meat cooking away in a boiler on a fire in the open. We all settle down in a circle around the fire, waiting for the pronouncement that it is ready to eat. Our party is too large to fit inside the house, so we will eat outside. At the same time, the farmer and his interested family join us, bringing with them bread and cheese and some liquor.

It is a fairly happy little party that sit and eat and laugh and talk. It must be about nine o'clock and completely dark by the time we finish eating. Our farmer friends suggest it will be a bit dangerous for us to try and make our way back over unfamiliar ground. Close by, there is a fair sized cavern that the animals often use as a shelter. We may use that for the night and he will provide a large rug to keep out the cold. We can then return to our camp in daylight.

This seems a sensible idea and we are happy to accept. He leads us to the cave which proves to be everything he says it is. It is large and roomy and effectively shuts out the cold night wind. The very large and heavy homespun rug is big enough for most of us to get under, provided we crowd together. With our boatmen claiming the sea is still running too high for us to make another attempt for Imbros tonight, this is as good a place as any.

There is only one problem and we do not find out about it until we enter the cave and try to bed down. The whole place is wall to wall fleas. We try to ignore them, but they refuse to be ignored. Some of the fellows cannot stand it and choose to stay out in the open. Towards the early hours of the morning, it grows bitterly cold and they creep back just inside the entrance. Sitting and scratching, with little thought of sleep, we spend a most miserable night. We are thoroughly glad to make our way back to our camp as soon as it is light enough.

Bob and his mate, and the three Officers, go back to their position to stand by their boat, which is still safely tethered. Our two boatmen, concerned at the non-appearance of their two comrades, announce they will go and look for them. They promise to bring some food back as well. With our boat safely tethered also, and that other boat still sheltering further up the cove, the scene is exactly the same as we had left it. We are not greatly concerned about the boatmen while the two boats remain with us. If the weather is good enough tonight, we will make the attempt to Imbros, with or without them.

We are laying back at our leisure, basking in some early morning sunshine, and recovering from our miserable night. Then we hear the unmistakable sound of a boat engine. As the area is totally isolated, except for ourselves, we know immediately that this sound has to have great significance for us.

From our excellent cover we are able to observe quite clearly. A Greek Caique with a German flag flying from its stern, still some distance out at sea, is heading straight in towards our position. Knowing that we are reasonably safe in our position, we watch intently for whatever is about to unfold. The Caique noses into our little cove, standing just off some rocks, while a couple of German soldiers jump ashore. They nose around the shoreline briefly. Apparently satisfied, they climb aboard again. But while doing so, they untie our boat and fasten it to the stern of the Caique, taking it in tow. They head straight out to sea again and, once clear of land, head back along the coast.

This behaviour completely mystifies us. If this is a routine patrol, confiscating unattended boats, why the hell have they ignored the other boat which is in plain sight up the cove? It seems ominous and we don't like it. Also, we have now lost one of our boats. As soon as the Germans disappear, we decide to find out whatever we can about the other boat.

We find that it is manned by a couple of ordinary Greeks who claim to be going to Turkey. Like us, they are sheltering, awaiting for the weather to abate. Will they be prepared to take us with them? Certainly, they will be glad to, as soon as the weather is clear.

Well, we have lost one boat, but manage to replace it with another. Somewhat mollified, we return to our former position, prepared to wait for the signal to go. These other boatmen are aiming to try and obtain some commodities that are becoming very scarce in Greece. In short, they are trying to do a little bit of smuggling. As such, they are ideal for our purpose. These blokes are older, more experienced, and also seem more trustworthy than our blokes.

We have just sorted our situation out, and are settling down again, when Bob and his mate come scrambling over the rocky outcrops from their position. That damn Caique has carried out the same manoeuvre and confiscated their boat. Again, a couple of Germans have stepped ashore, nosed about briefly, stepped back aboard and, at the same time, tying Bob's party's boat to the stern. They have sailed off without a backward glance.

Well, we still have one boat we feel we can rely on. If worse comes to worse, we will all sail in that. It does seem as if the Caique is on a routine patrol, just picking up unattended boats. But there is still that nagging doubt about this other boat further up the cove. Why have the Germans made no approach to that one at all? There is always the chance, too, that our boatmen might return, find their boats confiscated, and be able to go to the authorities and reclaim them.

We are mystified and rather worried, but feel we have to stick things out and see what develops. If only the sea would abate enough for us to make our dash. For the couple of days we have been here on the leeward side of Lemnos, the weather has been quite reasonable. But, clear of land, the sea is running high and dangerous.

The three Greek Officers are still back at their camp above where their boat had been tied. Bob and his mate return there to let them know what is proposed, and he will stay with them. It will be prudent to keep the actual size of the party, proposing to make the trip to Imbros, quiet from these new boatmen for the moment. Although separated and out of sight of each other, we can quickly join together if need be.

We keep a good sharp lookout for the rest of the day, but nothing untoward happens. There are intricate mazes of twisting, winding gullies behind us, and we plan to slip away, in the event of any threat to us from the seaward side.

Next morning at the very crack of dawn, we are awakened by the ominous sound of a Caique motor. Springing to our feet we see it, with its German flag at the stern, heading straight out to sea from our little cove. We know that it has already nosed into the shore. That means that, almost certainly, it has landed a patrol and we had better get moving.

We grab our few possessions and prepare to move away from the threat. While we are completely hidden from them, our position is such that we can see them quite clearly. There are, in fact, two patrols, each of about ten men. They have been landed at separate points, and each is making its way slowly towards us. While they are apart, they are maintaining about the same rate of progress. We can see them picking their way, rather slowly it seems, over the rather rocky ground just in from the shore. We are at a loss to account for the slowness of their progress. Often we are able to stand still for what seems minutes at a time, while keeping them in sight. They still haven't seen us, but are converging on where we have been. Obviously, they know where to look.

We see one of them, who appears to be an Officer, raise his arm in the air. From his raised hand comes a flash of light and an object flies up into the air. It is a flare. He has fired a Very pistol as a signal to someone.

We understand immediately what has happened. First, they have landed a patrol further along the coast to cut across inland, and get into position behind us. This is the reason they have only been dawdling along. This means that the unseen patrol, almost certainly, has landed in Bob's cove. If they have been caught napping then, almost certainly, they have been captured. At best, Bob's party will now be on the run. We have almost been caught napping ourselves and, in the confusion, have no time to warn Bob's lot.

We curse the Germans for their Teutonic thoroughness. Our attempts at secrecy are now blown. All we can do is make a run for it. They have the high ground while we will have to rely on those twisting turning gullies to prevent them getting a clear shot at us. Initially, we just take off in a dead run, but we quickly realise that this will be a test of endurance. We ease back on the pace a little, trying to conserve our strength. From the heights, they have now caught sight of us, and pound along in our wake.

We had thought previously that we could easily keep out of their way, without them knowing of our presence, just by keeping down in the gullies. If they had not been told that there are escapees about, this plan probably may have worked. Now, the plan seems as much a hindrance as a help.

On the commanding high ground, where they are, the land is fairly smooth with a finely grazed cover of pasture. From the high ground, the land falls steeply for about a hundred feet to the bottom of a gully where we are. The floor of each gully varies from two to three feet wide, before rising just as sharply on the other side. Covering the gully floors is small flow of water a few inches deep, as well as protruding rocks, large and small. Underfoot, the going is loose and stony. We have the advantage of the twists and turns, whereas they have the advantage of the smooth going.

All we can do is pound along and concentrate on our footing. The narrowness of the gullies forces us to move in single file, with George and I keeping together at the tail. Each of us now is too busy with his own plight to give much thought to the others.

From time to time, a shot or two is fired in our direction. I'm not too sure whether they are trying to hit someone or just hurrying us along. I have this feeling of being herded and that the gullies might cut out into flat country somewhere ahead. I begin to worry that some of us may be hit from a ricochet off the rocks, even though they may not intend to hit anyone. The thought of having to cope with a wound is just too hard to imagine. This worry gives me the idea to feign being shot, in the hope they will come down in the gully, looking for a wounded man. Such a ruse might even buy enough time for us to get away.

As the next bullet hits somewhere close to me, I suddenly throw my hands in the air and collapse in a heap beside a large boulder. My acting must have been realistic, for George halts, immediately, and runs back to me. He bends over me and says, "God, I thought you'd been hit."

I say, "Good, that's what I want them to think, too."

This little charade puts us out of their sight and we are able to move away again, without being seen. As we keep on running, we listen for any sounds to indicate if the Germans have fallen for it. But they have taken no notice and keep on with the chase.

By now we are feeling pretty distressed. Our physical condition has been poor for a long while. We have moved some distance away from the coast and have no idea what to expect in front of us. If these gullies do peter out, then we are sitting ducks.

As we pound along, my mind is racing, trying to think of a way out of our predicament. I say, "George, we can't keep this going much longer. We've got to find a hidey hole of some sort and lie low until they've gone." He agrees. But, with not much hope of success, we keep searching as we run.

Suddenly I spot a thin upright cleft in a rock outcrop that can only be seen from the gully bottom. It is about four feet high and about nine inches wide. And we may have missed it, if we had not been searching so desperately. Telling George to follow, I make a dive for it to see if it will suit our purpose. It is about six feet up the hillside from the gully bottom, and, to inspect it will use up valuable time. But we are desperate and take the chance. From dead in front, it doesn't look much, but I force my way in. It goes straight for about two feet, then turns at right angles to open into a quite roomy chamber or cavern.

It is a miracle. We could not have hoped to find anything as near as perfect as this. From right in front it looks unusable. We are sure the Germans will be unable to work out where we have disappeared to. Trying to control our tortured breathing, we stay perfectly still, waiting for them to pass.

After what seems like an age, they go noisily past without stopping. We feel safe for a moment, but realise they will backtrack, once they wake up to the fact that some of us are missing. We just hope the others will keep them busy enough to get them well clear of this area.

With a bit more time to think, we take stock to work out what we will do. We will stay put until dark, then try to find somebody friendly. We will need help to continue to hide, and search for food. On a small island, things will be much tighter than on the mainland where we can move about freely. If need be, we will just have to steal a boat to get to Imbros.

I discuss with George the real possibility of our recapture. We realise that we will have to go through some interrogation and we resolve not to do anything that may make it any rougher than necessary. If we have anything incriminating, now is the time to dispose of it.

All we have is that letter from the Greek schoolteacher for his son in Egypt. I pull it out and fold it into as small a package as I can. I find a thin crevice, about head high, hidden behind a small stone. I force the letter into it and replace the stone. We then settle down to wait.

A short time later, we hear the sound of several people approaching. We hold our breath until they go past. Instead, they stop right outside and a German voice calls out, "Come out with your hands up."

We cannot believe it. We are sure they would not have found us. Now they have walked straight up to our hideout. It is almost as if somebody has told them where to find us. Crestfallen, we squeeze our way out and put our hands up. There are three or four German soldiers facing us, with Tommy guns at the ready. Blinking a little, after coming into the sunlight again, we glance further up the hillside. Just above us and looking down, watching interestedly, stands an elderly Greek shepherd leaning on his long wooden staff. We cannot be sure, but, almost certainly, it is he who has told the Germans where to look.

Our captors motion us along and we head back towards the coast. At least they don't attempt to search our cave. If the shepherd also doesn't, then our hidden letter will be safe. They move us up to the high ground where the going is much easier. We mooch along feeling very subdued and saying nothing. As we near the coast, the farmhouse, where we had eaten our meal, comes into view. The direction, we are heading, will take us right past the front door. I am worried as to what might happen, for they had been our innocent helpers. If the Germans suspect them, reprisals can be particularly brutal.

As we near the house, the whole family can be seen lined up across the doorway. The abject terror written across their faces is so patently obvious that I truly believe the Germans must realise that they have in some way been involved.

What can I do to take the heat off? All I can think of, is to verbally abuse them in English, as if we have never ever been anything but enemies. This I do, only to see their look change from one of terror, to shock and the disbelief. Our captors march steadily on and totally ignore them. I have no way of knowing if my tirade has any affect at all. I just feel I have to try something. I am just scared that the Germans might confront the Greeks and us with each other, and start shooting.

We now begin to descend to the beach area of our little cove. The Caique with its German flag is tied up there and a fair number of soldiers are busying themselves round about. We are motioned to an area on one side, about fifty feet from the shoreline. We can see a lone figure standing there and, as we get closer, we can see that it is Bob. We feel a bit better in knowing that somebody else also shares our misery. We immediately ask what has happened to his group, to find that it is much the same, except they had been caught napping.

All were scattered about in various sleeping positions, and the patrol had just walked onto them. The two youngest Greek Officers had been caught first. They then pointed out where the others were sleeping. Bob and his mate had by this time become aware of the danger, and witnessed this betrayal. Bob was most upset at their conduct. So, the two of them had to make a run for it. Bob was quickly caught, but his mate got away. The patrol left one man behind to escort Bob back to the beach, while the rest carried on. With Bob standing to one side, the German bent down to search Bob's gear for weapons. With one against one, Bob decided to have a go for freedom.

He aimed a solid kick to the German's head with his heavy Army boot, in a bid to knock him unconscious. The German spotted the kick almost at the last moment, grabbed Bob's foot, twisting Bob off balance and throwing him to the ground. The German instantly had his bayonet out, with the point poised just inches from Bob's eyes.

Bob instantly gave up the struggle and, for a long moment, remained in this position. Then the German got up and motioned Bob to rise. When he had done so, the German directed him towards the shore, where they reached without further incident.

Bob points out to us the German concerned, and says he has made no move to retaliate. He thinks the Germans have accepted it as a natural reaction, and will let it go at that. George and I are a bit alarmed though, after deciding not to attempt anything like that ourselves. We can only hope the interrogation will not turn nasty.

Of the two boat loads that set out from Athos, only one Pom is still free from Bob's boat, while two Poms and two Cypriots are free from ours. The Germans have recaptured the three Greek Officers, Bob, and George and myself. We don't hold out much hope for the Poms, but feel that the two Cypriots may easily melt into the background. The likely success ratio of our bid for freedom looks pretty sick.

It is mid-afternoon before everybody is reassembled, and we are motioned aboard for the short trip back to port. We three are kept together on a portion of the boat, while there is no sign of the three Greek Officers. We are free to talk but keep it quiet, realising a nearby German, keeping an eye on us, almost certainly speaks English.

Our main concern is to make sure we all tell the same tale when the questioning starts. We really have very little to conceal. Bob has managed a word with the older of the Greek Officers, and he is adamant that our boatmen have gone to the authorities, and informed on us. We only hope that the involvement of the Monks and Athos can be kept quiet. But this information about the boatmen makes us feel uneasy, that the Germans already know about their connection.

It is only a short trip back to the port area of what appears to be a fair sized town. We presume it is the main town on Lemnos. We are marched off to a large headquarters building which is several storeys high. While there is no sign of the Greek Officers, we three are each put in separate rooms on the second floor.

My room is completely bare and fairly large. With the ground floor fully occupied and manned by German administrative services and, with their soldiers coming and going all the time, it is a very effective prison, even without bars.

We are given no food, just locked in solitary confinement and left to our own bitter thoughts. Slowly, the light fades until it becomes properly dark. With nothing better to do, I curl up in a corner on the bare wooden floor. Using my trusty jacket as a blanket, I try to sleep. With nobody to talk to, I am feeling pretty low and miserable.

In the morning, a Sentry unlocks the door and, telling me to come, herds me down and outside to the washing area. It is a trough with several taps over it, and seems similar to the standard schoolyard setup. George and Bob are brought down, too. We are able to have a bit of a natter together, before being returned to our rooms. This makes us feel a bit better and brightens us up a bit.

Next we are given coffee and a portion of bread. With something in our bellies at last, we feel better able to face whatever the day may bring. It is midmorning when my door is opened again, and a party of three or four enter. The leader is an Officer with the rank of about the equivalent of our Major. He begins talking to me in perfect English. Obviously the interrogation is about to begin.

I had expected that we would be taken, one at a time, to a sort of courtroom atmosphere and strongly questioned. Maybe a bit of force would be used. But this is rather mild, with the Major, proud of his fluent English, asking questions almost in a conversational manner.

After the preliminaries of name and number etc., his main point of interest is, where we had departed from. Although I am certain they already have this information from the boatmen, I have no intention of confirming it, if I can avoid it.

I wish to appear to cooperate as much as possible so that things don't turn nasty, yet without really saying anything. As his English is so perfect, I am at a loss as to how I can achieve this. Then it dawns on me that this is the answer. I can reply to his questions in an English, he can't understand.

His English is almost faultlessly scholarly English, and I judge he has probably spent some years in England at a place of learning, most likely at a University. If I reply in Aussie slang, almost certainly he won't understand.

Dropping into Aussie vernacular I say, "Look mate. I'm Australian. I come from the other side of the world. I don't know a thing about these parts. I haven't a clue where we left from. All I know, it is somewhere on the coast, with a bit of a hill on one side, and there didn't seem to be anybody else about."

The Major just looks at me for a long moment without speaking. Then he turns round, and the whole party walks out. I am nonplussed. I had expected a bit more probing than this. I cannot believe they will let things drop this easily. Now, I begin to worry that, maybe, I have been a bit too smart. I am left alone for the rest of the day, and can only wonder what the others have said, and how they fared. If only, we can get together and compare notes.

With nothing better to do, I spend most of my time staring out of the large windows of my room. I have been warned to stay clear of them, but feel, that if I keep about a foot away, I should be pretty safe. If I think I can hear anybody at my locked door, I quickly move further back into the room, before the door can be opened.

I can see a road leading out into fairly open country, with a lot of going and coming of Greek civilians. Next door is a large school, with the playground coming right up to the walls of my building. During recess the kids of all sizes are running about, playing games and calling to each other as kids do anywhere. I get a fair bit of pleasure out of being able to watch these activities. By doing so, I feel I am able to beat the solitary confines of my prison.

A day or two later there is a rattling at the door, and I move quickly to the centre of the room. Once again, the Major and his entourage enter and he comes straight to the point. "Ah," he says, "The Monks. What can you tell me about the Monks?"

I try to stall, and then reply, "Monks? What do you mean Monks?"

He immediately becomes irritable, and keeps repeating, "The Monks—You know—The Monks?"

It is just a reflex action on my part to pretend not to know what he means by Monks. I have sought to gain some time to gather my wits. Now, that I see him nonplussed, I determine to hold out as long as I can before claiming that, we Australians know them only as Priests.

His English is very good, but when it comes to explaining to me what a Monk is, he is gone. I continue to look dumb, and keep on with my ploy of not understanding. Finally I say, "Monks? I know monkeys, but I don't know Monks." Immediately, he blows up, turns on his heels, and storms out of my room with the whole party following.

I am left there wondering if I have had a small victory, or will be made to suffer for it later. Bob, whose room apparently is next to mine, is quite taken aback when the Major charges in and says, "I suppose you know nothing about the monkeys either?"

This is the full extent of our questioning on Lemnos. Our diet has developed into a wedge of bread, and a fair supply of drinking water each day. It is depressing and totally inadequate, but we are in no position to complain.

My window gazing has caught the attention of some twelve to fourteen year old kids in the playground below. A group of about eight of them will gather and stare up at me during recess, and I begin to signal back to them.

I have just received my daily ration, one day, when it becomes their recess time. The kids gather below and look up at my window. I show them my wedge of bread and, with much gesticulation and waving of hands, I manage to make them understand that this is all I get to eat each day.

They immediately go into a huddle, and there is much animated talk among themselves. They look up at me and wave from time to time, then it is class time again.

Next day, about midmorning the Major comes in and orders me to stay away from the window, or I will be shot. The kids had gathered a parcel of foodstuffs from their homes, and a delegation have asked permission to give it to me.

The Germans are acutely embarrassed when the kids present themselves, and do not know how to handle it. I think they are trying to maintain an outwardly friendly appearance to the locals and, while they can be firm with the adults, kids are a different matter. Needless to say, I receive none of their food.

One day, at ration time, a whole new procedure takes place. Instead of the usual bread, a couple of orderlies march in with a steaming Dixie and begin to dish up some soup. It is a thick creamy yellow type, somewhat like pea soup. I take to it with relish, and am pleased to find that I can back up for more, when I finish the first lot.

Then the Major walks in and offers me some cigarettes. I decline and explain that I am a non-smoker. He chats pleasantly for a while. He seems a pretty decent bloke. It just happens that we are on opposite sides. Emboldened, I ask if our diet is now to take a turn for the better.

"Certainly not,' he says, "We are being fed this way, only because it is Sunday."

We have been in custody on the island for about a week, when we are ordered out. This time we are all together again, and are marched under escort, down to the wharf area. We have a happy and animated time, talking our heads off and generally letting off steam. It seems our journey back is about to begin.

We are joined there by the three Greek Officers, who had been held somewhere else. We are put aboard a Caique, which is making ready to leave. There is a large contingent of soldiers also on board. It seems that they have been relieved, and are now returning to Salonika or wherever. We are just part of the cargo.

We are ordered into the diesel motor compartment. The engine takes up most of this small space, with just sufficient room for a man to move round its four sides. We six are crammed into this small space, with no room to sit or lie down. There is some consolation as the weather is cold and, in our half-starved state, we feel it keenly. The warmth from the motor is very welcome, but the one drawback are the fumes.

We get underway and quickly leave the shelter of the land, and enter into the open sea. The weather is still bad and, with medium to high waves running, there is a fair amount of pitching and tossing. Our boat is sturdy and I have no fears for our safety, but the fumes start to make me feel queasy. No bad weather of any kind has been able to upset me before, but the way I feel now, I just have to go up on deck and hang over the rail.

There is no opposition to my coming up on deck, and it is completely apparent why. Practically every German aboard is lined along the rail, heaving his insides out. I get a lot of satisfaction at their distress. As for myself, as soon as my head comes in contact with the clean salt air, it clears itself up. I am able to return to my position, and suffer no further discomfort.

We have a stop along the way at some small port to give the Germans a bit of relief from their ordeal. There is a Greek boat alongside us with bunches of onions hanging from its rigging. I ask a man aboard to give me one, which he does, subject to inspection by a suspicious guard, of course. I eat it like an apple, and it is the only time in my life I have been able to do so.

Every moment of our return journey is making me more and more depressed. All I can think of is how hard we had battled to get as far as we had, and how quickly we are being brought back to our starting point.

At Salonika we disembark and stand disconsolately on the wharf. Again the Greek Officers are to go to a different destination to us. This time will be the last we see of them. Escort parties are waiting for us both. The one for the Englanders moves across, and orders the Greek Officers to come with them. But the boat's Escort intervenes, and tells them they have the wrong lot. The Greek Officers are reasonably dressed, while we are ragged, dirty and look like ruffians. They have thought that no Englishman could look as bad as we do.

With the confusion sorted out, we are marched away to Gestapo headquarters. We are too low to worry much about what might happen there. None of us has any illusion about being able to withstand any solid questioning. We arrive to find it a very busy afternoon. There are lots of Greek civilians waiting to be processed, and from the inner room comes the sound of much shouting and bellowing. The Greeks are all peasant types and carry their belongings in a swag. They are made to leave their swags behind while in the inner room, and there is a great pile just outside the door. The interrogation seems to accept that these are people of no great consequence, and it concentrates on intimidating them and sending them on their way.

Our escort manages to break into the proceedings and gets us processed quickly. We are marched in and subjected to the same shouting and waving, and marched out again. Our escort tells us to pick up our swags and be on our way. All our belongings have long since gone, so none of us have a swag. George is the only one of us with sense enough to seize the opportunity to steal one.

Another short march and we are there. Dead in front of us is Salonika No. 1 Transit camp for POWs.

# CHAPTER 11

# Escape No. 2, again in Greece

It is with very mixed feelings that we again enter the gates of Salonika No. 1 POW Camp. The Administrative Block is in a long large building, just inside, and to the right of the entrance. Our escort delivers us here and leaves. What sort of reception can we expect here? Things had been pretty grim when we left Salonika No. 2, but that was some months ago. Maybe the changes will be for the better, although that doesn't seem likely.

We walk into a fairly large kind of orderly room where a cheery fire is burning in a small enclosed stove in the centre. There are a couple of prisoners, apparently on some sort of work, hovering round it and chatting away. Several German clerical staff are moving about also, and keeping close to the fire. It is all very cosy and informal, with one German, about the rank of Sergeant Major, seeming to be in charge.

He turns out to be the official interpreter. He has lived in America for more than twenty years, and seems to be more Yank than German. He begins talking to us cheerfully in a conversational way, without the slightest indication of any interrogation. His English is full of the wisecracks and sayings of normal everyday speech, and there is no way I can get away with my Aussie vernacular with this bloke.

He opens by asking, "Where did they pick you guys up?"

We know that all the details will have been sent on, so there is no point in trying to be evasive. I say, "Lemnos."

He says, "Jesus Christ, how the hell did you get there?"

I say, "We are trying to get home."

"It doesn't seem much sense going in that direction," he queries.

I retort, "If we had made it to neutral territory, maybe they would have sent us home."

He shakes his head and says, "I don't fancy your chances. Anyway, even if you did get through, they will only put you back in the Army and you'd be right back where you started from. You're better off safe here, with us, until the War is over."

There is a fair bit of badinage, back and forth between us. A British Sergeant Major walks in while we are talking, and, together with a German Clerk, they take down our particulars before passing us on. It is all very informal and has the air of slightly tardy stragglers being welcomed back into the fold.

I ask the Interpreter, "What happens now?"

He says, "Sorry boys, I'm afraid it's the cells for you."

We just shrug. We know there has to be something like this waiting for us, although everything seems much easier than what we had been prepared for.

The cells are large and roomy, and big enough to hold between twenty and thirty prisoners. They are directly below the Administrative Building and set below ground level. We know there is another cell alongside ours, about the same size, and more extend beyond that. How many, we don't know? They have heavily barred windows, at ground level, looking out onto a barracks square. By stretching a little, we are able to see out of them and take in the scene beyond.

We remember Salonika No. 1 well. We had spent little more than a week here before being moved to Salonika No. 2, because of the huge influx of prisoners from the south. Still, it was long enough to leave vivid memories, which we now begin to recall.

There was the incident of the man shot while trying to hang his shirt to dry on barbed wire. There were the many different nationalities with their many different customs. While we were searching for scraps of paper to wipe our backsides, the Hillmen of India were searching for a stone to do the same thing. Then there were the other Indians who used a can of water and a rag of cloth to cleanse themselves. We recall the incident of the diseased rat seeking refuge up the leg of a man's pants when it was disturbed.

Those memories are certainly not happy ones, and our expectations are conditioned by them. While the camp had been packed with hardly any room to move, now there are very few people to be seen. A barbed wire fence has been erected across the middle, with the camp now appearing to be cut in half. It seems that most of the POWs have been moved on into Germany, with only a few stragglers, such as ourselves, still remaining.

We are kept in the cells for a few days before being released into the camp proper. Our diet is the standard bread and water, and there are no further attempts at interrogation. We are now better able to see the revised camp layout. While the strong barbed wire fences and Guard towers are as before, the bisecting fence cutting across the middle has reduced its size, markedly.

The barracks buildings in the enclosed area are very long, and run from east to west. There are about eight to ten of them, one behind the other, and facing north. On the west side of them is the parade ground, with the main gate and Administrative Block in front of it.

To the east of the barracks is a two storey building running north to south in the opposite direction to the others. We are to learn that this building is out of bounds to the inmates, although it is in the camp area. The reason is because a road runs across the camp-front to the east, then turns south at the camp corner, and continues past the two storey building to a large stables area at the back. The Germans have a large contingent of horse-drawn transport and are using the road constantly. The outer barbed wire fence, unable to encroach on the road, has to end on one corner of the two storey building and restart on the other. These ends are considered vulnerable weak spots, so going anywhere near that building is strictly taboo.

We head for the nearest barracks which happens to be the second from the front. Inside we find it totally different to what we had experienced before. Back then we had been crowded together in a completely empty shell of a building. Now there are iron cots set up on both sides at regular intervals, with the centre space between being given over to tables and stoves. With a straw mattress to lie on, this is luxury indeed.

There are a few blokes sitting on bunks, with signs indicating that about two-thirds of them are occupied. As we enter, a couple of them get up and come to greet us. The foremost is belligerent in a vaguely familiar manner. It is that damned, objectionable Kiwi, we had encountered on Athos.

He immediately confronts us in a blatant standover way, making sneering remarks about his prediction that our pathetic attempts at escape will get us nowhere. He infers we are too dumb to turn round, and that the stupidest German could catch us blindfolded. He demands to know where we had been picked up.

Stung and nettled a bit, I tell him, "We got to the island of Lemnos, but were betrayed by some Greeks." He knows I am telling the truth and, while he is holding us up to public ridicule, it obviously makes his own efforts seem rather puny. It is the only time in the short period we know him, that he shuts his mouth and stops heckling anyone.

Immediately, the rest of the blokes in the room gather round and ply us with questions. They are all escapees, like ourselves, or evaders who had managed to keep out of the Germans' way, only to be picked up later. All have experienced the heartbreak of trying to find a way out of Greece. The fact that we had almost made it, excites their interest, and they are keen to know as much as we can tell them. The questions and answers are pretty animated for a while, then it is time for us to select a bunk for ourselves. We take good care to pick a position well away from that damn Kiwi. I have met up with and been associated with many Kiwis, and, without exception, they are damn good blokes. This one is the only throwback.

We quickly settle in and, over the next few days, we find out as much as we can about the routine running of the place. Apart from the check count parades, morning and evening, we are left pretty much to our own devices.

Our numbers are small and it seems we will remain here until there is a regular movement through to Germany. While we might receive some of the essentials we need from a permanent camp, in the meantime, we will just have to make do with what is available in this transit camp. While there is a QM Store of sorts here, administered by the British Sergeant Major, we had seen that the items available are so dilapidated that it is better for us to stick with the clothing we have. So, for the moment, we look pretty much the same as when we were on the loose.

There is an ambulance room, run by one of our blokes, with medicines supplied by the Germans. I front up one day to find he is giving out some black gritty powder for diarrhoea. I ask him, "What is it?" and "What is it supposed to do?"

He says, "It's powdered charcoal to bung you up."

"Suppose it doesn't work?" I ask.

He then shows me an object like a large pea and says, "I give you one of these pills."

I ask again, "What is that supposed to do?"

"Drive it out of your system," he replies.

So it seems that medical treatment is pretty much a hit and miss affair.

We are now fully determined that we are going to escape again. We had got too close the first time to let things stop there. We have no intention of going on into Germany, and will try our best to see it doesn't happen. I favour the idea of again jumping off a train, and I strongly urge to George and Bob that this be our plan. I point out that, with this way, we are instantly free and we don't have to negotiate any dangerous and chancy openings.

With this being more or less our plan, we have to wait for a movement by rail. As this may be sometime in coming, we feel we have to try and maintain a fair degree of physical fitness. Although we are by no means in perfect condition, our roaming about has kept us reasonably mobile. We may lose our mobility if we just laze about in the barracks. We, therefore, volunteer our services in cutting wood for the cookhouse fires.

Each day, we present ourselves at the woodpile, and hack away with the few tools available. The timber supply is tough and knotted, in the manner of just about all military cookhouses. Many pieces are virtually impossible to split and too big to be used as is. Nevertheless, we persevere and feel rather pleased with what we are able to achieve.

With our wanderings now common knowledge amongst the others, we have gained the rather doubtful distinction of being the most successful escapees so far. All these people think, live, breathe and scheme to escape. All ideas, good and bad, they will bring and share with us. While sharing their schemes, they caution us to be wary of the British Sergeant Major. In support of their suspicions, they tell us a bizarre story that only confuses us all the more.

They claim that he had been a member of the army of occupation, stationed on the Rhine, following WWI. There he had met and married a German girl. Under her influence, he became completely Germanised. After completing his service and being placed on the Reserve list, he was an unwilling starter when called up again for this War. He has a room, cum office, in the Administrative Block, where he sleeps and eats. He is on suspiciously good terms with all the Germans there, and enjoys all sorts of privileges.

This seems rather flimsy evidence to us. But all prisoners, particularly escapees, are a deeply suspicious lot, and are always on the lookout for anything that might suggest an ulterior motive.

All camps, too, are rife with rumours, and it requires a lot of level-headed thinking to sort the wheat from the chaff. In the case of the Sergeant Major, we decide to keep an open mind. We will be wary in any dealings we might have with him, just in case.

There has to be a senior man to act as camp leader. Both the Germans and our own military organisations demand it. The Sergeant Major, by his rank at least, would have to be the obvious choice. And, if those rumours are only half true, his knowledge of things German, would make it doubly so. But, says his detractors, "How come he's still here, when the great bulk of the prisoners have long since gone?" With only us stragglers left behind, there's not much left to be in charge of. So the doubters are still unconvinced.

The daily routine continues on its familiar pattern. Camp food remains pretty much as before, with bread being the main staple. Occasionally, one or two stragglers will be brought in, spend a short period in the cells, then be released into the main camp.

Always, everybody will gather round and eagerly question the newcomers about conditions and chances on the outside. Always, the objectionable Kiwi will thrust his way to the fore and browbeat anybody who has anything to say. Always, this has the effect of breaking up the gathering, with everybody just drifting away.

There are all kinds of nationalities amongst us, with even an Algerian having somehow been caught up and imprisoned. With us all being in the same boat, we generally manage to get on fairly well with each other. Language is not much of a problem, with English being the common language and spoken and understood by everybody, although the brogues are sometimes hard to cope with.

With us being occupied at the woodheap for most of the day, we generally don't catch up with the day's happenings until we get back to barracks after knockoff time. We return one afternoon to be told there has been a fight between the Algerian and a Scotsman. Fights are extremely rare and almost non-existent within our community. It is very much a case of us against the Germans, rather than against each other. Sometimes somebody might get hot under the collar, but it will never come to blows. As far as we can make out, this one is a misunderstanding between the Scotsman's broad twang and the Algerian's limited understanding of English.

It seems the Scotsman felt sufficiently provoked to cause him to punch the Algerian, who reacted by pulling a knife, only to be disarmed by some of the others at the scene. In the man-to-man confrontation, each had reacted in the manner normally adopted by their race.

The Algerian at a disadvantage, not knowing how to use his fists, began to get the worst of it. He closed with the Scotsman in a kind of wrestling manner and, in the scuffle, bit him on the upper arm. The bystanders now intervened and broke it up.

Now the Algerian is a rather forlorn figure down near one end of the barracks. He has none of his own kind to console him, and most of the sympathy is with the Scotsman because of the knife and the bite mark. To make things worse, the Scotsman claims the Algerian has syphilis, and the bite wound will not heal.

I feel sorry for the Algerian, as it seems to me that the fight is more of a personality clash than any wrongdoing. Things are bad enough in the predicament we are in, rather than have to cope with being ostracised by people you are forced to live with.

Without making a big deal of it, I begin to say hello to him and generally pass the time of day. He is noticeably grateful for at least one seemingly friendly face. Immediately after the fight, things are allowed to cool down by tacit agreement, and each endeavours to keep out of the other's way. There is still some aggravation from the Scotsman, who feels he has had some sort of victory, and he now keeps drawing attention to his unhealed wound. The rather meagre bitemark has barely pierced the skin. At its worst, it seems hardly worth taking notice of. True, it is taking its time to clear up. But, this may be as much a result from our poor diet, as any disease carried by the Algerian. We never ever find out if he really does have syphilis.

While we have our wood to cut, the other blokes are continually on the prowl, examining every last inch of the place and trying to find a weakness that can be exploited in an escape bid. One Australian, whom I have a particularly liking for, is a Military Policeman. He is a bubbly cheerful bloke with an infectious personality and is even more enthusiastic of escape than the others. He searches and searches without any success, and always discusses his thoughts and ideas with me. Once, he commented that the only sure way out seems to be through the front gate. I suggest that this is one way that is definitely not on. He tells me he has found out that it has been tried and almost succeeded.

Apparently, an English Lieutenant, reportedly the heir to the family who are the owners of the Hornby train empire, had some business to attend to at the Administrative Block. Upon completion, he is making his way back to the barracks and has to pass the main gate, on the inside of course. On the spur of the moment, he turns left and marches through the gate to the outside, saluting the sentry smartly as he does so. The bewildered sentry returns the salute, and watches as the Lieutenant marches at a steady, unhurried, pace straight ahead.

The space in front of the camp is laid out in garden beds on either side, with a very wide walkway stretching almost a quarter of a mile, before ending at the highway running past. The Lieutenant, still plainly in sight, has almost reached the highway junction, where he would have turned and been lost to view. A German Sergeant Major, roundly disliked by all of us, chooses this moment to walk out onto the raised patio beside the office, and pauses to admire the view. The German stares for a moment, then bellows like a bull at the sentry, who suddenly realises the enormity of what has happened. He drops to one knee and fires one shot. The Lieutenant is killed instantly.

My MP friend is full of praise for the Lieutenant's daring and resourcefulness. I have some trouble of getting through to him that it has cost the man his life. I urge him to take care and not be foolish. I further advise him to bide his time like us, and take his chances in a jump from the train. He promises nothing, other than he will keep looking.

A few days later, while working at the woodpile, another fight breaks out back at the barracks. News of it is conveyed to us by some of the fellows after the event. They tell me it is between the objectionable Kiwi and my MP friend. I am immediately worried and concerned for my friend. There is a marked difference in build between them, with the Kiwi the heavier by at least two or three stone. Our condition is such that it is an effort enough, just to go about our normal daily routine. The energy sapping frenzy of a bitter fist fight will take a long time to recover from. It might also bring reprisals from the Germans.

Our informants tell us not to worry as the MP has won, and, for this, I am grateful for two reasons. Firstly, my friend is okay and, secondly, that the already objectionable Kiwi will have been even more so, if he had won.

Later the MP drops round to the woodpile for his normal chat, chirpy as ever. There are patches of skin off his face and knuckles. Although the marks are raw and angry looking, he doesn't seem too inconvenienced. I ask him what had happened.

He tells me that the Kiwi had walked up to him in the barracks and began to verbally harass him. As was his wont, he had put his face close to the MPs and refused to be ignored. The MP had tried to ease away from him, but the Kiwi had manoeuvred him into a corner and blocked his escape. Because of their duties, all MPs have to put up with a certain amount of adverse criticism from the rest of us and become a little thick-skinned about it. But, in this instance, the Kiwi went really overboard. God knows what caused him to get off his bike this particular day, but he meant business and would not be denied. My MP friend says he really had no choice. The only way, he could move from there, was to fight.

A confrontation between the Kiwi and somebody has been building up for some time. It seems that this is the only way he can vent his frustration. It appears that the Kiwi has deliberately picked on the MP, because he is smaller in build, and felt he could handle him. He expects the general sympathy from the rest of us, will be on his side. But, by his conduct, he has alienated himself so badly from the rest of us, that we are pleased to see him get his comeuppance from anybody, even from the Germans. Besides, the MP is now one of us, an escapee first, and an MP second.

To do the Kiwi justice, he does not retire into himself. He continues to push his way into any group, as before. But now, he behaves in a more circumspect manner. Still, none of us can forgive him entirely for his past conduct, although there is a bit more tolerance toward him.

A few days later, we are informed that a large party of prisoners is on their way from round the Athens area. A Field Ambulance and Medical Unit has been employed there at a Field Hospital, taking care of our seriously wounded comrades. It seems that most of the wounded have recovered sufficiently to cope with the travel, and will come to Salonika, as a preliminary to moving to camps in Germany.

We are very pleased at this news, as it means that we will be moving on too, and our train jump is very much closer. Also security with the convalescent men will be much more relaxed, and our chances of making the jump safely, all that much greater. There is a frenzy of activity from the others, preparing accommodation for the new arrivals, while we carry on as usual with our job.

When the party arrives, it is a strange sight to see. While the wounded arrive on foot or in transport, the Field Ambulance Company marches in as a Unit, in full uniform and still with most of their gear. As Non-Combatants this is their entitlement, of course. The Germans, for their part, are usually rather punctilious in observing these niceties. They are fully aware of the great propaganda value to be obtained, as well as reciprocal rights for their own. For the Ambulance Unit, the brassard they wear of a red cross on a white armband, is their passport. And, of course, they carry no weapons.

Special treatment for the Ambulance Unit is immediately in evidence, for they are assigned the use of the two storey building that encroaches onto the road leading to the stables at the rear, and which up to now has been taboo to us.

The wounded are a wide cross section from all kinds of Units, mostly trying to come to terms with their injuries. Some are more mobile than others, and they help and support each other wherever they can, both physically and mentally.

There are a couple of Victoria Cross winners amongst them, and there is a great feeling of almost awed reverence in being in their presence. While it might be expected that they be big, tough men, in reality they are of small and average build, much like most of the rest of us. They, for their part, are slightly disconcerted and embarrassed at the open respect from us, and try very hard to still remain one of the boys. This, they can no longer do. From here on in, they will always be regarded as somebody special.

The story of one of them, a New Zealander, is told to us by the men. His Company was caught in a pretty hopeless position, and was being steadily wiped out by strong German machine gun and mortar squads. Somebody had to do something, so this man grabbed a satchel of grenades and crawled out under heavy fire. He crawled from position to position, wiping out each of them in turn with his grenades, until badly wounded, he could go no further. The Germans were so impressed with his bravery, that they recommended he be decorated, through the International Red Cross in Switzerland, as well as his own Officers.

When the award was confirmed by the International Red Cross, he was a prisoner recovering from his wounds at the Field Hospital near Athens. The German Command gave him a twenty-four hour parole, to go into Athens under his own steam, to enjoy himself any way he liked.

This is a typical point with our enemy. Just when you have worked up a good healthy hate against them, they do something special like that parole, that will make you grudgingly admit, that maybe, they may be human after all.

With the convalescing newcomers being housed in the barracks behind the one occupied by us escapers, and being within the confines of the camp, we have an easy and open access to each other. We escapers waste no time in visiting, seeking anyone we might know.

I find an Infantryman I know from my hometown. He is Slogger Kentish. While I am acquainted with him, he is more a mate of my Uncle Pat Fullick. Still, we have had several meetings and some good yarns. He had received some bad leg wounds and, although he is now mobile, he is still far from a hundred percent. He is typical of the condition of most of the others.

Some of the other blokes tell me that Slogger had been a batman to his Lieutenant. They claim the Lieutenant wasn't the greatest of performers, and Slogger virtually ran the Unit for him.

Three of the convalescent men have lost an eye, and it is the right eye in each case. They are still trying to come to terms with this disfigurement and they stick together like glue, in mutual support. These three are out walking by themselves in a quiet part of the camp, when we happen to come up behind them.

We are handling some blocks of firewood in a hand cart, when the cart makes a sudden, loud, rattling noise on a bad patch of road. It is heartbreaking to see their reaction. They panic and start to run, first to one side of the road, then to the other. One becomes separated from the others and, as soon as he realises it, flees back to rejoin them. Their hands and arms are extended as though trying to feel for something solid. All the time, their heads are turning from side to side, trying to use their good eye to get their bad side into focus as well.

Finally, they realise the strange noise, they have heard, has posed no threat. They just stand there, clinging to each other for mutual support. They are devastated. Their confidence is totally shattered. Before we came along, they had been pacing it out, jauntily and almost carefree. Now, they will have to go through the slow painful process of building up confidence again, and coming to terms with their disability. For us, the worst part is that we have been the unwitting cause of their pain.

All of us have been badly affected by the bombing, the shelling and the screamer devices on the Stukas. Any sudden unexpected noise, still sees us automatically dive for cover. Still, we have had the advantage of our facilities, and just as quickly recovered. But for these blokes, such an experience is terrifying.

Our somewhat dubious 'fame' of having almost made it through to neutral Turkey, and being recaptured on Lemnos, quickly spreads amongst the new arrivals. As reluctant and rather minor 'celebrities', we begin to be visited at the woodpile. We are eagerly quizzed by some of them on the possibility of their also making an escape. All prisoners, even the most introverted, are driven by that impossible dream of being free again.

One of these is a solidly built Officer of an English Regiment. If he had not been a convalescent, we would not have met him, as all Officers are kept strictly segregated from Other Ranks.

He tells me that he has worked his way round Canada. He has often worked splitting firewood there, and gives me a few pointers on how to handle some of our knotty problems. He gives a lot of thought to a possible escape and is a very serious contender. But, after discussing the pros and cons, and, with regard to his injuries, decides against it. Seeing that we are totally committed to another attempt, he says, "Here, you'd better have this. You'll make better use of it than I will."

He gives me an Army Prismatic Compass that he has managed to conceal. It may be invaluable to us later. I thank him sincerely and I carefully stow it away. My main concern now is to prevent the Germans from finding it.

Slogger makes a practice of visiting us most days, in an effort to exercise his wounded leg. Sometimes it is too painful and he will give it a miss. Another bloke to visit us is from the Ambulance Unit. The Ambulance blokes are fairly free to come and go amongst us, while the general restriction on us to visit their quarters still applies.

This Ambulance bloke is well known to George and me, as he had been a former member of our Unit. He is our former Sergeant and a Cook who had sailed with us from home. He had been deposed during our training days in Palestine, and his position taken over by Reg Jobber and Pee Wee. He had transferred out of the Unit, and we had no idea of what had become of him. Now he turns up as a Private in this Ambulance Unit.

He queries us about the chances of escaping, but seems rather half-hearted about it. I think he would like me to invite him to go with us, which I will not do. Instead, I point out that, as a Medical Orderly, he stands a very good chance of being repatriated in due course. An escape attempt will remove his non-combatant status and, upon recapture, he will be doomed to waiting out the remainder of the War like everybody else. He goes away and never broaches the subject again. All the people who speak to us have this implicit faith, that the next time we will make it through. It is very heartening.

Now comes a pleasant surprise. We are told that Red Cross Parcels have arrived. This is a major concession, almost certainly brought about by the Field Ambulance Unit and the convalescing wounded. We aren't too sure if we will be allowed to share as well, but hope for the best.

Ever since we had first been captured, we have had to put up with pretty atrocious conditions. All protests had received the same reply—that these conditions are only temporary. We are told that conditions are much better in the permanent camps, where we are to be sent to in Germany. It sounds too much like an empty promise in an effort to keep us under control, rather than to be true. Maybe these parcels may give some indication of what we can expect, if and when we do get through to those camps.

Nobody here has any idea of what to expect in these parcels, and there is some pretty wild speculation. We have a vague idea that, in due course, we will be permitted parcels from home, subject to censorship, of course. What will they contain? Food and clothing? Or just clothing alone? Will they be limited to whatever one's family can afford? Will the more affluent be reasonable well-looked after, while some receive next to nothing?

It seems to me that these parcels will be from one's home, and be addressed to each individual. That may mean a few will receive more than one parcel, while others receive none at all. Privately, I hold no hope for us escapers. While we have been on the loose, we will be listed as missing. And, with no address, nothing can be sent to us. Everything will be sent back, until we are located. While we have now been recaptured, not enough time has elapsed for that information to get through. Besides, if there is food in them, will it be stale or spoilt, like it sometimes is by the time it reaches us when in the field? It is rumoured, also, that there might be some mail as well.

Everybody dreams and fantasises in their own particular way. We carry on as usual at the wood pile, and return that evening to the barracks. We are told that a party of the able bodied men had been taken to the rail siding to unload the parcels from an enclosed rail truck. These have been returned to the camp, and are now safely under lock and key in the Administrative Block, in the care of the British Sergeant Major. He will make a distribution, as soon as the proper method is known.

We cross-examine the men in the work party to find out what, if any, we can expect to get. Their answers leave us wondering whether or not they are trying to pull our legs. They claim the parcels are cardboard boxes filled with all kinds of tinned food. A few have broken open and there is jam, condensed milk, meats, sardines, sugar, soaps and everything you can imagine.

Though finding it hard to believe, we know them well enough by now to know they are not lying. Our hopes and expectations begin to rise just a little bit. To their credit, the gang has not stolen even the smallest item. We will just have to wait for the handout to find out if we will get anything.

This is organised fairly quickly, and we are each given one of those cardboard boxes. Nobody, even at Administration, seems to know how long it will have to last. Some optimists claim we will get two a week, while others are claiming one. We aren't sure what controls the Germans might impose, for the arrival and distribution will be subject to their goodwill. Still, for now, we will savour what we have. The parcels themselves are exactly as the men have said, and fill us with amazed wonderment. They are packed and sent from England for a POW. They are an issue and not from one's family.

Again we are impressed. I don't think any of us had expected our authorities to come up with a concerted effort on behalf of POWs as is demonstrated here. We all know that the conduct of the War is taking all our people's energies and resources. We know, too, that food is rationed and is not very plentiful. Now, here, we have the widest range of all that the Country can produce, and all the best brands. There is a wider and better range than we have ever had on service.

Each of us handles and examines the precious cans and packets, over and over again. Each individual has to decide whether to splurge and gorge himself in an instant feast, or to carefully eke it out to last as long as possible. With the rumour that we might expect to get an issue once or twice a week, it seems we might be able to let our heads go. But bitter experience has taught us to be wary and generally expect the worst. So there is a little bit of splurging, and a fair amount of putting by for later. For we three, who have resolved to escape later, it is a matter of conserving as much as we can.

Together with the consignment, there comes some bulk foods from South America. Whereas the English cardboard parcels are packed as an issue of one per man, the South American bulk foods have to be shared among several. One item in the bulk stuff intrigues us very much. It is dried bananas. Dried fruits are a good and welcome food, but dried bananas is something we have not encountered before. They are compressed into a large square block and are dark brown to black in appearance. They have a typical banana smell and, when we receive our ration cut from the block, all we can think to do is just gnaw away at them. They taste good and, as they are sticky, this seems the best way to use them. That is all, except for the Algerian.

The Algerian, by now, has achieved a certain amount of grudging acceptance and has teamed up with a couple of Cypriots. This group keeps a low profile and pretty much to themselves. With the advent of the new arrivals, the Scot has moved to one of the other barracks to be with some men from his Unit. We no longer hear any whinges about the supposed syphilitic infected bite wound.

The Algerian with easy aplomb, puts his dried bananas in a pan with a little margarine and begins to fry them on one of the small barracks stoves. We all gather round fascinated. This is something new to us. We have not even heard of frying bananas before. We wonder how they taste and ask him.

With quiet dignity, he says, "Here, try some," and begins to offer bitesize chunks from the end of his fork to one after the other of us, who have gathered round. It is delicious, notwithstanding that all food is delicious to an undernourished POW. I protest that he will end up with none for himself. But he just waves this suggestion away with an easy gesture. This is a truly generous thing for him to do. In our society you share with your mates, but it goes no further. I am thankful that I, unlike the others, have no cause to feel any remorse as to my past treatment of him. This small tableau raises his esteem several notches with the others, and a new respect is accorded him from now on.

We are still buzzing with the impact of the food parcels when, next day, my MP friend visits me at the woodpile to tell me some momentous news. They have discovered an escape route and they intend putting it into use tonight. It is a little hazy as to who has actually come up with the idea, but there is a group of about eight or ten fully involved, with my MP friend one of the most active. He excitedly begins to spell out the details to me, while strongly urging us to be in it too.

The route is out through the two storey building, now occupied by the Field Ambulance Unit, and formerly taboo to the rest of us. We still have not been given permission to go there, but, with POW initiative, some have mixed in with the goings and comings of the Ambulance mob, and explored the layout themselves.

In the building there is a large central foyer that passes through to the roadway beyond. On the side facing the road, it is sealed off with extra-large double doors. The living quarters are on both sides of the foyer and upstairs. The stairway system includes a passage, connecting both sides of the upstairs section, and passing over the top of the foyer.

There are very large sealed windows admitting natural light to this passageway, giving an excellent view of the roadway and beyond. Study of the layout has revealed that the road is about twenty feet wide, with a low brick wall about three feet high at its far edge, in what looks like a former loading ramp and now used as a rubbish dump. Beyond the rubbish dump is a very wide stretch of heavily grassed land that finishes at the high fence line of the adjoining building. These adjoining buildings, similar to our own layout of barracks, are now being used by German garrison troops. Some distance to the right of the barracks is the large and busy stable complex at the rear. To the left, a shorter distance, is a fence fronting onto the main street.

The group has gone to work on the large doors and managed to get them open. They find that they are crisscrossed with single strands of barbed wire nailed to the outer frame. By taking care, the barbed wire can be pushed aside, allowing a man to slip through, and then spring back into place.

The escape procedure calls for each man to slip through the door and barbed wire, make a quick dash across the road, cross the rubbish dump, then cross the grassy area to the boundary fence. Then, by using the fence as a guide, move to the left until contacting the fence fronting the main street. By taking care not to be seen, you drop to the pavement, then walk boldly through the city to the outskirts. The MP, enthusiastically, sees it as quite simple and foolproof.

I am greatly alarmed and can see it as fraught with danger. They have ignored the German sentries and patrols, as if they aren't there. I tell him so, but he airily replies that they have that covered too. I ask him to explain. He tells me they have arranged a system of lookouts amongst the Ambulance men to watch at the high window. These men will give a signal when it will be safe for each man to make his dash.

I give thought about the German security system. To the left and right of the building, unlike the rest of the camp, because of the road, there are no elevated guard towers with mounted machine guns. Instead, the machine guns are set up at ground level. Supported by a searchlight, they are put in position each day at dusk and removed each morning to make way for the horse drawn traffic. A post is positioned at both corners of the outer perimeter, looking straight down the road that will have to be crossed. The one on the left of the doorway is located about fifty yards away, and the one on the right is about a hundred yards. As well, a patrolling foot sentry passes back and forth between them, with others patrolling the rest of the outer perimeter.

These two posts are so close together that I doubt that a lookout system will be efficient enough to allow for the lengthy dash that each man will have to make. The MP however, is supremely confident and will not be swayed. I point out that the Field Ambulance men might oppose the attempt through their quarters, in case it jeopardises their non-combatant status and special privileges. "No way," he tells me. It is they who have elected to man the lookout system.

Still worried, I urge him to reconsider, wait until the train trip, and drop off as we intend to. Equally strongly, he urges me to take this opportunity and break out now. Neither can sway the other, so there is nothing for it, but to wish each other luck.

Bob, George and I, don't do much woodcutting for the rest of the day. We just sit around and discuss the pros and cons of the escape. Each man will have to smuggle his gear into the Ambulance men's barracks and, if the Germans spot this activity, they can be ready and waiting to open up as soon as somebody makes a move. We are heavyhearted and feel it can only end in disaster.

We return to the barracks that evening to find that all the would be escapers have already slipped over to the Ambulance men's quarters. There is a noticeable gap now in our numbers but, at least, this is known only by those of us who are left. We just sit around talking quietly amongst ourselves, waiting for, but hoping not to hear, the rattle of machinegun fire that will indicate the attempt has been discovered.

It is almost full dark now and the searchlight beams are alight and probing. The newly installed guard is fresh and alert. Surely, they cannot miss catching the goings-on. Slowly, the minutes tick away and still nothing happens. Sufficient time has now elapsed for at least some of them to have made their run. A slight touch of optimism begins to creep into our thoughts, and Bob says, "You know. We are going to feel pretty foolish in the morning, if they get away with it, and we haven't had a try."

George begins to speculate in a like manner. We are regarded, undeservedly, as the escaping 'experts' and are expected to set the pace. With a fair group now gone, and us still here in the morning, our credibility will be somewhat dented. Of course, this doesn't worry us. Our shortcomings would have to be found out, sooner or later. Still, while we have credibility, the others are eager to share their ideas with us, and it gives us more scope than relying solely on our own ideas.

I point out that this plan is a risky one compared to waiting for a jump off the train. Bob points out, that with so many having tried it, maybe the Germans have worked out a counter to a train jump. "How will we feel then?"

Sensing the growing feeling of excitement in my two mates, I point out that it will mean us going into it unprepared. We, and all of our gear, are here, when we should already be at the Ambulance Barracks. Movement between barracks is forbidden after dark, and it is right on that now. We had not investigated the route, and will have to negotiate it blind, with only the MP's description to guide us. The alternative is the train idea. If it is to be this one, we will have to make our move now. "How do you feel?' I ask.

They slowly nod their heads, and it is up to me. I have to give the word. "Okay,' I say, "Let's go." We just stand up and grab our gear, while telling the others that we are going too.

The rest of the blokes are wide-eyed and silent. They, like us, are convinced that this one is too risky. But seeing that our minds are made up, they silently shake hands, in turn, as we begin to move towards the end door.

The Algerian is engaged in a little bit of cooking at the stove in the centre of the barracks. As I shake hands with him, the expression on his face tells me that he is genuinely sorry to see me go. Then with an impulsive gesture, he sweeps the civilian cloth cap that he wears, off his head and claps it onto mine.

I am deeply touched. I have no headcover of my own and the cap completes my appearance, giving me a more authentic Greek look and disguise. I have no time to dally or say anything. I just cling to his hand in a longer handshake, telling him with my eyes how grateful I am. He, in turn, tells me he understands, with his. Without a word being uttered, we continue on to the end door.

Now comes the first tricky part. There is an internal fence separating the Ambulance Unit building from the camp proper. It is a normal wire fence put there to indicate the demarcation zone, into which we formerly were not permitted to stray. Now that the Ambulance Unit has arrived, this has relaxed a little because of their comings and goings. To get to their building we will have to go in the opposite direction, straight ahead to the south for about seventy-five yards, round the end of the fence, then straight ahead to the north for about a hundred and fifty yards, before being able to turn into the building. Once we have rounded the fence, we will have to try and look like returning Ambulance personnel.

It is quite dark now at about seven o'clock, and strictly speaking any movement outside the barracks is forbidden. The presence of convalescing wounded and Ambulance personnel has caused this rule to be relaxed a little. Using the shadows and the rows of barracks buildings as cover, we negotiate the first seventy-five yards to the end of the fence. Upon turning, we are lucky enough to find about four or five ambulance Unit men stragglers, strung out and making a belated return to their quarters. We just fall in behind them, and stroll casually back as they are doing.

The searchlights play over us all, several times before passing on. Everybody continues unhurriedly, in the same casual way. We are carrying our gear in a bundle in our hands, so that it looks as if we are just bringing some ordinary mundane things back with us. Finally, we turn into the building to be the last to openly make this trip. We have made our move at the last possible moment.

Once inside, we go immediately to the door that opens onto the road. There is no light and the area there is pitch black. We become aware of a man hovering about and standing by the door. He is an Ambulance man and has taken over the role of opening and closing it behind each escaper. We ask him, "Where are the others?"

He says, "They have all gone and you are the last, unless any others show up."

I am shocked. My understanding was that they will be waiting until later in the night. The first ones must have gone before it was truly dark. We have nobody to observe as a guide, or to point out the proposed route. Without having reconnoitred it for ourselves, we will just have to go blind.

Desperately we try to remember all the information given to us by the MP. The doorman says he will give us word when to move. I ask him, "How will you know?"

He tells us, "There is another man at the large window in the passageway above you. He is keeping the patrolling sentry under observation. When the sentry turns and is moving towards the other end of his beat, the man above will signal the community singers and they will sing a certain song."

This song alerts the doorman, who is unsighted, that it is safe to open the door. In the confusion, we have barely noticed that there is some singing going on, somewhere above us on the second storey. The gang there are singing lustily, making a lot of noise to cover any movement we might make, after taking the cue of the special song from the window man. It seems like a rough and ready signalling system to me, but there is nothing we can do about it now. We just have to give grudging tribute to the non-combat Ambulance men for taking the trouble to get involved.

Suddenly, the doorman says, "Right", and begins to open the door. Ready or not, this is it. We have not had time to work out who will go first, so, as we are standing together in a loose group with George slightly the closest, it will be him, then me, and then Bob.

With the doorman whispering directions of, "Go straight ahead across the road, then go up the low brick wall onto the landing; then cross the rubbish dump and move on to the high fence." George crouches low down near the floor and eases his way through the barbed wire that criss-crosses the doorway. In an instant, he is gone. We listen anxiously for any sign of discovery, but none comes. We can't hear much because of the singing. Then it is my turn.

The doorman eases open the door, then touches me on the shoulder to indicate it's time to go. I crouch down and ease through the barbed wire. Once outside, I waste no time. I sprint across the roadway to the low brick wall, looking neither right nor left. After the gloom of the inside of the building, it seems very light outside and I can see easily where I am going. At the brick wall I make a leap to the top and almost stumble. It seems higher than I expected. On top, I reach the rubbish dump and start across. Jumping in wide spaced leaps to cross as quickly as possible, I am absolutely shattered to find I am in the middle of a vast heap of empty cans. Every footstep raises a tremendous clatter that sounds like a thunder clap. I am certain that the sentry, or those two nearby guard posts have heard, and I brace myself for their challenge.

None comes, so I pause for a second while my racing brain tries to decide whether to keep going and cross quickly, or slow down and try to pick my way quietly through this mess. Then I hear the same clatter that I had made. Somebody else is there, and I am sure it must be a Guard. But it is Bob. The doorman must have sent him right behind me without waiting. Bob is in the same predicament as myself.

Realising that it is Bob, who is with me, and we are both standing still, fully erect, the searchlight from the southern post swings full on us and stops, lighting us up like day. Bob makes the slightest movement, as if to dive out of the beam, and I instantly hiss at him, "Stand still. Don't move." For once, I am thankful for all that tedious training. It has taught me that if caught in a searchlight beam, keep still. The operators see movement, rather than objects.

For what seems like minutes the beam stays full on us without moving, and we remain frozen in our upright positions. Then slowly, it begins to move away as before, continuing its former slow sweep. We have not been noticed. It must have been a quirk, on the part of the operator, that has caused him to stop in that particular position. Wasting no time, and paying no heed to the clatter, we quickly clear the remaining obstacle of the rubbish dump.

We are now at a wide grassy area, stretching on both sides of us and reaching to the high fence of the adjoining German troops barracks. Bob veers away from me to my left, so as to be less conspicuous, and I go straight ahead. The grass is long and up to my knees. It is impossible to see what is underfoot and I just plough on.

Just short of the fence, my feet plunge into open space amongst the grass. I have suddenly fallen into a deep hole, apparently scoured out by rain water and completely obscured from view. I just lay there, slightly winded, with my head below the level of the grass tops, secure for the moment in my natural hidey hole. I abandon myself to the confused feelings of relief and excitement at the success of our breakout. George's low voice calling my name stirs me into moving again, and, with the three of us together, we make our way to the front fence leading to the street outside.

We stretch at full length, side by side, studying the layout before us. There is a drop of about eight or nine feet from our position to a narrow pavement below. The street we face is a very wide one, with electric trams running along it. When they pass, everything is dark again. Using the light generated by the trams to ensure there is nobody about, we carefully drop onto the pavement. With our gear in hessian bags over our shoulders to look like ordinary Greek workmen, we set off along the darkened street toward the lighted area of the city proper. We have no set plan other than to somehow make our way through the city and into the open country beyond.

We have no idea how much walking it will take us to get there, but now know the wisdom of the early breakout. We can move freely through the streets and appear to be just part of the population going about their business. With George leading, and Bob and I together behind because of the narrow pavement, we soon come to the lighted area and meet up with our first pedestrians. They are German soldiers coming towards us, and seemingly making their way back to the barracks behind us. Boldly we press on. We will have to meet this situation quite a few times if we are to make it through the city successfully.

We prepare to move aside and make way for them, hoping to make as little fuss as possible. They forestall us by splitting apart, with one or two hugging the wall, and the others spilling out onto the roadway to make way for us. They are talking amongst themselves and we just pass through without incident. They have not recognised us and, if no Greeks give us away, we just might be alright.

We continue on, not really knowing if we are going in the right direction, but trusting to the streets layout to guide us. From time to time, we meet and pass other groups of both soldiers and some civilians. Nobody pays attention to us.

We have been walking for what seems a fair while, when a good wide street, leading off from the main one we are on, seems to suggest it is leading through the suburbs to the outskirts. We turn into it hoping for the best. We continue on for some distance and, sure enough, it seems we have made the right move.

We are the only people about and feel a bit conspicuous. There is less light, but still enough to see fairly clearly. A fair way ahead we can see some kind of juncture, jutting out onto the roadway. For the moment, we cannot make out what it is. Then, we are alarmed to realise that it is a traffic checkpoint.

We have chosen the right road alright, for, beyond the checkpoint, there is seemingly open country. But how are we to get past this barrier? We look frantically for any side streets that might offer a chance of bypassing it. There are none. All that can be seen are rows of darkened houses on each side, shut up for the night.

We don't like the idea of turning back and looking for another exit. Besides to do so will look highly suspicious to the sentry at the barrier. With us the only ones in the street, we must have been seen by now. We walk on, but shorten our steps to the extent that we are almost marking time. We desperately try to think of a way out, but finally decide that we have no alternative but to brazen it out.

We now can plainly see the sentry's hut and the pole barrier that raises and lowers to open and shut the road. At the moment, it is up in the open position. There doesn't seem to be any light in the hut. But we don't take any notice of that, as we fully expect a curfew to be in force. With no alternative, we march straight up to the hut. It is unmanned and we cannot believe our luck. Our spirits soar and we march boldly on, straight out into open country.

Once in the open, we decide to press on as far as we can before bedding down for the night. We hope to put as much space as possible between us and any pursuit. It is well into the night when we finally come to a cluster of small houses under construction, off to one side. It looks to be some kind of new housing estate. The buildings are of concrete construction and, at the moment, just the shell of a house with a large basement or cellar underneath. Well-nigh exhausted, we crawl into one of the basements, collapse into a corner, and go instantly asleep. We are too done in to care much about anything. The sudden decision to escape, and the various crises, are just too much.

We awake a few hours later to find that we are stiff and sore. Dawn is just breaking. The promise is of a bright, sunny day, and, as our scrambled senses start to come together, slowly adjusting to our strange surroundings, the realisation fully hits us. Once again, we are completely free. We can go anywhere we choose, and it is absolutely marvellous. Our spirits soar, and this new day holds the promise of wonderful things to come.

We decide to get away from here as quickly as possible, as we expect workmen to be turning up at any time. Once clear of the place, we can stop and have something to eat. Light-hearted and full of optimism, we set out at a cracking pace.

We finally stop at a small grassy clearing surrounded by bushes at the side of the road. We decide to make this a good feed, as a sort of celebration. Among us, on the ground, we spread all the goodies from our Red Cross parcels that we have been hoarding. We are beginning to tuck in when we hear the sound of a truck engine, and it is almost upon us. As it sweeps into view from behind the bushes, I just have time to throw a cover over those tell-tale cans and packets.

It is loaded with German soldiers and, as now we can clearly be seen, all we can do is give them a cheeky wave. They casually wave back and pass on.

This encounter brings us back to reality. If we are to get through, we will have to be more cautious. Much as we would have liked to spin out those food parcel items, they are a dead giveaway and will have to go. We will use them up first. Without them, any search will have us seemingly to be just ordinary Greeks.

We eat, quickly pack up, then get underway. As we walk, we work out our plan of action. We will make our way back to Athos, as soon as possible. A boat still seems the best bet at getting out of the country, and Athos seems to offer the best prospect of getting another boat. Bob's experiences there were quite different to George's and mine. While we had wandered from Monastery to Monastery, asking and hoping, Bob and his group had been taken under the wing of some very influential senior Priests. His group had been housed and fed, and kept in one place, while the Priests set about trying to negotiate, along the coastline, for a boat for them.

This is infinitely a better way of achieving our goal, as the power and influence of this religious community spreads right across the country. All we can hope is that our recapture on Lemnos has not caused them too much harm, and that they are still willing to help as before. Bob feels certain that they will.

We have several days of walking ahead of us, as Athos is quite a distance from Salonika. Bob had originally got there by a slightly different direction than that taken by us. He tells of having come across a hidden Communist-built village, with town amenities of running water, and kerbed and guttered streets. George and I cannot believe him, as this is totally foreign in rural Greece. He urges us to detour slightly and see for ourselves. He feels sure that he will be able to find it again and, as it isn't too far out of our way, we agree.

It is early afternoon when we begin to approach a fair clump of trees, almost like a mini forest. Bob says, "There it is." But we think he must be mistaken, for we can see nothing but trees.

We are about ten to fifteen feet from the outer verge, when the outline of housing becomes visible amongst the greenery. Sure enough, as we enter the tree line, there in front of us is a narrow footpath, fronted by concrete kerb and gutter, with houses beyond the footpath. This is the closest to town-living that we have seen anywhere in Greece, outside the capital cities.

We have barely penetrated into this hidden wonder when several men approach, either to welcome or confront us. We aren't sure of either. Two men appear to be Communist advisory officials, and the other three, town officials of some sort.

In our fractured Greek, we explain who we are; we go into our usual spiel of begging for food, and a possible place to sleep for the night. The five men go into lengthy discussion, while we lean on our walking poles, awaiting the outcome.

The Commos obviously are the influential people, while leaving the townsmen to either accept or reject their advice. We figure that the townsmen's whole future will depend largely on how they follow this advice. We therefore, are rather impressed when the townsmen appear to take a different line to that proposed by the Commos. They politely decline any assistance to us, and request that we skirt round their forest cover, rather than travel through it. They are sure we will get assistance at another close by village, to which they direct us.

With no alternative, but to move on, we thank them and leave. They watch us out of sight, still talking back and forth amongst themselves. We have the feeling of things being not quite right and are happy to get going.

Once out of earshot, we begin to weigh up what we think the proceedings are all about.

Bob, whose Greek is a bit better than George's and mine, is convinced that the Commos had wanted to kill us and dispose of our bodies, in order to preserve the secrecy of the village existence. George and I know that some sort of restraint on our movements has been the subject of discussion.

It seems that the townsmen's objection was because of the difficulty of keeping such a drastic solution totally secret. As we are Allied soldiers, local sympathies can be expected to be on our side and, therefore, any hostile action towards us is likely to work against them. Their reasoning seems to be that, by letting us go, we will soon be out of the district, and of no further threat to them at all. We are very happy to get well out of that area.

We speculate on how the village came to be established and where the funding has come from. The strong desire to keep it a secret means that it is probably against the laws of the country, and certainly of the occupying power. It seems to us that it has been set up as a base from which to launch an insurgency when the time is considered right, and to also demonstrate a better mode of living under a Communist regime. We consider ourselves very fortunate in having to leave without any hassle. Otherwise, we may have been listed as having disappeared without trace.

We continue on towards Athos with George and I insisting that we make the Skite Xenophontos our first goal. As Bob as never visited there during his time on Athos, we convince him to call there first before moving on to the Monastery of Iviron.

It is several more days before we finally arrive at the border of where the Athos Peninsula joins the mainland. With growing excitement, we press on along the narrow track between the bushes and trees. All the time we speculate whether we will be remembered or not. Finally, we emerge into the clearing and there it is before us. We just stand there once again, taking in that magnificent scenic splendour. We gaze along the ridge to the mountain, the sea, the Islands, and back again to the mountain. It is almost like a homecoming. Now, to meet up again with our friends.

We are instantly recognised and greeted heartily. With the onset of winter, harvesting is finished and quite a few have returned to the parent Monastery, including our English speaking friend. But there still are many we met on our first visit. They want to know what has happened to us and we fill them in as best we can. They already know most of the details and that that damn boatman had got away with my watch and ring. They strongly condemn him and his helpers for their betrayal, and are loud with their expressions of sympathy at our having been recaptured. There is no indication from the Germans that anybody on the Peninsula is under suspicion. We are thankful for that.

With greetings over and done with, we are urged to stay overnight. As it is now well into the afternoon, we had intended to do this anyway. As the weather is now quite cold and, with a thick mantle of snow on Mount Athos, everybody retires to a large common room where a good fire is burning in the open hearth. We all sit around talking and soaking up the warmth. Later, a frugal meal is set out, after which we return to the fire.

Our hosts insist that we sample their wine. They make much of our having helped with the picking of the grapes. Now it will be justly fitting for us to taste the result. It has only been a short couple of months since that happened, so, obviously, they aren't too worried about waiting for it to mature.

Our knowledge of the fermentation process is nil, and we are a bit worried about its taste and potency. We figure to take things cautiously and just have a sip. But they won't have a bar of that. They insist on giving each of us a large tumbler full, and aren't satisfied until we have downed the lot.

The combination of the warmth of the fire, the wine, and our physical condition, takes almost immediate effect. The next thing I know is that it is a very cold morning, the fire is out, and I am stiff and sore from sleeping on the floor. We had all passed out and slept where we lay. Other than a little stiffness, there are no other effects.

Anxious to press on, we say goodbye to our friends and head off to Iviron. Upon arrival, Bob asks for his precious contacts and they quickly come forward to greet us. The main person takes charge and it is obvious that he has quite a lot of authority. He has a presence about him and, although dressed in the traditional priestly garb, it is of much better quality. Bob tells us later that he comes from a well-to-do Athens family.

He takes us to a small secluded house where we are to stay while he makes enquiries on our behalf. He will arrange for us to be fed and for a fresh change of underclothing, while the lot, that we are wearing, will be taken away and cleaned. This will be heaven for we have nothing spare, just what we are wearing. In all this arrangement, our priestly friend does nothing himself. He just gives the orders that have other priests scurrying to do his bidding.

We are asked to stay close to our house, be cautious, and not move around much. He will visit us regularly to let us know how things are progressing. He confirms that there has been no hostile move by the Germans against their community, and that they seem unaware of any assistance to escapers from here.

All we can do is settle in and wait for something to happen. Our Monk visits us regularly and, almost always, brings us a bottle of Raki, the spirit distilled by the Monastery. With the coldness of the season and the inactivity of just sitting around, we begin to take a regular nip to warm ourselves up. Little by little, I begin to acquire a taste for the stuff. Hopefully, we will be moving on before I become truly addicted.

With nothing else to do, we talk endlessly of our chances, and of any schemes we can think of to get away, no matter how hairbrained they might seem. We share all our thoughts and pass critical comment on each other's proposals. Gradually, I begin to sense just the tiniest bit of dissension creeping into our formerly harmonious partnership. George becomes alarmed at some of Bob's ideas as being too risky. A couple of times I find myself in the position of having to arbitrate in a difference of opinion, without causing a crisis.

George and I have been together since the formation of our Unit back in Australia, and our association has always been harmonious and clear. Our ideas on how far to push the escape issue are practically identical. The fact that I am an NCO from his own Unit may have influenced George's thinking to some degree. However, in the Australian way, he is always free to speak out and knows it.

As for Bob, it will be difficult to find a better companion to be with than him, and our threesome is a happy one. But his thinking is slightly different from ours in the matter of resistance and taking risks. He had demonstrated this in his efforts to fight his guard when captured on Lemnos. Our aim is to get back to our people in one piece. While we are fully aware of the risks involved, we are not prepared to increase them unnecessarily.

We had been disappointed at the Lemnos debacle and, while we readily understand that the odds were against us, this time we are determined to make no mistakes. George seems to be alarmed that there is a possibility that Bob might influence us into a drastic course of action. The sitting around, the waiting, and the inaction is probably getting at us, for there is no real friction. It's just that sometimes we tend to be a bit critical and snap at each other.

We have been in our hideout for about a week when one of the worker Monks hurries to tell us that we have to leave immediately and travel to the south side of the Peninsula. He will lead us to another house where we will wait. A boat is expected at any time and the people there will make arrangements for us to leave when it arrives.

Hurrying behind our guide, we make our way up over the ridge and partway down the other side. Naturally, we are excited, but Bob cautions us, not to get too carried away, as it may be a false alarm. The same sort of thing had happened to his party on their previous stay. Then, nothing had come of it.

At the new house, we are greeted by a new group of Monks, and Bob confirms that this is the same lot as before. We settle in and wait for three tedious days, expecting at any moment to be summoned to our awaiting boat. Then, the spokesman at our new location comes to tell us that he is sorry, but there has been a change of plans. The boat will not be coming, and we will have to go back to the former house to wait until another contact can be made. Back we trudge, heavyhearted and disappointed at this false alarm.

Our Monk seems a trifle disconcerted at our return. Things revert to what they had been before, with the exception that food has been less plentiful and a bit less to our taste. We distinctly feel that we might be a bit of a burden here. Still, with the faint possibility of a boat turning up, we just have to hang on. Then, to top it off, George gets sick and I am devastated. He awakes one morning, hot, flushed and feverish, and with swelling under his armpit that is causing a lot of pain. I get him to strip and raise his arm, which he does with difficulty. We closely examine his armpit to see if we can work out what is wrong, and how serious the problem is.

We have been living rough for so long, without bathing, that a fair amount of dirt has become ingrained into the skin. We all are the same, but, with George, the poor quality dye in the jacket, given to us by the Greeks at Pefkodassos, has run, mingled with sweat, and become ingrained too. Now there is a distinct lump under his arm, with angry red streaks running from it and down the side of his body. It looks very much like a case of blood poisoning. This highlights our unspoken and secret fear of being injured, or becoming too sick, to go on. George is in obvious distress, and a decision has to be made. Bob helps in our discussions, but, what to do has to be settled between George and me.

I try to weigh up all the possibilities. If George's sickness is blood poisoning, then he will have to have proper treatment very quickly. As far as I know, it only takes a couple of days from its onset, to its fatal conclusion. Where can he get treatment? In all our travels we have not come across one doctor. All the villagers, who are a pretty healthy lot, seem to muddle through by dosing themselves. In the case of my dysentery, it was the locals who had cured me.

If we alert the Monks, they will insist in going to work with the kind of primitive medicine, we had witnessed on the malaria victim, at Skite Xenophontos on our last trip. My own feelings are that it will at least require a tetanus shot, which is out of the question here. If the Monks take over, it will be out of our hands to try any alternatives.

So, where else is available to get proper treatment? There are the Greek civilian authorities, namely the Police, and the German Army Medical Corps. We know the German expertise to be top class, and that it would be a point of honour to them in giving proper treatment to a dangerously ill prisoner. But it will be a complete anathema, and unthinkable, to turn oneself in to them, after all the trouble we have gone to in order to get so far. Besides, the nearest Germans are many miles away, and George could be dead before getting anywhere near them.

This leaves only the Greek Police. They are an unknown quantity to us, but our opinion is that their attitude is generally favourable. We have avoided contact with them, not wishing to create a situation where they might have to put themselves at risk by defying the German Occupation authorities. Our information from other escapers, while back in Salonika, is of one or two instances of betrayal, but mostly a neutral attitude.

The Peninsula of Athos is a very large religious community completely isolated from the rest of the country. Although subject to the laws as set down, they have complete autonomy and manage their own affairs. All dealings with the outside world are conducted through the necessary officials who are located in the tiny township of Karyes. There is a police post there, staffed by one solitary policeman.

Karyes is located about midway along, on flat land, on the north side of the ridge. Although we have covered almost every inch of the Peninsula, we have strictly avoided the town. We hoped in this way to avoid coming under the wrong kind of notice. Our only knowledge of the place, therefore, is hearsay. And, as it is from the Greeks, it may be very suspect.

We could wait a day or two to see if George's condition settles down. But, if it is what I think, it could greatly lessen his chances of recovery. To leave the Peninsula and seek treatment outside, will involve several days' marching, an effort that seems, at the moment, beyond George's capabilities. Besides, we are still clinging to the hope of a boat turning up.

George and I talk over all these pros and cons exhaustively and, now, we have to come up with a verdict. I tell him, as I see it, that he must have proper treatment. The most acceptable way to achieve this, is to turn himself in to the lone policeman in Karyes. We figure that the Policeman's job there is a piece of cake, and he will do all in his power to protect it. If George demands treatment, the Policeman will find a way of getting it, by spiriting him off the Peninsula into police custody, while protecting the community as a whole.

It is drastic, but the only alternative is to hang on and hope that the condition will right itself. George himself has to assess how he feels and work out if this is a possibility. We both feel pretty bad at the suggestion of busting up our partnership, and we still try to think of another way. Try as we might, we cannot, and finally, George decides to turn himself in. It is only about an hour's walk into Karyes and George feels he can manage it alright. So, without further ado, he sets off. It is with mixed feelings that I watch him go. Prudently, we decide not to accompany him, while George will pretend that he is alone. If I had not had to consider Bob's situation too, I think I would have turned myself in also.

I am pretty despondent for the next couple of days. When our Monk visits us, we inform him of what has happened. He is non-committal, but our impression is that he isn't very happy. There is still no word of a boat, and we begin to feel there won't be. For one whole week, nobody visits us and the only food we have is a large earthenware jar of black olives. During this period, I learn a little bit of Bob's background.

Bob had been at school with the intention of going on to become a Doctor. In an assessment session, his Headmaster pointed out that, as he had been slacking in his studies, it would be prudent to aim a bit lower and become a vet. This he agreed to do.

At the outbreak of War, he joined the Royal Army Veterinary Corp, and had become a Lance Corporal before his capture. Composed mostly of country farm labourers, and supervised by practising Vets, they were given Army mules to look after. They were expected to serve in mountainous areas to transport supplies. His C.O. had taken Bob under his wing. With his help, Bob had been writing a thesis on an unknown sexual disease, discovered amongst their animals, as a means towards getting his degree. All this written work had been lost upon Bob's capture.

His Unit had been sent as far as Egypt, with the intention of going on to the mountainous areas of India, when the Greek business came up. Somebody got the bright idea that it would be just the thing for them to be used in the mountains of Greece. When the end came, all they could do was turn their animals loose and make a run for it. I had seen one or two mules killed on the side of the road, with others roaming the countryside, when we were making our run. They were fat, big and strong, and distinctly not Greek, and I was wondering where they came from.

While in Egypt, Bob had made a call on the British Ambassador, who was a friend of the family. The Ambassador told him that, in preparation for the Western Desert push, tanks were urgently needed. With the situation as it was on the Homefront, none was available from there. But a brand new squadron, of two hundred of the latest, had only recently been supplied to King Farouk. General Alexander had asked the Ambassador to intercede with Farouk, asking for their return on temporary loan, with all damages to be made good.

Farouk flatly refused and, with the situation rather urgent, the British got tough. In essence they told him, "Look, we put you on the throne, and we can bloody soon put you off." With very bad grace, Farouk finally complied.

I remembered, at that time, there were very strong rumours, that Farouk was about to declare his country neutral. Strong British pressure had been needed to make him change his mind. We heard that there was a very beautiful Italian woman who was a great favourite of his, and, under his protection, trying to get him to side with Italy. As Italy was making a very strong bid to invade Egypt from Libya, our troops would have been in a very tricky position, with Egypt conniving with our enemy, in our rear.

Bob's type of Unit, and his general background and outlook, is distinctly unlike the usual British Regimental attitude. His is free and easy, and almost Australian in approach, and we get on famously. It helps a lot in taking some of the misery out of the loss of my mate, George.

With nothing happening, food is getting tighter, and the cold weather advancing with the advent of Christmas. We think it is about time that we make some sort of move ourselves. We decide to head back to the side of the ridge, to that other house, we had been taken to, and find out if there has been any developments.

We arrive, and, our formerly friendly host stares at us in open dismay, and with almost terror in his face. We are nonplussed. Our intention is always to cause as little embarrassment as possible to these people, whose help we so sorely need.

He tells us that a boat had come in, just after we set out to return to the other side, on our last visit. A man had set off to try to catch us, but the boat had to leave before he could make contact. Now it is impossible to get a boat in all of Greece.

The boat had taken a few escapers and there would have been room for us. From his descriptions, it seems that one man had been recovering from a wounded leg. On our wanderings, we had been told of this man, and an offer had been made to take us to meet him. We declined as he was alone, and we felt that we might have to ask him to join us. Our reasons were that four was too big a party to travel with, and that his wounded leg might hold us back. It will be poetic justice if he is to make it through, while we are left behind.

With our welcome, rather bleak now, at both these places, we decide to revert to wandering from Monastery to Monastery as we had done before. With our hopes pinned to getting to neutral Turkey, and a wide stretch of sea separating us, we can only cling to the idea of somehow getting a boat.

Bob comes up with the idea that, if we could get any sort of boat, just something with a couple of oars, we could maybe make it across by island-hopping. First, we would make for Thasos which is almost at right angles to the direct route, then on to Samothrace, and finally to Imbros.

This is a much longer route, but capable of being made in shorter hops. We can rest up at each island, before pushing on in the next step. The more we talk about it, the more feasible it becomes. The miles of open sea we will have to traverse, will be a piece of cake. We even begin to calculate how many miles per day we can expect to cover, with each taking a turn at the oars while the other rests.

A tiny bit of reason begins to creep into my thoughts. I am prepared to take my chances in a scheme and, if things go wrong, well it can't be helped. Here, if we fail, we will be lost at sea with nobody ever knowing what has happened to us. I don't mention it to Bob, as I think he might see it as a sign of weakness. But I prefer to think it as being prudent. Anyway, with our sort of luck, we probably won't find a boat anyhow.

About mid-afternoon one day, we are making our way from one Monastery to another. Our intention is to arrive in time to make arrangements to spend the night. This will be no problem because of the unwritten law of welcoming travellers for the night. The winding track we are using, skirts the coastline.

As we walk, we take in the scenic beauty of the rugged rocky shores and lovely blue sea. As we advance, a small bay or inlet, begins to open up before us. Some distance away, just about where the inlet turns back to the sea coast, a small house can be seen, just coming into view above the surrounding shrubbery. This will be a small Skite or outstation from a parent Monastery and may contain from one to any number of Priests or workers, depending upon its size. Such isolated places are fairly common around the Peninsula and, although we generally are just as welcome to stay there, we usually opted for the slightly more favourable comfort of a Monastery proper.

Now our track takes us out into the open and along the edge of the inlet, which is about fifteen feet above the water's edge. With the bay now in full view, we can see a small row boat containing a Priest and two workers. They are busy setting a fishing net to close off a portion of the bay.

We have been led to believe that there is no boat of any kind on the Peninsula, and this one takes us completely by surprise. We feel slightly cheated at this information having been kept from us, and wonder how many other and maybe better boats, are hidden away somewhere. In our hearts, we know that, if there are, their loss will be a major disaster to the locals. With the large number of escapers gravitating to this spot, boats would vanish like flakes in a furnace.

Keeping out of sight, we pass a critical eye over the three men at their labours, paying particular attention to their boat. It appears to be about ten feet long and moves quite easily as it is rowed by one of them. Immediately, our island hopping scheme flashes back into our minds. Then and there, we decide that we are going to steal that boat.

Still keeping out of sight, we move round close to the house, take up a vantage point from where we can study every move they make, and the layout of the landing ramp. The house is on piers that are closed in, with timber, making a very effective boat shed. There is a sloping ramp leading from its interior, right down into the water. The slope is very steep, making a launching very easy.

Depending upon their fishing methods, they either leave the net out all night and pull the boat out of the water; or pick the net up during the night, or after a few hours, leaving the boat tethered close by.

We have to wait some time before they finish their job. The day is coming to a close when finally they come back to the ramp. We watch as they hook up a block and tackle to a ring on the boat's prow, from somewhere within the shed. Hauling on the rope, they pull it steadily clear of the water and up the steep ramp. When it is just outside the shed, they stop pulling and make it fast. They busy themselves with chores, cleaning up, then, with all three talking together, they move off and up into the house. The oars are left lying in the boat.

A light appears above, and preparations for a meal can be sensed. Their quarters are just above where the boat lies. So, we will have to take care not to be heard. We will not make a move until it is completely dark, preferably, after they have settled down for the night. The timing will depend on how things shape up. In preparation, we study carefully the layout. We will do our best to make absolutely no noise. There will be no stumbling and no talking. Each of us will know exactly what to do so that there are no slipups.

We select the path we will use to skirt the side of the building, and will approach the boat from the water. We both will take hold of the boat near the bow, and haul it up sufficiently to slacken the block and tackle. I will disengage the block, and lay it quietly on the ground. Bob will move closer to the stern on the opposite side, and secure the oars so that they do not rattle. With the boat free, we will gently ease it down into the water, so that there is no sudden rush or splash. We will quietly step aboard and, with me at the oars, slowly make our way round the set net, so as not to become entangled, and head out into the open sea. Although memorising the position of the net, we confidently expect the floats to show us where it is, because of the slight phosphorescence as the ripples move against them.

With the plan fully thrashed out, and each of us knowing exactly what to do, we turn our attention to the forthcoming journey. We will head for Thasos, making every effort to get there. But if it shows this is not practical, we will turn and make a landing somewhere along the coast. We will have to make do with the very small quantity of food we have with us. Water will be the most vital necessity, so we will fill all our containers while we wait.

In Greece, clear running water from springs abounds. This makes it unnecessary to carry any with you. We have long since lost our water bottles, and have been making do with one or two tins we have managed to latch onto, for those long journeys when locked away in cattle trucks. Now, we are acutely aware of how limited a supply, they hold. We will just have to make more landings along the coast. We don't like this, because of prolonging the trip. But, under the circumstances, it cannot be helped. For myself, the prospect of keeping close to the coast is pleasing, for I think it will be safer this way.

We have talked over every angle and possible faults in our plan, until we are confident that we have covered everything. We wait, patiently, while the night closes in around us. It is cold and clear, and there is no moon. Finally, with the chill creeping into our bones, we decide to wait no longer and set off.

Silently, we move along the path we have chosen, and skirt the house. We can hear talking directly above our heads, so they haven't retired yet.

We heave the boat up slightly and, without much difficulty, I remove the block, and lay it clear on the ground. Bob moves to his position, steadies the oars, and we begin to ease the boat down the ramp.

Now that we are actually handling it, we are able to see what kind of boat it is. We find it is a flat-bottom tub of a thing, constructed of thick heavy planking. It is the kind that the average small freighter carries and uses when in harbour, for chores such as painting the hull. A less likely craft, for our purpose, cannot be imagined. But we are committed, and just have to carry on. It will just have to do.

The stern begins to enter the water. We carefully ease the full length in, until just the bow is still on the ramp. As we prepare to push off and climb in, a slight swell lifts the whole boat, and the bow smacks down with a loud bang and clatter. There is instant reaction from the house above. Startled voices ring out and scampering feet can be heard, just above our heads. Abandoning any further attempts at silence, we climb in and push off.

As I thrust out the oars, I can feel water about ankle deep in the bottom. To skirt the net, we have to go parallel to the shore, instead of straight out. The three men, from inside the house, burst out onto a long balcony running along the front, and look down upon us. They realise, instantly, what is going on, and the Monk whirls and disappears inside. Seeking to confuse the issue, for some unknown reason, I stupidly call out some German swear words, I have picked up, as we pull away.

Now, the Monk reappears with something in his hands, and raises it to shoulder height. Suddenly, a great blast rings out, with a huge flash of fire. The object is a shot gun, and he is firing at us. Fortunately, we aren't hit. The three of them turn and clatter down the rickety stairs, and onto the water's edge.

By now, we have reached the end of the line of floats, rounded them, and headed away from the shore. Bob is sitting in the stern, as we had arranged, and water is sloshing round our feet. Precious drinking water has to be sacrificed, with Bob using the tin to bail, while I endeavour to put some distance between us and the shore.

With Bob constantly bailing, I make it out of the inlet, then turn parallel to the coast. We have to make sure we are gaining on the water before heading further out. The three men on shore set after us on foot with remarkable speed, along paths known to them intimately, while calling on us to stop and come back. Although I am working hard, I cannot outdistance the three on shore. Bob's bailing is making no headway and, in fact, seems to be losing ground. We make the decision that this boat is not a viable proposition. We will have to ditch it.

Then the three men begin to flag a bit, while the path veers away inland from the coast. They begin to fade from sight and quickly disappear. We keep going to put some distance between us. Then, when we judge it is enough, I turn the nose and we pull into a sandy shore. Hauling the boat safely out of the water, we quickly grab our gear and take off into the safety of the surrounding shrubbery.

There are no sounds from our pursuers. We know the area and realise there is a bush hut not too far away. We head for it, and spend what is left of the night, there. The whole episode has been a disaster. Although we could not be recognised, it won't take any great genius to work out that escapers are involved, as soon as news of what has happened begins to spread. News spreads so fast here, that it will be only a matter of hours, before the whole community knows. As probably the only two in this vicinity, we cannot evade being prime suspects.

In the morning, we sit and talk over the pros and cons of the situation. We probably have blown our chances of obtaining help in locating a boat. But, as a boat is the only real chance of getting out of the country, we feel we still have to brazen things out and keep trying. We know we will still be treated courteously, and given food and a place to sleep. We will have to continue wandering from Monastery to Monastery, and hoping that luck will allow us to become part of somebody else's plan, just like what happened to George and me on our last visit.

As for that boat, no doubt it will be very quickly found, and, almost certainly, is already back in the hands of the owners. We have not damaged it in any way, and we count heavily on the fact that they have recovered it intact, and for them to let the matter end there.

It is a couple of hours before we get moving. The anticlimax of the night before, and a slight reluctance to face up to the first of several people we will meet in the day, holds us back. Finally, we brace ourselves and set off. We need not have worried. Our first contacts greet us as before, as though nothing has happened.

We move on, and about midday we are nearing another Monastery. In common with most of them, there is a small inlet of calm water giving access to the sea, close to the outer walls. A small jetty about twenty feet long, which pushes out from the shore, is a bustling hive of activity, with Monks coming and going. Tied up alongside is a boat, and they are provisioning it. This is a real boat. It is sturdy and seaworthy, and is an identical match with the two we had set out in, when we got to Lemnos. We can see immediately that this is not an escape attempt that they are preparing for. It is some sort of trading venture where they will sell or exchange some of the products of the Monastery, such as the spirit Raki, for other goods needed by them.

We know that there is nothing here for us, but just stand there watching the busy scene. Presently the bustle slackens, with some of the Monks departing back to the Monastery. A couple of Monks left behind now ease the boat away from the jetty, and drop a small anchor. A line on the stern is tethered back to the wharf, allowing the boat to be pulled back for easy boarding, while still floating free. Then these Monks depart and the boat, fully provisioned for the trip, is left just sitting there.

I say to Bob, "You know, all we have to do is just stroll down there, pull the boat in, climb aboard and cast off."

"Well, I'm game if you are," says Bob.

"No, we can't do it," I reply, and I mean it.

My whole being revolts against the thought of stealing this boat. Almost all the people are so poor in material things that to acquire a boat is almost an impossible dream. For us to steal it, would break its owner and his family practically forever. We have been given so much simple but invaluable help with things such as food and water, that I cannot come at the idea. Last night's episode, I feel, has not been quite so barefaced and, therefore, more excusable.

The whole region fronts onto many miles of sea that undoubtedly has a large fish population. One may think that fishing and netting would be a major part of food gathering for the Monasteries. Yet, in all the time we have been here, the sole instance we have seen, is what we had observed the day before. Fish, of any kind, has never been on the menu in our experience. Maybe this is because of the total lack of boats.

Certainly, there are some fishing villages here and there along the coast, and certainly, they will have boats of some sort to carry out their calling. But they seem few and far between. Maybe the Germans have confiscated most of them. It is the fisher folk we had hoped the Monks could contact on our behalf. We had hoped they would be able to smuggle us through, rather than us having to take their boats and just abandon them.

All our movements, and comings and goings, up to now, have been concentrated in the central area of the Peninsula. We had entered in from the west and crisscrossed the ridge that runs its length to both the north and south side. The eastern end that soars up into Mount Athos, then falls away into the sea, is unknown to us. We understand that there are a few hermitages, containing small religious communities, dotted here and there, right round this area.

We now decide to head along the north side from where we are, skirt the base of the mountain on the seaward side, then come back along the south side. This will allow for the heat to abate on our indiscretions, while giving us the chance to explore new territory. Just maybe, there are hiding places along there, where a boat could be stored out of sight.

We set off, just following the tracks in the direction of where we want to go. In these new areas, our reception is always friendly. In fact, our advent introduces a welcome relief into the often lonely and humdrum life of these people. Their existence here is harder, and passers-by are almost non-existent. When we reach the base of the mountain area, we find the eastern end to be a vast broken rockslide of boulders of all sizes that fall right into the sea. There is a barely discernible goat track leading across it, which we traverse gingerly, half expecting to lose our footing and to plummet into the sea, some hundred feet below.

Once across this barrier, we arrive at a small hermitage. The Monk here produces a Visitors Book, insisting that we sign it, giving our names and home addresses. We give some thought to the prudence of such a step, almost deciding to write in something fictitious. The place is so remote and inaccessible, that we realise we need not worry. We sign correctly and, if the book still exists, our signatures will still be there.

We move on and begin to come back into the sort of territory that we are familiar with. One late afternoon, we spot a building some distance in front of us. We decide to make for it and spend the night there. Upon arrival we find it well locked and barred, with no sign of life. The building is in good repair and quite large. It seems that its regular inhabitants have moved out temporarily. We guess they have returned to the parent Monastery, as it is getting close to Christmas, and may return perhaps when the winter begins to ease. It is too late for us to move on and, as it is too cold to sleep out, we decide to break in. It is a bit difficult, but we manage to force an entry. Inside, we find lots of supplies, suggesting that the people will be returning at any time. All evening we half-expect somebody to walk in and catch us.

We decide to light a fire, and sort through the goods here to make ourselves something to eat. We boil some onions, mix in some tomato paste in water, and have a good bellyful. We use a long pine pole to keep the fire going all night, and bunk down in front of it. This one time, we are able to please ourselves what we do. It is likely we overdo things a bit, as Monks generally are very frugal. Also, the partial burning of the pole would be frowned upon. After our trials, we feel a little defiant, and in no need to be apologetic. Nevertheless, we deem it prudent to get an early morning start, to get well clear of the area, just in case somebody does show up.

Mostly, the Monasteries and their outlying Skites or Hermitages, are fairly close together, and a relatively short walk brings you to a building of some sort. But, on this particular day, we come across nothing until late in the afternoon. Then, coming into view, as the landscape opens up, is the familiar sight of well-cultivated gardens, laid out in front of a quite large Monastery. We judge that we are about halfway along the south side of the Peninsula, and that this Monastery is the landing point for visitors arriving by boat in peace time.

The approach to the entrance gate is along an unevenly paved path of natural stone. Above it is a trellis supporting a large grape vine. Just in front of the gate, a very large bunch of perfectly ripe black grapes hangs temptingly. It is all I can do to refrain from helping myself. We judge that we had better conduct ourselves with decorum, as the Skite we had broken into, more than likely belongs to this Monastery. The gateman receives us in the usual way and, after preliminaries, hands us over to some other officials. We declare who we are and, upon finding I am Australian, they tell us that one of their number had lived in Australia. They will settle us in, and bring him to meet us.

We are taken upstairs to what are obviously guest rooms for peacetime visitors. We had been shown nothing like this at any other Monastery. The rooms are spartan, but reasonably comfortable, at least to our lower standards. It seems that we are to be treated exactly the same as legitimate visitors. After dumping our gear, we return downstairs where the officials produce their man from Australia. He is well into his eighties and seems a bit senile. Yes, he has lived in Australia, in Melbourne. He asks me where I come from. When I tell him Newcastle, he asks, "Is that far from Melbourne?" I know immediately that there is practically nothing we can converse about. I had hoped to be able to get some information from him in our own language, as there is a lot we need to guess at with our limited Greek.

I try to explain to him, and also Bob, how very far away the two places are from each other. The man replies, "I have a friend, George, in Melbourne. Do you know my friend George?"

I answer patiently, "Sorry, I don't know George." And again, I stress how far apart the two places are.

He then thinks for a moment, then repeats, "But you must know my friend George." After a few exchanges like this, he falls silent. He then turns and walks away from us, mumbling to himself.

We are given food, eating together with the other Monks in the communal room. Afterwards, we retire to our room and spend a reasonably comfortable night. In the morning we gather our gear together, and are preparing to move on, when we are visited by the officials. In a very touching manner, they make a small presentation to us. At a before daylight service, they bless a small package for each of us. It will keep us in good health, and bring us good fortune during our travels. It appears to be a small quantity of cotton wool, carefully wrapped in plain white paper.

The explanation, as far as we can make out, is as follows. Our packages have been made sacred by coming under the influence of shavings from the original Cross that Christ had been crucified upon. At first we think the packages are supposed to contain some of the original shavings. Then we realise that this is most unlikely. It seems, more likely, that the original shavings are kept within a receptacle, that is contained in the altar, which makes it sacred. This means that all things and services, in which the altar figures, are doubly blessed, our packages included. The Monks are totally sincere in their beliefs, and we realise that these relics must have been held in veneration for hundreds of years. Any doubts, as to their authenticity, that we may feel, are insignificant in the face of the sincerity and the goodwill of the gift.

We tuck them carefully away upon our persons, make the appropriate expressions of thanks and, feeling rather chastened, make our departure. After this little episode, we rather regret our break in, of the previous day.

We cross once again to the north side, wander for a couple more days, each one just as unproductive as before. We are becoming rather fed up, but not quite sure what to do about it. Christmas has come, but not here on the Peninsula. Under the Orthodox religion, celebrations will occur thirteen days after the regular rites, as recognised elsewhere.

We awake one morning, after a very cold night, to find the Peninsula covered with a heavy blanket of snow. The mountain looks more beautiful than ever, but it is most unhelpful to us. As soon as we begin moving on, we find that all signs of a trail have disappeared. Soon, we are floundering up to our knees in thick snow, not knowing where we are.

After two hours of heavy going, in which we have covered a distance we normally do in about a quarter of an hour, we spot a building and head for it. It is almost at right angles to our path, but, although quite close, it still requires another half hour of floundering across open fields to get there. Almost totally exhausted, we keep banging for somebody's attention, refusing to be fobbed off.

Finally, a heavily rugged-up Monk pokes his head out. We tell him we are lost and demand that he help us. He takes us to a small barn and begins to build a fire, while we watch in fascination. With no paper, he cuts a small heap of very fine splinters from a block of wood, using a penknife. He gathers all the materials for a proper fire, close to hand, and then lights a match. Inclining the match, so that its tiny flame climbs up the wooden body, he carefully feeds the fine splinters into it, in twos and threes. Soon he has the tiniest of fires, and then he deftly feeds larger pieces on, until it is blazing brightly. Once properly alight, he scoops up some fresh snow into a pot and prepares a brew for us.

As the hot liquid begins to warm our insides, we take stock and mull over our situation. We decide that we have had enough of Aeyanoris and the Peninsula of Mount Athos. We will make our way overland and try to cross the border into Turkey, which we presume will be heavily guarded. Still, there must be some smugglers operating in that area, bringing in scarce commodities. We will make it our aim to contact some of that fraternity, and promise them high payment when they get us through.

We know that Greek Macedonia, through to the Turkish border, has been handed over to the countries immediately to the north. These new masters probably will be more zealous than the Germans, and this will make it harder for us. Still, it seems the only course we can now take. If we keep close to the coast, we still might be able to come across a boat.

With our minds made up on a course of action, we settle down for the night. By the time we are ready to move in the morning, the snow has thawed a little and the trail is a bit easier to find. The Monk steers us in the right direction, and we set off. We head up to the ridge and along it to the west. The snow has fallen mostly on the north side, with much less on the south. We keep to the easier going as much as possible, and avoid all contact with places and people. We are determined to quit the Peninsula this very same day.

It is late in the afternoon when we force our way through some shrubbery, much as George and I had done when first coming here. In front of us, we find the small fishing village we have been making for. It is the same village where the French woman had given George and I that lovely grilled fish meal.

We pause and take in the scene. There are about half a dozen sturdy boats riding at anchor, just out from the shore. Bob quickly suggests we revise our plans, and go back to our original idea of a boat. My whole being revolts once again at the thought of stealing such a vital possession from these people. I begin putting forward reasons that will make the idea impractical.

I explain that oars and sails will not be on board and, almost certainly, will be locked away. "Not so," according to Bob, pointing to a small shed near the water's edge, where these vital items are indeed hanging on racks on the side, in full view.

"What about provisions?" I point out.

"No sweat," says Bob, "All we need to do is to call at some of the Monasteries, and they will gladly stock us up, once we have our own boat. We might even get a few other escapees, who are hidden away there, to come with us."

The thought of returning to the Peninsula goes very much against the grain with me. Still, I grudgingly have to admit that the idea is a sound one. By now, we have come to realise that the locals are unwilling to take the risks involved in transporting us across to Turkey. To get there, we will have to do it ourselves, and this means stealing a boat, if you can find one. Here, there are half a dozen, almost inviting to be taken.

So the plan devised by Bob is this: We will put up for the night in the village. About two in the morning, we will sneak from our beds, take a set of sails and oars from the racks, wade out to one of the boats, get in, and shove off. We will be well down the Peninsula before daylight. I endeavour to temper the plan by suggesting that we see if any of them are willing to take us. Bob vetoes this idea, pointing out that they will guard against a boat being stolen, once they wake up to what we have in mind.

With the idea, more or less settled, at least as far as Bob is concerned, we venture into the town. We are greeted heartily by the people, with everybody being in a festive mood. Although Christmas has passed, they are still celebrating. We have missed out on the Christmas Day festivities, both on Athos and here, because of the difference in their calendar and beliefs. They try to make it up for us.

We are taken to a fair sized room, where several of the menfolk are gathered. They sit us down and begin plying us with titbits and drinks. Some women keep flitting in and out, bringing in different foodstuffs. This goes on for several hours until finally a couple of them rise, and take us to a house nearby. They probably notice that we are deadbeat. We have had a very tough day.

The accommodation offered to us is completely different to any that has been offered up to now. Whilst not elaborate, the degree of comfort is something we have not seen for a very long time. We have become inured to sleeping on floors, curling up in corners and on a bit of straw in a barn, if we are lucky. This place is a self-contained dwelling containing two cots. Usually most houses are primarily built for living in, with cooking, eating and a general living quarters; but here, we are faced with nothing but a bedroom.

On each of the cots is a new mattress, stuffed full of clean, fresh straw. The room itself is snug, which is important as the weather is very cold, even though all signs of snow have disappeared since leaving the Peninsula. It is a two person room, and we have it to ourselves. We will be able to slip out at any time without disturbing anyone.

As I take in the scene, I am very close to tears. It comes home to me how long it has been since last I have slept decently. After joining the AIF, there was a succession of camps, then the tent life in Palestine, and sleeping on the ground up in the Western Desert and through Greece, followed by the POW camps, and being on the loose. This simple setup seems like heaven.

We drop our gear, kick off our boots, and just fall into the cot and mattress, we are nearest to. It is like floating on a cloud. And oh! The luxury of being able to stretch fully out, to one's content! We begin to drop off immediately, while confused mumblings, of waking at 2.00 am, and carrying out our plan, come from Bob. I am too tired to argue against the idea, but feel that we will sleep so soundly, that it just won't happen. Besides, the mere thought of having to wade out in that icy water, possibly to chest depth, is more than I can envisage.

Doggedly, Bob manages to stir himself at the appropriate hour, and tries to rouse me, by first calling and then shaking me. Just as doggedly, I refuse to be stirred, while, at the same time, muttering pointless and inane excuses, as to why the exercise is not on. After a few minutes, Bob gives up, collapses back into his bed, and sleeps soundly for the rest of the night.

It is full daylight when, finally, we come back to our full consciousness. We are much refreshed, but the realisation that I have let Bob down, pretty badly, makes me feel remorseful. I rather lamely try to explain why I have backed out of our agreed plan. My excuses aren't very convincing, but Bob takes them in calmly, while at the same time telling me it doesn't really matter. There will be other times, and other plans.

By now, the whole village is awake. In the light of a new day, we decide that there is nothing further for us here, and we will push on with our plan to try and make it overland. Before we can move off, however, some of the menfolk insist on again taking us back into the room of the night before. They again ply us with little delicacies, and press gifts of money into our hands. The giving of gifts, apparently, is a required thing at this time of the year. I cannot help, but be thankful, that they are unaware of our intentions towards a boat. It helps to salve my conscience a little.

Once again we are on the road, and I feel there is a bit more purpose in our plans. My whole being refuses to even consider a return to the Peninsula, and those fruitless wanderings. We have not entirely given up the idea of a boat. Bob has an English banknote to the value of ten pounds carefully tucked away, and we propose to buy one if possible. This is a plan that I can totally agree with. We, therefore, set our course along the coastline and, if nothing turns up, we will press on with the overland idea.

While to buy a boat with ten pounds may sound a bit farfetched, it has to be remembered that the Greek currency has become practically worthless. The English pound at this time is the world's strongest currency. Ten pounds in this country is a small fortune. We have to be careful in making enquiries. If it becomes known that we have such an amount on us, we may quickly end up missing and dead.

Food is scarce and getting hard to come by. Although we are still being given something, as we beg along the way, the locals, themselves, have very little for their own needs. In lots of instances, their wheat has all been used up, and they are grinding corn to make into bread. The taste is pleasant, almost like cake, but the food value is much less.

We begin to learn something of the country that lay ahead of us, and some of the hazards barring our way. Greek Macedonia has been divided by the Germans, with a large portion being handed over for administration by Bulgaria. A natural barrier between the two parts is the River Struma. It is a wide, deep and fast-flowing river, now swollen by winter rains. The river rises in Bulgaria and traverses Greek territory before flowing into the sea. Somehow, we will have to find a way across. There are some road and rail bridges, but they are now heavily guarded by Bulgarians. Swimming is out of the question. Maybe we can get a lift in a small boat, round the mouth, where it enters the sea. But, on the Greek side of the river mouth, a very strong Police Post has been set up. We might have to explore the possibility of some aiding and abetting, by the Greek Police.

We find ourselves very close to a town called Stratoni, supposedly, the richest town in Greece. There is a nickel mine in the hills on one side, the source of its wealth, and the sea on the other. The nickel deposits are being mined at a great pace, with all the output being taken by the Germans for their war effort. To ensure against any production problems, a fair sized German garrison is stationed there. We are warned to give it a wide berth. Because of the geographical layout, we are unable to do this, without taking a very long detour.

Confident that our disguise is good enough to get us through, we decide to skirt the place, on the hillside and on the extreme edge of the town. As we negotiate the small back lanes, it is inevitable that we meet a few Greeks on our way. We greet them in the usual Greek manner and they reply in the same way. We are aware that they know who we are, although no indication is given. We just press on, anxious to be clear of the place as soon as possible, and hoping that nobody will give us away.

We are negotiating the last little bit, where we have to come round a small house, when a Greek man, in his late fifties, appears in front of us. We give the usual greeting, but the man stands square in front of us, barring our way and making no attempt to move. Then, in perfect English, with a strong American accent he says, "How will a large T-bone steak, smothered with onions, with French fried potatoes, followed by apple pie and cream, go right now?"

We give a tortured groan and say, "For God's sake man, stop teasing us."

He apologises saying, "I'm sorry, I'm unable to oblige. But if you come with me to my house nearby, I can at least give you something."

We go with him and he is as good as his word. He is eager to use his English again, and is glad of our company for someone to practise on. We tell him that we are a bit worried about the German garrison, and think that we ought to move on. He insists that we are safe here, and should stay the night. He claims that their main interest is the mine's output and, as long as that is okay, they don't interfere elsewhere. So we stay.

We find that he has lived in America for over twenty years, working there mostly in restaurants. He returned home with a moderate amount of money which became a small fortune here. He is able to live reasonably well and enjoys a bit of prestige amongst his neighbours. He has reverted to the Greek lifestyle in food and housing. All talk of Western food, is just that, only talk.

From time to time, as the night wears on, some of his men friends and neighbours, drop in. He proudly demonstrates to them his prowess with this foreign language. We, good-naturedly go along with this exhibition. We eye each of them warily, hoping that none of them will turn us in. He seems to trust them, so we have no alternative, but to do the same. When finally, we bunk down, it is a bit eerie to think that just up the street is a Company of German soldiers, who would just love to round up a couple of escaped prisoners.

In the morning, we are sitting at a small table having a snack before leaving, when our friend comes up with a proposal. He has been talking with some of his friends, and they have worked it out among them. He proposes that we wander no more, and stay here until the War is over. They will take us a couple of miles out of town, and set us up in a camp. There, we can work as charcoal burners, simply to give us something to do, and as a cover. They will bring us into town once or twice a week, so that we can get drunk, and provide us with the services of a woman.

It is a genuine offer, and we are a little taken aback by it. We have seen some charcoal burners at work, and know what is involved. You cut timber and roast it over a slow fire, while covered with a large mound of earth. When finished and dug out, all that is left is chunks of charcoal, much desired, in these parts, as fuel. It is a dirty job, ending with all the workers covered in black, much the same as coal miners. The getting drunk and sex offer is incidental, and designed to keep us from getting too bored. We know, instantly, that such an arrangement will be an open secret in no time.

We give him the courtesy of seeming to think the matter over. But, in reality, we won't even consider it. We explain that while on the loose, we are posted as missing. Our families have no way of knowing if we are alive or dead. For their sakes, and our own, we have to give it a try—even if we fail, and are recaptured.

He is a bit disappointed, but agrees, saying that he can see our point. We shake hands and depart, with him directing us to the path that will get us clear of the town, with the least likelihood of attracting attention. As we walk, we chew over the pros and cons of what might have happened, if we had accepted his offer. We both agree that the tedious wait for the War to end, possibly for years, would get us down. No matter how attractive the diversions seem, we would not have been able to stick it out.

We are about threequarters of a mile clear of the town, and walking across flat open fields, when we think we hear somebody calling out behind us. We look back to find half a dozen, of both males and females in their early twenties, waving and calling to us. We can see that they are young Greeks and, as there appears no reason for alarm, we wait for them to catch up with us. When they do, they tell us they know that we are English, and that they have come to help us get away. They ask us to come with them to a nearby barn, which can be seen just ahead, and to eat some of the food they have brought with them, while talking over this offer of help. We are rather sceptical, and feel a bit wary of the situation, but decide we have nothing to lose by listening to their proposition.

They approach the barn with a familiarity that indicates they know the place well. They open a large door in one side, and usher us in. The place is empty, except for a few bits of straw and some poles. They stand together in a group, while we two stand facing them. They close the door, produce a bottle of wine, and offer us some bread and cheese as well. Facing each other a little awkwardly, they try to appear cheerful and animated. They ask in what way they can help us.

We tell them we are trying to obtain a boat in which we can go to the neutral country of Turkey. The Greeks have very little love for the Turks, and this lot tries to influence us into going somewhere else. When they find they cannot sway us, they fall into discussion on the pros and cons of getting a boat. There is much animated talk among them, and we sense that there is no real ability to assist us. We begin to get the impression that they are mainly trying to delay us, and keep us here.

The conversation ebbs and flows, with a few awkward pauses in between. Their suggestions are all maybes, and quite vague. We indicate little or no interest. Most of the wine has gone by now, then one of the fellows points to one of the girls and asks, "Would like to have her?"

She is standing slightly aside from the others, as though with them but not of them. We now look fully at her, to see she is well build, rather comely, and fairly good looking. It seems that this one must be a prostitute, while the others are not.

We gravely decline the offer, while I privately think, "How the hell, do they expect anything to happen here in full view of everybody?"

The man now asks, "Don't you think she is nice?" We heartily agree and he asks, "What is the English word for girl?"

I give him the Greek word for 'good', and turning to a surprised Bob, I tell him, "It's not me talking, it's the wine."

After a bit more verbal sparring, the girl, seeing that her services are not required, leaves. We watch her, through the cracks in the barn, make her way back towards town. The others still keep offering suggestions, but come up with no real propositions. We keep rejecting them, pointing out the flaws in their reasoning. Finally, one of them says that he knows of a man who is just the bloke we are looking for. The whole group begins talking together excitedly, agreeing and saying, "Yes indeed, he is the man."

They exhort us to stay where we are, until they bring him back. It will take a little time, but they will indeed be back. In the meantime, they beg us to remain in the barn, out of sight. We are told to seal the place from outside entry by using the poles lying about, after they leave. We are to open to nobody, but them.

We watch them depart, then jam the poles against the doors. We don't know what to think. Are these just a bunch of young people getting carried away with a sense of adventure? Do they really know of a man who truly can help us? Or is this some crafty scheme that will end up seeing us recaptured?

We keep a sharp lookout and decide that, if we sight anybody we don't like the look of, we will slip out and hurry away, while keeping the bulky barn between us and them. About an hour later, we see the solitary figure of a man leave the edge of the distant town, and head towards us. As he gets a bit closer, we can see that he is wearing some kind of uniform. It is definitely not a German uniform. Then we make out that it is a Police uniform. The Police are still an unknown quantity to us, so we decide to stay put and keep quiet.

He approaches, then circles the barn, rattling the doors while trying to force an entry. Through the cracks in the timber, we watch his every move. While we can see him plainly, he can't see us because of the interior darkness. After a prolonged pushing and shoving, he stops. He circles the barn a couple more times, then heads back to town. We watch, carefully, until he is well clear of the barn, then we slip out of the door, and head off in the opposite direction. We have had enough of this caper, and decide that the only sensible thing to do, is to put as much distance as possible between us and this place. As we hurry off, we try to read some purpose into this strange behaviour. Up until now, the locals have been pretty trustworthy. These proceedings seem to be heading towards a sell-out.

We get out of the area as quickly as possible. This episode unsettles us a bit, and we now proceed with more caution. We try to size up whoever we come across, before sounding them out about assistance. We make one or two queries about buying a boat. Our prospects are greatly interested at the thought of some real money, but nothing eventuates.

We push northward, making for the area of the mouth of the River Struma and the Greek Police Post. We decide to look the scene over before deciding whether or not to contact them. While passing through a small village one afternoon, a Policeman appears in front of us, on the outskirts. It is too late to dodge, so we walk straight up to him. This is our first meeting with the Police, and we don't know what his reaction might be. We decide to ask for his help.

He speaks with us briefly, then places his hand on my arm in the classic come along with me grip. Angrily, I throw his hand aside, and ask, "Are you going to help us or not?" When no reply is forthcoming, we brush him aside and continue on.

This meeting gives us some serious doubts as to the possibility of any Police help. We are tired and in poor shape. Food is scarce, and it is raining. We have to do something. We decide that one Policeman isn't the whole force. We will take the risk, and see what our chances are at the Police Post. When we arrive, we pause while looking over the place. It seems harmless enough, just a small building with not much activity going on. At least in there, we are likely to be warm and dry and, maybe, there will be a little food.

We walk into a large open room, with about eight to ten Policemen either sitting or moving about. We announce who we are, and that we are seeking their help. They greet us in an open, easy going, friendly manner, and we begin talking together. We explain we have ideas of making our way across country to the Turkish border, then slipping across into neutral territory. We ask if they can help us to get round the mouth of the Struma, and whether they can tell us about the conditions in the area we have to cross. As well, we ask about the likelihood of food.

Several of them begin talking together, both to us and each other. They say that it is foolish to try, as the Bulgarians are very much on the alert. There is absolutely no possibility of getting round the mouth of the Struma. We insist that we are going to give it a try, anyhow.

They continue to talk and argue, back and forth. We say that in the capacity of their Police work, they must know of ways of slipping across the river. "Yes, but not here," they say. "Much further up there are bridges."

"What about the Bulgarian guards on the bridges?" we ask. They claim it is possible to get across, so we ask, "Will you show us how?"

They explain that it is a couple of day's walk from here, but it is possible. They say we are in luck as a regular foot patrol is just due to leave, headed in that direction, and we can go with it. Our visions of being warm and dry have to be put aside, and we move off once again. The patrol is of four or five men and, with us tagging along, the pace is not very fast. They have waterproof groundsheets, whereas we have the clothes we stand up in, and the rain keeps pouring down.

We plod on, with the surface water being about ankle deep. Our exertions make us very thirsty and we just scoop up water as we walk, in the tins we normally drink out of. It is muddy and unclean, but we are too tired to care. We come across an area where huge flocks of wild ducks have settled, as a rest stop on their annual migration. The air is full, with some ducks just landing, while others are taking off. The excited patrol members decide to bag some for themselves, and drop to one knee as they take aim.

Bob and I lean on our walking staffs and watch, taking a professional interest in their performance. The distance is four to five hundred yards, and they blaze away with four to five rounds each. There are that many ducks that it seems you only have to point your rifle in their direction, close your eyes and fire, and you cannot miss. But this lot never even gets one. I cannot help but think that wrongdoers have little to fear here, and hope their Bulgarian counterparts are no better. I imagine that the patrol will have to account for every cartridge used, so a duck or two would have made it worthwhile.

It is after dark before we reach another Police Post on our way. We are to stay here tonight, and move again the next morning. This is a much larger one than the other. There are two uniformed Officers in charge of the many people moving around. A place is cleared for us beside a cheery burning stove. Our gear is taken away to be dried out, but, apart from our outer garments, our clothing has to dry on our person, by the heat of the fire.

Once again, the debate flows back and forth between us and the police, regarding their ability to help us with our plans. With many more participating in the debate, it becomes more animated. Their sole attitude is that it can't be done, and that we are foolish to try. So, why not stay with them, until the War is over? We stubbornly insist, we will go on ahead, with or without their help.

One of the Officers keeps interjecting from time to time, firing at me a question in English. "Do you speak English?" he enquires.

I break off arguing with the others, turn to him and reply, "Yes, I do." I wait, expectantly, for him to carry on, only to find him lapse into silence. After this happens several times, my tiredness and irritability gets the better of me. I snap back at him in Greek, "Do you speak Greek?"

He draws himself up to his full five foot two and replies haughtily, "I am Greek."

I shoot back in English, "Well I'm bloody English."

He stares at me in shocked surprise. He probably does not understand what I have said, but my meaning is quite clear—If you've nothing to contribute, shut up, and stop making stupid remarks. Bob, trying to stifle a laugh, grabs my arm and says, "Take it easy. We need their help, not their antagonism."

Finally, they leave off their arguing, allowing us to settle down and get some sleep. We just curl up by the stove on the floor. There is much going and coming, and talking all around us, all night. It is a very fitful night we put in.

In the morning, our escort prepares to move off, and our gear is returned to us. I ask if it is all there, to be told, "Yes, everything." I check anyhow, to find a spare pair of trousers, I had been carefully hoarding, is gone. Clothing is impossible to obtain, both for locals, as well as us. And, this is a serious loss. Perhaps somebody had found it impossible to resist the temptation to help themselves. Surely, the Captain will order his men to search for them, and they will be discreetly returned to me.

The only sign forthcoming is a very expressive shrugging of Greek shoulders, indicating we know nothing. They all look at me, as if to imply that I never had a pair of trousers. And anyway, two pairs are more than enough for any man. I am fuming, and have no alternative but to push on with the escort.

Midway through the morning, more and more indications seem to bear out our suspicion, that we are heading for the town of Nigrita. We know this to be a large town in the area that contains a permanent German garrison. Do these fellows have it in mind to betray us? We stop, and flatly refuse to go any further, until they assure us that Nigrita is not our destination. They protest loud and long. "NO!NO! Nigrita is not where we are headed," they say. They argue that Nigrita is near where we have to go, and this is the only way. And they won't allow the Germans to know of our presence. We stick stubbornly to our suspicions, and it is some time before we grudgingly agree to move on.

We just plod on now, mostly in silence. We are tired and not prepared to make the effort that conversation requires. Besides, we are wrapped up in our own thoughts, wondering whether we will really get some help from these blokes. We had made the decision to go with them, and will see it through. If something concrete doesn't emerge pretty soon, we will tell them to shove it, take off on our own, and make our own way through.

It is late, about eight o'clock at night and quite dark, when we arrive at the edge of some sort of town. Our group is strung out, mostly in single file, with a few in front, Bob and I in the centre, and a few stragglers in the rear. There are lights, here and there, and it is fairly easy walking as we pick our way along the street. A fair sized building draws our interest as we approach and pass it. It is set back from the street line, while a large entrance gate appears to be guarded by two sentries. They are uniformed Germans. So then, this must be Nigrita.

Our escort pays no attention to the Germans, and we dare not kick up a fuss here. We will reserve that for when we arrive at wherever they are taking us to. They have lied to us, and we want to know why. We arrive at a large and obvious Police building. We are taken to a second floor where there is a row of unoccupied cells. The door of one is thrown open, and we are ushered in with the door remaining open. Well, a cell is as good as anywhere else to sleep, and we are used to putting up with far worse than this.

We dump our gear, then turn on our escort, and really tear into them. They protest that they had no alternative but to come to Nigrita, as it is so late. We counter, by telling them, that they had no right to lie to us. After about ten minutes, back and forth, we say anyway, "Where's the toilet?" A couple of them take us along the passageway to two cubicles, side by side, and without doors. We enter to find that these two stand on guard outside, keeping us under observation. Then, and only then, we realise that we are prisoners of the Greek Police.

We are dumbfounded at their perfidy, and our own stupidity. Because they are Greeks, we had taken it for granted that we could count on their help. At least we had expected that they would let us know where we stood. But, they have strung us out all along, and allowed us to willingly capture ourselves. We are fuming, and resolve to get out of this situation as soon as possible. There is simply no way that we will allow ourselves to stay in their hands.

By next morning, our plan has been formed. We will demand to see their Officer-in-Charge. We will deal with nobody else, but him. He will release us immediately, or we will insist on being handed over to the Germans. We have committed no crimes against the Greek people, and they are holding us illegally. As Prisoners of War, the Germans, only, have that right. We are determined to be free again, and, if that means another escape, then it will be better from the Germans than the Greeks.

Most of our escort has disappeared by now, probably to other duties. But we lose no time in making our demands to other rank and file men here. They protest long and hard, and plead with us to change our minds. We refuse to cooperate, unless our demands are met. Finally, they say it will be some time before their C.O. arrives. We say, "No matter, we will wait," and continue with our stubborn stand.

Sometime during the morning, we are told the C.O. has arrived. Once again the men plead with us to reconsider our stand. This time I really tear into them. I tell them that we had come to their country as Allies to help them fight their enemies. We have risked our lives for their sake, and all we get in return is treachery. They have betrayed us, after we ask for their help. They are thieves as well, for they have stolen my trousers from my personal pack, while pretending to dry it after being wet in the rain. They are no longer worthy of our trust, and we want nothing further to do with them.

My tirade is highly dramatic stuff, and takes all my ingenuity to get it across in my fractured Greek, signs and whatever. It hurts them deeply, for there are protests of, "No, No," from them, at each point I make. At the mention of my trousers, one of them rushes off, and returns with a pair of his own and tries to force them upon me. They are heavy corded khaki breeches and, by their quality, must have been his very best. This would be a great sacrifice for him. Scornfully, I reject them, drawing back from touching them, as if they are poisoned.

They are so generally upset at my harangue, that I am a bit remorseful for having laid it on so thick. Still, we have to make it as near impossible, as we can, for us to stay in their hands. How on earth can we bring ourselves to escape from people who, in the main, we still consider our friends?

There are no further attempts to sway us and, in genuine sorrow, we are taken to see the C.O. in his office. We make our demands to him to either let us go on our way, or hand us over to the Germans. In talking to the C.O. we find we can converse in a common language. Once again, Bob's French becomes the medium. While Bob puts our case, the C.O. replies in a matter-of-fact, man-to-man manner. He tells us that to release us is out of the question. Too many of his men know of our capture. To do so will give them too big a hold over him. To maintain his authority, he can't allow that. There is a German garrison in the town, but he avoids contact as much as possible. He considers we will be better off with his people than with them. But if we insist, as is our right, then he will ask for someone to come and collect us.

We insist and, while waiting for a German response, we sit casually in the C.O.'s office. We do not return to the cells. There is no attempt of any kind at interrogation. The German squad, when it arrives, consists of an Officer, a Corporal and two privates. The Officer is a tall young second Lieutenant, in his early twenties. He sits in a chair, slightly to one side of us, while we all face the C.O. sitting in his chair, with his desk in between. The German squad stand in the background.

The Greek C.O. acquaints the Lieutenant with our demand. The Lieutenant asks us why we insist on being handed over. We tell him we have no desire to be held in a Greek prison amongst criminals. If we have to be imprisoned, we prefer it to be a POW camp, amongst our own kind. He asks us a few questions, but we stick to this line. We have no desire to embarrass the Greeks in front of him. Finally, he agrees, rises to his feet, shakes hands with the C.O., and tells his Corporal to take us in tow. Once again we are in the hands of the Germans. They march us out of the Police Headquarters and through the town. We are taken to an area, where there are several quite large buildings, one of which has been taken over as a barracks.

We have placed them in a bit of a spot. They have no prison accommodation to hold us in, so we will have to be kept in their barracks. While the building has been taken over, all the rooms are quite small. Their men have to room together in twos and threes, like a large boarding house.

In our case, we are given a room on the second floor, in one corner. It is just past the head of the stairs and, with occupants all around, would be difficult to escape from. It is completely bare, except for two very well filled paillasses on the floor, and scrupulously clean.

We have no idea how long we will held here before being shunted back to Salonika, nor of the routine. Neither have they. This is a new situation for them, as it is for us. They lock us in initially. We expect that this is how it will be, except for the toilet, washing, and maybe some marching around under guard, for an hour or so, for exercise.

It becomes evening meal time. The door is unlocked and thrown wide open, while we are handed ours on a plate. It seems that what they have, we have. Several of them sit around in the hall, and on the stairs, eating and talking together. They motion us to relax as well, and join in their conversation. The food is a bit more our style, rather than what we have been having, with boiled potatoes very popular. A couple of them speak English, and slowly the ice begins to thaw.

After eating, we arise and go to re-enter our room, preparedly to be locked away again. They tell us to stay. There is plenty of time for that later. One of them gets up, goes inside, and returns with an accordion. He sits in the hall with his back against the wall, and begins to play. And he is damn good too. There is singing, laughing, and chaffing, much the same as any bunch of soldiers anywhere, except that this has a more Germanic flavour.

We study them with interest, and can tell, by their treatment of each other, that they are a pretty decent average bunch of blokes. Grudgingly, we begin to feel that, if we are with them for very long, we may not help but get to like them.

The English speaking blokes ask us about this and that, where we had been captured, where we had been to, our home life etc. Gradually, the others draw around while the English speakers relay the gist of what is said. The music stops and we find ourselves the centre of attention. We begin to ask questions of them in return. We find they are a Company of occupation troops that move in after a country has been overrun. Their job is to restore some semblance of order, and get essential services running again. In this way, they have travelled through several countries before ending up in Greece.

They had left Germany many months before, and travelled more than eight hundred and fifty miles, always on foot, and with horse drawn transport. The best of everything is reserved for their combat troops. These blokes have to be satisfied with second best. There are no fanatics here, just a tightknit group who rely on each other.

They ask us, "Who is going to win the War?"

Of course we reply, "We are."

Nobody seems to think it strange that a couple of prisoners can skite to their captors about the War's outcome. They reply that they believe they will, as they have already overrun most of Europe. But they want to know why we think we will win. We now have to consider a reasonable argument to back up our boast.

We tell them that it is only a matter of time before America comes in. And, even if they don't, their industrial capacity is so great that they will keep our people well supplied. We also have access to raw materials to keep our effort going, while their side has to struggle for everything, and often has to make do with a substitute. True, Germany has had great success up to now, but are greatly stretched everywhere. A lot of their effort is concentrated on hanging on to what they have taken. We think it will be unlikely that they will be able to invade England, and that they will end up alone, facing the rest of the world. It might take some time, but the result is inevitable.

They listen to our argument quietly, and with great attention. They point out one or two areas, where they feel they have to disagree. They can understand the logic of our thinking, and our belief that we will win. Still, in their opinion, the result will end up going their way. We cannot help but feel that this calm, almost academic discussion, of what is going to happen to the world, is bizarre and totally unreal—especially, when it seems that two prisoners are imposing their views on their captors.

With the fate of the world taken care of, we get down to more mundane things of ours and their home life and families. Soon photos begin to appear, mostly on their side, as we have long ago lost most of our possessions. We cannot help but marvel at the similarity of interests between us. Our interest in what they have to show is genuine, and not perfunctory.

Trying to return the favour, we search our pockets for any half-forgotten item that we might have tucked away. Anything at all we have, they study with great interest. Then, in one corner of my wallet, I come upon that tiny aluminium medallion, in the form of a Coptic cross, that had been given to me by an Arab trader in Jerusalem. The English speaking German gazes at it in awe. He stares for a moment, then pulls out a silver cross that is hanging on a chain inside his shirt. He begs me to trade him for it. I protest strongly that it would be a totally unfair trade, biased greatly in my favour. My medallion has no monetary value at all, while his cross, being made of silver, must be worth quite a lot. The Arab trader had given it to me for free. This proves how worthless it is, for an Arab never gives anything away.

He is unmoved, and just pleads all the harder. In his eyes, the fact that my cross comes from Jerusalem, makes it more valuable than his cross. Mine does have Jerusalem stamped across its centre in tiny letters to prove it. With reluctance, I finally agree, and we make the swap. I fully realise that he is in the position to take the damn thing anyway. It isn't until very much later that it occurs to me, I may have a very tough time explaining how I come to be in possession of a German religious cross, if found in a body search.

It is quite late when we all retire for the night, with both sides feeling we have had a very interesting evening. They seemingly forget to lock us in again, and deliberately refrain from doing so for the rest of our stay with them. They include us in their routine, as if we are welcome visitors from another regiment. We all rise at reveille, go and wash together, eat together, then go along to their headquarters building, in a group. While they have various duties to perform, we stand around, basking in the wintery sun, close by the cook house. Regularly, one of the cooks will come out to us with a titbit from the kitchen. Often it will be a heap of potatoes boiled in their skins, and so hot that he has to carry them before him in an apron. We will stand there, peeling and eating, while several of them will stand around and talk, then move away to carry on their duties. It is all very informal, and there never is any parade, or marching, as such.

We have no contact at all with the Greeks, with one exception. The exception is a young, mature girl, about nineteen. She is very good looking, with a beautiful figure. She speaks German and has been co-opted to act as interpreter, in dealings between her people and the Germans. She is on duty every day and, while waiting for her services to be called upon, just stands around, much the same as we do. Initially, she tries to be friendly and talk to us. But, maintaining our anti-Greek pose, we refuse to have anything to do with her. Rebuffed by us, she stands to one side, and seems a bit lonely and forlorn. The cook will appear with his apron load of potatoes and a half-smoked cigar in his mouth. He will unload the potatoes into our waiting hands, then, on the way back, grab her breasts. She will half turn away and shrug off his mauling hands. There is no attempt at romancing on his part—just an attitude of total belief in his right to fondle, if he feels like it. This callous behaviour contrasts sharply with his care and concern on our behalf. We find it hard to come to terms with the rather Jekyll and Hyde nature of the German character. We rather pity the girl in her lonely isolation, and feel sure that she must deeply regret the situation she now finds herself in.

Our own situation just has to come to an end and, finally, after the best part of a week as guests rather than prisoners, we are notified that we will be transported back to Salonika. There is a regular truck service carrying supplies and exchanging personnel, and this time we will be on it. At departure time there are handshakes all round, and genuine expressions of regret at our leaving. With good luck wishes for the future from both sides, our little idyll ends, and we climb aboard the truck. There is wooden seating down both sides, and a canvas canopy over the frame. With about twenty men, including us, making the trip, they quickly move aside to make way for us.

With Bob opposite me, we are seated about midway along each side. There is no obvious sign of keeping us under guard, but the seating arrangement takes care of that. We are a little subdued as we gaze out the back, and watch the ice-covered road speed rapidly away behind us. Bob breaks the silence between us and says, "You know, we could just stand up, jump over the tailboard, and make a run for it."

I contemplate the idea for a moment, then veto it. I agree that we can probably make it over the tailboard alright, in this relaxed atmosphere. But, it's what will happen, more than likely afterwards, that makes me say no. We are going at least forty m.p.h., and will have to make the jump facing the wrong way. We almost certainly will injure ourselves in the fall, then face the ignominy of instant recapture. With visions of maybe twisted or broken ankles, to curb our mobility, that is the last situation we want for ourselves. But, even if we manage to somehow survive the jump, the landscape, on both sides, is wide, bare and snow-covered, with nowhere to hide. All that our guards have to do is stop the truck, drop to one knee, raise their rifles and shoot. They couldn't miss.

Bob reluctantly agrees. I point out that we cannot afford any injuries. As long as we are in one piece, we are free to take whatever opportunity that may present itself. But it has to be a real opportunity, not a desperate one. This lot of Germans, we are with now, are not any of those we had been rooming with, except for the Corporal in Charge. Although they are friendly enough, we are certain they will not hesitate to shoot if we do make a break for it. The Corporal has been the one exception who has kept completely aloof from us. He has pointedly avoided speaking to us, or communicating with us in any way. As such, he is an unknown quantity to us.

The truck continues on without incident, and we reach Salonika just before nightfall. The Corporal leads the way, still without speaking, and, with a couple of men around us, we expect that we are heading for the POW camp. But this proves not to be so. They have decided to give us one more night in their care, then take us through in the morning. We are taken to their barracks somewhere in town, given a meal, then shown to one of several tiered bunks in a fairly private part of the building. There has been no sign of any Officers, and we have no idea whether this is a procedure they have decided upon themselves.

We are tired and depressed at the prospect ahead of us tomorrow, and very soon we climb into our bunks. We fall into a fitful sleep, only to be shaken awake with all lights blazing, at about 3.00 am. It is our aloof Corporal and he is pretty drunk. He has a colleague with him, and it is obvious they have had quite a session. Now he decides to show us off to him. Where before he had spoken not one word, now you can't shut him up. He talks and talks, mainly on how great the English are. He finishes by boasting that he is more English than we are. To prove it, he strips off his uniform to disclose that his entire undergarments are army issue, socks and all.

We can't believe it. They seem brand new, and it is many moons since we have seen any. All we have is what the Greeks had given us. While sturdy and adequate, they aren't the same, and we are envious. For a moment, we think he might be of a mind to outfit us. But, if he has any more, he gives no sign. After quite a while, he allows us to return to our bunks for what is left of the night.

In the morning, with the Corporal nowhere to be seen, two soldiers arrive to escort us back to Salonika No. 1. We set off through the streets, and soon begin to pass through the busier part of the town. More and more civilians pass us by, with more and more young females amongst them. In Salonika, the young females, as a group, are outstandingly beautiful. More and more our escort stops, turns and openly stares at this wonderful display.

Our progress through the city becomes painfully slow, as we have to stop, and wait for our escort to catch up. These Germans must have been fairly new here. This is ridiculous and finally, we have to stop, and give them a good tongue lashing. This straightens them out a bit, and they speed up. At last, we arrive within sight of our destination. There in front of us is the familiar sight of Salonika No. 1, from which we had escaped. How long ago is it now? This is getting to be too much of a bad habit.

# Chapter 12
# Welcome to Stalag VIIIB, Germany

We mount the steps of the Administration building, and enter the large orderly room. Here we are, prisoners, and back inside once again. This is getting monotonous. With another abortive escape, we are faced with the prospect to having to do it all once more. We are resigned to a period of taking stock before making our next move.

The very familiar scene is almost identical to what it had been when last we were recaptured. The people are the same and, with that cheery stove burning brightly in the centre, most of them are hovering closely around it. Instinctively, we make straight for it too.

The German Sergeant Major Interpreter with the American background, chides us once again on our damn foolishness for having made the "hopeless" attempt. He says we should know by now how well-guarded all the borders are. He points out that the whole of Greece is very short on food, while at least the camp rations are regular. While they might not be to first class hotel standards, at least they conform to Geneva Convention standards. Of course, once we move on into Germany to a permanent camp, then they will be much better still. There will be Red Cross parcels, ample opportunity for sport, and activities of all kinds.

We tell him that we are fed up and just want to go home. Again, he gives us the argument of this desire to be useless, claiming that we will be shoved straight back into the Army. We are quite happy to keep this badinage and banter going, back and forth, as long as possible. It delays our inevitable return to the cells, while giving us the blissful delight of the warmth from the cheery stove. Besides, we figure we are giving just as good in the exchanges, as we are taking.

The German Sergeant Major has given us each a mug of hot coffee, and it is good to feel the unaccustomed warmth inside our bellies. We are dressed in mostly Greek civilian clothing, are bedraggled and scruffy, and feel the cold keenly.

Suddenly, the German Sergeant Major says to me, "For God's sake man, don't do that. You look like a bloody Greek." I then become aware that I am shrugging my shoulders, gesticulating, just like the locals. It is a habit we have actively cultivated to better fit into the background. Unconsciously, it has become part of me. "And here," he says, "We had better get rid of this."

He picks a pair of tongs and, with them extended in front of him, he advances towards me. Mystified, I hold my ground, wondering what he has in mind. He gingerly takes hold of the cap on my head in the jaws, removes the lid of the burning stove, drops the cap inside, then replaces the lid. It takes me by surprise, and is done before I can even raise a protest. I had greatly prised that cap, for it had been given to me in a magnificent gesture by the Algerian. True, in our wanderings, it had become greatly dilapidated, greasy, and probably vermin ridden. Still, it was the only headcover I had. I hold very little hope of being able to get anything as a replacement. Obviously, the German has believed it to be infected, and decides to take no chances.

While still trying to come to terms with my loss, the English Sergeant Major, who is acting as liaison officer between the POWs and the Germans, wanders in. He begins talking to me, while the German is talking to Bob. I am a little surprised to see him, as the great bulk of captives have long since moved on into Germany, except for a few stragglers such as ourselves. Still, he has a pretty good setup here, having his own quarters in the Administrative Block and, seemingly, an adequate food supply. He would be a damn fool not to prolong it, as much as he can.

His attitude to me is friendly and confidential, and our conversation is strictly between ourselves. Remembering those unsubstantiated rumours relayed to us, when last we were here, that this man is somewhat pro German, I am on the defensive, while trying to appear friendly. I choose my words carefully. He asks me where we were recaptured, and who by. What is the level of help that can be expected from the locals, in both food and getting out of the country. I am able to answer most of it truthfully, as this information is already known to the Germans.

Then he asks me, "What is the best route to aim for, to get clear out of the country?" I take my time with this one, carefully fitting it in with the already known data. As we had been picked up at Nigrita, which is well inland, I tell him we think it is best to go overland to Turkey, and slip across the border. It is already known that we had been picked up last time at Lemnos, trying to get through by the sea. In reality, the overland route is a tentative alternative that we had elected to try, because of our frustrations in trying to locate a boat. By sea, is still our preferred option.

He asks, "How did you intend to cross the border?"

I reply, "We have no idea; we have been nowhere near that region. We intended to meet that problem when we got there."

He then tells me, "I think I will have to try to make it through there, too. I've hung around here long enough, and it's about time to make a break."

Suddenly, I feel sorry for him. This man is a Sergeant Major, and he should have all the loyalty and respect of every man in the camp. Instead, he has practically none. The Germans are quite happy to use him, but will drop him, completely, the moment it suits them. Although most outward signs of respect are shown to him, in reality, he must be a pretty lonely man. I am not prepared, indeed cannot, tell him anymore. After leaving this room, I never see him again. I never do find out if he really does attempt to escape, nor if there is any truth in those rumours of his suspect loyalty.

Having become fairly thawed out and warm, the German Sergeant Major decides it is time for the next move. He says, "Well, of course, you know you will have to go to the cells."

I respond, "If it's all the same with you, why not save the bother, and we'll just go straight over to the barracks."

He just smiles indulgently and replies, "Don't worry. You won't be there long. There's a draft leaving for Germany this afternoon, and you'll be on it." This is very disturbing news.

We had expected the usual short term in the cells, followed by a return to the barracks where we could mix freely with the other prisoners. We had felt certain that the prisoner numbers, still to be transported through, would have thinned out by now. But, it has not occurred to us that their numbers are now so few, that we will be moved straight on, without delay. So now, there is no time to organise anything. Another escape plan might have to be postponed, until sometime later.

We are escorted downstairs, and the cell door is opened. We are ushered inside and told to make ourselves comfortable. When it is time to move, we will be taken straight out and put on the draft. Once the cell door closes, we go straight to the ground level window. We are aware of some sort of activity going on in the parade ground, just beyond. There are some three to four hundred men formed up, under guard. They probably are the last of the prisoners still in Greece. A routine contraband search is being carried out. Anything found is placed on the ground to one side, and is steadily growing into a reasonable pile.

While watching these goings-on, we begin to take stock. At the moment, it looks like our best option is a train jump. As an escape method, this is much favoured by me. It is so simple. You are instantly free, with little chance of the Germans being able to do anything about it. Bob again points out that this method has been used so often, we have to expect that the Germans have worked out some sort of counter. While I agree that he does have a point, for the life of me, I cannot see how that is possible. If we do jump, where will it be. Will we give Greece another go? Or wait for somewhere further along the way? Maybe, even in Germany itself?

The thought of another ramble through Greece makes us baulk. On the plus side, we know the area well, and can expect some support from the locals. But then, there is the downside. On our last foray, we had become completely frustrated at the negative results. Boats are practically unobtainable, and we have practically worn out our welcome at our haven of Mount Athos. With the season, deep into winter, food is scarce, and we can no longer help ourselves to food crops as we go along. The overland route that we had attempted, as an alternative to the sea escape, while still mostly untried, had turned out to be a bit of a disaster for us.

If not Greece, where then? The Continent is an unknown to me. All I know is that every country here is under the domination of Germany.

The only neutral territory seems to be Switzerland. To get there seems almost impossible. Another attempt from Greece to reach Turkey still seems reasonably attainable. However, as Bob is English, the further on we go, brings us much closer to his home. Without his saying so, I gain the impression that he would prefer to wait. To do this will put us into continental Europe, and into one of maybe half a dozen countries already under German domination.

As an Australian, I'm not too keen on this idea. It seems to me that the governing factor for an escape, has to be in an area that gives us the best chance of getting through to our own people. Our escape planning involves a dual effort, and each has an equal right to have his say. Our experiences, so far, have shown that Bob is inclined to take what I would term as "foolish" risks, in his efforts to get away. The further we go on, the more likely it will be Bob calling the shots. While this point really doesn't worry me, the outcome does. It has always been my deep-seated resolve that, somehow, someway, I am going to get back home. Any setback to that, cannot be for doing something stupid.

As we mull over the pros and cons of what to do, we stand at the window watching the searching and preparations out in the parade ground. There is a great deal of movement, backwards and forwards to the toilets, and general milling around. This is typical POW procedure, designed to confuse the guards. It gives us some amusement.

We become aware that there are some people in the cell next door. Their cell is exactly the same as ours. There has to be some mystery about its occupants, for our gaolers have made no mention of any other captives. If there had been other escapers, our jocular German Sergeant Major would have told us that we had other company.

We manage to find out that they are three middle-aged Greek women. The fact that they have been thrown into a POW prison, rather than a civilian one, seems to point out that their future looks pretty bleak. We feel for them in their plight, and it depresses us a little more, for it seems to indicate a hardening in the German attitude. After we leave our cells, we never find out what happens to them.

About mid-afternoon we are taken out and attached to the transit party. Still undecided on what we will do, we look them over carefully. There is nobody we know among them. It looks as if the camp has been cleaned out and these are the final lot, gathered in from here and there. We are to move in half an hour, so we just stand in line waiting. Time drags on. When it becomes obvious that we will be held up for a while, the Guards decide to have another search, just to pass the time.

With a fair sized heap of contraband already stacked on one side, this seems to be a useless exercise. And the prisoners protest loudly. But, this time the guards strike a bonanza. The first pile pales into insignificance. The new lot is about three times as much. The heap is about fifteen feet in diameter, and about three feet high in the centre. On the very top is a German bayonet, in its scabbard, that somebody had managed to conceal first up. It is unbelievable that so much escaped the first search. But, this success leaves the guards almost speechless. It simply doesn't seem possible for so much to be concealed on so few men.

When finally the word to move off is given, one or two of the incorrigibles, still make a last minute grab at the heap. At the rail siding the usual arrangements are in force, and we are herded into cattle trucks, with about fifty assigned to each one. As a concession to winter, two bales of straw are thrown in, which we are told to break open, and spread over the floor. These trucks are the same type from which George and I had escaped before. This time, no special attempts are made to make them more secure with barbed wire etc., so we take this to mean that the Germans don't particularly care. This doesn't look too good.

The numbers crammed into each truck means that there is no spare room. If you lay full length, your head touches one side while your feet touch the other. For a measure of comfort, half the men have to line one side of the truck, with the rest on the other. When everybody lies down, you have somebody's feet on either side of your head, while your feet are alongside somebody's head on the opposite side.

The usual makeup of the train is for passenger cars to be at the front and rear, with the trucks containing prisoners, between. The Guards, generally, are from a Unit going home on leave.

As the train moves off, we shuffle ourselves into position, settling down with your mate alongside. There are no toilet facilities, and no room for them anyway. Some men have dysentery, and practically all have stomach problems of some kind. Bob and I are lucky, for we have achieved a measure of stability while on the loose, sustained mainly on a diet mostly of bread, hard boiled eggs and goats milk cheese.

As the diarrhoea pangs start to take effect, we have to work out a system to cope. Miraculously, somebody has managed to conceal a steel helmet. This, together with our arms, is the first thing the Germans confiscate. Yet here, after months of capture and many searches, is an almost perfect potty. A handful of straw placed in the bottom copes with the main job, but, as it is too small to urinate in it at the same time, somebody hands over a jam tin, he has saved, for this function.

A user has to balance himself in a squatting position, against the swaying sides of the cattle truck. With the tin hat on the floor, he has to hold jam tin in position with one hand. His neighbour on each side, will avert his head, trying to shut out the smell, and afford him at least a token measure of privacy. Disposal involves passing the contents, hand over hand, to the man nearest the trapdoor window. He will open the flap, empty the contents outside, then pass the utensils back to the next user. It is degrading and humiliating, but, under the circumstances, there is nothing else we can do.

It is late afternoon when the train pulls out and, with steady progress, darkness soon begins to set in. Bob and I, still undecided, keep mulling over whether to jump or not. Because the railway runs through central Greece, the prospect before us involves a hike of many miles to get back to the coast again. With the bleak food outlook and wintery landscape, a jump is becoming less and less attractive. We finally decide to wait through the night, and see what the new day brings along.

Mentally fagged out, worrying whether our decision to wait is the right one, we are pretty well exhausted. We fall into a fitful sleep, with the one consoling thought. If anybody else tries a jump, we will quickly find out if the Germans have worked out a countermeasure.

The night passes without incident, and we awake just as the train is pulling into a small station for a brief stop. I push my way to the window, look out, and see a man in a station attendant's uniform. I ask him in Greek, "What is the name of this place?" He replies immediately, so I deduce we are still in Greece, although the name of the place is unknown to me. I figure that we must be very close to the Yugoslav border.

A day's travel, before the cover of night, gives us another opportunity to jump, deep inside Yugoslavia. But, to jump then is considered undesirable. We have heard that the Slavs have split into two factions—Royalists and Communists. They usually spend more time fighting each other than fighting the Germans. For us, to fall in with either lot may see us swept up into guerrilla actions, of hit and run raids, make-do weapons, hard forced marches, etc. In an atmosphere where brother cannot trust brother, a couple of strangers could disappear without trace. So reluctantly, it appears, we are committed to going all the way through to Germany, unless something else turns up.

As we progress, the cold begins to get more intense. We have no body fat, and feel it keenly. We huddle closer together, drawing a little warmth from each other's bodies. Snow begins to appear. The further we go, more appears, until finally the whole landscape is completely covered. Remembering our ordeal of having slogged knee deep through the snow at Mount Athos, we have no desire to go through that again.

We become steadily more miserable in this frozen tomb of a cattle truck. Our breath begins to condense on the roof and sides, until the entire interior is coated in white frost to a depth of two inches. At midday, when the day is warmest, the whole lot melts and rains down on us for about an hour. Then it refreezes, building up again, until the next warm period.

We are given low priority in rail movement, and often spend hours on side tracks without moving. While stationary, we scream for the Guards to let us out to relieve ourselves. Always, they ignore us. In retaliation, sometimes a guard can be caught, walking and testing door fastenings, while stopped. Our jam tin will be emptied out the window, at what is judged the perfect moment. A great torrent of abuse in German rings out and, for a fleeting moment, we feel a great satisfaction. We do not try this very often, as there is too much danger of reprisals.

From the time we left Salonika, we are locked in for five whole days. Then, one morning, while stopped at a siding, the doors are flung open and we are ordered out. As we sort ourselves out, we are ordered into the field alongside the truck, and told to relieve ourselves.

There is a broad pathway alongside, running parallel to the track and separating us from the field. Along this pathway a steady stream of civilians, both men and women, are making their way into the small nearby town. The depth of snow on the open field is about one and a half feet. Although some of us balk at exhibiting ourselves in front of the townspeople, after being locked in for five days, we feel we have to try, just in case we are not given another chance. So we plough our way through the thick snow, choose a spot, kick a hole with our feet, and squat, keeping as much clothing around us as we can. This is really more for warmth than modesty.

The townspeople are obviously disgusted. They show it plainly in their manner and talk, even though we do not understand what they say. Quite plainly, the plan is to get as much propaganda as possible, by putting on a show. There is a certain amount of dirt in the straw and this, mixed with the melted frost drippings, has left us filthy. Our clothing is ragged and shapeless, with as much as possible draped around exposed skin areas. Trying to cover exposed parts, has taken away all semblance of Military smartness. We are a rabble, and look it. We can only concentrate on keeping going, and will not gain our self-respect until we get new clothing and a bath.

The Germans have brought up a covered van, while these goings and comings and milling around are going on. Some of our blokes are being carried to it on stretchers, and placed aboard. We enquire from the others to find that two men have died.

The van has brought up some new supplies. While most of it is for the Guards, there is some for us too. It is always the same—loaves of bread to be shared around and some drinking water, if you have the means to carry it.

About five hours later, we are locked in once again. Sometime later, the train moves on. From now on, whenever there is a lengthy delay, the guards will open up and allow us to use the open space nearby. Thinking back, those first five days of being locked in were probably taken up traversing territory the Germans consider unsafe.

After several more days, we halt at another siding, but the procedure here is different. We had halted sometime during the night. In the morning we are all ordered out, and are told to form up for a march into town. We are told that we are going to be given a hot meal. This seems too good to be true. Anyway, it is a good diversion.

We shamble along, herded by the Guards, into what is obviously a fairly large town. It is Graz. We march through several streets, finally arriving at a large building in what seems to be the town square. We enter into a large barnlike room and, sure enough, there are large cauldrons of steaming soup, ready and waiting for us. It appears to be a canteen set up for the use of troops in transit, and is serviced by some middle aged women. We lineup in an orderly queue and, this time, there is none of the usual milling around. It isn't the time or place to try and confuse the guards.

We present our food containers, receive a generous helping, plus a chunk of bread. There is a small apple for each of us, too. The soup is thick and creamy, and very tasty. We 'hoe' in, ravenously at first, and then ease off, making it last longer. We savour every last drop. We are humbly grateful for this unexpected treat. The warm atmosphere inside the building, plus the warm food in our bellies, makes us feel almost human again.

We linger on here as long as possible, but the Guards finally give the order to move back to the railway. It is a cold Sunday and, as we march along, there is almost a total absence of people on the streets. One exception is a girl of about nineteen, who pauses on a street corner for us to pass. As we do, she spits contemptuously into the gutter. This gesture loses its impact, however, for, although she is nicely dressed and rather good looking, she has a cold. Her nose is shiny red and dripping continuously.

Once back aboard the train. We have to wait out the rest of the day. Sometime during the night, we begin to move on again. Our journey continues on for several more days. We begin to lose track of time. Although conditions are still the same, the Guards are letting us out during the stops, on a much more regular basis. However, there are no more hot meals forthcoming.

Just as we begin to think that we may never get off the train, we come to a halt. We are roused out of the trucks, and told that we have reached the end of our trip. It has taken us a fortnight, when a reasonable timetable would have been four or five days. The whole area is flat and bare, with a stand of pine trees some distance away. Everything is deep in snow. It is bleak and looks like a completely forgotten part of the earth. We have to march a little over a mile to get to the camp, which is to be our destination.

Finally, there it is—Stalag VIIIB at Lamsdorf in Ober Silesia. It is huge, and we can only guess at its size from where we are. But, we can see it is well-organised and permanent. Maybe here, we will be able to get some regular food, and be fitted out in decent clothing.

We arrive at the administrative and processing centre. Farther over, we can see rows and rows of huts, in which the prisoners are housed. There is smoke coming from round pipe chimneys, which poke through the hut roofs at regular spacings. There are regular comings and goings of what seems to be, well-kitted and clean prisoners.

The outer walls consist of the usual two, widely-spaced strands of very high barbed wire fences. In between are mounds of loose barbed wire, up to about chest high. Guard towers are spaced at regular intervals, and overlooking the camp. The inner area is divided off into compounds, with admittance being allowed through high barbed wire gates, manned by sentries. Guards are everywhere, and we expect them to be very efficient.

Now, begins our processing. We are herded into a large barnlike building to be documented and searched. There is an Officer-in-Charge, with a large staff to do the work. They move into a smooth and well-practiced routine. This is good, for all we have to do is to 'innocently' disrupt this routine and they will be completely lost.

We are lined up on one side of the room and moved in queues through a line of desks where English speaking Germans take down our particulars. Then we are to line up for a body search. Simple enough, but the Officer seems to be working to a timetable. We are able to disrupt things enough for him to order his men to get a move on, thus, allowing them to do only half the job.

I still have the prismatic compass hidden away, and given to me by the English Officer back in Salonika. I am not worried about the consequences of it being discovered on me. As an escapee, I will have to face up to a trial and detention of some sort soon. It will only be just a little bit more to add to the total. Its value here, however, will be tremendous, and I do not want it found.

Our disruptive tactics are kept to a minimum at the documentation stage, for this is important. We are listed as Missing in Action, until this data is sent through to our people. When my turn comes, I give my particulars, and am asked if I have any money on me. While on the loose,

I have acquired some money, mostly in Greek bank notes. It isn't worth very much, but I hand it over knowing it will not be much use to me now. The German clerk hands me a receipt for the amount, on a printed form. Even though I never expect to see it again, it is encouraging to see the proper formalities observed.

By the time I line up for the body search, we have got so far behind that, all I have to submit to is a token pat. My compass is safe. I don't think they would have found it anyhow. With the German Officer hurrying his team through the last of us, we are again formed up for movement to our overnight quarters. This is to be in a holding compound, and we are to go through a thorough delousing tomorrow. We can't wait to experience the luxury of more space, after the cramped and inhuman conditions of that damn train.

The compound, we are taken to, is for Indian troops. Our hut is on one side, and we and they are very interested and curious to know about each other. They show compassion and sympathy at our poor condition and dilapidated appearance. One or two individuals offer pieces of food to some of us. Like bees to honey, we are irresistibly drawn and gather round their doorway. They keep handing out bits to us from their meagre stores. There is no pushing or shoving, just a pathetic sort of dignity in giving and taking.

I feel the situation deeply. The quiet compassion from these men, considered in some quarters to be an inferior race, is something to see. I cannot help but remember how the beggars had pestered the life out of us in Colombo, on the way over to the Middle East. Now our roles are reversed. Need is a great leveller. These men too, because of their religious beliefs, cannot eat some foods. I feel pretty sure that the Germans will make no special effort to see that their needs are properly catered for. There will be little chance for us to return the favour.

In the morning we are off to the delouser, and a chance to find out about the inner workings of the camp. All the internal chores are carried out by the prisoners, with very little interference by the Germans, other than for security. As we line up in the outer area, one of the workers asks if there are any Aussies from Newcastle. I tell him I am, and he tells me he is too. He says, "Of all the men who have been through here, you are the first I have come across from home." He fills me in on what is to happen.

Our hair will be cut, and we will have to remove all our body hair. We will strip completely and shower, while our clothing and gear will be put through a fumigator. Once the process is finished, we can dress again and then be taken to another compound. We are warned not to try to cheat, for the good of the camp.

The Germans are very nervous too, for they have just got the all clear after three months' quarantine. There has been a very bad outbreak of typhus, and many have died. It had started in a badly overcrowded Russian compound, where they were crammed in like cattle. The Russians are regarded by the Germans as subhuman, and they do not bother to document them. Their food ration is much less than ours, which is bad enough, and they have no way of supplementing it, as we do with Red Cross parcels. With the general practice of a comrade collecting rations for a sick man, nothing would be said when a man died. The collection would continue, with the body being kept, until the smell alerted the authorities.

They were heavily infested with lice, and, when typhus broke out, it spread like wildfire. The Germans panicked and moved in quickly, before it spread to the rest of the camp. The Russians were moved away to another area, while those who died were buried in a long deep trench nearby. It is said that the trench was scooped out by a bulldozer and the bodies tossed in by their comrades. In some instances, although pretty far gone, a few were still not quite dead. The whole lot were heavily covered with lime, then covered in by the bulldozer.

A high level enquiry had taken place, and now the German medical staff are wary of any more trouble. It is said that the death toll was about three thousand.

We are the first lot of prisoners to arrive, after the quarantine has been lifted. Everybody is anxious for the improved procedures to be a success. We are told that we will be here for most of the day, so we will be served our midday meal while being processed.

I am pleased at the prospect of a haircut, until my Newcastle friend advances to do the job. The clippers are horse clippers and he proceeds to take the lot off. Next, it's over to the shower, and for our decisions, whether to remove our body hair, before or after our bath. I decide to shave after, but this is a mistake. There is no hot water, and the cold shower is quite an ordeal. With deep snow outside, the temperature is about thirty-six below, whereas the atmosphere inside the building is quite reasonable. We need a bath badly. But the shock of that cold water on our bodies, makes us almost chicken out. Mostly, we just stand at the fringe, splash small areas at a time, and try to get some sort of lather with the Ersatz soap.

We dry off as quickly as possible, then tackle the body hair with safety razors. Legs and torso aren't too bad, but when it comes to our tender parts, our skin is so shrivelled from the cold water that it is impossible to avoid nicks and cuts.

There is no clothing available other than what we have. This is put through a steam process, and is snug and warm when we put them back on.

About midday several large boilers of soup are brought in. It is our first prepared meal in the camp, and we are interested to find out what kind of food we can expect. My Newcastle friend tells me it is turnip soup. It is a kind of amber colour, completely clear and without body. We help ourselves to a generous helping, and get stuck into it with relish. It is lukewarm and quite pleasant to taste. When we have finished, there is still about threequarters of it left. Enthusiastically, we back up for another lot, and some for a third, and some even for a fourth. After all this, there is still some left. All this time, the fellows on the working staff have stood back and let us go our hardest. Now that we have eased off, they advance to take a share for themselves. But not before making sure that we have had enough. When they are certain of this, they dish out their own, then begin to wash their socks in it. We are dumbfounded.

My Newcastle friend explains that, with a camp such as this, it is almost impossible to get enough fuel for heating water. True, there is an allocation from the Germans for the camp use, but this is strictly controlled. Every day, the midday meal is soup, always the same consistency, but, occasionally, a different taste. After a few weeks on this diet, the prisoners usually ease off, leaving a fair amount untouched. Somebody had got the idea of using the lukewarm leftover for washing. And the idea has spread. He predicts that after a while, we will do the same. Privately, we cannot believe we will ever be able to do so.

We ask what the rest of the rations are, and the reply is—a cup of hot water, or Ersatz coffee, and a wedge of bread for breakfast; the soup for dinner; and some boiled potatoes in their jackets, plus a cup of hot water, or Ersatz coffee, for tea. Red Cross food parcels are the mainstay, with the standard issue being one per man per week. As these have to come by rail from Switzerland, there are regular delays, in the cluttered system, when none can get through. Despite these periods, often for several months at a time, everyone just has to get by on the standard camp food.

We are intrigued at this information, and are eager to get out into the main camp and examine, for ourselves, what is really going on. By mid-afternoon, with early darkness closing in, we are almost finished with our delousing job. All that remains is for our gear to be released from the special fumigator. Any blankets, haversacks, or spare clothing that we own, has to remain inside for several hours, while being impregnated by a special gas designed to kill the vermin.

Finally, this device is opened and we are able to retrieve our gear. It is a long metal tubelike thing. We had just crammed our packs inside, without opening them. We had not wanted them to become hopelessly mixed together by being loose. This seems alright by the Germans, who just gave our gear a bit more time for the gas to penetrate.

We are given a couple of issues before moving out. One is a pair of clogs. These consist of a wooden base about one and a half inches thick, shaped like a one-piece sole and heel. Across the front is nailed a piece of leather, extending halfway up the instep, for the toes to fit into. Two squares of calico, like large pocket handkerchiefs, are to act as foot cloths, instead of socks.

We had noticed some of the delouser staff wearing these clogs, and felt pity for them for not wearing boots. We also noticed that they were able to move about very well in them. For ourselves, we can only see them as a poor substitute for a proper pair of boots—just good enough for the Germans to claim that they are supplying us with proper footwear. As for those foot cloths, any claim that they are equal to socks, will fool no one. We feel we will never get used to the clogs, and, probably, will never try to wear those foot cloths.

We are issued a Red Cross parcel to be shared by several men. This is to tide us over until the next proper issue, when we will get one each. We are impatient to get away to where we can open and examine them, and then share the goodies in these parcels. We are to go to a separate compound for the night. We will be here for a few days until given the all clear, healthwise, and then pass into the main camp area to be absorbed into the huts there.

We form up quickly, with a couple of Guards up front leading the way, and others down both sides. We move out into the bitter cold, and a short march brings us to a gate leading into our compound. A sentry opens the gate to lets us through, and we lose no time making for our hut. Our party is the only group in this compound, so we have nobody to familiarise us as to the general layout. It is now almost dark, but, with the electric lights on inside, we can see for ourselves. We presume the lights are controlled by the Germans from the administration area.

There are rows and rows of three tier wooden bunks with straw-filled paillasses. There is a good ablutions and toilet centre, all under one roof. With no need to go outside to use them, this is all we need to know. So, quickly we select ourselves a bunk. There are a few cast iron heating stoves spaced along the centre of the long hut. With nothing to burn in them, we just have to suffer the cold. At least it is better than inside those damn cattle trucks. We just close all the windows and doors, and settle down to our Red Cross parcels.

They are magic. They have all those foodstuffs we have so long yearned for and dreamed about. Bob and I, of course, already have some knowledge of their contents because of the issue back in Salonika, following our first escape, when the wounded soldiers were being shuttled through. These parcels contain condensed milk, jams and several kinds of meat as well as bully beef. There is tea, some dried fruits, and some chocolate too. The sharers work out their own methods of dividing up the spoils. Sometimes it is you take this, and I'll take that. Often, it is opened up and divided into portions. With the opening and dividing, it is impossible not to taste and try. And everybody samples some of their portion. But, with typical POW caution, always something is tucked away and saved for later.

It has been a long, eventful, and tiring day, and now our tiredness catches up with us. Almost as one, we turn into our bunks, open our packs, shake out our blankets or whatever cover we have, and climb into bed. Most of us fall asleep immediately, and sleep soundly for a short while. Then I, like a lot of others, rouse into a fitful state of half asleep and half awake. I toss and turn on my paillasse, feeling the discomfort of the bed boards beneath. I begin to feel a bit queasy in the stomach and regret indulging in unaccustomed, rich, parcel food. I try to put it out of my mind and go back to sleep. Gradually, it gets worse, until I am in danger of being sick. My head begins to ache, and am feeling real bad. Then, I become aware of moaning, coming from the other bunks. Somebody is up and moving from bunk to bunk. It is a Medical Orderly, who is part of our party. He is trying to tend to the, by now, many distressed men. Suddenly, he strides to a window and smashes it. At the same time he calls out for a sentry, stationed somewhere outside. One comes running and, for a moment, it is touch and go, before the Orderly can get through to him, and convince him that there are many sick men who need a doctor.

Immediately, the alarm goes up and Germans come from everywhere. The whole hut is thrown wide open to the outer air. Two uniformed Doctors come, and order everybody out into the open, with the less affected walking the sick, up and down. As one of the affected, I have a man supporting me by each arm, and walking me back and forth. As I begin walking, my head begins to clear. Within seconds, I am almost back to normal. But the German Medical Officers insist that the walking is to continue.

I had put my clogs on and, as this is the first time I have tried them, I find it very hard to manipulate them. I just stumble along, with first one, then the other, falling off my feet. Then I retrieve them, as a man, on each side of me, keeps urging me on.

The German MOs order all the hut doors to be thrown wide open. The bitingly cold night air sweeps the place clean, as it had done to my head. It is now apparent what has happened. The gas which is said to have a cyanide base, had penetrated our tightly packed gear, with some of it being trapped inside the folds of the cloth. When we shook out the folds to prepare for bed, it had escaped into the room, well-sealed to keep out the outside cold. It then, was only a matter of time as to when, and how badly, we would become affected.

In clearing out the hut, it is found that two men have died. While most of the others have suffered to a greater or lesser degree, luckily, one of the least troubled is our Medical Orderly. His actions, undoubtedly, saved a few from any serious harm. It is a long time before the Jerry MOs consider it safe enough to return to the hut. There are a dozen or so men who, they insist, have to be kept for further observation. I am one of them.

Feeling much better now, I try to argue my way out of it, but they will not have a bar of it. So, along with the observation cases, I am sent off to the camp hospital.

The camp hospital is large and roomy, and has single beds rather than our three-tiered bunks. All our gear is taken from us to be properly aired. I am left with only my clogs, and given a pyjama coat that reaches only to my navel. We are kept here for a week before the Germans are prepared to allow us to return to the rest of the party. The hospital contains a fair sprinkling of cases, apart from us. There appears to be little in the way of medicines, and food is standard camp food.

The recollections of my stay are embarrassing. To go to the toilet, I have to traverse a very long and draughty corridor, with only that coat to try and cover myself. It is a slow drawn out trip, with my skinny legs trying to manipulate those clogs. I feel so humiliated that I try to avoid going at all costs. I am forced to stay in bed most of the time, for warmth as well as modesty.

Finally, we are given the all clear. Our clothing is returned to us, and we lose no time dressing. I personally, have never been in hospital in my life, and I am busting to get out of the place. In such a huge complex, I suppose it is necessary to have a hospital of some sort. Except for a bit more space, this one seems very little different to the general camp quarters. We have to wait awhile for some Guards to come and escort us to our hut.

We set out about midmorning and we shamble along as best we can. With snow everywhere and roadways ice-covered, there are a fair few of us who have no prior experience of this kind of winter. We find it difficult to keep our footing. It is a long trip back and, in my clogs, I soon find myself at the tail of the column. The further we go, the more I lag behind. The Guards can see I am in trouble and just let me make my own pace. They look back occasionally, see that I am following, and continue on with the main bunch. Soon, I am about twenty yards behind and completely on my own.

Up ahead, I become aware of a large group assembled on parade, on the roadway along which we have to pass. There appears to be about three hundred of them. They are formed up in a column of threes, with guards stationed front and rear, facing them with rifles at the ready. The row of Guards are about ten or twelve feet apart. I can see by their prison garb that they are Air Force men, and realise that this must be some kind of check or search. From the way they are assembled, it looks as if the Germans mean business.

As a newcomer, I can only dimly sense what this is all about. Later, I am filled in as to the special arrangements the Germans have enforced for captured Airmen. These fellows are mostly Air crew, who have been shot down and captured. They are highly trained and difficult to replace. While the Germans make it difficult for anybody to escape, for Air crew they try their damnedest to make it impossible.

A special Air Force compound is set up in the centre of the camp, with the rest of the Prisoners' Compounds surrounding it. They are not permitted to mix with the rest of the prisoners. Access between their compound and the rest of the camp is restricted to a gateway that is guarded day and night. To be on the safe side, the Germans are prone to make a sudden, unannounced search, seeking contraband. This is what I am seeing now.

As I near the parade, I watch the goings on with interest. By this time my party has passed them, with me trailing about thirty feet behind. I am completely on my own. The Airmen are stamping their feet in the cold, swinging their arms and milling around in the usual confusing POW fashion. Suddenly, one of the Airmen calls to me in a guarded voice, "Hey! Do you want a French overcoat?"

Desperately short of clothing of any kind, I reply, "Yes." Instantly, hands shoot out and grab me, pulling me into the centre of their ranks. Swiftly, an overcoat is thrown on, buttoned up, and I am thrust back out onto the road, in what seems like two seconds flat.

I stumble along, now with an overcoat on, where I had none before; and those Guards, watching intently for anything suspicious, have not seen a thing. Some captured French Uniform supplies are occasionally doled out by the Germans to those POWs, where a clothing issue becomes necessary—mostly overcoats. French overcoats are much roomier than the standard British ones, and of thinner material. With some tailoring and dyeing, they can be made to look like a civilian suit. If found with more than the one issued, an Airman is an instant candidate for the cooler.

I finally make it past the paraded Airmen and, just ahead, our Guards are waiting for me at the gateway leading into our compound. The Guards notice nothing different in my appearance. The rest of the party has passed inside and, when I finally make it, none of them notice any difference either. I go inside the hut and tell the others what had happened. They just cannot believe it. But, my newly acquired coat proves that it did.

I reunite with Bob and quickly check for any happenings in my absence. The rest of our party have been kept in this holding compound, until we have rejoined them—other than that, nothing of note.

The next day, we assemble with all our gear, and march into the camp proper. What a different world it is! There are rows and rows of huts, the kind we are now becoming familiar with, covering a vast area. Estimates of the number of men in the camp vary from ten to twenty thousand. At any one time, a big majority will be out at different locations on working parties. So, the actual number inside is less than that. But, at all times, there is still a large and busy population, moving purposely about.

Your hut is the centre of your world. A typical hut is a very long wooden building, with toilet and ablution facilities at one end, and a fairly roomy compartment for the Hut Commander and his staff, at the other. The very large space between is taken up almost entirely by three-tiered bunks. The small cast iron stoves for heating are spaced at regular intervals down one side of the hut. Naturally, there is also one in the Commander's room. These stoves are the centre of social activity in this bleak winter weather. There always is a small group gathered round here, while somebody is heating a can of water, for a shave or a brew.

Fuel for the stoves is very much a problem. There is an allocation, by the Germans, of coal for the whole camp. The distribution procedure for each hut's quota, is issued to the Hut Commander. His job is to issue it fairly. With the quota being totally inadequate, there are daily periods when stoves cannot be lit. The wherewithal to relight them is almost impossible to come by. Yet somehow, or someway, this is able to be managed. Generally, there are at least a couple alight for the use of a few. To beat the cold, many spend a lot of time in their bunks.

The internal organisation of the camp is exceptionally efficient and lowkey. We newcomers have the tremendous advantage of just having to slot into what already is a very well-oiled machine. God knows how much heartache and strife has gone into establishing proper guidelines and procedures between us and our captors. Always there is a constant testing on both sides, as to what is permissible and to what is finally and definitely not allowed. These fellows have the work procedures all sorted out, and for the supply of materials to keep the place clean. Food issues are made direct to a large cookhouse staff, and distributed from there. Each Hut Commander is responsible for seeing that a carrying party picks up his hut's rations at the appointed time. They are brought back to the hut and distributed from there.

This camp has been established to contain, as much as possible, those types of prisoners who the Germans most want to keep confined. It is known as a hard camp, and is for NCOs and other ranks. It has been set up deep inside Germany, and close to the Polish border, to discourage a breakout. It also contains captured Air Crew and most of the recaptured escapees. Officers are never ever a part of our numbers. They have been taken away to a separate location.

Stalag VIIIB has been constructed from scratch by men captured at Dunkirk in France. By various means they have been transported here, a goodly proportion arriving on foot. Upon arrival, they were told to pitch in and start building. The sooner they finished, the sooner they'd be out of the weather. These men are regular British troops, who were left behind to fight a rearguard action. They are solid, well-disciplined, and come from many different and famous Regiments. Their ability to remain cheerful, and make the best of any situation, gives us a tremendous lift. It is a lead that we will do our best to follow.

There is a Company Sergeant Major, the most senior NCO, as the nominal head of the camp. The Hut Commanders are Sergeants, answerable to him. Their staff is picked to cover the cleaning chores and food distribution. They are responsible for discipline within the hut, and for assembling the men on parade at the daily check counts. There is great cooperation from everyone. As these men have been captives for a year since capture, their organisation is immensely smooth and efficient.

Our Hut Commander fills us in on what is required of us. It is surprisingly little. We will have ample time to fill in, and there are all sorts of activities we can occupy ourselves with. There are lectures being given on almost every conceivable subject, by experts in their particular field. Some of the tutors are even Oxford or Cambridge Dons. There are theatrical activities, with all sorts of plays being attempted. Some of them are very ambitious indeed. A symphony orchestra is in the process of being formed. Permission is being sought from the Germans for a pit to be dug, as the proper medium from which it can perform. There are dozens of jazz groups, or string quartets, needing players. The opportunity to study, or to complete study courses already undertaken and still to be completed, is almost limitless.

There are working parties away from the camp, in factories, mines, saw mills, and on some farms. It is reasonably easy to get onto one of these, but not very easy to get back. Care has to be taken before committing oneself. On a working party, the food is supposed to be better than in camp. There is also the opportunity to trade for necessities. Also, there are better chances of escaping.

Our Commander tells us that he might have to ask for our help, from time to time, on a matter that may seem a bit frivolous. Always there will be a very good reason. He gives us an illustration of collective might. The theatrical groups, in setting up their stage facilities, need some solder for their electrics. Solder is completely unobtainable in Germany. Where to get it? The order goes out to every man to hand in the foil seal from the top of his cigarette issue. Cigarettes come in as an issue through the International Red Cross. They are in round tins of fifty, vacuum packed, and sealed with a foil seal. The air hole in the seal is closed off with a tiny blip of solder. With all the seals handed in, enough solder is obtained to more than cover what is needed.

He also briefs us on work practices, in case we decide to go on a working party. The policy is for no obvious disruption or confrontation, just a subtle botching up where possible. Some fellows, who have been sent on working parties, give us a rundown of the practices and antics that they have got up to, and been able to get away with.

One bloke had been sent to a construction site to work on the erection of a new building. Timber had to be carried up an inclined ramp and stacked on the ground floor. He was required to pick up a baulk of timber, about the size of one of our railway sleepers, trot up an inclined plank with it on his shoulder, and then deposit it on the stack. Somehow he could not make it any further than halfway up the plank, before falling off—with the baulk on one side and him on the other. The exasperated German workman, gave demonstration after demonstration, of how quickly and easily it could be done. Try as he might, our man just could not manage it. He did, however, manage to give the German workman an admiring pat on the shoulder for a job well done.

And there was another job of tightening up nuts and bolts, for holding steel girders in place, several stories up. If you dropped your spanner, you would have to climb all the way down to retrieve it. If somebody you disliked was passing down below, you could delay calling out a warning, until the last moment. This is not recommended, as it cannot always be made to look accidental.

Another bloke had been working on a farm. They had been planting potatoes. The farmer would open a furrow, and a prisoner would walk behind, dropping seed potatoes at regular intervals. Another prisoner would be coming behind, and filling in. The second man would grab all the seed he could, hiding it under his French Greatcoat, which trailed the ground. This gave extra rations, but a failed food crop.

Any rights, we have, are covered by the Geneva Convention. The Germans are anxious to give the appearance of at least a token adherence to its principles. Most prisoners know very little about its laws, but quickly pick up on the things that, they think, may work to their advantage. The two things that are always uppermost in our minds, are food and work. For food, we find that we should be entitled to a large percentage of the basic civilian ration. Whether this is two thirds or threequarters, we aren't sure. But we are adamant that, if we are required to work, we will, at least, have to get the amount of food that we are entitled to.

NCOs cannot be forced to work, but they can volunteer. Privates can be required, or forced, to work, as well as Lance Corporals. This situation creates a bit of a dilemma for Bob and me. Bob, as a Lance Corporal, and me, as an Acting Corporal, are on different sides of the fence. While I seemingly have a choice, Bob doesn't. Then there is the uncertainty of the position of my own rank. What if my C.O. has gone ahead with the recommendation to wipe my Acting rank? That will wipe out my freedom of choice. He may have done it after the Crete show, and word of it delayed from getting through, because of my wanderings.

With the opportunity to study, and also take exams here in camp, it may be a good idea to stay put and study. It will be a good way of putting to use all that dead time as a prisoner. This could be a valuable option for

Bob, who was well into his studies, and on the way to becoming a vet, when he joined up. He might even be able to rewrite, from memory, his thesis, which had been lost in the Greek debacle. Again, maybe, even I could find something to study.

We have promised ourselves that we are going to escape again. To take up any courses, will automatically put that idea on hold. If one of us, and Bob is the most likely, decides to do it, then the position will be the same. We both feel keenly that, having been through so much together, the interests of the other has to be considered, just as carefully as his own.

All POWs firmly believe that in a month or two, something decisive will happen, and we all will be on our way home. Optimistically, it may happen before we have time to get into a course. Few can even consider being captive beyond a fortnight. It just cannot go on any longer. Then comes the sobering thought, that the Dunkirk boys have been here for over a year.

Decisions, decisions! We have plenty to chew over. What should we do? There is still the prospect of facing up to trial for escaping. We go to our Hut Commander and ask if we are likely to be overlooked. He tells us, "No, it will be fairly soon. Just as quickly as a sufficient group of offenders can be gathered together to make it worthwhile."

We agree that we will put off a decision to escape for the moment. I am pretty determined not to take any chances in such bleak weather. Getting free is no great problem, but it is about what happens then. Chances of help seem pretty poor to me. My reasons for escaping still remain the same—to get back to my own people. But, there is no way I am going to take the risks, just to be a nuisance.

So, for the time being, we settle into the camp routine of everyday life. We are badly undernourished and, with the winter weather to continue for several more months, all we can think of is food, and trying to keep warm. Mindful of my dodgy stomach, I am greatly heartened on visiting the latrine. I find it is a great, long, one-piece, bank of wooden seating, where one can sit in comfort. I have vivid memories of the despair I have felt, at having to squat in my weakened state, in some pretty hopeless situations. My joy is tempered a little, upon lifting one of the lids. The excreta falls into a pit below and, in this cold weather, it has frozen into a huge pyramid, with the peak finishing exactly level with the seat top. A quick inspection shows every opening is the same.

While the lice situation is pretty much under control, there still are some about. A few of the men have taken to washing their shirts and hanging them outside the hut. Quickly, they freeze solid. To make sure, some shirts are left out for a fortnight. That should fix them. But it doesn't. As soon as the shirts are thawed out inside the hut, those damn lice become active once more.

In trying to straighten out our thinking, Bob and I begin to take walks around the compound. There is a kind of circuit beaten out just inside the wire. The outside air is keen and bracing, and its freshness on the face is good to feel. However, the bitter cold makes numbers involved in such walks, few and far between. We are on one of these walks, deep in conversation, when a man approaches, circling in the opposite direction to us. Like us, his hands are deep in his pockets, and the only exposed skin is the round oval of his face. As he comes abreast of us, he stares intently at me. He suddenly says, "I know you. You jumped off a train in Greece, didn't you?"

"Yes, that's right," I reply.

He says, "I was one of the three who jumped before you. As we were waiting to get out of the trapdoor, I distinctly remember you telling your mate, We have to go. We will never get a better opportunity than this one."

I vividly recall the incident. George was with me then. Bob, of course, is mystified, as I didn't meet up with him until later. I quickly explain the circumstances to Bob, of what had caused me to speak to George in such a way.

We fall into earnest conversation and compare notes. He is Doug Robbins, a Staff Sergeant in a Field Artillery Unit from Victoria. I ask him how they had fared after jumping? He tells me, "It was an instant disaster." One of his mates had fallen back under the train, and had been decapitated. All they could do was lift his body clear of the line and leave it to be found by the authorities. This event took all the sting out of things for them and, with little heart to continue, they were picked up after three days.

I tell him that I had foreseen the chances of such a thing happening, and urged George to make his way round to the buffers, pick a spot, then jump clear. In this way, we had no problems with the jump.

After this meeting, we frequently meet again while out walking. He tells us that he has just about given up the idea of escaping again, and will sit it out until the end of the War. It will probably send him off his head, but he cannot see any other alternative.

One of the greatest events in the life of a POW, after food issues, is the arrival of mail from home. The suspense, while waiting for your name to be called out, is heartbreaking. To miss out, brings bitter recriminations against those thoughtless people back home, who surely couldn't care less if you lived or died. Although, in your heart, you know this to be untrue, still, you cannot prevent yourself from railing away, anyhow. Those who miss out, just stand aimlessly around, trying to share a little of the joy of those who don't.

A few days after transferring over to the main camp, our first mail delivery comes through. Our Hut Commander prepares to dish it out. Our train group is still largely together and, although Bob and I know very little about them, nor they of us, we still consider that we are part of the team. Bob and I crowd round with the others, hoping against hope.

We know that we only have a very small chance of scoring a letter. Without some sort of a reasonably permanent address, no notification could be relayed back home. Our escape attempts have left us in a kind of limbo, which will rule us out. Still, maybe for us two, there is just a faint glimmer of hope. After recapture on Lemnos, and then being sent back to Salonika, we had remained there for a period. While this was only a short time before our second escape, maybe it was long enough for the usually efficient Germans to send our particulars through. It is enough to give us hope.

As the names are called, the lucky receivers stretch out their hands for their priceless treasure. There is nothing for us, and we are bitterly disappointed. We have to concede, it is a forlorn hope anyway. As we just stand there in a group, those with mail rip it open, and begin to devour every word. It is a curious fact with POW mail. It is almost community property, with the receiver often reading passages aloud to anyone within earshot. The overwhelming pride, relief, and longing, just has to be shared with someone; And, who better than a fellow sufferer, who truly understands its poignant impact. You might not even know the bloke, and he might even come from a different country. It is a special kind of sharing that is spontaneous.

We are still grouped loosely together, when one of the blokes says, "Here you are. What do you think of this?" He goes on to read aloud the following, "I have returned my engagement ring to your mother. I am no longer engaged to you. I am now engaged to a REAL man, an American. I have no time for anyone who would put up their hands to the enemy." The reader is a young man in his early twenties, from Melbourne, Victoria.

For the moment, there is stunned silence. Then, as one, we all instantly rally round, trying to give him words of support. We tell him that he is better off to be rid of her, and it is just as well he found out, before it is too late. But the deep shock and helpless feeling of being locked up here, when grave and important things are happening so far away, is very hard to take.

A couple of those, who have received nothing, remark that, at least, they do not have to put up with bad news. It is a lame attempt to ease the pain somehow. Then another young fellow, a New Zealander, about the same age, says, "Don't worry. It wouldn't happen to me. NOBODY will write to me." He has been standing quietly, back a little from the others, just on the fringe of the group.

His hopeless tone makes us try to cheer him up. We tell him that at least his family will. He replies, "No, they least of all."

Mystified, we ask, "Why?"

"Because I shot my brother," he replies.

We are dumbfounded and ask him what were the circumstances. I think he gets some solace from sharing his burden with some sympathetic listeners. He explains that he, his brother and a couple of friends had been out deer hunting. They had spread out and were advancing, out of sight of each other. Suddenly, seeing movement in some bushes, and certain it was a deer, he fired. It was his brother.

Badly hurt, they tried to make the brother comfortable, while one raced off to get help. Well out in the scrub, it took time. When he returned with the police, they would not allow the man to be shifted, until they satisfied themselves that it was accidental. By the time they gave the OK, he was pretty far gone. It was too late, and he didn't make it.

The young Kiwi is bitter—believing that the long wait, almost five hours from the time of shooting, allowed his brother to bleed to death. We say, "It was a tragedy. Surely, by now, your family will understand."

He replies, "No, they can't stand having me around. It was almost a relief for the War to break out, so I could enlist and get away."

Our anger, frustration, and helpless bitterness, together with the deep sympathy we feel for our two comrades, make it almost a personal hurt. It is a gloomy first mail delivery, and takes us several days to get over it.

Then our Hut Commander calls Bob and me in, and informs us that we are to present ourselves for our court martial. We can leave our gear with him for safe keeping, and it will be returned to us when we return.

On the appointed day, we are marched off to one of the administrative buildings, arriving there about nine o'clock. We are taken into a fairly large anteroom, and told to wait until our names are called. There are some other fellows waiting already and, by the time proceedings begin, there are about fourteen or fifteen of us to be tried. We mill about, talking to each other, trying to assess the seriousness of each other's offence. As far as we can see, our crimes are sufficient to net us a fairly heavy penalty. Not knowing what to expect, this worries us a bit. Some of our fellow felons, who seem to know the procedures, advise us, "Don't accept your sentences. Give them an argument against it."

This puzzles both of us a bit. We wrack our brains, thinking back over our various detentions. We try to remember anything that might count in our favour as mitigating circumstances. The men waiting are quite a cross section of nationalities, although all are British. To me this means that, although we all are pretty much the same, there is sufficient difference to make this gathering rather interesting.

One of the fellows is a medium tall, clean cut person, with a sort of presence that draws your attention. He is an English Private, and inquiries, by the other Poms, reveal his name. This information is conveyed in a manner suggesting that he is well known, and a person of note. The respect and acceptance that I have, by now, gained for the Pommy serviceman, leads me to accept their personal assessment of him without question. Besides, Bob has been my travelling companion long enough, for me to get to know their worth. So I quietly question them further, as to who, or what, he is.

They tell me that he is a Liverpool Irishman from a tough Liverpool area. He is damn good to his friends, but very deadly to his enemies. He is definitely not a man to cross. He is a man to keep on side with. I ask if he is an escapee, too. They tell me, "No, his brother is."

He and his brother were together on the same working party. His brother is to stand trial for escaping. But, he had fallen deeply in love with a Polish girl, whom he had come in contact with, while on the working party. If he is brought back and made to serve a sentence, it will be almost impossible for him to return to that same party, and his girlfriend. So, this bloke changes identities with his brother. He will serve his brother's sentence, and will take his chances on being able to get back together again.

The proceedings start, and we felons begin being called into the trial chamber, one at a time. Finally, it is my turn. I am about middle of the bunch, with Bob to follow. The trial room is bare, except for a plain medium sized table and three chairs. The Presiding Officer is seated on one chair behind the table, a Records Clerk sits on the other to his right, and an Interpreter is seated to his left at the end of the table. There are several Guards standing together, on one side.

I am escorted to the front of the table, and face the Presiding Officer. The Clerk reads aloud the details of my misdemeanour, while I stand to attention. While he is reading, I am able to observe the Officer. He is in such an alcoholic haze, that I fully expect him to fall off his chair. He does not seem capable of being able to take in what is said. But, when the Clerk has finished, he remains silent for a moment, then stirs sufficiently to utter a few words. These are, "Twenty-eight days detention."

Mindful of the advice to argue against the sentence, I protest that this is unfair. I argue that I have already served fourteen days solitary confinement on Lemnos and in Greek civilian gaols. The Interpreter translates my protest to him. Again, he remains silent for a moment, still seeming incapable of understanding. Then he amends the sentence to fourteen days detention. It has been so easy, that I silently curse myself, for not having claimed the full twenty-eight days.

With the sentencing completed, I am marched back out into the anteroom. I quickly relay to Bob the argument, I had used to get my sentence reduced. He is next in line and when he re-emerges, he has managed to secure the same sentence. So, we will go in and come out together, and avoid separation.

Now, we are taken back to our hut where our Hut Commander is informed. He will look after our interests while we are inside. We then march off, under Guard, to the detention cells.

The cell block is a long wooden building in a special compound. It looks rather grim and forbidding, with the snow piled fairly deeply around it. There is an exercise yard in the open, with a circular path beaten in the snow. Inside, we are lined up and quickly assigned, one to a cell. There is a long central corridor, with cells running off both sides of it. The cell door is solid and substantial, with a small opening at eye level, secured by bars and a trapdoor. The cell is about five feet wide by seven feet long, and about ten feet high. In the top righthand corner is a sealed and barred window for light. The only furnishings are a bare wooden cot with two baskets of synthetic material, a bucket for toilet facilities and a metal water jug.

There is one redeeming feature, in that the whole block is centrally heated. As the Guards quarters are incorporated in the building proper, doubtless, it is mostly for their convenience. Still, the system is extended to cover all the cells as well. At least none of us will freeze to death, unless they decide to cut the heating off as some form of punishment. Each cell has one of those pipe grill contraptions, with hot water sealed in and running through them. It occupies the small space at the foot of the bunk. It is possible to sit with your back against it, and remain reasonably warm.

Now for the rules—we will remain in solitary confinement, except for two exercise periods of half an hour, one during the morning, and one during the afternoon. There is to be no fraternising or talking amongst the prisoners. Our food is to be bread and water for two days, then standard camp food every third day. Each prisoner will empty his toilet bucket under escort, first thing in the morning. He will then scrub out his cell and the passageway immediately in front of it. During this period only, he will be permitted to exchange items of a personal nature, with a fellow prisoner. Mail and letter writing for the period of the sentence is forbidden, and books are not allowed.

With nothing to do, I spend my time keeping warm, until the exercise period. At the appointed time, the doors are open and everybody is herded out into the exercise yard. Despite the bracing cold of the outside, it is something to look forward to. Everybody is rugged up with everything he has, and headgear pulled down over his ears. There is animated talk and laughter as we trudge round and round the circuit. Everybody wishes it would last a bit longer, despite the relief of getting back inside to the warmth.

At clean-up time in the morning, the whole place is a hive of activity. First, our cell doors are thrown open, with the guards urging us out with the familiar call of, "Raus, raus." A group will be taken to empty their buckets and have a wash, while the rest will sweep out their cell and wait for their turn. When the first group returns, they will start scrubbing their floors, while a new group goes to empty their buckets etc. The cleaning gear is kept stowed away at the end of the corridor. So it is necessary for a few to go and collect it. It will then be passed from group to group and, when finished with, returned to the store.

Always, we make the cleaning and scrubbing spin out as long as possible. It gives us an outlet for our pent up energy. With luck, we can waste time until almost morning exercise time. And we are able to make a complete mockery of the no talking, or fraternising, order.

We are sensible enough not to make things too blatant. We concentrate on seemingly legitimate requests, such as, "Pass me the scrubbing brush please." Or, "Have you finished with the bucket yet?" We always manage to achieve our goal of organised chaos. It is a perfect cover for anything secret that needs to be done, and everybody combines enthusiastically and without question.

On my first morning, I find a large chart has been placed on the outside of my cell door. It gives my name, number and length of my sentence. The sentence is marked off in fourteen squares, labelled Monday, Tuesday etc., with every third day showing my entitlement to camp food. Everybody else is the same, and I watch my sentence unfold, as religiously as the Guards.

My first bread ration is a pleasant surprise. I had imagined it will be the standard camp issue. But, when it comes, it is three times bigger. With this large dollop of bread and plenty of water, at least my stomach feels reasonably full. In fact, when my days of regular camp food come round, I quite seriously think I would be better off with bread and water.

Two days after our sentence begins, we are all roused out of our cells and made to stand to attention just outside, with the door open. It is about 1.30 pm, still too early for our afternoon exercise, and we are mystified as to the reason. Then, at one end of the corridor, a group appears, consisting of all the German NCOs in charge of the Guard, as well as the Duty NCO, and a couple of men dressed in civilian clothes. It is to be an official inspection. Quickly, the whispered news is passed from prisoner to prisoner, "It's a Swiss delegation from the International Red Cross."

Slowly, they make their way along the corridor, peering into each cell, talking among themselves, but not to any of us. Finally, they reach the end, pause for a moment, then ask, "Are there any complaints?"

This takes us by surprise, and there is complete silence for a moment. We wrack our brains trying to think. It will have to be something reasonable, and not frivolous. Then an English Sergeant in the end cell, close to where the delegation now stands, speaks up. This man had already been in here when our lot arrived. He says, "Under the Geneva Convention, as prisoners, we are allowed to write home and receive mail. While in here, we have been denied this right. Also, as prisoners, we are allowed books to read and study. This too, has been denied us."

The Germans look slightly uncomfortable. The Swiss speak quietly to them. Then, after a few moments, one of the Swiss speaks aloud to all of us, "We will see what can be done." Then they leave.

For the next few days we look carefully for any reprisals against the English Sergeant for speaking out. If there is to be any, we will protest. But there is none. Once the Swiss have gone, we expect that the Germans will do nothing. Still, they are sensitive to criticism, and try to maintain an illusion of fairness, especially in front of an independent observer.

In the morning, with nothing further having been said, we are issued with the official letter cards, enabling us to write home. Some of the fellows receive mail, too. Then a stack of books are brought in from the camp library, and quickly passed around. Our Swiss friends have certainly come good. This alters our routine completely. It allows us to utilise our dead time, while alone inside our cell, making the solitary aspect, almost non-existent.

With the advent of books and letter writing, we have a legitimate excuse for a bit more disruption at our morning clean-up time. We now have to borrow a pencil to write with, as well as swap books with each other. All letter writing has to be in indelible pencil, as the use of ink is forbidden. The suspicious Germans suspect that we might use the ink as dye, for staining the khaki cloth of our uniforms. When stained, they can be made to look very much like civilian clothing, when escaping.

With the official issue of four letter cards and two letter forms per month, our writing time is minimal. Most of our spare time is taken up reading. We are not allowed lighting, so we have to rely on the daylight coming through our cell window. As the light starts to fade, I will stand on the end of my cot, holding my book as close to the glass as possible. I'll maintain this position until I can no longer see. As it is now midwinter, this occurs about 4.00 pm. Then, I have to settle down for the night.

In the solitude of my cell, I cannot help thinking how bizarre my present situation is. I am in here under strict supervision, limiting my freedom of movement, and with severe restrictions on my diet. This is meted out to me as punishment. In fact, the mere suggestion of freedom of movement in a POW camp is farcical. The overcrowded conditions of the general camp, while bearable, make it impossible to get any privacy. And, the superior attraction of camp food, is in the German mind only.

So here I am, in my private centrally heated quarters, occupying my time, by matching wits with my captors for a couple of hours each morning. My food, such as provided, is being brought to me, rather than having to queue up for it. Two half-hour sessions each day are spent outside in the bitterly cold, but crisp, fresh air to break the monotony. Then, for the rest of my spare time, I am curled up with a good book. I don't know if I'm going round the bend, but my punishment is beginning to seem better than my freedom.

My sentence finally comes to an end. Together with Bob, we are escorted back to our hut. We have just missed out on a Red Cross Parcel issue, but our Hut Commander has held ours over, knowing that we were about to be released from detention. This is just another example of the efficiency and honest discipline, that is a great feature of the organisation and internal running of this camp—all due to these Regulars captured at Dunkirk.

There is a small parcel of prunes in the parcel and the Hut Commander says he is quite happy to trade us for them, if we wish. We ask him what he does with them. He says that they boil them up to make a kind of jam. The trade offer is cigarettes and, as neither of us smoke, we decline. A cautious Bob says to me privately, "If he can do it, so can we."

We are completely in the system now, and we have to make whatever meagre resources come our way, stretch to the limit. With our punishment behind us, we settle into the general camp routine. We now have to the difficult decision of what our future is to be. We have several things gnawing at us. We are perpetually cold and hungry. Whatever we decide to do, will inevitably be influenced by these problems.

The more, we try to rationalise our situation, and think a proposal through, the more, a serious obstacle seems to emerge, in making this line of action a doubtful prospect. Since being thrown together, Bob and I have become real friends, as well as partners. Each of us agonises over what he, himself, desires. It has to be something that won't let his partner down.

Escaping again is no real problem. But getting clear is. There are too many miles of hostile country to cover. We will be faced with the need to continually steal our food, and to find adequate shelter at night time, or whenever exhaustion catches up with us—always, without being discovered. But firstly, before any of this, we have to come up with a reasonable target to aim for. And there are none that we can think of. As for me, our present location seems a pretty hopeless, offering little prospect, with regards to getting away. But, I have to remember that this place is much closer to home for Bob than mine. This factor may make it worthwhile for him to give it a go. If we are to come up with a reasonable sort of plan, in a partnership such as ours, I may find it almost impossible to say no.

If we put escaping on hold, should we stay in camp, or go on a working party? Bob may be made to work, whereas my Acting Corporal rank seems to have me protected. So maybe, a decision there could be taken out of our hands. If Bob is sent anywhere, I could volunteer, so that we remain together. But this seems a bit dicey. For us to go on a working party, before being forced to, doesn't seem very attractive. The gossip about some of these, that have been relayed to us, makes them seem unappealing.

The option of staying in Camp, and becoming involved in some of the educational pursuits, means the almost impossible struggle to find fuel of some kind to keep warm. Also, it means continued hunger during those periods when Red Cross Parcels fail to get through. While Bob has something to aim at in the educational sphere, I don't. For me, this means the soul searching business of existing from one day to the next, waiting for something to happen.

While we are agonising, a very persistent rumour begins circulating in the Camp. Because of the severe winter, and we can attest to that, a desperate shortage of fuel for both domestic and industrial use has come about. This means that coal production from the nearby Polish mines, has to be greatly increased. This will require many more POWs to augment those already working there. If sufficient volunteers are not forthcoming, then the guards might round up everybody they can lay their hands on, and force them to do the job. If true, it seems to imply that the rights of NCOs to choose to work, might be ignored.

I am fiercely determined that there is no way I am going down a coal mine. My Dad and all his family had been miners, and all my Mother's family too. The area I come from is a solid coal mining area. While I, myself, have never worked at it, I know that it is a very dangerous occupation, even under good conditions. With the sort of approach, I imagine will be taken here, it may be almost suicidal.

Discussions of the coal mining proposal are talked over and debated quite fiercely, over the next few days. A group of us are arguing in the hut about it, with the consensus proposing to dodge it at all costs. A little Welshman in the group has been taking it all in, while saying very little. One of the fellows turns to him and says, "How about you, Taffy?"

Quietly he answers, "I think I'll go."

Amazed, I turn to him and reel off some of the many life threatening problems, I imagine that these mines will be beset with. Then I ask him, "Why will you go?"

He is quiet for a moment, then he answers in his beautiful, lilting, Welsh twang, "Well, you see, I'm a miner." For the Welshman, there is nothing further to be said.

The next day, still confused, I am walking along thinking, when a couple of fellows approach, so that we are face to face. One of them is very well-known to me. He is Norm Shute, a Sergeant from my own Unit. It is unbelievably good luck, and we begin to compare notes. Both of us have long since lost all contact with any of our Company. Norm had been detached and seconded to a Greek Unit as an Instructor. After the fall of

Crete, and his subsequent capture, I am the only person from our Unit, whom he has come across.

With the exception of George, I lost all contact with the others, when I jumped from the train. It is now some time since I parted from George, and I have no idea what has happened to him. "Have you seen George?" I inquire.

No, Norm hasn't, but he does have word of the Sims brothers, who are both from my home town. After their capture, the younger of the two had become so shocked, that he found it difficult to cope. His older brother had to watch over him, and almost spoon-feed him. They had got through to Germany and gone out on a working party to a coal mine in Poland. Now, the older brother has been killed there.

The story is that coal, stored in a large steel hopper, had become frozen to the sides. He had climbed up and prodded it from the top, trying to free it. But it would not budge. He had climbed down inside, trying from there. Suddenly, it came loose, burying him. By the time they got him out, he was dead.

He was given a proper military funeral, and some photos were taken. Norm takes me to see them, and we may purchase some, if we desire. At the time, we cannot see much point, as we feel certain that the appropriate notification, plus the photos, will have been sent on through the International Red Cross. The Germans are rather punctilious about this sort of thing. The view we see is of a uniformed German party firing a salute over an open grave, with the bareheaded younger brother looking into it. I cannot help but wonder, how he is coping.

I tell Norm of my fear of ending up in a coal mine. He asks, "Why not come out on a working party with me and my mate? It's in the process of being formed now. It's an all new, all volunteer NCOs' party to work in a timber mill."

Norm has teamed up with George Passmore, a West Australian, from a Field Engineer Unit like ourselves. They have made extensive inquiries about this party, and believe it is one of the better ones. Those already accepted seem a pretty good bunch of blokes, and an Aussie Sergeant Major is to be in charge. While there are a few vacancies, these are expected to be filled within the next couple of hours.

Faced with a quick decision, I tell Norm and George that I have to first work it out with my partner, Bob. I will get back to them within the next half hour. I hurry back to Bob with my head in a whirl, trying to figure out what this decision will be. When we had previously discussed the pros and cons of what to do, it was in the sense that we had time to work it out. Now, it is crunch time. The decision, we now will make, has to be instant and final.

For myself, it seems a good move. There is the chance of a little extra food, and also to escape when the time seems right. While the escaping bit has lost some of its attractions, because of the difficulty of getting clear from this part of the continent, the food bit is most attractive. I am eternally hungry, and the mere suggestion of extra food is enough for me. Besides, I haven't exactly enjoyed my stay in Stalag VIIIB, since arriving here. A change of scenery will be welcome.

For Bob, the decision is difficult. While he can see the attractions, a working party is still an unknown proposition. Maybe, we will be worse off than here. Then there is the study bit. To take that on, he will have to stay here. With Bob, seemingly unwilling, and me eager to go, Bob finally says, "You go, and I'll stay." We both still argue the pros and cons a little, but this statement really settles the matter.

I hurry back and confirm whether a position is still open for me, and then inform Norm and George that I am a goer. Then I return to Bob to divide up our common property. There isn't much. Now that the parting of the ways has come, I decide that Bob may make better use of my prismatic compass than me. I insist on giving it to him, and tell him to use it if he can. But, if he decides not to escape, then dispose of it in any way he thinks fit. In this place, such an item, is a very valuable commodity.

The next day, it is with mixed feelings that I trudge out with the rest of the party. We have a very bleak, snow swept hike of about two miles to the rail siding. There are about fifty-four in the party, plus an escort of Guards, and we are bound for somewhere in the Sudetenland. The one happening, that makes things seem brighter for me, is that Doug Robbins is also a member of the party. With another friendly face to count on, I can only hope that I have made the right decision.

CHAPTER 13

# Working Party Days at Mahrisch Trubau: Episode 1

IN DUE COURSE, WE ARRIVE at our destination to find it is a place called Mahrisch Trubau. This, of course, means nothing to us. We are too intent on climbing down from the cattle truck, and getting the stiffness out of our bones, to pay anything more than a passing interest to the place. It seems to be a reasonably compact, small town, set in undulating country. It is surrounded by heavily timbered hills. Obviously, these will be the source of supply for the sawmills where we are to work. Everything is heavily snowed under and, to an Australian at least, the outlook is bleak and unattractive.

With the party formed up, we are moved off by the Guards. The Guard contingent is of about six or eight men, with a Corporal in control. They will be stationed here permanently also, with the job of keeping us under control. They are mostly men, no longer fit for frontline or active service. Some had been wounded, and now recovered from these wounds.

We trudge through the streets, slipping and sliding on the icy roads. The locals, sensibly, keep inside, and there is barely a soul to be seen. After about half an hour, we are led to a medium-sized house, the end one in a row, opposite a fairly large timber mill. It is on the outskirts of town, with snow swept open fields behind it. The first thing that strikes us is that this is not a barbed wire prison compound. True, there is some wire, but that only closes off the rear yard. The front façade is exactly the same as the nearby houses, giving the illusion of everyday living.

Inside is very spartan. There is one fair-sized room for the guards, one for the mess room and cooking, and two into which we fifty-four have to cram. The toilet and washing facilities are in a little annex, jutting out into the backyard. Our quarters are crammed full of three-tiered wooden bunks, with just sufficient room to walk between. We take in the scene at a glance, and waste no time in selecting a bunk. We have learned by now, that your bunk area is your own little private domain. It is the only place you have for yourself, and everybody has a preference. For some it is the lower, for some the middle, and some the top. I prefer the top.

To climb into the middle, you have to stand on the side of the lower; and for the top, you stand on both the lower and middle. At the top, you suffer none of these disruptions. Then too, as hot air rises, you get a little extra benefit from the warmth generated by those close packed bodies. As for getting too hot in summer, right now, it doesn't seem possible for the temperature to rise sufficiently for this to be a problem.

As a last minute joiner of this working party, I know nothing of the other members. So, I stick close to Norm and George. I now begin to see how efficiently, it has been put together. Bill, the man in charge, is an Aussie Sergeant Major. His official Interpreter is a Palestinian, named Wally. Three or four of their associates will be the Cooks and Cleaners. This group will remain at home running the place, while the rest of us go out to work. Jack, an English Sergeant Medical Orderly, will treat any minor problems we might have. Anything major will require us to be sent back to Lamsdorf, where there are better facilities.

Bill is about six foot three, and of slim build. He is tough, fearless, and uncompromising. In dealings with the Germans, if he wants something done, he doesn't ask for it, he demands. He has four or five close friends he mucks in with, all of lesser rank. He is a natural leader. There is some suggestion that he has been a policeman, but had left the force. True or not, it does tend to enhance his authority.

Wally is about five foot seven, quiet and rather studious, and of an almost academic personality. He is a Jew, who had fled Germany to Palestine, when the Nazi came to power. He had been studying at the

University of Vienna at the time, and is better educated than most present day Germans. As an Interpreter, he is invaluable to us.

I am surprised to find that a Unit of Palestinians exists. Arab-Jewish troubles had been raging in the country for some years pre-war, requiring a garrison of regular British troops to keep them apart. I did not think the authorities would trust them enough, to arm and train them. Maybe the work they were required to do, was of a Pioneer nature, rather than frontline stuff.

It is easy to understand their wish to have a crack at Hitler, as well as using their military service as a lever, to force the British into recognising their right to exist in Palestine. In being taken prisoners, it must have been a great shock to them, wondering what the Germans may do to them in reprisal. The Germans, to their credit, have accepted them totally, as bona fide British troops.

The German Corporal in charge is named Kapitza. He is shrewd, cunning, and calculating. He sees this appointment as his sinecure. He doesn't particularly care what happens, as long as it doesn't affect his position here. He will endeavour to keep both sides as happy as possible, while always protecting himself.

The kind of life, we will have to live here, depends on the interplay between these three. It will be a battle of wits and wills, between Bill and Kapitza, and the shrewd verbal skills from Wally to get the message across.

This is an entirely new all-volunteer party, with only a few having been on a working party before. The experienced ones have some harrowing tales to tell of conditions, that we are not prepared to tolerate without a fight. It is extremely important that we lay down the rules from the outset, as anything we accept now, will be virtually impossible to change in the future.

Our workforce is to service three sawmills, a cement products factory, and a small engineering works. The number of workers required for each place is known; therefore, the only criteria we have for selection is, whether those numbers allow us to be with our mates. Our mucking in system consists mostly of twos and threes, with the odd person on his own. Mostly, this doesn't present much of a problem. However, in my case, I have to separate from Norm and George.

The mill we have elected to go to, only requires an extra two to fill its quota, by the time our turn comes round. So I drop out. It is the mill directly opposite our house and, because it is so close, is the most favoured as a work place. With one man too many, trying for a spot on its workforce, as a late comer, I am the logical man to go.

While there is a wide range of nationalities in our party, the differing origins have very little bearing on our ability to work in together. There are Australians, New Zealanders, Palestinians, Welsh, Scots, and English. But we regard ourselves as all British, while the Germans regard us all as English. Nationalities, therefore, have no influence in the allotment of jobs.

With the other worksites being unknown and unseen, the only assessment we can make of them is the size of the complement required. It is very much a question of pot luck. I finish up teaming with Doug, and going to the mill that requires the least number of men.

With the manning requirements sorted out, we end up spread around as follows—For the Home Mill, opposite, there are eight men; for the large Berg Mill, there are twenty; for the small Kollas Mill, where Doug and I elect to go, there are six; for the Koldas Cement Works, there are ten; and for the Engineering Works there are four. At home, there are three to act as Cooks and cleaning staff; and the administration staff of three are Bill, Wally and Jack.

Bill is adamant from the outset that the Cooks, cleaning, and administrative staff, are not to be interfered with. Any shortages in the workforce, due to sickness or injury, will have to be made up by new recruits from Stalag VIIIB at Lamsdorf.

We retire for the night, wondering what treatment we may expect from the locals we have to work with. We are determined that we will not allow them to stand over us. We have the comfort of Bill's promise and Wally's readiness to come and sort out any trouble spots, as they occur. At least, it is warm in our home, with a coal fire burning in the central stove. The coal supply, which is strictly rationed, appears adequate, at least for the moment.

In the morning, we line up and have the food distribution system explained to us. For breakfast, we will get a wedge of bread and some Ersatz or make-believe coffee. A very wide range of all sorts of food, clothing, and many other things, comes as a substitute for the real thing. They are referred to as Ersatz, one of the first German words we learn.

For lunch there will be potatoes boiled in their skins, and more coffee. For tea, it's some of the thin watery soup, maybe, if it is available, and again coffee. There will be monthly rations of very small amounts of sugar, jam and cheese—all Ersatz, of course. All this is in line with what the German civilians receive. The only consolation, we get from this news, is that we will be coming home for lunch, and not stopping away until nightfall.

I personally, do not relish the prospect of going outside to work in the snow. Surely, the Germans won't expect much in this God forsaken climate. To add to my woes, my clothing is well worn and threadbare, and offers little protection from the elements. My treasured black jacket, that had been given to me by the Greeks back in Pefkodassos, and protected me for so long, had been taken from me back at Stalag VIIIB. In its place, I was allowed to pick over a large heap of discarded uniforms that had been picked over many times already, by thousands before me. The boots I wear came from a similar heap. My old sandshoes, that stink to high heaven, have long since fallen apart. The pair I chose from the heap, still have the sole firmly fixed to the upper, but, these soles have a deep wide crack, clear through, and right across. One step outside, makes the snow and slush come through immediately. For hand protection, I have a pair of mitts, cut out, and made up from several layers of khaki cloth. These are standard issue. My privations have caught up with me, to the extent that I am physically at a low ebb. The cold is right through to my bones. I am constantly shivering and cannot stop.

Because of my escaping, I have little or nothing in the way of surplus gear, as most of the others have. All the clothing, I own, is on my back. I have to live in it, work in it, and sleep in it. I have nothing to change into, once I return home from work. All I can do is to try and dry out, as much as possible overnight, before having to wear the same things next day.

I have done this to the best of my ability. I can afford to take off a little bit in the warmth of the room, as a straw-filled paillasse, plus two blankets, is issued to each man. The paillasse is sturdy enough, although it is woven from string, made out of paper. The blankets, however, are thin, and feel like a sheet of calico. They are Ersatz, and probably made from paper, too. I cannot help but compare them with our Aussie issue blankets, which we were forced to dump, when we evacuated from Greece. Any one of those is better than a dozen of these.

So, here I am, half dried out, a mug of warm coffee and a nibble of bread in my belly, a prudently saved half, from the earlier bread ration. I am feeling totally miserable, with my whole being revolting at the prospect of facing the outside elements. I am too wrapped up in my own miseries to give any thought to anyone else, as indeed they are. Then comes the call to turn out.

We form up as best we can, while the Guards, suitably rugged up, sort us into our proper parties. We will all leave together, but, as our worksites are in different directions, we will turn off almost immediately. The parties are arranged, so that this chore, only requires the services of three Guards.

The Home Mill group are shepherded across the road to their job, and left in charge of the civilians there. The Engineering Works and the Kollas's Mill groups, my job, will go off in one direction under one Guard. The large Berg's Mill and Koldas's Cement Works lot, under two Guards will head off in another. They have to make their way through the centre of town. A Guard will stay on the job at each of these work places, and bring them home at the appropriate time.

Our party, under one Guard, will drop off the Engineering group into the care of the civilian employees, then continue on to Kollas Mill with the rest of us. He will remain with us until it is time to return, then pick up the Engineering lot on the way back.

All this rather complex procedure, is finally sorted out with the help of Bill and Wally. We will be back for lunch and a short break, then return to work until knockoff time, when we will return home for the night. We wonder if there is any advantage to be gained, by being under the care of a civilian or Guard. We will just have to wait and see.

Once outside we feel rather cowed in the half-light, with the bleak landscape all around us, and houses, streets and everything, half-buried in snow. The dark, leaden sky, presses down upon us, seemingly determined in preventing the sun from ever getting through again.

We trudge, with our heads down, wondering if we could possibly survive to get out of this. The Home Mill mob drops off, then the Berg and Koldas lot turn away, and finally, our mob is left alone. The Guard is just at our rear, with his rifle slung on his shoulder, when a civilian approaches, walking along the street towards us.

As is the German custom, the civilian greets the Guard with the standard, "Heil Hitler', thrusting his right arm forward and up, in regulation salute. Our Guard replies mechanically at the same time. To us, this offensive gesture, is just rubbing salt into our wounds. It is just too much, and more than we can stand. The same thoughts must have struck all of us at the same time, for there is no prompting from anyone, as we all roar out together, "Fuck him."

The startled, nonplussed Guard and civilian, have no idea what we have said, although our meaning is unmistakeable. The slightly cowed civilian hurries on his way, while the Guard just plods along in our rear. We don't give a damn what reprisals might be forthcoming. We have to get back at these bastards somehow. We have to let them know that, although we are prisoners, we are still not beaten.

We are still half-starved, poorly clad, and heading off into an uncertain future. This act of defiance, however, gives us a lift. Whereas before, each man was silent, and wrapped in his own thoughts, now we begin to talk and chatter among ourselves.

Whether this blasphemy ever is reported to anybody, we never ever discover. Certainly, we never suffer in any way because of it. Once the others catch on, they quickly keep the practice going. With everybody becoming used to it, civilians included, the use of this kind of salute becomes much less practised.

The Engineering Works proves to be a very small establishment, when we come to it. The fellows, who are to work here, are handed over by the Guard, and we continue on. Soon we can see the unmistakeable layout of a sawmill, with the logs, stacks of timber, and the mill building with its smoke stack, from which clouds of steam or smoke are emerging. We can hear the sounds of the machinery in action, so work is underway before we get there. With most of everything covered in the all-enveloping snow, we just hope that, somehow, we might be able to wrangle a job in the warmth of the engine room.

With our determination to stick to the more or less menial jobs, so as to give as little assistance to the German war effort as possible, we are a bit apprehensive, as to how much confrontation, we can expect from the locals. We need not have worried. They have no intention of allowing us near any machinery, nor the chance to sabotage anything.

We are met by Frans, the foreman, a small, energetic, and bustling man in his fifties. He wastes no time in handing us over to various workers, who indicate what jobs each of us is to do. He does this by pointing to each of us and indicating, you go with him. By keeping together, Doug and I manage to be accepted as a two man team, and are handed over to a man called Josef.

Josef is something of an enigma in this place, as he is no older than in his early thirties. All men of his age are serving in the armed forces. Somehow, he has managed to remain a civilian. He has the puckish face of a joker, with plenty of laugh lines around his eyes and mouth. We feel a cautious, but instant rapport with him.

With much talking and waving of arms as a means of communication, he asks us our names. We tell him, Doug and Arthur. He says that is too hard for him so, from now on, we are to be re-christened. Doug is to be Max, and I am to be Moritz.

Telling us to come with him, he takes us well down the yard to a quiet section, and indicates that our job is to be stacking cut timber. To be sure we get it right, he gives us a demonstration of what he wants us to do. He leaves us to it, saying that he will be back later to see how we are going.

While we have not known what to expect, we imagined that somebody will be standing over us at all times, telling us to do this and do that. We were ready and prepared to resist this kind of treatment as much as we could. Now, we find that, we have been given a job, and left to our own devices.

There is no boundary fence here. The land stretches away for about a quarter of a mile, into what may be open fields, if not for the damn snow, before coming to a very good road, which leads into town, one way, and into the unknown distance, the other. All we have to do is walk away, keeping the timber stacks between us and observation from the yard, and we can be well gone before anyone is the wiser. It is so easy. Now we know why the advice back in Stalag VIIIB is that, if you want to escape, go out on a working party. But where will we head for? By placing us deep inside Europe and close to the Polish border, we will have to travel thousands of miles, in any direction, to get right through.

We mull over the pros and cons: the hostile country, troops swarming everywhere, the hellish wintery conditions, and the almost impossible chance of obtaining food. In our uniforms we stand out like a sore toe. Even if we are able to steal civvies, it is well-nigh impossible to travel from one place to another without proper papers. Anyway, in our emaciated state, it is a task that is quite beyond us. Our malnourished bodies just cannot stand up to it. Maybe, we will make our attempt in the future, when we get our strength back again. And maybe, when this accursed snow goes away, and the sun begins to shine again.

Reluctantly, we come to the conclusion that escape is out, at least for the time being. This is something of a relief, as the mere thought of the hardships involved, are exhausting enough.

We turn to the job in hand. It is simple enough, and Josef has given us a good demonstration. We are to carry on with a just started stack, and just keep on building it up. The end result will see a pile of boards, all the same type, length and thickness. The stacks start building on heavy, three by two type timber, a metre wide. The rows of boards are separated by slim, metre length sticks, offcuts from the mill waste. This allows air to circulate freely, so that proper seasoning can take place. The boards are delivered to us by small trolley, pushed along a set of rail lines, after being cut in the mill. A couple of other blokes have this job.

We find a couple of small pieces of board to stand on, to keep our feet out of the snow. We stack a couple of layers of boards, before the cold gets to us so badly, that we just have to head off to the warmth of the engine room. We are unaccustomed to working in our loose fitting mitts, and find it clumsy going, sometimes losing them in the process.

We use the excuse of needing more metre sticks, or looking for the toilet, to enable us to get in the engine room. With Josef elsewhere, we stay inside until chased out by the foreman, Franz. In this way, we fill in the morning, by first stacking, then a little warm up. Then it becomes time to head home for lunch.

It is time for the civilian workers to knock off for their lunchbreak too. We haven't given much thought to what our hours of work will be. Now that we are on the job, we can see that it will have to tie in with their hours. This will make it pretty much the same, as we are used to, back home. It looks as if we have chosen the best possible working conditions, when we elected to come on this working party. There have been a few minor brushes with Franz, the foreman, mostly by the other blokes. They, like us, tend to make for the warmth of the engine room, at every opportunity. Having to chase them out again, understandably, tends to exasperate him somewhat.

The language barrier is the main stumbling block, and tends to keep tempers short on both sides. He will try to tell somebody to do something, and they will do the wrong thing, or in the wrong way. Then he will just explode. He will charge off and find the Guard, usually in the engine room, pour out his woes in a torrent of German, and with much waving of arms. The Guard, although sympathetic, cannot do anything, for we cannot understand him either. Anyway, he is there only for security reasons. He is not a work supervisor.

As for our man, Josef, he just gives us free rein. He comes round, from time to time, to see that we are going alright. But always, his instructions are more as a workmate, filling in a couple of new hands on the procedures. There never, ever, are any orders. The more we see of him, the more we get to like him.

With us all assembled, the Guard heads us off back home. Part of the way along, he directs us to make a slight detour. He wants to have a few words to a colleague, who is on another working party in the town. But, we are happy to be on the move back home, as this tends to get the circulation moving better. And we can look forward to a break inside, in the warmth. We are a bit unhappy at this proposed delay, but are intrigued at maybe finding out something from, whoever these other people are.

We arrive to find it is a French working party. Their quarters are bigger, better, and more comfortable than ours. Now that France has fallen, it is regarded by the Germans as a part of the Greater Third Reich. These men, who had been captured some time before, now only have token supervision, and are allowed to come and go at will. We can only guess at the privileges this semi-freedom allows them to enjoy. There doesn't seem to be any of them about. Our Guard tells us to wait in a passageway, while he goes looking for his mate.

A strong smell of cooking food drifts in from somewhere, as we stand there. My nose seems to indicate that it comes from around a corner in the passage. We all are half-starved, with me, perhaps, being a little worse off than the others. Saying nothing, I just slip away, irresistibly led on to this smell. The passageway turns the corner, and leads into a large room. It is the kitchen. There are two large vats, steaming over separate fires, with a Frenchman at one, stirring with a large paddlelike ladle. A couple of others, obviously staff, are moving about, further down the room. This food, obviously, is far better than what we are heading home to. Without a second thought, I beg for some.

I know I only have a few seconds before the Guard returns, but I don't care. I just have to have some of this food, even if it is only a mouthful. I am far beyond suffering my hunger with dignity. I will beg, even grovel, if I have to, in order to get some. This lot seems the sort worth going for, on hands and knees.

We have no common language to communicate in, but, to the Frenchman, my needs and wants are unmistakeable. Doubtless, he has been in the same condition, early in his captivity, and knows, full well, how badly you can be affected.

Silently, he takes a bowl and, with his ladle, fills it to the brim, from the hot, steaming vat. It is like Irish stew. It is full of chunky vegetables, and there is some meat in it too. And the broth of it is something to smell and savour. In the French way, it is laced with garlic, and, although garlic is not a food I am used to, this seems to make it all the more exotic.

Instantly, I am at a disadvantage. The cook has not offered me a spoon to eat with, so I will have to drink it straight from the bowl, and scoop out the pieces with my fingers. Also, it is bubbling and boiling hot, and has not quite finished cooking. I make a tentative sip at the liquid, and I am instantly burned. Resolutely, I attempt another. There is no way I will allow the scalding to put me off. Then there is a scurry of feet from the passageway, and in bursts the agitated Guard.

He has returned in my absence, found me missing, and tried to find out from the others, where I have got to. They just shrug their shoulders, and don't understand. There is no way they will tell him anything. Thinking that I have taken the opportunity to escape, he is frantic. If I have, he knows he is in big trouble. Telling the others to stay put, he hurries off in a quick search. Just as quickly, he finds me. As he bursts in, he takes in the situation at a glance. The relief at finding me, coupled with a little compassion, makes him react the way he does. He just says something that seems to indicate, "Hurry up and get on with it. You're holding us all up." I do my best to oblige, even though my mouth and throat are severely burned. Trying to ignore the pain, I am most upset when, finally, I have to give up, leaving some still unfinished broth in the bowl.

Mumbling my heartfelt thanks, I hand the bowl back to the cook, and with much shaking of hands. A couple of others from my group have drifted in to see what is going on. When they realise that food is involved, they are torn between hating my guts for scoring, and kicking themselves for not realising the opportunity on hand. When you are starving, you cannot stand for someone else getting something, while you miss out.

We march off again, with me trying to ease my scalded mouth and throat. The others ply me with questions as to what it was like, what was in it etc. At the Engineering Works, we pick up the others, who have been kicking their heels waiting for us. They are quickly filled in on the good food the Frenchmen are enjoying. Everybody is sure, that we have made a wise choice, in coming here. Surely, it will only be a matter of time, before we get the same treatment. After all, access to more food is the main reason for coming on this party.

We arrive home to find the other parties already here. We quickly collect our rations of potatoes and Ersatz coffee, and join the fellows we muck in with, in our spartan dining room. We have just a little time to compare notes with each other, before heading back to the job, and out once again into that bitter cold. The Home Mill party disclose, that they have managed to establish the principle, of being allowed to come home by themselves.

For the Berg Mill and Koldas work parties, however, there have been some bitter confrontations. Our fellows feel that anybody and everybody there, seems to think, that they have the right to order them to do whatever that particular individual, doesn't want to do himself. As volunteer workers, our blokes feel, they have some rights in determining what they are prepared to do, particularly, in the tricky business, of what may be helping the German war effort.

It seems that those Frenchmen, whose cooking I have sampled, were the main labour force manning these industries, prior to our coming. While they and the civilians have worked out an understanding of what the Frenchmen's duties are, it does not necessary follow, that our lot will follow the same pattern. Their country has been overrun, and they don't have much choice. Our blokes tend to feel that they do. It is hard to say whether, or not, the civilians just want to carry on as before, or seek to unload some of the menial, undesirable tasks onto us, in the transition. But there are lots of jobs, that our blokes are just not prepared to do.

With the language barrier, there is no room for persuasive finesse. Every disagreement is a head-on confrontation, with much red-faced shouting and waving of arms, that threaten to come to blows. With the seriousness of the situation, threatening to get out of hand, Bill, Wally, and Kapitza, are forced into a busy role on mediation.

They have been sent for by Herr Berg and Herr Koldas in turn, to sort out our lot. Hearing, from both sides, on what the disputes are about, and coming to a compromise, involves some tricky negotiations. Bill is determined to establish a fair working system for his men and, in this, he has a surprising ally in Kapitza.

Kapitza is determined to hang onto his job as Working Party Commander, taking advantage of any lurks and perks along the way. As long as this can be achieved with a minimum of fuss, and a certain amount of harmony, then he doesn't much care which side, if any, gains an advantage. Indeed, he is prepared to bring some pressure to bear on his countrymen, if necessary, to achieve it.

Wally's total command of the language, enables a satisfactory formula to be worked out that, finally, almost eliminates these blow ups. It is almost a POWs' trade union.

On the Berg Mill and Cement Works jobs, the civilian foreman is the only person empowered to direct a POW to a job. Any civilian, who needs assistance, will ask the foreman. He will direct one or more of the POWs to help. In the event of a dispute, the POW job leader, or Arbeit Chef, will work out something with the foreman. (The POW Arbeit Chef, or work boss, is a senior ranked man, to be selected from amongst the work crew, and elected or chosen by the others). If still in disagreement, then Bill, Wally, Kapitza, and either of the two owners, are to work something out.

Of course, all this takes some months to sort out. On this first day, there is only the bitter arguments, with Bill, Wally, and the others called in to mediate. With the Home Mill party, Kollas Mill party, and the

Engineering Works, there has not been any need for upset—perhaps, because they are small compared to the others.

The bitter cold, our intense hunger, and the inadequacies of our clothing, force our spirits to a low ebb. On this first day, a few are so disillusioned that they want us all, as a body, to refuse to turn out for the afternoon. The majority opinion, however, is that we stick it out, at least for a while. Stalag VIIIB, at Lamsdorf, is certainly no better; whereas here, we have the advantage of a regular supply of fuel. With a regular issue of coal, we can at least, be warm at home. At Stalag VIIIB, it is a scramble to find anything at all. Then too, here, we expect to be able to trade with the civilians for food. And really, food is the great and commanding reason, that has prompted us to come here. With my experience at the French camp, there must be some available. We will just have to figure out a way to get onto it.

We take our potato ration, eat some, and save the rest to concoct some sort of an evening meal. Whoever gets home first, starts the preparation, using whatever resources we have. It looks like Norm or George will do most of the cooking for our group, as it is unlikely that I will beat them home. However, we have the advantage of having a representative on two separate parties. This should give us a wider field for any trading.

All the little groups have adopted much the same system of pooling as we have. By now, it has become pretty much automatic. We, who had been captured in Greece and Crete, have been prisoners for something like eight months now. Some of the Pommy boys with us, had been taken at Dunkirk, so they were in the bag twelve months before us. I, of course, have managed to vary this a bit, by being on the loose for something like half of that time. But, in all cases, the treasured bits and pieces, we have managed to put together, is truly amazing.

Empty tins have become cooking and drinking vessels. Here and there, somebody has managed to scrounge a discarded cooking pot of enamel, with some holes in it. Somehow they have managed to repair it. Such a magnificent implement makes them the envy of all the others. Some of the blokes will wait until the owners have used it, then beg to borrow it, to use in turn. There are profuse promises of the care and cleanliness that will be taken, with the owners grudgingly complying. For most of us, our acute hunger is too great to allow us to wait—especially, as the pot owners will make their use, as long drawn out as possible, to discourage the borrowers.

The frenzied confusion of the midday meal break, coupled with the stories of the happenings on the various jobs, are soon disrupted by the Guards' hated call, to turn out once again. Very, very reluctantly, we drag ourselves back out onto the road, for the march back to work. It seems even more cold now, than before. The instant I walk outside, my whole body again shakes, uncontrollably. In miserable silence, we trudge back to our places of torment.

Josef greets us, Max und der Moritz, cheerfully once again, and saying, "Come," he takes us away to help him shift some boards. To me, the dark, leaden sky, and the total absence of any sun, makes this just the most miserable place on Earth. After this small task, he takes us back to our stack, and leaves us to carry on as before. Somehow, we get through the afternoon, and it again becomes time to head for home.

This time there is no detour to the French camp. Indeed, we never ever go there again. Instead, as we trudge along, we begin to hear the sound of voices calling out, and even laughing. We come to an area, where we can see across to a hilly slope. There are dozens of civilians, grownups and children of various ages, cavorting and carrying on, at high jinks in the snow.

The slope is enclosed on three sides by dark, sombre, and threatening forest. There is no bush here, as we know it. Each and every tree seems to have been handplanted, so that they are all exactly the same distance apart, and in row after uniform row. They are big and substantial, and all pines. All the people are well-rugged up against the cold, but the cheeks of their pale bare faces, are lit by a bright, rosy glow. There are a few runny noses, but all of them are having a great time. This amazes me greatly. I cannot see how anyone can be so stupid to venture out into the biting cold, unless forced to. These people demonstrate, quite plainly, that they actually like being in the snow.

When we arrive home, we find there has still been some more confrontation and argument, on the larger parties, between our blokes and the locals. This is depressing news. If it keeps up, the only alternative that we can see, is for the whole party to be sent back to Lamsdorf. It doesn't seem likely that they will split us up, and allow the fellows in the smaller places to stay on. In any case, we feel we cannot allow that. We will stick together as a body, no matter what.

Once inside for the night, the place is a hive of activity. Everybody is occupied in doing something. There is a cooking set up, of a stove and a medium sized hot plate, as distinct from that used by our staff for the regulation meals. The staff have a good fire going in the grate, and the amateur cooks are crowded round, trying to conjure up something for their mates—from the spuds they have saved from dinner time, plus anything they can add from their horded stores. Almost every square inch is taken up with a tin, can or pot, while their amateur chefs hover close by, keeping a critical eye on their masterpieces. There are others in the background, waiting to claim a space, as soon as one appears. With fats of any kind being unobtainable, the cooking is very rudimentary. It has to be watched to ensure it doesn't burn, and also to make certain that it doesn't end up in somebody else's clutches.

While waiting to eat, most of the others are involved in trying to clean themselves. There is a large copper in the corner of the wash room, and the staff have a good fire going under it. This means we have a bit of relief from the bitingly cold water. Still, as the only soap ration is a small cake of Ersatz soap once a month and, as that has never lasted any more than three days, our efforts tend to be only partially successful.

Then there is the battle to dry out your gear, before having to turn out next morning. With only what we stand up in, and nothing to change into, it is a big problem. It requires great judgement, and jostling for a spot, to be able to get some degree of dryness, before having to don them again. Boots are the worst. If you place them too close to a heat source, the leather will stiffen, then crack when flexed.

In footwear, we have some relief at home. We still have those clogs, we had been issued with, and now they are a godsend. The accursed things are still as difficult for me to manage, but, strangely, those footcloths prove even warmer than a pair of socks. Anyway my socks have to be dried out again for the morning. Our feet always are wet through, minutes after stepping outside into the snow. Our greatest misery is the endless dead feeling, that reaches to our calves, and, to which, no amount of foot stomping can ease.

Our overcoats, that help to keep us warm to some degree outside, and on the job, have to be dried sufficiently to serve as a blanket during the night. At least a lot of snow can be shaken off before penetrating like water, but any warmth, even body heat, is sufficient for it to get through.

Eating, cleaning and drying out, keeps us busy for two to three hours after getting home. Then, we have a short period to compare notes, before turning in.

Norm, George and I, talk over the day's happenings, while we eat what we have managed to put together. They are first home, and have beaten me by a half hour or more. Their work conditions seem to suggest that there will not be much room for complaints there. Their group has managed to establish a pattern of procedure with a minimum of argument, much as we have done on our job.

As far as we can make out from the fellows on the larger jobs, the main problem is that they are told by one civvy to do something. Then, while they are doing that, another civvy will come along and tell them to stop. He will tell them to do something different. They will start on the new task, only for the first bloke to come back and abuse them, for not doing what he has said. After an argument, they will go back to the first job, only for the second bloke to come back, and repeat the dose.

No wonder Bill, Wally, and Kapitza, have been so damn busy. The civvies for their part, refuse to concede their right to order about these 'stupid' Englanders, and tell them what to do. Our blokes, for their part, do their best to point out that nobody can do more than one job at a time, and for the 'stupid' Germans to get their act together.

We three feel that these disagreements will eventually sort themselves out. In the meantime, we will try to become friendly with some of the civvies, in order to trade for food. I feel that in Josef, I have already managed this to some extent. We will have to feel our way before testing how receptive they may be to the idea, before putting on the bite. Then we will have to decide what, if anything, we can afford to sacrifice from our meagre possessions, in order to satisfy our overwhelming craving for something to eat.

It has been a pretty heavy day for all of us. Everyman has suffered in some degree, from the uncertainty of new surroundings, the petty arguments, and the general physical discomforts. We all are glad to retire to the haven of our bedspace at lights out, to chew over in our minds what has happened. We are crammed in so tightly, that it is almost possible to hear each other think.

Soon somebody begins talking to somebody close by. Then somebody else chimes in. Quickly, a general conversation begins to ebb and flow, until finally, our tiredness catches up. And the subject is food. The last thing I can remember, before falling asleep, is a graphic and minute description of the delights of roast beef and Yorkshire pudding, amidst the agonised groans and calls to "shut up" from those within earshot.

Next morning, we are roused out early for a repeat dose of what had gone on the day before. It is damned hard to face up, once again, going out into the snow. At least we have the good news of finding that we are only required to turn out half a day on Saturday, and not at all on Sunday. The only exception to this will be that, if a rail truck comes in, it has to be loaded. It seems that a load of boards, occasionally has to be dispatched somewhere by rail. Because of the tight rail schedules, once the empty truck has been shunted in, it has to be loaded immediately. The Germans insist that there can be no compromise when this happens. If it occurs in normal working hours, then the job has to continue until finished, even if it means continuing beyond the normal knock off time. If it happens at the weekend, then we will just have to turn up regardless. We gloomily are prepared to bet that, somehow, the Germans will manage for this to always happen on a Sunday.

Back on the job, we begin to take a lot of interest in the people we are to come into daily contact with, and this spreads through all parties. The owner of our mill, Kollas, is a medium tall man in about his early forties. He is lean and healthy looking, and would normally be in the Army, but for his occupation. Evidently, the timber industry is sufficiently important to exempt him, or he has some sort of clout.

We are interested in the setup, in order to get some sort of an idea as to its importance to the War effort. If it is important, then we want to know how, just in case there is something we can do about it—perhaps by refusing to handle something, or maybe even a little sabotage. Early on, we are suspicious of everything. We feel certain the Germans will do their damnedest to put it over us, and that they will lie and cheat anyway they can. It is these suspicions of ours, and theirs about us, that help to fuel the arguments.

In time we learn that Kollas had inherited the mill by marriage. His wife's people had owned it, and it has been left to her. He worked for her father, and managed to catch the eye of the boss's daughter. When dad died, he was able to take over. They live in a house on one side of the mill, and have a couple of school age children. She is in her mid-thirties, and the first thing we notice about her, is her wild, untidy mop of black hair. She looks like a floozie, as if she has just got out of bed and hasn't had time to comb it, no matter what time of day it is. This is in marked contrast to most other females we see.

With Kollas being occupied in mostly policy and administrative affairs, we don't see a lot of him. When we do, however, we often see her come up to him, and she will speak in a manner, indicating that she has a lot of input and clout in the running of things. Her demeanour seems to indicate that she is of easy virtue. While this, in itself, is of very little interest to us, for we are too hungry to be interested in sex, it might mean we may catch her out in something that may turn into food.

The small civilian workforce are men too old for military service, with the sole exception of Josef. They pay outward marked respect to Kollas, as a man of influence and power. But inwardly amongst themselves, they seem to think of him as a jumped up Johnny come lately.

The very efficient running of the place, is in the hands of Franz, the foreman. He is a very active man, who may have scraped into military service, if he had wanted to. When something is said to him along these lines, sometime later, he whips off his cap, bends his head and points to his scalp saying, "I got that in the last war." It is a deep furrow-like scar, where a bullet had creased his skull. How it had missed penetrating through bone, and into the brain, is one of those miracles that seem to happen in wartime. We have a bit more respect for him after this.

Then there is Josef. Everything about him, makes him eligible for service. He is single, seems physically okay, and his job, though seemingly important, is not sufficiently high enough up the scale, to warrant exemption. He had been called up several times, but managed to talk his way out of it. He is a first class conman. The more we see of him, the more we like him, and likewise, he and us. He is always calling out to "Max und der Moritz", to come and do something or other. And, always, he manages to find ways of making things easy for us.

These are the people, whom Doug and I come into immediate contact with, and, if we are to do any trading, it will have to be through them. Of these, Josef seems our best bet.

There is a morning tea break, halfway through the morning, when everybody stops for a little food. We, of course, have nothing, so Josef gets into the habit of sharing his with us. It is food, and we are grateful. But it is totally different in concept to what we would have back home. We are fascinated by what they produce, and how they eat it. There is always a chunk of bread, generally with something else to go with it. The something else might be a dob of melted fat, in which case, the chunk of bread is cut into two, with the dob in the middle. It might be a small block of fat, that has been cut from between the rind and the flesh part of a piece of bacon. It might be a small heap of cooked up crackling.

Everybody owns a pocket knife, and will hack off a mouth-sized bite of bread, and spread a smear of fat. For crackling, a piece is put into the mouth, together with a bite of bread. Often the bread is placed in the mouth, and then the bite is sliced off close to the lips. Always the blade will be in the hand, which conveys the food to the mouth, and sticking upwards. Always we expect somebody to stick themselves badly, or gouge an eye out. But it never ever happens.

Our concept of slices of bread with butter, and with different types of spreads, seems unknown. In any case, a lot of things that we take for granted, are simply unobtainable because of rationing. Sweet stuff, like jams and honey, and dairy foods such as cheese, are very scarce. These only become available in very small amounts, and at very infrequent intervals.

It seems that all we can trade for, is the basic commodities such as bread and potatoes. There is no meat as we know it, and certainly not the typical Aussie steak. We really need some more variety in our diet to help us get back some of the stamina we have lost. We soon find out that Josef can't help us very much in the way of food, other than what he shares of his own. He may be able to purchase some for us elsewhere, but the currency will have to be cigarettes.

Cigarettes are a fairly regular issue to us—some by the Germans, and some from Britain via the International Red Cross. Those from Britain are usually good quality Players brand, in sealed tins of fifty. Those from the Germans are very strong and rough French Army issue, of Gauloisie brand, in standard paper packs of twenty or so.

As a new party, our supplies distribution is lagging behind a bit. All the regular supplies will go first to Stalag VIIIB at Lamsdorf. They will have to be sorted out before issue there, and then sent on to the various working parties. There will be a time lapse, before they catch up with us. In the meantime, with little or no currency, we will just have to tough it out. One advantage we have is that neither Norm and George, nor I smoke. We can use all of our issue for trading.

The Rules of Warfare and treatment of POWs, had been hammered out after World War I. Known as the Geneva Convention, most of the major nations had signed the Treaty, agreeing to abide by its code of conduct. Germany is a signatory, and is at pains to appear to be abiding by it.

Our knowledge of those rules is very vague and rudimentary. But that doesn't stop us in the slightest from claiming to know all about them, especially in the way they apply to our present predicament. One of the rules, apparently, is that we are to be paid for our labours. We take it for granted that a formula for how much, and the type of work, will be part of that rule—and the Germans will comply, only where they have to.

Payment is made in Camp currency, as distinct from the regular kind. It is in the form of coloured slips of paper, not much larger than the tram tickets we use back home. They are in denominations of one, two, five, ten marks etc. Officially, we can use it to buy things we need. But actually, it can only be used within the camp, where all we can buy are pencils and paper, and not much else.

Our great need is for food and, as there may be some available for purchase in local shops, it is deeply frustrating to have some 'so called' money in our pockets, and not be able to use it. Bill and Wally, through Kapitza, try hard to convince the rationing people that it is official currency, and therefore legal tender. We ought to be given authority to purchase extra supplies as a group, similar to the townspeople. They argue that their distributions are so efficient, that there is little or nothing surplus left to distribute. They can't very well admit that the damned camp stuff is worthless.

So here we are, starving and in desperate need of food we cannot get, and with money we cannot use to buy. We know of an alternative currency that is certain to get us something of what we want—cigarettes. But, with the supply lines not yet established, its arrival is sometime in the uncertain future. Our clothing is tatty and threadbare, and inadequate to keep out the bitter cold. To keep reasonably clean and dry, is a never ending struggle. In a God forsaken place, in a seemingly unending twilight, and half-buried in snow, it seems we have reached a very low ebb. Our mood and thoughts are close to being suicidal. How long we can stand this sort of thing, doesn't bear thinking about.

Gradually, ever so slowly, the days begin to creep by, one at a time. While totally absorbed with our hunger and general misery, we begin to take in some of the life around us, almost unnoticed. The population is made up of females, elderly men, and young boys. All men of military age are away on service. All the gaps created in this way are filled by conscripted or forced labour, mostly from countries overrun by Germany, and now considered to be part of the empire. All of these people have to wear a cloth patch sign, sewn to their jackets, denoting from whence they come—P for Poland, OST for the East etc. People from the East are regarded as Russians by the Germans. While this is true, they in turn cling to their district identity of Ukrainian etc. The people, whom we come in contact with here, are conscripted civilians—not soldier prisoners like us. With the German belief, or attitude, that Russian soldiers are subhuman, they are kept confined, and not allowed on working parties. These people, therefore, are able to live a much better lifestyle, although their movements are fairly restricted.

Mahrisch Trubau is a smallish town with four or five small rural villages close by. These villages are within a radius of one and a half to five miles from the town, making it the general administrative centre of the area. These conscripts are scattered throughout, with the males working on the farms, and some females as well. Other females are employed as housemaids and general helpers for residents in the town.

The living and working lifestyle of this area is practically identical with that as practised by the conscripts in their home environment. This makes them an ideal source of labour, and exactly the kind needed to live reasonably well, with a minimum amount of supervision. We begin to come into contact with some of them, when they come to the yard with their employer to pick up some timber.

With the cloth patch system, control of the conscripts' movements is relatively easy. No special force is needed, other than the local police. In some cases, members of the Hitler Youth, similar to our Boy Scouts, are known to apprehend offenders, who have strayed from their home territory.

In such a small close-knit community, where everybody knows everybody else, it is just a matter of routine to stop any strange face, and demand that they produce their identity papers. With this similar right of demand being accorded to young kids, the lift to their self-esteem is such, that they pursue their perceived duty with great zeal. It is an added hazard to escaping and, for those conscripted workers caught without their patch or papers, it means pretty serious trouble.

The conscripts and their cloth patches, and us in our uniforms, become instantly recognisable to each other. Both consider the other to be on his side, and therefore, a friend and ally. Whenever we are able to meet, great interest is shown in each other. For the moment, the language barrier restricts our ability to communicate, and, therefore, to learn very much. Still, we do envy their greater freedom of movement.

From our observations, it seems that the locals, who need a bit of timber for something or other, need some kind of authorisation order. There are occasions when people will approach Kollas without such authority. They will plead their case very persuasively, seemingly offering inducements of some kind to agree. After much haggling, usually he will come to some arrangement. Sometimes, however, he refuses.

One day, an extremely well-dressed, short, plump man, with a distinctive bearing, and in his fifties, approaches Kollas and attempts to speak to him. Kollas does his best to avoid the man, and refrains from even speaking to the stranger. Kollas's behaviour draws my attention and intrigues me, to the point where I just have to watch for the outcome.

The stranger is finally forced to turn away with his request unfulfilled. As he does so, I see him front on for the first time. On the left breast of his very expensive tailored suit, and, at least more than six inches square, is a Star of David in gold braid. In its centre, is the word JUDE, also in gold. With the word JUDE being German for Jew, I understand Kollas's reluctance to be seen to be even talking to the man.

I have no way of knowing from whence he has come, but deem it has to be close by and local, because of his immaculate appearance, and because he is afoot. I can only speculate at the difficulties that he and his family have to face on a day by day basis. And that we, even in our miserable state, are better off than he. This is the only time I see, or hear, of the man.

Czechoslovakia runs roughly east and west in Central Europe. The Sudetenland, where we now are, is a narrow strip of land abutting its northern border. Mahrisch Trubau is about fifteen kilometres from the Czech border, and there are several Czech civilians working amongst the civvies we come in contact with daily on various jobs. On the pretext of coming to the aid of their nationals in the Sudetenland, the Germans tricked the Czechs into surrendering their country without a fight. With the economy virtually intact, and a Nazi administration to run things, the country is producing at full blast. The world renowned arms factory of Skoda, is now producing farm products as well. With some products finding their way into our area, it gives us a bit wider scope for trading.

The Poles and Ukrainians, we come in contact with, all have much the same story to tell. After their home areas were overrun, a general roundup has seen them sent through to here. Some had even been grabbed off the streets, while going about their daily business. In such cases, it might be a few months before they are given permission to write home, alerting their families that they are still alive.

The fellows on our party are made up of a wide cross-section of captured British forces. There are Australians, New Zealanders, Palestinians, Scots, Welsh, and English. The Englishmen are from several different counties. We colonials are virtually new chums at this working party business, whereas, the British are old hands, having been captured at Dunkirk.

Almost all of us are NCOs, although rank means very little here, other than for our leader. We are all individuals just trying to survive. The blokes, we muck in with, are generally known by nationality, and, or, Unit. Our service life has taught us to work in well with each other, so our relations are fairly harmonious. We are still going through the process of getting to know each other as people.

Every common little item, taken for granted elsewhere, is in short supply here. A toothbrush to clean one's teeth, a blade to shave with, are possessed by only a few. Then there is no shaving cream and no soap.

You become irked, irritated, and enviously frustrated, while having to do without.

Free time can be used in cards, draughts etc. But the great favourite is reading. For this, you can retire to the warmth and privacy of your bunk, and perhaps escape from your unhappy surroundings for a while. Most have managed to hang onto a book when quitting Lamsdorf, so, for the moment, there is a fair selection that can be swapped around.

With the constant climbing up and down, needed to gain access to the various tiers of bunks, it is necessary to stand on the edge of your neighbour's bunk or endure his standing on the edge of yours. With calls of nature, personal chores and the like, making this a constant and troublesome traffic, we manage to accept it as just part of our life.

We have fixed a piece of board at each end of our bunks as a shelf to keep some of our cans and utensils out of our way. This leads to leaving our things in full view of everybody, even to some foodstuffs. While recognising this to be a bit foolish, we feel that we are in such close contact, that nobody can take anything without being seen. We know that some of us are so desperate, that the temptation to steal might prove too much. Still, the risks of being caught should be enough protection. This turns out to be wrong.

The mad scramble to turn out each morning has led to a revision of our bread issue procedure. It is much easier and more convenient to dole out this issue at the evening meal time. The round loaves, shaped something like a cow pat, with flat bottom and raised centre, have to be cut in wedges by the kitchen staff. The time involved makes this change a necessity.

There are a few, who resist the temptation to eat their issue immediately, and save it for next morning's breakfast. The prudent ones of these few take care to hide their wedge away amongst their possessions. One or two, however, elect to just leave it amongst the cooking and eating cans on the shelf at the foot of his bunk. Nobody would dare try to take anything while the lights are on, because they are constantly under observation. If an attempt is tried after lights out, the loose cans will give the game away. Or so we thought.

One bloke, places his wedge in a can on his shelf, so that it is still partly visible. Sometime during the night, it disappears. The theft is so expertly done, that not a sound of a can rattle, or any footsteps has been heard. We are deeply shocked at the knowledge that one of us is a thief. But who?

The whole place is abuzz at the discovery. Condemnation is loudly and freely expressed. Suspicious eyes are roving everywhere for any sign of the loot, or the culprit. Although there are some blokes, still with wedges of bread, these all appear to be their legitimate ration. We are crammed in so tightly, that it seems impossible, for damaging evidence of some kind, not to turn up. The worst part, is the uneasy suspicion each of us feel for somebody, we think, might be capable of such a deed. Such thoughts cannot be bandied about, without something to go on.

The usual morning turmoil, before moving off to our jobs, is even greater with all these intense feelings in the air. Doug and I chew them over and over at work, but come up with nothing other than one or two possibilities. As these are only gut feelings, they have to be kept to ourselves. We each resolve to keep our eyes open for any repeats. But, this seems unlikely because of the intense feelings aroused.

Day follows day, while Doug and I watch suspiciously. We notice a few individual quirks and foibles, but nothing of any consequence. Doubtless, a lot of the others are as much on the same watch as we are. When nothing happens, it seems that it was a one-off occurrence, and best forgotten. Then it happens again.

It is almost a fortnight after the first episode. Everybody has relaxed so that conditions are exactly the same as before. But again nothing is heard, nor can the culprit be found. Again everybody is deeply upset. Now people with bad bowel conditions are becoming afraid to make the necessary trips during the night. They resort to making a lot of noise, so that they cannot be suspected. This, in turn, tends to waken everybody and disturbs us all. The turmoil this time lasts much longer than before. The pressure, to find out who, is intense. Still there is nothing to go on. The one or two possibilities, whom Doug and I suspect, seem above suspicion. We are just as baffled as everybody else.

Trading is beginning to improve, so that several of the men are regularly bringing home extra pieces of bread. A few more are beginning to keep their ration overnight, until breakfast time. Several of these begin leaving it amongst their cans on the end of their bunks, seemingly daring the thief to have another go. Either he has become less desperate or more cautious, for these baits are ignored.

Days pass by, until it is almost a month after the second theft. With more and more adopting the habit of leaving their bread amongst their cans, it seems that, finally, the problem has disappeared. Everybody relaxes, and almost forgets it ever had happened. Then, again, he strikes. This time, it is me, who is the loser. Because the position of my bunk, the top one of three, is in an exposed and busy area, I am certain that it is now safe for me to leave my ration on the shelf. I awake one morning to find it gone. I am devastated, and my hunger pangs seem twice as bad. But it is gone and there is nothing I can do about it.

At breakfast, Norm and George want to share some of theirs with me, but I cannot allow it. It is my own stupid fault for thinking it can't happen to me, and they shouldn't be made to suffer. On the job, Doug queries me closely from any angle he can think of. But it is no use. I don't have a clue about how it has happened. I take the loss pretty badly, and it takes me some time to get over it. We all feel bitter about the Judas in our midst. Watch as much as we can, nothing comes to light. Realising I am not as smart as I thought I was, I gradually get over this nasty episode. My ration loss turns out to be the last one we have.

Then a few things start to trickle through from Stalag VIIIB at Lamsdorf. It is an issue of Red Cross parcels and a bit of mail. Because of the winter conditions, and the heavy War usage of the rail system, we are warned to make the best use of our parcel issue. Nobody knows when we can expect another lot.

Oh! The wonder of those Red Cross parcels! I had thought that food parcels would have to come from one's relatives and families, and addressed to one personally. I had imagined that your people would have to gather what tinned foodstuffs they could, and post them on. The distance to be covered, the organisation required, would make this a very expensive operation, only feasible if the Germans cooperated. I had thought that the financial standing of each person's family, would determine how well he would survive. Surely, some would fare better than others. From the very first letter I was able to write home, I had asked everybody, I could think of, to send me food. I had asked for mostly dried fruits. They are sustaining, light to carry, and ideal for escaping. When the parcels do start to trickle through, I find my preconceived ideas to be totally wrong.

The odd issues that I have received up to now, first in Salonika and then Lamsdorf, I thought were a gift from the International Red Cross. I had thought they would be issued for a short time only, until our supplies from home could catch up with us. To realise, now, that they are of a standard content for regular issue to each and every man, makes me, as well as he others, feel humble and grateful.

They arrive in cardboard boxes about nine inches wide, by fifteen inches long, and about five or six inches deep. They are packaged in England and, according to the Poms, the brand names indicate they are the country's best. With rationing there, how can they afford to send them to us? The goodies they contain—how we gloat over them. One Pom scores a tin of condensed milk. He punctures it with two holes, then lays back on his bunk, just sucking away, until it has all gone. We use the cardboard boxes to store our possessions in.

Later on, Red Cross Parcels are packaged in Canada, in a superior corrugated cardboard box, that prevents any breakages or damage en route. The contents, while still by and large the same, now have North American brand names, and also contain some salmon.

The mail that begins to trickle through, leaves some men high in the clouds, and others down in the depths. The extraordinary yearning for contact with those at home, is almost unbearable. Those with letters almost devour them. Those without, just ache and fume. My escaping has put me out of circulation for so long that there is nothing for me. I rant loudly at missing out. All around me blokes are reading excerpts to anyone, who will listen. Their happiness is so great, they just have to share it with someone. Sharing with them is something, but, not having my very own, is hard to take.

Several mail calls come and go, with still nothing for me. By now, I am about the only person, who has received nothing. I am becoming increasingly more bitter, and say so, loudly. I blame everybody I can think of, including my family back home. In my heart, I know they will not desert me, especially my Mum. I know my Dad cares just as deeply, but all the communication will come from her.

I wait and wait, but still no mail. I am becoming more and more despondent. The fellows around me try to cheer me up. The Pommy boys are especially helpful. They point out that Australia is so far away, that I have to expect some delay. I point to the other Aussies already receiving theirs. Norm and George share theirs with me, and that is some consolation. But, when Doug receives a letter, that is a bit much. We had escaped at the same time, and in the same manner, so it doesn't seem right. Still, I had made another escape, after recapture.

Then comes a mail call and my name is called out. There are three or four letters for me, and I give a great whoop. But they aren't from Australia; they are from England. They are from girls I do not know, and contain personal photos. Some of the Pommy boys had sent home my name and address, asked for it to be passed around, and this is the result. I am so deeply grateful.

The girls are from different areas, and not known to each other. Their photos show them to be personable young women, and their letters are bright and cheery. At last, I have somebody to communicate with, at least until something comes through from my family.

Now that the regular process of contact between us and Lamsdorf has been established, it is just a matter of a little extra time, for what is available there, to reach us here. We can rely on the efficiency of Bill and Wally to see that we get our share. One of their rights, that has been established, is the need to keep in personal contact with the administration there. This means that they will travel back to Lamsdorf, for briefings and to arrange supplies, on a regular basis. Kapitza or one of the Guards will escort them per train, making these trips officially correct.

In this wintery wilderness, where our great need is for adequate clothing and footwear, supplies coming through from Official British sources, are still just a trickle. Now the Pommy boys begin receiving personal parcels from their homes, containing shirts and underwear. It seems that uniforms will come from Army sources, while underclothing comes from home. With big Armies to equip, we gloomily predict that POWs will just have to come a bad last.

How this damn winter drags on! It seems it will never end. To all of us, it is unthinkable that we are in for a prolonged captivity. Initially, we thought it may be a couple of weeks, and certainly no more than a month, before a big push would be mounted. In a couple of days, we would be free! Now, we just cannot accept that it may take longer than this.

Of course, we are receiving plenty of news regarding the progress of the War, mostly German propaganda and not much else. With their sweeping advances, and gains into Russia, the news is mostly bad. Still that is in the other direction. We are looking eagerly for news of our mob's big push, from the west.

Then one magic day, it happens—mail from home. How marvellous it is—all the mundane, little, everyday goings and comings of my sisters and brother, as well as Mum and Dad. All the ordinary things are so important. We crave so much to keep in touch with normality, while languishing here in this bizarre existence. The happenings, my two married sisters' children, our friends, and everything, is so important and meaningful. And, gratefully, it seems that I am still accepted as part of the family.

It is a dark period for all of us. We are subject to wildly fluctuating mood swings. There are half-mad fits of lightheaded highs, and deep dark pits of despair. When in the pits, the very real urge to provoke a Guard into shooting to kill, seems greatly desirable. The understanding of the fellows around you, helps you to ride out these extremes.

Then comes the tell-tale signs of a thaw. The dark gloom is the same and the snow as thick as ever, but the icicles, hanging under the eaves of the houses, begin to melt and drip. It is a slow painful process. Hardly has it started, than a cold snap reverses the trend. Then the thaw starts again. Little by little it increases, until the snow is half gone. Now it is worse than before. The clean white look is replaced with a dirty, ragged unkemptness. The streets are a sea of slush. Our feet that have formerly been cold and wet, are now cold, wet and filthy. Everything finds its way through the cracks in our boots, no matter what we do. It seems that some perverse being is watching over us, determined to drag out our misery as long as possible.

We trudge backward and forward to our jobs, go through our cleaning routines at home, and half-heartedly occupy ourselves with the business of keeping on going. Things have improved ever so slightly, but we are still very hungry and poorly clad. Home is our haven, though still a poor one because of the shortage of food. The trickle of comforts that had come through from Lamsdorf, have come and gone, almost as if they had not existed. Maybe, it was just a dream to tantalise us. Then we become slowly aware of something strange.

At first, it is just an odd feeling, that we can't seem to pin down. Whatever it is, it gives our spirits a lift. We begin to take more notice of the things around us. And, they are changing. A few small birds begin to appear. Those gaunt, sombre forests, soften, and seem almost appealing. Stark dead trees and bushes, sprout fat leaf buds almost overnight. That deep ditch, that twists its way through the timber mill, has a trickle of water in its bottom, increasing by the hour. Those dead, dark fields, that have become exposed after the snow melts, now are turning to a faint green. Spring is upon us.

Seasonal changes are something we all know about. But to me, this one is something special. Back home, the changes are very vague and hardly discernible. Here, they can actually be seen. Green is the predominant colour. But what a green! At home it is hard and dark, while here it is pastel, pale and light, and, above all, young. The feeling of a new beginning, a new birth, is infectious. My feelings begin to soar, and my optimism to creep back.

Soon the march to and from the job becomes enlivened with chatter. Sure, it is often ribald and coarse, but no longer silent and morose. Each day, the weather improves, and the sun comes out for gradually lengthening periods. Even the odd spring shower is welcomed as a change from a snowfall.

The supply situation from Stalag VIIIB is improving, and becomes almost regular. Food parcels, some clothing and cigarettes begin to appear. A few men, fed up and restless, manage to have themselves sent back to Lamsdorf, to be replaced by others, so that there is no loss of manpower. Some of the Dunkirk boys have formed the habit of returning to VIIIB for the winter, then volunteering for a work party in spring. They claim this regular change of scenery helps to break the monotony.

One of the first lots of clothing to appear contains several pairs of pyjamas. Bill has the task of deciding who, amongst us, should get them. With only a few sets, there has to be a lot of disappointments. I long to be one of the lucky ones, but I dare not do any lobbying. If I do and am successful, it might look as if Bill is favouring the Aussie connection. I just pray and hope. Really, out of a very poorly equipped mob, I am pretty near to the bottom. Still, this is no guarantee that I can expect to be preferred. I am surprised, and thankful, when I score a set.

Straight away, I know that these pyjamas will have a big bearing on deciding my future behaviour. To escape, I will have to travel light. Pyjamas are a useless encumbrance. If I go, I will have to leave them behind. It has been so difficult to get them, that this would be very hard to do.

Now that I have pyjamas to change into, I will give my hard pressed underclothing a bit of relief. I will be able to wash them more often and, maybe, even get them reasonably dry, before having to put them on again. I begin to feel that I have made it—all because of a pair of pyjamas!

As the weather improves and we get a bit more sun, our interest in day to day doings quickens. We are picking up a few German words and phrases, and increasing our communication skills as best we can. While cigarettes are still in short supply, smokers amongst us are doing it hard. They crave a smoke almost as much as they crave food.

All the civvies, we come in contact with, are themselves heavy smokers. With their own supplies hard to come by, they are most willing to share with any of us, either by gift or trade. Some of the smokers, working on their jobs, manage to make contact with one or two of the Czechs, who are in touch with areas where tobacco is grown. These Czechs manage to obtain a small quantity of homegrown leaf for their own purpose. They are prepared to trade to the smoker prisoners, the unwanted leaf stalks and thick veins.

These hardheads decide they have to give it a go. Using a razor blade, they sit and slice these coarse pieces into the very finest of slivers. Using whatever paper they can find, they roll this lot into cigarettes, then try them out. The result is so strong, that they can only do so, by sitting down. Coupled with our half-starved state, the effect is to make their heads swim, and almost causes them to blackout.

On the job, Doug and I begin to find out a bit more about Josef. He has, more or less, taken us under his wing, as far as that is possible under this situation. He is a bachelor in his early thirties, and lives with his married sister, in a village close by. As one of the very few eligible men around, he can pick and choose from a wide range of lady friends. This is kept in check, however, by a persistent and long-time girlfriend. From time to time, she will drop in and visit him for a short time at work. She seems a decent and attractive enough woman, a good marriage prospect, and we tell him so.

She obviously thinks the world of him, and has made up her mind, that he is for her. She is possessive, and does her best to steer Josef away from any other females, who might be around. She firmly believes, that she has a commitment from him, although Josef is a bit non-committal about it. Their arrangement is a longstanding one, and they live close to each other in the same village. Although this setup has existed for something like five years, their frisky behaviour seems to suggest, that it has only just started.

We find that a solid commitment between a man and a woman, usually, is the norm here, along with the acceptance of 'marriage', even resulting in several children, before the actual ceremony takes place. It seems that many cannot afford the cost of even the most simple of ceremonies, so they get on with their lives, until they are able to do so, sometime in the future. There are instances of a family of four or five children before a marriage takes place, while the first born may be as old as fifteen. While they are able to accept such a situation without question, we can only marvel at their commitment. In most of the instances that we are familiar with back home, where children are born out of wedlock, it often results in the father shooting through, and leaving the mother to get by as best she can. Josef, it seems, has managed to avoid the final commitment of a child.

One day, a teenage girl of fifteen comes to the mill, and marches straight up to Josef, where he is busy in the yard. She talks to him for a moment, while handing over a parcel, obviously of food. He calls Doug and I over, and introduces us to her. She is his niece, Elle, and she has brought his lunch from home. We are a bit awkward and uncertain of our reception by a German youngster. After all, we are the enemy. She greets us warmly, in the old German way of shaking hands, where the clasped hands are lifted high, then brought down low and instantly disengaged. She is pleased to meet Max and Moritz, and, although the reply is formal, she means it. I get the impression that she has deliberately set up this visit, more to meet us than to bring Josef his lunch.

She is a typical, bubbly, full of life, teenager. And, with a teenager's honesty of commitment, she accepts us totally. She is an attractive, healthy girl, and we are her friends. She openly seeks us out, and stops for a chat any time she can, whether Josef is about, or not.

Fraternisation is strongly discouraged by the Germans, and there are some strict penalties for anyone caught at it. We try to be a bit secretive so as not to get her into trouble. But, she refuses to be intimidated. She accepts us as her friends, and she doesn't care who knows. It gets to the stage where she can be walking along the main road into town, about a quarter of a mile from the mill yard, and she will spot us stacking boards. She will start waving from the moment she comes into sight. She will raise her arm fully, and sweep back and forth, until she gets our attention. We, of course, wave back.

She is like a breath of fresh air to us, and we love her for it. But, because we do, we begin to worry. Here, in the yard is one thing, where people could turn a blind eye, if they are close by. But out on the highway is something else. There, her greetings are open for the whole countryside to see, and we fear that some sort of an example might be made of her.

We collar Josef and ask him to please explain our fears for her safety, and to please be a bit more circumspect. It is damn hard, with our limited German, to get through that we value her friendship, but fear that an open exhibition by her may get her into trouble. He nods his head in agreement, and promises to tell her. The outcome shows little difference than before. She still wants her independent way, as if defying anybody, to do anything.

Then an incident occurs that is viewed by our large party on their way to the Berg Mill and the Koldas Cement Works. Our group is returning to their workplace after lunch, with their route having to pass through the centre of town. In the main Square, they come upon two German women, chained to two policemen, for all to see, and being paraded round town. Their hair has been cut off, and placards hang around their necks, detailing their sins. They have been caught dallying with two French POWs. Public ridicule is the punishment for betraying their Aryan blood.

There has been a great deal of propaganda, instilling the concept of the purity of the German bloodlines into their people. The necessity of maintaining their "Aryan" heritage of a master race, is fairly well known. We had heard of it, but, up to now, have accepted the tale as being a bit of a myth, of the crackpot variety.

We, of course, did not see the spectacle, and query at great length those who did. What were the women like? Were they good sorts? How about the Frenchmen? Was there any sign of them? But, as our blokes had only seen the women in passing, they cannot tell us anything more. One thing, we all agree on, is that the French must be better fed than we are. We know from experience, starvation kills the sexual urge. We think that, if any of us had been in a similar situation, those ladies would have been disappointed. We just would not have been able to perform.

Again Doug and I are worried about Elle's open display of her friendship for us. Still, she continues on in the same vein. Whether the authorities realise the stupidity of their attitudes or not, it is hard to say. But Elle is never questioned, nor do we ever come across another such instance, the whole time we are here.

With the spring and summer weather now upon us, there has been a steady movement of a few men back to Stalag VIIIB, to be replaced with other new men. While the majority of us are happy to stay put, there always seems to be a few restless souls who just have to keep moving. The movement of prisoners, back and forth, between their home Stalag and a working party, is definitely not allowed by the Germans. It requires a lot of ingenuity, and working of the system, to enable a man to present a seemingly legitimate reason for being sent back. It usually has to be because of some kind of sickness. However, to get out onto a working party is easy. It just requires volunteers to fill the gaps created by the leavers.

Three new arrivals to Mahrisch Trubau are South Africans captured in the Western Desert. They had been taken while on operations against the Italians, not long after we were taken on Crete. One of them is a dark, sombre, morose man, who, more or less, blames the other two for his capture. One of the two explains to us that the three of them were surrounded by young, very nervous Italians, with rifles pointed from six feet away. The morose man wanted the three of them to charge the Italians, and to try and make a break for it. But the one talking to us, ordered him not to try anything, and for the three of them to surrender. The other of the two concurred with this decision.

Upon joining us at Mahrisch Trubau, these two muck in together, while the morose man elects to keep to himself, even though he is willing to be part of the threesome. His general attitude puts him at odds with most of us, and an incident at the nightly cook up, soon after, only serves to widen the gap.

A Scotsman has managed to do a trade for some local sausage. He elects to skin it and flatten it into patties, like rissoles. He proceeds to cook them, barbeque style, on the hot cook top of the communal stove. We all envy him greatly, as anything in the meat line is almost impossible to obtain.

We watch fascinated as the four or five patties cook. While most of us keep our council, the morose man cannot. He asks the Scotsman what is in them, and where did he get them. It is almost an unwritten law amongst all of us, that there is to be no interference, or questioning, in another person's trading. This is a breach of the code.

The Scotsman is a dour man and, with a perfectly expressionless face, tells the morose South African in a confidential tone, that he has brought home a little bit of sawdust from the mill, mashed some of his potatoes, mixed the lot together, and this is the result. The morose man nods gravely and goes away. It is obvious to those of us, who have heard, that the morose South African believes what he has been told. The composition of the sausage is such, that with a bit of a stretch of the imagination, it looks as if it may have come from a mixture, such as the Scotsman claims. Sure, upon reflection, we think he should realise he is having his leg pulled, and just forget about it. Next evening, we have our answer.

Amidst the flurry of activity around the cooktop, the morose man is busy trying to cook patties. It is obvious they aren't much of a success. The Scotsman is busy also, but this time more in line with the rest of us. The morose man points to his efforts and asks the Scotsman, "What is wrong?"

The Scotsman stoutly claims, "You're using too much sawdust." It is only then that the morose man realises that he is being made a fool of. Without saying a word, he gathers up his efforts and departs. No doubt, he feels deeply humiliated, particularly, as he knows that most of us are aware of what has happened.

In such a crowded setting, it is not possible to keep entirely to yourself. The morose man, however, withdraws further into his shell. His countrymen do their best to snap him out of it, and try to include him in activities, wherever they can. He, steadfastly, maintains his solitary attitude, and avoids mixing as much as possible.

About this time, a group of four or five Poms arrive as workers. Right from the outset, they let it be known that they will not be with us for very long. Their sole purpose of coming here is to escape. They are not very secretive, and are quite open about their plans. They ask anybody, who will listen, for the general layout of the area, and for any advice that may be relevant.

They are a friendly happy lot, and we are only too happy to oblige. They have wrangled it to come to this area, because it is close to the Czech border. They intend crossing into Czechoslovakia, hoping that the local Czechs will be able to give them the help they need. As a matter of course, we have already gathered the information that gives us a good idea of what is involved.

The Sudetenland is a narrow strip running parallel to the Czech border for most of its length. The Czech border from Mahrisch Trubau is fifteen kilometres due south. We reckon the country that way, is too settled to make a straight run through. We advise them to make a wide detour, using whatever forest country for cover as possible. In that way, when knocked up with fatigue, we know they will have somewhere to hide until their strength returns.

Behind our house there are open fields for about five miles, until the forest line starts. Although this is due north and directly away from the border, the forest line sweeps in an arc westward, and continues in an unbroken line, back across the border. Although this means a trek of something like twenty miles, those first five will be the critical part. After that, it will be a piece of cake. The Poms, straightaway, declare that this will be their plan.

My experience tells me that you gather all the information you can, and then work out your own plan. These fellows are quite happy to go along with the general thoughts of the rest of us. Magnanimously, they invite any others, who feel inclined, to be in it, too.

To a prisoner, escaping, and the thought of being free, is infectious. Very quickly, quite a few of the others, suddenly get the urge to give it a go. I, myself, will not consider it. Neither will Norm or George. Doug, too, isn't interested. It seems, that if nobody backs out, then half our entire party will take part in the attempt. This will leave a big hole in our workforce that will have to be filled from Lamsdorf.

With such a large upheaval, it is anybody's guess as to how the Stalag VIIIB authorities will react. They might get fed up, close the place down, and return the rest of us back to the Stalag. With the established principle, that it is our duty to escape, any reprisals will probably take the form of a spell in the cooler. I had already gone through that, so it is no big deal to me. No doubt, the escapers may be reflecting upon the uncertainty of what might happen to those who stay.

No firm date is set for the breakout. The principals decide to wait until more into the summer, to take advantage of better weather, and more growing food plants that they may steal. With everybody being privy to what is going on, the planning and preparation is open for all to know. It seems that every man and his dog must be aware.

The actual method of breaking out of our house is still a bit vague. At the moment, it seems that the favoured option, is to squeeze out of the toilet window to enter the outer yard, and then cut a hole through the barbed wire. After that, the twenty mile hike, across Sudetenland to the Czech border, can be completed. They are sure they can make it, but I am sure they won't.

I don't like their proposal at all. It seems to me that they are putting too much reliance on Czech assistance. They speak confidently of Czech partisans operating against the Germans. They reckon it will be easy to contact some of them, and be passed from band to band, until they are out of the country. In reality, we have heard nothing of partisan operations, even from the couple of Czechs, we come in contact with on the job. We know the country is running smoothly under German control. If there are such operations, it seems to me the escapers best bet would be to make firm contact from here, before making a move.

A big fault in their scheme is for so many of them to go at once. Although they intend to go in groups of twos and threes, and, therefore, be split up, the impact on the countryside of providing food and assistance, will be much the same, as if they are together. Doug and I talk over their plans while at work, as each new development comes up. Our opinion is that it is a fizzer, and not worth the effort.

In the meantime, the country round us is getting more into summer, and looking lovelier every day. We are still hungry, but the irregular advent of food parcels has taken some of the gnawing pangs from us. We are now pretty well versed in stretching out what we have, and what we can trade for.

The locals are getting more used to having us around, and seem to accept us as part of the scene, without question. There is much less of the "Heil Hitler" greeting, when we are around. On our daily journeys, back and forth, we see German housewives spread their white linen washing on small bushes in the open. From time to time, they will water the linen lightly from a watering can to again dry it out in the sunshine. This drying, watering, and drying, produces a dazzling whiteness, that is hurtful to the eyesight in its brilliance.

One day, a small elderly lady on this errand, walks so close to our ranks, that she actually brushes us in passing. It so happens that I am in the centre of the squad, and in the outside file, and it is me she actually touches. Quickly, she thrusts something into my hand, and just as quickly I cover it up. It is done in a fraction of a second, without most of the squad, and especially the Guard, knowing anything has happened.

Waiting for a little while to ensure that we have not been discovered, I open my hand to see what it is. In my hand is a piece of bread. Doug and a couple of the others know that she has slipped me something, and they are eager to know what it is. I tell them, and the news quickly spreads right through the squad. We cannot help but marvel at the happening, and the compassion of this little old lady for a fellow human being.

It just doesn't make any sense. Here we are, captives wanting desperately to go home, and here they are, the Germans, honest and hardworking, and wanting only to make a decent living. Who the hell do you blame for this kind of predicament? How the hell do you make it come unstuck? All we can do is blame it on Hitler, while railing, bitterly, at the circumstances that have brought us here, and wondering, desperately, if we will ever get out of the place.

Working together, Doug and I get to know each other's background. We are always reminiscing about the ordinary mundane things—happenings of no great importance, yet, from this perspective, of oh, so great significance. My thoughts are taken up with my family and the girl I am "going out" with; Doug's thoughts are of his newly married wife, whom he misses badly. He comes from a farming background, where his people had fallen on hard times, had to sell up and move to the city. Here they had to split up, and get work wherever they could.

He still has several uncles in the farming game, and their daily doings provide us with some humorous stories. There is the eccentric one, who is a great blacksmith. If a neighbour wants to borrow some of his machinery, always, it is broken, and he will show it to prove it. When he needs to use it himself, miraculously, it is welded, and operates as good as new.

Then there are the two, who are wheat farmers. After the harvest is in, they have three months with nothing to do. They have an old but reliable motor vehicle, which they will load up with a sack of potatoes, a sack of onions, and a kerosene tin full of dripping. They will then head off into the bush, and will live off the land on anything they can shoot or catch—not putting in an appearance until it's time for the next planting. From here, that kind of lifestyle seems the ultimate.

We share other highs and lows, which, in our state, can swing from one to the other like a pendulum. We work up a great rapport. Doug, however, is never at his best, first thing in the morning. I know him well enough to let him be, until he comes round. One of the others in our work squad doesn't, and Doug suffers badly because of it.

Doug hates getting up in the morning, and often is still in bed, when we are forming up, ready to march off to work. We will delay proceedings, while our Guard is trying to get us formed up, before giving us the order to march. Miraculously, as the door is opened, and the order given to move, Doug will be there, fully clothed, silent, and in a deep black mood.

Left alone, he will gradually come out of it, and be almost his old self, by the time we get to work. Another squad member decides to take him to task one morning, for his tardiness. As soon as we get outside the door, the man's remarks are half jocular, and easy to shrug off. Doug's bitterness, deep emotions and frustrations, overwhelm him. He savagely and verbally castigates the man, leaving him speechless and silent. We continue in silence for the rest of the journey. Nobody ever tries this caper again.

On our small Kollas party, there is not much scope for trading, as there is on the others. Through our contacts, we begin to understand how the locals go about the business of feeding themselves. Every single person, male or female, young or old, is into food production in some shape or form, no matter what their regular job may be. Everybody tends their garden plots, as well as raising geese, chickens, and even rabbits. The rabbits are kept in backyard hutches, and take surprisingly little room. To get through the winter, it is necessary to store hay. The ordinary households, that do not own any fields, are allocated roadside verges, from which they cut and store the grass. The spring and summer growth is very prolific, and the resultant crop is generally enough to get through, at least for the rabbits.

The roads, too, are lined with trees, spaced at regular intervals. In our area, they generally are cherry trees. When ripe, the townspeople can harvest this crop and, although the quality is ordinary, at least it is something providing a bit extra.

The real farmers and professional growers always have wide fields of various crops under cultivation. With both amateur and professionals alike, engaged in food production, the whole countryside has a neat and tidy appearance, which contrasts sharply with the bleak, bedraggled, winter outlook.

Josef's sister and her family, own only a rather small field, which produces barely enough for their own needs. They supplement this by helping some of the larger producers, in a deal that returns some of the harvest, in exchange for their labour. This is a custom that prevails widely, hereabouts, involving just about everybody. Whether this is government inspired, or general local practice, it is hard to tell. Everybody just pitches in when needed. In this way, there is a steady supply of most things. The real shortages are the luxury items such as sugar, meat, soap, jams, etc. Although there are regular issues of these things, such issues are very small, very few and far between, and always Ersatz.

Our life has fallen into a regular pattern, not exactly enjoyable, but at least a general routine. The Official War news, as put out by the Germans, indicates that they are rolling along in a seemingly invincible manner. The civilians are a trifle smug and patronising, often commenting to us on how well their side is doing, in contrast to how badly ours is. This we find hard to stomach, and fiercely determine to combat, as best we can, with propaganda of our own. In trading, we will ask for impossible to obtain items, then castigate them roundly for not being able to supply—always claiming that the self-same item is in ample abundance back home.

As the Germans are seemingly poised to invade England at any time, they claim to maintain a tight blockade of all foodstuffs entering there. We are able to counterclaim by producing bits and pieces from our infrequently arriving food parcels. A great clincher is a packet of coffee. With tea being our preferred brew, occasionally, a small packet of coffee will arrive. When it does, it almost ends up as a major trading item, as well as a top counter propaganda one, also.

Real coffee is perhaps the thing that the locals miss the most. They have a good supply of an Ersatz variety that tastes something similar, but in reality is only a poor substitute. With the evidence there before their eyes, and our insistent urgings that they are being fed a pack of lies, gradually, the seeds of doubt begin to gather in their minds. To keep the façade going further, we strive to dress particularly well, whenever having to make a trip amongst the population. The quality of cloth in our clothing, is noticeably superior to that of the Germans. The more we can emphasise this, the better it is to our liking.

It is sometimes necessary for a man to receive medical attention for such things as eye or dental care, where the services of a proper practitioner is essential. With such services being available locally, or in nearby towns, it becomes the practice of sending the patient, plus a Guard and Interpreter, there to receive treatment. Of course, we are willing to push this kind of service as much as possible. However, it is our belief that the German authorities, while willing to use these practitioners, probably will not pay their fees anyhow.

The outing itself, always, is an interesting diversion from the norm, for everybody, including the Guard. It sometimes involves riding on public transport, such as a train. Always, the people, we encounter, pay great attention and interest in the prisoner. It is essential that the prisoner maintain a good bearing, and be dressed as well as possible. Clothing issues still have not caught up with us, so it is necessary to borrow from each other, to put on a public front.

One popular item is a shirt owned by an Aussie named Ken. Before the war, he was a boundary rider cum station hand from the outback. He is about six foot, well built, and typically resourceful. The shirt, in question, had been worn continuously throughout the Desert Campaign and Greece and Crete, as well as after being taken prisoner. The back of it has rotted away, leaving only the collar and front intact. When this, similarly, has happened to the rest of us, we have discarded the shirt as useless. But not Ken. He has fashioned and sewn some tapes on. It is now possible to put the thing on, with the collar in place and the front smoothed down, to be held in place by the tapes tied behind one's back. With a smart khaki tie, the type we used to wear when going on leave, the outfit looks impressive and authentic, when worn with a jacket.

Ken's shirt, always, is the first item to be borrowed. Using the best of what we can muster among us, we are able to prove to the locals, that they are being fed a pack of lies. Can they not see, that our clothing and uniforms are superior to theirs? Can they not see, that we are better provisioned and fed than they are? Of course, we prisoners are not faring so well. But then, that is the fault of our captors.

The mail situation has eased quite a lot by now. We are allowed to write two letter cards and four postcards home each month. Ink is not allowed, only indelible pencil. Now that the home mail is coming through, the English girls, who had written to me, begin to ease off, and finally stop. Then comes a letter from an English girl, somebody who has never written before. I am intrigued at the strange name and Manchester postmark. The writer introduces herself to me, claiming she has stolen my name and address from one of the other girl writers, whom she considers a bit of a nong.

It is her express purpose to cheer me up, and keep my spirits from flagging, from now until I am free again. I am to write constantly, and pour my troubles into her sympathetic ear, no matter what they are. If they happen to be of a boy-girl nature, then she is quite happy to handle this aspect, too. After all, she is a girl too. The letter is ribald, spicy and greatly entertaining. I will just have to reply, to find out if she really means what she has written.

From now on, a nonstop correspondence begins between us, this will continue until I am free again. She is magnificent. True to her word, she is entertaining. She has an uncanny knack of being able to reach my innermost feelings, when I most need a lift. The photo she has sent of herself, shows her to be a little on the plump side, reasonably good looking, but above all – feminine.

In this place, things feminine, hold sway in importance over lots of other things. While the letters are mine personally, and I do all the correspondence, they are too good to keep to myself. Apart from Norm and George, others around us share them too. Frank and Allan, two Field Engineers from Victoria, who work at the Home Mill with Norm and George, are just a couple of them. Allan is moved to compose a poem concerning those letters, which he pins on the notice board for all to see. He titles it, MANCHESTER GIRLS, and it goes as follows:

> Marion swiped Arty's address from young Bobby,
> And there and then dropped him a note.
> It was snappy and cheerful and not a bit sobby,
> And Arty said roll on the boat.
> The letter of course, passed to one or two more,
> Most of them Aussies like Arty,
> And now it becomes an unwritten law,
> To show them to all of the party.
> Cliff and young George sent their names back at once,
> Came letters from Doe and Big Nan.
> A photo was sent by George, the big dunce,
> Now Nan writes to Frank, what a man.
> Today mail came in, briefs for all of the gang,
> Except the original Arty.
> They like the Greek God, (Frank), the rest can go hang,
> He got more than the rest of the party.
> Of course as you know, they say like calls to like,
> And Marion says Nan is quite bandy,
> Frank's legs, of course, are really not Gleich,
> Pardon the word, 'cos its handy.
> Doe is still mine, but I'll bet that one day,
> She follows the other two's lead
> Just mark my words and hear what I say,
> She's just like all of the breed.
> But there's the consolation if to England we go,
> Frank surely can't take on them all.
> They say you reap what you sow,

So we'll wait till we give them a call.

This English lass, who is married, and whose husband is serving somewhere overseas, has quite an impact on the sanity and the stability, of quite a few of us at Mahrisch Trubau. It takes a fair bit of juggling by me, to maintain contact with home and Manchester, within the limits of my allocated cards and letters. I will not be allowed to drop my letters to her by the other blokes, even if I may want to.

It is now well into the summer and the weather is just great. We have taken to working outside with our shirts off. The nastiness of the winter and snow, seem remote and like a bad dream. We have almost forgotten what the interior of the engine room looks like. We still are hungry, but ever so slowly, our trading and food parcels are taking some of the edge off this. Now the Poms, who plan to escape, begin to get down to some serious planning.

They have been quiet for some time now, and it seems that they may have had a rethink, deciding to stay put. All of a sudden, the urge to get going bursts forth, and again, the whole lot of us become swept up in their plans. Their leader approaches me one day, asking for my opinion of what they have in mind. As a sometime escaper, I have the somewhat dubious regard of being something of an expert. Their plans are basically what has been suggested to them, when first they came here—through the toilet window, go north until they reach the forest line, then follow in an arc around to the south, and cross the border into Czechoslovakia.

I ask him, who is going and in what order, they intend to leave. There seems to be about twenty men, anxious to make the attempt. They plan to start leaving about midnight, in twos and threes, at fifteen minute intervals. I point out that with the earlier sunrise, the last to leave will find it hard going to make it across the open fields, to the shelter of the forest, without being discovered. Once the tail is discovered, the Germans will know what has happened, and cut off the rest at the border. A quick discovery will make the effort a useless exercise, so they will be better off not even attempting it.

He insists, doggedly, that they are determined to go, and asks if I can offer any suggestions that may help. Together we go over each phase, while I pick out what I consider to be flaws, that need rethinking. Their plan has them committed to getting into Czechoslovakia, so that has to stay. What he needs to do, is to give the lot of them, the best possible chance of making the twenty mile hike in the first night.

I don't like their idea of leaving by the toilet window. It is terribly small, and will be hard going for each in turn to squeeze through, plus their gear. There will be a bad bottleneck there, even with fifteen minute intervals. To give everybody the best possible chance, they really ought to leave at the same time. But from what point of exit? Then it comes to me. Why not the front door? He immediately balks at the idea, considering it too risky, as the Guards' quarters are in the room adjacent to it. I stick to the scheme, countering each of his fears, as he puts them forward.

As the Guards' complement occupies the room alongside the front door, they maintain no outside Guard, and rely on their position there, to ensure security. Access to their room always is closed off by nine o'clock each night, when they settle down to their own chores and prepare to sleep. Mostly, they are second-class physically, and can be expected to sleep soundly. Access for us to the front door is via a short passage of about ten feet. The only hazard to negotiate is the closed door to the Guard's room, located right alongside the front door.

I propose that, at the given time, they move silently to the front door, unlock it, slip out in a body, relock it behind them, turn into the fields at the back of us, then hightail it for the forest line. As a diversion, we will prepare the toilet window to look like the exit.

The Pom leader says, "If we are seen leaving in a large group, the alarm will be raised immediately."

I explain, "Not so. We have been marching in groups, in and out of the house, backwards and forwards to work for so long now, that we've become part of the scenery. The locals are used to it, and hardly even notice the solitary Guard in our rear. If they spot only one or two leaving by the front door, then they will catch on immediately."

He considers this and replies, "Well then, to get out the front door, we will need the key, and the guards have the only one. How do you overcome this?"

I suggest, "We can either steal the key, or make our own. But, stealing only adds to the risks, so we will make our own."

None of us has ever handled the key, but from observing the Guard, we know it to be a large old fashion type. We will have to get an impression somehow, and take it from there. This proves much easier than expected. When returning from our jobs, it is the custom to stop at the bottom of the house steps and move aside, allowing the guard to come forward to unlock the front door.

On this day, seemingly without thinking, we march straight up to the door, and pack the steps. With the steps packed, and the guard needing to force his way through to do the opening, we call for him to pass the key and we will do it for him. He hesitates for a moment, apparently deciding that there can be no harm, then hands the key over.

We pass the key, hand over hand, to the bloke at the top, then chiack him loudly at his clumsy "attempts" at opening the door. Somewhere along the way, an impression is taken in a piece of soap. Once we have manoeuvred the Guard into handing us the key, we continue the procedure, so that no suspicions will be aroused.

With the impression taken, and the whole party privy to what is going on, there are enthusiastic offers of help on making the key. Ken is working at the small Engineering Works and is pretty sure he will be able to come up with what is needed. He has managed to get himself a fair amount of freedom of movement on his job, mainly because of the girl who works in the office there. She is about nineteen, and wears thick heavy glasses because of her poor eyesight. She is incredibly shy and awkward, and very sensitive about her appearance. She has fallen hopelessly in love with Ken, and takes every opportunity to come into the factory, just to gaze on him from afar. If he speaks to her, even to say hello, she will retire in utter confusion.

Ken is good looking and personable, and has cultivated an Errol Flynn type moustache. To this utterly shy, small town girl, he seems to represent the personification of an unobtainable, romantic dream. Ken, for his part, conscious that he is the cause of her confusion, does his best not to embarrass her, in front of her own people. As the situation is patently obvious to all, they respect him for his forbearance. As a result, they allow him a fair amount of freedom of movement within the workshop, including access to some of the machinery.

Some of those discarded and holed cooking pots, that we had scrounged, are fixed and mended by Ken. Often, some of the workmen will help with suggestions and materials. As for the office girl, her besotted admiration is a deep dark secret, known only to herself. Or so she thinks.

It takes almost a fortnight of undercover work, before it feels that the substitute key is just about right. Now it is time for the test run. This is no problem, for our packing of the front steps, plus the hand-over-hand passing of the key for one of us to open the front door, has become standard procedure. This time, when the key is passed up, the Pom leader uses the substitute, and it works like a charm. Now, all that is required is to set the date of the breakout.

The Pom leader seems in no great hurry, and sets the date for about two weeks away. I want them to make their move at 9.30 pm, which is half an hour after the Guards have closed up for the night. The leader thinks this is stretching it a bit, and decides on ten o'clock. It is their decision, so I just leave it to them.

Now that the plan is set, I am a bit worried that somebody might spot them outside the front door, before they can turn away into the open fields. Previously, I was convinced of the soundness of my argument, that an observer will think it is just a routine thing. I had convinced the Pom leader of this. Still, I am a bit worried.

With everybody being aware of what is on, there is an undercurrent of subdued excitement throughout the whole party—half with the idea of, "What the hell! I'll give it a go."; and the other half thinking, "You damn fools, you're just wasting your time." Although we are evenly divided on the idea, nobody attempts to influence anybody else. Always, it is one's own personal decision to make. Now that it is definitely decided that the break is on, the whole of us help in any way we can.

About this time, one or two personal items go missing, or are mislaid, by various men. While it is worrying, the impending breakout, tends to push this problem into the background. The stolen bread ration thing re-emerges. It had faded into the almost forgotten past, so we all hope that it is a careless misplacement on the part of the owners. Other than reporting the loss to Bill, nothing much else can be done. We, most certainly, don't want that air of mistrust returning at this stage. We feel that we are very much a united group now, and want no part of the earlier suspicion.

Then, an infrequent mail delivery comes, and in it is a clothing parcel from home for the Pom leader. Upon opening it, he is ecstatic. It contains mostly civilian clothing. The big item is a blue civvy shirt, quite distinct from the khaki colouring of everything else we have. Immediately, he decides he will wear that shirt on the breakout, which is set to take place two nights hence.

He insists showing his shirt to all and sundry. He points out how perfect it is for the job ahead. He feels it is a good omen, which means that their bid will be successful. After just about boring the lot of us, he tosses it, still in its folded state, onto his bunk, while he goes about the business of eating and a few other chores.

The usual comings and goings, and milling about, that are a feature of our life after work, have been going on, as bedtime approaches. The Guards have carried out their nine o'clock close up. Soon, we will turn out our lights, and bed down ourselves.

The Pom leader can be seen roaming about, with a worried expression on his face. His manner now is so much in contrast to a few hours before, that it attracts attention from quite a few of us. We ask him, "What is the problem? "

He says, "I can't find my shirt."

We just cannot believe it. He has only just got it, so it has to be here somewhere. Surely he must have left it with some of the others, whom he had been showing it to. "No," he claims. He has looked everywhere he can think of, without success. Anyway, he is certain he had left it in full view of everybody, just lying on his bunk.

Now, a few friends go with him, and look in any likely place they can think of. Their searching turns up nothing. It becomes painfully obvious that the shirt must have been stolen. Those of us close by, feel the gloom and depression of this awful discovery. We all have to pull together. We just cannot afford to have this kind of suspicion amongst us. What do we do now? Just forget about it? That is a decision, the leader will have to make for himself.

A very worried man, he decides to talk it over with Bill, who hears him out, then states the obvious. The shirt has to be somewhere in our quarters. Since it cannot be found, the only thing to do is to have a full scale search.

Bill will do it himself. Every man will stand by his bunk, while Bill starts from one end and works his way through.

With the whole party fully aroused and feeling pretty glum, Bill starts. It so happens, he begins in our area. The Pom leader's bunk is just across and against the opposite wall from mine, so it will be best to clear this part first. Bill is pretty thorough, and works his way from each three-tiered stand to the next. From where we stand, we can see everything he does. He goes through the personal belongings, then the blankets, then under the straw mattress. As we have few possessions, this is very quickly done.

In only a few minutes, he has arrived at the bunk stand opposite mine, and next to the Pom leader's. There, unlike the rest of us, the morose South African is lying full length on his bunk. "Come on," says Bill impatiently, "Move! You're just the same as the rest of us," while attempting to search around him.

The morose South African is most unwilling to move, and seeks to satisfy Bill by rolling his body from side to side. Bill is adamant, however, and insists he moves. He grudgingly rolls into a sitting position, with his legs dangling over the side. He occupies the middle of the three-tier, so, with his head bent over his shoulders, hunched by the rail of the top one, all his weight prevents Bill from examining under his mattress, except at each end.

Again Bill says, "Come, you've got to move." Finally, with Bill's shoving, he rolls a little, and there beneath the mattress, where he was sitting, is the missing shirt.

Bill's reaction is instantaneous, saying, "You bastard." He sails straight into him. The morose man, protesting his innocence, covers up as best he can, while drawing back into the relative safety of his middle placed bunk. With the bunks placed sideways against a blank wall, the only way to get at him is from the open side. To do so, Bill has to crouch over, while throwing punches. Although the morose man is a difficult target, very quickly blood starts to flow freely. Then Bill reaches in, and pulls him out onto the floor.

Everything has happened so quickly, that the rest of us have stood where we are, without moving. The fellows in the other room standing by their bunks, now come running in to see what the commotion is all about. The morose man is swaying on his feet, with a bloodied face, and now surrounded by the rest of us. The situation looks decidedly ugly.

Suddenly, the door to the Guards' quarters bursts open, and in they come. They are in various stages of undress, obviously alerted by the noise and pandemonium. They are startled, and unsure what to make of this sudden outbreak of violence amongst us. Bill settles it quickly by saying, "Take this bastard out of here, or we'll kill him." While a couple of Guards help the morose man into their room, another collects his gear. Once again, now that it is all over, they close up for the night.

Over, but certainly not forgotten. For a long time, we just stand there, talking over what has happened. Most are pretty sure that justice has been done. Those personal items that some thought had been misplaced, are now adjudged to have been taken by this Judas. Maybe he hates all of us because of his humiliation over the rissole affair, and has done these things to get back at us.

As we calm down and begin to think more rationally, I begin to wonder, "What if his claim of innocence is true? What if somebody else has stolen the shirt and hidden it under the morose man's mattress?" But then, he is the only one reluctant to cooperate in the search. So, he must have been guilty. Then I begin to think, "Hell, what if he had hidden it under somebody else's bunk to be retrieved later?" My bunk is opposite his, and it would have been easy to hide it there. If this had happened, how the hell would I have explained it away? By and large, most of us are damn glad the incident is over.

Next morning, the morose man is kept well away from us, and is still in the Guards' quarters. Kapitza, not understanding what the ruckus is all about, is nonplussed as to what to do with him. Bill's reply is, "I don't care, just get him out of here. We refuse to have him with us anymore."

Sometime during the morning, while we are all at work, he is hustled away and taken back to Lamsdorf. He is swallowed up by the big contingent held there and, we neither see, nor hear of him again.

I think about the happening quite a lot, and wonder if Bill has acted a bit too rough on him. Upon reflection, I feel Bill has done him a favour. By sailing into him, he had made it a one on one situation. If he had held back to let the mob take over, there is no telling what might have happened.

With all the commotion and upset, I would have thought that the Pom leader would have a rethink and reset the breakout date. It seems more prudent to wait until things have settled down. But he doesn't see it this way. He insists they will leave as planned.

Now, I begin to wonder whether the morose man may have tipped off the Guards as a final gesture of getting even. Then, I decide, "He wouldn't do that." I have a gut feeling that, basically, he is a straight bloke. I think, really, that those thefts were made for something to trade with, as a means of staying alive. To tip off the Germans is a big "No, No" with everybody. I feel certain that this includes him. I trust my gut feeling, for it has stood by me, so far.

The night of the breakout arrives, and all those going, standby with their gear at the ready. There is a buzz of excitement from those of us staying behind, as well as those leaving. The Guards close up, punctually, at nine o'clock. The goers move into position, just inside the passageway that leads to the front door. Ever so slowly the time drags by, until finally it is ten o'clock, and time to move.

The Pommy leader moves silently to the front door, with his key at the ready. He unlocks it, and quietly swings it open. Now the others move forward, in an orderly body, and slip through the opening. Quickly, the door is closed shut, then locked again from the outside. Disposal of the key has already been arranged, so that, if needed later, it can be retrieved.

We wait for any sign of discovery, but none comes. As the minutes tick away, it becomes obvious that the exercise is a complete success. With so many having departed, the place looks noticeably empty. The rest of us will just have to wait and see what the German reaction will be, and if there will be any reprisals.

In the morning a stunned Kapitza is allowed to find out for himself that a lot of men are missing. It has to be reported, with the usual procedures being that the Guard Commander be moved elsewhere in punishment. A desperate Kapitza can see his sinecure slipping away from him. He searches urgently for a plausible excuse to serve up to his superiors.

Bill provides one by claiming that it had to be expected. We are crowded in so closely, that everybody finds the living conditions intolerable. Not being able to stand it any longer, a lot of men have decided to take off.

Kapitza must have been able to convince somebody along those lines, for he is allowed to stay on, and comes back with a promise to extend the place in the near future. We just take this promise with a grain of salt. But there are no reprisals, and our work party is not closed down.

Word is to filter back to us later, that all the escapers made it to the timberline unseen, then made their various ways onward from there. The whole effort, however, is a complete failure. Everyone has been rounded up. None have remained free longer than three days, with most being captured on the first or second day. They all are returned to Lamsdorf to be swallowed up there, after the usual procedures of trials, followed by stints in the cells.

With the big escape being a total fizzer, we gradually settle back into our normal routine once again.

CHAPTER 14

# Working Party Days at Mahrisch Trubau: Episode 2

THE GAPS IN OUR WORKFORCE are quickly filled by more men from Stalag VIIIB at Lamsdorf. The business owners for whom we work, lose no time in demanding that their workforce, again be brought up to scratch. We, who have remained behind, have a new lot to get used to, and they seem to fit in with us.

Although the escapers have left a large gap in our numbers, most jobs are not very inconvenienced. With the newcomers having to be spread around, some of the old hands elect to move to a different job. Then the new chums are slotted in wherever there is a vacancy. The Home Mill, where Norm and George were placed, has established itself as the pick of the places to work. There is a freer more open atmosphere there, and the locals seem easier to get on with. But, as nobody from that lot had joined in the escape, there are no vacancies there. For myself, I decide to stay where I am. I have a good mate in Doug, a good association with Joseph, and occasional meetings with Elle.

This new lot of arrivals maintain the broad mix of nationalities, and fit in harmoniously. Most of them have been on other working parties, and have a good idea of the routine. It only requires a slight adjustment to get the hang of how things are done here. As always with new men, there are interesting stories of happenings on other jobs. These new arrivals, and our regular contacts with Lamsdorf, fill us in with the latest War news. Everywhere the seemingly unstoppable Germans, are pressing strongly ahead. There is no sign of our mob mounting an invasion. Indeed, it looks strongly that England is in great danger of being invaded herself. With the prospect of release, still seemingly a long way off, we can only concentrate on what is happening around us.

There are a couple of things constantly gnawing at me. What has happened to my escaping mate George? Have those two wounded men, I sent on to hospital in Athens, made it through? Have they managed to survive? Then there is that tin of souvenirs I had posted home from near Benghazi. Has it managed to get back home? With George, there isn't much I can do from here, other than hope, somehow, that somebody, who may have made contact with him, might turn up. As for the other problems, word about the tin of souvenirs, can be ascertained in mail from home. With regard to the wounded men, I might be able to clear this up in the same way.

My home mail has settled into a regular pattern, with my Mum doing most of the writing. I will just have to keep asking for word about the tin, and for her to make enquiries about one of the wounded, Keith, a Newcastle mate. There should be some word of his fate sent to his family back home. As for Paddy, the other wounded man, who had also been my fuse man on the Tobruk job, he is from Sydney. I have no means of contact. I just have to hope that he and Keith had stuck together. In any case, the process of finding out is a slow business. For me to ask something in a letter, then receive a reply, involves a round trip of something like three months—apart from the time taken to make enquiries, before a reply can be sent.

The beautiful sunny weather is well into full swing now. The crops are well advanced, and ripening daily. The fields are sprinkled liberally with wild flowers of all colours. Soon it will be time for harvesting. Doug and I have adopted the habit of taking our shirts off while working, and just lazing the balmy days away in the sunshine. We talk and reminisce, and do perhaps a little more work than we may have done, chiefly for Josef's sake. One day he asks us if we would like to come home with him one Sunday, and help with the harvesting.

We jump at the idea. We welcome anything at all that can give us, at least, a brief illusion of freedom. But how can it be arranged? We rather doubt that official permission will be granted. If it is allowed, we two will be the first to be given such permission. Maybe there will be that many restrictions put on our movements, that it won't be worthwhile. Josef says, "Do not worry. Leave it to me. I'll arrange it."

For the next few days, we are emotionally up and down, not sure which way things will go. We know that a lot of farms nearby are undermanned—with menfolk in the services, and women coping as best they can with conscripted labour. Usually, when crops are ready for harvesting, they need extra help to get them in. With food vital to the German economy, surely they will accept help such as ours.

But we wonder about Joseph's setup. He isn't a farmer and, indeed, the land in question belongs to his sister. Then, again, it isn't a true farm, just a small plot on which they grow whatever they can. Without getting too buoyed up, we will just have to wait and see.

A few days later, Josef tells us that everything is fixed up, and he will pick us up on Sunday morning at about 7.30 am. Sure enough, at the appointed time, he just walks up to our front door. He speaks briefly to Kapitza, who ushers us outside into Josef's care. We have been ready and waiting, and Kapitza tells him what time to have us back by. Josef readily agrees, saying it will be no problem. Then off we go, out onto the road, and down the street—the three of us walking along, and talking together. There has been no asking for our parole, or anything like that. It just seems that Kapitza takes it for granted, that a trust given, will be a trust not betrayed.

It is a strange feeling walking along, as we have done so many times before, but this time not to our regular workplace; instead, a journey into completely different territory. We are deeply grateful to Josef for having taken the trouble to set up this break for us. It has been entirely his own idea. It had never occurred to us that such a thing would be allowed. His sister's place is in a village just about a mile and a quarter outside town, and just beyond our workplace. For him to come and pick us up, and take us back with him, is a round trip of almost five miles. To return us in the evening, will necessitate another one of the same distance. It is a lot of trouble for someone, who is supposed to be your enemy.

Ambling along, and in no great hurry, we talk and take advantage of the lovely sunny day. Finally, we arrive at our destination, and Josef formally introduces us to Mary, his sister. Elle and Josef's girlfriend, of course, we already know. Elle is her usual bright and friendly self, while his girlfriend is much less formal than when we met her at the mill. She is very possessive, and there is much chaffing and playful goings-on, between her and Josef. With introductions over, Mary invites us in, and we all sit down to coffee.

The coffee, though Ersatz, is much more palatable than what we manage to turn out from the same stuff. We look around us with interest, taking note of the neat and tidy kitchen. Mary moves about in an efficient and practiced manner. This ordinary mundane scene, brings home to us, poignantly, what we have left behind—emphasising much of what we now badly miss.

We linger long over the coffee, with much talking and attempts to understand each other. In due course, and with Josef giving the signal, we all set out to the nearby fields. Farm work, mostly, and especially grain crops, is unknown to me. But, in Doug, who has grown up in this type of farming back home, I have an able teacher.

It takes him less than a minute to catch on to the method used here. Back home, most of this work is done by machinery. Here, with mostly small holdings, it is labour intensive. The long wheat stalks are cut down by scythe, then gathered by hand and tied into bundles. These are stacked in a particular way, into what Doug calls stooks. This allows the wheat to dry out more quickly in the hot sunshine. If the stooks are stacked correctly, any rain will just run off, doing little or no harm to the grain. When the drying out is considered right, the threshing begins.

Doug shows me how to gather an armful, then with a few stalks, make a tie to bind it together. We then stack them, on end, in bundles of three, so that they support each other, and not fall down. With the grain ears uppermost, the drying will be efficient and clean.

We all set to work, with the females doing the scything, and we three men doing the bundling and stacking. It is all pretty light-hearted, with much calling out and laughing. It is treated more like a picnic than work. We know we have ample time to get the job done, so we just take our time. As we expected, they could have done it without any help from us two. By arranging this outing, Josef has changed a chore into a happy event, whilst giving 'Max and Moritz' a very welcome change to their soul destroying routine.

We work for a couple of hours, then sit down to enjoy the food brought to us by the females. It is bread, fats, cheese, and some fruit, together with cold coffee. We relax light heartedly, for some time, before turning to the harvest, once again. After a few more hours, the job is done, and we slowly trek our way homewards.

When we get back to the house, Mary busies herself with the evening meal. Doug and I eat with them, before returning to our place. Josef seems in no great hurry to get us back. In any case, with the long twilight, darkness does not set in until almost 11.30 pm. We can always claim that the job took longer than expected.

While waiting, Josef's girlfriend indulges in a little playful wrestling with him, while we just stand and watch. Then he detaches himself and, beckoning us, says, "Come." He leads us to the side of the house and up to an open window. Pointing inside, he invites us to look, and tells us that it is his room. Interested, we peek in. Instantly, we are struck speechless. It is the barest, bleakest, living quarters, outside of institutions, we have ever come across. The room itself is reasonably sized, but just a bare concrete cell. All it contains is an iron cot and a small cheap wardrobe. The only things that make it superior to our own accommodation is that it is private, and that its occupier is free to come and go as he pleases.

Josef can tell that we are affected, and adversely disturbed, by what he has shown us. While not understanding why, he does not press us for any comments. He just lets the matter drop, and never mentions it further. It gives us a bit of an inkling, into the hardships and kind of life that these people have to put up with; and maybe, a bit of understanding at some of the pressure that has caused this War to come about.

Our hot meal is a typical soupy stew, with lots of vegetables, and a trace of some meat of some kind. Afterwards, it is time to head back to our quarters. We say our goodbyes, with much shaking of hands all round, then set off for home.

It has been a fairly mundane day, with nothing very eventful happening. We have enjoyed it immensely. The feeling of freedom we have experienced, is, far and away, sufficient recompense for our time. Still, the fellows back at our quarters, will insist on a ball by ball description—and their fertile imaginations will be running riot already, as to the kind of high jinks they feel sure we got up to.

By now, some of the edge of our hunger has gone, and there is a gradual awareness and growing interest being taken in the female sex. The fellows imagine that our outing, surely is an opportunity for some pairing off and romping in the hay fields. Should we tell it like it was, or embroider it a little, to add some spice, just for their benefit?

We decide to jazz up the story a little bit, and discuss between ourselves, what form it should take. We think it best to suggest that quite a few, young and attractive females take part, with them practically fighting amongst themselves for our attention and favours. Of course, with so many around us, there was no chance of pairing off. Adding colour to our story, we will argue mildly as to the attractions of one imaginary girl against another, while expressing our own personal preference.

With our prepared story just about sorted out, we arrive back at our quarters. It is just about eight o'clock when Josef hands us over to Kapitza. Once again we shake hands with him, giving him our heartfelt thanks for a great day. We enter our rooms, while the fellows come clustering round, demanding to know what we have been up to.

Before I can say a word, Doug launches into a lurid tale of how he had occupied the attention of all the females, allowing me to disappear behind a haystack, for over an hour with one of them. He makes it quite plain that there is absolutely no doubt as to what has happened, and that the girl was a willing participant. I do my best to protest, that what he is saying, is untrue. They will not believe me. They want it to be true. That damn Doug has put it over me, and just stands back grinning. From time to time, he will add a little bit more to the tale, and this reinforces their belief.

Try as I might, I just cannot convince them, that it is all just a tale. Finally, I give up. It is an undeserved reputation and I will just have to wear it. For months afterwards, Arty's romp in the hay keeps surfacing, while many envious comments are expressed.

Back to our routine again, with the days passing pretty much the same as before, mail is coming through, both from Manchester as well as home. With issues of clothing coming as well, we are gradually getting knitted out again, and aren't too badly off, at least for the summer. All gear is British

Army issue, which simplifies our complex distribution system. While we would prefer our national uniforms, we are glad enough to get anything. Underwear is supplemented by clothing parcels from home. I have also asked my Mum to see what she can do about an Aussie uniform, and an especially good pair of gloves for the coming winter.

The Koldas and Berg gangs, seem to have better access to local news and gossip, than we do on the other jobs. They now bring home news of two American girls living in the neighbourhood. With one of them over six feet tall and the other of medium height, we naturally christen them, Big Yank and Little Yank.

Enquiries as to how they came to be in Germany, is the same for both of them. They had taken cheap boat passages, available for people of German descent to visit the Fatherland. War had broken out while they were here, and now they are trapped. While they know each other, they live in separate locations, and meet only occasionally.

Big Yank came to visit her aging father. Apparently, she had migrated to America, while he chose to live here permanently. She now lives with him, and is accepted as a German citizen.

Little Yank had come to pay a visit to her Grandmother who owned a farm. A short while after the War began, her Grandmother died. As Little Yank is the only relative, she inherited the farm. She is now required to run it, and contribute to the economy. This is quite a problem, as she is only in her early twenties. Still, the very efficient German organisations see to it that production is kept up by helping with labour and plantings. She is virtually just a nominal owner, with not much say in anything.

Both Yanks are keen to speak to any of our blokes, given the opportunity, for they are keen to speak English again. They regard their present circumstances s only temporary, and can't wait to get back to the States. Because of their peculiar situation, they are pretty circumspect in making any approaches. They also have very little contact with each other.

It so happens that Little Yank, in running her farm, has need for some timber. Armed with the necessary requisition orders, she turns up at the Home Mill to get her requirements. She comes into contact with Norm, and they strike up a great rapport with each other. There is a mutual healthy attraction between them, where both just long to talk together, in their own language. The need to talk becomes irresistible for them both.

Soon little Yank begins manufacturing excuses that see her turning up at the mill. They quickly become firm friends, and derive pleasure from their regular meetings.

We are learning a bit more about the background of the locals, we are in contact with. We have found them less hard towards us, than we expected. It seems that there could be a reason. Most of them had belonged to an Infantry Regiment, raised in these parts during the First World War. Most of their fighting had been against the Russians. Quite a few had been captured, becoming POWs, as we are now. They were put to work on farms, living with and sharing with their host families. With most of the Russian men away, the prisoners got on famously with the women—so famously that there are cases where a Trubau man will pull out a faded snapshot, gaze at it wistfully, while declaring that he should have stayed there, and not come back.

With the end of summer approaching, there is much activity in the surrounding fields, getting in the harvest. For us, that also means the oncoming winter, with its miserable conditions, is not too far away. While I for one, am not very happy at that prospect, I have to concede that I am better prepared this time. I am reasonably well clothed and shod, and am hoping my Mum comes good with those leather gloves I asked for. I still haven't come to terms with working in the snow, and still have nightmares about the bone-numbing cold and shivering of my first winter here. Then Kapitza asks if any of us will help to get in the harvest, using Sunday, our spare day.

It seems that the harvesting work is running a bit behind time, and they could use some extra labour. Mindful of our status as a volunteer NCO work party, Kapitza is at pains to point out that there is no compulsion. It is purely a volunteer effort.

His request gets a fairly mixed reception from the blokes. Firstly, we have dropped into a routine of letter writing, clothes washing, and personal chores on a Sunday. While we can rearrange these things to some extent, it is a disruption, and we aren't too sure if we like this.

On the other hand, it will be a brief taste of freedom in the open air, with the prospect of a home cooked meal as bait. Then there is that business of Arty's romp in the hay to remember. Maybe the opportunity will occur for somebody else to get lucky. In the end, there is a reasonable proportion of volunteers, with Doug and I deciding to give it a go.

Bill, Wally, and some of the cleaning staff, whose work keeps them mostly around our home, elect to opt for an outing. Theirs is a pretty confined existence, other than trips down the town to collect our supplies. Doug and I tag into their team, reasoning that they will probably get the pick of what is on offer.

The farm, where we are to go, is owned and run by a German woman in her thirties, who has the help of some conscripted labour. Using our previous outing with Josef, as a guide, Doug and I figure that we will be gathering wheat stalks, bundling and stooking them. We know that this will be a work chore, and not the light-hearted, picnic atmosphere, we had experienced then. There will be some form of payment for our labour but, as this will come to us in camp money, it will be practically useless.

With the prospect of a long day in the sunshine, of gathering and bundling, the experienced Doug warns me to be sure to wear trousers and a long-sleeved shirt. He warns that there will be countless scratches and cuts from the sharp grain edges. Those opting to work in nothing but shorts, which most do, will be rueing it for days after.

Bill, Wally, and the administrative blokes, spend most of their time indoors. Now that they have the opportunity to be outside, they cannot resist stripping off and getting some sun on their bodies. As Doug has predicted, they soon pay the penalty with numerous cuts and scratches.

In our home environment, such things can just be ignored. Being healthy, they will just fade away. But here, it is different. With nothing to treat such things, we have this great fear of something going wrong—something that will see the others moving on, while you are left behind.

As the day wears on, the unaccustomed labour, and our poor physical condition, reduces us to little more than plodding robots. It is backbreaking toil, and we take every opportunity to stop for a break and a drink of water. Doug and I cope a bit better than the others, but not by much.

There are a couple of conscripted labourers working, who seem to be Ukrainians. One bloke, in his early twenties, is going around giving orders, and seems to be a boss. Obviously, he is the fellow who lives and works on the farm on a regular basis. They work together as a team, keeping mostly apart from us. They have been hard at it for some time before we arrive and, because of our late start, they seem to think that we have favoured treatment. The fact that we have a Guard with us too, may have influenced them to keep their distance. They cope much better than we do. It really is their line of work.

It is about 5.00 pm when finally we are told to knock off, and come to the farmhouse for a meal. We have had some bread and fruit during the day, but we are now looking forward to something a bit more substantial. This meal is the sole reason for Doug and I being here.

Our Guard ushers us into a fairly large, open style kitchen, and he motions us to sit up to a long, bare wooden table. When we are seated, the farm women begin to dish up the hot dinner, with the assistance of a Polish or Ukrainian girl of about eighteen. It is the standard and typical German food of a stew containing plenty of vegetables, with a hint of some kind of meat. There is bread to go with it, and it looks and smells, inviting and sustaining.

There are six of us, plus the Guard, the German woman and the girl. The Ukrainians seem to be being looked after somewhere else, or dining later. Then the boss Ukrainian, who works here permanently, comes in as a late starter. He plonks himself down at a position, reserved and obviously regarded as his, picks up his spoon and sails straight in, while talking between mouthfuls.

He obviously regards himself as a sort of de facto man of the house, rather than the hired help. The German woman resigns to putting up with his attitude, as a necessary evil. There is absolutely no indication of cohabiting, as some of the locals had enjoyed with Russian women, during the First World War.

We all have felt rather awkward, waiting for a lead from the other faction, to begin eating. The Ukrainian had no such inhibitions. With him breaking the ice, the rest of us begin to eat also, but with a markedly different style. We stare fascinated, as he sets about the job, with efficiency and speed. The sole utensil provided is a dessert spoon. He grasps the handle with a fully closed right hand, with the business end pointing straight towards him. He lowers his mouth to the same level as the rim of his plate, and just shovels the stew straight in.

With us adopting a more civilised, leisurely manner, he obviously finishes his meal, before we have barely started. The females, for their part, eat in a fashion more after our style. He sits back for a short time, talking to anyone who cares to listen. As nobody seems interested in responding to him, he soon grows tired, rises and leaves us to rejoin the others, wherever they are.

With the long twilight continuing until almost midnight, there is ample light to keep on working for several more hours. But, Bill has had enough by now, and decides to call it quits. He tells the Guard flatly that, as our normal finishing time is four o'clock, and it is now six o'clock, we are long past our knock off time. He considers we have been more than fair, and have honoured our commitments. Now it is time to go home. He insists that the Guard take us there, without delay. The startled Guard, not knowing what other course to take, is only too happy to comply. The whole business has been a bit of a drag for him too, as Sunday is normally a free day for him. We start off and head back home, while the rest of the workmen just carry on.

We arrive back and tell Kapitza, flatly, that we have finished for the day. He accepts this without argument. There is no attempt this time to embellish the story for the others' benefit. With so many involved, it wouldn't have worked anyway. Besides, there was almost a total lack of females of any kind. As an outing, the day was a fizzle, and we didn't like it. For any of us to be involved in such a project again, it certainly will not be as a volunteer.

Back to the grind, and the fretting at the slowness of our side's military progress. We revile them bitterly at their lack of get up and go. We worry constantly about mail and parcel deliveries. We wonder about family happenings back home. I receive word from Mum, that my girlfriend Jean is seriously ill. She was in hospital and having to undergo a major operation for women's complaints. She is recovering slowly, but with little indication of what the effect might be on her future life.

Winter arrives, and the constant ups and downs make you swear. Up to now, I have been fairly circumspect in my language. With no reason to hold myself back, I just let myself go. The fellows around me understand, so it doesn't matter. The locals don't understand English, so it doesn't matter when I use it, even in front of females. The depth of feeling, of course, is a different matter. Everybody understands clearly, what I feel.

Frank and Allan, two Aussie Engineers from Victoria, like Norm, George and myself, shake their heads and say, "Arty, you'll have to do something about your language. It's becoming so much a part of you, that, when we get out of this place, you won't be able to stop. You'll be in all sorts of strife, when we get back home." I appreciate their concern, but I do not care. I prefer to think, I'll be strong enough to drop it, whenever I want to.

Whenever I am most down, a letter will turn up from my Manchester girl. She never fails me, and treats me as her own special commitment. Always they are bright, breezy, and sexy. They are intimate between her and me, but too good to keep to myself. I always share them with my little group. They won't have allowed me, not to share. They in turn get almost as much pleasure from them as I do. It gets to be that, at every mail call, everybody will line up seeking firstly, something for themselves, then calling out, "Hey Arty. Did you get anything from Manchester?" My mail call is almost as important to the others, as it is to me.

Naturally, we avidly follow the progress of the War. None of us ever doubts that we will win. What irks us badly, is our side's inability to get going. We always think of our imminent release as being just a matter of weeks. As for a month away, we just cannot bear thinking about.

But all the news is bad. The German war machine just seems to roll on to success after success. Then, when the Japs come into it, they seem to be doing the same. It seems more like a competition to see which of them can outdo the other. Even the tiniest initiative from our side is something we hope and pray for. Sadly, there is precious little we can cheer about.

We are pretty well up to the minute with everything that is happening. Firstly, radios are everywhere in Germany, being a required installation in most work places. Being the prime medium for disseminating news and, of course, propaganda, broadcasts are very much required listening for the locals. Our Guards have one that they play into our dining room from their quarters, enabling us to hear some music occasionally.

Every Stalag is fitted with its own public address system, enabling the Germans to broadcast whatever and whenever they choose. When they have something to crow about, they lose no time in telling it to the world. Naturally, the BBC mounts a strong counter offensive, telling their version of any particular happenings.

The BBC's broadcasts are designed to be heard right across Europe. They are eagerly listened to in all the occupied countries, although such an activity is forbidden. A lot of Germans themselves, listen regularly, and draw their own conclusions between the two presentations.

Naturally, POW ingenuity sees to it that we have access to the right information. A goodly proportion of this comes from the office at the Home Mill. Frank, our Victorian colleague, has formed a friendship with the German girl, who manages the office there. Frank is tall and handsome. The girl, in her early twenties is also good looking. She is generally attired in folk or semi-folk dress, which makes her appear very feminine. Their friendship is firm, and mutually agreeable. She is what we blokes consider to be a "nice" girl.

Most people know the timing and the tuning to the BBC's broadcasts. Frank's girl, as we call her, does also. At the appointed time, she will tune in the office set, give Frank the nod that the set is on, then walk off to somewhere in the plant, leaving him to it. We are able to "fanoogle" access to the Guards' set, from time to time, as well.

Further information comes to us from the great clearing house of Stalag VIIIB at Lamsdorf. With the regular movement of men to and from working parties attached to Stalag VIIIB, some of whom eventually trickle through to us here at Mahrisch Trubau, we are privy to most of what is going on within the system as well. Bill's regular visits back there to report, keep us abreast of the official British line within the prison camp.

It is widely rumoured, and firmly believed by all, that the Senior British Warrant Officer in charge of the camp, is under secret orders not to escape. Supposedly, he is to stay at his post, and keep the internal camp organisation running smoothly and efficiently. His job is to keep morale high, and to call on other Senior NCOs around him for their help, when he considers it necessary.

With a large Air Force compound in its centre, being part of the Stalag VIIIB complex, the shot down Air Crew are trickling in at regular periods. By virtue of their being in England one day, and prisoners the next, they are a great source of the latest news from home. Although the intermixing of Airmen with other prisoners is not allowed, there are ways of getting round this ban. Therefore, we have a good idea of what the real situation is, as opposed to the official line.

Separation of the real from the phony, is absolutely vital to every POW. All of us has suffered, to some degree, by official misinformation and bullshit. Often, it has been a contributing cause leading to our capture. None of us put much reliance on official handouts, and always seek to unravel the hidden truth behind them. Anything relayed by our internal, camp organisation, in our eyes, is considered to be reliable and trustworthy.

The Commando raid on Dieppe is a case in point. When it occurs, the news is flashed throughout Stalag VIIIB, in an official news broadcast. Within a few days, it is relayed to our working party at Mahrisch Trubau. We have heard the claims and counter claims on the news. Some of the captured Commandos have been sent to Lamsdorf, so we are able to learn the truth of what has occurred, and the intention behind the raid.

The Germans have been taken completely by surprise, and are very disturbed by it. This sneaky, stab in the back, seems almost unethical to them, while they are involved in Russia. They are deeply incensed by it and seek to make capital out of any conduct that may be construed as questionable.

Their version is that the Allies have sought to establish a Second Front. In doing so, they have engaged in practices that are nothing short of piratical. Their very large force has tried desperately to hang on, but has been driven out by the victorious forces of the Reich, forcing the enemy to abandon much heavy equipment, such as tanks and field guns, and to suffer heavy casualties, in killed, wounded, and captured prisoners. Also, much documentation has been captured from the raiders, that confirms the illegal and piratical practices they had planned to implement. The Germans claim that a captured Field Order sets out the enemy objectives, which states that all prisoners are to be handcuffed. This, says the Germans, is contrary to the Articles of War.

Our side claims that the raid is nothing more than an ongoing test of German defences, as well as the testing of new equipment. Both sides confirm that the main participants are the Canadians.

We find that there has indeed been a raid, in strength. The aim has been to test new landing craft, and their ability to transport and land heavy equipment, such as tanks. Further, it has been to test our ability to capture and hold a position, large enough for a beach head. A further aim has been to capture documents and prisoners, and for these to be transported back for processing by our intelligence service. The raid had planned to hold on for three to five days, then evacuate.

As in all these types of adventures, there are a few slipups in the planning and doing of the job. Some of the Canadians seem to think the raid has been a bit of a shemozzle, pointing out bad faults here and there. But, the main aim seems to have been achieved, with some important prisoners being taken back in handcuffs.

The handcuffs business particularly incenses the Germans. Their News service launches into a tirade of condemnation, spreading it right throughout Europe and the Occupied Territories. This, they claim, is in marked contrast to the humane and strictly correct behaviour of themselves. Such practices leaves them no alternative, but to retaliate in kind. Therefore, all POWs in their Stalags will be handcuffed, daily, and made to suffer the same indignities, as the Allies have sought to inflict upon their German captives.

On the face of it, these proposals carry a serious, almost sinister threat. However, they end up in the form of a Keystone comedy, causing the Germans untold headaches and trouble. We immediately see that such an order could not apply to a working party. Handcuffed men simply cannot work. We will refuse, if an attempt is made to force us. Civilian plant owners, with output quotas to maintain, simply won't tolerate that kind of interference. They will find ways of not complying, if ordered to do so. Therefore, it can only be implemented in the main Stalags.

Instead of the ominous threat, as imagined by the Germans, to the men in the main camp, it offers the promise of great entertainment. As a relief to their normal monotonous existence, they could unite in a vast battle of wits, against their Guards. As it is an Official Decree, the authorities have to make a serious attempt at carrying it out. First, they have to come up with the handcuffs. This takes several days, delaying the start by almost a week. With metals of all kinds being in critically short supply, God knows how they manage it, but a large assignment arrives at Stalag VIIIB.

On the first day, the prisoners are paraded and ordered to don their handcuffs. They refuse. They claim that, if they are to be manacled, then the Guards will have to do it. After some hesitation, this they proceed to do. In fact, some of them rather enjoy the prospect of slapping handcuffs on a prisoner's wrists. But when the job extends into thousands, it becomes a nightmare. To top it off, the prisoners set about their own satanically devised, disruption.

Nobody objects to being handcuffed, except for an official protest from the Camp Leader. In fact most POWs seem eager to get in the lineup. While the Guards expect the relatively simple task to take no more than an hour or so, it becomes obvious that it will be a never ending chore. Anything the men can think of to mess up proceedings, they will do. Some get themselves handcuffed, wander off, then return quickly to say they urgently need to go to the latrine. With their hands cuffed in front of them, they cannot wipe their backsides. They demand the cuffs be unlocked, then refastened with their hands behind their backs.

Others find that, with a little bit of tinkering, the cuffs can be unlocked with such things as a sardine can key. Those blokes will dump their cuffs then get back on the line for another go. In some instances, a Guard is certain that the man now before him, had been handcuffed before. The Guard then has to concede that he must be mistaken.

Realising that they are in a losing situation, the Guards seek to lighten the burden, by suggesting some exceptions. There are many tasks that have to be carried out for hygiene, cooking etc., where the men involved cannot work in handcuffs. Then, too, those key personnel of the Camp Commander and his staff can be exempted. They flatly refuse, insisting in being treated in exactly the same way as the rest of the men.

The Guards try valiantly for two or three days, even though it is obvious the whole idea is unworkable. Then, without any announcement, they just drop it. It is a victory for the POWs and the German administration avoids making fuss about the matter.

In our relative backwater, here in Mahrisch Trubau, it is still very important to us that we are privy to all that is happening back in the main camp. Whatever applies there, will inevitably spread to us here. And we want to be sure that we tackle the problem, in the same way.

In Stalag VIIIB, there is a constant battle of wills on both sides—with the German Officials and the Guards, maintaining a constant flow of propaganda, aimed at breaking prisoner morale. The prisoners retaliate by tearing apart the announcements, and exploiting any flaws, real or imagined, that they can find.

The usual practice is for the Germans to call a full camp parade, where a formal announcement will be made, usually for another great Military victory. Sadly, they have plenty to throw at the Prisoners. Apart from the fall of Russian cities, there is the astounding successes of the Japs, when they enter the War. The apparent ease of their sinking of Britain's two great battleships, seemingly without retaliation, and then the fall of fortress Singapore, doesn't seem possible. Singapore the impregnable, so we thought. It takes weeks to grudgingly concede that there seems to be some truth in this news. With the annihilation of the American Fleet at Pearl Harbour, the entire Pacific is theirs—and Australia becomes under imminent threat.

It is hard going for the POWs, but they generally manage to get back at their tormentors in some way, even in the face of these obvious disasters. Then comes further announcements of Jap air attacks on the Australian mainland. We Aussies just hope the vastness of our country, will make for minimal damage. The first announcement covers the raids on the city of Darwin, to be followed by another special announcement of a raid on the pearling city of Broome, in Western Australia. The German Officer making the Broome announcement, is speaking into a microphone, while standing on a raised dais at the head of the assembly.

Immediately, there are laughs, boos, and catcalls from the Australians, quickly supported by the other POWs, although they're not sure what the noise is about. Word is quickly passed around that Broome, far from being a city, is nothing more than a small pearling port, on a very isolated part of the north west coast. Its buildings are no more than a dozen or so, corrugated iron shacks, with a population of two or three hundred at the most. The Aussies are certain that any attack there, is a total waste of time.

As the noise from the Prisoners becomes more strident, the German Officer announcer becomes more incensed. Finally, he steps down from his position, orders his deputy to dismiss the parade, and stalks off with as much dignity as he can muster. Not knowing what the hullabaloo is about, the Germans choose to ignore the incident.

At Trubau, we just get on with our work and chores, noting the diverse little happenings around us, while chewing over the latest happenings relayed to us from Stalag VIIIB.

We are well into winter again, and soon we will have to prepare as best we can for Christmas. Just to think about it, depresses me. Although we have reached a reasonable measure of nutritional stability, and have a reasonably friendly relationship with the civilians around us, as well as a good, harmonious rapport with the rest of our fellows, this is definitely one Christmas that I am not looking forward to.

Since arriving overseas, my Christmases have been pretty lousy. The first was up in the Western Desert outside Bardia, the second while wandering round Mount Athos like a tramp, now the third is to be behind bars. While circumstances have improved a little, the location really does get me down. I think of the many occasions back home, when all of our family would get together— and of the wonderful dinner put on by my Mum. I can see her basting the fowl, while we watch in anticipation. They were times of laughter and happiness.

Then I think of my ups and downs since leaving home. As I think over my experiences, I have to concede that my spirit, if not broken, is pretty badly bent. I have just stumbled on from one disaster to another, despite everything I have tried.

There was the failed Bangalore Torpedo job at Tobruk. That hurt. In Greece, I felt responsible for Cocker being killed in the air raid. Then there was the nightmare of quitting the country, after being left behind by my Unit. There was the sinking of the Costa Rica, and the attempted evacuation on Crete. To almost make home from there, only to suffer the devastation of capture was a crushing humiliation. Then followed the movement from one bad prison camp to another that weakens your mind, body and spirit. There was the exhilaration of escape, only to be followed by the devastation of recapture. There was the inhumane rail trip through to Lamsdorf, and the near death experience by the gassing overdose from the delouser. Then I spend time in the confinement cells and finally end up here at Mahrisch Trubau. What I have been through, hits me hard.

God, I hate the prospect of this Christmas. I just cannot stomach the celebration of special events and dates. My bitterness tells me that my feelings, in this regard, are totally dead. But I am trapped. I will just have to get through somehow. The Germans may not have harmed us physically, but mentally, I, for one, have taken a beating.

While I am feeling sorry for myself, others are fiercely determined to put on a show, if only to spite the Germans. The most determined of our lot are the Poms. The Pommy Regulars have this uncanny knack, of being able to set themselves up, just about anywhere. In no time, it seems they can always come up with a workable system of everybody pulling together. If they want something to happen, it usually does.

We Colonials, the Aussies and New Zealanders, are intent on going our independent ways in most things, and do things differently. We are often nonplussed at each other's method of attacking a problem, but, by and large, we manage to work in with each other, without much fuss. While we Colonials are content to concentrate on food, the Poms are insistent that there has to be decorations as well.

With no real leaders, there are just general suggestions, from here and there, to make our own decorations. There will be paper chains, Merry Christmas signs, and anything to promote the Christmas feeling, that anybody can think of. Sheets of coloured cardboard will be bought, using our camp money for the purpose. As for food, we will receive the standard fare from the Germans, with maybe a little extra. We will conserve whatever we can from our own food parcels, with some electing to try and concoct a kind of Xmas pudding. Each little group will try and trade for something in the meat line, maybe a rabbit, or a chook.

In our meal times, there is community food and group food. Community food is the standard German ration prepared by the cooking staff. Group food is anything extra you can come up with yourself. You prepare this yourself, in your groups of two or three muckers. It is strictly your property, and not shared with anybody else. For our Christmas fare, this system will still operate. There is simply no way we can come up with a bulk of food, sufficient to make it a communal feast.

Frank and Allan, our Victorian colleagues, muck in together, as do Norm, George and I. Frank is pretty sure he has the contacts to trade for a rabbit. He suggests that we five combine together, to share the trade and the feast. This we readily agree to. They all work at the Home Mill, with me being the odd man out at Kollas Mill. They handle all the negotiations among them, while I'm not called upon to do much of anything.

From now on, most leisure time is taken up with the preparations. The diligent ones knuckle in, making their paper chains etc., every evening after work. Nightly, there will be a few working away at these tasks in our common room cum mess room. From time to time, they will hold up their handiwork, and invite comments and suggestions. While not involving myself, I really cannot knock what they are doing. But the sight of them producing their cardboard boxes, in which they stow their gear, depresses me. No matter how good the job, to me, it is still make-believe and homemade.

With the standard routine, carrying on as normal, it is a relief to be able to go to work at the mill. There is the friendly face of Josef, and occasionally Elle will show up to brighten our day. Some of the local citizens, who regularly come to buy timber of some kind, have, by now, nodding acquaintances with us. It is all so peaceful and domestic, almost as if we are becoming fixtures in the place.

We are better equipped to cope with the rigours of this winter. Our clothing and boots are British Military issue, of good quality materials. In addition, my Mum has managed to get good quality underwear through to me in clothing parcels from home. A big bonus is a pair of leather, gauntlet like, gloves. This is a prize indeed.

My Mum informs me that she has become a member of a group known as Mothers of Prisoners of War. It seems that a fair number of men from Newcastle, have been captured. With the proliferation of committees raising funds for something or other, the mothers, wives and girlfriends, have decided to form their own committee, and raise funds for POWs. She has become a member of the Executive.

The President of the group is the mother of a friend of mine from my Unit. I am now able to learn that a lot of my friends and acquaintances, have, indeed, ended up in Germany, in other Stalags. The big news item is that Keith, one of the two wounded, whom I had rushed to hospital in Greece, has made it back home. And, that tin of souvenirs, that I despatched by mail from up in the Desert, has also made it home, intact.

It is just before Christmas, and the snow is fairly thick. Doug and I are stacking as usual, but the snow doesn't seem to bother us much now. One stack, in a fairly quiet part of the yard, has a hole like the mouth of a burrow, showing from one side. With the snow around it fairly deep, there are animal track signs of some kind. I show it to Josef and ask him, "What is it?"

He says, "It is a weasel."

I have only a vague idea of what a weasel looks like, but I keep a lookout in the hope of seeing one. I look and look, but am unable to spot any animal at all. I almost forget about it. Then, just before knockoff time, something stirs close to my feet. I am standing almost on top of the opening, and the animal is attempting to leave the burrow, which extends under the stack. As it pulls itself clear, I raise my boot and quickly stomp down, pinning it underfoot. With a thick carpet of snow beneath, there is no danger of hurting it. Doug comes to inspect it too, and we can see it is a long bodied animal, almost certainly what we call a ferret. Its fur is thick, sleek and glossy. It obviously is a fine specimen, but, what shall we do with it?

Its teeth and claws are sharp and businesslike. Both of us are loath to attempt to grab it in our bare hands. If we do, all we can do is put it in a cage. That would make it a prisoner, just like us. As far as we know, they are no good for eating. We look at it and can see that it is certainly a fine looking animal. Spontaneously, we both say, " Let it go." I lift my foot and away it scampers. We see it often after that, frequently with its mate. Often they will romp together in lively games, twisting and turning in the snow. It is cheeky, and seems to accept us as part of the scenery. Somehow, snow doesn't seem such a hardship anymore.

Christmas Day arrives. The paperchain makers have hung their handiwork the night before. All that is required now, is to get into the Christmas spirit. In reality, I suppose, the enthusiasts have done a pretty fine job. The trouble is, the restrictions of our situation, weighs heavily on our minds—and the stark contrast of what may have been, had we have been back home. Without belittling the effort, to me, the decorations still come over as amateurish and second rate. Again, they tend to emphasise our plight, rather than detract from it.

Frank has been successful in his trade, and we do, indeed, have a rabbit for our Christmas dinner. Now, this is something I can really get enthusiastic about. While none of us profess to be any great shakes as a cook, by necessity, we all have had to become reasonably proficient at it. As provider of the carcase, Frank will do the honours, while us other four, particular his pal Allan, hover around, advising how it should be done.

There is plenty of good-natured banter, while the preparations are under way. Fats for roasting or frying are almost unobtainable. We have to call upon our very limited supply of margarine. So there is a fair amount of monitoring to make sure Frank doesn't go to excess. Naturally the rabbit will have to be stuffed. Among us we have managed to obtain the necessary ingredients. Frank's method requires chopped up liver, heart and some lightly fried onion. This is combined with some seasoning and a poultice of damp bread. This is all thoroughly mixed together and crammed into the body, sewn up and ready for baking.

We all help and harass Frank, in these vital preparations, imploring him to be sparing with the marge, to ensure there is enough left, for the baking. Frank just calmly carries on, fully determined to make as perfect a job as he can manage.

With most of the other groups having also scored a trade of some sort, the stuffing and sewing up becomes a pretty busy scene. Most of the hangers-on, just hover around the stove. The frying, and then the baking, fills the air with an almost unbearably, tantalising aroma. The wait, until the tasting of the finished product, is almost more than we can stand.

The Germans have permitted and arranged for us to buy some bottled beer with our camp money. The thought of sampling such a world famous brew, is almost too exciting for the long deprived drinkers amongst us. Some of the old hands warn that it isn't worth the trouble. And so it proves. Restrictions on the use of proper materials because of War needs, have produced a flat, non-alcoholic concoction, little better than coloured water. It is German beer in name only.

Still, we do have our rabbit, and a couple of other goodies we have managed to save from our parcels. Frank has done us proud, with our help of course. We tuck into our banquet, savouring every last moment of it. We will be short on margarine for a while, but that will be in the future. For the moment, all we can concentrate on, is to eat. Then we again go over the feast, right from the preparation, through to the eating. We sit and talk about our dinner several times over. We just sit there, lazily taking it all in. I guess, all things considered, we have had a fair Christmas. But still, nothing like home.

While preparing for Christmas, some thought has been given, as to what can be done about the new year. It is decided to hold a New Year's

Eve concert. Personally, I cannot see much sense in foregoing our normal sleeping habits, just to see in the New Year. If there has been some great military achievement, that gives the promise of leading us to our freedom, then surely I may be able to get enthusiastic.

Back at Lamsdorf, there is loads of talent, of every conceivable kind. Quality stage plays, dramas and revues are in constant production. Musical instruments of all kinds are readily available, having been purchased with camp money. There are many prisoners with the professional expertise to cover all aspects of what is required—be it producing, directing, staging, lighting, acting, orchestral, arranging, or whatever.

Knowledgeable Poms, can rattle off name after name, of some of the world's best musicians who are held there. The word is that most of Victor Sylvester's orchestra had joined the RAF, and are now in Stalag VIIIB, after being shot down. At this time, Victor Sylvester's dance band, is acknowledged as the world's best.

With all these experts about, and with all the time on their hands, a lot of raw talent is steadily being coaxed along, amongst the rest of the men. However, that is back at Lamsdorf. Here in Trubau, we have nothing. There is one bloke, who has elected to try and teach himself the trumpet, and is a pain in the neck to everybody. Apart from him, we are just your average bunch of people.

After some prodding and coaxing, several agree to either sing or recite. It will be a concert in name only, with one exception. Kapitza insists on putting on an act. All activities and happenings within our quarters, naturally have to be cleared with the authorities. The Authority here is Kapitza and he, more than anyone, is keen for everything to run smoothly. By now we have become accustomed to his agreeing to just about any reasonable request. We just take it as a polite formality to ask. Now, his insistence on performing, intrigues us. We will just have to see what transpires.

Those of us, who have, more or less, made up their minds to bed down as usual, feel interested enough to front up, just to see what is going to happen. The show gets underway, with Bill making most of the announcements. One after the other, the performers climb onto the small stage, which we have constructed in one corner of our mess room. They do their best, and the dutiful audience applauds in kind. Then Bill announces, rather unenthusiastically, Kapitza's turn.

He states, "This famous artist from the cabarets of Berlin, will perform for us. He is known as the One Armed Fiddler." Kapitza enters with a solemn face, carrying a violin and bow in one hand, with his other hand hidden under his jacket, and with his hand tucked inside the waistband of his trousers. Still maintaining his solemn expression, he makes several flourishes with the instrument in his one free hand. He tucks the heel under his chin in the normal position. Holding it there with his chin, and with the bow in his hand, he plucks at the strings with a finger, testing and tuning. Suddenly, and very theatrically, he is smitten with an uncontrollable desire to sneeze. He will have to take his handkerchief from his pocket to smother the sneeze. Being one armed, with the bow in his hand and the violin under his chin, how can he do this? He makes several gestures, emphasizing his dilemma. Then suddenly he whips the bow across the front of his pants, where miraculously it is held firmly, allowing his free hand to reach for the handkerchief.

He has thrust the forefinger of the hand hidden in his pants, through the open fly. This is what is holding the bow. He noisily blows his nose, then bows to the audience, and that is it. Kapitza himself, thinks his turn is hilariously funny, and almost falls off the stage laughing. The rest of us, we diplomatically applaud lightly, while hardly knowing what reaction to take.

By now, we all have had long experience of the German character, and know them to be a fairly humourless people. Certainly, they can laugh, but joking, even in a mild form, seems beyond them. We have learned early, not to be too jocular with them, as they take everything so seriously. You just don't become too flippant, with the man holding the rifle. Now Kapitza and his turn has us nonplussed. This is a side of him, we have not seen before. Maybe, he is an exception to the rule.

With the concert finished, we all are happy enough to turn in. In its way, this Christmas and New Year period, has been some sort of a milestone. Although a somewhat unhappy one, for me, the thing to focus on, is that wonderful roast rabbit.

The recent War news has been rather patchy. Our side seems to be doing little more than, just hanging on. The sweeping gains that have been the norm for the Germans, seem to be slowing down. Maybe this is because it is winter, or, hopefully, because their momentum is spent.

There is a fair amount of bombing of the German mainland by our mob, but land warfare seems to be getting nowhere. In some instances, we seem to be losing ground. The sector, that hurts us badly, is the Western Desert. All the gains, we had made in a couple of weeks, have been wiped out almost as quickly. On top of that, they have pushed us further back, until there is a real danger of the whole of Egypt falling.

True, a strong garrison is holed up like 'Rats', in Tobruk. We know it can be supplied from the sea, and that the fortifications make it well-nigh impregnable, whilst in the hands of a resolute defender. Maybe it is a ploy to make Rommel overextend himself. Then Tobruk falls. This is a personal affront to us, who had taken it in the first place. Doubtless the authorities are greatly concerned with the grave threat to Egypt, but all we can think about is the hard slog needed to get the damn place back again.

News from the Russian front, is much less available to us, than from elsewhere. We have to sift the official German version, and try to make some sense from that. It seems to us that the Russians are resisting fiercely, and stubbornly, and that the Germans are beginning to have trouble there.

Waiting, fretting and hoping, all we can do is carry on as usual. It is a relief to leave our quarters and go to work. Then, it is a relief to leave the bleak winter environment, and return to the warm comfort of our home. Always, the pressure on our nerves is constant and steady, and it is a miracle, there aren't more stressful blow ups.

Slowly the days pass, the winter begins to wane, and once again comes the approaching spring. Now, at last, we get word that the Germans are preparing to extend our quarters. This has come about as a result of Bill's contention, that our cramped conditions, had been the reason for that escaping foray.

Materials begin to arrive to do the job, which will be done by German workmen. The walls are to be constructed of cement and cinder blocks, of the type being produced by the fellows working at Koldas's Cement Works. By the time work finally gets underway, winter has gone, and we are coming into spring.

The new work abuts onto the existing building, with the knocking down of the connecting wall, being left to last. This is for security reasons, to deny us access to the half open building while work is in progress. When the connecting inner wall is finally knocked down, the workmen work late to complete the job. The finish is an all-over plaster, though looking good, it seems to be made of very poor materials. They depart, leaving it unset, and still damp.

All of our blokes return from work and inspect the results with interest. They test the surface finish and, upon realising how easy it will be to demolish it, sense that a breakout at this moment would be a piece of cake. There is a fair amount of excitement in their conversation, as the fellows busy themselves with their usual evening chores. As the night wears on, the realisation that, practically an open door is staring them in the face, begins to have its effect on their actions. The frustrations, hopes, and yearnings to be free, is just about too much. About a dozen decide, that they cannot stand it anymore, and will take the opportunity to break out.

There is no real planning, just an opportunity, followed by a sudden decision. Travelling companions of twos and threes, quickly group, without any thought of compatibility. Their plans are quite hazy, and will be developed, once the groups are underway. The activity is feverish, as gear is assembled. All that most of them want to do, is get out and keep going. Having made arrangements for the disposal of any possessions left behind, the committed escapers, settle down to wait for a suitable time to go. They have decided, who will be first and, with a little bit of assistance from one or two not in the break, the actual breakout will be at about 11.30 pm.

Just after ten, and when the guards have locked up for the night, a couple of the impatient ones, start to work on the plaster finish, just in case it sets too quickly. It just falls off in large chunks, exposing the new brickwork underneath. This is too easy. But they will just have to wait to tackle that—for the removal of the bricks will leave an exposed hole, clearly visible from the outside, before it is prudent to leave. Now, they begin to worry, if they have made their move too soon, in case a Guard takes it into his head to take a last minute internal walk through. The larger portions of peeled off plaster will be a dead giveaway.

Finally, it is time, and they are ready to depart. Once the first large block is removed, the others follow quickly. The opening is made in only a couple of minutes. They certainly make a job of it. Stacking the blocks on each side of the hole, they aren't content with just a small hole, that a man would have to stoop and crawl through. They make it big enough to walk erect through, carrying all one's gear.

They are all gone in a matter of minutes and, with no alarm having been raised, the rest of us just settle in until morning. Again, I have decided, that this is not for me. The problem still is, where to head for, once out.

It is broad daylight by the time the damage has been discovered, and we are all astir. A worried Kapitza comes rushing in, and he is clearly shaken at such a large opening. He then departs to inform the authorities. In his absence, Davy, a Scotsman from the Black Watch Regiment, and a member of the cleaning staff, puts a mouse trap in the centre of the opening. Upon his return, Kapitza, despite his worries, has to laugh at such a ridiculous gesture.

With the birds flown, there is no alternative but to call the civilian workmen back to reseal the opening. This they do in very quick time. We are worried that we might not be allowed to use the new section, after all the trouble that has been caused. But, once the Germans are satisfied with the finished work, we are allowed to spread out. These changes make a great difference to our personal comfort. We now have more room around our bunks, a proper wash and bathing room, and greatly improved toilet facilities.

As for the escapers, we all know, as well as them, that there is absolutely no chance of them getting away. It will be, more or less, a competition, to see who can stay on the loose the longest. For them, it is a way to break the monotony, and relieve their frustrations. Anyway, somebody just might get lucky.

Once again, it will be a big test on Kapitza, to see if he can wrangle it, to avoid being moved elsewhere. While this outcome may take a bit of time, the rounding up of the wayward ones, takes no time at all. Once again, the longest anyone has been out, is three days. There is one big difference on this occasion. This time, three of the men are allowed to return to our working camp, without punishment. The practice has always been, to return them to Lamsdorf after recapture, to be dealt with. Previously, we had lost all contact with them after their escape. This time we have someone to question, and to make up our own minds whether the exercise is worthwhile.

These three are two Poms and an Aussie. Although they are friendly with each other, they aren't your usual tight knit group. The two Poms are muckers, but the Aussie looks after himself. They just spontaneously grouped together on the night.

Once outside, the escapers adopt the preferred camp plan, and head straight across the fields, due north to the tree line. Buoyed by the exhilaration of the escape, they set out at a fast pace. They are soon strung out, but keep together in their individual groups. The five kilometres, or so, to the tree cover, quickly becomes a hard slog. By the time they reach the trees, all the little groups have become well separated. This lot never sees the others again.

Once amongst the trees, they turn south, after a breather, and head for the Czech border. On this first night, they are glad to call it quits, and hide out in the woods, while still well inside the Sudetenland. This is the normal pattern, as the adrenalin drive keeps you going, until fatigue catches up; then you collapse.

On their second night, they estimate they have made a reasonable distance across the border, before hiding out again. This time they pace themselves better, but are still knocked up before stopping. During the morning, they move to the edge of the trees, to find that they are beside a large, open, partly cultivated field. The layout seems to confirm, that they are indeed across the border.

After resting for a while, one of the Poms, feeling decidedly crummy, decides to risk having a wash, before moving on again that night. He moves along a nearby stream, well away from the others and under the cover of some bushes. He decides to go the whole hog, strips off, and begins having an all over bath. He is well into it, when he realises, he is being watched.

A woman has been working in the field, and he had not noticed her, until now. She is standing watching him with unabashed interest. His clothes are in a heap on the bank near her, and they are unmistakeably British Battle Dress. He is greatly upset and concerned at being discovered, so soon after their escape. All he can do is try to reason with her, beg her not to give him away, and, hopefully, prevent the other two from being discovered.

In his completely naked state he climbs out of the water, advances and tries to talk to her. Neither can understand each other, so he figures, she must indeed be Czech. This is encouraging, as they are generally pro-British.

She eyes him all over, and the invitation is unmistakeable. She doesn't care, who he is, or where he is from. He is a man and she is a woman. There is he and there is she, and let nature take its course. And it does.

After a while, and when some sense and reason has returned, he dresses awkwardly, and slowly departs while she watches him out of sight. After such an encounter, he has no fear of her turning him in. He goes straight back to rejoin the others. He feels a bit ashamed of what has happened, and thinks it best to keep things to himself for the moment.

Upon his return, the anxious second Pom, takes him to task for being away for so long. "Where have you been?" he asks. The first Pom mumbles something about it taking longer than he thought. The second Pom then announces that he, too, will go along and have a bath. The first Pom, alarmed, tries to dissuade him—putting up weak arguments, which the second Pom brushes aside. If it is alright for the first bloke, the second one cannot see any harm in repeating the move.

The second Pom is gone for a reasonably lengthy period, and returns with a rush. He bursts into an excited tale of an encounter with a very willing female, on the verge, between the stream and the field. His story is almost identical to what has happened to the first bloke. The first Pom now speaks up, and relates what had happened to him.

This is unbelievable, with the disappointed Aussie feeling very much the odd man out. "Dammit!" he decides. He will just have to try his luck too. And off he goes. When he returns, he tells how he has just walked up and asked. She willingly obliges.

Shortly after, they move on from there. Next day, they are quickly sighted and rounded up. This is pretty much inevitable, as the very efficient German organisations, make any movement virtually impossible, without being challenged.

Now that they have joined us, they cannot wait to tell us about their adventure. This tale, knocked the story of Arty's romp in the hay, into a cocked hat. But is it true? I know that my supposed romp is just a tale.

We set about cross-examining them, from every angle we can think of. Try as we might, we cannot shake them. Grudgingly, we begin to believe them.

"But what about the woman? What was she like?" we ask.

They tell us, "She wasn't exactly young, and she certainly wasn't old. She was reasonably good looking, and quite shapely. She looked the type, who would have no trouble forming an attachment, if she wanted to. There just can't be any men about."

"What did she say? Did she say anything?" I persist.

The Aussie, mimicking her voice as best he can, says that all she said to him was, "Me, Romantica." The depth of feeling he puts into it, seems to indicate, that she was disappointed that there were only three of them.

This story and fantasy proves very unsettling to the rest of us. Whereas before, food has been the great focus of our attention, now the opposite sex assumes a much higher profile in our sphere of interest.

There are some Polish girls working as housemaids, whom some of the fellows have become acquainted with. But, we regard these mostly, as comrades in adversity. Although they have more freedom of movement than us, they still are pretty much captives, as we are.

Much talk, speculation, and blatant signs of interest, in the German females in town, is exercised by most of us on those constant marches to and from work. With the scarcity of young mature males in the place, there are encouraging signs that some are prepared to return this interest, although with great caution.

New arrivals, to replace those escapees returned to Lamsdorf, bring tales of their working on parties, where there are large contingents of Polish girls nearby. These girls, allegedly, are quite willing to pair off with some of our blokes. These tales stir the general unrest even further. Frustrations at the slowness of the military scene, plus our continued captivity, accentuate these feelings. However, we have achieved good working conditions, and a great deal of harmony here, compared to some other places and newer fields.

I have enough sense not to be carried away with all of this. I know that we will still be prisoners, no matter what working party we are working on. Freedom to go and come, will be no better anywhere else than it is here— probably less so. The only way I am prepared to risk copping a bullet, is in a genuine escape bid—not fooling around with some girl, Polish or German.

I have already decided that, escape from here is not on for the moment, because of our location. I have no intention of moving from here. I cannot stand it, back at Lamsdorf, so here I will remain. But, for a change, I decide to make a move to one of our other working parties. It means severing ties with Josef and Elle, but I console myself by remembering that, when the time comes to get out of this place, I will be doing this anyway. For the moment, my move is a soft option, because I still can keep in touch with them through Doug. I am the means of Josef getting some of those French issue Gauloisie cigarettes, that he dotes on. I always save most of mine for him, from the infrequent issues supplied to us from the Germans. They are the standard French Army issue to their troops. Now that the Germans are in control of this supply, most of our blokes will smoke them, only at the last resort—their quality is that bad. But to Josef, they are great.

I prefer to go to the Home Mill to be with Norm, George, Frank, Allan, and the others. However, there are no vacancies there. Regarded as the best work place, nobody will move. I will just have to go elsewhere.

Moving from one job to another is no problem. The old hands here just move into the vacant spots, if they wish to move. The new arrivals then just fill in the remainder. So, if a certain job appeals to you, it is just a matter of biding your time until the present holder moves on.

One particular reason why I want a move, is to familiarise myself with the town proper. Our route to and from work is through back streets that skirt the town. The Berg and Koldas workers go through its centre. They all speak, familiarly, of this and that feature. I want to see for myself. When I eventually take off, I want to know which way to go. I choose to work a short stint at the Koldas Cement Works, before moving on to the Berg Mill.

Meanwhile, our combined intelligence services, of radio and information from Stalag VIIIB, both official and unofficial, further stirs our unrest. There is a heartening lift to the military news for our side. The former, seemingly unstoppable advance into Russia by the Germans, has taken a battering at Stalingrad. A really bad winter, together with bitter fighting, has seen the whole German Army plus its General, fall captive to the Russians. Other Russian cities are also putting up a tenacious resistance. For the first time, it begins to look as if the Russians might be a match for the Germans.

And, as for what we regard as our War zone, the Western Desert, our mob seems to have, finally, managed to overcome Rommel, and are chasing him back across North Africa. Yanks are landing in Algeria, and are set to head him off from that end.

On the Air Front, heavy day and night raids from Britain, are hammering the hell out of German factories, towns and installations. Coastal towns like Hamburg, or anywhere submarines or naval forces might operate from, are given special attention. There are POW camps for captured British Naval personnel in this vicinity, and they have to be evacuated. Quite a few find their way through to Lamsdorf.

The Germans try to counter this heavy air raid activity, by branding the aircrews as "Murder Fliers". They resort to this type of propaganda, after several large cities are devastated by fire bombing attacks, that result in heavy civilian loss of life and property damage. Of course, we say, "Good on 'em. Look what you Germans did to England."

The propaganda output results in some shot-down aircrew being lynched, and killed by irate citizens, before security forces can take them in tow. When word gets back to England, the Airmen are armed with revolvers when on a mission, as a means of protection against these hotheads. Once the German security people arrive, the Airmen, as a matter of course, will surrender and hand over their weapons.

However, the greatest piece of information is that there is a very strong move for a Repatriation of Prisoners. A medical committee has been set up, under the auspices of the international Red Cross, to investigate people for possible exchange. Sick and wounded, together with non-combatant medical personnel, naturally will have first preference. The exchange will be made through neutral Sweden. While the numbers have not been decided, at least a large shipload is almost certain.

Good God! Does this news create a furore? Here is a heaven sent opportunity to get out of this hellhole, without having to wait for a painfully slow military victory. Every single person, who hears of it, craves, with all his being, to be one of these to make it up the gangway.

Everybody wracks their brains, trying to conjure up some disability, either real or imagined, that will give them an edge. From Lamsdorf comes the news of many sudden cases of insanity, with people doing all sorts of odd things—like digging a hole and piling up the dirt, only to dig another hole to bury it; and, pushing heavy loads round and round in a wheel barrow, while staring vacantly and paying no heed to anyone.

These "insanity" cases go at it with fierce dedication, so that even the sceptics begin to wonder that, indeed, they might be mad. Others attack old wounds, trying to make them flare up again. For myself, I have similar feelings and fleeting wild hope, before common sense prevails. I have no sickness or injury, and am too far out of the picture down here. Although I know I haven't a hope, I sure can dream about it.

It seems unlikely that authorities will comb through working parties. It seems certain that the best place to have a chance, will be back at Lamsdorf. If there are insufficient sick and wounded, will they make up the difference with able bodied men? What then will the criteria be? Will the Germans insist on making such a selection? Length of captivity may have to be taken into account. If so, then the Dunkirk men will walk in. They had been captives for a year by the time we were taken.

The possibilities are endless. The urge to return to Lamsdorf to be on hand, just in case, is overwhelming. The terrible uncertainties, have us all in a turmoil. The only thing to do, is for each man to fight it out, within his own thoughts and conscience. Some do return, but the majority can see, that negotiations and agreement to conditions, may be a long drawn out process. With the hotting up of the war, surely it will be over soon, and we will be released anyway.

Our assumptions prove half right anyway, for negotiations are long and drawn out. Still, an exchange eventually is made. By the time it happens, most of the steam has gone, and it seems just a passing incident. Eventually, this one lot does beat the rest home, by almost a year.

With all the turmoil, significant changes occur in our party. Kapitza goes and, about the same time, Bill and his mates decide to move on, as well. Bill has achieved much in laying the groundwork, that we now live by. With everything running smoothly, he has become bored and decides to look for another challenge. He thinks he might try a party with access to all those Polish girls, whom we have been hearing about.

Wally, too, goes with Bill. We will never get another interpreter as good as him. His intellectual capacity and knowledge of German, which, after all, is his native language, has smoothed the way for us, remarkably. One or two are suspicious of the ease with which he is able to work with the Germans, to the extent of hinting darkly, that maybe, he is in cahoots with them.

Of course, this is ridiculous. Wally is a German Jew, who had to flee to Palestine, when the Nazis came to power. He is risking a lot, just by being here. Still they doubt. Then, there is the fact that he is a Jew. Even here, that age old hostility and prejudice, affects some. Even the slightest hint, cannot help but be felt, in our close packed community. Maybe this is enough to make him move on. Anyway, I am sad, for he is a truly nice guy.

Just before Kapitza goes, he demonstrates to us the sadistic type of discipline, practised in the German Army. We are sitting at a noisy lunch one day, when suddenly the door to the Guards' Quarters is thrown open by him. As we hush to a dead quiet, he launches into a tirade of abuse. One of the Guards has committed some sort of misdemeanour, and is being chastised.

The poor sod is forced to stand there at attention, while Kapitza circles him slowly, at the same time lashing him with a verbal tirade. The victim cannot move or talk back. He has to endure being publicly humiliated in front of his comrades. To make it doubly hurtful, us prisoners are allowed to also witness his discomfiture. For our part, we think it to be, too barbaric a practice for words.

Despite all the mental ups and downs, that we have been through, we are still stuck here at Mahrisch Trubau. And, like anywhere, the mundane day to day things just carry on, regardless. We have jobs to go to, and we just turn out as usual.

I am quite happy to march off with the combined Koldas and Berg crews, on my first day. For me, this one is something of a new beginning. Traversing a route, where I have never been taken before, I look around with interest. Everything seems new and exciting.

I drop off at Koldas's with the rest of the workers, while the Berg crew continue on. The job, I have scored, is making cement and cinder building blocks. The moist mixture, after being mechanically mixed, is wheeled into our workroom by one of the other blokes. Using a steel mould, I will shovel the mixture in, temp it tight with a wooden tamp, then unhook the mould, which is in two parts. And hey presto! There is a building block. Easy, there's nothing to it.

As the blocks have to be left for several days, to cure and dry out, it is essential to set up the mould in the best position. Care has to be taken to ensure that there is sufficient clearance to unhook the mould, without damaging any newly formed blocks—not too much clearance, for our workspace is limited. Spillages have to be cleaned up as we go.

We are working on a smooth concrete floor, from which the dried out blocks are easy to remove. But, as this cannot be done for a couple of days, we have to utilise the floor space, so as to work as comfortably as possible.

The fellows, whom I am working with, have the job down to a fine art. They are able to place the mould, fill and tamp, with a minimum of physical energy. They warn me that they are sticking to a quota of fifteen blocks, per man, per day. I take my cue from them, trying to copy their every move. I know by experience that such jobs require a physical knack, that not everybody can achieve. If I can, it will be easy. If I can't, it will be damn hard work.

Privately, I think fifteen a day will be a piece of cake. Actually, I find myself struggling and, for the first few days, manage only about thirteen. We have our ways and means of slowing things down, without appearing to do so. But I need to try myself out, for my satisfaction. I want to be in fair condition, when it becomes time to move on. But, this work is heavier than anything I have done for quite some time. Phew! Then and there, I decide I won't be staying.

Apart from the toil, the work is all inside. The workroom may be cool and pleasant in summer, but, probably, deadly cold and freezing in midwinter. And I hate those cold winters. I will stick it out long enough to enable me to move on to the Berg Mill.

Koldas's had been the one place where there had been much confrontation, between us and the Germans, when first we came to Trubau. Thanks mainly to Bill, Wally, and with the help of Kapitza, all that is in the past. With all the work practices now well established and, more or less, agreed to, Koldas is resigned to obtaining the rather meagre output he is now getting. But, he has been negotiating, and trying to find an agreeable method, to raise it.

Our fellows maintain that the work is physically hard. Our condition is poor, due to our hardships and lack of food. All things considered, the amount of work being turned out, is exceptional. Anyway, if they do manage to turn out a few extra, what benefit can the workers expect in return?

Koldas has wheedled and cajoled, and promised extra money. "No good," say our fellows. "That is only Lager money, and it can't be spent on any of the things we really want to buy. How about some extra food?"

Koldas protests that this is beyond him. All food is strictly rationed, and all distribution is strictly monitored, so that there can be no cheating.

"But isn't there some way you can get your hands on some local stuff, produced for the townspeople's own consumption?" we query.

Apparently, that, too, is taken into account by the authorities. The regular ration is reduced to each household, according to the amount they produce for themselves. With both sides, seemingly, unable to find a solution, the issue has reached a deadlock, when I begin to work here. Koldas is stuck with us as his workforce, and he will have to work out something to increase output, or just let things continue on as before.

Finally, one of our workers suggests, "Why not try piecework?" Once the men have met their quota, they can return home. This idea seems better than nothing, so Koldas begins negotiations into what a reasonable quota might be. He thinks twenty-five will be a fair target. Our fellows loudly protest that this is far beyond their capacity. After much haggling, a final figure of twenty is agreed to. This new system starts just after I move on.

The first day has seen the expert men reach their quota of twenty, and then demand to be returned home. It is just eleven o'clock. The shocked Koldas agrees that they have, indeed, fulfilled their side of the bargain, but have made it impossible for him to keep his side of the agreement. He points out that it will be patently obvious to all, that some sort of rort is being connived. He suggests that it will be to the advantage of both sides, for the men to remain on the job, until sometime in the afternoon.

The men grumble, but can see the wisdom in his proposal. It ends with Koldas getting a bit more production, the men being able to take it easy, without reprisal, after filling their quota, and still getting an early mark during the afternoon.

In moving to the Berg Mill, I have decided that I will not work at stacking boards. I have opted for a change, and there is more scope here, for Berg Mill is the largest mill in town. It employs a greater number of our blokes, than any of the other places of work.

It is situated alongside the railway, and there is a siding for shunting rail trucks in for loading. These come in only occasionally, and were the source of our early fears, that we would have to turn out on Sundays to load them on our scheduled day off. But, it's an unfounded fear.

At a new place of work, in this prison fraternity, it is important not to upset the status quo. Work practices, already hammered out, may easily be upset by an unthinking act. My first few days are spent getting to know the layout of the place, and what is allowed from a prisoner's point of view, of course.

There is a log yard on one side, then mill buildings in the centre, with the grading and stacking area on the other. The mill buildings cover the engine room, and the saw or breaking down area. The saw setup is totally different to what we are accustomed to back home, where the practice is for all the sawing to be done by circular saws, with frequent back and forth passes through the log. Here, the cutting is done by a machine called the Big Gatter. A series of vertical saws are set up in a frame, that moves up and down under engine power. These saws are set to trim a log to a certain thickness in one pass. The saws are then reset to cut the trimmed log into finished boards, in one more pass. The engine power to run the show is fuelled by mill waste, even the sawdust.

To me, the method of fuelling the engine is ingenious. The firebox is mounted in a deep pit, about eight feet below ground level. It is a movable steel box, on wheels for easy cleaning. The box is about ten feet long by about seven feet wide. Inside the box is a series of baffles, set horizontally, somewhat like a staircase leading down. The baffles are about nine inches wide, and set about a foot apart. Once a small fire has been started, all that is required to keep it going, is a basket of sawdust at regular intervals.

All of the sawdust from the cutting, collects in the pit area beneath the saw. One of the locals gets a wicker basket full, and just tips it into the firebox. The sawdust will land on the baffles, in no particular fashion. With the burning of the fire, and the natural draft, the sawdust is sucked in. This is sufficient to keep the fire burning fiercely, and provide sufficient steam power to run the whole show.

All the mechanical and technical jobs are handled by the locals, while all the labouring jobs are handled by us prisoners. Small jinkers on a light rail system, bring the cut logs into the mill, and transport the finished boards out to the grading area. From there, they are taken away for stacking. The two man job, I have scored, is transporting boards from the mill to the grading area.

Dave, my workmate, is an Aussie Infantryman and, like me, is also new to the job. While I am an old hand in Trubau, Dave has only just recently arrived with the latest bunch of newcomers. Before arriving at Lamsdorf, he had been in a Stalag near Munich. We strike an instant rapport with each other, and become great mates. We decide that we will just go along with the present method of doing things, then change the procedure later, if it suits us to do so.

While getting the feel for the job, we get to know a bit about each other. After Crete, Dave, along with most of the Australian contingent, had ended up in Austria. Eventually, due to pressure of bombings, and large groups of prisoners coming up through Italy, many had been moved out to other Stalags. Dave had ended up in Lamsdorf. The way Dave tells it, things had been pretty good in Austria. The Austrians had been fairly friendly, and conditions for the POWs were reasonably good. It seems that there had been some truth in those tales the Germans had told us, early in our capture. In those dark days through the transit camps, when we were in a bad way, the Germans always countered our bitter complaints with the story, that we will be much better off, when we reached our destination.

Maybe, I have been a damn fool to risk everything in escaping. If I had gone through with the others to Austria, I may have recovered much sooner. With all that had happened, I may have saved myself a lot of heartache.

Then I think about those carefree days, of wandering across Macedonia, helping ourselves to food along the way; of sleeping out and enjoying the warm balmy days of summer; the tranquillity of Mount Athos; the exhilaration of getting a boat and sailing off; the wonderful Greek peasants and the help received from OUR village. Yes, even after the disaster of recapture, it has been worth it.

Dave claims that early on in Munich, crews were put to work cleaning the streets. It quickly developed into an easygoing, almost light-hearted affair, where they got on friendly terms with proprietors of businesses, along their beat. It was on one of these occasions that Dave actually saw the German leader himself, Adolf Hitler.

One day, about midmorning, there came a ripple of excitement among the locals. The streets suddenly cleared of traffic, and the passers-by crowded the edge of the pavement. Then a cavalcade of about half a dozen cars swept into view. The wondering prisoners paused, stood in the gutter, leaning on their brooms etc., to see what was going on. A large, open car in the centre, contained a bareheaded, solitary figure, lolling comfortably in the back seat. It plainly was Adolf Hitler. Dave said he looked a picture of health, was tanned, and seemed totally relaxed. Apparently, he was returning to duties, after spending some time at his mountain retreat.

The small cavalcade swept on, and was gone, almost as quickly as it had come. There was no special fuss, nor emphasis on security, and everyone could plainly see who it was. It seems strange that this man is responsible for bringing us halfway round the world, and is the focus of so much hatred and enmity, from our side. Yet he turns out to be a rather small, healthy, ordinary man in appearance, not much different to ourselves.

Dave and I always manipulate our working time, so that there is always a little work, interspersed with a greater degree of loafing. In good weather, loafing time is spent in the open sunshine, behind a log stack, out of general sight. In bad weather, or in winter, it is spent in the drying room. This is a long narrow room, part of the mill complex. It is just behind the Berg residence and ducting from the engine room conveys warm air into it. Its purpose is to assist in the drying of timber. But in this season there is very little need of that. There is a large box kept there, where blocks of timber ends are kept, ready for Berg residence fires.

These loafing rights, we enjoy, are the result of hard fought gains from the early days at Trubau. Although there is no actual agreement, it is tacitly accepted. The POWs work their own warning system to ensure there is no hinderance to work generally. If manpower supplies for any of the stages of the workflow are getting low, a man taking a break from his particular job, will warn the appropriate man or crew, that it is time for them to turn up again. In this way, there are few arguments, and everybody seems reasonably satisfied.

In the job, Dave and I are doing, of transporting cut boards to the grading area, we have very little loafing time. The way the cut boards come off the Big Gatter, after the second pass, keeps us hanging around. As it is also our job to return the trimmed logs, from the first cut to the bench in readiness for the second cut, the only loafing time we have, is when the Big Gatter saws are being reset for a different cut. We decide that we will have to do something about this.

We manipulate the workflow, until we are able to load a huge pile of boards onto the jinker at one time. While the trolley itself is strong enough to take the load, we both sometimes have a tough time, heaving and pushing the heavy load out to the grading and stacking area.

Our civvy workmates often shake their heads at our behaviour, but make no comment. Work practices have developed to the extent of letting us do what we have to do, in our own particular way. Working in this fashion, Dave and I toil intensely for ten minutes to a quarter of an hour, then go off and loaf, doing nothing for an hour or more.

The work keeps us in good nick, and the bludging time leaves us free to just loaf, or maybe even trade. It is great to stretch out in the sun, out of view, behind a pile of logs, clad only in a pair of shorts, boots and socks. With your forage cap over your eyes, you can even sleep. Always, somebody will give you a nudge when you need to turn up, again.

Having settled into the work pattern at Bergs Mill, we look around to see if some other jobs appeal to us more than what we are doing. We both agree, that the job we finally want, is log hauling. This entails rolling the required logs off the log stacks onto a jinker, then pushing them along the rail track into the mill. There, it is a simple matter to roll them off the jinker onto the log platform, alongside the Big Gatter.

There is a team of two working on the log stacks, getting the required logs into position for the jinker. These two and the log haulers, work as a team of four, and are a very close knit bunch. The logs aren't overly big in diameter, and it requires much less time to load the log platform, than it does the cut boards. A saw reset can take one and a half to two hours, by the saw crew, during which time you need do nothing. This is the job we aspire to. We just have to wait until the present holders feel the urge to move on. We know this is only a matter of time and, my seniority at Trubau, should see that we get first pick.

While all the mills work pretty much the same, the method of doing things differ in some instances, from mill to mill. When moving to a different workplace, you automatically adopt the new method of doing things, always prisoner inspired. You don't rock the boat. New men are always instructed on what is required of them. Despite the different nationalities and personalities amongst us, there is little or no friction, and the system works well.

Our new camp leader is a New Zealand Sergeant Major, named Arthur. He is a good natured, happy sort of a bloke, who has been with us from the beginning of our stay in Mahrisch Trubau. Knowing all the inner workings of what has transpired since we arrived here, the transition is smooth. The new interpreter is a Pommy Yorkshireman, also an original here at Trubau. He has made it his business to become as proficient in German as he can. He is nowhere as good as Wally, but still good enough for the job. By now, we all have become good enough to make this service almost unnecessary.

The new Guard Commander, a Corporal, arouses our suspicions and wariness, right from the start. He tries very hard to get really close and friendly with us—to the extent that he sort of implies that he prefers to be one of us, rather than a German, although not saying so in actual words.

He makes it his business to wander into our section of the quarters. He will stop and enter into casual conversation with anyone he comes to. He will offer facts about his personal and family life, while enquiring about ours. His favourite ploy is to walk up to a group of three or four, and just start talking. He never ever seeks any military information, and only mentions the War situation in a general way.

Some take him at face value, but most are suspicious of his motives, and are guarded in what they say to him. We cannot fathom out a reason for the way he is acting, but decide to be wary in our dealings with him. He seems to prefer our company to that of his own men, if this is possible.

One personal fact that comes to light, is that he has been married only two years, yet has a son aged fifteen as well as four other children. We tax him about it, and he refers to it as the common German practice of being unable to afford a church ceremony. The church bit has to come later, when they can afford it. We still marvel how they stick together, while our experience is that the bloke shoots through, after only a short time together. Here, there seems to be none of that, and their commitment seems to be total.

There has been a change in the Guard Complement as well. Before, there had been a couple of reasonably young blokes, recovering from wounds. Normally, they would have served on, somewhere in the relatively quiet back areas, away from frontline service. They have disappeared, and have been replaced by local older men, in their fifties and sixties. These oldies wear civilian clothing, with an armband to denote their status. They are armed with a rifle while on duty.

We have always been on good terms with our Guard Contingent, and these older locals are more friendly still. One day, we have an incident, where an old Guard, in charge of a party, is returning them home for their lunchbreak. He collapses with a heart turn, in the street in the centre of town. Our fellows carry him into a shaded doorway, loosen his clothing and make him comfortable. They prevail upon some locals to summon the proper services to take care of him, hand over his rifle, and march themselves back home.

He is off work for a week, and returns fully recovered. Upon his return, he is loud in his praise of treatment and care, given to him by the prisoners. He declares openly that he trusts us, more fully, than he does his colleagues.

We attribute the change in the Guard personnel to some reverses at the front, and the need to bolster their forces, regardless of how fit the replacements might be. For us, this is a good sign. The sooner the Germans are beaten, the sooner we will be out of here.

With the change in our leadership, as well as the Guard formation, our former fairly easygoing relations, become even more relaxed. It is the right atmosphere to push for some more privileges. We know that the forced labour workforce of Poles, Russians and Ukrainians are able to stroll freely about, and meet with each other on Sundays, their day off. They usually meet up at an inn, in a quiet place in the nearby countryside, sit about chatting, and having a quiet beer. As there isn't a great deal of difference in their status and ours, why can't we be granted a somewhat similar privilege?

With Camp Leader Arthur leading the way, we manage to get permission for Sunday afternoon walks, under supervision of course. While it is an added chore for the Guards, Sunday being their relaxing day, it is a great boon for us.

We grow to love these Sunday rambles. The alternate fields and forest groves, the rolling countryside, are truly picturesque. The long grasses waving in the breeze, are liberally speckled with blues, reds and pinks of flowers growing wild, such as cornflower, poppy etc. It doesn't seem possible that this is the very same place, I had cursed as being bleak and God forsaken, when first we came here.

The inn proves to be roomy and comfy, without being pretentious. The beer is just the same old fashion type, which is just as well. With a little alcohol inducement, certainly, some may take the opportunity to disappear. This would mean the cancellation of these walks, almost as soon as they begin.

We receive a couple of footballs from Stalag VIIIB, as an issue of sporting equipment. After a bit of pressure from us, we are allowed onto some flat ground, alongside our house barracks, to kick a ball around. We have a little trouble with some of the townspeople here though, as our activities trample and flatten the grass. All grassed areas, road verges etc., are allotted to certain families for the cutting and storing of winter fodder. It is an important resource for feeding their animals. Our activities ruin that. Our Guard Commander ignores their protests and just brushes them aside.

Upon our Sunday rambles, we have passed a stream that broadens out to form a decent sized hole. Some of the locals are swimming there. With the late summer heat being very warm, we too, crave an opportunity for a swim. After some urging, we get permission. But this creates a minor problem. As it is a public place, we will have to wear a swimming costume of some sort. Such an item just isn't available for a POW. So, we will have to improvise. Shorts are still a hard-to-get commodity here, with British Battle Dress being our regulation uniform. Shorts, generally, have to be sent in a clothing parcel from home, which is a long, slow, involved process.

I solve the problem by using a very long woollen scarf that has come to me as a Red Cross issue. It is about eighteen inches wide, and I am able to wrap it around myself three times. I sew it together down the side, then tack it together in the centre, allowing sufficient room to get both my legs through. The result is a passable pair of trunks. While we enjoy the dunking, the fresh water is icy cold, even in midsummer, and quite a shock to the system.

Now it is proposed that we buy ourselves a bath. This surprising suggestion comes from Togo, one of a group of three New Zealanders, who muck in together. We refer to them as the "Three K's", because their surnames all start with a "K". They are originals of our group, who first came to Trubau. Togo is another of those, who shake their heads in despair at my swearing habits.

Togo is half Maori, and a big man in the Maori tradition. His voice is musical after their style, and he has a cheery disposition, with an infectious laugh. His imposing bulk is such, that if he makes a suggestion, you generally tend to listen—and that goes for the Germans too.

There has been a terrazzo bath, propped up in a corner at Koldas's Cement Works, ever since we came here. Togo had done a stint there, noticed it, and made judicious enquiries from Koldas, of its availability for sale, and, if so, the possible price—while, at the same time, concealing his interest as a possible buyer—as if anybody would believe this possibility, anyhow. Armed with this data, he puts it to Camp Leader David, to push it through.

The plan is to pool our Lager money, which is practically useless to us anyway, and make the purchase with that. While officially it is legitimate currency, Koldas knows it is useless, but he cannot admit it. Togo feels, that if we make an official request to buy, Koldas will not be able to refuse to sell. The blokes are all for the idea. This Lager money has been slowly accumulating for a while. With nothing else on offer, this is a good way to get rid of the stuff.

There follows a fair bit of negotiation, with us not being too confident of success, Finally, a deal is struck, and we have ourselves a bath. What a boon this is. We install it in a corner of our ablutions block, close to the inset copper. With an abundant supply of coal, hot baths are now a reality for all. The fire under the copper is lit by our cleaning staff, at about three o'clock. It will be hot enough for bathing by the time the first workers arrive home. As the Home Mill men are the first, Norm and George, always have an early claim. Either will be first, followed by the other. I usually arrive in time to follow behind them. With a little topping up, it is the practice to go three to a bath. Then another lot will follow on. This bath makes a tremendous difference to our wellbeing. Finally, we feel that we have conquered the fleas and the lice, for good.

Camp Leader Arthur, is maintaining those regular trips back to Lamsdorf, as had Bill. The internal information he brings back, informs us of a new dodge dreamed up by the Airmen, to get out of the place. Because Airmen are forbidden to go out on working parties, their chance of escaping, are much more restricted. The Germans are immovable about this, for they know, only too well, how valuable an Airman is. In the case of a soldier, you put a gun in his hand and, almost immediately, he is ready for war. For an Airman, it is much more complicated than that. The technical training and knowhow he must have, is lengthy and costly, and makes him a very valuable resource.

With us ordinary mortals, escaping is very much a matter of one's own initiative. With Airmen it is pretty much a required procedure. Part of their briefing before a mission, concerns what to do and where to make for, if they are downed. There are clandestine escape routes across Europe, where members of the various undergrounds, will pass them from one group to another. Their uniforms, in some cases, are said to contain maps printed on silk, but are sewn in as indistinguishable linings. Their buttons are magnetised, and can be used as a makeshift compass.

While us blokes are privy to much of his information, naturally we cannot take any advantage of it. With the Airmen confined to the Stalag, neither can they. At least, not until they have come up with this new idea. Simply put, it is to change identity with a soldier.

There are a sizeable number of men, who have decided to just stay put in Stalag, and wait out the War. With the top class educational courses available, they can put in their time by increasing their knowledge. It will give them better employment prospects, later on. Airmen canvass among these stayers, for anyone willing to exchange identities.

Once a willing partner is found, a lot of procedure has to be ironed out to ensure the swap will not be detected. As mail, and now photos, involves much traffic back and forth to our homes, all of which is censored, care must be taken. Ingenious ways informing the respective families have to be worked out. For once Bill Smith, Airman, becomes John Brown, soldier, that is it. Once the counterfeit soldier is free to go out on a working party, from which he escapes, is captured, or killed, the counterfeit Airman must stay put, and cop any reprisals if his cover is blown.

In due course, one of these Airmen turned soldier, arrives at our working party. Why he chooses to come our way, we cannot fathom. It is possible to arrange to join a working party, in whatever location you fancy. Our party seems well away from any possible contacts, to help him on his way.

Our Airman has arrived with a very capable looking bloke, a real soldier, as his escort and minder. The Airman himself, though, is a wide-eyed, baby faced, youngster, with a sort of shocked and bewildered air, as though he still has not come to terms with his situation. In our rough and tumble world, he is completely out of touch.

They explain their situation, in a private word with Arthur, right from the outset. Arthur passes the word on to us, explaining only what is necessary, and asking us to give them any assistance we can. To cover for anyone, is a matter of routine with us, anyway.

We know that they will only be with us for a very short time. Then, after a few days, before we even get to know them, they just slip away from a worksite, and are gone. They're picked up in next to no time, being free for only three days. The usual routine for escapees in our area, applies in this case too. They will be returned to Lamsdorf, do their time, and maybe give it another go. But we never hear of them again.

The system of swapping identities is badly dented by the advent of Douglas Bader. He, with his tin legs, is a world famous top fighter pilot, and is considered a top prize by the Germans, after being shot down over France. He was forced to bail out, and in the process, having to cut himself free from one of his tin legs, leaving it behind in the plane.

The Germans extend a lot of old time courtesies to him, while exploiting the propaganda value of his capture, to the full. They contact his home base, and arrange for a spare leg to be flown over and parachuted down, so that he can be mobile again. Any Officer of note, particularly Air Force men, make it their business, to come and have a chat with this famous prisoner.

He tries several times to escape, but, because of his tin legs, he is unsuccessful. In due course, he spends some time in Lamsdorf. He is an abrasive man who makes it his business to verbally castigate anyone whom he considers is not making a sufficient effort to escape, including the

Camp Leader. He demands to know what schemes are being used to help escapers. When told of the identity swaps, he insists on being part of it.

We are told that, in due course, he goes on a working party. Every party has to walk one to two miles, to get to the rail head, and often longer from the other end, to get to the barracks. With his tin legs, this is beyond him. When he begins to falter, the blokes around him, support and half carry him. Upon arrival to the worksite, it is obvious that he is in no condition to go out and work. The Party Leader then arranges a cleaning job for him, that allows him to stay around the barracks.

A week or two later, a high ranking German General turns up at Lamsdorf for one of their periodic inspections. He insists on meeting and talking to the celebrated prisoner. The counterfeit Bader, who is brought before General, obviously has real legs, not tin ones.

Meanwhile, the real Bader is getting along alright at his working party, with a lot of support from the fellows around him. One day a small group of German Officers turns up and orders every single man out on parade. When all are assembled, they are ordered to drop their pants. Bader knows immediately the jig is up. Stepping forward he says simply, "I'm Bader."

Eventually, a very sophisticated tunnel is dug from the Air Force compound, allowing for regular escapes to take place. It is lined for its entire length with bed boards. The string from around Red Cross parcels is woven into their hammocks, as a replacement for these bed boards. The Camp electricity system is tapped to provide lighting. A good blower system provides ventilation, and a wooden track allows trolleys to be pulled back and forth.

Here in Trubau, we continue on in our normal daily fashion. There are rumblings and indications that our side is beginning to have some successes. To us, they are painfully slow, and not very decisive. All we can do is fret and fume, and get whatever relief from our drudgery that we can devise. We have a touch of light relief one day, after lunch.

We are on our way back to Berg Mill and are going through the town square. Several townspeople are passing through, also, going about their normal daily business. From the centre of our group, in an outside lane, is a chirpy little London Cockney, called Tosh. Suddenly, he shoots out a greeting, from the corner of his mouth, at a tall thin female passing close by. "Hi ya, Babe," he says.

We simply do not attempt to speak to any of the female population in public. So, this blatantly familiar attempt, takes me by surprise. Her reaction is even more surprising. She replies in the same fashion, with, "OK, Big Boy."

The strong American style of chatting up a female, tells me that this must be the Big Yank. It is the first time I have seen her. I have seen Little Yank, Norm's friend, but only from afar, and never to talk to. This encounter leaves me with a fit of the giggles. What seems so ridiculous is that Big Yank's "Big Boy" would be hard pressed to come up to her shoulder. Still it is only a clandestine, passing greeting, and we each continue on our way.

About this time, one of my teeth starts to play up. I put up with it for a while, thinking I might have to be sent back to Lamsdorf. The aching gets to a stage where I have to do something about it. I report it to Jack, our Pommy medical Sergeant, who tries to look after all our problems with virtually no supplies. It seems there is a practicing Dentist here in town, and arrangements can be made for me to have treatment there.

The local Dentist is a Czech, which is good news to me. Somehow, I don't fancy a German having a go at me. Will I have it filled or pulled? I figure that proper materials will be hard to come by for filling, and less likely to be used on a prisoner. I make up my mind to have it out. Besides, when the time comes to get out of here. I will have enough problems without the handicap of chronic toothache.

Now that a regular Dentist has been found, Tosh decides to come along too. He has a troublesome tooth and decides on a filling. The two of us, plus a Guard and Interpreter, present ourselves at the Surgery. The Dentist is a kindly, middle aged man, and he places us, side by side, in two dental chairs. He fusses about us, and we get the impression that he considers it a privilege to be working on 'Englishmen'. He examines us both, tells Tosh that his tooth is too far gone, and will have to come out. Mine, he says, is a good one, and can be saved.

I make a quick decision, and decide the best alternative is to have it out anyway. He fills a syringe and injects Tosh first. From my position, I can see Tosh's eyes bug out, as the needle goes in. This makes me chicken out a little. Then it is my turn. Once again, he pleads with me to reconsider. But I say, "No, pull it." Reluctantly, he does the job.

Once it is completed, we leave and go back home. I have no idea how the work is paid for. I presume the German authorities will have some kind of an arrangement, where the dentist will be reimbursed by some kind of government instrumentality.

Having established that it is possible to receive expert professional treatment, without having to return to Lamsdorf, (and the probability of being unable to return to Mahrisch Trubau), the way is open to claim attention for other problems, both real and fancied.

The big attraction is a day off work, a trip away somewhere, the chance to dress up, and put a show on for the locals. Then there is the cost. We get a perverse pleasure out of causing the Germans to have to pay attention to us, their Prisoners. I decide to try for a pair of reading glasses.

Reading is a favourite leisure pastime for all of us. By overindulging, I begin to get a few headaches. In our rather crowded conditions, you tend to retire to the privacy of your bunk, for a good read. While the atmosphere is right, the lighting is not the best—especially in summer, when the Northern Hemisphere twilight, extends to 11.30 pm and beyond, before true darkness sets in. You tend to stretch your reading a little too long. I decide my headaches are caused by eyestrain.

There is no local eye Doctor, so this time I will have to be taken to the rather large, nearby town of Svitavy (Zwittau). This is better still. It means a train journey, and a more pleasurable outing. It will also give me a chance to show off my newly acquired Aussie uniform, probably the only one in Germany.

As soon as regular communications became established with my hometown, I have continually pleaded with my Mum, to try and send me a full Aussie Uniform in a clothing parcel. For a long time, only the regular, and very welcome items, such as underwear etc. came through. Then, at long last, comes a full Aussie Uniform.

This whim of mine has been sparked by the fact, that the various items allowed to be sent to us, are really of a military nature—so, why not a full uniform? I am hoping that the Parents of Prisoners of War Association, that my Mum has joined, will be able to have enough clout to get whatever permission is required to do it. While it doesn't work out this way, I do get my uniform. It is a gift from my mate, 'Pee Wee' White. He gives Mum his own uniform to send on to me. He is a member of my own Unit, and we have long been associated together, both in peacetime, and now in the regular Army. The Uniform comes complete with colour patches, badges, insignia, and even the regulation slouch hat. While our builds are pretty similar, he is a bit more robust than me. Coupled with my weight loss, it is too big. The job of taking it in is a bit beyond my skills. But, one of the Guards, old Kneifel, had been a tailor. I do a deal with him, in return for a payment in cigarettes. The finished job really looks smart.

The Interpreter, a Guard and myself, go to the rail station for the trip to Zwittau. What a difference this trip is. Instead of a closed cattle truck, I ride as a real passenger, in a real carriage, together with all the other passengers. In my uniform I am unique, and stand out like a sore thumb, slouch hat and all. The other travellers sidle up as close as they can, trying to make out who, or what, I am.

They can plainly see, that I am under escort. With the Interpreter in regulation British uniform, I am obviously some sort of prisoner. What kind, they cannot fathom? Half aloud they will try to read out from my shoulder badges, who I am. In their own fashion, it comes out—"Ows – tray – lya. Hah! Australia." Then there is animated talk, trying to identify, where such a place exists. To most Continentals, our country is as remote, and unheard of, as Siberia is to us.

With the Pommy Interpreter and myself, maintaining proper military bearing, the rather ordinary clad Guard, tags along, just behind. Whenever presenting ourselves publicly, it is a matter of principle, to put on, as good a show as we can. It impresses the ordinary citizens greatly, and the propaganda value is enormous. This is a really outstanding occasion.

My examination is routine, and without fuss. Then it is back to the station for the return journey. There has to be some standing around, waiting for connections. Again comes the jostling of people, trying to make out, who I am. Through it all, the Interpreter and myself, act as though we are oblivious of any furore, we might be causing.

The outing has been a great success, both politically, and in personal satisfaction. In due course, a pair of spectacles do arrive for me. They are a rather plain, steel-rimmed pair. I am never sure, whether they are a real help, or not.

At Bergs Mill, I am getting to know more about the people, as well as the place. There is a rather plump and pleasant Polish girl, of about sixteen, working here as a live-in maid. She is a forced worker, like most of her people, and we all come into daily contact with her. All Poles consider themselves to be prisoners of the Germans, as much as we are. Therefore, we are comrades in arms, whether civilians or soldiers.

For Maria, the maid, working conditions are quite good, and she has a lot of freedom of movement. This enables her to have other Polish girls, in a similar position, to visit with her, frequently. Through her, we get to know about half a dozen of them, quite well.

They all have their duties to attend to and, as long as their work is done, they seem to have a lot of free time to mix amongst themselves. As long as the "P", for Polish, cloth band is in place on their chest, there is no restriction on their moving about. Our Maria is the youngest of the group, with the others' ages ranging up to their mid-twenties.

As they are working for the well-to-do families in the town, they are well-fed and have access to some surplus food and cigarettes. Frugality has long become a way of life for them, as it has for us, and they never waste a scrap. They are in the habit of parcelling whatever they can get, cigarette butts included, and passing them on to some of us. One girl begins giving an occasional parcel to me.

Her name is Janina, which I think is rather pretty. But her friends call her by the abbreviation of Janka, (Yanka), which I think sounds much less attractive. We became acquainted one day when she visits Maria at the Berg Mill. I say "Hello" to Maria in passing, and she automatically introduces us.

She is about nineteen when first we meet, attractive and rather shy. Her voice is husky and throaty, a la Marlene Dietrich. Just to hear her speak, fascinates me. I make it my business to talk to her on the few occasions she is able to visit Maria. This isn't very often, for the family she works for, is a professional one, with a large house in the centre of the town. They have no contact with POWs at all.

I ask her how she came to be here. And, the story she tells me is typical of what has happened to the other Polish girls. Her mother had sent her down the street to get a loaf of bread from the bakery. While on the street, she is passed by a group of forced workers, being herded to the rail depot, for transport through to Germany. A Guard forces her into the group, despite her protests. To all intents and purposes, she just disappears. She ends up being sent to Mahrisch Trubau to work for the family she is now with. It was three months, before she was able to get a letter back to her home, letting them know what had happened to her.

As she tells me her story, tears well up in her big, brown eyes, and trickle down her cheeks. It is a sight to melt a heart of stone. With the occasional parcel, we both are a little awkward and embarrassed, at giving and receiving. I feel like discouraging her, although I am grateful for her help. I fear, that in the gathering of various items together, she might get caught, resulting in big trouble for herself. She regards that possibility as a non-event, not worth considering.

I suggest discontinuing the association to my muckers, who also share, but they won't have a bar of it. Frank, in particular, wants those cigarettes, butts and all, to continue. With the Red Cross and German issues, often having big gaps between them, it is vital that cigarette supplies be at their maximum, both for their use, and as a currency for trading.

Berg Mill is just about the biggest business in the town, and as such, has a sizable office. There are three females running it, and all are reasonably friendly. Two are married, with their husbands away, serving in the forces; and, the other is single, about nineteen. This one is a real Goddess. She is medium tall, outstandingly beautiful, and has a stunning figure. She is a brunette, with thick glossy hair, well below shoulder length. It is naturally wavy, and she has the slenderest waist, that any of us has seen.

Once, when she came through the mill on her duties, the German-in-Charge of the Big Gatter, happened to be putting some logs through. Part of his job is to take the mean diameter of each log, and enter it in the records. The instrument, he uses, is a rather large set of adjustable callipers. On the spur of the moment, he just turns and measures her waist. It is just nineteen centimetres. He holds the callipers up for all to see, and repeats the measurement aloud. She just shrugs and goes on her way.

On the occasions it becomes necessary for her to appear in the yard, the fellows hang around her like flies around a honeypot. They all claim that she is pining for a love affair. Each and every one of them, display their interest, and just hope that they will be the chosen one. There seems to be some truth in this belief, when one day she declares she can speak English. As usual, she is in the midst of a group of POW admirers, when she makes the claim. As they are prone to express their feelings about her, aloud in English, this makes them pause a little.

Ernie, a decent likeable Yorkshireman, a married man himself, speaks up on behalf of all the others. "OK then, say something."

She replies with, "I love you." All who hear are stunned into silence. These are the words they all want to hear—but for their individual ears only. Now what?

However, that is it, and is all she knows. She must have learned it at school, or picked up the phrase somewhere. It is pretty much an anticlimax, and the fellows just drift away. Just after this episode, she disappears for a while. We are told by some of the locals that she is on holidays for a couple of weeks. Then she returns, and we are told, again by the locals, that she is pregnant. "How come?" demand some of the fellows.

Those secret dreams they have nurtured, give them the right to know, so they believe. Their previously unattainable Goddess, has fallen to the dubious status of a tainted rose. How has this happened so quickly, and clearly with no male of any kind in the offing? It seems that an official Government decree, has asked for an increase in the population, and with the aim of maintaining the purity of the Aryan strain. As part of the program, suitable young German girls, are invited to volunteer themselves for a love-in, with an S.S. soldier whilst he is home on leave.

The stigma of illegitimacy will be removed for any offspring, by law. And, Adolf Hitler will be certified as Godfather. S.S. Units about to come home on leave, will be allowed to advertise in the papers for a companion to live in with them, usually for a fortnight. The Government has set up suitable flats, where the two people can live together. After a fortnight, he will return to the front, and she to her hometown.

For the S.S. men, it is something to look forward to, after the mauling they have been receiving on the Russian Front. For the girl, who answers the advertisement, it gives her a patriotic feeling of helping in the growth of her country.

Now that we become aware of this scheme, the ribald imaginations of the fellows run riot. The thought of a prolonged, sustained, officially sponsored, sexual session, seems full of merit. If only we can sell the idea to our people, once we get out of this damned place.

The movement of men, restless for change, sees the log hauling job, that Dave and I aspire to, becomes vacant. And we grab it. One of the chaps, who had worked here, was the Arbeit Chef, or Work Boss, and was the spokesman for the prisoners in their dealings with the Germans. Now that he has gone, somebody has to replace him, and the position falls to me.

The previous fellow was a tall Pommy Corporal, who has been on the job from the outset. With much confrontation in the beginning, he has had to maintain a fairly high profile. As a result, he is well known to all in charge, including the boss, Berg himself. The Pommy Corporal is a very decent bloke, who had maintained his dealings with dignity and fairness and, as a result, had gained quite a measure of respect from all of them.

Originally, our party had been an all-volunteer, all NCO's one, which allowed us to gain pretty good conditions. Since then, Privates or non-NCOs, have been replacing those leaving, for various reasons. Conditions have remained the same, although the personnel have changed. As Corporal, I am now one of the more senior on the job. And, as it is the Pommy Corporal's work position that I have moved into, I sort of, just inherit the job.

There is a Sergeant senior to me—Togo the big half Maori. But he goes out to the forests each day with the timber jinker crew. As he is away all day, he can't very well act on the Prisoners behalf. So it has to be me. As things have been running smoothly for so long now, I decide to keep a low profile, and only come forward, if needs be.

There are a few chores that go with the job, and which I have to administer. I have to run the roster that supplies the gang for loading the occasional rail truck. This hated task keeps the men at it, until the job is done—hence the roster to ensure that everybody gets a fair deal.

Another chore is to notify the office daily, if there are any absentees, due to sickness etc. The methodical Germans keep their records in order, at all times, and this is part of the process. I have to pass this information on to one of the two married office workers. She is a rather nice woman, and is the older of the two, by a couple of years. She is cursed with very poor eyesight. To combat this, she is forced to wear very thick lensed glasses, all the time. Without her glasses, I think she may be quite attractive. She speaks a little English, and is keen to try it out, whenever she can. As her duties keep her confined, pretty well within the office, most of her dealings have to be with the Work Boss. This is now my job and we become reasonably friendly.

With me keeping a low profile, it takes a little time for the Germans to realise that the original Work Boss is no longer with them. Berg himself only finds out, when an infrequent rail truck arrives for loading. He comes looking for the Pommy Corporal to notify him that he needs a loading crew.

As is his usual procedure, Berg comes into the mill, tells the nearest prisoner to find the Pommy Corporal, and inform him that he, Berg, wishes to speak to him. The prisoner informs Berg that the Pommy Corporal is no longer with us. There is a new Work Boss, who is me. Instead of sending for me, Berg comes looking himself. He informs me of his requirements, and I agree to have a crew ready for the job. In this way, he gets to know me, and I him.

In keeping with his profile of being the most important and influential man in town, he keeps aloof and distant from our blokes, at all times. The fact that he personally seeks me out in the first instant, is quite a condescension on his part. And we, the prisoners, are impressed by the significance of this act. In his dealings with me, he always is courteous and dignified, and never overbearing.

A couple of months after the beginning of my tenure as Work Boss, I enter the office after arrival at work, as usual, to inform the young woman about the day's absentees. I find her dazed and bewildered, and really uncomprehending. The other girls inform me, she has just received word, that her husband has become a POW of the British.

She then plies me with questions. "Where will he be taken? How will he be treated? Will he be properly fed? What is the likelihood of her ever seeing him again?" It gives me some insight into what my people had gone through, when I was taken. And I had prolonged their agony by going on the loose, with nobody knowing whether I was alive, or dead.

I cannot truthfully answer any of her questions. I just don't know. No Army ever really plans for prisoners—they just happen. I mumble lots of assurances, relying wholly on the British sense of fair play. I scuttle out of there, as soon as I decently can. I know, that any prisoner's chances of a fair go, is totally reliant upon the individual enemies, with whom he comes in contact.

For some days after, she keeps seeking reassurances from me, as if, in some way, I will be able to guarantee his safety. All I can do is tell her to hang on, until she receives a letter from him, through the International Red Cross. When one finally does come through, it doesn't tell her much. Still, she seems to think that, somehow, I have been able to do something, and she becomes almost sisterly to me.

We are notified from Lamsdorf, of an Official change in our camp title. Instead of Stalag VIIIB, it is now to be known as Stalag 344. We are mystified, trying to think of a reason for the change. All we can come up with, is that, too many adverse reports must have filtered back home, and the Germans are trying to clean up their image.

That repatriation and prisoner exchange gig, has finally taken place. Maybe that has had something to do with it. News of that event, slowly filters through to us, after the happening. All the earlier furore and excitement, has long since faded, and we accept it as just another news item.

CHAPTER 15

# Working Party Days at Mahrisch Trubau: Episode 3

WE ARE NOW IN A period of relatively calm stability. Our situation seems as if it can remain this way, for a long time. It seems that, in our calm little backwater, life will just proceed serenely, as though the War will never touch these parts.

True, the Russians have managed to achieve a small measure of success, while our blokes have managed to clean up North Africa. The Yanks have arrived, and are making loud noises, like the world beaters they, undoubtedly, think they are. They have even managed to make a landing in Italy.

Still, it is painfully slow stuff. Every move that our lot makes, the Germans seem to be able to stop in its tracks. We have envisaged our lot making a quick dash across the Channel, then a lightning campaign of a couple of weeks, followed by a total collapse of the German forces. This just doesn't seem likely to happen.

In contrast to what the Germans have achieved, our side's efforts seem ineffectual. German forces had swept across country after country, in four to five days. True, they had the advantage of surprise, and those countries unpreparedness. Given the, now, changed situation, it still seems reasonable to us, for our mob to be able to speed things up, considerably.

The general feeling amongst the locals, however, is that this is just of a temporary holdup. And, at any moment, their forces will resume their spectacular thrusts, as of old.

Looking at our chances, we weigh up the opposing forces, as best we can, with what we know. Taking the Battle of Crete as a yardstick, we feel that we are better than the Germans. We were sure that we had beaten them, when given the order to fall back. What had beaten us was the lack of supplies and equipment. As that situation ought now to have been reversed, then we should be on top.

On our side, we know the Poms, the Kiwis and the Aussies. We have no worries there. We don't know much about the Russians, and less about the Yanks. The Russians are a bit of an enigma. They had signed a Treaty with the Germans, before fighting, which had seemed an advantage to both of them. However, when fighting commenced, the Germans had gone through the Russians, like a hot knife through butter. Now, after a couple of spectacular battles, the Russians seem able to match the Germans. They seem able to do this by mass of manpower, and relying on our side for their armament. We feel that, if the arms supply keeps up, they will prove a match.

As for the Yanks, we don't know what to think. We are well aware of their great capacity to turn out the hardware, and that this has been a great factor in Britain's ability to fight on. Still, in the First World War, as well as this one, the fighting had been going on for a couple of years, before they had come in. Now, with Japan taking them on in the Pacific, and having plenty of first up success, can the Yanks maintain much of a pressure on this front? Had their First World War success been because they were fresh, while their foe was almost on his knees? Our assessment of the probabilities has us greatly perturbed. We feel the Yanks might prove the big difference. However, the European situation has to be settled first. To us, any other approach, is unthinkable.

What about these Yanks? Does anybody know how they perform? One of our fellows, a Pom Commando, says he knows a bit about them. He had come in contact with them in the Desert, just before he was captured.

This fellow's Unit of about three hundred strong, were holding down a very quiet sector of the Western Desert. Nothing much had happened for several weeks, when they receive word that they are to be relieved by an

American outfit. Just on dusk, a great flotilla of jeeps, trucks and vehicles of various kinds, comes charging up, amidst clouds of desert sand. They are about three thousand strong.

The Pom's Commando mob, are to pull out the next morning. The Yanks ask if they have any unusual activity to report. The Commandos tell them there is nothing, and everything around there is very quiet. Then, as an afterthought, the Poms say, "Well, there is one thing of slight interest. There's this ancient Italian bomber plane that comes over every morning just after sunup, on a reconnaissance mission. It makes the trip every day, and flies very low, always at the same time, and always on the same flightpath. We Commandos ignore it, and just keep our heads down, until it has gone. The Italians don't know, that we are here."

"Right," say the Yanks. "We'll prepare a reception committee." They get on the blower, and during the night a heavy Ack-Ack Unit rolls up, and rings the whole area with big guns. When the old bomber lumbers over at first light, every gun opens up and blows it clean out of the sky.

There is instant pandemonium. Every single one of the Yanks pile onto vehicles, and charge across the desert to where the plane has crashed, about a quarter of a mile away. In minutes, all that is left has been ripped to pieces, as all of them grab something to take home as a souvenir.

This doesn't sound too encouraging. We just hope for a bit more commitment, when the serious stuff is at hand. Still, we are pretty much on top in the air. We, who had suffered so much because of the lack of aircover, know only too well how vital this aspect is. The sustained bombing programmes have disturbed the Germans greatly. It has caused the closure of some POW Stalags in the northwest, particularly the Stalags for Naval personnel around the Hamburg area. A couple of these sailors have found their way to our party at Mahrisch Trubau.

At sea, the Germans still seem to have a formidable Navy. We hope that ours can match it, at least. Convoys and goods, still seem to be getting through, so we have high hopes there. To show that our Navy is at least still active, one of our sailor comrades tells us of the raid on St Nazaire, where he was captured.

The German Pocket Battleships have been creating havoc with the Atlantic convoys from America. With their formidable firepower, they outgun practically anything Britain has. But, if she can get at those ships from the air, then Britain will have a distinct advantage. As the ships range far out into the Atlantic, they are out the bomber range. If the planes cannot get to the ships, then a way has to be found to bring the ships to the planes. If their Battleships can be forced to use the Channel, then our land based planes will have a field day. So, the bright idea is devised for the raid on St Nazaire.

It seems that a Battleship can only operate for three months at a time, before having to be docked for cleaning. While there are excellent facilities in Germany, this will require a dangerous trip up the Channel. The alternative is to use French port facilities along their Atlantic coast. The only drydock capable of handling such a ship is at St Nazaire. Destroy this facility, and the Battleships will be forced to come up the Channel.

Reconnaissance, and intelligence reports, conclude that the raid cannot be done effectively by airstrikes. So it will have to be a Naval Commando job. The planners go to work. Their idea is to fool the Germans into thinking, that the Commando Force is one of their own patrols, returning to port. These patrols are of a Destroyer and nine or ten Motor Torpedo boats. Upon leaving and returning to port, the Destroyer will be seen leading, with the MTBs in single file behind. In keeping to this pattern, it is hoped the Commandos will be well inside defences, before being discovered.

There are a few tricky bits. The aim is for the Destroyer to crash itself, well up into the mouth of the dock. Hopefully, a massive charge will destroy both the ship and the dock. But to get into the right position, the ship will have to navigate a shallow marshy area, normally too shallow for its draught. To do this, the tides will have to be right, and much of the guns and armaments will have to be stripped from her, to lighten the ship. With no guns and no ability to fight, it's practically a suicide mission.

Then, for the MTBs to reach their target position presents a problem, as it is well beyond their normal range. It means that they will have to be towed most of the way. With their crews and the heavily armed Commandos aboard, this will be a most miserable trip.

The port itself is heavily fortified with masses of troops everywhere. It will have to be a complete surprise for any chance of success. There comes the night, and it is just that. The fake patrol penetrates well inside the port, before the Germans become aware of the daring raid.

Our Sailor comrade is an Oerlikon gunner on one of the MTBs.

"An Oerlikon gun—What the hell is that?" we ask.

He says, "It is a Swedish made quick-firing, cannon type gun." Gosh! It seems that current technology is getting away from us.

Two of the Commandos, aboard his boat, are assigned the task of cutting off a barracks of three thousand Germans, from crossing a narrow bridge. To do this, they have a Bren gun and some hand grenades.

The raid is a success. In the fighting, our comrade is wounded, his craft sunk, and he becomes a prisoner. The delayed charges explode about midday next day. With the Destroyer and the Dock subsequently destroyed, the German Battleships are now forced to use the Channel, and the rest is history.

Inside information, such as this, gives us much heart. But, the fact that we are still a long way from getting out of here, frustrates us greatly. It seems that, while on one hand our people distinctly have the ability, on the other hand, transferring that ability into action, is a slow painful process. Meanwhile, we will just have to sweat it out, the best way we can.

We continue our daily routine, immersing ourselves in our standard activities—trading for food, keeping abreast of the situation, and doing a little work with a lot of loafing, while on the job. Our leisure time is taken up with cards, reading, cleaning, washing etc. We do ask the guards to see if they can find a local woman to do some washing for us, without much success. We had hoped that the fact that we can supply proper soap for the job, while their own supplies are practically nil, might be enough inducement to arouse somebody's interest. But nothing much comes of it. This is one chore we will happily drop, if we can.

Now, a Pommy serviceman from one of the Guards Units lands amongst us. He announces that he is hell bent on creating some sexual activity for himself, with some of the girls working locally as forced labour. We tell him that he has picked the wrong party to come to, as there is none of that sort of activity here. He is undeterred, and adamant that he will look-see, for himself.

Doubtless, spurred on by tales of such activity occurring in industrial complexes, where fair-sized groups of both sexes work side by side, this bloke has decided to involve himself in this kind of action. The trouble is that this is a rural township, and there is none of those manufacturing complexes, around here.

He seems to consider himself free to pursue his own activities, regardless of the rest of us. Nevertheless, it has to be brought home to him that he is on his own, as far as we are concerned. We have achieved a situation of relative low profile surveillance from our Guards. It is vital that this shall continue, and not be risked by some damn foolish, nightly tomcatting, by him. When it is necessary to leave here, we expect a breakout will be simple. If he is allowed to have his head and is caught, (which we consider a certainty because of his antics), then procedures here will be tightened up considerably.

Somewhat chastened, he modifies his attitude, to the extent, that he will devise his own method of getting out of the place, as distinct to those places, we consider group property. Also, he promises to be careful in setting up any trysts.

He manages to get one of the other fellows interested enough to help him in his preparations. They get hold of some hacksaw blades, and go to work on the steel bars guarding a back window. The bars are about threequarters of an inch thick, and the job requires a fair bit of hard going. They accomplish the job, on their own, without help from anybody else. When finished, they doctor the cuts, then invite anybody to inspect the job and pass judgement. As a former escapee, I am invited also. Search as I may, I cannot detect a thing, even though the approximate area is pointed out to me.

They have cut a bar completely through, top to bottom. It is now possible to grasp that section, and pull it away. The hole left, is big enough for any of us to slip through, easily. The doctoring holds the bar in place, so that the time needed is only a fraction of a second.

We are impressed and, with a mutual softening of attitudes, it is decided that this route will be held back for a probable final breakout. In the meantime, if he deems it necessary to go out at night, he can use one of the other easy routes—such as the toilet block window, which cuts out the need for re-doctoring.

Now that some rapport has been achieved, we ask him why he has chosen to come to our party, when, obviously, it is not what he has been looking for. He says he just grabbed the first opening that was on offer, and he wanted to get away from Lamsdorf. He claims the place is now ruled by razor gangs. He asserts that groups have banded together and, with the use of cutthroat razors as weapons, they virtually rule the place. We have heard nothing about this sort of caper, despite being privy to the latest information from there. Camp Leader Arthur's regular trips back there, have brought no mention of any such happenings.

We know it is possible to buy cutthroat razors, with German approval. They can be purchased with camp money, and it is one way of getting rid of the stuff. It seems that these gangs just take what they want. Our Guardsman, obviously, believes what he has told us. But to us, well, we just don't know.

The Guardsman and his helper, do try one night time outing, some months later. They claim to have had a tryst with two Polish girl farm workers, whom we haven't heard of. We see these girls later, so it seems they do in fact exist. The tale of the night's happenings is quite lurid. But, as it only happens once, we are inclined to disbelieve it.

One day, at work, I am moving a log with a Pisa, a wooden lever pole. In doing so, I manage to jam my finger against a steel machinery fixture. My nail is torn away and left hanging. Quickly, I bandage it, and, when I return home, I show it to our medical orderly, Sergeant Jack. It is pretty sore, and angry looking. It is obvious, that the torn piece of nail, should come off. Jack decides, it is a doctor's job, and he makes the necessary arrangements with the Guards.

Again we dress in our best gear, and our party of four, M.O. Jack, the Interpreter, a Guard and myself, make the rail journey to Zwittau. It is a military type surgery where we attend, consisting of a large room, that is quite crowded. There are a lot of German servicemen lined up in the passageway. The Doctor, the only one in attendance, is a rather short, tubby man. He is dressed in a well-tailored uniform, and is bustling about, giving sharp orders to the patients.

Our party is ushered into the room, where a place is made for us on one side. Interested in the proceedings, we look around, and notice another party of a Guard and Prisoner. This one is a Russian, with both hands heavily bandaged.

The Doctor is attending the German soldiers first. As he calls their name, they will spring to attention, march through the hallway door, then stand to attention in front of him. One such man, recites his problem to the Doctor, and in reply to the doctor's sharp question, opens his mouth and points inside. From my position, I am able to see a large blister, about the size of a shilling, on the back of his throat. The Doctor sharply orders the soldier to open wider, while standing in front of his patient, with both hands by his side.

Suddenly the Doctor makes a quick lunge inside the patient's mouth, with one hand. It is only then, I notice that his hand holds a scalpel. Still standing at attention, the soldier's eyes almost pop out of his head, as the Doctor lances the blister with one quick thrust. The Doctor instantly orders him on his way, and the poor man stumbles out, the best way he can.

The Doctor now decides to attend to the Russian, and orders him forward. He orders the Russian to hold both hands, pointing upward, in front of the Doctor's face. The Doctor then proceeds to unwrap the bandaged hands, each in turn. The wounds are several days old, and the blood-soaked bandages are set solid. They have to be torn away in sharp tugs, layer by layer.

The Russian is a little man in a bedraggled uniform. He just stands there with an expressionless face, and speaks not a word. He seems completely devoid of any feeling. When the unwrapping is completed, we can see that he has lost most of his fingers on both hands. We are told that he had caught them in a brickmaking machine. All the Doctor does is put fresh bandages on, without dressings, while the Russian continues to hold both hands in front of him, as before. Then he is sent on his way.

Then it is my turn. I am thinking, "My God, what have I got myself into, here?" I would gladly have left, but it is too late. I need not have worried for, with me, he could not have been gentler. The fact that he regards me as "English" seems to put him on his metal. It seems he has to prove, he can do a good job. He carefully removes the torn piece of nail, leaving the quick only half-covered, with what is left. He carefully bandages it, and we are on our way.

I have several days off as a result, although my hand is in fairly good shape. Then, as the finger starts to recover, the quick starts to grow over the stub of the nail, that had been left. Jack reckons that this will have to come off too. This time, it is decided that a minor operation will be needed. It will have to be done in a hospital. There is a small one in our town, run by, what seems to be, Roman Catholic nursing Sisters.

With the appointment having been made, our party of four set out for the hospital. As it is local, this time, no train trip is involved. We will march there and back. We know a fair bit about Mahrisch Trubau, by now, but the hospital is something we haven't known about. It is pretty small as hospitals go, but enough to cater for a small town. A Sister meets us at the entrance, by opening the main door and ushering us in. She is dressed in a dark, Nun-like habit, with large white, stiff and starched collar and headdress, with wide "wings" on either side.

Illnesses and injuries are an unspoken worry to us, all the time. There is a fear that treatment and standards may be inadequate. After all, we are POWs, and as such can't expect much. Our great dread is being incapacitated, when the time comes to get out of this place. To be left behind, for any reason, is something we just cannot bear to think about. So, I anxiously face up to my minor operation, hoping sincerely that it will remain just that, and go no further.

The first thing I notice about the Sister, is that she is wearing rubber gloves—the type you wear as protection for operations. She appears to have been working, before she meets us at the door. She does not remove them. She handles door knobs, shakes hands, and whatever, with the gloves still on. I immediately wonder what their postoperative rate of infection might be. She gives me the impression of putting her gloves on in the morning, and not taking them off until the end of the day. She seems to think the gloves are for her protection, and not the patients.

I am whisked into a fair-sized room by the Sister, and lay prone on a bare, metal table. There is some equipment, but, otherwise, the room seems pretty bare. Quickly, I am given a whiff of ether. Seemingly, in the next instant, I am being helped to my feet, and stumbling from the room. With Jack and the Interpreter supporting me, we are ushered out the front door by the smiling Nun, still with her gloves on.

I am gagging and stumbling, and wanting to be sick, while Jack cheerfully comments that it is a normal reaction after a whiff of ether. He predicts that, by the time we reach home, most of the effects will be gone. My finger is bandaged and feeling rather numb. So, for the moment, I can't tell what shape it is in, or how sore it will be. Future dressings will be taken care of by Jack.

Of course, after a "surgical" operation, I will have to remain off work, until the wound recovers. This means that I will be confined to barracks for a while. As the numbness wears off, the throbbing starts. By nightfall, it is giving me the gripes. I have a hell of a night, and am glad when daylight comes.

For the first few days, with Jack regularly dressing my wound, I am pretty miserable. With most of the fellows, other than the cleaning staff, at work, time drags, and just about sends me up the wall. Then a change in the military situation gives me something to focus on.

We have managed to manipulate the Guards into believing that their radio is faulty, and has to be serviced regularly. We, of course, have an expert, who will fix it for nothing. As a gesture of goodwill, this expert, who, in fact, does not exist, is supposed to be a member of the cleaning staff. It is this fellow's habit of taking the set into our quarters to tinker with it, after his morning's work is done. With everybody at work, there seems no harm in this arrangement. It is just a coincidence that both the tinkering time, and the BBC broadcasts from England, happen to coincide. I am able to take note of the news, and read it out as a regular bulletin. Our "expert" will re-doctor the set, and return it to the Guard Room. Tinkering involves the loosening a couple of terminals, so that the static becomes pretty bad.

The military news is about the Anzio landings. Our mob have been finding it very tough going against the Germans in Italy. In an endeavour to speed things up, they have made a seaborne invasion, landing behind the enemy front, at Anzio. Supposedly, this will cause the Front to collapse, the Germans to be routed, and forced into a full scale retreat.

Actually, the Germans counter so effectively that, for a long time, it looks as if this invasion will be repulsed completely. The confusion of claim and counterclaim, coupled with completely unfamiliar placenames, keeps me busy recording, and serving it up to the blokes.

I am in the middle of a bulletin at a lunchtime break, when the Corporal in charge of the Guard comes in and wants to know what is going on. The unusual quiet, while the blokes listen to me, has attracted his attention. When he spots me reading from a sheet of paper, he is doubly suspicious. All regular announcements are normally made by Camp Leader Arthur. His queries are diverted by our Interpreter, luckily, without raising any suspicions.

We always study the information that comes our way, very seriously. Our situation is such, that we have to. We are too experienced to be taken in by the official guff. Most of our energies are directed towards trying to estimate what is the true situation.

In due course, my finger recovers sufficiently for me to return to work. I am damn glad too. It has healed well, and there is no sign of infection. The news continues to flow, of course, but the regular bulletins cease. The Italian situation now appears to be at a stalemate. Neither side seems to be able to get an advantage over the other. Once again the mighty push, that may set us free, has come to nothing. It is worrying too, for once again, we are faced with the onset of winter.

In our hearts we know that winter will see a slowing down of military Operations. While much fighting will still be done, it will be the summer before anything of real significance can be achieved. There's a bit of urgency in our assessment of the situation. We talk seriously of what may happen when the end comes. Either, our side will roll into town one day, and we will be free; or, we will have to move out on the march, when the fighting nears. If they roll into town, there will be no sweat. But, if we have to move out, we realise that we are poorly equipped to go on an extended march.

In the process of our capture, escaping, and moving about, most of us are without essential and vital kit items. I am short of a haversack, a water bottle, and a knife suitable enough to cut bread, and open cans. We turn our energies toward rectifying this situation.

If we do march out, which way will we go? It will be either East to the Russians, or West to the Yanks and British. We decide that West is the way home and, even if the Russians look like making it through first, that's the way we will go. We do not consider our Guards in this scenario, at all. Providing they decide to move us, in the direction we wish to go, we will allow them to think that they are in charge. If not, we will just pack them off quietly, or allow them to tag along with us, until they drop out. We are confident there will be no violence, and are certain of our ability to have them do what we want—especially in the kind of chaos, we expect to be ruling at the time.

Now everybody gets busy, with needle and thread, to make those items, he is short of. By utilising old uniforms and blankets etc., he does, as best a job, he can. I manage to get hold of a suitable bottle to carry water. Most of us take the time and trouble to make a good job of our sewing. We realise that, once we get out of here, we will have practically no chance of making running repairs. So our work has to be good, right from the outset.

The knife is a different matter. I will have to make one up, somehow. It has to be good enough for what I want, but without looking like a weapon. The boys at the Home Mill are on pretty good terms with the Engineer there. Norm feels that he will be able to persuade him, to make up what I want, provided I draw up some sort of a diagram, for him to work to. This is great news. He has access to materials and tooling, as well as the knowhow. Anything I might try myself, would be hard going, and at best, just a makeshift item.

The Engineer makes the knife, exactly as I want. He fashions it from a piece of high grade steel, used on wood cutting saws, and puts a nice edge on it. Norm fashions a handle from a piece of beechwood. With two rivets through, it is light and strong. I treasure the thing and, hopefully, I will take it all the way back home with me.

With all these "just in case" preparations going on, a sort of infectious fever, spreads amongst the blokes. Some of them, at the Home Mill, decide that they have to get into some sort of practice, of what to do, when they arrive home. They decide to practice walking down the gangplank, and greeting their families.

One of the medium-sized outbuildings there, is used to store wood scraps and blocks, for use in household fires. Its floor is about four feet above ground level, and is reached by a sloping ramp, and through a wide, open doorway. They fill an old sack with wood blocks, to represent their kitbags, sling it over their shoulders, and stand in the doorway—supposedly, at the head of the gangway of their imaginary liner.

The other blokes spread in a semicircle at the foot of the ramp, representing the welcome home committee. The bloke, at the head of the "gangplank", begins to wave and call out, "Hello Ma, Hello Pa," while the welcoming committee, cheer and clap. He walks down the gangway, calling to sisters and brothers, and to be greeted by much backslapping, and more wild cheering. Their performances are very enthusiastic.

The German civilian workmen look on in amazement. They can't make head nor tail of it, and are quite sure the blokes have all gone mad. The civilians' assessment isn't all that far from the truth, with few, if any of us, able to claim to be normal. The wild, enthusiastic, practice run is a great relief for pent up feelings. Afterwards, a mixture of poignancy, pathos and heartache, brings on a sad opposite reaction.

The local German population is quite unconcerned about the direction of the War, and just carry on as usual. We seem to be the only ones concerned. Things are so normal that Berg sees fit to pause one day, on his way to the mill, and have a few words of conversation with me. He indicates that he is happy with our work and, if we are prepared to stay on after the war, he will be happy to employ us. He assures me that the wages will be good, and there will be no problem with accommodation. I just tell him, "No thanks. We will not be staying. We will be going home."

It is a totally surprising conversation, initiated by Berg himself. It is all very amicable, with no attempt at point scoring by either of us. His approach is of an employer to a prospective employee. There is not the slightest suggestion of a German captor to a forced prison labourer. As such, it is quite a decent gesture by him. It also points out that he can see a change in circumstances and, at the cessation of hostilities, Germany will be in control. He goes on his way with a sort of tacit feeling, that the conversation will be renewed, when peace returns.

My feelings are decidedly mixed. I have to appreciate that Berg's offer is for an assured future. He seems to think that here, in a new country, it will now be mine by adoption. However, my whole being is primed for the fact, that I am going home. The only point in question is, when? There just isn't any point of coming together, for such totally opposed points of view.

I recall the wistful looks on the faces of some of the locals, as they look at faded photos of Russian women left behind, after stints as POWs in the First World War. There is the suggestion that, if they could have a rethink, they may have stayed. Berg's offer puts me in the same boat. At least, it doesn't offer regular female companionship and a booze up, such as I had been offered by the Greeks near Stratoni. Presumably, we will have to look after this sort of thing, ourselves.

The reaction to Berg's offer, amongst the rest of the fellows, is as mixed as mine. We do not know whether to be pleased or insulted. We are quietly conscious of the fact that we are working at only a quarter of our capacity and, at the type of work that anybody can do. We have insisted that we will stick to labouring work, only; whereas, the Germans have ensured that their civilians always handle any machinery. Could it be that Berg senses that we are capable of much better? Or is he genuinely satisfied with what we are doing now? Whatever the reason, it just highlights how completely, we have come to be accepted, as very much a part of everyday life.

The decision of not to be involved with things mechanical, is general. However, it is, more or less, up to each individual. Our reasoning is that, if we do this job, then a man will be released for military duties. As long as what we do seems to be non-war production, then our labouring work doesn't matter. This complicated reasoning leaves a few grey areas, and often an uneasy compromise.

Now, a situation arises that is hard to define. The crew, who brings the logs from the forest to the mill, consists of two Germans and two prisoners. One German drives the tractor that pulls the loaded jinker. The other is the Loading Boss. The two prisoners help in the loading. Each day they will climb aboard and head out to the forest, and then return with a good load. It is essential to keep the mill going. They have worked together for some time, and are a pretty harmonious bunch.

The prisoners are two New Zealanders. One is Togo, and the other a Maori named Jackie. With just the one load per day, it is almost idyllic. It entails a long slow ride through the countryside, a leisurely lunch in the forest, then the long slow return trip, in time to finish for the day.

One day the tractor driver isn't able to come to work. This creates a minor crisis, bringing about a situation, that Togo and Jackie cannot tolerate. They cannot stand the thought of being confined to the mill, after the comparative freedom of their trips to the forest. Togo says, "No worries—grab another prisoner to make up the crew, and I'll drive."

The Germans baulk for a while, unsure of whether it will be safe to entrust the tractor to Togo. The Loading Boss has seen Togo do a bit of manoeuvring with the tractor, out at the loading site. He urges them to agree. Reluctantly, they do; and, for everybody, it is a case of wait and see.

At round about the usual time, the tractor and jinker heave into sight. It turns into the yard, with Togo perched casually in the driver's seat. The Loading Boss busies himself in the usual unloading procedures, helped by his offsiders. When all is finished, a knot of both Germans and prisoners gather around to query how things have gone. Togo's verdict is an airy, "Piece of cake." The Loading Boss and the others, heartily agree.

The regular driver, an older man, misses so much time that Togo comes to be considered as the regular driver. The position of the extra man, needed to make up the crew, is so highly prized, that it has to be rotated among those, who can be spared. As Work Boss, I, naturally, have to "force" myself to take a turn, and spend a blissful happy day, away in the quiet of the forest.

The forest sections cover all the hilly areas around, and close to the town. All timber is selectively felled, then hauled to a loading area at the forest's edge. On my day, we journey to this area, load up, have lunch, then return. Nominally, it is the Loading Boss who is in charge, dictating how the logs will be stacked. Actually, it is Togo who calls the shots, and he really knows his stuff. The work of loading, under the skilled Loading Boss, isn't too hard, and allows a pleasing testing of one's own strength. Everything is done in a leisurely fashion.

Occasionally, the tractor crews arrive back late at the mill. Then the Loading Boss will escort the prisoners back home. On my day we are on time, and I return home in the usual fashion, with the rest of the fellows.

It is coming into summer, when the great and exciting news, hits us. The Allies have landed in France. The long awaited Second Front has finally been established. All those impregnable defences, set up along the French coast, of which Rommel had been in charge, have been overcome. With cries from the Russians, for many months past, to get on with it, and take the pressure off their beleaguered Armies, it has seemed, this may never happen. Now it is a fact. This, surely, will be the end. In a few weeks, maybe a month at the most, it will be all over, and we will be free.

We are agog with excitement, and pleased that our preparations for moving out, are well in hand. On the job, we are a little bit cocky with the locals. For their part, they are a little bit concerned, but not too worried. They have been through years of outstanding conquests by their forces, and believe this to be just a setback—a serious one perhaps, but they feel no cause for alarm.

We steel ourselves for the severing of our lifeline, our Red Cross food parcels. We know that urgent military rail traffic will take priority, and make it virtually impossible for them to get through. We will conserve what we can of our tin goods, to carry with us, if we are forced to march out.

Then follows this slow agonising wait—as first days, then weeks and finally months begin to slip by, while our mob are still contained in the small perimeter, they have established. Why haven't they got moving? Militarily, we know our Forces will have to build up arms and supplies before advancing. But they have landed so decisively, we cannot believe it will take so long. What if the unthinkable happens, and they are pushed back into the sea? We hardly can bear to think about it.

Slowly, our life here drops back into the old normal pattern. The interference in food parcel arrivals, is now being interpreted as the normal erratic thing, we are accustomed to—and not the beginning of the end. As needs dictate, we cull over our meagre hoard of cans. In the end, what is being held in reserve, by almost everybody, is canned salmon. Good food it is, but it is also the most difficult for us to conjure into a meal.

Camp Leader Arthur's usual commuting back to Lamsdorf, is awaited with interest. Maybe, there will be some clarification from that quarter. But they are no better informed than us, except that a couple of things are in view there. For years, the Prisoner Administration at Lamsdorf, has been pressuring the German Administration, for permission to dig out a swimming pool within the Prison Camp grounds. And, for just as long, the Germans have refused to consider it. Both sides know without stating so, that large earth moving jobs can be used as a mask for illegal tunnelling. Now, the Germans have agreed for the project to go ahead.

There is no apparent reason for their sudden change of heart. However, with the Prisoners hoping the situation in France is the beginning of the end, there doesn't seem much point in going ahead with the project. But, after so much urging, the feeling is that they may as well get on with it.

Another item at Lamsdorf concerns the great wealth of musical talent, confined there. With some of the world's best musicians having formed symphony orchestras, jazz groups, string quartets etc., pressure has been mounting for permission to allow some of this music to be taken out to the working parties, for their entertainment.

The Germans consider themselves great lovers of music, and have a soft spot for it. They had baulked at the idea of prisoners, although under escort, travelling fairly freely around the countryside. They now, grudgingly, decide to allow some entertainment on a limited scale. A concert for several of the work parties in our area, is to be given in the near future.

With this kind of news, obviously, the Germans are just carrying on as usual. With no signs from them of any change, despite the landings in France, it seems that for us, life is to continue on, pretty much as usual.

The arrangements for the concert are, that it will be an after work, evening concert, in a nearby town. With half a dozen work parties scattered around the area, each will be transported, to and from the venue. As it will be too late for the musicians to return to Lamsdorf, they will be billeted at the working party barracks for the night.

We generally, are unaware that other British parties are nearby, and we welcome the chance of a get-together. But, when it comes to a night's billeting, we find the others most uncooperative. It has been presumed that groups, of four or five, will be taken care of by each party. But each, in turn, argue that it is out of the question for them. The reasons advanced are overcrowding, strain on food resources, etc. With all POW activities, there are always hidden motives, as well as the obvious ones. For we all know, this caper may be a cover for something that may be vital. In any case, the effort deserves better than a cancellation.

With the imminent prospect of the concert being cancelled, our lot decide that we will take them all in. After all, it will be for one night only, and we can surely put up with that.

On the night, we are taken to a medium-sized hall, with a stage and a curtain, at one end. The group of about twenty musicians are assembled on stage, busy tuning and preparing their instruments. The POW patrons, pretty well, fill the hall, with their Guard contingents scattered round as well. Then it is time to start, and the music begins.

Everybody likes music of some kind, with each having their preference. For myself, I consider I am about middle of the road, being fond of light stuff, but not too much into classical. These serious men, bury themselves into their music. They put on a performance that transports us, and just carries us away. There are no ribald sketches, just music. And, it gets to us, like nothing else can. Each retreats into the only private domain, he has left—his mind. Those pent up longings swell up, the frustrations, the hopes—all are buoyed, by the ebb and flow of the music. To me, it is just about the most memorable event, that I have experienced.

All too soon, it is over. We have to snap to, and come back to reality. The various parties climb into their transport, and depart for home. We are delayed a little, while the musicians pack their gear. We all jam in as best we can, and are last to leave.

Still under the spell of the music, we cannot treat these men, as we would any other prisoner. Although they are in the same predicament as us, they are, somehow, kind of special. When we arrive home, we practically fall over ourselves, trying to be hospitable, and make them comfortable.

We show them through our quarters, and the first thing, that takes their eye, is our bath. Wistfully, they say that they haven't seen one, since they left home. "Would you like a bath? No problem, we will start heating the copper. It will take about an hour. Then you can each have one, in turn." Willing hands set to work, to get this chore underway.

While waiting, brew kits are produced for tea, coffee, or cocoa—whatever our guests prefer. Beds are allocated. As we have to cater for an extra twenty-one, it will be a tight squeeze; but not for our guests. We will double up, while they will each have a space to themselves.

Upon being given a bunk, one of their number, a Doctor, gives us a lesson in sleeping comfort. Without saying a word, he takes a cake of soap from his pack, folds back the blankets, and begins dabbing here and there on the exposed paillasse. He is removing the fleas. They are pressed into the soap and cannot escape.

We are pretty happy with the cleanliness of our quarters, and feel sure we have the fleas and lice beaten. We are unaware that we still have a problem, and are surprised at the number of captures he makes. Before settling in for the night, first one musician, and then another, tends to his instrument. There is a cleaning of a mouthpiece here, a tending of string tension there, followed by a final tootling of the scales, before putting it away.

In our close packed quarters, the musical notes draw us, irresistibly, like moths to a flame. A silent knot gathers round the man with the instrument. With this encouragement, after the scales, he will carry on a bit further. His mate, alongside, will join in harmony with his instrument, and, once more, we are wrapped in beautiful music.

Groups of three or four musicians, surrounded by a close ring of silent listeners, are spread right around our quarters. With the bathing, the brewing, and the listening, there isn't a wink of sleep to be had anywhere, by anyone, the whole night. When morning comes, we reluctantly tear ourselves away, and prepare to go to work.

This has been a tremendously rewarding experience for everybody. The musicians are uplifted by our spontaneous enthusiasm for their work. As for us, our grateful pleasure at their performance, will be hard to forget. When we return from work, they will be gone. Neither they, nor us, regret our sleepless night. They can catch up on the train trip back to Lamsdorf. We will make it up on the job.

Now we are made aware of a special facility in the town, that we haven't previously been aware of. It is a heated, indoor swimming pool. Arrangements are being made for us to be able to use it, one night per week. There is little about Mahrisch Trubau that we do not know, but the existence of this pool, takes us by surprise. We can understand the locals insistence on keeping it for themselves, and certainly not sharing it with prisoners. But this offer seems spontaneous, as though the townspeople have accepted us as part of their community. We jump at the offer of its use, but wonder at their viewing of our standing in the community. It worries us a little to think that, in their eyes, it seems they expect us to be here for keeps.

On our first night, we are marched in a body to the place. On "our" night, the pool is for our exclusive use. No civilians are allowed, so there will be no intermixing. We have no idea what to expect, and are surprised at the size of the place. It is well appointed and tiled, right throughout.

With only us in attendance, there is no need for costumes, and we swim naked. We dive, swim, splash and enjoy ourselves immensely. With winter coming on once again, we consider the opportunity to use the place once a week, as a marvellous boon.

The Guards on these outings, just stand back and allow us to cavort and splash about, as we wish. A small group of females get to know, and will gather at a screened doorway, ostensibly to talk to the Guards. Actually, they are ogling and perving on naked male bodies running about. But that's as far as it goes. There may have been some opportunity to fraternise, but we are unwilling to risk cancellation of these swimming outings.

We view the onset of another winter with mixed feelings. Our side is moving, laboriously slowly, and winter will slow things down, even further. The Russians are the only ones, seemingly, advantaged by the harsh conditions. Still, we are at least settled comfortably here, and can stick it out for another Christmas.

We go about our preparations, as usual. This time, however, we expect to have a little alcohol. One of our recent replacements from Lamsdorf, is a bloke deeply wrapped in distilling. He assembles a collection of containers and metal tubing, and sets up a still. He is continuously experimenting with various mixtures of ingredients. By and large, the rest of us do not know what to expect.

The resultant liquid is always clear and waterlike in appearance, and he always assures us that "this lot is a good drop". He keeps testing with a small, tubelike, glass bottle—just a couple of drops at a time. He seems always slightly dazed, so we have no reason to doubt its potency. Very few of us feel the urge to accept his invitation for a taste of the raw spirit. Most agree, it is best for the bottled stuff to age a little.

We enter into this Christmas, with rather mixed feelings. Our forces have managed to get moving to some extent, and have broken out of their bridgehead. Our expectations of quick decisive thrusts, just don't seem to happen. They are advancing alright, but still seem to be labouring. Progress is slow in Italy, although the Italians have tossed it in. In France, our side has turned away from us here, and are headed for Paris. We can see the enormous political advantage in this, but we fret at the time wasted, before they turn about, and head our way. We are deeply conscious of being so far inside Europe. Our mob will have to cross the whole of Germany to reach us. In our hearts, we feel that this will take a long time.

Patton, a Yank General, supposedly a whiz tank man, seems to be having the kind of success, that the Germans did at first. He also seems to be getting at cross-purposes with his associates. Eisenhower, seems to be using a lot of his time in smoothing things out between the various Allied factions, appeasing firstly, to De Gaulle, and then to Montgomery.

"Monty" appears to be particularly abrasive. There seems to be some friction between the Yanks and the British, with each competing against the other, for territorial honours. We don't much give a damn, who gets the kudos, as long as they all get moving.

This Christmas, our five manage to score half a goose, in our trading. So food wise, we don't fare too badly. The slightly aged liquor turns out to be rather strong, and the taste, not so hot. I am drinking and talking to Alistair, a Scot, when I turn my head to speak somebody behind me, for a fraction of a second. When I turn back to Alistair, he has disappeared. Search as I might, I can't find him. This is ridiculous. It is impossible for a man to be lost in the close confines of our barracks.

We eventually find him, two hours later. He has passed out from the grog, fallen over backwards, and rolled under the mess table. He is still unconscious when we put him to bed.

The liquor gets to some, enough to start them singing. After the din has been going on for a while, a couple of the Guards come in and ask us to sing 'Silent Night'. This is a favourite Christmas hymn with them, as well as us. As the voices swell out loud and strong, the Guards stand there with tears running down their cheeks. What a miserable Christmas! They miss being with their people, almost as much as we do.

Our pattern of life continues on again, after our short Christmas break. To tell the truth, it is always a relief to get back to the mill. The marching to and from work is always a great diversion, and we make sure to make things entertaining, and not overtaxing, when we get there.

As the days pass, and the snow starts to leave, camp Leader Arthur, makes another administrative trip back to Lamsdorf. He returns with news of a very great mystery. The swimming pool that the men have built there, naturally had frozen over during the cold weather. Now with the thaw, the ice has melted, and a body is found floating on the surface.

The body has been in the water for two months or more, and is swollen, black, and unrecognisable. It is fully clad in a British uniform, and could be anyone. Full checks by both British and Germans find nobody missing, or unaccounted for. Speculative rumours suggest it might be a stooge, planted by the Germans, to ferret out information. Somebody may have found him out, killed him, and dumped him in the pool, which had then frozen over. But there are no indications of how he has died, and the Germans insist, he isn't one of theirs.

One of the prisoners had been a Detective in the Fingerprint Department of Scotland Yard. With the cooperation of the Germans, he is put to work to try and solve the mystery. With everybody's fingerprints on file, he spends weeks checking, but still isn't able to come up with an identity. It just has to remain a mystery.

A few weeks later, on a Sunday rest day, a Guard comes to seek me out. He tells me that I am wanted at the front door. Somebody wants to see me? Things like this don't happen to a POW, and I am mystified. When I go to the door, it is Josef from Kollas's, and he is in uniform.

He wants to know if I can let him have some Gauloisie cigarettes—those strong, black, French troop issues, that our blokes avoid, but are greatly loved by Josef. Since transferring to Berg, I have not been in contact with Josef, nor have I seen Elle. Whenever I have had some to spare, I send a few of the Gauloisie to him, via Doug. Now fortunately, I still have a couple of packs left in our latest issue, so I quickly fetch them and give them to him.

While the fags are mine, they also are part of the resources of our group. Cigarettes have become a universal type of currency and, in lots of instances, are more valuable than money. They are our principal trade medium. I will have to clear their usage with the other four. But in this instance, I don't quibble. I can tell them later.

After I return with the fags, now the questions. Josef's demeanour is more serious than his usual self, and he, obviously, is a rather unwilling soldier. Despite his protestations, he has been inducted into the Army. He has been away for training for just over a month, and is home on leave. He is about to return, and will be posted, probably to the Russian Front.

What a queer situation! My friend Josef, whom I have not seen for a couple of months, comes and asks me for a few packs of cigarettes, before they send him to the Russian Front. But I am a British POW held captive by his people. Strictly speaking, he and I are on opposite sides, and should be enemies.

After a short talk, we shake hands awkwardly, and wish each other well. We both know that we possibly will not see each other again. He turns and walks away down the road, while I watch him. The Guards, quite decently, have left us alone to talk together. Now that he has gone, I think of a dozen different things I want to ask him, but won't be able to—principally, had he married his girlfriend, or is she still waiting?

Josef had no desire to be in the services, and has done all in his power to keep out. He was completely happy with his lot, and wouldn't change his life for anything. Up to now, he has been secure in his civilian role, but the government has stepped in and grabbed him. This suggests they are beginning to draw on their final reserves. Maybe, just maybe, there is some light beginning to appear at the end of the tunnel, for us.

A couple of weeks later, I am at work when one of our blokes comes to me, to tell me that Berg wants to talk to me. Actually, our log-hauling gang of four are bludging behind a stack of logs, in some rather weak sunlight. Mystified as to why he wants me, I just hope it isn't to tick me off. I go into the mill building, where he is waiting for me. He is standing a little apart from all the work going on, but in plain view of everybody. I go up to him, and he begins to talk. He says that he has been directed by the government, together with other prominent citizens, to report for a fortnight's physical work, to help the war effort. Their job will be the digging of a massive tank trap, for the protection of their Eastern Front, against the Russians.

During his absence, he hopes we will just carry on, in our normal fashion. He will be back shortly. He hopes that all this will soon be over, and that all of us can return to our homes. As he finishes, he reaches out, takes hold of my hand and shakes it. This is the first ever physical contact, between him and any of us. And, it is done in an area, where all can see. For my part, I have just been standing, formally, in front of him, and his words and actions take me by surprise. In reply, I just nod to signify that I have received his message, but offer no spoken comment of any kind.

All who observe our meeting, both POWs and Germans alike, are greatly intrigued, as to what has passed between us, especially the handshake. Of course, I pass the message on, and it causes everybody to wonder, even more.

Obviously, things are going badly on the Russian Front. While this is a significant boost to our blokes, it is a sobering and grim prospect for the others. Our township, and its surrounding area, is so economically structured, that it could just roll along in this backwater, without feeling much of the impact of what is happening, until invasion arrives at its back door.

Another trip to Lamsdorf by Camp Leader Arthur, brings news of another new development. The Germans are seeking volunteers from amongst the British POWs to form a Brigade to fight against the Russians. They promise that such a Brigade will be used only against the Russians, and not our own people. They try to make the point, that Russia is, as much our enemy, as theirs. If Germany does fall, then certainly, we will have to fight Russia anyway. They offer all sorts of perks and inducements to make the prospect enticing, as opposed to the drab POW existence. Their recruits, if any, are very, very few.

With things seeming to be moving, although very slowly, Big Allan, our partner and Frank's mate, are faced with a troubling situation. For some time, he has been suffering badly with piles, which he jocularly refers to as the "heaps". He really needs an operation, urgently. He can have an operation, if he elects to go back to Lamsdorf. If he does though, there is a fair chance that he will not be able to return here at Mahrisch Trubau. If he elects to stick it out here, and we are marched out, he could collapse along the road somewhere, with no chance of medical attention at all. If he decides on the operation, he may be a convalescent, and still have to march out—or worse still, be left behind. It is worrying to all us muckers, but it is the decision that he alone will have to make.

Another pointer to a change in thinking, is the attitude of the half dozen or so Polish girls, we have got to know. With the odd exception, we are friendly, without much indication of any serious involvement, on either side. Now the girls make a serious decision to focus their attention, on one particular bloke. Evidently, they have decided amongst themselves, who that one will be. Yanka decides on me.

They step up their food and cigarette parcels, passing them on, so that everyone gets to know that a parcel, from such and such a girl, is intended for her particular bloke. In this way, she becomes "his girl". On Sundays, when they all walk out together, in their spare time, they begin to pass by outside our barracks. They will stop outside, where the windows front onto the street, and call out to "their boy" by name.

Naturally, there is a fair amount of ribbing from the other fellows, for the chosen few. For myself, I'm not anxious to be part of it. I cannot see any future in crowding to a window, and waving through the bars, like a monkey in a cage. Still, the others won't let me be, particularly, my mucker, Frank, who is keen on those cigarettes. While I try to disappear somewhere out the back, he will call out loudly, "Come on Arty, here's your girl."

The girls can hear these calls quite plainly, so for decency's sake, I feel compelled to comply. Once, I determined to tough it out, and not show. But, with the fellows' calls ever louder, I have to relent. When I appear at the window, Yanka is standing slightly apart from the other girls, on a slightly rising bank, on the other side of the road. Big tears are slowly starting to fall down her cheeks. As I appear, she brushes away the tears, and breaks into a smile. She waves, and I wave back. Just like the other fellows and girls, we just look at each other, wave and smile. Then they go on their way. What a lousy situation! Still, I have to admit that these food and cigarette parcels are most welcome. And it will be stupid to do anything to cut off their supply.

These girls are decent and certainly not promiscuous. In the main, we have little contact with them at all, with this Sunday's walk past being the nearest thing to a meeting. Certainly, it is with Yanka and me. We have been able to talk to each other face to face, only two or three times since I have been here—unlike the other blokes, who come into contact with "their girls", fairly frequently. But, because Yanka's family and place of work have no contact with us POWs, it has to be on the odd occasion, when she comes to visit her friend Maria, at Bergs.

Obviously, the developing situation, has caused this new interest in us by the girls. They know from past history and bitter experience, what their lot will be, when Germany falls. Russia has to sweep across Poland to reach German territory. Once they occupy Poland, it is most unlikely, that they will give the country back. These girls and their families will be subject to famine and rape after rape. There isn't much the girls can do for their families. But, if they can attach themselves to one of us, they might stand a chance of a new life, when we head off towards the Americans in the West. It is a lousy dilemma they are in, and it is impossible not to feel compassion for them.

I am just coming to terms with Yanka's expression of interest, when another intriguing episode begins to unfold. While at work one day, some farm carts go by. They travel along the road that passes the mill, and continue on through the town. Horse drawn farm carts constantly go back and forth along this road, and are very much a part of the passing scene. But this lot is different.

They have household furniture piled aboard. A man is driving and, what looks to be his wife, and also two or three children, are perched up there, too. There is a name and a village, painted on a plate on the side, near the front of the cart, denoting ownership. The village is unknown to us, and definitely not from around here. For a few moments we are mystified. Then it dawns on us. These are refugees fleeing from the War zone.

This is the first real evidence that things actually are moving in our direction. Everybody dreads the coming of the Russians. During the German advance into Russia, their treatment of the locals, reportedly has been very harsh. Now that they are being beaten back, one can only guess at the devastation and reprisals, they will leave behind them. It only stands to reason that an implacable Russia, will react in kind. It will be most unlikely that anybody, who can make a move, will stay behind to see what will happen.

At this stage, it is only one small isolated group, and they very quickly are gone. We realise that when there is a constant stream of refugees, either our Guards will make a decision for us to move out, or we will have to make one ourselves. By then, we expect wayside pickings, food wise, will be very slim indeed.

As we keep a close watch, the days slip past, without any further sign of an exodus. Berg has returned from his labours, and taken up again, from where he left off.

To prevent any panic, we worry, that the authorities may have decreed, that any movement, made by people, is to take place only at night. At Bergs, during the daytime, all traffic has to pass by us. With our home being on the outskirts of the town, we will be unaware of any night time happenings. We might lose our freedom of choice on what to do. However, everything around us keeps on progressing in the same old way.

We study the military situation even more closely than before. Allan is worrying about his "heaps", still undecided what to do. Our mob is moving with a fair bit of momentum now, while the Russians seem to be taking their time. The Germans had made a serious push against us in the Battle of the Bulge, which our mob has managed to hold. This seems to be their last big effort there. Now they seem to be concentrating on trying to hold the Russians. With the attempt on Hitler's life, the mood of the population becomes serious and sombre. More refugees come through, still only in small parties, and not yet in a constant stream.

We are becoming edgy and frustrated at the slow progress. Although we realise that we are witness to the slow disintegration of a nation, and while we urge it on, we are disinterested in the historical aspect—just concerned with the human factor, and our part in it.

Then a new development arises about mid-afternoon one work day. We are treated to a sound that we have not heard, up to now. It is a siren sounding off. It seems that we are to be subjected to an air raid. There have been no prior drills or training, and the civilians are a bit panicky. Our geographical position seemed to rule out such a prospect. Now, nobody is prepared.

Then into sight, they come. A great Air Armada, heading from the southwest, over us, and onto the Eastern Front. Flying, evidently, from fields in Italy, they are bringing assistance to the Russians.

The bombers are flying about six abreast, in an endless stream, to the horizon. Fighters are darting over and around them, as escort and protectors. There is no challenge of any kind, either by aircraft or groundfire. Then, from here and there amongst them, tiny objects float away, and begin falling lopsidedly, towards the ground. There are only about six of these objects and the locals are sure they are being bombed. We know differently, for they have fallen straighter and truer. Also, their bulk is too big to be a standard bomb. We reason they must be auxiliary wing tanks, needed to give the fighters the extra range. They are jettisoned when empty. This is what they prove to be, for we see some later.

The massive flypast takes one and a half hours to pass over, by which time the leading elements begin returning, their mission completed. The air raid alert lasts for three hours, before the all clear. On the few subsequent raids, it is the practice to drop the empty wing tanks in our area.

Now we add our loud protests to the already jittery local officials. We demand bomb shelters to protect us. In reply, they point to a deep canal, that runs diagonally across the bottom end of the mill yard. Usually dry, they tell us to use that. We flatly refuse. We point out that, if a bomb lands in the canal, its blast will be channelled along its course, and kill everyone in it. They promise to look at other alternatives.

Again, there follows a period of relative calm. While things are progressing militarily, they are remote and far away. The air raids have practically petered out, and refugees still haven't become a flood. There are indications of German difficulties. Red Cross parcels are failing to get through. Without them, we are back to the basic potatoes and bread, and we will lose some of the stamina we need for the march out. It is a few months now, since last we received any. We might reluctantly have to turn to some of our salmon.

Mail seems to be unaffected. My Manchester girl, always one to give me a boost, writes that it is the ambition to meet a returning POW as he lands, and take him to a quiet place in the country, lock the door behind him, then not reappear for a fortnight.

With this period of stability nagging at us, Allan makes the decision to go back to Lamsdorf for the operation on his "heaps". He has been suffering quite a bit, and obviously something has to be done. We all hope, he has not delayed the problem too long.

The departure of Allan leaves a vacancy at the Home Mill—the first one to have come up so far. I decide to take it. By doing so, I will be together with my partners, Norm and George, and less likely to become separated when the end comes. We just hope that Allan can make it back to rejoin us.

At Bergs, I am much more informed with what is going on. To leave means that I will have to rely on somebody else's assessment of the situation of what is happening. This is no big deal, as we all share in the current situation. Still, it does give me a feeling of being less in control of my own destiny. In moving from Berg Mill to Home Mill, I gain something and lose something, and this is a little unsettling.

The changeover makes very little difference to me jobwise. The tasks performed are pretty much the same. The big advantage is the nearness to our barracks, which gives me a bit more leisure time to myself. We are always home well before the others. We get first pick at bathing and cooking facilities.

I have been at the Home Mill, for just a couple of weeks, when a sudden, very strong, radio broadcast bursts forth. It is a pirate broadcast announcement by the Czechs, telling all, that they have staged an uprising in Prague. Prague is the headquarters of a large, powerful, radio network. Strong broadcasts are being put out constantly in English, announcing repeatedly, that the Czechs have risen against the German Occupation Forces, and are in complete control of the station. They appeal to the Americans to push through and link up with them, and also to drop them arms and ammunition.

All this is taking place a long way from us. It is just another incident, in a series, that will hopefully set us free. Meantime, we are in the box seat to monitor the broadcasts, and see how the Czechs get on. As we see it, the Czechs are making a play now, to try and establish some sort of credibility as a nation—and, therefore, have some say in their future. Even though occupied, it may be interpreted that their behaviour is a fairly passive one. Even with our close proximity to the Czech border, we have heard nothing from the Czechs, we regularly come in contact with, of any partisan activity there. Arms production from the giant Skoda works seems to proceed without interruption. Maybe, they just have to try something to be credible.

For three days, the broadcasts are strong and confident. The reaction from the Yanks is totally nil. They don't even acknowledge that they have heard the Czechs, although it seems certain to us that they must have. We wait anxiously for the German reaction, which, we know, must come. From a military point of view, such a rebellion has to be hit hard, and swiftly. The Germans, being hard-pressed in both the West and the East, we know they will waste no time.

To us, and I guess to most of the world, the progress of the war, seems a straight out contest of arms. We expect that our mob will keep going from the West, and the Russians from the East, until both sides meet somewhere. Which side gains the most territory, will depend on the degree of opposition each encounter. The mood of the German population, both military and civilian, tells us that they fear the Russians the most. If all else fails, the Germans will do their damndest to preference the Americans.

Nobody knows, of course, that the three world leaders, Churchill, Roosevelt and Stalin, have already carved up Europe at a secret conference. The boundary lines of their advance have been set, beyond which, they have pledged not to go. Spheres of interest, determining who takes charge of which country, have already been decided among the three. If the Czechs had known this, they may have saved themselves the heartache of a costly, futile exercise.

On the fourth day, the broadcasts seem to get progressively weaker. A note of pleading begins to creep into the appeals for help. Still there is no reaction from anywhere. Obviously, the Czechs expect the Yanks to push through to Prague itself. The Yank spearheads are somewhere close to that sector, and we, as well as the Czechs, expect them to take up the challenge. But nothing happens.

On the fifth day, the broadcasts are very weak and intermittent. The appeals are now begging, to the extent of, "Please help us. We can't hold out much longer." Time stretches out between each one, and several times we think the end has come—only for yet another, weak, hardly audible appeal to come through. Sometime during the afternoon, the broadcasts cease altogether. We know then that the Germans have crushed the rebellion.

For us now, the exercise of going to work, is just that—an exercise. We are too taken up with the situation, and do only what is necessary. The difference of approach on the two Fronts, is quite marked, and causes us some speculation. Whereas, our side seems anxious to push on as far and fast as they can, the Russians seem content to just take their time methodically, making steady gains.

With no response by the Americans to the Czech appeals, it seems certain to us that the Russian advance, is the one that concerns us the most. Their slowness makes us a little despondent. Nevertheless, we keep full check on our preparedness to move, when we consider that it is time.

Norm and the Little Yank have made plans, that see them taking off together. Norm is determined to get her through safely to the American lines. They plan to use pushbikes, carrying only a minimum of supplies. This form of transport is universal here, and will attract little attention.

The Little Yank has her own bike, but Norm will have to steal one. He already has one earmarked. He will steal the Engineer's bike. It usually is propped up against the wall of his house, just inside the mill yard.

The refugee stream from the Russian Front, according to the Berg men, is now fairly constant. But there are still no signs of anything military. When uniformed men begin to be part of it, then the end will be close. Somehow, we are not too anxious to hand ourselves over to the care of the Russians. We want out, and that is towards the West.

Some Ukrainians, working for some of the local farmers, come to the yard to pick up some timber. As is usual, they swap confidences with us, and reveal they are very worried. They produce pamphlets printed in Russian, allegedly dropped by Russian planes in their area. The pamphlets exhort them to do nothing to help the enemy and, wherever possible, seize arms, and actively attack him in the rear.

Often the closeness of working together, has generated a high degree of mutual respect between the farmer and his workers. With food and living quarters being good, most are happy with the arrangement. The prospect of attacking, and killing their "friends", is something the Ukrainians cannot contemplate. Failure to comply with the order, can be equally uninviting. There never is time for explanations in war. The ruthless Russians will regard their own nationals as collaborators, when found in this situation. This usually means shooting out of hand.

I awake one morning to great excitement throughout our barracks. There has been an air raid on our town, by Russian planes on Sunday night, and I have slept through it. In the excitement, everybody had crowded to the windows to watch. Nobody notices that I was missing. I am disgusted with myself. Everybody is anxious to get to work to find out the extent of the damage.

I closely question the others as to what has actually taken place. I come to the conclusion that it is a relatively minor thing, with, maybe, only a couple of bombs being dropped. This proves to be the case, and perhaps explains how I have managed to sleep through it.

We are just about ready to leave for work, when we, the Home Mill crew, are told that we will not be allowed near the place. There is an unexploded bomb just inside the entrance, and any movement near the area is strictly forbidden, until the bomb has been removed.

This is disastrous. We have this panicky feeling that somehow things will happen, that will see us left behind, while everybody else takes off. It is absolutely essential that we keep our freedom of movement, and not be cooped up here in the barracks. It is absolutely vital for Norm's plan, that he keep track of the whereabouts of the Engineer's bike. This bomb has to be moved as soon as possible, to allow us to get back on the job.

Our Guard Corporal had been recalled some time ago, and for several months we have been waiting for his replacement. In the meantime, old Kneifel, who is a Lance Corporal, is temporarily in charge. Old Kneifel had altered my Aussie uniform for me, and has been with us for a long time. He is elderly and cautious, and stubbornly refuses to take any initiatives, on his own bat. The authorities have said, that there is to be no movement, in or out, of the mill, and that is that.

We argue with him, and put forward everything we can think of. "If the bomb has to be moved, then, where is the bomb squad? They do have one, don't they? In England, bomb squads are everywhere. Don't tell us, the Germans are so backward, that they don't have one!"

We, Field Engineers, know this is just a routine task, and is part of our everyday duties. We would have the bomb out in no time. Old Kneifel just turns our arguments aside, saying only, that he will pass them on.

We badger and badger, cajole and cajole. We even say that, if it is left to us, we will have the thing out of there in five minutes. Still, the only reaction, from old Kneifel, is that, he will pass it on. After a couple of days, our sarcasm, at the lack of German initiative, is ever more biting and offensive. Then, about midmorning one day, a small delegation arrives, and they confer with the Guards. There are two in civilian Police uniform, and a couple of what seems to be Civilian Officials. The Home Mill Engineer has tagged along, too. One of the Policemen seems to be the leader. The badges on his uniform seem to indicate he is the local Chief of Police.

After a meeting with the Guards, for about half an hour, old Kneifel comes out and asks our Home Mill crew to come in, as they want to talk to us. All our other blokes are at work, and only the cooking and administrative staff, and us, are at home. Usually, all official decisions are relayed to the whole of us. But, seeing that they only want to talk to us Home Mill blokes, we think they may have come up with a solution. Not knowing what to expect, we line up in the Guard Room.

The Police Chief does the talking, and says, quite candidly, that they have nobody to call on, who will be able to remove the bomb. Since we have stated, that we have the knowhow, will we remove it for them? And, what will we require in payment, in return? The Home Mill Engineer adds his plea, saying, that he and all his family have been ordered out of their home, and will not be allowed to return, until the place is made safe. The bomb is just outside his front door. They have nowhere to go, and they cannot even get to their clothes, and have no way to feed themselves.

We are completely stunned. What a bizarre situation! What are the ethics of our position? Our captors, are asking us, to help them. Should we say "yes", or an implacable "no"?

Then there is the practical side. We do want to get back our freedom of movement. If we don't do it, will the situation remain a stalemate, until the Russians blow into town? We cannot stomach the thought of being caught like that. We want to be able to go, when we feel the time is right.

To give ourselves a bit of leeway, we can ask for an impossible payment, then quite cheerfully refuse, when our request isn't forthcoming. What is an impossible payment? What is it, we crave the most? It doesn't take too long to decide this. What we want most is a bloody good steak. It is the stuff of our dreams.

Meat, as such, in Germany, can only be found in small bits and pieces, usually in soups and stews, and generally is pork—and never for a POW. Beef as such, we have neither seen, nor heard of. Strictly rationed, the better-off civilians are able to get a little, only occasionally. It is impossible to obtain, even on the black market. "Yes, we will consider it, for payment of about ten or twelve kilos of beefsteak. It will have to be calves flesh, not some tough old cow, that has seen better days."

Satisfied that we have arrived at a suitable stalemate, we put our proposition to the Police Chief. He says that he will go away, and see what can be arranged. He will come straight back with an answer.

We figure, that the answer will be "No". We think, that somewhere in the town, a man in a uniform will come to light, game enough to give it a go—especially, as they are now prepared to offer a payment for the job.

The Police Chief returns about an hour later to tell us, that our terms will be met. We can have our payment before, or after, the job is done.

Although, if we are prepared to wait until afterwards, it will give them more time to organise the butchering.

The Chief is affable and straightforward. He speaks to us in man-to-man style. It is obvious, that he means what he says. Now that our bluff has been called, we have to respond. We say, that payment afterwards, will be good enough.

We are still not sure, that we are going to do the job, although the chief is certain in his mind, that he has achieved an agreement. He wastes no time escorting us to the bombsite, while we, for the first time, begin to give some thought to the device itself. What if it is a sophisticated delayed action type?

True, as Field Officers, bomb disposal may be one of the jobs, we have to deal with. In actual fact, what we know about the job, is purely theoretical. Having been locked away from actual service for almost four years now, this theory may be well out of date. If the bomb DOES happen to be on the sophisticated side, we won't have much of an idea of what to do.

Not knowing what to expect, we walk as a group to the site. Without getting too close, the Chief points and says, "There it is." We look, and what we see, is the crudest aerial bomb, we have ever seen, or expect to see. It has ploughed into the ground at an acute angle, leaving the soft earth furrowed to a depth of about two feet. Almost the whole of the bomb is clearly visible. It is immediately obvious, why the thing has not exploded. It is meant to be detonated by an aluminium plunger, which had bent because of the angle of ground entry. In its bent state, the bomb was rendered completely useless.

The casing is of cast steel, about two feet six inches long, and about twelve inches in diameter. Its appearance is such, that it suggests the Russians are using them, also, as a shell projectile, but with an alternate type firing mechanism. The aluminium plunger is a one piece casting of thick metal. A large, round, flat disc, with a pencil-sized shaft coming from its centre, sees the shaft leading through the nose and into the bomb. Almost certainly, it is spring loaded, so that to fire, all that is required is direct pressure on the flat disc. If the bomb is perpendicular, firing will be no problem. However, as all aerial stuff enters at some degree of angle,

I conclude that the majority of this type is wasted. On this one, the shaft has bent at the bomb nose, so that the disc is pressed against the casing.

As we survey the situation, the Home Mill Engineer, again pleads for our help, for both him and his family. We are a crew of four. With nobody actually saying anything, we pick up some wooden slats, and begin poking at the soft earth. Once started, our professional interest is roused, and we plan what we propose to do. We will clear all the soil away on both sides, pass two ropes around the body, then lift it clear. Once clear, we will put it on a canvas stretcher for transport away to the fields. There it will be safely detonated.

As we begin work, everybody else clears away from the site, to what they consider a safe distance. This is quite a fair way from us. Starting about a foot away from the body of the bomb, we work two men on each side. The thin slats move the soft earth easily. We start gingerly and carefully. But, as we work, we become bolder and bolder. By the time we have opened up a large trench, deep enough to pass underneath, I find I am working right against the casing. Frank suddenly says, "Careful Arty, you moved the bloody thing then!" And indeed I have. But this is the only scare we have.

With the two furrows for the ropes finished, and most of the earth alongside the bomb cleared away, we are ready to lift the thing clear. We fix the ropes in place, then signal the Chief for the stretcher to be brought up. This is quickly done. Using a stout pole, with two of us on either side, we lift the bomb from its position, then lower it onto the stretcher. Our job is now finished. From here, the small group of civilians and police, will manhandle the stretcher to a safe place out in the fields.

With our stretcher party leading the way, we amble along with the Police Chief, chatting casually. He offers us cigarettes, which are a good quality German make. With our one smoker accepting, the rest of us decline, explaining we are non-smokers. We reach a point where we stop, while the stretcher party is about a hundred yards further on, in a slight hollow which hides them from sight. This is to be the detonation area.

We cannot see who does the actual detonation, but the bang is hardly more than a muffled blast. With it all over, the whole party troops back again, and we are delivered back to our barracks. True to the Chief's word, the slab of meat is delivered to us there.

For myself, I cannot help but wonder why nobody else was game enough to tackle that bomb. They had cheerfully carried it away, once it was on the stretcher. And somebody had the knowhow to detonate it by using explosives. But, initially, the thing itself had them bluffed. The gratitude of the Home Mill Engineer, is almost embarrassing. He thanks each and every one of us, profusely. If he had only known, that the one big reason for doing the job, is to make his bike available to Norm, when the time comes for us to move out.

Now that we have the meat, we find it a bit of an embarrassment. With no facilities to keep it, we will have to use it up quickly, before it goes bad. We figure that we have earned a couple of meals out of it. But as for the others, we have neglected to ask for enough for everybody. We do give some of it away. But, with our steaks spread out cooking barbeque style, amongst the meagre offerings of the others on the hot stovetop, we are rather relieved, when it is all gone.

The way is clear now, for us to return to work—not that we are interested in working. But those Ukrainian workers, whom we come into contact with there, may have a bit more information with regard to the situation.

The single bomb turns out to be the only one dropped in this area. With no significant damage, hereabouts, I begin to feel, that the planes that flew over, were bound for somewhere else. And that single bomb, had been accidently dislodged on the way.

Reports from the Berg Mill crew indicates that the refugee flow, seems to be almost a regular stream now. But, it still doesn't seem significant enough, for us to elect to move out. The military situation has the Americans, seemingly, to be stationary, and the Russians, the only ones, still on the move. The British are far to the north, well away from our sector. Some of the fellows think they can faintly hear the sound of Russian big guns. If so, this will put them about twenty to twenty-five miles away.

We are edgy, unsettled, and uncertain. A couple of days later, we tune into the BBC broadcast. Pandemonium seems to have broken out, with us being almost unable to get a clear word. Always the static has been at a minimum, and the news flows in those famous, measured tones. Now, when we need to know what is going on, it looks as if our radio is going to let us down.

Then the noise becomes muted, and fades to the background, as the Announcer takes over. His words, more or less, are to the effect, that what we are hearing, are the wild celebrations raging throughout London, at the news, that the War in Europe is now over. The lights in this part of the world can, once again, be relit, after years of darkness.

We are absolutely stunned. How can the War be over, when we are still Prisoners? We are deep inside Germany, with Russian guns still banging away, about twenty miles from us. It remains now, to convince the people out here. At least, a decision has been made for us. It is now time to pull out.

# Chapter 16
# Escape to Freedom

So the War in Europe is over. Well in our sector, it isn't. First thing to do is confront the Guards, and see what they know. If anything, they know less than we do. Old Kneifel maintains he is awaiting instructions from Headquarters. Camp Leader Arthur, our usual source of official instructions, can find out nothing. Obviously, there is some trouble with military communications—how much, we can only guess. Maybe this means that our links with our home Stalag, at Lamsdorf, are severed. What this may mean for our mate and partner Allan, who has gone back there to have his "heaps" fixed, is something we don't like to think about.

Now, some of the aspects of the removal of that bomb, begin to make sense. With the spring-loaded aluminium plunger, bent hard back against the casing, it is obvious for one and all to see, that it is harmless. It didn't need an expert. Any damn fool could have shifted it. Any military man, from Private up, knows that. But we haven't seen any military men, other than our Guards. Their military expertise has been culled, so severely, over the past six months, that what has been left, is little different from the civilians.

The delegation, that had conferred with us about the bomb removal, are all Civilian Administration Officials. There was no Army representation at all. These people had done it off their own bat. In such a matter, normally an approach will be made to the nearest Military Official. They had come directly to us. This means that the Military Officials have gone, or are now out of communication. This seems to mean, that our little enclave is left to its own devices.

With all the uncertainties, the best thing to do, seems to be, is go downtown, and see what is going on. Davey, a Scotsman from the cleaning staff, and I propose to do this. All work has been suspended, with everyone confined to barracks. Davey and I just march up to old Kneifel, and demand that he open the front door for us. We tell him that we are just going down the town, and will be back in an hour. Without demur, he opens up.

We head through the main part of town, to where the principal road cuts through to the west. Here, the refugee flow is very solid. But there's still nothing much in the way of uniformed men. We decide to cast about for areas just off the main road, to where a Unit on the move might pause for a rest. We find a small transport Unit, complete with several trucks. Any soldier knows, that if you want to know what's going on, you get more information from an ordinary soldier, than from anywhere else. We amble over, squat, and begin to talk to these men.

They treat us as if we are visitors from a sister Unit. They produce some schnapps, and offer us a drink, as we begin to talk. Schnapps has always been plentiful around these areas. It's usually homebrewed, and with a wide variety of tastes. This lot tastes pretty terrible.

They cannot tell us much. They have been moving on pretty aimlessly for the past couple of weeks. With the rapidly changing situation, they are having trouble making contact with their Headquarters. We let them know that radio reports from London, claim that the War in Europe is over, and that Germany has capitulated. While we cannot speak for the Russians, we advise them that their best move will be to head for their homes.

Feeling that we have obtained all the information we are likely to get, Davey and I head back to our barracks, about half an hour's walk from here. We have to walk along the road for the first part, then take a shortcut across the fields direct to our home. This shortcut is used daily on our journey to and from work.

We start off briskly along the road, but, by the time reach the shortcut, the rather potent schnapps begins to take effect. We are really staggering, with each trying to support the other. Our eyesight is affected, so that the flat path seems to be undulating in waves. As we attempt to place a foot in a trough, it suddenly becomes a crest, and we will stumble badly. While our faculties still seem to be with us, we just cannot make our brains control our limbs. And our eyesight continues to play outrageous tricks. It takes a long while for us to negotiate this shortcut. By the time we reach home, we really need help.

Our shortcut ends in a drop down a bank, of about six or seven feet, to a roadway which passes in front of our barracks. As we two sway alarmingly on the top of the bank, all our fellows are crammed against the windows, calling for us to stay back. Only then, we become aware of a small Company of horse-mounted Infantry, assembled on the roadway, just to one side of our barracks. The fellows are scared of what may happen, if these soldiers take exception to us two wandering about.

There are several satellite villages bordering our town. It seems that this Company has billeted for the night, unbeknown to us, in one of them. They are now preparing to move out. Moving out, with them, are two village girls of about sixteen. Each is mounted behind a soldier, clasping him around the waist. The girls have evidently decided to take their chances, on the road, with their own kind, rather than the Russians—only a slightly better choice.

To ride behind the saddle, the girls have to hoist up their skirts, way up to the thigh. This marvellous display of lovely legs, by two well-proportioned girls, immediately raises a tremendous whoop from our fellows at the windows. Despite themselves, both soldiers and girls, burst into smiles. This breaks the tension and, as they pass, our mates rush out and help us inside.

By now, we are complete cot cases. We cannot control our limbs. We mumble out our assessment of the situation, as some of the fellows help us to our bunks and roll us in. We immediately fall into a deep sleep, and are to stay that way, until next morning. When we awake, we are amazed to find, that we have been out of it for so long. We had drunk very little, so the liquor given us, must have been almost pure alcohol. Luckily, we feel OK, and there are no after effects.

While we have slept, the entire work party, after bullying the Guards, have gone downtown and mixed freely with the townspeople. We have longed to do just this for the entire three and a half years, we have been here. For all the time, that we have passed to and fro amongst the people, it has been as captives. Somehow, it made us feel a little inferior. Now that it has happened freely, Davey and I have missed it all.

Few, if any of us, have scores to settle. Many, have cause to be grateful to someone, for a special act of kindness. It is a last chance for final meetings, before pulling out. Then there are the Polish girls. Our fellows tell me that the girls are also out, mixing freely. As our blokes show up, the girls quickly seek out their own particular friend. Yanka has been looking for me. The fellows tell her, that I am drunk and I have passed out, and that I am now asleep in bed. She cries, bitterly, with great tears coursing down her cheeks. She is a very attractive and lovely girl. But she sure is a weeper. She must have decided, that I am too unreliable, and so we never meet again. While I am disappointed, I realise it is probably for the best.

Norm has used the occasion to quietly steal the Engineer's push bike, and meet up with Little Yank. He does not return with the others, and I am unable to make any final plans with him. He is determined to get her through to the American lines. While I can only wish him luck, I think he is taking a big risk.

Over the last few days, the Big Yank has also decided to get out. Her situation is a little different from the Little Yank, as she has been living with her father. Little Yank has only herself to worry about. For Big yank, her Father is a local resident. Here is his home. It is a tough decision. She asks some of the fellows for advice. Big Togo, airily says, "No problem. Come with us." To me, this is asking for trouble. Physically, he is a big man. I can only hope, that he can handle it.

With nothing further to keep us here, we, unanimously, decide that now is the time to go. We can wait for the Russians to show up, but, home for us, is in the opposite direction, and we have many miles to travel. The sooner we take off, the sooner we will get somewhere.

A body of us go to the Guard's Room, and tell them that we are leaving. Old Kneifel still half-heartedly insists he is waiting for orders. But we are adamant, and insist this is it. We tell them that, if they are undecided what to do, they can tag along too. It will look as if they are still in charge, although we make it quite clear, that we are taking no more orders from them. Anyway, we will be going away from the Russians, and they are free to go, anywhere and anytime, they want.

Leaving them to gather up their gear, we all start to make our own preparations. We do not have a lot of packing to do, but in the last three and a half years, we had accumulated enough to make it impossible to carry everything on what will probably be a long hard footslog. Some sort themselves out quickly. Moving to the door, they order the Guards to open up. In their little partnerships and cliques, they begin to leave.

While gathering mine together, I agonise over the gear, that Norm has left behind. In the middle of his bunk is a wallet, plain for all to see. It contains lots of photos that, I know, have been very precious to him. In the end, I reason that he will have taken them with him, if he really wanted them.

In the middle of making up my mind, in wanders the Home Mill Engineer. He is very upset. Somebody has taken his push bike. Do I know where Norm is? I tell him that Norm has already gone, and that I know nothing about a bike. He pleads with me. He tells me that he must have a bike, in order for him and his family to survive. It is the only way, he can get to outlying farms, and trade for food. He is a pretty decent bloke, and I am sorry for him. But there is nothing I can do. I point to the clothing and gear left behind by the departing men, and tell him, he is free to help himself. Ours is of much better quality, and superior to theirs, and he is grateful. But he is still lamenting about his lost bike.

Packed and ready, we move to the door. Leaving behind us a fair slice of our lives, we move out without a second's hesitation. As we pass through, we are met by the Big Yank and her Father. Each is heavily laden, and have very large suitcases. We immediately look for Togo, but he has disappeared. Big Yank, determinedly, attaches herself to us. Herding her aged Father along too, she heads off, together with our group of about seven.

I am furious about this turn of events. I silently curse Togo for his airy promises, and his willingness to leave it to somebody else to carry them out. As we plod off, I stubbornly resolve to myself, to be of as little assistance to these two interlopers as I can. The other fellows don't seem to mind at all. The whole gang, bar a few still behind us, are spread widely across the open fields, heading west. I determine that, if and when, we catch up with Togo's lot, I will do all in my power to see he is handed back his responsibilities.

With summer approaching, the weather is fine and warm. By mid-afternoon, it becomes fairly hot. As we walk, we speculate as to what seems our best course of action. We are in German territory, with hordes of refugees both in front and behind us. There is still only a light sprinkling of uniforms amongst them. Given the German treatment to the Russians, we expect the Russians to be fairly merciless in return. If they resort to aerial strafing, this lot, with us included, will be sitting ducks.

Some fifteen kilometres to the south, and at right angles to the direction we want to go, is the Czech border. Even though we expect the refugee stream to be pretty much the same, we reason that the danger of aerial strafing will be less likely over Czech territory. There too, the Czechs have much more reason to be friendly to us, and we can expect some assistance, whilst in their territory.

Plodding along, with Big Yank and her Dad slowing us down only slightly, most of the fellows help cheerfully, with those cumbersome suitcases. Me, not at all. I have to admit to myself, grudgingly, that they are doing a good job of keeping up. We have the great spiritual lift of knowing that we are on our way home; whereas, they are carrying the burden of leaving behind one life, and facing the uncertain future of another.

Our three or four Guards, by this time, are following somewhere in the rear. They have given up any semblance of trying to direct us. In the heat of the afternoon, some form of transport begins to seem very attractive—and this, on our first day, when we have many hundreds of miles of territory, still to cover.

Without thinking much about it, we have automatically accepted Frank as our leader. As a Sergeant, he has the unanimous trust of all of us. There is no way we will, or can, accept anything else. We are going home. And, this is too serious a business, to allow ourselves to be swayed or coerced by any damn fool.

The decision, to make our way across Czech territory, appears the more attractive option than across Germany. We speculate about the best way to get there. We figure there is still some rail travel into Czechoslovakia, so we decide to make our way to the nearest rail junction. Slightly to our north is the fairly large town of Zwittau, where, as a prisoner, I was taken to see the eye doctor. So we head for there.

We reach Zwittau in the late afternoon. The rail station is just on the edge of town, and there is a lot of hustle and bustle, but no signs of obvious panic. We have no preconceived plan, but just to get aboard a train. Just inside the barrier leading to the platform, a German Military Policeman is standing on duty. He looks a bit formidable in full uniform, with his steel helmet, and, on his chest is a badge of office of steel plate, suspended by chain, round his neck. We hesitate for a moment, then all in silent agreement, march straight on in a body. Surprisingly, he never says a word.

There is a train standing at the platform, with engine coupled and steam up, awaiting for departure. We head straight for it, clamber aboard, seat ourselves in the nearest available seats, and settle down. It is good to relax our tired limbs. We have not asked the train's destination, but guess it has to be somewhere across the border. We have not attempted to buy tickets, and have no intention of paying anyway.

We are grateful to be able to rest. As we look around, we find our carriage contains mostly German soldiers in uniform. The carriage beyond seems to be mostly civilians. Nobody seems to take any notice of us, other than knowing we are here. Shortly after some more soldiers and civilians get aboard, our train begins to move. We are accepted completely, as just a few more travellers.

As the train picks up speed, I silently think of the wonderful aerial target, it would make. However, I decide the comfort is worth the risk factor, which is constantly at the back of all our minds. After all we've been through, we have this silent fear, that something will knock us out, on this last leg of going home.

Having settled down for the trip, people start chatting amiably with each other. If it wasn't for uniforms, it may have been a mundane peacetime journey. As is the case in most train journeys, the odd person or two begin making their way along the corridor, and into other carriages. We have been under way for more than ten minutes, when a civilian with a rather foxy look, comes along, cradling a small suitcase in his arms. He is stopping frequently, lifting the lid to show the contents, and saying something as he moves along. When he nears us, we find it is packed with tobacco and cigarettes. He is a black marketeer, working the trains. Some of the soldiers show interest, and try to negotiate a price. But there seems very few buyers. He passes on, and disappears.

After a while, he makes his way back. This time the soldiers surround him, firmly take away his case, and pass out its contents among themselves. He protests loudly, only to be told, he is a parasite. He is then threatened with being forcibly thrown from the train. He disappears with his now empty suitcase, still lamenting loudly.

I cannot help but recall a similar incident, amongst our own people. We were aboard the train for Alexandria in Egypt, en route to Greece. Some Arabs had climbed aboard the train, trying to sell bottles of fake Johnny Walker whiskey. Some of the men took to the bottles, grabbed hold of the Arabs, and tossed them clear of the slow moving train. The Arabs, with robes flying, tumbled head over heels in the sand. Unhurt, they jumped to their feet, shook their fists, and screamed abuses at the disappearing train. It seems there isn't a great deal of difference among soldiers anywhere.

After a short trip of barely more than half an hour, we come to a small town. As the train stops, everybody rises, and begins to disembark. It is obvious that this is as far as we go, so we climb down too. We are at a small town, just inside the Czech border. The station is decorated and festooned with flags and bunting. There is a festive air of celebration. Obviously, the locals are celebrating the supposed end of the War, too.

Quickly the passengers disperse, probably to join the columns on the open road—although there are a fair sprinkling of Czech civilians, who obviously live nearby. We pause for a moment, to gather our bearings, then decide on our next move.

We become aware of a girl of about nineteen, hovering in the background, nearby. Nobody remains on the station, except us and the girl. She is medium tall, very beautiful, and with a stunning figure—a real knockout. To her, there is some doubt as to who we are. We all are dressed in standard British battledress, except me in my Aussie uniform, which I hadn't been able to bring myself to leave behind, and also Big Yank and her Dad of course.

The girl walks up to us, and asks if we are English. We say, "Yes." All British troops are considered, universally, as "English".

She says, "Follow me."

I, being the closest, then say in English, "Lead on sister. I'll follow you anywhere."

She turns back to me, and in perfect English says, "What did you say?" I could have bitten my tongue off. It turns out that she is a local school teacher, put here by the Czechs, to round up any of our blokes, who come through by train.

She takes us to a large house in the town, where we are welcomed by a group of about half a dozen, both men and women. They are efficient and well-organized. They ask, "What are your plans?"

We tell them, "We think it best to make for Prague, and then go on to the American lines." They agree, but say that we can go no further by train from here, as the rail lines have been cut by partisans. They suggest we stay the night, then move across to a nearby town, where they think that we may get a train to Prague.

We ask how we can get to this other town. They say that they might be able to arrange a car. Although everything that rolls has been confiscated, we don't doubt their ability to provide one. They say that the driver will have to be paid, and ask if we have any money. We demonstrate, we have little or none. They say, "No matter, we will provide you with some."

They feed us, and we bunk down for the night, happy to know we have a concrete plan to work to. While we are happy to pile in anywhere, they automatically arrange separate accommodation for big Yank and her Dad. By now, these two are automatically accepted as an integral part of our group. The people we come in contact with, accept them at such, without query or question. Most of my hostility has evaporated by now, but I am still dirty on Togo for having saddled us with them, and I will let him know, as soon as we catch up with him.

We are woken early, just after daybreak. As we are preparing to move, Big Yank comes to Frank and me with a problem. She has two passports, one an expired American, the other a current German one. She asks, "Will it be wise to get rid of one, or both?"

This is a very tricky one to answer. Really, we know nothing about passports. As soldiers, we have no need of them. We still have a long way to go, and cannot foresee what situations may arise. While she is with us, it doesn't seem to matter. Still, somewhere ahead, somebody may demand identification, or even make a search. They may even decide to separate us, and we may not have any say in it. Any trouble will probably rub off onto us. It is pretty decent of her, to take it up with us. She could have kept quiet, making her own decision. We end up telling her to decide for herself, and we will abide by it. Our lack of knowledge is no help for her at all. She never mentions it again, so we have no idea whether she stashes them away, or dumps them.

Our overnight hosts take us to a nearby complex, that looks like a public school. They hand us over to a group of four or five young men, whose apparent leader is a man in his early thirties. He is dressed neatly in ordinary civilian clothes of tweed jacket and grey trousers, and is hatless. The others are similarly dressed. There is no sign of any badges or emblems, and they look for all the world like a group of school teachers, engaged in harmless chitchat before commencing work. There are no arms anywhere. Of course, with no children in sight, they may belong to some kind of civil administration.

We stand around and discuss our desire to proceed to Prague. Although nothing is said, we gather the impression that this is the headquarters of the local resistance, with orders and decisions being made by the man in the tweed jacket. He appears to have the ability to make things happen.

He tells us that all major rail lines to Prague have been cut by the partisans. He thinks there just might be a chance to get through on a minor line, from a nearby town, about twenty kilometres away. He has made arrangements for a car to take us, and it will be along in a moment. He is sorry that it is parallel to the way we want to go, but is sure we will get all the help we need from there. He tells us to make ourselves known to the civil authorities. He gives us ten thousand of the local currency notes, to pay the driver. Frank takes charge of it.

When it arrives, the car is a rather large sedan. We quickly cram inside and are off. Instructions are given to the driver, so we just sit back and enjoy the ride. As we are not heading west, the roads are practically empty. In very short time we arrive at our destination, in the small town of Litomysl. We scramble out and unload our gear. The driver has delivered us to the Burgomeister's Headquarters. We scarcely have time to say a word to the driver, as he quickly turns round and heads back—anxious to get his vehicle under cover before it can be confiscated.

After the driver leaves, and we are getting ourselves together, Frank suddenly pulls the bundle of notes out of his pocket. He says, "Damn! I completely forgot to pay him." We can only hope that everybody will realise it is an honest mistake, and not hold it against us.

The Burgomeister and his people tell us immediately, that there is no chance of a rail link to Prague from here—maybe from another town, but no closer than where we are now. Once again, the work of the partisans is the reason. Each official knows the situation in his own area, but is unsure what has happened in his neighbour's.

Understandably, we are impatient to keep moving forward, and balk at the idea of moving sideways, from one small town to another, and getting no further. As we talk over the pros and cons, the Burgomeister offers us a solution. He says, "The Russian tanks are just two hours away, and advancing steadily. Why not wait until they arrive, and hitch a ride with them?" We demur, explaining that with the language problem, it will be hard to communicate our wishes. He offers to negotiate with them, on our behalf.

We had hoped to make our way out ahead of the Russians, as they are an unknown quantity to us. While we don't actually fear them, we think they may channel us back through their lines, into Russia proper. And it may take months to get back to England. Then there is the Big Yank and her Dad, too, to think about. The alternative is to go back on the road, and take our chances in the column of refugees. Grudgingly, we decide to leave it to the Burgomeister.

With our decision made, the Burgomeister immediately begins to organise a reception. They have been preparing an official welcome by the townspeople to the victorious Russian troops, with our little interlude being only a sideshow. He asks for two of us to go with one of his men, to watch out for any more of our people coming through. The others are to stay put until the tanks come.

I, and another of us, volunteer for this. We are taken to a building alongside the main street which passes through the town. Everything moving has to use this street. We are taken up to the first floor, and seated in comfortable armchairs, at a very large window with excellent views of the hordes of refugees passing below.

There is an endless tide of people, all on foot, and all heading west. They are almost all civilians, with still no sign of any uniformed men amongst them. It is rather grim to see them, plodding along, just bent on getting away from the Russians. A few have been on the road for some months, while others have only just recently joined the column. All have abandoned their homes, possessions, and everything they had, to get away. The meagre few items, too precious to leave behind, they carry on their backs, or in little carts, they pull along behind them. There is hardly any vehicular transport. Occasionally, we see a farm cart pulled by a horse, but nothing motorised.

We sit at our vantage point watching. The time passes slowly, with no letup in the crowds below. After what seems about an hour having passed, we suddenly spot two fellows from our work party amongst the throng. We race down, pull them out of the crowd, and return to our watching post. They had become separated from the other fellows on the first day, and have no idea of what has happened to them. We tell them of our proposed plan, and they are happy to go along with it.

After some time has passed, during which nobody else in British uniform comes through, the streams of people thin out, noticeably. Then we get the word to go to the Town Square. The Burgomeister and several of his officials are assembled ready to greet the Russians. Most of the townsfolk have gathered also, with many carrying bunches of flowers. Our little party are assembled together, plus the two newcomers, immediately behind the Burgomeister.

We have been waiting expectantly, for little more than ten minutes, when the tank column cruises into the Square, in single file. The lead tank containing the Commander, pulls up in front of the Burgomeister. Immediately the townsfolk rush forward, surrounding the whole column and showering the men with flowers. Here and there, food and bottles of spirits are handed up. A great show of relief at their liberation, is put on. The Burgomeister makes a welcoming speech, then speaks at length with the Commander. Then it is our turn.

The Burgomeister explains who we are, our desire to get to Prague on our way home, and hope they will be good enough to give us a lift there. The Commander readily agrees, saying, "Climb aboard my tank." We had thought, they may stop in the town overnight, then proceed the next day. But, after half an hour pause, for speeches and welcome, they decide to press on. It is then about two in the afternoon.

Our party scrambles onto the tank body, and space themselves around the open turret. We are able to stand and hang onto a handrail. We tie Big Yank's two suitcases firmly to the rail, and we keep both hands free for a firm grip. We have no idea how fast, or rough, a trip it will be, and can only hope for the best. The Commander gives the order to move, and away we go at a steady cruising speed of about twenty-five to thirty miles per hour.

The Czech road system is very good. Our road has a good surface and is fairly wide, with a U-shaped ditch on either side. The day is bright and sunny, and, with summer upon us, is pleasantly warm. My position on the rail, places me in close proximity to the exhaust grid, across the back of the tank body. The powerful motors needed to propel this heavy mass, gives off a fair amount of heat. So I am content to hang on with one hand, keeping as clear of the grid as possible.

The refugees are pretty scarce now, and we are able to cruise steadily for almost an hour, before catching them up. Our Commander just eases into the tail of the column, which parts to either side. Our progress is slowed considerably. After about a quarter of an hour of this slow progress, the Commander becomes impatient. He suddenly veers off the road to the left, and onto the open field. The road here is about five feet above the surrounding plain, with the road edge falling away steeply, at an angle of forty-five degrees.

His sudden manoeuvre catches us by surprise. As the tank leaves the road at an angle, it tilts sharply to the left. I, being on the low side, am jolted off the body onto the ground. Instinctively, I cling my one-handed grip onto the handrail. As the tank bottoms and levels off, I make an almighty leap back on, just managing to clear the spinning tracks by a fraction of an inch. Badly shaken, I redouble my grip, keeping close to the turret, despite the heat from the grid. Everything had happened so fast, that nobody else seemed to notice what had taken place. I am only too grateful for a leap that, under normal circumstances, would have been beyond me.

Although we are on the way out, I'm not totally convinced that we are going home. I have this niggling fear that something may happen to prevent me, personally, while the others carry on. This incident leaves me shaken, and unreasonably scared.

As soon as we reach the flat ground, the Commander opens the throttle, with the other tanks following. And "boy", can these monsters go! Speeding across the open fields, parallel to the cluttered road, we maintain this speed for about half an hour, then turn suddenly, and charge back onto the road.

Once we are back on the road, the tanks pull to a halt. We have bypassed a lot of the clutter, and the traffic has thinned considerably. The people here are all uniformed men, plodding on as before, but no civilians.

With a temporary stop, we climb down to stretch our legs. We are immediately surrounded by German soldiers. They want to know who we are. We tell them that we are English. They say, "Thank God." They dread that we might be Russians. They are stunned when we explain that we are ex-prisoners from one of their POW camps, making our way home, and this, indeed, is a Russian tank column.

Fearfully, they ask us what they are expected to do. This puts us in a bit of a spot. If they are to be regarded as prisoners, it will have to be of the Russians. The Germans speak no Russian, and the Russians speak no German. So, somehow, we will have to find out the Commander's wishes, and relay them back to the Germans.

The only Russian word we know is "tovarisch", meaning comrade. This is spoken while raising a clenched fist to shoulder height. Somehow, with signs, waving hands, or whatever, we finally deduce what is required. The Commander insists he is not interested in prisoners, and just wants to press on. As for the Germans, he wants us to tell them to throw away their rifles, and go home.

So this bizarre scenario is played out, for about a quarter of an hour—with British Ex-Prisoners of War, instructing German soldiers, at the behest of Russian Forces, that they are to dump their weapons, and head for their hometown. At first, they are unbelieving, then in ones and twos, they drop their rifles and head off. The tank men don't even bother to collect the dumped weapons.

With the Commander impatient to get moving, we again climb aboard, leaving the milling Germans, to accept or reject the instructions, we have just handed out.

We press along the road, once again at cruising speed. Soon we begin to catch up with more traffic. Now they are Russian troops, who have commandeered anything that moves—from push bikes, horse-drawn farm wagons, dilapidated and ancient motor vehicles, of all types. Their driving skills and mechanical knowhow are very limited. So, for things motorised, they usually commandeer a German driver as well. They have no respect for road manners. The just spread across the entire road, each striving to pass the other. The forward progress now, seems to have degenerated into a badly organised race.

The heavily cluttered road slows us down. At one temporary pause, a lone Russian soldier asks for a lift. He is just told to hop aboard. With us mob, all crowded around the turret, there is actually no place for him. We expect him to board one of the other tanks. However, he climbs aboard ours. He sits squarely on the exhaust grid, as it's the only space available. The heat and gasses given off are tremendous, as the grid is only nine inches above the motors.

He is clad in standard Russian uniform, of light blouse type tunic, breeches and high boots, and a forage type cap. I would not have been surprised to see his clothing start to smoulder. But he just sits there, his Tommy gun across his knees. He stoically endures the torment, for almost fifteen miles, before electing to climb down at another stop.

We have made steady progress all afternoon. Now evening darkness begins to close in. Just ahead we can see a small village and, on the outskirts, a small group of four or five men, crouched down by the edge of the road. As we come abreast of them, we find they are Germans, manning a Panzer Faust position. A Panzer Faust is the German equivalent of the American Bazooka—an Infantry manned tank killer. Luckily for us, they decide not to fire, and we roll straight past.

We are badly shaken at the incident, acutely aware of how vulnerable we are. We decide to climb down, spend the night in the village, and plan to continue on the next day. We signal our intention to the Commander. He lets us off, then continues on his way, as we wave goodbye.

In the summer of most European villages, there are ordinary cottages with a few farm houses mixed in, stretched out along the road. We select a large farm building, and move to ask its Czech owner for permission to stay the night. We find the owner to be a young lady in her early twenties. She is quite happy for us to stay.

Continental farms are built in a square, with living quarters fronting the street, and the barns for housing cattle, down both sides and across the back. There is a large open courtyard in the centre. In the larger farms, the living quarters are two storeys high. This type of layout is necessary, as the severe winters won't allow the cattle to be free ranging, as in our country.

The young woman says that Big Yank can stay with her, then she takes us up to the first floor, to a large bare room. Already, there are about twenty to thirty other fellows there. They are British Ex-prisoners, on the road out, the same as ourselves. They are already bunked down.

The young Czech woman is sorry she cannot do much for us in the way of food, but gives us some bread and two bottles of schnapps. We select a position for ourselves, in the now crowded room. We share the bread and schnapps all round, settle down, and quickly go to sleep. It has been a very eventful day.

Halfway through the night, we are woken by the very tearful young woman, knocking on the door, and asking us to come out, as there is trouble. As last in the room, we are close to the door, so we open it to see what is the problem.

She says the Russians have arrived, entered the farm house, and are threatening to rape both her and Big Yank. She pleads with us, for someone to come down, and try to explain the situation to them. I am closest to the door and, after being told, I relay the message to Frank, who, by this time, is on his feet. Frank is further inside the room, and he will have to do some fancy footwork to avoid the prone bodies, in order to get to the door. A few of the others are sitting up by now, and we decide somebody had better go down, to try and sort things out. As I have received the message, I volunteer.

Upon leaving Mahrisch Trubau, one luxury item I have allowed myself while on the road, is a pair of pyjamas. It allows me a change each night for sleeping, instead of having to do so in my uniform. I am now in my pyjamas. Needing covering of some sort, I grab an overcoat hanging on a hook behind the door. It is Frank's coat, with three chevrons, denoting the rank of Sergeant. I figure it is best to give the impression of something of authority.

Still, thinking it is probably only a misunderstanding, I step outside to find Big Yank there, too. As we move down the hallway to go downstairs, in a shocked voice, in English, she tells me, "They have a German woman in the room down there, and they are raping her."

Now fully awake, I can see that things truly are serious. When we reach the bottom floor, I find two or three Russian soldiers standing idly by a small room close by. One is leaning against the door jamb, cradling his Tommy gun, with the door half open. Two or three, what look like

German refugee men in their forties, are standing by another door, leading out into the courtyard.

Saying, "Tovarisch," and making my clenched fist salute, I move, casually, as if to enter the little room. The Tommy gun man does not budge, and says nothing, so I back off, and stand to one side. There are noises of activity inside, but no talking. I have no illusions about preventing any Russians from doing as they wish. I just hope, that my presence may influence them, to postpone their business.

After about a quarter of an hour, there comes the sound of feet moving about. Shortly after, a fully clothed woman in her mid-thirties walks out. Her face is set, and expressionless. She clutches the waist part of her dress, holding it well out from her body. Saying not a word, she walks over to the German refugee men, and they go out through the door, back into the courtyard.

Then a Russian comes out. He appears to be in charge and, almost certainly, is the rapist. Whether he is an Officer or NCO, I cannot tell. Doing my "Tovarisch" bit, I try to tell him, I am English. This involves pointing to myself. And saying "English" in a dozen different ways. Finally, he seems to catch on. Then I point to the farm owner, saying "Czechoslovakia", and he catches on to this, as well. Suddenly, he becomes excited, speaking to her in Russian.

It seems that the Russian and Czech languages are very similar, and that it is possible for them to converse and understand each other. That might account for our Burgomeister friend being able to convey our wishes, so completely, to the Tank Commander. Now the young woman asks him to slow down, so she can follow what he is saying. Soon, she is able to make him understand the position at the farm. When she finishes her explanation, they are acting almost like old friends. I then beckon him, saying, "Come." The whole party of us troop upstairs to our temporary bedroom. I open the door, and call on our fellows to sit up. I indicate that we are all English and the Russian nods in affirmative agreement. He then spots the empty schnapps bottles, and asks for a drink. I demonstrate, regretfully, they are empty. He nods once again, then goes away, leaving us alone. We are not disturbed for the rest of the night.

When morning comes, we all gather our gear together, troop downstairs and wash up at the tap in the courtyard. With the other British Ex-prisoners making their own arrangements, our little group keeps together. With Big Yank and her Dad to think of, we decide that our best bet is to cadge another lift. Because of what has happened, during the night, we realise that the main body of the Russian Army has caught up with us. We hope to have a better choice of transport, than the previous day.

As we are planning our next move, the lady farm owner, together with Big Yank and her Dad, come across to us in the yard. The young lady singles me out, plainly grateful for the happenings during the night. As she begins to talk, Frank says, "Look time's moving on. We'll leave our gear here, go and arrange a lift, then come back." Off they go, leaving me, alone with her, to mind the gear.

She asks me if I would like some coffee. I say, "Yes," so she goes back inside, presently emerging again, with a mug for me, and one for herself. We sit in the morning sun and talk. I ask, "Where's the rest of your family?" She tells me that she is on her own. The farm had belonged to her father and mother, but they both have died, leaving it to her. She has to rely on getting help to run it, and most of this is assigned forced labour. With the end in sight, and the collapse of German authority, they have all shot through, fearing Russian reprisals. She has allowed refugees to use her premises, as temporary overnight accommodation, letting Germans and their farm carts stay in the courtyard and barns. It is from one of these, that last night's victim had been selected.

I suggest to her, that perhaps it may be wiser for her to exclude any Germans in future. I caution her to try and make it plainer, that this is Czech property, and that she, herself, is Czech. I know that things can happen too quickly for any explanations, so I ask, "Do you have a Czech flag?"

"Yes," she says.

I tell her to hang it at the front of the farm, where it will be visible from the street outside. We are conversing in German, and suddenly I have to stifle a ridiculous urge to burst out laughing. It has just occurred to me, that Aussie slang, for an intimate part of the female anatomy, is "fanny". This too, is the phonetic sound of the German for "flag". So, here am I, telling her to protect the one, by displaying one. Happily, Frank and his gang return to say, they have secured a lift.

I shake hands with her, wish her well, and away we go. As we make our way to the meeting place, Frank fills me in with the arrangements. Our transport is an open tabletop lorry. The Russian in Charge is some sort of Political Official, and they will be going all the way through to Prague. When we get to the meeting place, the Russians are ready to move.

The Politico is tall and in his early twenties. He has two soldiers riding in the cab, with a captive German soldier acting as driver. The majority of Russians seem to exist on Vodka. It makes them dangerous and unpredictable. These two in the cab, seem to be just happy.

I cannot tell if our Politico has any particular rank, or not. His men pay the kind of attention to him, that we normally do to an Officer. With this type of function, unknown in our Army, we just have to accept, that he has sufficient authority to get us through. He is cheerful and pleasant, and seems to consider it a privilege to have us British aboard. He ushers us up into the truck, motioning us to stand while hanging on to the frame at the back of the cab. With all aboard, he takes up his position, standing on the footboard alongside the driver. We immediately start to move.

The main body of troops have indeed caught up with us during the night. All that can be seen now are Russian soldiers, with the odd German captive pressed into service as a driver, as is the case on our truck. With the great urge to press on to Prague, the road is one huge swarming mass, all moving in the same direction. The same chaotic conditions of yesterday, still prevail. But, with more people competing for the same amount of road, it is just that little bit worse.

Our driver is good and competent and, although the conditions are so bad, he manages to keep us moving along with the minimum of fuss. The morning is sunny and pleasant, and we enjoy our trip, despite a few minor stops and starts. With the undisciplined road manners, we know there has to be a major traffic jam, sooner or later.

We have been travelling for over an hour, and are moving at about forty miles per hour, when a truck, similar to our own, draws up alongside and attempts to pass. It is loaded with Russian soldiers, with the Russian in Charge, riding on the footboard, as is our Politico. They draw up alongside and attempt to pass. But our Politico orders our driver, not to let them pass. So he presses on. The Russian leader is furious and orders his driver to again overtake, and, as they do, he orders our man out of the way. This time he emphasises his determination by drawing his heavy automatic pistol, and waving it threateningly. Undeterred, our Politico, again orders our driver on.

The Russian leader refuses to be denied. As he draws level with us, he speeds along beside us, waving his pistol, and is almost beside himself with rage. Our driver becomes more anxious at each attempt. Our Politico is adamant, and orders our driver on. We pray for one or the other to concede, before the next inevitable stoppage. But neither will.

Then comes another traffic jam. The two trucks, forced to stop, pull up side by side. The Russian leader, beside himself, instantly jumps to the ground. He pushes aside the Politico, leans through the open window and, with pistol in hand, deals a backhanded blow, with all his force, to the face of the German. The heavy pistol butt, trigger guard and barrel, crash, sickeningly, across the side of the man's face. Blood spurts instantly.

The Russia leader then, turns on our Politico, to let him have one too. His Russian soldier companions rush round, pleading with him to stop. However, he is too strongly committed, and refuses to take heed. Our Politico starts to argue bitterly with him, trying to assert his verbal authority. The furious argument rages on. From the gestures made in our direction, we deduce that our Politico is accusing him of disgracing the Russian Army, in front of us. No doubt, he points out that we are British Allies, and threatens him with all kinds of punishment. The Russian leader, in turn, threatens all kinds of things back, saying, "Damn the British." His soldier companions, circling warily, finally manage to grab him. They drag him away, still struggling madly.

Meanwhile, our shocked driver pushes his way along the seat, forcing one of the two men riding up front, to get out and come round to the driver's side. Trying to stem the blood flow, these two fuss over him, all the time saying soothing things, in the hope of calming him down. In terms of authority, our Politico, obviously has much greater clout. The Russian Leader, however, is obviously a dangerous man to tangle with. His men are very, very, cautious about laying hands on him, doing so only when he is completely distracted. Once they do, they half run him back, along the way he has come, all the time pleading with him to calm down.

We are spectators only, in this dust up. We hope the Russian leader's men will be able to contain him long enough, for us to get away. I, personally believe, any further confrontation, may lead to shooting.

The traffic jam has cleared itself, and the traffic has moved on. With a clear road, our Politico gives the order to move again. The two Russians up front move to make way for the German to drive. But he flatly refuses. One of the Russians then takes over the wheel and, with the German between them, we move off.

Both Russians are three parts sozzled, and concentrate all their efforts on soothing and appeasing the German. The still badly shocked and traumatised German wants no part of it. With the incompetent temporary driver, concentrating more on the German than on the road, we are now subject to the most frightening ride of our lives.

On both sides of the road is a deep ditch, with a depth of about five feet. As the driver moves off at a fast pace, the truck shoots to the edge of the drop. We brace ourselves for the inevitable rollover that will, at the least, see some of us badly crushed. As the leading wheel is about to go over the edge, the driver jerks the steering wheel sharply, causing the vehicle to shoot across to the opposite side of the road. As he does so, he again turns his attention back to the German. Now out of focus, we are again poised to shoot over the edge of this opposite side of the road. Again, we brace ourselves for the rollover, and again he swerves sharply to the opposite side of the road, at the very last second.

Usually, when a poor driver swerves sharply away from danger, then swerves sharply back again, he generally straightens up to hold a fairly even course. This fellow never does. I do not know, if he is demonstrating to the German, how to stop other traffic getting through. But he continues these tactics, for at least fifteen miles. He never once uses the brakes, and maintains a fast pace all the time. The truck is continually veering sharply from side to side. It is just a question of time before his drunken judgement causes the inevitable crash.

None of our group, utter a single word. We are all too busy hanging on, while being swung, first one way, then the other. For myself, I am petrified. Again, I have this unjust fear of being wiped out on the last leg, after those long years of waiting and hoping.

The road, hereabouts, is practically free of other traffic, with nothing to interfere with our progress. We pray for any type of stoppage to put an end to this nightmare. But nothing happens for that long fifteen miles.

Then, ahead of us, appears a town. As we approach, there is a backup of traffic. It is a massive traffic jam and, gratefully, we pull to a halt.

Our Politico climbs down from his perch on the footboard, and walks ahead to see what the holdup is. He had remained there, on the footboard, throughout our scary zigzag ride, being jolted about, but saying nothing. The soldiers on the other truck have been left well behind. His attitude seems to suggest, that all of that business, is just a forgettable incident. With our truck now at a standstill, we gradually begin to calm down.

We have pulled up in the centre of the road. There are different types of conveyances on both sides of us—all commandeered from somewhere, and all Russian soldiers. Right alongside us on our left, and at the edge of the road, is a fairly large, black sedan car. From our higher position on the body of our truck, we are able to see clearly down into the interior. There in the front seat is the driver, a Russian soldier, and in the centre of the back seat is an Officer of about Lieutenant rank. On either side of the Lieutenant is a civilian girl.

The Lieutenant is lolling back in style, and the two girls are draped, one on each shoulder, fawning over him. He is in his early thirties and half drunk; they are in their early twenties. They are fairly pretty and well-shaped. It is difficult to tell what nationality they are, but it isn't Russian. It is obvious they have attached themselves to him, probably preferring to take their chances that way, rather than to stay behind, and become the sport of the bulk of the Army. For his part, he appears to accept it, as his right.

This is a massive traffic jam, with everything locked in tight. It is obvious that it will take some time to clear itself. After a while, the Lieutenant and his girls take leave of their fawning and pawing, and begin to take some interest in what is around them. They spot us and, as we are noticeably different, they apparently begin to speculate, as to who, or what, we may be.

After a while, the Lieutenant climbs out to stretch his legs. Then one of the girls gets out too. She comes and asks, "Where are you going?"

"Prague," we answer.

She points to my slouch hat, and says she would like to borrow it. She will return it to me, when we reach Prague. It is the only Aussie hat on the Continent, and I am very much attached to it. Normally, I would have told her to go and fly a kite. But in view of the unpredictable behaviour, we have witnessed, and the rape incident, where we had been lucky, I hand it over, without a murmur. She climbs back in the car, wearing my hat, and leaving me bare in the sun. The Lieutenant, mildly amused, just paces up and down.

We have been locked in for about an hour, when an unarmed German NCO marches up smartly, and salutes the Lieutenant. He shows all the proper deference to the new masters of his country. He asks, respectfully, if it will be possible to obtain some food for his men, as they have not eaten for several days. The Lieutenant ignores him.

Some Russians, standing idly by, drift closer as the German makes another try for rations. The Lieutenant swings round, draws his pistol from its holster, and clouts the German on the side of the head. He then raises the gun to a firing position. The Russian idlers close in, spin the German round, urging him back the way he had come. The startled German breaks into a trot, and disappears. To us, the future for things German looks pretty bleak. The incident brings home to us the fact that we have never been given any food by the Russians, nor have we seen any of them eating. It is to be like this, all the time we are with them.

The jam is locked in for over three hours, before finally disentangling itself. When, finally, we clear the town, we emerge to an open road. Our former driver, still refuses to take the wheel. The Russian substitute, though still erratic, manages to steer a much straighter course. We speed on, completely alone, for over an hour. Then we are flagged down by a car, standing by the roadside.

There are two Russian Officers of fairly senior rank, standing alongside the vehicle. As we pull up, our Politico jumps down from the footboard. He begins to talk to them in a respectful manner. We know that they must be important. Their tone of voice and manner is enough to earn them respect.

After a few minutes conversation, during which our Politico seems to get very apologetic, he indicates for us to climb down. We are to continue our journey in the car. From what we can make out, the Politico and his men are to report back to their Unit. It seems that they have overstepped themselves, by agreeing to take us into Prague. The Politico ushers us across into the car, while the two Officers maintain their stance on the side of the road. They never once speak to us.

As we climb in, we take stock of the vehicle and its occupants. The car is a very large, open Mercedes Benz, German staff car. There are two Russian privates, well-sloshed, lolling back alongside the driver in the front seat. The driver is tall, blond, and obviously German. He is bare headed, and wears a plain fatigue uniform, without camouflage markings. The car has obviously been for the use of very high ranking, German Officers in the field. Even with our large party aboard, it is still roomy and very comfortable.

The Senior Officers give instructions to the privates, and away we go—leaving the two Officers still standing on the side of the road. While they are quite sober, and seem not to have had a drink, most of the rank and file seem always half sloshed and unsteady on their feet. While we wonder about this, we can see it makes little difference to their efficiency. Meanwhile, our Politico and his crew have turned about, and disappeared back from whence they have come.

Our trip now becomes a real pleasure jaunt. Our road ahead is devoid of all traffic. The two privates in the front seat fall asleep in the warm afternoon sun, while we pass the time talking to the driver, as we speed effortlessly along. He had been a racing driver before the War, and it is quite obvious in the way he handles the car. We tell him that, after Prague, we expect to link up with the Americans. Wistfully, he says he would like to come along. For a while, we discuss the pros and cons of taking him with us. Then we dismiss the idea, as pushing our luck, a bit too far. There has not been one query about Big Yank and her Dad. They have been accepted completely as a legitimate part of our group. However, taking a German soldier, could be quite another matter.

In the late afternoon, we enter the outskirts of the city. Then, after a short drive, we finally pull up in the main City Square. Stiffly, we climb down, and unload our gear. The two privates stir, and climb down, too. I turn to one and shake his hand, as a thankyou gesture for the ride. He immediately grabs me by the shoulders, plants a big slobbery kiss, first on one cheek, and then the other. I am a bit embarrassed, and more so later, when I find out, that I should have returned the gesture. Neither of us can speak each other's language, but, it is plain, we have their wholehearted good wishes.

They climb back into the car, the driver turns around, and they disappear back the way we have come. We deeply regret, that we cannot continue on in such super comfort, until we reach the final end of our journey. It has been the best part so far. Now, we have to make contact with the Czech Red Cross. We had been given these instructions by both the Burgomeister and the Resistance Chief. We find the location, quite close by.

The Red Cross people take down our particulars, then explain the situation regarding our further movement. All journeys to the west have to be sanctioned and approved by Russian authorities. They have to be made at night, and cleared by several checkpoints, on the way. They are to be made in a fully enclosed vehicle, with the occupants remaining strictly inside. All negotiations are to be conducted by the Red Cross. While we are here, we should keep very close to our assigned base, as movement approval can occur at very short notice. They earnestly ask for our cooperation, as the Russians are very suspicious, and tricky to deal with.

After our briefing, we are given a guide to take us to our temporary accommodation, until a more permanent one can be found. We hope, we won't be here long enough, for the second move.

As we walk along the street, we look with interest, at the buildings and the people we meet along the way. Prague is a very beautiful and imposing, old world, European city. The architecture is solid and mostly stone. Everything is clean and tidy. We ask our guide, if the city has suffered much, in the German occupation. He says not too much, structurally, but the people have had it very tough.

The Germans had based their administration in the city, taking over most of the important buildings. Any opposition to their orders, was firmly dealt with. Anybody seen as a threat, was quickly hustled off to a concentration camp. He tells us of the attempted overthrow, when the Resistance had taken over the radio station. He speaks of the repeated appeals for the Americans to come to their assistance, and of the inevitable ruthless countermeasures when the Czechs could no longer maintain their position. We tell him, that we had heard their radio appeals back in Mahrisch Trubau. The Czechs cannot understand why the Yanks had not come. They somehow think that the Yanks must have had their hands full elsewhere.

Once the War ended, however, the Czechs took a bloody revenge. He points to the street lamps, spaced at regular intervals along the kerb. They appear to be cast iron, with an enclosed lamp at the top, and a short arm sticking out at the base of the light. I presume that the arm is there to support a street name. Apparently, any German caught in uniform, was strung up and garrotted on that arm. He claims there were very few lamps without a body swinging from it. They were left there for several days, before being taken down. The German women were taken to the huge city square, given a toothbrush, forced to their knees, and made to scrub every inch of it.

We finally arrive at a very imposing building, and our guide ushers us inside. It is the Hotel Opera, one of the truly grand hotels of Europe. He hands us over to the staff, and tells us that he will probably see us next day. The staff usher us into a lift, whisk us up several floors, then begin to assign us to a room, two to each one. Tommy, my roommate, is a West Australian, who had come to our party at Mahrisch Trubau, just a short while, before we left there.

We two are overwhelmed. Never in our whole lives have we been privy to such a grand lifestyle. Coming after the hardships of service and POW life, we can only stare in open-mouthed wonderment. Our suite is huge, with some doors leading off to other parts. It is a bridal suite. The ornate plaster ceiling of the lofty room, is decorated with cupids and hearts entwined. The double bed is enormous and inviting. Through one of the doors we find a bathroom. The huge raised bath has two taps, obviously one for hot, and one for cold water. Despite the bath's size, it takes up only about a quarter of the huge area. Again, we can just stand, open-mouthed, in disbelief.

Then we begin to notice some flaws in this paradise. Over by the window, the wall is pitted with bullet holes. From the angle of fire, the shots had obviously come from street level below. Several windows are smashed, almost certainly from those bullets. It seems that the uprising had been pretty fierce, while it lasted. We try the bath taps to find that cold water comes from both. The hot water service is not working. We are pretty happy with our new digs, despite the flaws. Thinking that we two must be the lucky ones in the allocation of rooms, we check with the others, to find that theirs is almost identical.

We decide to have a bath, and clean up. It is almost dark and, with the evening chill, we find the water too cold to suffer for long. With food rationing in force, there is not much on offer, other than Ersatz coffee and bread—certainly, no grand dining room meals. We will just have to wait and see what tomorrow brings.

Physically tired, and emotionally drained, we have no desire to explore, so we opt for an early night. We fear that, if we wander about, we might anger the Russian authorities in some way, and they might refuse us permission to travel. We are on our way home, and again comes the fear of being chopped out, on the final leg.

This beautiful inviting bed, proves to be not as comfortable as it looks. It isn't the fault of the bed. It is just the fact that we have been sleeping rough, for so many years now, that our bodies cannot adjust. The broken windows allow the night breezes to blow around our large lofty room, until the temperature seems to drop below zero. We are glad when daylight comes, allowing us to prepare for another day. Perhaps we might even get permission to travel on.

Once cleaned and dressed, we go downstairs to the hotel dining room for breakfast. The large dining room is almost empty. There appears to be only about a dozen civilian guests, other than ourselves. Just a couple of waiters hover in the background. Obviously, the hotel is still going through some very lean times. Perhaps they are happy to accept groups such as ours, if only to keep their now skeleton staff busy.

The civilian guests are grouped together in one corner of the dining room, so we choose a section a little apart from them. We are still unsure of what our conduct should be, in these strange surroundings. We are served a continental breakfast of Ersatz coffee and rolls. There is no butter, margarine, or jam. The ingredients, in the rolls, appears to be of poor quality. Still, we seem to fare just as well as the locals, and are happy enough just to be here. While we remain at the hotel, all meals served are quite plain, and spartan. We never know, if costs are borne by the hotel, or the Red Cross.

After breakfast, we go round to the Red Cross to check if there are any developments, only to find there is nothing yet. A couple of young men invite us round to their flat for coffee. We say "OK", so they pick us up at the hotel at about eleven. A short walk, of about ten minutes, sees us at a fairly roomy, comfortable flat. Half a dozen of their friends are also there. After a few generalities, the conversation turns serious. They earnestly seek our opinion of what their country's future prospects might be.

This is pretty sobering stuff, and we talk it over at some length. We all add our little bit, with them shooting a few possibilities back at us. We suggest that Russia probably will control their destiny, with very little chance of them being allowed much input. We think the Russians will take the view, that they have forfeited any rights, by submitting, tamely, to the Germans in the first place—and ever since then, by producing arms and food for them. The Czechs point out, that their Resistance had assassinated the top German Administrator, Reinhard Heydrich, and in doing so, suffered the reprisal of the razing of an entire village, plus the extermination of its entire people. Won't this count in their favour? We doubt it, thinking that the Russians might expect that this is the very least, they have achieved.

They chew over our assessment, grudgingly agreeing, that this is probably the way things will go. They regret not having fought the Germans, when invasion first threatened, even though defeat had been inevitable. If so, their position, now, may have been that of a conquered nation, rather than a seeming collaborator, thus improving their bargaining position. The young Czechs are genuinely worried about their country's future, and we feel sorry for them. But we feel that, barring the Allies going to war against Russia, that's how things will end up.

We return to the hotel, settling into a pattern of sticking close to our quarters, and checking for movement details. After three days, the Red Cross tells us, that we are to be moved to other quarters, nearby. We move out, with each of us taking some printed postcards as souvenirs, which the hotel provides for mailing by their guests. We are taken to a comfortable building nearby, that has been used by German troops as a barracks. We are to remain here, until given permission to travel.

This time we are on our own. Big Yank and her Dad, are taken off to somewhere else. We have not been forewarned, and there are no goodbyes. We figure they will be alright, as they have been accepted completely, as Americans caught in Germany, because of the War. The only hiccup had been that threatened rape business, and that had been explained away. There is still a fair way to go, and maybe we will come together again, when sent on, from here.

In the beginning, I had been resentful of these two, with their large suitcases, and the certainty that they would slow us down, and almost certainly become a great burden. Now I am missing them. I have to admit to myself, that they were in no way near the trouble, I had expected. In fact, they have been an asset. Their presence to some extent, has helped influence us to negotiate the various lifts, we have enjoyed. The only walking we have done, was in the beginning, from Mahrisch Trubau to Zwittau. There have been some hairy spots, but our progress has been good up to now. However, I am still crooked on Togo, thinking it was his responsibility to take care of them.

Our new quarters are a typical barracks set up. There is a fairly large, long room, furnished with single iron framed cots, down both sides. Washing facilities are just outside and, although it is fairly comfortable, there are no frills. This is the kind of thing we are quite used to. Although we will not miss our hotel, we will always remember its lavishness, with affection.

Again we occupy our time, constantly checking with the Red Cross for our travel orders. With nothing much else to do, we can only hang about our quarters. We dare not wander away too far, in case word comes through, and we may miss out. The unreasoning fear of something happening to you, individually, causing you to be left behind, while the others move on, is terrifying. After a week of this tedious waiting, comes the electrifying news. We are to move out this night. We are told early in the day, and just have to sit tight, waiting for the call to move.

We gather our gear together, making sure that nothing, we value, is left behind. Now we become aware, that another group has been moved into the room next door, into a barracks setup, similar to our own. We investigate to see who they are. There are some twenty to thirty, all in bed. They are Americans, and we ask them, if they are sick. They say, "No, just starving." They have had no Red Cross parcels to keep them going, like we have.

I quickly tell them that we have not seen a Red Cross parcel for at least six months. Anyway, at this stage of the War, their own sense should tell them that Red Cross parcels are a thing of the past. I ask them how they came to be here. They tell me that the Red Cross has put them here, and left them. Nobody has been near them for two or three days.

I point out that the whole city is under food rationing, with food being doled out only by proper authorities. The Red Cross has a pretty tough job negotiating for supplies, and also the movement of people with the Russians. It is unlikely they have the time, or the personnel, to spare, in order to take care of every small group that turns up. It is fair to expect somebody may be overlooked. I suggest that, if they want to survive, they had better get off their tails and make contact, as we have done.

The fellow I am talking to is in the first bed, nearest the door. He now climbs, rather weakly, from his bed, and a little shamefully, supports himself by hanging on to the side. I tell him that we will be only too glad to help them, but we are moving out tonight. I suggest, they select two or three of those most able to move around, and have them keep in constant touch with the Red Cross. And, if they have any wounded or sick needing attention, ask the Red Cross for medical help. I explain that the supplies of food, and movement back to their own people, can only come from the Red Cross. And this can only be done by negotiation with the Russians. In this situation, they just have to keep in touch with the Red Cross, and not wait for the Red Cross to come to them.

We part, with me wishing them luck, and he promising to see they get better organised. I comment, "The sooner you do, the sooner you will be in American lines."

As darkness approaches, the tension starts to build up for us. This is to be the last leg of the trip to freedom. Sometime during the night, or early in the morning, we should be with the Americans. We are restless and fidgety. Secretly, each of us worries, in case anything goes wrong at this late stage. We just hope the Russians do not cancel, for we feel our nerves won't stand it.

It is about eight o'clock, when a guide takes us to the loading point. At last, our move is really on. In the darkness we can just make out the shape of our conveyance. It is a trailer, about the size of a standard truck body. It is completely enclosed by a canvas cover, with open flaps at the rear. It is hooked onto a farm tractor, with a man in civilian clothes as driver. We are the last to arrive, and scramble aboard, sitting on the floor, close to the tail. With only a short delay, the word is given, and we begin to move.

The tractor's speed is slow. It seems to be moving at about fifteen miles per hour. Looking around us, we can see there are about fifty people aboard. They are all civilians with the exception of us. It looks as though our small group has been added, to make up the load. Big Yank and her Dad, are not among them. There is no talking, with only the occasional subdued whisper to be heard. Nobody attempts to look out. Nobody wants to offend the Russians.

With the slow progress over the dusty roads, clouds of smoke begin to be sucked into the back. I take out my handkerchief, and tie it across my nose and mouth, as was the normal procedure under similar conditions we followed, up in the Desert.

We lose track of time, as each of us becomes wrapped up in his own thoughts. After what seems about an hour, our tractor begins to slow, in a preliminary to stopping. We become aware of voices outside. As we come to a halt, footsteps move to the rear of our vehicle. Suddenly, the rear flap is thrown aside, and two Russian sentries look in. It is the first checkpoint. As they shine a torch about, checking that all is in order, one becomes aware of me, with my face covered.

I am sitting in the last-man-in position, right at the tail. I suppose it may seem that I am concealing my identity. They clearly become agitated, and I realise I must do something quickly, to calm them down. Frank also calls from his position opposite me, "For God's sake Arty, take that bloody thing off." I yank my handkerchief down, making a big show, as if spitting out dirt. I grab their free hand, one at a time, shaking it warmly and doing my Tovarisch bit. This seems to calm them down, and after a few more minutes, they give us the OK to move on.

I make no further attempts to keep the dust out, determining to put up with it for the rest of the trip. We roll on, through another two checkpoints, without incident. We have been rolling along for quite a long while now, and I have sunk into a kind of half-stupor. It seems to be sometime in the early hours of the morning, when we come to another checkpoint. But this one is different. The voices outside the rear flap are American. We quickly rouse ourselves, and reach out to touch them, just to make sure they are real.

After a quick inspection, they pass us on further to their rear. We don't remember much after this. I just have a hazy awareness of reaching some kind of camp, falling into a camp bed, and dying, for what is left of the night.

When we come to, we find that we have arrived at a large American transit camp. We feel refreshed and eager to move on. There is no sign of the civilians, we came through with. We suppose that they must be being cared for elsewhere. The ordinary Yank Servicemen, we are now quartered with, are friendly and sympathetic to us as ex-POWs. We are free to make use of the camp facilities. There are no parades. Food is in abundance, and the fellows are constantly offering us cigarettes and candy. Often cartons of their K rations will be brought in and broken up. Their contents contain unbelievably wonderful meals in our eyes, yet are scorned as commonplace, and uninviting, by the Yanks.

We have nothing to do bar, eat, sleep, and clean ourselves up. We are told that as soon as transport can be arranged, we will be sent on, eventually to England. As soon as we begin to take notice of the men around us, we find the Yanks to be a very unhappy lot. A new word has just been added to their Service vocabulary. It is "redeployment". It means that, now that the War is over in the European sector, the Units here will be sent out to the Pacific, to do battle with the Japs.

The Yanks are most upset with this. They claim that, after being over here all this time and risking their necks, they should be allowed to go home. Anyway, sooner or later, they are going to have to fight the Russians. Now that they are here and ready, they should be allowed to do it.

We sympathise with them, asking, "How long have you been away?"

"A whole six," they answer.

Mystified, we ask, "Six what?"

We are told, "Six months," making it seem like sixty years.

I am afraid our disgust gets the better of us, as we reply, "Christ mate, you haven't started yet! We've been away six years."

Our reaction to their situation, clearly disconcerts them. It simply has not entered their heads, that there can be an opposite view. Their feelings on the matter are universal—nobody, among them, thinks any other way. We begin the think, they seem very reluctant soldiers. We begin to wonder, how can it be possible, that the tremendous military successes, they have achieved, can actually be the work of these reluctant men?

Apart from our comment on their wish to go home, we make no further mention of their situation, and we remain good friends. However, as this is our first contact with the Americans, we are greatly intrigued at their ideas, and the way they do things.

One morning I decide to have a shower, and am leisurely making my way to the shower lines. Some thirty yards from them, I become aware of a large group of about thirty people. As I come abreast of the group, I can see a female in Service dress, seated in the centre. The rest of the group are Yank Servicemen, forming a solid block on both sides, and behind her. We have heard of women in the Services, but, other than a few Russian women, this is the first one I have seen. I half-stop to get a better look, but quickly resume my way because of the obvious hostility of her self-appointed guardians. As one, they all stare balefully at me. The unspoken warning is quite plain. Keep away or else! I continue on, deciding to postpone my curiosity, until later.

Upon reaching the showers, I enter and strip ready to bath. The installation is a single pipe, with four showerheads on top, pointed in different directions. The idea is for bathers to cluster round it together. There are two black Yanks showering, just taking their time. I have heard, vaguely, of American segregation of blacks and whites, but this means nothing to me. So I move to get under, too. They refuse to make way for me, deliberately prolonging their shower, and making me wait, until they are good and ready.

I decide that my best reaction is to just fold my arms, stand back and watch them. After all, they can't stay under the shower all day. I have no way of knowing what their plans are, but I have plenty of time, and can wait longer than they can. There is an air of arrogance in their stance, as they continue to make me wait. I continue to stand, arms folded and watching them. After some seconds I can detect some anxiety in their demeanour. A few seconds more and they decide to get out. Then I get under the shower. Not one word passes between us during this time.

In our Forces, there are a few Aborigines and many Maoris are with the Kiwis. We always accept them as equals, with every bit as much rights as we have. They bleed and hurt the same as us, and we are damn glad to have them along. I will always remember the way the Indian POWs had doled out precious food scraps to us, when we arrived at Stalag VIIIB. The Maoris in particular are our friends, sharing all the hardships of POW life. I have heard of white discrimination against the blacks, now I have actually experienced, black discrimination against a white.

We continue on with this group of Americans for a week, before receiving word to move out. We have been in a kind of limbo, just waiting, and anxious to move on. Now, we are to be taken to a flying field, and flown to France. The prospect of flying gives us a tremendous lift. This will cut the journey time considerably. Maybe, they may even decide to fly us back home.

The trucks arrive early, and we are at the flying field at Regensburg by about 9.30 am. It is a vast open area, and is said to have been a Luftwaffe fighter base. It is entirely grass covered, with not a sign of the smallest bit of debris. There are no buildings. But, on the side where we are, there is a small area of brick foundations, either waiting to be built on, or where buildings have been torn down.

There has been a steady build-up of released POWs and, with typical Yank efficiency, a big contingent has been assembled here for the airlift to France. There are hundreds of men gathered, waiting for the planes to arrive. Following instructions, we all sit on the ground together, on one side of the airfield—not daring to move, for fear of obstructing their landing.

It is a beautiful sunny day and, as the morning moves on, we begin to feel the effects of the heat. There is no sign of any taps or water, and we have brought none with us. And, we dare not go looking for any, for fear of being left behind. We strain our ears, constantly listening for planes that do not come. The tension is tremendous. We are too damn scared to move, in case we miss that plane. I begin to get a headache. By midday it is the mother of all headaches, where my scalp seems to crawl down over my eyes, making it difficult for me to see. I finally reach a point where I seem to have lost the capacity to feel. I can only observe and experience, in a detached automatic fashion.

It is about two-thirty in the afternoon, before the sound, we have waited so long for, becomes audible. In next to no time, a fleet of Dakota transports appears, lands, and rolls to a halt on the far side of the field. The access doors of the Dakota opposite us open, and from the body of the plane step two "Hollywood Stars". They are dressed in cool, casual, designer slacks and skirts, incognito in gold rimmed dark glasses, and chewing gum, of course. To us they appear like creatures from another planet. They completely ignore this motley sea of humanity awaiting them.

The word to board comes from somewhere. We line up, and file aboard in a pretty subdued fashion. Meanwhile, these two "Gods" disappear somewhere in the cockpit area. There are long fixed forms, down each side of the plane. We all take a seat. There are no frills, and we don't expect any. One of the "Gods" checks the door fastening, then prepares to disappear again. As he moves forward, one of the blokes asks nervously, "Is there any danger of crashing?"

The Yank replies offhandedly, "A couple crashed yesterday."

"What happened?"

"They were all killed," says the Yank, then vanishes into the cockpit area.

Most of us have never flown before and, under normal circumstances, the trip may have excited us immensely. But to me, at least, it is just another happening, as mundane and automatic as getting out of bed in the morning. I notice that, contrary to appearances from the ground, once in the air, and in formation, we tend to drift up and down, in anything but an orderly fashion. It is only a short flight, that seems to be barely half an hour.

We shape to land, fly in and touch down. As we hit the ground, there is a tremendous noise and clatter. For a terrifying moment, we think we are about to crash. Then the plane rolls on, and we all know we are safe, though the noisy clatter continues. The noise, we hear, comes from vast rolls of chain wire mesh, pegged to the ground, and is caused by the heavy plane rolling over it. These clever Yanks make instant flying fields, by rolling out chain wire mesh on any reasonable flat stretches of ground. When it comes to move on, they roll it up, and take it with them.

We are in Rheims in France. From the airfield, we are moved to what seems to be a very large rest and recreation area. We are told to prepare ourselves for bathing, before moving to our overnight sleeping quarters. This is to be a kind of preliminary delousing. Our little group still keep together, although we are only a small part of the crowd, that has now come together.

We are lined up in queues, facing a mobile field shower unit. We strip, leaving our clothes behind, shower, then don fresh clothes on the other side. We are allowed only three minutes to shower—one minute with the water on to get wet, one minute with the water off to soap up, then one minute with water on to rinse off. We have never seen such a contraption before, and can only marvel at the Yanks' efficiency to get things done.

The unit itself is on a long trailer, so that it can be taken anywhere in the field. A single pipe passes along the centre, just above an average man's height. From the pipe, showerheads point to the truck sides, at regular intervals along its length. It can handle two queues at a time. With eight to ten men in each queue, something like twenty men are going through at a time. Yank NCOs are in charge, keeping the line moving.

As we wait our turn, we are able to look at what is going on around us. I notice that all physical work is being done by uniformed German soldiers, unarmed, of course. The Yanks, as conquerors, are using the Germans as their labour force. Some distance away, I can see a line of them working continuously as barbers, shoe shiners, tailors and pants pressers. Any Yank who feels like it, can just stroll up, flop in a chair, and tell the prisoner to get on with it. And there seems to be a steady stream, doing just this. I, personally, feel rather dubious about this attitude. I just hope that this scene is not being set for World War III, because of the humiliation being heaped upon these Germans.

As it comes closer for our turn to shower, a Yank Sergeant is having trouble getting his orders through to a German labourer, who is bringing cartons of fresh clothing for us. The Sergeant wants him to open the cartons, stack the clothing alongside, and put the used clothing back into the cartons, then take them away. Neither speaks the other's language and, the German, anxious to please, keeps doing the wrong thing. The Sergeant, getting more furious, finally calls out, "Does anybody here speak German?"

I say, "I speak some."

"Well tell this God damn son of a bitch, what I want done," bellows the Sergeant.

I go forward and speak quietly to the German. He does what is required with efficiency and dispatch. He skittles away as quickly as he can, glad to escape the Sergeant's loud bellowing. Then it is our turn to shower.

After showering, we dress in used, but freshly laundered American Uniforms. We keep only our very few personal items. I am sorry to leave behind my Aussie uniform, but realise I will have to part with it somewhere, in the interests of hygiene. From the showers, we are moved to the area where we are to spend the night.

We are taken to what appears to be a large University, or Municipal Headquarters of some sort. The building is huge and imposing. The very wide and lofty façade is supported by ten or twelve massive columns. Wide flights of steps lead up to the entrance, from which many figures, in Yank uniforms, are coming and going. The Americans have obviously taken it over, as their Headquarters. As we look, we become aware of something printed in huge letters, right across the front of the building. Immediately above the entrance for all to see, it reads, "THROUGH THESE PORTALS PASS THE BEST DAMN SOLDIERS IN THE WORLD". We can only stare open-mouthed.

On vast lawns in front of the building, is a sea of tents, containing fairly comfortable army cots. It is just a case of take your pick. With K rations freely available, there are no worries about food. We settle down for the night, too emotionally and physically drained to even consider exploring.

As I doze, I recall the incident of the Yank Sergeant and the German labourer. I suddenly realise that I am the only person to admit to speaking some German, although there must have been at least fifty within earshot, as good as, or better than me. It slowly comes home to me, that all things German are definitely out of favour right now. It will be wiser for me, to prepare for my homecoming by cutting any casual allusions from my thoughts and speech. We have long formed the habit of including a German word or two in our casual conversations—such as "Arbeit" instead of "work". This will have to stop, too.

Next morning, we waste little time preparing for yet another move. With a minimum of fuss, we again move out to the airfield. The planes land about 11.00 am. They are British Lancaster bombers. They have been stripped of their armaments, and pressed into service for our benefit. The crew, all dressed in regulation, shapeless flying kit, fuss around us, solicitously, like old hens. The Captain apologises, seriously, for being so late. He explains that it has been a big job, getting the plane comfortable for us, after combat. He promises to fly low over the coast, and give us a good look at the D-Day landing areas.

It is a mixed Commonwealth crew, and there is much sorting out of, "Who's English, Aussie, Kiwi?" etc. Amidst all the handshaking, they talk to us. They ask questions, and all the time they apologise for the spartan conditions. They fuss over us, getting us on board, and stowed away as comfortably as possible. A man is placed in each of the mid and rear gunner's turret. These are the pick of the positions, with a marvellous view, and a comfortable, fully rotating seat to themselves. I score a seat on a short form, fixed to the side of the plane, and about in the middle.

When this happy scramble has died down a little, our pilot gives the word, and we prepare for take-off. There does not seem to be any organised schedule, just pick up your load and get going. The big motors roar, and quickly we are up and away. Once we are fully airborne, a crew member opens a big hatch in the floor, so that those of us in the body of the plane, can see better. The hatch opening is at least three feet in diameter, and the door is very heavy. Some men cluster round the opening for a better view. My position is on the end of the seat, so close to the aperture, that I am able to look straight down in comfort. The crewman stays in position, pointing out different features as they come into view. True to his word, the pilot descends, as we near the coast, giving us a first class view of the area stretched out below.

I am amazed. I had expected almost total devastation, but the damage is very minimal. The bomb craters are few, and widely scattered. I see no evidence of wrecked tanks or vehicles, or any sunken ships. Maybe this had been a quiet sector of the landings, or a very good job of cleaning up has taken place. On our flight from Regensburg to Rheims, we passed over what had been a very large industrial town, which had been destroyed by heavy and concentrated Allied saturation bombing. The craters there are lip to lip, and overlapping. The destruction is total. For the D-Day area, I have expected something similar, if not as bad.

As we clear the coast, the plane is caught in a slight downdraft, and drops about fifty feet. As I am leaning forward, this has the tendency to pull me out of my seat, and into the gaping hole at my feet. Again, I am overcome with irrational fear. In a split second, I can visualise myself falling through that gaping hole, plummeting to my death below. For a moment, I am seized by panic, fully convinced, that I am to be cheated out of my freedom, on the very last lap. As the panic subsides, I look around. Nobody else appears affected in any way. Nevertheless, I take a firm grip, with both hands on my fixed seat, and take very little interest in the scenery, from now, until we land.

We have no idea where this will be, except in England. Our little group from Mahrisch Trubau, is still together. We have finally made it. We climb down from the plane, and walk slowly towards a reception area. There are groups of Servicewomen, bareheaded and dressed in Army working dress, rushing forward as each plane stops, helping the men with their gear. There is a bank of Newsreel cameras on tripods and, with arc lights shining, standing to one side. We have no gear, so the Servicewomen turn, from us, to some of the others. The cameras pay us no attention, no doubt having captured the same scenes many times already. Something exceptional will have to be needed, for them to consider using any further film.

We pass through to reception, being deloused, with grey DDT powder, on the way. This involves blowing the powder inside our clothing, through arm, leg, and chest openings. As soon as a load is assembled, we are placed in a covered truck, and whisked away to temporary overnight quarters. With no idea of our whereabouts, I begin to look for signposts. Suddenly, I spot one I am able to read. It reads "Bicester". I ask, "Does anybody know where By-sester is?"

A very English voice, from somewhere inside, answers in a disgusted tone, "Not By-sester—Bister."

I know then, for sure, we have finally arrived. At our overnight quarters, facilities are made available for us to cable home. The messages are all standard, saying briefly, "Arrived in England – Safe and well – See you soon". We supply the home address and signature. And so it ends.

## Chapter 17

# Freedom – England

OUR LOT ARE COMPARATIVELY LATE arrivals from captivity, with quite a few having already been repatriated home. Procedures for our reception, care, and housing, are, therefore, well organised and running like clockwork. Nevertheless, while we appreciate the organisation, we find it strange in coming to terms with our new situation. We herd together like cattle, and just go in the direction in which we are pointed.

Arrangements for our billeting are set up at the coastal town of Eastbourne, not far from London. In pre-war times, Eastbourne had been a very popular holiday resort, and had many boarding houses that catered for visitors. These had been mostly boarded up, while the threat of invasion was on. Now, they are ideal for the rest and recuperation of us lot, exclusively for Australians. We imagine that the Kiwis, and other nationalities, have similar setups, somewhere else.

A large building, staffed by Australian Comforts Fund people, is Headquarters for the area. From here, we are allocated our quarters, and everything necessary to our needs, no matter how remotely obscure, is covered with ease. Travel arrangements, advice mail, anything at all, comes from here. We are attracted to the place by necessity, and it automatically becomes our temporary or unofficial home, while our billets are just somewhere to sleep.

The former boarding houses are all several storeys high, and side by side in rows. Frank and I, still together, are allocated beds in an upper storey of one of the houses. Our room is rather large, and contains about eight beds. They are individual iron cots, and quite comfortable. The furnishings are nice, without being elaborate. We have been doing it rough for so long now, that this sudden transport to comfort, is something we aren't quite ready for.

Messing arrangements see us attending a large dining hall, close to our quarters, where meals are served to us at regular hours. While the whole of England is still under rationing, our government has supplied mountains of the best of food, just for us. Pommy messmen cook, and serve it to us, and are under instructions, that it is for us, alone.

With food and lodging taken care of, our next priority is moving on. We are rather dismayed to find, that we may have to wait for some time. It seems, that we will have to remain here, until a ship can be made available, and for sufficient numbers to have gathered, to make the trip worthwhile. After flying from Germany to France, and then on to England, we had rather hoped, that we might be flown all the way home.

Our first duty is to fill out a printed statement, giving details of our capture, treatment, and any relevant facts, that may be significant for official records. This is done, fairly informally, at our Comforts Funds Headquarters. We are too experienced old hands by now, just to do as we are told. We have to think of what may happen, if we are to report something controversial. We are sure that may mean keeping us back here, while the facts are being checked and rechecked. To us, this would be intolerable. Therefore, our answers are honest, but guarded.

With this duty out of the way, one of our first priorities is to check on the well-being of all our friends, and the people we know from our group at Mahrisch Trubau. This place is a mine of information. Big Allan has made it through, but without the operation on his "heaps". It still has to be done. Norm and Little Yank have made it, with Norm somewhere in England. My main concern is Togo. I am still determined to chew him out for saddling us with Big Yank and her Dad, although things turned out alright. It is from Norm, that I learn about Togo and little Alistair, and the rest of their group.

The news is short and to the point. Togo and his group, travelling on foot much the same as our own little group, rounded a corner onto a road, and were spotted by a Russian tank column, from about a quarter of a mile away.

The Russians, seeing them in a strange uniform, considered them enemy and opened fire, before it could be established, that they were English and not German. Togo is dead, and Alistair, the little Scotsman, is gravely wounded in the head. Although the Russians did everything they could, it is felt that Alistair has very little chance of pulling through.

I am stunned. We have lived together on our working party for about three and a half years. We have shared the bad spots, and the fits of black despair, that regularly plagued us. The rough humour and the sharing is all gone. Alistair, a little man with a wry sense of humour, had endeared himself to everyone. Togo was a big man, and his bigness earned him respect. But he was no bully. His infectious laugh, his great capacity for humour, and his soft musical voice, probably stemmed from the Maori side of his forebears.

Now, all I can think of are the good things. My petty whingeing seems stupid. It just isn't right for things to end like this. It takes a fair bit of skin off our new found freedom. Much later, we hear that Big Yank and her Dad, have made it through to America.

With each national group being taken care of by their own people, the information available to us, concerns mainly the Australians. My first concerns are for my two escaping mates—George, my Aussie mate, who turned himself in on Mount Athos, and Bob, the Pom, who had come through to Lamsdorf with me.

I learn that George is in England, but nothing more. At least he has come through alright. As for Bob, I cannot find a thing. Two of our old Newcastle contingent, Dave and Arthur, are here too. This gives me a slight sense of satisfaction. When George and I had tried to team up with them for the train trip through to Germany from Salonika No 2, they had given us the brushoff, claiming they had their own plans of escaping. I would be mortified, if they had succeeded, when our own efforts had fallen down.

I meet with Arthur soon after our arrival. In common with all of us, he is checking at Comforts HQ, for mail and movement orders. He is pretty busy, and says he has to be off. He can spare me only a few minutes to talk. He and Dave are being cared for, as guests of the management of Lysaght's English Works. They have been in England for some time. They had gone up to London, and chanced to meet with Parry Okeden in the street. Parry, being the General Manager of the Australian Plant based at Newcastle, our hometown, has arranged with the English Management, for special treatment to be given to his men, who have just been released from German POW camps.

Arthur and Dave say, that Okeden had fallen all over them, insisting on taking them with him to Lysaght's English Works, where he is scheduled to hold talks, regarding the future of the Australian Plant. Before the War, Dave was a Superintendent, and Arthur a Staff Member of the Newcastle Plant. The English Management has responded by installing them in one of the best hotels, where they are waited on hand and foot, with everybody falling over themselves, looking after ex-POWs.

They are feted and cared for to such an extent, that they have overstayed, missing the previous ship home. Arthur is here now, checking on movement orders, before heading back to their luxury accommodation. As a Lysaght's workman myself, albeit of lower echelons, I know there is sufficient in this tale to suggest, that it may be true. Still, I don't know whether to believe it, or not.

Then he tells me of Wally, one of our Unit mates. The story is bizarre and unbelievable. Wally had gone home on the previous ship, in a pretty bad way. As an incorrigible escaper, he had ended up in a concentration camp. I find out later, from Wally, that while this is true, the story is fanciful and way over the top. It seems that a lot of information, we are receiving, can be relied upon, but some of it is a little suspect.

This brief talk with Arthur is unsettling. As I had been promised my job back at Lysaght, when I enlisted, it forces me to give some thought to "afterwards". The War is still very much on in the Pacific, against the Japanese, although our mob seems to have them on the run. My great yearning is to get back to my Unit, and to meet up with my mates again.

I long to see Harry, Joe, Billy "the Wog", Moby Dick, and all the others. And Taffy—what had happened to him, after we left him behind in Alexandria, after being knocked down by a taxi? I know, intuitively, that he is still around somewhere. For I would have "felt" it, if anything had happened to him.

And what about Lenny, Old Bill and Ayrt Onyons? God! What a marvellous gabfest we will have, as soon as we are together again! We will swap half-truths and lies, as if there is no tomorrow. The time will just roll away, as if we had never departed.

Then, gradually, it seeps through to me, that we have been departed for four long years. Things just can't be the same anymore. It will be impossible to get them altogether in one place again, like in the old days, even if they all are still around. My doings, and the happenings since that time, have been totally different to theirs. Although the interest in each other will still be there, the rapport and understanding, brought about by shared experiences, will be gone. That closeness has ended, perhaps forever. I feel more bitter than ever about my capture. If only, I had made it through to Turkey back then, instead of being recaptured on Lemnos. The parting would have been only temporary, a mere six months. Then everything would have been as before.

The disturbing realities of our freedom, trying to reconcile the past, facing an uncertain future, are upsetting hurdles for all of us. Ours is a kind of brotherhood, where we feel safe amongst our own kind, but unsure, when we are parted. We cling to our friends, and those we know, rather than try to re-establish old acquaintanceships, or Unit associations. Thus, Frank and I continue to keep together.

There are no parades, no drills, or military procedures of any kind. We have somewhere to sleep, but can sleep elsewhere, if we wish; likewise with meals. We are free to go and come, as we wish. We are entitled to one free rail pass to anywhere in the country. We are given the drum to apply for one from Lands' End to John O'Groats. That is, from the very bottom to the very top of Britain. With it, we can break our journey anywhere, stay a while, then continue on.

But, freedom of travel, is denied us for the moment. We are deemed to be "unproperly clad". While we have been fully outfitted, the finishing touches, Unit colour patches and some badges, are still to come. Until these arrive, we will just have to wait.

But, let it be understood. If we feel we want to go here, or do that, we will. We have just walked out of a prison camp, deep inside Germany, defying our Guards, crossed Europe, arriving in England in the ultimate escape. There is no way that being told, we can't go on leave, will be sufficient to hold us. The defiance won't be open, we will just melt away, and do our own thing, if we feel like it.

What keeps us put, is the possibility of a ship becoming available, at short notice. Until we are able to assess for ourselves, how short this notice may be, we will have to rely on official news. This means fronting each day, only to be told, "Nothing yet."

After a couple of days, we begin to realise that nobody is making any great effort to have us moved on. This being the case, we may be here for a few weeks, or a month, or more. Of course, the War in the Pacific takes first priority. As much as we hate the idea, we will have to wait our turn. With ships being badly needed over there, it may be a long time, before one becomes available for us, here.

Once we come to terms with the situation, we begin to look at what options are open to us. We can make day trips up to London, when we are granted our leave passes. Comforts HQ has many holiday offers available. These range from a day or two billeting with private families, in towns and cities across the country, to a week or two on country estates, with horse riding facilities available.

Then there is my Manchester connection. My Manchester girl, in the last letters, I had received, had practically ordered me to go straight there. Those intimate letters promised much, and were great morale boosters, while we were captives. Now that we are free, just what can I expect? It was me, she focussed her attention on, and me she wants to see. While Frank will be welcome, also, not knowing the situation there, I just don't know what to do.

The facts I have about her, while irrelevant before, now are of some significance. I know that she is married, and about three months, or so, pregnant. Her husband is overseas at the moment, after a short leave—hence, the baby. She has a son, about ten. While I have to remember my commitments back home, it doesn't look like I can get into much trouble here. Anyway, until I am granted leave and a rail pass, Manchester looks to be out of the question.

We had thought that slipping back into everyday life, will just happen, with a minimum of fuss. How wrong we are. We are aliens in a strange land. Being in friendly territory, our pattern of behaviour has to recognise, that we are now among friends. We can no longer take or steal anything. Rationing is very much in force, and quite incomprehensible to us. If there is something we think, we will buy, almost always we can't, because of the coupons needed. Money is another thing. We have substantial credits in our pay books, but after getting by for so long without any, we have no idea about prices. So, mostly we overdraw, just in case.

Frank has an Aunty just outside London, and more relatives in Bristol, whom he just has to visit. And there is the ex-POW Sailor, from our Mahrisch Trubau days, whom we have to look up in Bristol too. While we can fit the Aunty in at the moment, the Bristol lot will have to wait, until we are granted our rail passes.

We like the idea of mixing with the people, and talking freely again in our own language. While the Pommy twang isn't always easy to understand, we have mixed so much with them as prisoners, that it isn't a problem either. Mostly, we just want to mix with females—talk to them and just listen to their chatter, from the very young, right through to the old. For myself, I have to keep close watch on my swearing. The more control I gain now, the easier it will be when, finally, I meet up with my family and Jean, the girl I left behind.

Our first outing will be a visit to Frank's Aunty. He has phoned and alerted her, that we two are coming to visit. We go by train up to London, then out to the suburb, where she lives. She has insisted that we come to lunch, and is very excited at the prospect of our coming. I gather that, although she is a relative, she is almost as unknown to Frank, as she is to me. She turns out to be pretty much as I expect.

She is medium tall, slim and fair, in about her early fifties. She greets and fusses over us like a mother hen. She has gone to great trouble, to make this a special treat. The table is set in an open sunny room, and is resplendent with napery and all the trappings, so dear to the heart of your "nice" household manager. It has been years since we have been treated in this fashion, and we will have to struggle, to regain these almost forgotten skills. For our meal, there is to be something special. She has been saving her food coupons for some time, in expectation of Frank's imminent release. Triumphantly, she announces, it is to be salmon.

Back in Mahrisch Trubau, where we had been eating together for some years, taking turns to conjure up a meal from what supplies we had, the one food item that plagued us was salmon. Our Red Cross food parcels, latterly packed in Canada, always contained a tin of salmon. It was the one item we found almost impossible to turn into a palatable meal. Consequently, when stockpiling food to cover shortages, almost always, the item set aside was salmon. For the last six months in Mahrisch Trubau, we had received no food parcels at all. So, we had to cut into our supplies—salmon of course. By the time we left Mahrisch Trubau, as far as possible for a POW to do so, we were heartily sick of salmon. Now, this very nice lady has stretched her resources to the limit, for our special benefit. What can we say?

Making suitable noises of appreciation, we sit down to a truly enjoyable experience, notwithstanding the salmon. The grateful feeling of everyday ordinariness, is something to savour. We chat with our hostess, and there is much discussion of family relationships, with explanations for my benefit. When it comes to leaving, she makes us promise to return, if it is at all possible. We do so on the understanding, that she will not squander her precious food coupons on items, such as salmon, for our benefit.

With the first outing under our belt, we really can't stop ourselves from continuing. The urge to keep going is irresistible. We continue our excursions up to London. We decide to see some of the sights, such as Big Ben, the Houses of Parliament and Westminster Cathedral. We are greatly entertained by just walking, observing the comings and goings of people, and just talking to some of them. There are servicemen everywhere, and servicewomen too, although the latter are very much a novelty to us. We are still having difficulty coming to terms with the idea of women in uniform.

The wide range of nationalities represented by the people, brings home to us, just how many countries are involved in this War. A lot of the overrun nations, have governments in exile, functioning here in Britain. Most of their nationals, who have managed to get clear, are formed into Armies to fight on, such as the Free French, Free Polish etc. They wear mostly British Battle dress, with their own distinctive badges and headgear. Other than some Air Force men, we are the only Aussies hereabouts.

Of course, there are large numbers of Yanks around, and we seem to come across them everywhere we go. We are intrigued greatly, to find that a great many of them have, what seems to be, some sort of high decorations, dangling from their left breast pockets. The ribbons are wide, about six inches long, but instead of medals, they have purplish bulbous things, hanging on the ends. We ask what they are, to be told, the award of the

Purple Heart. Now, we can indeed see, that the things on the ends, are shaped like hearts.

We know that the Yanks, like us, have a system of bravery awards, with their highest, the Congressional Medal of Honour, roughly equivalent to our highest, the Victoria Cross. Still, this Purple Heart has us beat. We just can't figure out what it has to be for. On asking, we are told that it is for being wounded in battle. We make the appropriate noises of being impressed. But, privately, I think it is a lot of hoo-ha for doing your job.

Getting a little bolder, we decide it may be an idea to sample some of the night life. We are advised to try Piccadilly Circus. About six o'clock, we arrive at Eastbourne station, for the trip to London. Directions, of how to get there, are given by our friendly female porter. She finishes by adding, "And watch your step." We realise then, that sex will be on sale there, too.

Being Britain, we know there will not be an area where brothels abound, such as we were used to in Egypt. Being wartime, we also know that there will be some sort of trade going on. Usually, where there is such trade, small bars abound with food and drink. It might be interesting to see, what goes on here.

We find the place and look around. There are very few people moving about. The area appears to be a quite respectable business area. We can find no cabarets, clubs, or any places dispensing drinks. We wait, knowing that there must be some sort of activity going on. We are just about to give up when, about nine thirty, a couple of girls appear. As if by magic, a couple of fellows appear. They are pounced on by the girls. The girls wave their hands, and a taxi comes from nowhere. The two girls and two blokes climb in the back, and the taxi moves off. In what seems like only five minutes, the taxi returns, and they all get out. It seems that the taxi acts as a roving brothel, with the girls signalling, when they need him. A quick run round the block, and they are ready for business again.

By this time, we've had enough, and are ready to head back home. We are emotionally and physically exhausted, and cannot last much after dark. Here, nothing much happens before ten, with everything then speeding up, and running through to dawn. We just don't have the stamina, to match this kind of schedule.

Back at Comforts HQ, I run into Norm, and am very pleased to meet him. While I had heard that he made it through, I am anxious to talk to him myself. I am keen to get the real story of how he and Little Yank have fared. As he had left Mahrisch Trubau before us, I am able to tell him that we had brought Big Yank and her Dad out with us. For Norm it had been pretty straight forward, with him leaving Little Yank with the first bunch of Americans, they came across.

He asks me, anxiously, if I have brought out with me his wallet, containing photos and personal papers. I have to tell him, "No". While I had seen it lying on his bunk, when we were about to leave Mahrisch Trubau, I had thought that he had discarded it. I should have brought it, for I know it means a lot to him. I have let him down, and I feel bad.

Norm tells me that he is off to meet up with a bloke from our Unit, a South Australian named Doug, who is an NCO like us. He had spent his captivity somewhere else. Norm had told Doug of the circumstances of his and Little Yank's escape. Doug's family in South Australia are involved in the newspaper publishing business. One or two reporters, known to him, are here in London. Doug had passed the story on to the reporter, with Norm supplying some of the details. The reporter had relayed the story back home, and a rather coloured version has appeared, as a full page item in the Australian Womens Weekly. It is a romanticised version, portrayed as a true love story. Naturally Norm is rather embarrassed by it all. The purpose of this further meeting with the reporter and Doug, is to try and get the reporter to tone it down a bit. The reporter wants to push it on, and have Norm marry the girl.

I wish him luck, but don't expect the reporter to be too helpful. After all, he has to justify his presence here, by sending stories. So, this one of Norm's escape with Little Yank, is a good one, especially now that most of the action has moved out to the Pacific. Norm asks me if I have been to Manchester yet. I tell him, "No, I am still being held up over my rail warrant." We part, knowing that we will be together on the same ship, sailing home.

The first time, when we were freed, we loved to observe and talk to females, just to listen to their chatter. Now, a new element begins to appear in our association with them. It's an unspoken, irresistible attraction, that draws a girl and a fellow together. Without rhyme or reason, it begins to overtake some of us. The most casual passing conversation, will see two passing strangers, just magically be drawn to each other. An inner yearning of the one, will find total rapport with the other, and create a hopelessly enamoured state. There is nothing sexual about it, though, obviously, this may come. It's just that two strangers will meet, be absolutely gone on each other within minutes, without any conscious attempt by either of the two.

Returning to Eastbourne after our outing, we witness such an encounter. We are travelling in one of those box carriages. Frank and I are sitting in one corner, and another Aussie is seated diagonally opposite. Facing Frank and I, is a good looking, decent girl, of about nineteen.

Our wanderings, by now, have made us pretty knowledgeable about girls. We can tell instantly if a girl is respectable, friendly, or a pickup. This one is respectable and nice. The other Aussie is a quiet, decent bloke, of about forty. He is a lean man of about middle height, and gives the appearance of probably coming from a small country town.

Frank and I are sitting together near the window, with the girl on the seat opposite ours. The Aussie is sitting in the corner, on the same seat as the girl, with about four seat spaces between them. The trip to Eastbourne takes about half an hour. In no time a conversation just starts naturally, between the girl and us two. She asks a few questions and, with the ice broken, gradually the quiet man, in the corner, is drawn in.

From the moment the girl and the quiet Aussie speak directly to each other, they turn all their attention to themselves. They still maintain their seating positions, but obviously these two strangers are gone. They can't help themselves. They are so wrapped up in each other, that they are practically oblivious to us two.

To us, it comes across as a total mismatch. The age difference, the fact they come from two different countries, could mean a cultural gap, that may be too hard to bridge. It is also obvious, they are beyond being reasoned with.

We are concerned at how easy it is to get carried away. We decide to be very cautious in our own dealings. Frank is engaged, and intends being married, as soon as he gets home. I'm not that deeply committed, but I still have obligations to my girlfriend Jean. Besides, my Mum, Dad, and the rest of the family, will be greatly upset, if I commit myself over here. A big factor, in our managing to get through all those hard POW years, is due to the support from back home. To get involved and marry here, will be almost like abandoning those, we have depended upon so deeply, for so long.

And another thing—involvement here, means staying here, at least for a while, when our great yearning is to move on. We want to be with our Unit and mates again. This amorous sort of thing may see the abandonment of our yearning to be home. We just want to be normal again. But every which way we turn, and every simple thing we do, brings us complications. We are getting well and truly fed up.

God knows what happens between the girl and this quiet Aussie man. But, there are many who end up marrying. My old escaping mate George, succumbs and marries an Irish girl. Of course, there is nothing wrong at all, with such unions. But, if things go wrong for any reason, all it may lead to is terrible heartache. I'm not too sure, we have the ability to cope with that.

In succeeding days, there is still no sign of those bits and pieces of uniform, that will allow us to get a rail warrant, to allow moving further afield. Then comes word of a garden party, by the King and Queen at Buckingham Palace. Some volunteers, from amongst us, are needed to attend. This is the last straw. We are fretting enough as it is, without something like this.

We visualise spit and polish, parading and marching—something we can't stand. Then I get the flash of a brainwave. If we are to volunteer, the Brass will insist that we are properly kitted out. If we are OK for the King, then we are OK to travel.

I put the idea to Frank and, after a bit of thought, he agrees it is worth a try. With everybody convinced that the preparation for the show is the sort of chore to be avoided like the plague, we are accepted as volunteers, with no problem at all.

We wait for the call to parade and march, but nothing happens. We are resigned to having to put up with restrictions on our movements. But this doesn't happen either. We just continue on as before, almost as if the whole thing has been forgotten. The closer we get to the event, a growing trickle of interest begins to get to us. After all, he is our King, and it is Buckingham Palace, where we are to visit. We begin to wonder what to expect, apart from the spit and polish bits. I begin to wonder what the food will be like. I expect that the cutlery and china will be exclusive, and certainly with the Palace crest. We know there will be a lot of people there. Just how will they stop anybody from souveniring something? Probably, it will be a sit down affair in one of the great reception halls. We have experienced too much to be overawed by the occasion. Anyway, we probably will only see the King from a distance.

All our fears are completely groundless—No parading, no marching, no polishing. Our only instructions are a simple matter of protocol. Under no circumstances are we to speak to Royalty, unless spoken to first. We then are to answer, "Yes Sir, no Sir", as the case may be. As the King is the Head of the Armed Services, we are to observe the military courtesies, and stand properly to attention, while being addressed.

On the day, we aren't even taken to the Palace by transport. We make our own way there, coming to London from Eastbourne, then walking up the Mall to the Palace gates. The very wide Mall, bordered by lawns and gardens ablaze with flowers and the shrubs, is very attractive. As we near the entrance, we speculate whether we will be challenged by the sentry. We aren't, and just pass through.

With a couple more POWs, our small group is just one of several similar small groups, making their way in the same direction. Those, we have seen so far, are mostly civilians. So, it is to be a mixed affair. In common with these other groups, we just stroll up the steps leading to the main entrance doors, which are open. Liveried servants, spaced at intervals, indicate which direction to take, without speaking or moving a muscle. They just remain in the background, as unobtrusive as a piece of furniture.

Passing through the doors into a broad wide hall, we move on for twenty feet or more, to an exit doorway. Passing through this, we descend another broad flight of steps, into a large courtyard, that is almost entirely a beautifully kept green lawn. This surprises me. Viewing the Palace from the outside, I had thought it to be one huge solid building. Now, I am able to see that it is a four sided affair, with a huge but empty central courtyard. I presume that, originally, it almost certainly was built as a castle. Having to withstand foes on all sides, it needed lots of space in the centre for goods and supplies.

We cross the courtyard, mount steps on the other side, and again pass through a broad wide hall. We emerge to another flight of steps, leading down to a large parklike expanse of lawn, beyond which are shrubs. All are beautifully kept, appearing to have not one blade of grass out of place.

We pause on the landing to take in the scene, before descending. There are quite a few people already here, moving about in small knots, talking to each other. Over to our left, just adjacent to where the garden beds begin, several booths are set up. They are dispensing tea and refreshments, and bear prominent signs, declaring them as from Lyons Corner Tea House—so much, for my expectation of the Royal cutlery and china.

Over to our right, at a further more discreet distance, is an enclosure that obviously is the urinal. It is set up on the lawn, and consists of long poles wrapped in hessian—definitely not a permanent establishment. There is a fair amount of comings and goings, so, obviously, it is getting plenty of use.

Somewhat disillusioned, at the ordinariness, of what we had expected to be something rather special, we descend and walk across to the refreshment booths. The busy staff hand us our tea choice, in standard functional cups and saucers, branded with the Lyons crest. We help ourselves to the small triangular sandwiches with various fillings, and just stand by, taking in the scene.

There are still small groups arriving, who, like us, will move over to the refreshments, after first looking. By now there is quite a fair crowd of people, moving about, or just standing and talking together. There seems to be more civilians than service people present, and the two distinct groups, just naturally, keep slightly apart.

The assemblage maintains this order, for quite some time. Still, there is no sign of any of the Royals. After a while, I say to Frank, "Come on, let's go and piddle on the King's lawn." We go to the enclosure and, after negotiating the winding entrance, we find two large sanitary cans standing in opposite corners. Despite the signs, some people haven't bothered to use the cans, We do our bit, and wander out again. There are plenty of ladies in the crowd, so there certainly must be facilities for them also. We aren't interested enough to find out where.

We had been standing around for some time, when a gentleman appears on the landing through which we had come. He calls for the large crowd, now about three thousand, to form a semicircle. He announces that Their Majesties will shortly appear and circulate, after we are in position.

The Queen will start from one end, and work round to the other, while the King will do the rounds in reverse. In this way, each and every one of us, will have ample opportunity to see them both, without leaving our position. This is a polite way of telling us, not to push and shove.

He also says there are some amongst us, who are experienced in the procedure of a Royal Tea Party. He asks that they organise, and assemble, their nationals into position. Several people begin gathering groups around them, and forming up. We Australians are being called together by a Gentleman, whose face is familiar to me. I have seen his photo often in papers back home. He is one of our former Governors, Sir Philip Game.

There are about fifteen of us altogether, a mixture of Airmen and Soldiers. Several of the Airmen are on crutches, so we manoeuvre to give them a good position. The former Governor has learnt his stuff in Australia alright, for he is informal and friendly. He tells us, the function is to be fairly relaxed, and is the King's way of saying "Thank You" to some, who have helped, so much.

The crowd is quite orderly and good natured, and quickly into position. Another short wait follows. Then a small knot of people emerge, from somewhere within the Palace, and gather on the landing, from which we had descended to the lawn. It is the King and Queen, and the two Princesses. They mill together for a few moments, then descend the wide steps to the lawn proper.

With the semicircle focused on the landing, the two ends are fairly close to where the Royals are now standing. This nearness is just too much for some of the ladies, and several of them break ranks, rush forward and quickly curtsey. Just as quickly, they are ushered back into line, and the King and Queen prepare to begin their walk and talk.

It is quite leisurely, with their Majesties pausing for a word, with just about everyone. The Princesses follow about four or five paces behind, with their hands clasped in front of them—Margaret behind the Queen, and Elizabeth behind the King. At this pace, it will take a bit of time for them to reach us in our position. It will be first the King, and then the Queen. To us, the occasion is an interesting experience, but no more. We can't get excited or carried away for, to some extent, we are emotionally dead. Certainly, we are capable of intense and deep feeling, but only for something that affects us deeply.

When he arrives, the King speaks directly to us. He obviously is aware that we have been POWs, for he asks, "Where were you taken prisoner?"

Frank answers, "Crete Sir."

The King says, "That would be the first of June 1941, wouldn't it?"

We both answer, "Yes Sir."

He then says reflectively, "So much has happened, that it is hard to remember the dates." He then moves on.

The impression I get of our King is of a very human, caring man, one of deep concerns. He has a quiet air of dignity, without being pompous. Dressed in Naval Uniform, he is handsome. I feel a warm liking for him, and I am glad I have come. Princess Elizabeth, a short distance away, says not a word. At all times she maintains her spacing, looking straight ahead.

About halfway round the circle, the paths of the two groups, naturally cross. Upon coming together, they stop their promenading, with the four giving their attention to each other, for a moment. It is all family, very human, and totally natural. In its warmth, it seems to indicate that peace, indeed, is with us once more. Finally, the Queen reaches us.

She is dressed as usual in her own distinctive style, and is all peaches and cream. She tends to be a little offhand in what she says, to put people at ease, and dispense with formality. She says, "It is good of you to come, and now that you're here, you might as well have a good look at the old place," waving her hand, airily, towards the Palace, as she speaks. Then she moves on.

When next she pauses, it puts Princess Margaret, following silently behind, directly in front of us. There is an Airman, alongside me, with a smashed foot, balancing as best he can on crutches. He blurts out of the side of his mouth at Margaret, "Don't you get fed up with all this bull?" Without turning her head, Margaret gives him a strong sideways stare, but says nothing. The Queen then moves on again, with Margaret dutifully following behind.

Finally the circuit is completed, and the two lots come together at the ends of the semicircle. Then the Royals wander over to the refreshment booths, to be served their afternoon tea, exactly the same as we have been. They stand there, sipping, eating, and talking to each other. It is obvious, the show is over.

The semicircle drifts apart again, with little knots of people still banding together. Several move to be closer to the Royals, reluctant to call it a day. The Queen, for her part, indicates that enough is enough, acting a little like a mother hen protecting her brood. She seems ever mindful of the wellbeing of her husband, and I am impressed with this.

It is time for us to go, and we begin to move back the way we had come. This time we take more notice of the Palace interior, mindful of the Queen's invitation to "look the old place over".

The broad wide halls open up to become great, expansive chambers. We pause to examine what is on show there. We come to a large area, housing a vast collection of clocks. There are dozens and dozens of them, closely bunched together. They are in all shapes and sizes. They are set in models of various things, such as an old time Galleon in full sail.

We stare and marvel. Then, just to one side, I spot a large ornate volume, on a pedestal. Moving over to see what it is, I find it to be a Visitors Book. I immediately think of the many illustrious personages, who must have signed it. Curiously, I stretch out my hand to open up the cover, and see what is inside. As my hand is about to make contact with the cover, I suddenly freeze. My God! This is Buckingham Palace, the realm of Kings, Queens, and important personages. What I am attempting to do is sacrilege. It is unthinkable, and I withdraw my hand. As I do so, I hear a slight rustle behind, and to one side of me. I look round to find a liveried footman, whom I had not noticed before, moving back to his former position against the wall. He has moved to intercept me, but returns when he realises, I have changed my mind. He says nothing, and he is half smiling, almost as if he has read my thoughts. We move on, leaving the Palace, and make our way back down the Mall.

With the Royal Tea Party behind us, we again make an application for a travel pass. This time we are issued it, without fuss. With freedom to move, we have to decide where to go. The only firm commitments, we have, are to see my Manchester Girl, and Bristol to visit Frank's relatives. In Bristol, we have to look up Ginger, a Pom Navy man, who had been a POW with us in Mahrisch Trubau. We had promised to visit him, when we got through.

We know, that if we go to Manchester first, we won't get any further. We have an obligation to go to Bristol. It does seem, too, that now we are in England, we should see a bit of the country before moving on. Signs indicate that we cannot expect a ship, for at least a week or two. We decide to head well up north, maybe to Scotland, then back to Bristol, and then Manchester.

With a tentative plan, we enquire at Comforts HQ, about billeting up north. Of several on offer, we choose overnight accommodation at a private home in Edinburgh. We will stay there for one or two nights, while deciding whether to go on further, or come back to Bristol. With plans settled, we waste no time getting on our way.

The train journey is pleasing, if only, because we are going somewhere. The renowned British Rail system, sees that our journey is comfortable, even though War restrictions are still very much in force. The endless procession of towns and hamlets, the neatness and order of the countryside, is impressive—quite different to back home.

In Edinburgh, we have to find our accommodation, so we take a taxi. We hand the driver the written down address, and settle back, looking around us with interest. Along the way, the driver points out and explains several features to us. We find it a lovely old city, with beautiful gardens along the entire length of the main street, Princes Street.

At the house, we find it fairly typical, with daytime living areas below, and bedrooms upstairs. As this is our first experience at private billeting, we aren't too sure what it may entail. Unable to put up with much stress, we have decided to move on, if we do not like it.

As we walk up the short pathway from the front gate, the front door opens, and a Serviceman comes out. He is a Yank, and he is just leaving. As we pass, he stops long enough to give us a warning. He claims they are nice people, but won't stand any liquor in the house. That doesn't worry us, for we aren't too fussy about the taste of Pommy beer. Unlike the Yanks, we aren't into the hard stuff at all. Besides we aren't able to cope with it yet.

We find that our hosts are a widower in about his fifties, and his daughter, about nineteen, who runs the household. He has the girl show us to our room, and where we can wash up. He tells us to come down, as soon as we have settled in, as supper will be ready soon.

We eat, quite well, then follow our host into the living room, where he settles into a comfortable chair in front of a cheery fire. He bids us to sit too, when he finds that we have no intention of going out. It seems that most of his guests prefer the night life, usually not returning until very late. We are just too tired and done in, to even consider this.

We help the girl with the washing up, chatting all the while, then all of us settle in front of the fire. With the talk just flowing naturally, it is otherwise quiet, and peaceful, and heaven. The homey atmosphere is something we have been without for years. We won't upset it for anything else.

The girl is sitting on a rug on the floor, right in front of me. As we relax, she naturally leans against me, until I am supporting most of her weight. She is young and attractive, and her fascinating Scottish accent, just flows over us with a compelling charm. As night wears on, that irresistible attraction, begins to work on both the girl and me. And, of course, it is pretty evident to Frank and her Dad. When our tiredness catches up with us at about nine thirty, and we are forced to head for our beds, it is like breaking a spell.

In our room, we had gone through the preliminaries, and are just about ready to climb in, when a knock comes to our door. It is our host, and he is carrying two tumblers of a hot steaming liquid. He says, "I've brought you something for that bad cough. It's a whiskey toddy."

Ever since coming out of Germany, the two of us have been plagued by a bad cough, which we can't seem to throw off. Every few minutes it just bursts out, without us being able to prevent it. We haven't realised it is so evident to other people as well.

We each take a glass from him, saying "Thank You", expecting him to leave it at this, and depart. But he just stands there, insisting that we start drinking. We take a preliminary couple of sips, hoping this will please him. Still, he doesn't move. Obviously, we will have to drink the lot.

Neither of us are any great shakes as drinkers, especially spirits, even after our four years in Germany. We are now almost back to being teetotallers. We gag and gulp at it, finding the taste terrible. He is unmoved and not satisfied, until it is all gone. Taking the empty glasses, he assures us we will be completely cured, when we wake up in the morning.

We roll into bed, instantly falling asleep. I personally have been worried that I may not be able to keep the stuff down. We sleep like logs, and upon wakening, find his prediction completely true. Our coughs have disappeared, and he is quietly pleased, with the effectiveness of his medicine.

After the warning by the Yank, that liquor is completely unacceptable here, and then, for our host to produce some, completely surprises us. Possibly, somebody has gone overboard in the past, prompting the ban. It seems, he has accepted us two enough, to waive it in our case. It turns out that he, himself, works at a large local distillery, and fully believes in the quality of his product.

With the new day, we are faced with the prospect of filling in our time. It seems appropriate that we should go, and see some of the sights. The girl suggests that we might like to look at the Forth Bridge. This large bridge, that spans the Firth of Forth, is said to have some bearing on the design of the Sydney Harbour Bridge.

Well this seems as good an idea as any, so away we go. The Bridge, its setting, and its surrounds, are impressive. But it is obvious to us, that we just aren't into sightseeing. We are too emotionally fatigued to be interested. At this moment, even if the Seven Wonders of the World are to be paraded in front of us, for our inspection, the amount of interest, that we are likely to conjure up, may be, "Oh well, so that's them. So what?"

Unable to sustain interest in anything much, it is obvious that it will be best, if we move on to Bristol. Keeping on the move, and without any restriction, is, seemingly, the only thing that affords us a measure of peace. Then again, there is the danger lurking here, of that irresistible attraction. Another dose of it, and I may find it impossible to break the spell.

We inform the girl and our Host, that we will be returning south on the evening train. We tell them we have to see relatives in Bristol, and that we are afraid to be away from base too long, in case we miss our ship. We thank them very much for their kindness, and the wonderful feeling of home.

As a billeting home, they are used to irregular comings and goings, where guests may stay for a day or two, and often a week. They accept our moving on without a fuss, although the girl is rather serious and noncommittal.

We move south again and arrive in Bristol. With two commitments here, we decide to see Ginger first, and then Frank's relatives. We figure, that a bit of a letdown with Ginger, will do us good.

Ginger, a Navy man, had come to us at Mahrisch Trubau, with about half a dozen other Navy men. Navy POWs had been held in Stalags around the Hamburg area. Intensive Allied bombing, had forced their removal to other Stalags. This lot ended up with us. Ginger is one of those blokes, liked by all, and without an enemy. We do not know, if he has made it out of Germany, but feel sure of his ability to do so. We look forward to comparing notes, and checking on the welfare of any others from Trubau.

We have very little trouble finding his house. It is in a row that fronts directly onto the street. There is no front yard, just a step at the front door, right on the pavement. We knock and wait, speculating on the pleasant surprise, he will get, when he sees us.

There comes no sign from within, so we knock again, while hoping we have not missed him. After a while, we hear some stirring. Finally, the door opens just a small crack. A female peers through, and demands curtly, "Yes, what do you want?" We say we are looking for Ginger. She demands to know, who we are. We explain our connection, while she still keeps the door open, just the same small crack.

We hear some further rustling from inside, and some whispered talk, between her and somebody else. Then there's a cautious examination, from a slightly visible face, which we are just able to recognise as Ginger's. There is some further fierce whispering, then the door half opens, and Ginger cautiously steps outside. He flashes a quick glance, both ways up the street, and says, "Come on. I know a quiet place, where we can talk," and takes off, with us closely following.

Nothing much is said, until we get to Ginger's "quiet place". It is a small pub, with only one or two others there. Ginger orders beers and, as soon as it comes, downs half of it, without stopping. "God, I needed that," he says, then relaxes into the old Ginger, whom we know.

Rather apologetically, he begins to explain the reasons behind our odd reception. He had arrived home, and word quickly circulated that he was back. Friends and acquaintances from near and far, had flocked to his house. They insisted on taking him to the pub, to celebrate his safe return. Day and nights for weeks now, it is booze, booze, booze, until his wife is just about up the wall. At first, Ginger is happy to go along with it. But quickly, his POW weakened constitution, finds it more difficult than he can take. He is now desperately anxious to avoid any further demands, as he and his wife, seek sanity.

With relations rather strained at home, when they should be otherwise, Ginger's wife is fiercely determined to fend off any would be celebrators, at least, until Ginger has time to come down to earth. Then, we have come along, and spoil things again. We talk about Trubau a bit, then walk him back to his house, and leave.

From this rather sobering interlude, we move on to Frank's relatives, and to a completely different atmosphere. His Uncle and Aunty are open and friendly, and deeply family orientated. Whatever they do, is done as a group, with always half a dozen or more, moving about together. There are sons and daughters, cousins and friends, and, although we get to know each and every one of them by sight and first name, we have difficulty fitting them into the family pattern.

They just include us as part of the group, without being anything special. They just go about their everyday goings and comings, taking us along with them. They just explain the relationships, as we go along. Sometimes, it is just as necessary for some of the others, as it is for us. One relative, a very beautiful girl in her early twenties, had been engaged to a fighter pilot. He has just been killed, and she is still in some shock about it. They do their best to include her in everything, so that she is surrounded as much as possible with her own people, in a bid to snap her out of it.

They accept us both, equally, as if I am just as much family to them, as Frank is. Frank's Uncle, a fine sturdy gentleman with thick wavy silver hair, is retired. For us, this business of being part of the family, does more for our sanity, than anything else can.

Then, we have to move on again. This time it will have to be Manchester. I am both eager, yet apprehensive, at the prospect of finally coming face to face with my Manchester Girl. We know each other intimately by correspondence, and now will come the crunch. While we have photos of each other, and know what to expect, it will be a bit of an ordeal.

After arriving, we leave Manchester station and begin to walk up the street. As we do so, we come face to face with Cliff, an Australian, who is another one of our people from Mahrisch Trubau. He is on his way back to our Headquarters. His first words are directed to me. He says, "Have you been to see her yet?"

I reply, "No."

He says, "Boy, are you in trouble. She has put the word out, right across the country. Everybody is trying to find Tommy."

With my penchant to always sign my full name, "Thomas Arthur Dawson", she just naturally calls me "Tommy." There doesn't seem much point in trying to get her to switch to my second name, even if she wants. While the rest of the Mahrisch Trubau crew are familiar with our relationship, she in turn has a working knowledge of them, from group photos I had sent to her. When Cliff refers to my Manchester Girl as her, it isn't necessary to elaborate. We all know, whom he is talking about.

In her last three letters to reach Germany, she has ordered me to make straight for Manchester, as soon as I get through. With her marital status and pregnancy, I have presumed it may be more diplomatic, if I just turn up casually. The contents of those letters have been pretty intimate, leading me to believe the people at home, here, will know very little about me. It seems that my existence is anything but secret.

With Cliff on his way back to check on mail and movement orders, we pause long enough to swap experiences, and check on friends. Then, it is on our way again. We find our street, and are almost there, when three Australians come toward us. As soon as they come within earshot, one of them calls out, "Are you Tommy?"

"Yes," I answer.

"You'd better get down there. She's waiting," he replies.

All this is very intimidating. It looks as if I am heading for a fair sort of a tongue bashing. We reach the house and turn in, to find a large group of other people there, with my Manchester Girl, sort of in charge. She recognises me immediately and, ignoring everybody else, comes forward to greet me.

She immediately wants to know where I've been. What has kept me? Why haven't I been in touch? In turn, I try to explain that we were held back, waiting for permission to travel, and we had commitments regarding Frank's relatives. This, back and forth, just concerns the two of us, with the others being completely ignored.

She is openly concerned and reproachful, as if I am her property. It is almost as if we are lovers, which, of course, we are not, and, that I am backsliding, and am required to explain my absence. After a few minutes, we ease off, and pause to take each other in. We silently eye each other off for a few moments, comparing the mental with the real image.

She is exactly as her photo portrays her. She is a little on the plump side, without being fat. There is little or no signs of her pregnancy yet. Her voice and mannerisms are as her letters have led me to expect. She is my Manchester Girl alright, and I am pleased enough with the real thing. All I can hope, is that she will be pleased enough with what she sees.

We have no firm plans of what we intend to do. We have waited until we arrived here, before making any decisions. Just as well, for my Girl immediately takes charge of the organising, accommodation, feeding and entertainment. For the first night, we will sleep at her parent's home, which is nearby. Her young sister has just moved out. There is a spare bedroom, we can share with her brother, an Airman, who had been shot down over Germany. He, too, is a just released POW. I had not known about her brother, and am surprised she hadn't mentioned him before.

We are taken round, introduced, and shown our room. While we will be putting our time in here, her brother will be putting it in elsewhere. He has plans of his own. Like us, he is still trying to come to terms with his new found freedom. But, he will be back to sleep.

Our first night is a confusion of people and talk, with a few beers thrown in. They note and remark on our distaste for their Pommy beer. We agree, explaining that it is so unlike our own. Besides, it has practically no kick in it. My Girl promises to rectify this on our first outing, by introducing us their "half and half"—half beer and half stout. Apparently, it is a much favoured drink here, which we have yet to try.

In due course it is bedtime. Her brother has returned, so we three retire. We all will be required to share a double bed. As somebody has to cop the middle position, it somehow falls to me. We are too done in to do anything, other than pile in, and go to sleep. Sometime, during the night, I awake, boiling hot. The close proximity of three bodies, generates more heat than I can stand. Naturally, the person in the middle, will be the worst affected. I climb from under the bed clothes, and just lay on top, still in the middle. While I am reasonably comfortable, the others are not.

Frank and the brother have also been affected by being overwarm. They would like to throw some of the bed clothes back, but can't, because I'm lying on them. In their sleepy state, they haven't realised what has happened, so they just put up with it. Now they are feeling not too bright, and a little miffed at me.

My Girl comes round early to see how we have fared. I tell her, it hasn't been much of a success. She says, "No matter." She has already made arrangements for us to stay at a friend's house, opposite to where she lives. The friend is a widow with a large house, and is quite happy for us to stay. My Girl says she may have put me, personally, in with her, but thinks it may not look too good. This new arrangement will allow us to spend more time together, as I will have my own key, and can come and go as I please, day or night.

During the morning, we put some time in around town, getting to know our way about. Her brother starts off with us, showing us which buses to catch. We get off the bus in the city, when her brother drops to his knees, searching and exclaiming, "I've lost my golden Caterpillar."

We had noticed this fairly insignificant clip, pinned just above his left jacket pocket. It is a thin wriggly shape, like a caterpillar. We realise that it must have an important meaning, but have not known what for. With all three of us on hands and knees, searching frantically before the bus moves off, he briefly explains its meaning. It is the badge of an exclusive club called, naturally, the Golden Caterpillar Club. To become a member, a person has to have saved his life, by parachuting from a crippled plane. Naturally, it is his proudest possession. Luckily, we find it on the bus's outside step.

After wandering around a bit, we go back to the bus stop, find the right bus, and return home. We have been meeting various members of My Girl's family, and now I meet her son. He is a lad of about eleven or twelve, a real fine lad. He and I get on famously. He has a problem, and asks if I can help him.

For sport at school, he is required to wear gym shoes (our sandshoes). The trouble is, due to wartime rationing, they are practically unobtainable in Britain. They are on issue to the services for leisure time wear—but, of course, in adult sizes. He thinks that a serviceman with a small foot, may be agreeable to sell a pair, which he may be able to make do.

My foot size is just about as small as they come in the Army, and I tell him that I have a pair, I haven't worn, in my kit at Eastbourne. He can have them, if they suit. From then on, we have our heads together like a pair of conspirators. I warn him they are a brown colour. But, he says that will be no problem. We discuss ways and means of making them fit, if they are too big.

On my first return trip from Eastbourne, I carry those sandshoes like something precious. I badly want them to be a fit, but doubt they will, and this proves the case. I think I am just as upset as he is. But I leave them with him, saying, soon or later, they will fit.

During the afternoons, My Girl's Dad, who is retired, is in the habit of visiting the pub around the corner. He takes Frank and me with him, and it is a thoroughly enjoyable ritual. He is nicely dressed, and wears his bowler hat. The atmosphere inside is quite unlike anything to be experienced in our pubs back home. Mostly, Frank and I will buy the drinks, and that upsets him badly. He tries to insist that he should buy for us, not us for him. These are quiet interludes, that we enjoy very much, just being part of a family again. We like being with Pop, learning something of the Englishman's ways, and his institutions. We will have only a couple of drinks, relax in the homey atmosphere, then go home for tea.

My Girl has taken it upon herself, the task of organising our entertainment. It just doesn't stop at Frank and myself. Those other three Aussies, we had first met on our way down the street to her house, are also catered for. Always, there is somebody to take us about. Always, there is a good mix of male and female, with ages pretty compatible, too.

With this type of mix, there always seems to be a fair jumble of people, doing nothing in particular, just associating and being together. Entertainment is mostly at night time, going out to pubs and clubs. This consists mostly of music, drinking and talking, and lasts well into the night. Then we'll return home and sleep until late.

On our first outing, the girls introduce us to their "half and half", as they promised. It is an improvement on beer straight. Being new to us, it is a bit more potent than we expect. We haven't yet learned to pace ourselves, and inevitably overdo it. later in the night, I go out to the urinal, and get disgustingly sick. I'm not much good for the rest of the night, although I at least know what I am doing.

It is the first night under the new sleeping arrangements. Being a bit under the weather, and unfamiliar with the house layout, I am worried that I will make myself unwelcome. However, I manage to find my bed without too much trouble, and sleep like a log until quite late.

I awake, and am just lying there for about ten minutes, when my hostess, the widow, comes in with a cup of tea. It is a wonderful reviver, and I drink it, gratefully. Then we talk for a while, during which time it comes out, that her electric iron needs repairing. With everything in short supply, it is impossible to get things repaired. I tell her, that if she has a screwdriver, I'll have a look at it, and see if I can fix it.

I get washed and dressed, come downstairs, and sit at the kitchen table, while the widow produces her iron and screwdriver. I begin to work on it, only to find I have a very bad attack of the shakes. It is impossible for me to control my hands properly. I am battling away, trying to make the screw driver do what I want it to, when in comes My Girl. She is upset and worried. I was to have breakfast with her. It is now eleven o'clock, and I have not shown up.

I am truly surprised at the time. I explain, and demonstrate the difficulty I am having with the screwdriver and the iron. One of the wires had blown, and it is a simple case of reconnecting. I tell her that, as soon as I can get it done, I will be straight over for breakfast. Somewhat mollified, she sits down and waits, while I work. After the rough night I have had, she must have thought that I cried quits, and shot through, when I didn't show up.

The job takes me about three times as long as it should have. But My Girl waits patiently, until it's done. Then, together we go over to her place, where she cooks me a big breakfast of eggs and bacon, plus the trimmings. This is the first time, the two of us have been alone, together.

It is quiet and peaceful, and we can talk and compare notes. We both know each other well from our correspondence, now comes the physical reality. There is a rapport between us, that makes us happy to be in each other's company. There is an understanding, that allows me to talk about my worries, and misgivings about my future.

It is extremely important to me at this time, that I have a sympathetic listener to talk to. I am stuck here in England, waiting for transport to move on, after years as a POW, plus a hairy escape to get here. I have the feeling of being caught, and of surrendering my newly acquired freedom of movement.

As a POW, I had the freedom to make my own rules of conduct and movement, within the confines of that situation. Now, I am forced to obey and follow the rules, of an ordered society again—and a military one at that, although a benevolent one, at the moment.

We are all plagued with doubts and confusion, as to what our future moves will be. We all are determined to exercise whatever control we can, to ensure that these moves are in the direction "we" want. We have to decide if, for us, the War is over, or move on to the Pacific against the Japanese. Then, there are personal relationships, both here and at home. Having been deprived of them for so long, they are now vitally important.

While the Military system has their plans for us, we have no doubts at all, about our ability to manipulate the system into complying with "our" wishes. Our great trouble is in trying to decide, what "we" want.

We can contrive to "unfortunately" miss the ship home, when it turns up, giving us more time here to think our problems out. To do that, will probably make it impossible to get back to our Units, and to be in it at the finish, against the Japs. What the hell to do? There is one thing I am certain of—I have had a gutful of getting sick, and ending up with the shakes. From now on, I will pace myself very slowly, and see that it doesn't happen again.

Time again for a quick trip back to Eastbourne. My Girl is worried that, once I leave, I may not return. She takes me aside, and makes me promise to come straight back, after checking in.

These returns, turn out mostly to be the same—a check in at Comforts HQ, and your digs, a lunch at the dining room, then filling in time, awaiting the train departure to wherever you are holed up.

Frank decides he has covered all he needs to in Manchester. From here on, he will stick to his relatives and Bristol. Now, I will be on my own. We decide on a bite to eat, and go to a picture show, while waiting until train time.

Our Eastbourne dining room caters for two hundred or more at a sitting. With the fellows free to come and go at will, the Pommy catering staff has no way of knowing how many to cater for. As the food supply is for newly freed POWs, they are under orders to cater for a full house, and this they do. All food, turkeys, hams, etc., has been supplied from Australia, for exclusive POW consumption.

Frank and I enter the dining room to find maybe only twenty of us here. The cooks have prepared a magnificent roast turkey dinner. We have a fabulous meal, then prepare to leave. We pause to thank the orderlies cleaning up, on how much we have enjoyed the meal. As we do so, we discover they are throwing whole, untouched roast turkey carcasses into rubbish bins. This distresses us greatly. I chide them for being so wasteful, only to be told that there is nothing, they can do about it.

They regret it as much as we do. But their orders are very strict, and they dare not disobey. This food is for Australian POWs only, and our government has extracted a promise from the British government, that none of it will be diverted, elsewhere.

This highlights the difference between the Pommy and the Australian servicemen. The Poms obey orders strictly, while we obey them, only, as long as they make sense. When an untenable situation arises, we always feel free to choose an alternative. We don't actually disobey, we just bend the rules a little.

In this instance, we are sure we will have found some way to divert the surplus food to civilian use. We just hope, that some of the mess staff, are mentally tough enough to do something about it. It grieves us greatly to see any food wasted, so soon after our release—especially, as the tough British food rationing, makes it almost impossible to obtain luxuries of any kind, for their people.

Still upset about the food waste, we go up to London, looking for a picture show. We decide to pick something special, after being deprived for so long. As the ultimate entertainment venues, movie theatres are doing booming business, and sessions follow sessions. If we want, we can stay on for a repeat session. If there is time to kill, we might do just this.

The show we pick is reportedly a good one, with top actors and actresses taking the lead roles. We settle down amidst a packed house, and the old familiar pattern begins to unfold. The lights dim and the show begins, firstly with a newsreel. This mostly is War related, so is something we are familiar with. Then begins the feature. As it seeks to establish its storyline, and outline its characters, more and more, we become restless and unsettled. While this is the top Hollywood of its day, it comes across to us, as so nauseously phony, that it is unbearable.

Our perceptions have become so sharpened, that we can pick how a scene is put together, how the storyline will develop, how the actors will react, and what they are about to say. We just can't stand it, and have to get up and walk out. We just have to resort to some aimless mooching about, until train time. Then, with Frank on to Bristol, and me on to Manchester, again we are on our way.

I catch My Girl a bit on the hop when I arrive, as she hasn't expected such a quick return. She suggests I go to the shop around the corner, pick up some fish and chips for tea, while she prepares things at home. She flatly refuses to allow me to buy, and insists on giving me the money.

I go round the corner, and up the street, to easily find the shop. The aroma quickly identifies it. There is a long queue, of mostly British housewives, stretching back from the door and along the footpath. They are a happy, middle-aged, cheery lot, gossiping together, while they wait. I fall into line, on the end of the queue. Instantly, those nearest to me take me to task. With words and pushes, they propel me to the head of the line, and into the shop itself. They insist that I am special, and have to take first place. The proprietor, busily serving, agrees, and takes my order. When it is ready and I try to pay, he flatly refuses to accept my money. These wartime British people are truly wonderful.

I am quickly back into our pattern of living, and we go on as before—out every night until late, and always as part of a fair-sized group. During these outings, all problems are put on hold, with a lot of us content to just let the time pass, and not worry much about anything. During the day, when I find time alone with My Girl, and we do some serious talking, then the doubts and worries will start to creep back.

A few more days, then it is back to base again to check. As always, I go first to Comforts Fund Reception, then back to my quarters to see if any mail has been left for me, here.

Just inside the entrance to our quarters, there is a sort of communal parlour. Here, we can gather, meet with each other, or with any visitors we might have. With fellows scattered far and wide, always the whole building is quiet and empty. In the dormitories, you might occasionally strike one or two of the others, who just happen to pick the same time as yourself, to return to check. This time, I am surprised to find a woman, seated in the parlour, waiting, as I pass through.

She pays me no heed, nor I her. But, I am able to instantly gather a pretty full impression of what I see. She is medium tall and slim, and typically English country gentry. She is thirtyish, neither young nor old, but good looking. She wears a conservative, serge suit, of jacket and skirt, with a white silk like blouse. Her well-kept hands, are folded resignedly in her lap. There is an indefinably tragic, almost hopeless look, on her face. She looks straight ahead, paying no attention, and with an air of just eternally waiting.

Mystified and wondering, I climb the stairs up to my quarters. When I enter, there is another fellow there, also apparently back for a check. He is rummaging amongst his gear, and I decide to ask him if he knows anything about the mysterious lady below. Before I can speak, however, he asks me if I have seen her. When I tell him "Yes", he begins to pour out a tale of woe.

Having no contacts, and not knowing what to do with himself, he decided to take up one of the many offers available at Comforts Fund HQ. A lot of the landed gentry, have offered Aussie ex-POWs, the chance to spend some time in the country on large estates, amongst horses, and amidst the kind of atmosphere, they imagine, a lot of us have been pining for. The one, he chooses at random, provides just this.

He is treated as a privileged house guest, with his own room, and everything possible is done to make his stay thoroughly enjoyable. The lady of the house takes particular care, to see he is looked after. His first day is a busy one, and a very tired man is glad to head for his bed, as soon as he decently can.

He is barely tucked into bed, when his considerate hostess comes to check that everything is in order. She also is prepared to retire, and is in her nightgown and housecoat. Then it happens. This irresistible attraction takes over, and they both are in bed together making love. He claims that neither of them can help themselves. Nor is it premeditated. They have no idea how it happens. Now she has left home, following him here to Eastbourne. She has been sitting there in the parlour, for a week now, and he is at his wits' end, trying to work out what to do.

He seems very glad to have somebody to talk to about it. While I understand and can sympathise with him, all I can offer, which isn't very helpful, is, "Sorry mate. It's your problem, and you will have to sort it out."

It is a hopelessly complicated situation, where emotion and common sense are fighting against each other. For the moment, emotion has the upper hand. And, until common sense returns, there is no way out.

Because of both person's commitments, it has to be resolved. No matter what happens, people will be deeply hurt, particularly on the lady's side. I can imagine my colleague being upset at having been the cause of so much heartache.

I leave him, and walk downstairs, past the lady in the parlour, still with a forlorn look. I head back to the station, to return to Manchester, and my own problems. I do not come across him again, and never find out what happens to the lady.

For me, there are a few more trips, to and return from Manchester. Finally, the inevitable happens. A ship has arrived, and we are to sail from Liverpool in a few days' time. Further leave is cancelled, while frantic efforts are made to contact those men, scattered across the country, who are unaware of its arrival, and the sailing date. The War is still on, so there will be no fanfare, with departure day, time and date, kept secret, as much as possible.

My Girl and I have already made our plans, for how we will handle it, when the time comes. I will get a message to her by letter, and she will understand. This I do, and so we part.

# Chapter 18

# Homeward Bound

OUR SHIP IS A BIG one, even bigger than the Orcades, on which we had sailed from home, so long ago. On the Orcades, we had first class accommodation, but I don't exactly expect the same on this ship. However, I reason that, because we are ex-POWs, it should at least be reasonable.

There is a fair-sized contingent of Air Force personnel, together with wives and children, sailing also. Quite a few have married over here, and this will be one of the early batches, bound for their new home. Obviously, the women and children will have first priority. We will take potluck, with what is left.

The business of embarking, always is a lengthy and tiring one, particularly with a bulky kit to be lugged aboard, by each individual. High spirits, generally enables a person to pass through this phase, without really noticing it. In this case, however, while we are happy to be moving, we still haven't come to terms with our feelings. Almost nobody can decide, whether or not to go, or to stay behind. Part of us are anxious to push on, to be reunited with our mates, our families and our friends. Another part of us wants to stay, come to terms with this new lifestyle, and pick up the pieces. Then, again, there is the War. They are still hard at it in the Pacific, and we have to remember this.

By the time I get on board, the Air Force contingent has been placed, plus a fair few of our blokes. Norm is somewhere ahead of me. He meets me on the upper deck, and tells me that we have been assigned very cramped quarters, well down below. Then and there, I rebel, saying with feeling, "They can shove it up their arses. I'm staying here!" while throwing my gear down on the deck. The place I have selected, is inboard from the rail, and against the cabin superstructure. There is a further deck overhead, that will give some shelter from the elements, and the position is approximately amidships.

Norm says, "Save a posse for me, while I go and get my gear." A few others do likewise, and there we stay. This is my camp, throughout the entire trip. I never ever go below, even to view my assigned quarters. We know that, whatever route is taken, we will be in for a lengthy spell in the tropics. And life below, will be hell.

We are resentful, unhappy, and don't exactly like the way things are shaping up. We have become stubborn and intractable, fully determined to go our own way. We don't exactly rebel, or put on a demonstration. We just do those things we feel, we want to, and flatly refuse anything else. After all, what can they do to us? Put us in gaol? Hell, we've just done four years as POWs. Anything this lot can dish out, will be a piece of cake, after the Germans.

These feelings are spontaneous, and affect us all. Nothing is actually said, nor any attempt to form a concerted front. It is just the way we feel. Our mood is pretty obvious, for we are left pretty much to our own devices. There is no attempt to impose any sort of discipline.

Once we are underway, and well clear of land, we can see we are not part of a convoy. We are on our own. If attacked, we will just have to do the best we can. With the Germans taken care of, there isn't much to worry about here. This problem may arise later in another ocean. We speculate in what direction we might be headed, pretty well convinced that it will be via the Suez. This is put to rest by the Captain, sent to escort us home.

From the outset, the Captain, apparently from an Infantry Unit serving in New Guinea, makes it quite clear that, to him, we are nothing more than a damn nuisance, he can well do without. He bitterly resents being detached from his men, and made nursemaid to us lot. I can respect him for his attachment to his men, but it doesn't help our position. Throughout the trip, he is to have as little contact with us, as possible. Now he informs us, that we will be returning via the Panama Canal. By the time we get home, we will have travelled round the world.

My first night sleeping on deck is reasonably comfortable. With the new day, we fall into a pattern of passing our time. We have established our eating and washing setup, now that we get to know some of the ship's layout.

We tend to be drawn like a magnet to a promenade deck area, shared with the Air Force Married Quarters. There are two little girls there, sisters of about eight and ten, who play and chatter together. It seems that they come from Glasgow, and their Scottish brogue, absolutely enchants everyone, who hears them speak. Their area is out of bounds to us lot, but, by crowding close to the boundary, we are able to hear and observe them, quite well. It is a sad disappointment to us, if they don't happen to be there.

Each individual begins to find a few familiar faces, amongst the motley group aboard. Before sailing, we have heard about this or that person, or even met a few. While we are interested enough to be pleased, they have made it through, safely, we are too occupied with our own situation, and trying to come to terms with it, to actively seek out mates and colleagues. Now that we have the time, our feelings still remains pretty much the same. We are pleased enough to meet and speak with them, then lapse into our individual preoccupation.

As well as Norm, others from my Unit are Les Lockhart, Doug Dolman and of course, George Wade. All have spent their time in other camps, and in other places. In George's case, after turning himself in on Mount Athos, the blood poisoning I had greatly feared, had not eventuated. The Greek Police put him in a Greek prison and kept him there for a couple of months, before eventually turning him over to the Germans. It was a bit hairy there. Some of the prisoners had been taken out and shot, from time to time. George reckons that they were mostly Greeks, who had done something wrong. He, himself, was treated fairly well. But, it was a bit upsetting not knowing what their intentions were.

While he was with the Greeks, they gave him no treatment, at all, for his swollen armpit. It just righted itself. This makes me feel pretty bad. I was so certain that my diagnosis had been correct. I have this guilty feeling, that it was my say, that had influenced him to turn himself in. Perhaps, I had unconsciously adopted a Corporal to Sapper approach, where he had to obey, what he perhaps saw, as an order—whereas, I was only trying to make it a suggestion, and that he had to decide.

Anyway, it is all water under the bridge now, ending up much the same, had he stayed with me. He ended up in Austria, made several escapes from there, trying to get to Switzerland, none successful. He got to England, well ahead of me, met up with an Irish girl, and married her. She is expected to follow him home soon, on another ship, with a lot of other War Brides.

Amongst some New Zealanders aboard our ship, there is another familiar face in Jack Brooking. "Jackie", a Maori, had been a workmate with us at Mahrisch Trubau. Mostly the nationals kept to their own groupings. Despite these friends and acquaintances, around us, we still tend to keep to ourselves, weighed down by our own thoughts and problems.

The days at sea just follow, one after the other, in much the same vein. After leaving England, we begin to give some thought to Australia, and our people at home. A general feeling begins to spread, that we should endeavour to take home a few presents. We had been unable to do anything in England, as coupons were needed for everything, and we weren't entitled to any. We all have varying amounts of English currency on us, and this is good worldwide. But, certainly, there will be little in the way of ports of call, where we can spend it. We will have to rely on what the Ship's canteen can provide.

Our ship, a cruise liner in normal times, has a well-stocked canteen run by the ship's personnel. Much of what is stocked, is unobtainable in Britain. It is available here, only because the ship has been able to buy, and stock up, in open ports.

Goods sold at sea, generally are not subject to duty. If we can determine what we want, we should be able to buy at bargain prices. For several days, a steady stream of men search amongst what is on offer, but without success. What is there, we consider is priced too high. So mostly, we refuse to buy.

With one, after another, commenting on the high prices, suspicion begins to build that the ship's crew see us as easy pickings. It seems they are indulging in a bit of profiteering. On learning that the Head Purser is responsible for the canteen, complaints are made to him regarding the charges. He claims they are fair and reasonable—but then, wouldn't he?

Totally dissatisfied, a deputation is formed, and requests our Army Captain to take it up with the Ship's Captain. In due course, a reply comes from the Ship's Captain, stating that he has examined all aspects, and is satisfied that no improprieties have taken place. There it has to lie.

Still unhappy about the situation, we think that the Ship's Captain may lean on his people, telling them to take it easy for a few days. We watch to see if there is any change. There is none. We will just have to wait until we reach a port. As we are heading for Panama, and, as they are not involved in the War, surely, we will be able to buy whatever we want, there.

In due course, we arrive off the port of Colon, at the Atlantic entrance of the Canal. There is a wait, before we can move in dockside. This is done in the early hours of the morning. We awake to a new day, alongside the wharf, with the tying up procedures still being completed.

After the boring days at sea, several of us early risers hang over the rail, taking in every aspect of the hustle and bustle on the dock below. There are stores and supplies to come aboard, and several workers are moving busily about. One is a man in his forties to fifties, who appears to be a foreman. He proves to be a Yank. A couple of our fellows call to him, asking what sort of a town is Colon.

The Yank, a pretty cheerful sort of bloke, calls back telling us that it is great. There is plenty to eat, plenty to drink, and lots of nice girls. All the time these exchanges are going on, he keeps bustling about. A few more of our fellows come to the rail, one of them wearing his slouch hat. The Yank looks up, sees the hat, and stops dead in his tracks. He calls up, "Say, are you guys Australian?" On being told "Yes", he replies, "Then you won't get ashore here."

Those of us who hear this exchange are completely mystified. We cannot make any sense of it. There is no known reason why Panama and Australia can be enemies. The Yanks are running the Canal anyway. Surely, they must be on our side. From what we have heard, the Yanks are practically running riot in our country. Finally, it just seems to us that the Yank is pulling our legs.

As the morning wears on, and stores begin to come aboard, we begin to fret a bit. We feel that this kind of activity is odd, while we are on leave. There are comings and goings of Officials associated with our port clearance and passage through the Canal. It is about midmorning before we are officially told that we will not be permitted ashore. For us, the place is out of bounds.

Naturally, we are in a pretty rebellious mood, and seek to find out why such an inhumane order is forced upon us. We are told, officially, that it is because of the strict orders of the Military Commander of the Canal. As such, they cannot be disobeyed. Still mystified, coupled with the desire to buy gifts to take home, which before had been a vague afterthought, it now becomes an absolute necessity to go ashore. But these damn Yanks are intent on depriving us of this right.

By questioning some of the local workmen, busily loading stores, the word begins to filter back to us of the real reason. It quickly spreads to everyone, and tends to make us more incensed. Basically, the story goes like this—We had been preceded three months before, by a shipload of returning ex-POWs. They had arrived just as we have done, and were given leave. They were told that certain sections of the town were out of bounds to them. Under no circumstances would they be permitted to go there. Our imagination tells us that this is the only place to be. Our forerunners had decided likewise. They probably decided that the Yanks were trying to keep the best for themselves. A fair sized group was seated at tables in a bar, in the forbidden zone, having a quiet drink. A jeep containing a couple of MPs on patrol, charged up to the front door. The MPs crowded the doorway with batons in hand, and ordered everybody out of the place. Nobody moved. The MPs then pulled out their revolvers, and waved them about. Again, they ordered everybody out.

A lot of ex-POWs had German revolvers of their own, that they were taking home as souvenirs. Thoroughly stirred up, they pulled out their own weapons, and hit the floor. They upturned tables to act as a shield, and prepared to defend themselves. More Yank MPs rushed up, and quickly the battle was on.

We can only imagine what took place. But, supposedly, six MPs are still in hospital there. With that sort of news, it is obvious there will be no chance of the "no leave order" being reversed.

Official delegations demanding the right to go ashore, get nowhere, as do the pleadings and appeals to reason. The excuse of wanting to buy presents to take home, only gets the reply, "Use the ship's canteen." We are bitter, and feel trapped. We are helpless and can see no way round the problem. It is almost, as bad as, when we were first taken as Prisoners of War.

Then, an announcement is made telling us that a musical revue will be put on, especially for our benefit, at eight o'clock tonight. It will be put on by mostly American office workers, working here locally. There will be chorus girls, dancing, and singing, etc. That's all we need—amateur theatricals. Then and there, large groups determine to boycott the show.

The loading of stores goes ahead, while unhappy passengers watch the day slowly fade into night. Several attempts are made to infiltrate into the loading area, and thereby attempt to make it into town—all fail. Just after dark, and during the teatime period, when most are otherwise occupied, a raft is dropped into the water, on the open side of the ship. These large rafts, are mounted on steeply sloping ramps, on both sides of the ship. Their purpose is for their use, as a vitally quick means of saving lives, in the event of the ship being sunk. All that is required to release them, is the cutting or release of a single rope. Now, a small group go quickly over the side, making it into the raft.

They push off, making for a section further down the wharf. Harbour water patrols quickly move in, having rounded them up, before they can even get there. They are back on board, under escort, before most of us know what has happened. Of course, there is hell to play. Much is made of the interference with such a vital piece of life saving equipment. The raft is hauled back aboard, and again made secure. Threats and reprisals against the perpetrators, are just shrugged off. After four years of somewhat like treatment, it just doesn't mean much anymore.

When concert time approaches, the performers start to arrive, and are quickly escorted to their dressing area. There are, indeed, some young and attractive girls amongst them. A lot of blokes begin to have second thoughts about that boycott. Of course, there will be no chance of fraternisation. This will be too much to expect for a riffraff like us. While most of the fellows do change their minds about the boycott, I, together with a small group, stubbornly refuse to go. We are due to move on into the Canal tomorrow, and I, personally, will be glad to get out of this place.

In the morning, just before we are to sail, an announcement is made. As a special concession, to compensate for not being allowed leave, the local authorities have agreed to allow us to come ashore, and move round to the next wharf, where there is a canteen. This canteen will be opened, especially for us, and we can purchase whatever we want. We brighten considerably.

In next to no time, everybody is organised, and the first lot begin to move down the gangway. We are met by the most insulting display, that can ever be mounted by a supposedly friendly country.

Armed Yank servicemen are lined up, shoulder to shoulder, in two lines facing inward, about eight to ten feet apart, their rifles at the ready, across their chests. We are herded, between these two lines, round to the canteen, which is only a few hundred yards away. All that can be purchased there is Coca Cola, and toiletry items such as soap or toothpaste. As we can already purchase these items aboard, it is a useless exercise anyway.

We are seething. We have never experienced anything like this, even from Hitler. Good, decent, mild, and friendly Norm, whose tolerance is practically unshakeable, is marching alongside me, and nearest to our Guards on that side. He savagely goads, and verbally lambasts them, in a manner that keeps me open-mouthed and quiet. The Yank Guards, for their part, remain stony-faced and unmoved. No amount of provocation can stir them. The slightest, nearest response, may have triggered an immediate riot. In the end, all we can do is return to the ship. Quite quickly, we cast off and get underway.

The passage through the Panama is quite different to Suez. Here, there are stretches of fairly open water, then narrow locks, just wide enough to take a single ship at a time. In the locks, sometimes you may enter with the sides high above you, and be unable to see anything but the sky. The ship will rise with the gradual swell of water as the pumps go to work, until you are floating high and free. Then you will sail on into open water again. In due course, the reverse will happen, and you will sink to a new level.

There aren't a lot of ships making the passage. Sometimes, we have to standby for one that has priority. One fairly narrow section has thick heavy jungle, running right down to the water's edge. Our Army Captain, who is wet nursing us back home, exhorts us to take a good look. He says, "That is the kind of country, our fellows are having to fight through, in New Guinea. Only there, the constant heavy rain makes conditions much more miserable."

We are too wrapped up in our own problems, to pay more than a passing glance. However, the constantly changing pattern of scenery, enables us to put the unhappy business of Colon, from our minds.

In due course, we arrive at Panama, from where we exit the Canal into the Pacific. It is a busy place with many ships in port. We make a short stop for clearance, and a few traders in small boats cluster round. I manage to buy a Panama silver dollar to take home as a souvenir.

Now, we sail on, gradually losing sight of land. It will be many days before we see any other land. We know we cannot make it through to Australia, without having to replenish supplies somewhere. There is much speculation as to where that somewhere may be. From here onward, our journey will get ever more dangerous, the closer we come to the War Zone. Given this situation, there aren't many places we can head for. We, therefore, are very happy, when it is announced that we are heading for Tahiti.

Tahiti is well down in the Pacific, almost as far as you can get from hostilities. It is world renowned too, for its free and easy lifestyle. There should be absolutely no reason to refuse us shore leave there—unlike the Panama Zone, where we grudgingly have to concede, there might be a case for tight security.

For a few days, we are happy. Then comes a further announcement. Word has been received that a Japanese submarine is lurking down in that part of the Pacific. Therefore, we will not be heading to Tahiti. Instead, we will be heading for Hawaii. This sobers us completely. Hawaii is American territory. Now, we don't know what to expect.

Day follows day at sea, as we sail on. We are still pretty mixed up in our minds, as to what our futures will be. Given our experiences to date, there seems no point getting excited about visiting Hawaii. It will only be a stopover point anyhow. Time and restrictions will probably curtail any pleasure to be had there.

At long last, early one morning, low down on the horizon, a bank of cloud comes into view. As we get closer, the cloud becomes land, growing larger and larger. It is Hawaii. We crowd the rail watching, as the landmass climbs higher out of the sea. Then points of interest become ever more recognisable. Finally, we head into port and tie up. We are in Pearl Harbour. We stare about with interest, looking for whatever signs there might be of the devastating Japanese raid. Everything has been cleaned up so thoroughly, that there is little or nothing to see. It is almost as if it hadn't happened.

We are granted leave here, but only for as long as it is necessary to take on stores. We will have approximately twelve hours, and will have to be back on board by midnight. US currency only is accepted by the locals, so we will be permitted to make withdrawals from our pay books, in the appropriate dollars of course. The maximum permitted withdrawal, will be ten shillings. While it may look as if they are letting us loose, they definitely are keeping the leg rope on.

We are allowed to wander off, pretty much under our own steam. This indicates to us that the Yanks have everything under control, and there isn't much mischief, we can get into. Four of us from our old Unit, wander off together. There's Norm, Doug Dolman, Les Lockhart, and myself.

We aren't sure how we are going to pass the time. We find outside the wharf area, the place is very neat, very clean, and completely urbanised. In all respects, this is your normal America. Any grass huts that once might have been here, have long since gone.

Our first problem is to extend our dollar capacity. We solve this by heading to the nearest bank. They are willing to exchange some of our English currency, long regarded as the world's best, for the appropriate dollars. We feel smug and quite pleased with ourselves, over this deal. It is good to feel we have outsmarted those who have power over our movements. We have sufficient in our pockets now, to have a moderately good time, if we so wish.

Our ideas and knowledge of the place are very vague. All that I know of the place is what I had gained by reading shipping brochures in my first job, some sixteen years before. It told me that Waikiki Beach is supposed to be the world's best, and the Royal Hawaiian Hotel, is the premier hotel.

We wander on, taking in the scene as we go. We have gone just a short distance, when a threatening thunderstorm, suddenly bursts above us. Taking our cue from the locals, we just stand under awnings for about twenty minutes. The storm is short, sharp and fierce. Just as quickly, it is gone. Again the sun is bright and strong, so the weather won't worry us very much.

We have hardly moved on again, when we are approached by a young Yank sailor. He has recognised us, instantly, as Aussies, from our uniforms. This isn't always the case with Yanks. Mostly, they seem wrapped up in their own kind. Anybody else merits only passing interest. Their unspoken attitude seems to be, that they are being forced to clean up the mess, created by their Allies, and they don't much care for the idea.

He tells us, that he has spent a lot of time in Australia. This surprises us, as he looks so young, and we think, that he has only just joined up. He says, that he had been in Sydney for a while, and also visited Coolangatta. He liked it very much down there. "Do you know those places?" he asks. On being told that some of us come from Sydney, he tells us of his first encounter with an Aussie serviceman.

He is standing on a street corner in Sydney, when two of the biggest guys, he has ever seen, walk up to him. They say, "We're the Desert Rats. Give us a quid." He quickly reaches into his pocket, pulls out some notes, then hands them over. This done, he takes off, as fast as he can go. Despite this, he still thinks the place is great.

And Coolangatta—"Do you know Coolangatta?" Without waiting for a reply he says, "Oh boy, that Coolangatta," with rolling eyes, and an expression that tells us much. It is obvious, that all the delights, a serviceman on leave can wish for, are pretty well catered for in Coolangatta.

To us, Coolangatta is just a name. It is pretty obvious that this surfing beach area, south of Brisbane, has grown and boomed, since we were away. While we know nothing about the place, it seems obvious the Yanks have made it their own—how much to the exclusion of us locals, we can only imagine. The thought disturbs us a little.

We tell the sailor that we are just passing through, and only have limited time at our disposal. With no idea of where to go, and what to see, what can he recommend? He says, "There's nothing here in Pearl. You will be better off going into Honolulu. There's much more to see and do there." We have pretty much decided, that there is little of interest here, but have no idea of which way to head. Now, that we have his firsthand advice, this is what we will do.

It isn't far from Pearl to Honolulu, and we are soon there. We decide to wander about, to take in the scenery and the people. The place itself is clean, spacious and picturesque. The people are a fascinating mixture of all kinds of racial backgrounds, who seem to come together in a harmonious blending.

We see a fellow, obviously different, in a quiet section on the footpath, selling some kind of goods from a large metal cabinet. Intrigued, we go over to see what it is. The cabinet is insulated, contained ice for cooling, and the goods are bottled milk for sale. We haven't seen anything like this before, and can't see much future in this kind of business. We buy some, and stand there talking to the fellow. We find him to be an Australian, who has lived here for about fifteen years. He tells us, that he likes it here. He says, he may go back home for a visit some time, but he will be back. We leave him and wander on.

We come to a business area, and are passing a photography studio, when we are accosted by the proprietor. He urges us to have our photos taken, and they will be developed while we wait. We agree and go in. He has a local girl as an assistant. She dons a hula skirt to pose with us, and add some colour. While three of us stand at the rear, the other sits on a chair in front, with the Hula girl sitting on his lap. We rotate round, so that each of us has a turn on the chair, with the girl.

This is pretty mundane stuff, hardly any more, than filling in time. We have to find something a bit more interesting. We chew it over, and come to a decision. We will go to the Royal Hawaiian Hotel and have a drink. Then we will hire a bathing costume to have a swim at Waikiki Beach. There isn't much point in stopping over in one of the world's most famous spots, without sampling some of the things, that make it so.

We don't have much trouble locating the Royal Hawaiian. You can pick it out from some distance away. The surrounds are picturesque, with lovely grounds, accentuating the island's atmosphere. There are palm trees and an imposing entrance façade. A large sign advertises the current resident entertainers. They are two of Hollywood's long time stars, Mary Brien and Charles Ruggles.

My mates are dawdling a bit, so I cross the road with its imposing drive, and stand on the corner awaiting them, just at the entrance to the hotel. It is a private road and there is no traffic. Now, a jeep comes along from nowhere, makes a U-turn, then pulls up in front of me. Its occupants are all in uniform. There are two ordinary seamen in the rear, and two female Officers in the front. The driver, one of the females, is seated right alongside, close to where I stand. She and her mate eye me up and down, quite clearly ogling. The seamen don't like it, not one little bit.

The driver asks, in an outrageously exaggerated southern drawl, "Say guy, where you all from?"

"Australia," I reply.

She then asks, "How looong have you been awaaay?"

I reply, "Six years."

She then says, "Myy, that's a miiighty looong tiiime!"

Females in uniform, being a new thing to me, I say to her, "What are you supposed to be?"

She replies, "Ahm a Waaave."

Before I can stop myself, the words just blurt out. I say, "Well I'm Bondi Beach. Come roll up on me!"

She just stares blankly, totally uncomprehending. Now the fellows on the other side of the road, step off the kerb on their way to join me. Hastily dismissing her, I say, "Here are my mates. I'll see you later." We all turn away towards the hotel, leaving her still sitting there in the motionless jeep.

The fellows want to know what that was all about. I tell them, "Just a Yank sheila, wanting to know where I'm from, and how long I've been away."

As we had expected, the hotel has tasteful décor, and is comfortable inside. We find ourselves a bar, and order our drinks. Habits and conduct differ somewhat, in different parts of the world. We aren't too sure whether our dress, and conduct will be acceptable here. But, we are accepted without question.

After a leisurely interlude, we find our way to the beach, and costume hire stand— as expected, in the American style, one is readily available. We lose no time in changing, and prepare for our swim.

It is truly a lovely setting, with the beach curving away for some distance. The hotel is set in about the middle of the beach, with its beachfront edge only about fifteen feet from the water. The waves in majestic and uniform rollers, about thirty feet apart, sweep to the shoreline. The water is warm and inviting. The sand, however, is coarse, pebbly-grained, white coral, with knobs of solid coral, protruding about every ten feet. Care has to be taken to avoid stubbing your toes on these knobs. Upon entering the water, we find the coral knobs, just a big nuisance. We enjoy the interlude, but agree, as beaches go, we much prefer our own. We decide we have had enough, and it is time to head back. The break has been different, and has given us a spell from being wrapped up in our worries.

We are well within our time limit, and stroll leisurely back along the wharf. Although Pearl is a huge Naval Depot, there are hardly any ships, other than our own, berthed here. The odd one or two are very small, seemingly with crews of only between fifteen and twenty. They all have their own film projector and screen setup, with just a handful of men watching the film being shown. We marvel at the seemingly limitless amenities, the Yanks deem necessary for their men. We just cannot see the sense in such expensive outlay, which we deem unnecessary to the job in hand.

Sometime during the night, we are on our way again. There are no dawdlers; everybody is back in time. We are getting into the last leg, with the next stop being Auckland in New Zealand. Here the Kiwis will disembark, with the next stop being Sydney.

More days at sea, then finally Auckland. We have some time ashore, while the Kiwis are disembarking, even to attending a local dance evening. We are too close to home now, and too much on edge to take any part in the dancing. The Kiwi girls aren't too interested in us blokes anyway. Then it's the final leg to Sydney.

There isn't a lot of sleep after Auckland, with most watching out ahead, from daylight onward, for the first sight of the Heads. It doesn't matter much if the famous landmark into Sydney doesn't show on the first, the second, or even third day; somebody will be watching. As it turns out, we arrive off the Heads, sometime in the early hours of the morning. The ship heaves to, and we don't actually proceed into the harbour, until after daylight. By this time, every person aboard is glued to the rail, watching every inch of our rather slow progress.

Our emotions are very mixed up, with every man aboard going through his own mini hell. One moment you are quietly glad, the next deeply apprehensive. How much change has there been after six years? Will we be able to cope with that change? We were totally out of our depth in England. God, let it be different at home.

We worry about our families. We are about to come face to face with them once again. Their letters and interest had sustained us during the hard times, and, despite photos received, the images, we carry of them, is as they were. Will we find a difference, that we don't particularly like?

How much will they see in us, that they don't particularly like? For we have changed. That is for sure. We just agonise, and worry.

Our slow progress is deliberate. I figure, it is probably because we are scheduled to berth at a particular time, and the need to allow for some sort of a welcome home ceremony. With the War still on, it probably won't be too elaborate. About halfway up the harbour, a speech of welcome, from the Governor General, is read out to us over the ship's public address system. Some are a bit miffed, that he hasn't seen fit to deliver it in person. Others are pleased that, at least, some bullshit has been dispensed. Some begin digging into what happened here, when the first lot of POWs had arrived home.

The story, we are able to piece together, is very disturbing. It seems that the Governor General, the Duke of Gloucester, the King's brother, had arrived in person to make a speech of welcome. Due to pressing engagements, his arrival was delayed for over two hours. The whole disembarking procedure was held up, until he arrived. The fretting and fuming returnees were so pent up that, when he did, they exploded with profanities.

They called him everything they could possibly think of, from a bastard onwards. When he tried to speak, they derided his affected English upper crust voice, in the most obscenely and derisive way, they could think of. His Regimental dress uniform of rather peculiarly cut checked pants, got the same kind of treatment. In the end, a red-faced, and thoroughly demoralised official party, had to retire in utter confusion.

We, ourselves, can actually feel their fury and indignation, just in the retelling. We actually shiver at the thoughtless agony inflicted on our mates, by mindless bureaucracy. In turn, we are fiercely determined, that we will not stand for any similar treatment.

We need not have worried. Our predecessors had done the trick. Before we tie up, we know exactly what the procedures will be. First off the ship, will be all men who have to travel to another state. There will be transports to the railway, where trains are waiting to take them, there. New South Welshmen will be last off. They are warned, that this will be late, because of the time needed to have the interstate blokes attended to. While we aren't exactly happy, we can see the fairness in this method. While we, basically, have arrived home, the other blokes still have a long way to go.

Then begins the wait. The ship is moored at Circular Quay, with the wharf area and immediate surrounds, a sea of humanity. As time wears on, the already dense crowd gets even bigger. Despite being packed closely together, they remain in good humour. There is a Guard at the foot of the gangway, ensuring nobody can come aboard, and only those, who are authorised to do so, can leave. When at last the first of the interstate men begin to go ashore, a fleet of buses is standing by to whisk them to the railhead.

Norm and I have taken up a position against the rail, from where we are able to watch proceedings. It is a substantial height above the wharf, and we are able to overlook the scene, almost with the detachment of neutral observers.

When our turn comes, we will part company here, with me getting away first. I am New South Wales country, and will have to travel by train, while Norm is a Sydney local and, therefore, one of the last to get ashore.

We talk quietly together, trying to assess our military future. Without giving much thought to it, we had expected to be taken to a camp or depot, from where we would be granted leave, after a day or two. But, our leave and pay arrangements are already taken care of. Once we go ashore, we will be on our way, only to report back after leave. With no Unit to report to, it will have to be at Headquarters, here, in Sydney. Norm insists that I am to make his home my base, while ever I need to report. With his Dad working, and his sister Betty in the Air Force, we probably will have the place to ourselves, anyhow.

During the morning, from here and there in the crowd, people begin calling to us lining the rail. They are trying to make premature contact with those of us, they have come to meet. In this way, a bare handful are able to do so. When this happens, there will be a calling out back and forth between them, then a wild scramble by the soldier to force his way down the gangplank. It also elicits an equally mad scramble, through the good humoured crowd, by his greeter on the wharf. A brief meeting follows at the foot of the gangway, then the soldier will return to await his turn to disembark.

With a couple of successful get-togethers, all of us listen intently, hoping to hear our own name being called. Then a name is called that sounds like "Dawson". With the distance involved, it is hard to make out what is called. It may have been "Dawson", "Rawson", or "Lawson". I stretch and strain, trying to see from whence it comes, hoping to pick out a familiar face. I find none, and my hopes fade. Weighing up the pros and cons, I decide, it is most unlikely, that any of my family have been able to make it, from my home in Newcastle, to be part of this crowd on the wharf. In fact, I find out later, that my sister Clare was part of the crowd. She had asked somebody with a powerful voice to call out for her. Now, we both feel disappointed and let down, that no contact was made.

It has been a long, tiring, traumatic day, when at last, it is my turn to go. I half-carry, and half-drag my gear, which feels as heavy as lead, down onto the wharf. By this time, darkness is beginning to set in. Without any assistance, I struggle aboard a double decker bus, that has just pulled up. Almost as quickly, it moves off. We are close behind the one in front, to be followed, just as quickly, by the one behind. With this close shuttling, only a few men are able to board each bus. There are only about six on this one of mine.

None of us speak, or pay much attention, to where we are going. We have a vague idea that we are being taken to a central place to meet some of our people. For myself, I doubt that any of my family will be there. I cannot see that the authorities will have arranged for them to be informed of my arrival, and then have arranged transport for them from Newcastle to Sydney, and out to a central point, which probably is the showground. With the War still going on, and the transport difficulties, it doesn't seem possible. So, I have a sneaking doubt of their ability, or willingness to do such a thing.

We are too done in, both physically and mentally, to pay much attention to anything. We just look unseeingly ahead, waiting for the bus to stop, and our next move. It is quite dark, and most of the street lighting is on, when finally our bus stops. We pile off, and are pointed, pushed and led, towards a very large marquee. There seems to be a lot of people about, mostly in civilian clothes. We halt in single file at an entrance, halfway along one side. With a few ahead of me, I am able to observe and take note of the procedure.

A bloke at the entrance takes your name, and passes it on to another bloke, inside. This second bloke will announce it over a microphone. You then start to walk round in a large circle, until claimed by somebody from the very large crowd, gathered inside—something like a parade of animals at a circus. It is an ongoing thing, with each of us following quickly behind each other.

When I reach the outside bloke, I give my name, then move inside the tent. The bloke inside calls it out, and I begin to move round the circle. The sudden blaze of light makes it difficult to pick out anything much at all. The fellow in front of me has not gone far, when suddenly, he is swamped with people hugging, kissing and lifting him off his feet. I ease off to give them a chance. Then the fellow behind me is given the same treatment. Caught between them, I and my gear, am pushed, pummelled, and trampled on unmercifully. I disentangle myself from one lot, only to be swamped by another. There is no sign of my people. I struggle on, finally finishing the circuit, still finding nobody I know.

That does it. My nerves have had enough, and I literally can't drag my gear another step. I go just outside the entrance, and slam it down in a heap, alongside the canvas side. I go back to the bloke on the mike. Then, gesturing to the lined up POWs to hold back a bit, I order him to call my name again. I make sure he gets it right. I pause for a long second, before starting on my second round of the circuit—this time, without my gear.

Still unsure, if there is anybody here to greet me, I resolve to head off to the station, and make my own way to Newcastle. My manoeuvring has created a bit of space, so that I am the lone figure in the spotlights, and now clearly visible. I have hardly taken a half dozen steps, when there they are: My Dad, as always, solid, quiet and dependable; My Mum, just as dependable, but quite emotional; My sister, Clare, and my brother, Ted, a boy when I left and now a fully grown man, excited, exuberant, and boisterous; and my girlfriend Jean, standing quiet and shy to one side, with her sister Edna in support. My God! After six years, this is all of them alright, but there are some changes. Will I be able to cope with this? Will they be able to put up with me? At the moment, this will have to be sometime in the future.

On this first night, the whole crew of us, stay in Sydney, putting up with distant relatives, whom I hardly know. I just drift along, with all decisions made for me. Conversation is animated and constant, much of it over my head. It is relevant to local stuff, and as such, fairly foreign to me. There are some questions of course, but you cannot wipe away six years in five minutes. I struggle, mightily, to curb my bad language, being only moderately successful. For the moment though, any lapses are overlooked.

The house is overfull, with makeshift sleeping arrangements having to be made. Some will have to stretch out on the floor. They want me to have a comfy bed, but I refuse, explaining I have slept on deck all the way out, and won't be able to use a bed. I just pick a spot on the loungeroom floor, and stretch out there. They all are a bit disconcerted about this, but raise no arguments. With the day's proceedings having been a very big strain for all concerned, we finally turn in.

The next day, with some of the pressure off, we make our way to the station, and finally arrive home. There it is—the place I had left six years before, and hardly changed a bit. I silently pick out, this and that, as something stirs my memory. I am feeling daunted at the thought of picking up, where I had left off. But then, I am still in the Army.

There follows an extended leave, with frequent returns to Sydney Headquarters. For my stays in Sydney, Norm's home becomes, in fact, my second home. With Japan on the backpedal, it is only a matter of time before the War ends. This means our Army service will be drawing to a close, unless the Authorities decide to hang onto a sizeable force for the time being.

Norm and I are just marking time, uncertain whether to push our energies toward becoming civilians, or remaining soldiers. His sister, Betty, comes home on leave, just as uncertain, as to her future. While we are unwilling to pull out, all indications from Headquarters seems to be, that we are expected to demob. While standing by, we buy ourselves some civvies clothes, and start going out to some entertainment. Norm and his girlfriend, and Jean and I, start seeing some of the picture shows. Jean stays with her Aunty, some of the time, while I am in Sydney. Betty and some of her girlfriends even persuade Norm and I to try some ice skating—even though I had vowed never to go near snow and ice again.

For me, there is a welcome party in Newcastle, which I have to attend, but quietly detest. In this way, several months are to pass. Then Japan finally capitulates. It is all over, and we have no alternative. We will have to take our discharge. We never make it back to our Unit.

# Chapter 19
# An Unexpected Reunion

In various ways, I am able to meet up with some of my special mates, and get some idea on how our Unit fared, while I was on the run or confined inside the prison camps. Sadly, I have to concede, there wouldn't have been many familiar faces, even if I had made it back to our lines.

I am stuck with the painful, bewildering business of becoming a civilian, once again—trying to accept the mediocre and mundane, as being significant and important. However unwilling, I may feel, my future is now mapped out for me. I now have to try and make my way in this kind of jungle. But, ever so slowly, and little by little, it begins to happen.

Work is easy to come by, and I try a few things. Then I go back to the industrial complex, I had left at the outbreak of the War. I begin to climb the ladder a little, and achieve a slight measure of importance. I continue to prosper, even to the point of penetrating the Works Staff System. Some of the workmen have even got round to addressing me as Mister. And so, a couple of years roll by.

As a civilian, the tracking down of the old gang of my former Unit, takes months after my discharge. But I manage to establish, and make contact with some of my special mates, especially Jock. I find him, back in a single hotel room, close to his beer supply. We talk and try to fill in the missing years, since he, and most of my gang, managed to escape from Crete. All too soon, I have to leave him.

After a while, small snippets of news filter through on the grapevine, about Jock. He is still in his hotel room, still drinking, but now, without rationing restrictions. From time to time, some of the old gang will drop by, and seek his company.

Then, one day, about midmorning, I am sitting in my office, in my comfortable swivel chair, when the Departmental Superintendent calls me in. Because of my standing, we talk as equals. He says, "Do you know a man named Jock?"

Startled, I say, "Yes."

He says, "Well, you'd better go down to the Watchman's Office, and find out what he wants." God! It is Jock. Without another word, I just turn and take off.

My office, located in my particular works sector, is about a quarter of a mile from the Watchman's Office, which is located at the outer front fringe of the plant. I break into a run and, as I do so, I remember that running on the plant is forbidden for safety reasons. So, I alter my pace to a brisk stride. I keep to this for about a hundred yards, then I say to myself, "What the hell. It's Jock down there," and break into a run again.

When I arrive, I find Jock and a young bloke, obviously a companion, and the Head Watchman, standing guard, over the two of them. Several others of the Watchman's staff, are seated at their desks, a short distance away—half attending to their records, and half ready to back up their boss, if needed. I walk in, wave the Watchman away with a brief, "It's OK," then turn my attention to Jock.

Our greeting is unmistakably special, and the Watchman observes our antics with some surprise, and a little awe. Then the Questions follow:

"How did you find me?"

He remembered, I had told him, I worked here, pre-war. So he just took a punt.

"Do you want a job? No problem, I can arrange it," I offer.

"No, I am just passing through," says Jock.

"Where are you staying?"

"The Sports Ground," he replies.

Ah! That figures. He is on the "Wallaby".

"Who is your offsider?" I ask.

He is just a young bloke, whom Jock has teamed up with, for the trip.

"Where are you heading?" I query.

"To Queensland for a break," he announces.

"How did you get here?" I inquire.

"We walked," he grins.

From the Sports Ground to here, is about five miles.

"Do you have any money?"

"No," he says cheerfully.

I dig into my pocket and pull out all I have on me. "Here," I say, "That's for now. There will be more later. What are you're plans for the moment?"

"Nothing much, other than head back to the Sports Ground."

Now for some planning with others of our Army mates, who are working at this, and other nearby plants. We arrange for a get-together after work, when everybody can be free. The venue we choose is the pub near the Sports Ground. Satisfied we are organised, we part—me, to my office; Jock and his young offsider, to the Sports Ground.

Back at the office, I get on the blower—connecting with some; leaving messages with others. This done, I sweat out the time as best I can, before heading for the pub. The thought that keeps turning over and over in my mind, making me feel immensely proud, is the fact that it is me whom, Jock has taken the trouble to seek out.

At the pub, within a short time, there are at least a dozen gathered to see him. Each and everyone is so damn pleased, and make a tremendous fuss. Meanwhile, his young offsider hovers in Jock's background, a bit overwhelmed at this display of genuine affection.

There is talk, laughter, and rough badinage, from where we have taken over a corner of the bar. And, of course, the beer flows. Onlookers can only be amazed, that this nondescript man is so much the centre of attention to this personable looking group.

After a while, amidst all the hubbub, somehow there is just Jock and me, alone together. We eye each other intently, and it is Jock who speaks first. He starts with, "Do you mind the time when we… ?"

I interrupt mockingly with, "Do I mind the time? Of course, I mind the time. I mind every bloody time."

He gives me that old quizzical half-smile, half-grin, in amusement at my heckling. Suddenly, the years just roll away, and we are back where we had been. We just look at each other, and the emotion takes over. And it hits me hard. Without another word being spoken, it dawns on me what this is all about.

Escaping from the rigours and stresses of civilian life, by a session with Jock, is a temporary therapy for the fellows. But for Jock, it has now become a nightmare. He has reached crisis point, and is running away. Somehow, he hopes that I, a non-drinker, can help him. That's why he has sought me out.

I instantly know that to do this, I will have to drop everything, walk away and go with him, leaving all this civilian crap behind. There can be no turning back. There will be hungry times and sleeping rough. Big deal! We'd done plenty of this before. I'd be walking away from my position, and what I have achieved. So what? But now, there too, is my wife and young son, my comfortable home with its undischarged mortgage. When I disappear, she will have to cope with this.

Then the coward in me, asserts itself. These civilian comforts, suddenly become attractive. And, I chicken out. In doing so, I also realise, that I have become, completely, a civilian. Our rapport is such, that without speaking, Jock knows that I have weighed up the situation, and that I have turned him down.

We carry on at the pub, long after we should have left. We have a whip around, contributing more than we should. We buttonhole his offsider, fiercely instructing him on his duties, and cares to this special person, our mate. We threaten dire consequences, if he fails our trust. When we can think of no more, we dribble out and leave.

I am a bit difficult to live with for a week or so. But, one thing I have been forced to accept is that I have made a choice, and this is to be my lifestyle. At least, Jock has settled this for me.

I hear no more of him for about eighteen months. The word, then, is that he had disappeared inside Queensland for a period, but is now back in Sydney, in his hotel room. I know this is too short a period to have been effective.

Then, no more, until one day a query gets an answer, "Oh Jock? He died a couple of months ago. His body was found in a park, an empty flagon by his side."

"He was buried in an obscure suburban cemetery. Nobody knows where, and nobody knows if there were any mourners. Certainly, nobody will be tending his grave."

"Ah well! I guess it had to happen. In the broad scheme of things, I guess he was just another bloke—nobody to really cry over. Just a drunken no hoper," as the man said.

Then why is it that, every other day, I see him standing there—wearing that quizzical half-smile, half-grin, on his face, in quiet amusement, while being badgered? Well, despite his personal hardships, he was a mate in our Unit, and, in a troubled world, one of the many, who did their best for King and Country.

www.ingramcontent.com/pod-product-compliance
Lightning Source LLC
Chambersburg PA
CBHW030257080526
44584CB00012B/347